Canadian
Book
of the Road

Canadian Book of the Road

Third Edition

The Reader's Digest Association (Canada) Ltd.
Montreal

Canadian Book of the Road

EDITOR: Andrew Richmond Byers
ART DIRECTOR: Lucie Martineau
ART ASSOCIATE: Andrée Payette
RESEARCHERS: Wadad Bashour and Penelope Body,
   Gladys Pollack, Lillian Reinblatt and Karen Evoy
PICTURE RESEARCHER: Rachel Irwin
COPY PREPARATION: Joseph Marchetti
PRODUCTION: Holger Lorenzen
COORDINATOR/INDEXER: Marilyn Ghadirian
CARTOGRAPHY: Aéro Photo Inc. and
   MapArt (Road units 76, 78, 84 and 97)

CONTRIBUTORS

RESEARCHER/WRITER: Martha Plaine
ILLUSTRATOR (Bird's-eye Views): Murray Hay

Canadian Cataloguing in Publication Data:
Main entry under title:
Canadian book of the road
3rd Canadian ed.
ISBN 0-88850-175-7
   1. Automobile travel — Guide-books — Canada.
2. Canada — Description and travel — 1981—   —
Guide-books. I. Reader's Digest Association
(Canada)
FC38.C355 1991   917.104'647   C90-090348-1
F1009.C36 1991

ACKNOWLEDGMENTS

The publishers acknowledge with thanks the assistance of the
following organizations:

Calgary Tourist and Convention Bureau
Canada's Capital Visitors and Convention Bureau, Ottawa
Department of Development and Tourism, Newfoundland and Labrador
Department of Economic Development and Tourism, Saskatchewan
Department of Industry, Trade and Tourism, Manitoba
Department of Tourism, Alberta
Department of Tourism and Culture, Nova Scotia
Department of Tourism and Parks, Prince Edward Island
Department of Tourism, Recreation and Heritage, New Brunswick
Edmonton Tourism
Environment Canada/Canadian Parks Service
Fredericton Visitors and Convention Bureau
Greater Montreal Convention and Tourism Bureau
Greater Quebec City Tourism and Convention Bureau
Metropolitan Toronto Convention and Visitors Bureau
Ministère du Loisir, de la Chasse et de la Pêche, Québec
Ministère du Tourisme, Québec
Ministry of Environment and Parks, British Columbia
Ministry of Tourism and Recreation, Ontario (Ontario Travel)
Ministry of Tourism, Recreation and Culture, British Columbia
Saint John Visitor and Convention Bureau
St. John's Tourist Bureau
Tourism Halifax
Tourism Regina
Tourism Vancouver
Tourism Victoria
Tourism Yukon
TravelArctic, Northwest Territories
Winnipeg Convention and Visitors Bureau

Thanks is expressed also to federal and provincial parks departments,
and regional tourist associations and tourist bureaus, city and
municipal offices across Canada.

Foreword

This vast country of ours is endowed with a network of roads
few others possess. Roads that link Atlantic to Pacific, small
communities to bustling cities, populous heartland to solitudes
of the Far North. Along these roads beckon countless natural and
man-made wonders, warm welcoming people and historic places
—opportunities for discovery, adventure and recreation.

Canadian Book of the Road shows you where those opportunities are and how to make the best of them. It travels well-
known highways, main streets, wilderness roads and country
lanes. Its maps span the nation from the surf-washed beaches of
Pacific Rim National Park on Vancouver Island to Signal Hill,
the majestic rock overlooking St. John's harbor. They range north
of the Arctic Circle to Tuktoyaktuk and south to Point Pelee, at
the same latitude as northern California. Virtually every region
you can reach by car is covered.

In these pages you will find major historic, scenic and
recreational attractions as well as unique or especially interesting
local features. Here are more than 2,300 entries illustrated by
1,000 photos and sketches. And there is an element not usually
included in motoring guides: a portfolio of bird's-eye views
by Calgary artist Murray Hay. His striking renderings show
five different regions from the air, a vivid panorama of our
diverse land.

Essentially a vacation planner and on-the-road travel guide,
Canadian Book of the Road can also provide hours of pleasurable
browsing. It offers a wealth of background information and little-
known fact that will not only enhance your travel enjoyment, but
also broaden your knowledge of Canada.

The Editors

How to Use the Book

Canadian Book of the Road is a complete motorists' guide to virtually every part of Canada you can reach by car. This 428-page book takes you along more than 48,000 kilometres (30,000 miles) of highways and byways across Canada. It leads you to great recreational locations, awesome scenic wonders, secluded beauty spots, sites where history was made, quaint villages where traditional customs and crafts survive, and bustling, dynamic cities.

Canadian Book of the Road presents all these attractions in 184 road units. There are 172 units that trace routes through country regions and 12 that describe major cities. The road units, numbered from 1 to 184, fill 376 pages. There are 180 double-page road units; those for Vancouver, Toronto, Ottawa and Montreal have four pages each. (The book has no page numbers.)

Preceding the road units is a 14-page atlas section showing where the various road units are located. By referring to the atlas maps, you can select road units in areas that interest you.

Name of the region dealt with in the road unit.

An inset map, taken from the atlas section, showing the road unit in relation to its surrounding area. By turning back to the atlas map, you can locate adjacent road units.

A detailed strip map of the road unit. The route is marked in red. Route lengths range from 50 to more than 500 kilometres.

A compass sign.

A miles/kilometres conversion scale.

Symbols identify all the attractions on each road unit. Symbols for various attractions in a specific area are grouped under the name of the nearest city, town or park. There are 45 symbols in all. They are explained in one common legend (see box below, right).

Black figures between two black dots indicate point-to-point distances.

Red figures between two red dots indicate accumulated distances.

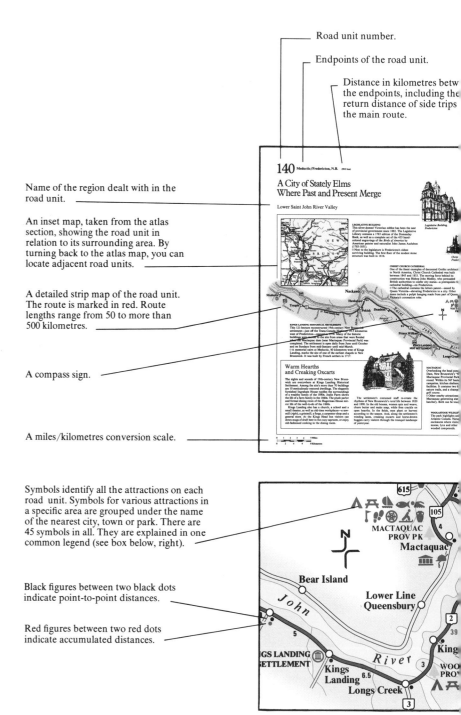

Road unit number.

Endpoints of the road unit.

Distance in kilometres betw the endpoints, including the return distance of side trips the main route.

City Road Unit

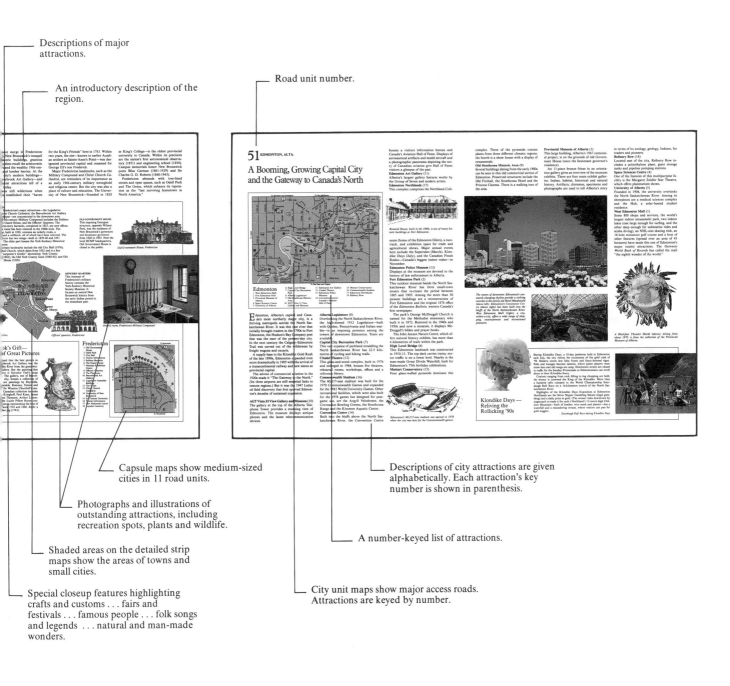

Descriptions of major attractions.

An introductory description of the region.

Road unit number.

Capsule maps show medium-sized cities in 11 road units.

Photographs and illustrations of outstanding attractions, including recreation spots, plants and wildlife.

Shaded areas on the detailed strip maps show the areas of towns and small cities.

Special closeup features highlighting crafts and customs . . . fairs and festivals . . . famous people . . . folk songs and legends . . . natural and man-made wonders.

Descriptions of city attractions are given alphabetically. Each attraction's key number is shown in parenthesis.

A number-keyed list of attractions.

City unit maps show major access roads. Attractions are keyed by number.

Map Features and Symbols

The legend explaining the features and symbols on the detailed strip maps is on the foldout page at the back of the book. By leaving this page unfolded, you can refer easily from any road unit to the legend. A chart showing the distances in kilometres between major metropolitan centers is also included on the foldout page.

Five Canadian Roads from the Air

An Artist's Impression

This specially commissioned pictorial section of *Canadian Book of the Road* comprises five bird's-eye views of Canada by Calgary artist Murray Hay. Each view depicts the overall appearance and the predominant physical features of a region described in a particular road unit of the book. Each shows a different aspect of the natural diversity of our country—soaring mountains and spacious plains, rugged wilderness and sparkling lakeland, meandering watercourses and scenic ocean shore. A diagram with each view provides a key to the main features.

A Year-Round Route Through Our First National Park

The 60-kilometre stretch of the Trans-Canada Highway between Banff townsite (*far right*) and Lake Louise (*upper left*) runs through the Bow River valley. This view of Banff National Park (Road Unit 34) looks northeast from the Alberta side of the continental divide, whose slopes form the park's western boundary. Until the First World War, the park could be reached only by rail. The first rough road from Banff to Lake Louise, built in the early 1920s, opened what was then a relatively remote wilderness to a few adventurous motorists. Today, for more than 3 million visitors annually, the Trans-Canada Highway offers year-round passage through this majestic region of towering peaks, glaciers, wild rivers and alpine meadows. Originally created to preserve the local hot springs, Banff became our first national park in 1887. In 1985, the United Nations Educational, Scientific and Cultural Organization (UNESCO) bestowed the status of World Heritage Site on Banff and the adjacent Jasper, Yoho and Kootenay parks.

1 Lake Louise
2 Castle Mountain
3 Bow River
4 Pilot Mountain
5 Johnson Canyon
6 Massive Mountain
7 Mount Cory
8 Lookout Mountain
9 Mount Edith
10 Mount Norquay
11 Vermilion Lakes
12 Sundance Range
13 Cascade Mountain
14 Cave and Basin Centennial Centre
15 Banff (townsite)
16 Sulphur Mountain
17 Lake Minnewanka
18 Mount Rundle

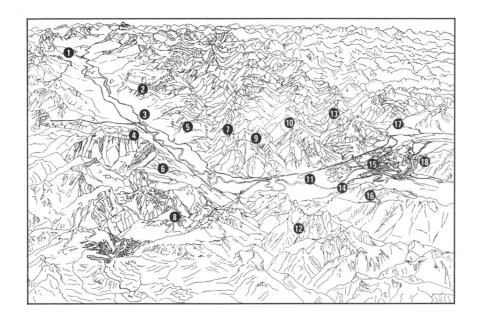

Murray Hay

A Hidden Valley in the Heart of the Prairie

Some 11,000 to 12,000 years ago, glacial meltwaters flowed across the prairie, carving out the 430-kilometre-long trench that is today's Qu'Appelle River valley in Saskatchewan (Road Unit 65). Its wayward path east to the Manitoba border disrupts the orderly grid imposed on the landscape by the rectangular grainfields and road network. The valley, as much as 140 metres deep and 2.5 kilometres wide in places, is the region's most conspicuous natural feature from the air. But from the road it is almost completely hidden. After a long drive across flat farmland, the abrupt descent into this strikingly different realm of water and woods can come as a delightful surprise. The chain of lakes at Fort Qu'Appelle (*upper left*) has long been a recreational playground for people from Regina and elsewhere in southern Saskatchewan.

1 Pasqua Lake	7 Katepwa Lake	13 Crooked Lake
2 Qu'Appelle	8 Indian Head	14 Stockholm
3 Echo Lake	9 Melville	15 Grenfell
4 Fort Qu'Appelle	10 Qu'Appelle River	16 Round Lake
5 Mission Lake	11 Sintaluta	17 Esterhazy
6 Lebret	12 Wolseley	18 Broadview

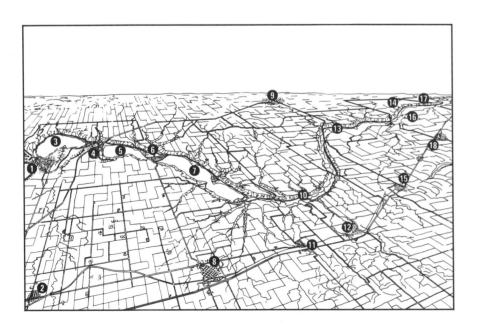

Murray Hay

A Famous Ontario Waterway on the Fringe of the Shield

The Kawartha lakes (Road Unit 100) lie on the fringe of the Canadian Shield, which runs diagonally across southern Ontario from Brockville to Georgian Bay. The southern Kawarthas, such as Sturgeon, Pigeon and Chemung lakes, stretch into the rolling farmland around the busy communities of Lindsay, Peterborough and Lakefield. The northern lakes press against rocky, wooded shores, a popular setting for summer cottages and resorts. But the true Shield country—rugged and sparsely settled—begins north of the lakes, where roads curve and climb through rocky outcrops to Minden and Haliburton (*upper left*). The Kawartha Lakes had long served as an Indian waterway when French explorer Samuel de Champlain canoed and portaged through here in 1615. Today's uninterrupted travel from lake to lake is the legacy of the region's 19th-century settlers, who began the task of linking the lakes with canals and locks to the larger Trent-Severn waterway system, which joins the Bay of Quinte to Severn Sound on Georgian Bay. Originally built for commercial shipping, the scenic waterway today welcomes thousands of pleasure craft in summer.

1 Minden
2 Balsam Lake
3 Haliburton
4 Shadow Lake
5 Coboconk
6 Cameron Lake
7 Fenelon Falls
8 Sturgeon Lake
9 Lindsay
10 Bobcaygeon
11 Pigeon Lake
12 Buckhorn
13 Buckhorn Lake
14 Chemung Lake
15 Burleigh Falls
16 Stony Lake
17 Clear Lake
18 Katchewanooka Lake
19 Lakefield
20 Otonabee River
21 Peterborough

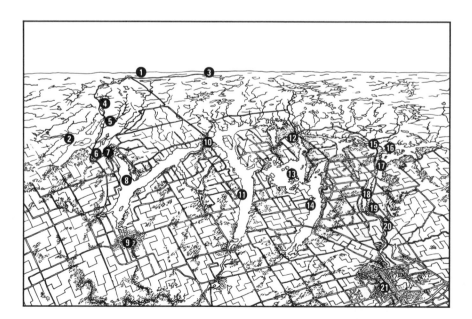

Murray Hay

A Panorama of Shore and Shield Along a Mighty River

Quebec's Charlevoix County lies along the southeastern margin of the Canadian Shield that bounds the wide St. Lawrence (more than 25 kilometres wide at this point). The shoreline from Baie-Saint-Paul northeast to the Saguenay estuary (Road Unit 128) embraces bold green hills (some rising more than 600 metres), forested plateaus, narrow valleys, deep gorges and swift-running rivers. Seen from the air, these scenic wonders merge to form a lush, knobbly landscape veined with roads and watercourses. Two coastal roads connect the quaint old farming and fishing villages of Baie-Saint-Paul, Saint-Joseph-de-la-Rive and Les Éboulements to the famous resort center at La Malbaie. At Saint-Joseph-de-la-Rive, travelers can take the ferry to Île aux Coudres (*foreground*), roughly 11 by 4 kilometres in extent, where the atmosphere of 18th-century New France is well preserved. From the coast, roads lead inland to a thinly settled area, where Saint-Urbain, Saint-Hilarion and Notre-Dame-des-Monts nestle among the highest peaks of the Canadian Shield.

1 St. Lawrence River
2 Baie-Saint-Paul
3 Rivière du Gouffre
4 Saint-Urbain
5 Notre-Dame-des-Monts
6 Saint-Hilarion
7 Saint-Joseph-de-la-Rive
8 Lac Sainte-Agnès
9 Saint-Aimé-des-Lacs
10 Lac Sainte-Marie
11 Les Éboulements
12 Île aux Coudres
13 Clermont
14 Mont Grand-Fonds
15 La Malbaie
16 Pointe-au-Pic
17 Saint-Irénée
18 Gros Cap à l'Aigle
19 Saint-Siméon
20 Baie Sainte-Catherine
21 Saguenay River

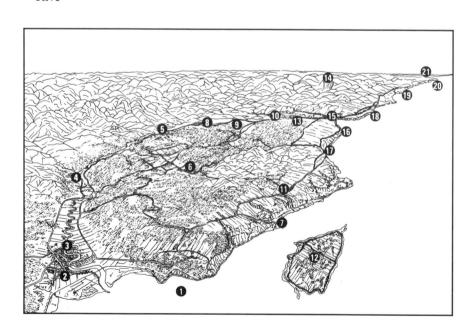

Murray Hay

Across Prince Edward's Isle to Our Finest Beaches

The hilly central section of Prince Edward Island is roughly 25 kilometres wide. This view looks southwest across Northumberland Strait to the headland of Cape Tormentine, New Brunswick, where visitors can catch the ferry to Borden on the southern shore of the island. The crowded patchwork of fields is a reminder that tiny Prince Edward Island is our most densely populated province, with the greatest proportion of its people still living on farms. One of the compact island's prime attractions is the narrow coastal strip along the Gulf of St. Lawrence from Tracadie Bay to Cavendish Beach (*foreground*). This is the site of 32-square-hectare Prince Edward Island National Park (Road Unit 150), which preserves a shoreline of sand dunes, high sandstone cliffs, saltwater marshes, freshwater ponds and some of the finest beaches in North America. From the provincial capital of Charlottetown (*upper left*), half a dozen roads lead to different destinations in this national park; no drive across this part of the "Garden of the Gulf" takes more than 30 minutes.

1 Tracadie Bay
2 Dalvay Beach
3 Stanhope Beach
4 Brackley Beach
5 Rustico Island
6 Gulf of St. Lawrence
7 North Rustico
8 Orby Head

9 Cavendish
10 Cavendish Beach
11 New London Bay
12 New London
13 Darnley Basin
14 Charlottetown
15 Hillsborough Bay

16 Northumberland Strait
17 Cape Tormentine, N.B.
18 Borden
19 Bedeque Bay
20 Summerside
21 Kensington
22 Malpeque Bay

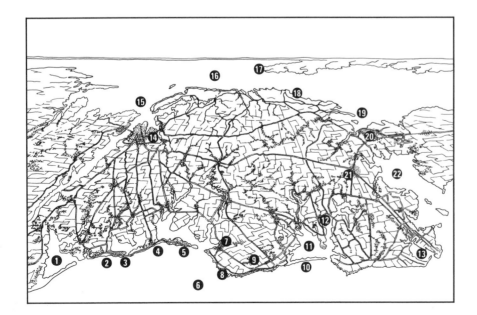

Murray Hay

Road Unit Atlas

This atlas consists of seven maps of Canada. The general map of Canada (I) divides the country into six major regions, which are shown in more detail on the regional maps II to VII. The regional maps locate the book's 184 road units and identify each unit within a numbered box. The route of each road unit is shown in red. The following list groups the road units according to their location on the regional maps. The list also gives the endpoints of each road unit.

IV. THE CANADIAN SHIELD/THE GREAT LAKES

75. Kenora/Kakabeka Falls, Ont.
76. Red Lake/Shabaqua Corners, Ont.
77. Thunder Bay/Rainbow Falls Provincial Park, Ont.
78. Nipigon/Terrace Bay, Ont.
79. Hawk Junction/Thessalon, Ont.
80. Espanola/South Baymouth/ Little Current, Ont.
81. Sudbury/Parry Sound, Ont.
82. Penetanguishene/Owen Sound, Ont.
83. Tobermory/Wiarton, Ont.
84. Milverton/Orangeville, Ont.

85. Kapuskasing/Kirkland Lake, Ont.
86. Englehart/North Bay, Ont.
87. North Bay/Renfrew, Ont.
88. Grand Bend/Rondeau Provincial Park, Ont.
89. Windsor/Wheatley, Ont.
90. Hawk Cliff/Shakespeare, Ont.
91. Doon/Guelph, Ont.
92. Long Point Provincial Park/ Blair, Ont.
93. Hamilton/St. Catharines, Ont.

94. Niagara-on-the-Lake/Thorold, Ont.
95. Dundas/Black Creek Conservation Area, Ont.
96. Toronto, Ont.
97. Pickering/Aetherley, Ont.
98. Barrie/Dwight, Ont.
99. Dorset/Burleigh Falls, Ont.
100. Haliburton/Lakefield, Ont.
101. Warsaw Caves/Trenton, Ont.
102. Belleville/Amherstview, Ont.
103. Kingston/Smiths Falls, Ont.

V. THE ST. LAWRENCE VALLEY/THE MARITIMES

104. Mill of Kintail/Manotick, Ont.
105. Ottawa, Ont.
106. Aylmer/La Pêche, Que.
107. Gananoque/Johnstown, Ont.
108. Iroquois/South Lancaster, Ont.
109. Williamstown/L'Orignal, Ont.
110. Coteau-du-Lac/Lachine, Que.
111. Papineauville/Saint-Eustache, Que.
112. Montreal, Que.
113. Sainte-Rose/Parc du Mont-Tremblant, Que.
114. Terrebonne/Pointe-aux-Trembles, Que.
115. La Prairie/Hemmingford, Que.
116. Lacolle/Saint-Ours, Que.
117. Rougemont/Stanbridge East, Que.
118. Magog/Georgeville, Que.
119. Sherbrooke/Victoriaville, Que.
120. Sainte-Marie/Lac-Mégantic, Que.
121. Boucherville/Sainte-Croix, Que.
122. Trois-Rivières/Saint-Tite, Que.
123. Cap-de-la-Madeleine/Neuville, Que.
124. Quebec City, Que.
125. Bois de Coulonge/Cartier-Brébeuf National Historic Park, Que.
126. Sainte-Pétronille/Saint-François/ Saint-Pétronille, Que.

127. Beauport/Cap-Tourmente, Que.
128. Baie-Saint-Paul/Baie-Sainte-Catherine, Que.
129. Lévis/Rimouski, Que.
130. Hébertville/Alma, Que.
131. Larouche/Petit-Saguenay, Que.
132. Tadoussac/Moisie, Que.
133. Sainte-Flavie/Saint-Joachim-de-Tourelle, Que.
134. Anse-Pleureuse/Penouille, Que.
135. Matapédia/Gaspé, Que.
136. Mount Carleton Provincial Park/ New Mills, N.B.
137. Jacquet River/Burnt Church, N.B.
138. Saint-François-de-Madawaska/ Grand Falls, N.B.
139. Drummond/Woodstock, N.B.
140. Meductic/Fredericton, N.B.
141. Marysville/Nelson-Miramichi, N.B.
142. Baie-Sainte-Anne/Moncton, N.B.
143. St. Stephen/Letete, N.B.
144. St. George/Chance Harbour, N.B.
145. Saint John, N.B.
146. Oromocto/Saint John, N.B.
147. Kingston/Hillsborough, N.B.

148. Alberton/Bloomfield Provincial Park, P.E.I.
149. Summerside/Portage/Summerside, P.E.I.
150. Kensington/Parkdale, P.E.I.
151. Scales Pond Provincial Park/ Charlottetown, P.E.I.
152. Southport/Georgetown, P.E.I.
153. Mount Stewart/Cardigan, P.E.I.
154. Yarmouth/Digby, N.S.
155. Deep Brook/Bridgetown, N.S.
156. Bridgetown/New Ross, N.S.
157. Port Williams/Mount Uniacke, N.S.
158. East Medway/Pubnico Beach, N.S.
159. Voglers Cove/Prospect, N.S.
160. Halifax, N.S.
161. Advocate Harbour/Bible Hill, N.S.
162. Joggins/Balmoral Mills, N.S.
163. Pictou/Port Hastings, N.S.
164. Minasville/Eastern Passage, N.S.
165. Lawrencetown/Auld Cove, N.S.
166. Margaree Valley/Englishtown, N.S.
167. Port Hastings/North Sydney/ Port Hastings, N.S.
168. Sydney/Louisbourg/Sydney, N.S.

VI. NEWFOUNDLAND

169. Channel-Port aux Basques/ Deer Lake, Nfld.
170. Wiltondale/L'Anse aux Meadows, Nfld.
171. Badger/Gambo, Nfld.

172. Glovertown/Bonavista, Nfld.
173. Goobies/Heart's Content, Nfld.
174. Bay de Verde/Outer Cove, Nfld.
175. St. John's, Nfld.
176. Donovans/Petty Harbour, Nfld.

VII. THE NORTH

177-184: A note on the northern road units precedes map VII.

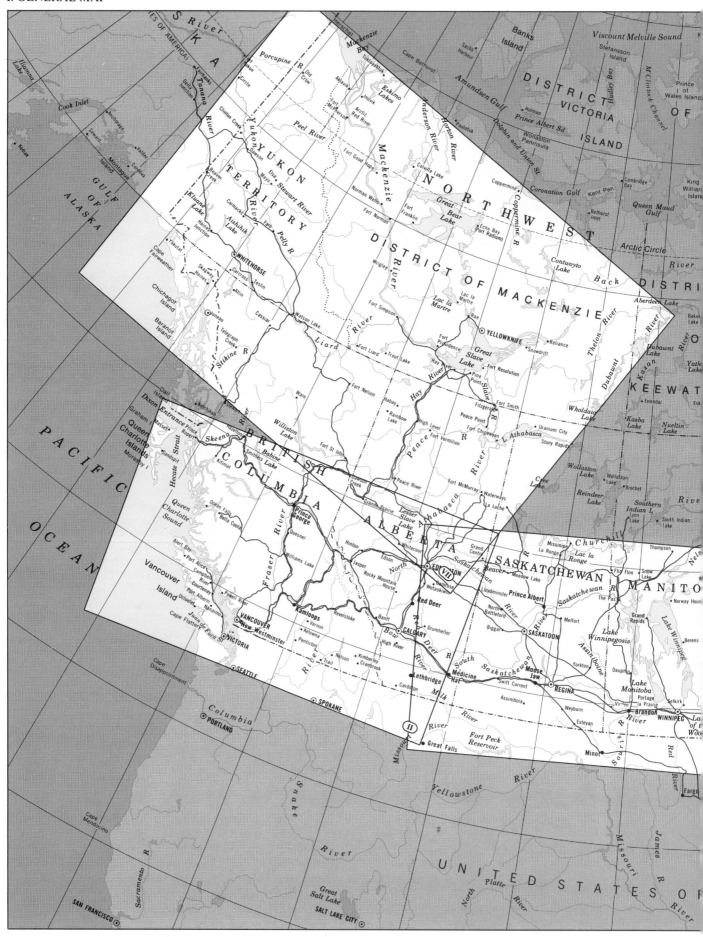

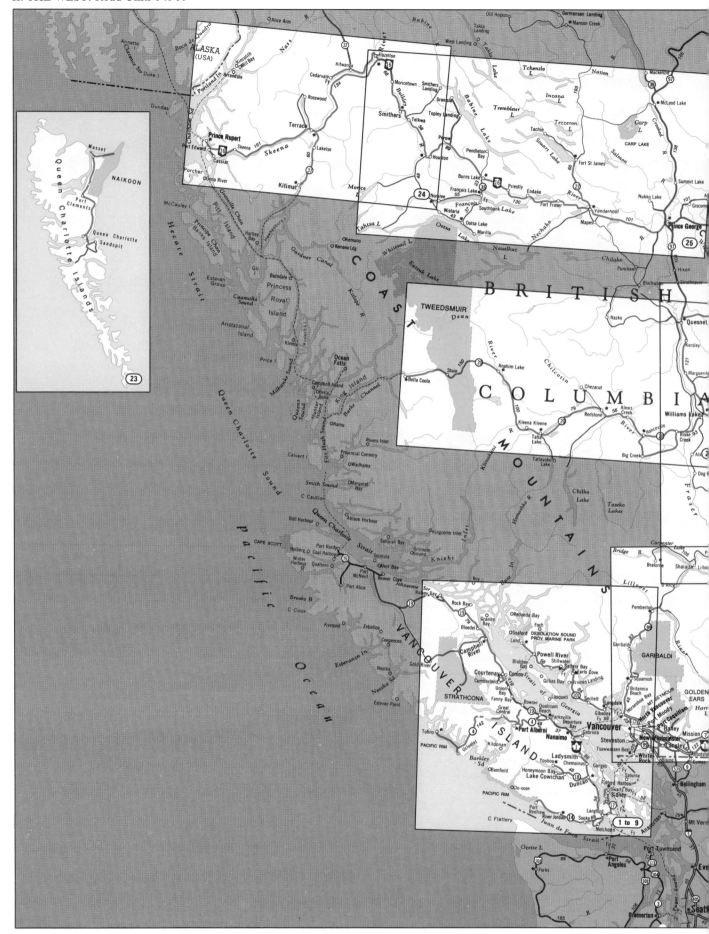

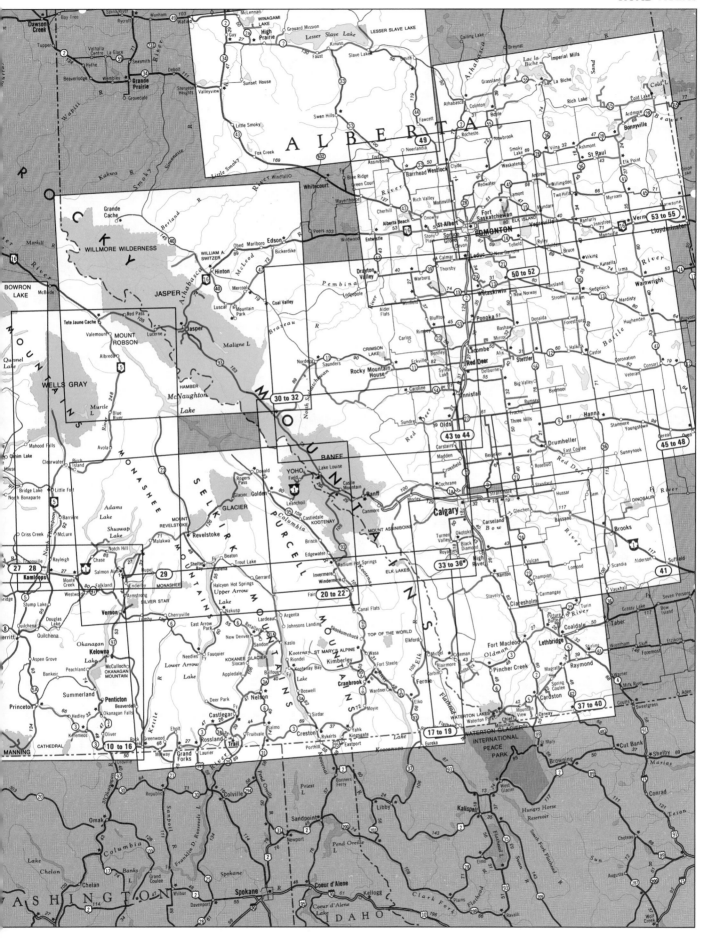

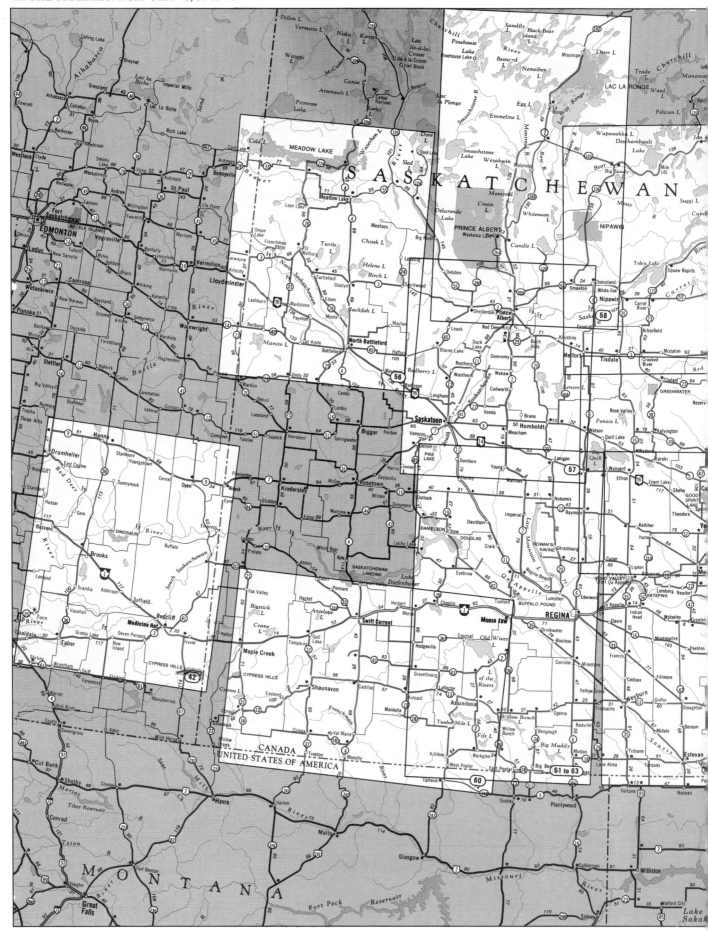

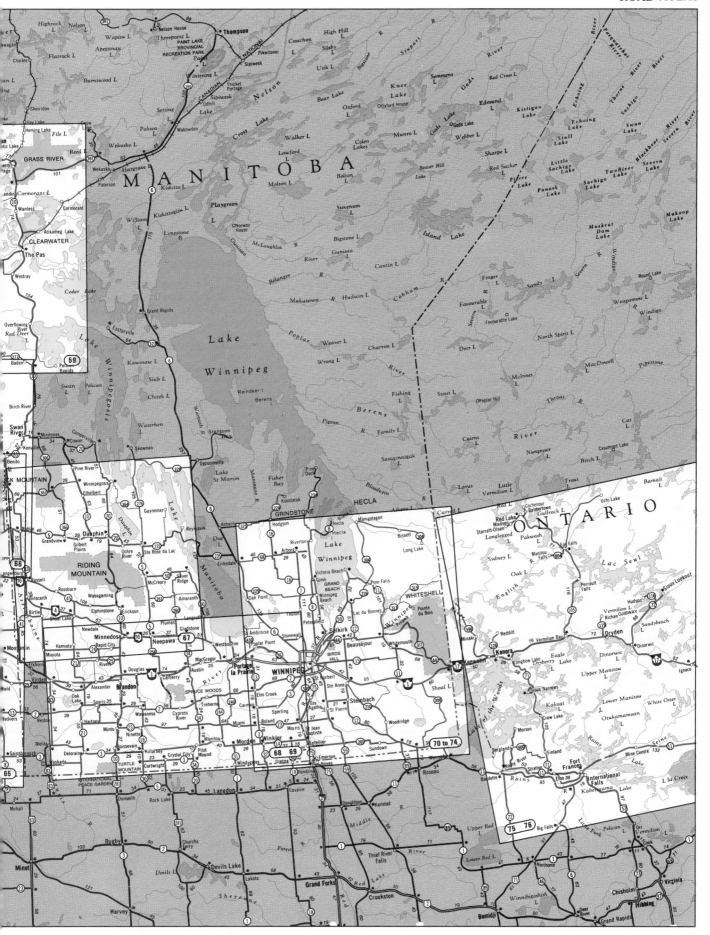

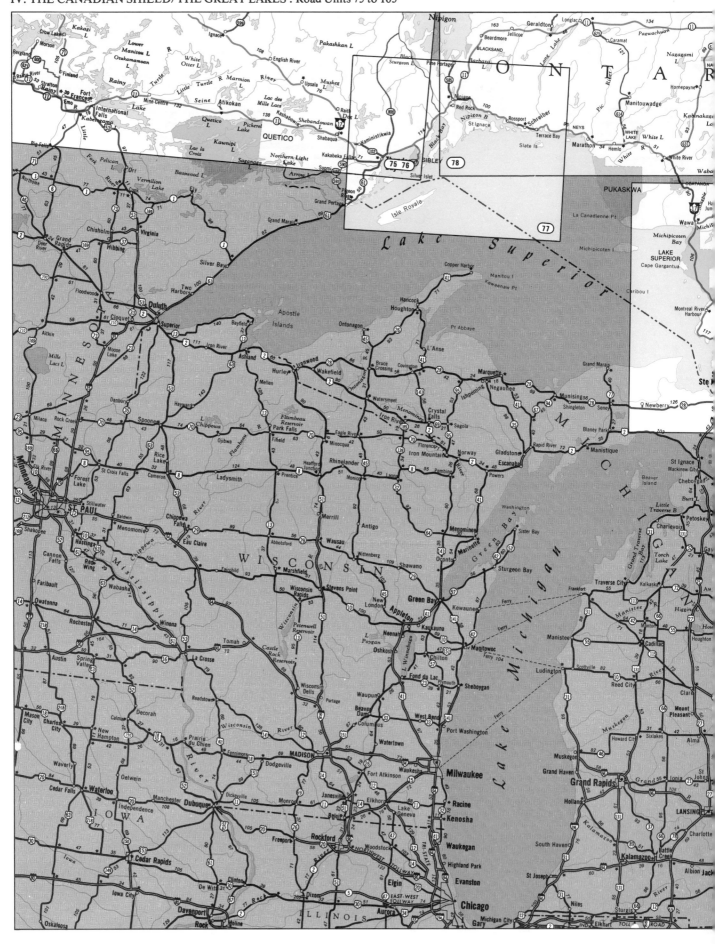

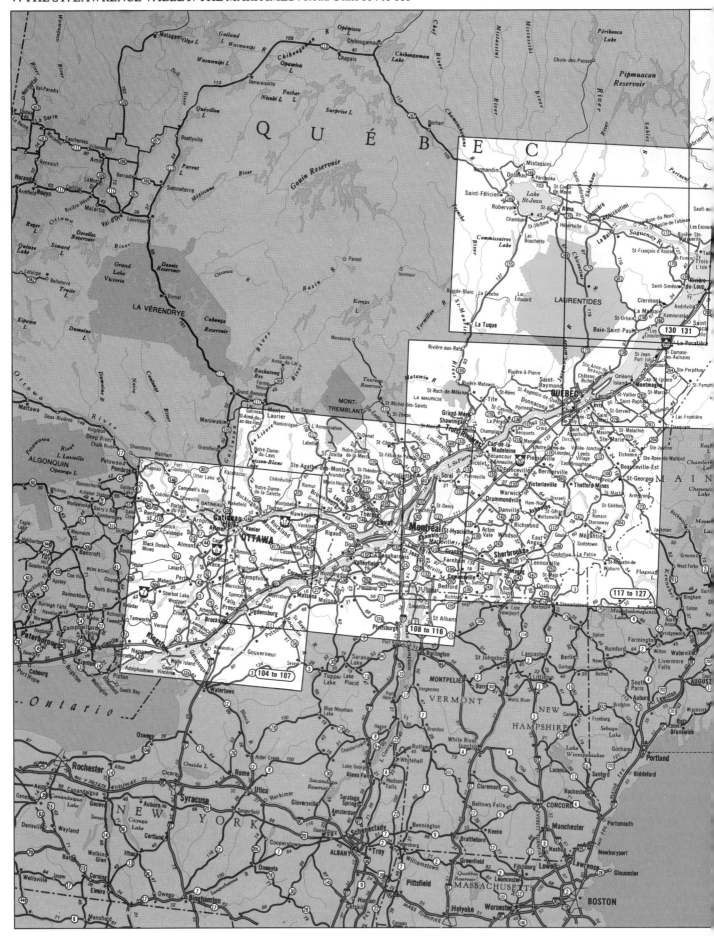

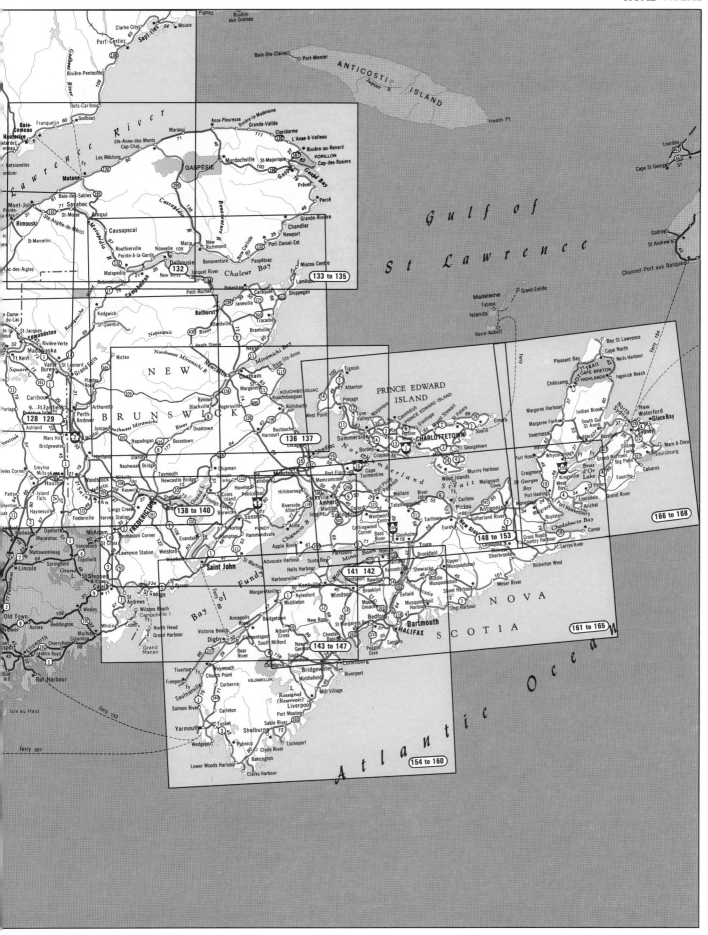

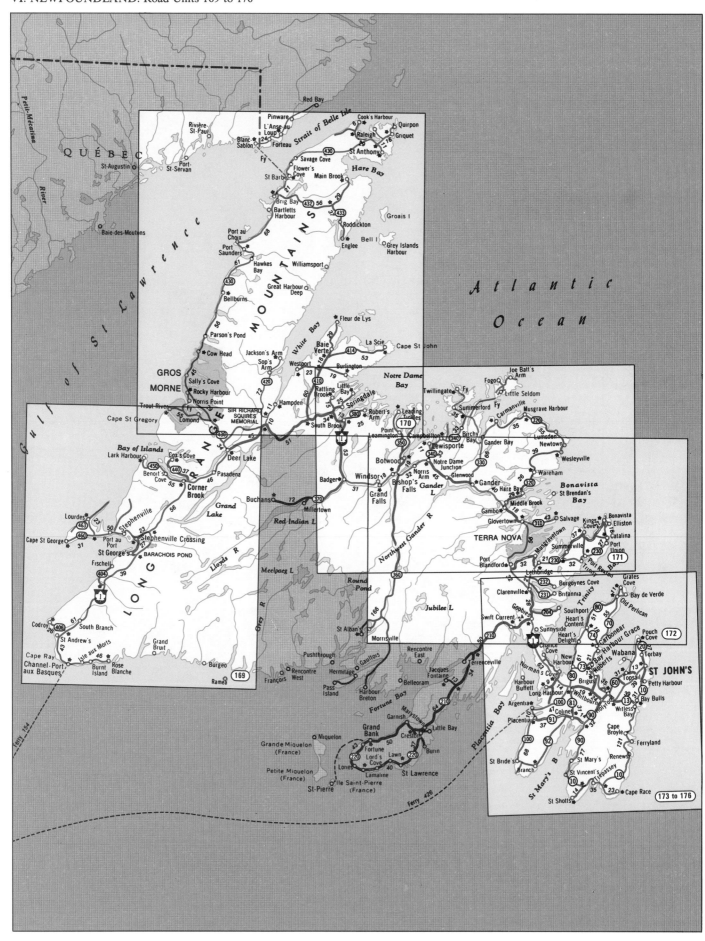

The North

The routes of the northern road units, which are listed below, run through a vast and rugged territory—once impossibly remote, but now increasingly attractive to the adventurous traveler. They include some of Canada's most challenging highways: the Alaska, the Dempster, and the Mackenzie. Map VII (*overleaf*) pinpoints these routes.

Driving North

The unpaved highways stretching across Canada's Northwest are often described as hazardous. In fact, they are well engineered and well maintained. With planning and care, the traveler can minimize the problems they present.

There are long distances between northern garages and accommodations. You can check the location of the services along your route at tourist information bureaus. Make reservations well in advance because accommodations are limited. (If you intend to drive north in winter, contact the territorial or provincial tourism departments about road conditions.)

The main difference between summer driving in the north and elsewhere in Canada is the need for protection against gravel and dust. A northern garage will prepare your car before you set out. Headlights should be fitted with clear plastic covers. A wire-mesh screen across the grille will shield it and the radiator.

Flying gravel can easily damage the gas tank: inserting heavy rubber matting between the gas tank and its securing straps provides adequate protection. Substituting metal fuel lines for rubber underneath the car helps ensure against ruptures.

Dust is worst in construction areas and where heavy rain has disturbed road surfaces. (After a prolonged downpour, highways may be impassable; check with the nearest RCMP detachment, road maintenance office or tourist information bureau.) To help keep dust out of the car, close the windows and turn on the fan. Filters in the heating and air-conditioning systems keep out some dust. Mosquito netting placed over the air intake keeps out more.

Do not drive fast on gravel roads. A speeding car throws gravel and a cloud of dust, creating a hazard for other vehicles. At high speeds you can easily lose control of your car if you hit a pothole or begin to slide over the small, loose stones. Speeding on gravel will also wear down tires quickly and lead to a blowout. Do not be tempted to drive in the middle of the road, where the surface may be smoother. An oncoming vehicle, also in the middle of the road, may appear unexpectedly.

It is advisable to carry an extra tire, a tow rope or chain, tools and spare parts, a first-aid kit, and extra food. If you have a breakdown, stay with your car and flag down a passing driver for assistance. Do not venture more than 100 metres from the road; you can easily become disoriented and lost.

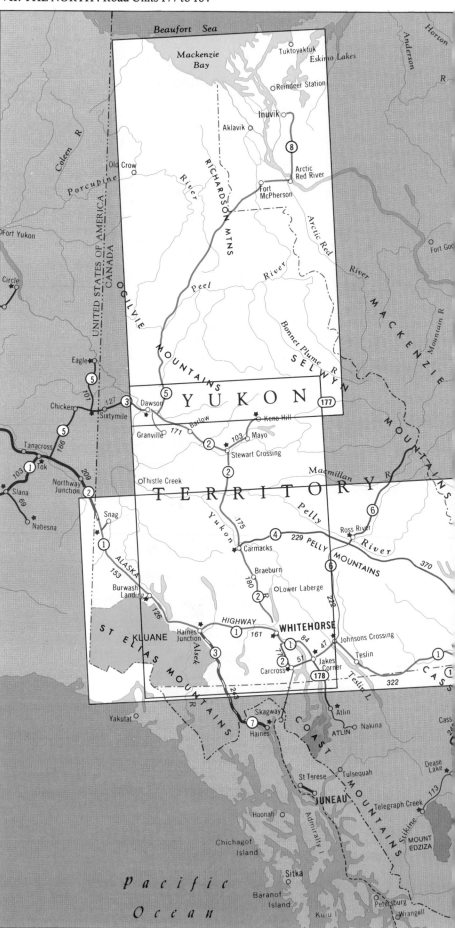

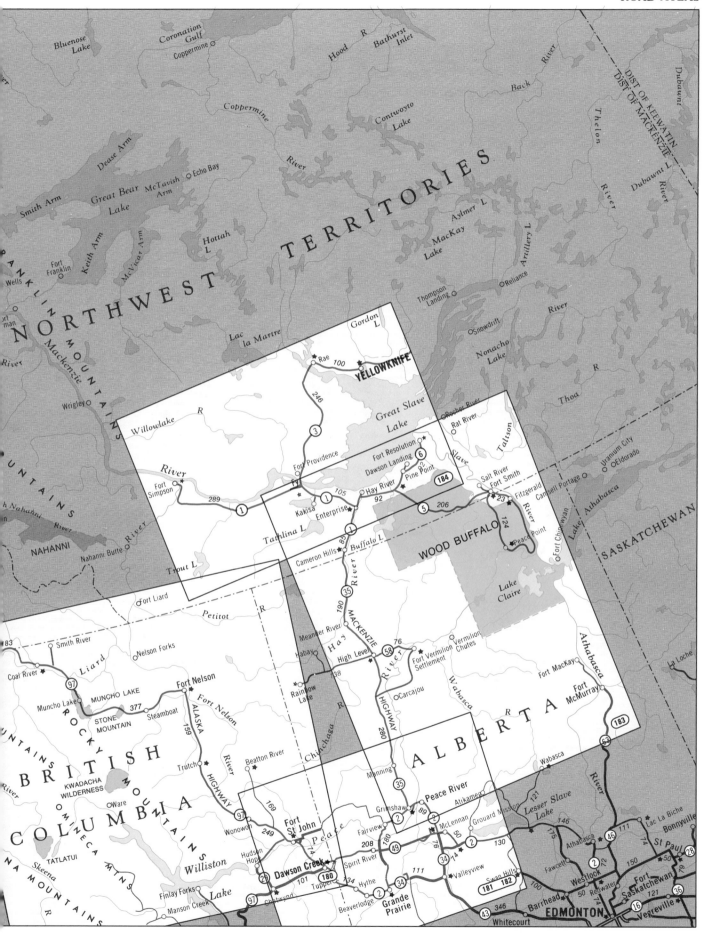

Restless Tides and Dense Forests Along a Mist-Shrouded Coast

Vancouver Island

Winding along the coast of southern Vancouver Island, Highway 14 is one of Canada's most breathtaking drives. Echoes of the past are everywhere: old coach inns, forts, lighthouses, churches and monuments. The scenery varies from the pastoral to the spectacular: beaches and headlands, neat fields and wild forests, the mountains of the Olympic Peninsula high and hazy across the Juan de Fuca Strait. Fog and mist often envelop this landscape, bestowing a quality of deep mystery.

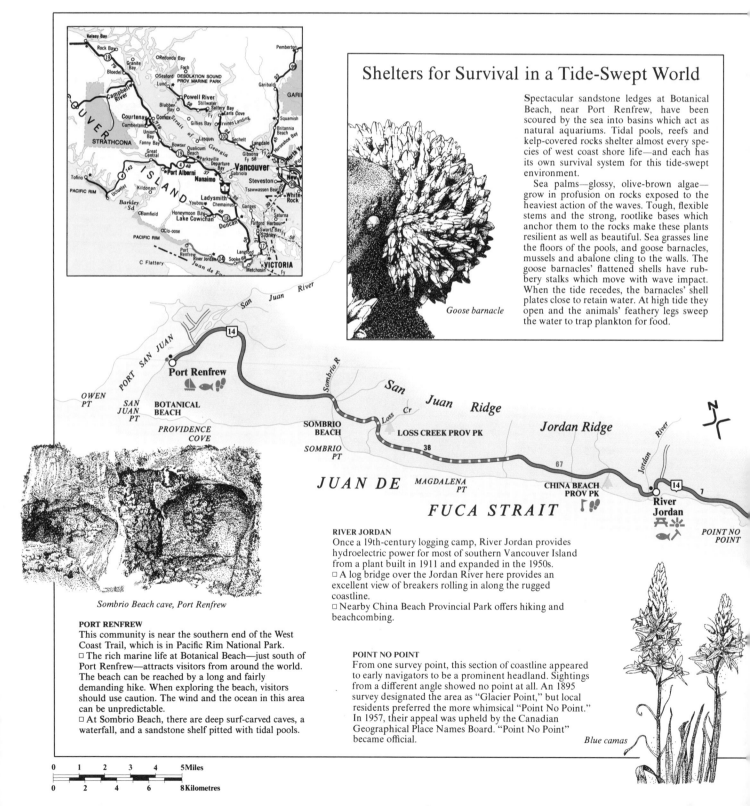

Shelters for Survival in a Tide-Swept World

Spectacular sandstone ledges at Botanical Beach, near Port Renfrew, have been scoured by the sea into basins which act as natural aquariums. Tidal pools, reefs and kelp-covered rocks shelter almost every species of west coast shore life—and each has its own survival system for this tide-swept environment.

Sea palms—glossy, olive-brown algae—grow in profusion on rocks exposed to the heaviest action of the waves. Tough, flexible stems and the strong, rootlike bases which anchor them to the rocks make these plants resilient as well as beautiful. Sea grasses line the floors of the pools, and goose barnacles, mussels and abalone cling to the walls. The goose barnacles' flattened shells have rubbery stalks which move with wave impact. When the tide recedes, the barnacles' shell plates close to retain water. At high tide they open and the animals' feathery legs sweep the water to trap plankton for food.

Goose barnacle

Sombrio Beach cave, Port Renfrew

PORT RENFREW
This community is near the southern end of the West Coast Trail, which is in Pacific Rim National Park.
□ The rich marine life at Botanical Beach—just south of Port Renfrew—attracts visitors from around the world. The beach can be reached by a long and fairly demanding hike. When exploring the beach, visitors should use caution. The wind and the ocean in this area can be unpredictable.
□ At Sombrio Beach, there are deep surf-carved caves, a waterfall, and a sandstone shelf pitted with tidal pools.

RIVER JORDAN
Once a 19th-century logging camp, River Jordan provides hydroelectric power for most of southern Vancouver Island from a plant built in 1911 and expanded in the 1950s.
□ A log bridge over the Jordan River here provides an excellent view of breakers rolling in along the rugged coastline.
□ Nearby China Beach Provincial Park offers hiking and beachcombing.

POINT NO POINT
From one survey point, this section of coastline appeared to early navigators to be a prominent headland. Sightings from a different angle showed no point at all. An 1895 survey designated the area as "Glacier Point," but local residents preferred the more whimsical "Point No Point." In 1957, their appeal was upheld by the Canadian Geographical Place Names Board. "Point No Point" became official.

Blue camas

0 1 2 3 4 5Miles
0 2 4 6 8Kilometres

Sooke harbor

The intricate coastline was well known to 18th-century Spanish explorers, who anchored their ships here in search of gold. Later, homesteaders fought the dense bush, but eventually they drifted away, abandoning their hard-won clearings to the forest. When Highway 14 was completed in 1957, the riches lay not in gold or farming, but in lumber and fishing.

Some 200 species of birds and 20 types of mammals inhabit the sea and shore—some seldom seen because they are nocturnal or attuned to the dense, often impenetrable forest. At Botanical Beach, near Port Renfrew, receding tides reveal a rich variety of marine life in tidal pools.

The coastline here is a winding and a twisting of waterways, a confusion of islands and bays, inlets and cliffs whose flanks slip sharply into the sea. In places, the forest opens up to sweeping views of the Juan de Fuca Strait, a hint of the broad Pacific beyond.

ROYAL ROADS MILITARY COLLEGE

James Dunsmuir, a premier and later a lieutenant governor of British Columbia, invested much of his personal profits from coal, lumber and shipping in the most opulent estate in western Canada. Sandstone and granite parapets crown the stone Hatley Castle (1908). Promenades pass Italian, French and Japanese gardens, game courts, stables and guest cottages. Following Dunsmuir's death in 1920, the property was purchased by the federal government, which established Royal Roads Military College. The estate's botanical gardens are open to the public.

Hatley Castle, Royal Roads Military College

SOOKE

This important logging, farming and fishing center has Canada's southernmost harbor.

□ The area's first settler was Capt. Walter Grant, who established a farm here in 1849 under contract to the Hudson's Bay Company. No dedicated farmer, Grant and several of his tenants were soon lured to the goldfields of California. But Grant did leave a lasting mark on Vancouver Island. During a winter trip to Hawaii, he was given several broom seeds by the British consul. Planted on Grant's farm, the hardy broom eventually spread throughout the island.

□ All Sooke Day, held in July, features logging competitions such as high rigging, sawing, birling (log rolling), and ax throwing. Food is prepared at the fairground the way prospectors cooked during the 1864 gold rush at nearby Leech River: beef is roasted in a pit of alder coals, and salmon is grilled over open fires.

METCHOSIN

St. Mary the Virgin Church, a simple black and white frame building (1879), is the "Easter Lily Church." In spring, masses of dogtooth violets spread a white mantle among the headstones of pioneers buried near this church that they helped to build.

Black oyster catcher

Columbian black-tailed deer

Fisgard Lighthouse, Fort Rodd Hill National Historic Park

FORT RODD HILL NATIONAL HISTORIC PARK

Fortified in 1895, Fort Rodd Hill was an important coastal defense battery for many years. A battery of six-inch cannon protected Victoria Harbour and the Royal Navy yards at Esquimalt until the fort was declared obsolete in 1956. The cannon are gone, but their bunkers remain—huge cement horseshoes on a grassy knoll overlooking the ocean. Visitors can inspect the fort's command post, the warrant officers' quarters, the smith's shop and forge, the canteen and the guardhouse.

□ Adjacent to the fort is Fisgard Lighthouse, a 14-metre column that has guided ships through the Juan de Fuca Strait since 1860. Its light is visible for 16 kilometres in clear weather.

□ A herd of tame Columbian black-tailed deer roams the 18-hectare park surrounding the fort and lighthouse.

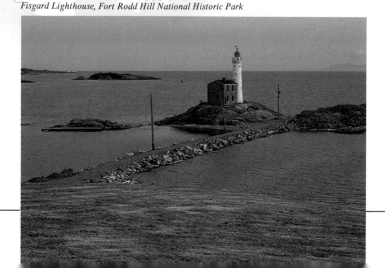

2 VICTORIA, B.C.

A Gentle City That Preserves Its Totems and High Tea

In the beginning it was a fur-trade post, then a booming gold-rush town. Now it is Canada's gentlest city, a civilized place of unhurried streets and enchanting gardens where flowers bloom year round.

Victoria, capital of British Columbia, is also Victorian, a bit of England consciously preserved amid the primitive beauty of the Pacific coast. Some of this is to please the tourists—the double-decker buses and tallyho carriages—but most of it is natural. The people and the city are mostly British in origin; this is reflected in fine shops selling tweeds and bone china, white-clad lawn bowlers behind the Crystal Garden, high tea in the Empress Hotel, and the crack of a cricket bat in Beacon Hill Park.

Victoria is elegant and modern, but its past is well preserved in museums, art galleries, pioneer homes and great mansions. In Thunderbird Park, near the dignified Parliament Buildings, is a forest of totem poles that evokes the highly developed Indian cultures of the Pacific coast.

The city moves at a quiet but steady pace, its inner harbor dotted with pleasure craft and its streets bustling with strollers.

Art Gallery of Greater Victoria (18)
Canadian artists represented include A.Y. Jackson, David Milne, Homer Watson

and Emily Carr. Also displayed are Auguste Rodin's bronze statue, *Mercury Emerging from a Cloud*, and Pier Fiorentino's painting, *Madonna and Child with Saint John*. In an outstanding Oriental collection are por-

Among Victoria's attractions are Beacon Hill Park (right) and its 38-metre totem pole (detail below), and the Royal British Columbia Museum (below right).

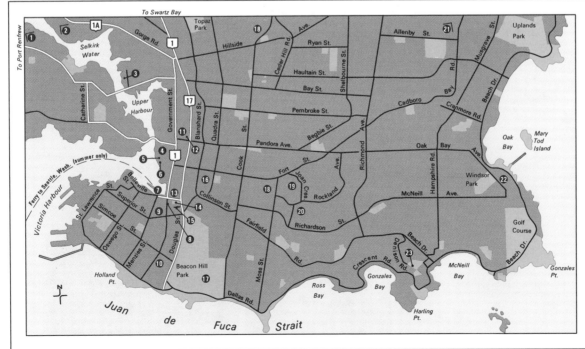

Victoria

1 Craigflower Schoolhouse Museum
2 Craigflower Manor
3 Point Ellice House Museum
4 Bastion Square
5 Maritime Museum of British Columbia
6 Tourist Information
7 Pacific Undersea Gardens
8 Royal British Columbia Museum
9 Parliament Buildings
10 Emily Carr House
11 Centennial Square
12 McPherson Playhouse
13 Empress Hotel
14 Thunderbird Park
15 Helmcken House
16 Christ Church Cathedral
17 Beacon Hill Park
18 Art Gallery of Greater Victoria
19 Craigdarroch Castle
20 Government House
21 University of Victoria
22 Sealand of the Pacific

The Parliament Buildings (above) were built of local stone and slate in 1898. A weathered, 19th-century totem (right) is preserved in Thunderbird Park.

celain figures and intricate jade carvings.

Bastion Square (4)
The restored 19th-century buildings adjacent to Bastion Square (the site where Fort Victoria was established in 1843) include the city's first jail and the first Provincial Court House, now the Maritime Museum of British Columbia (5).

Beacon Hill Park (17)
Expansive lawns, rose gardens, a cricket field and an outdoor theater grace Beacon Hill Park, which was given to Victoria by the Hudson's Bay Company in 1882. Here are a Chinese bell cast in 1627, a 38-metre totem pole and a plaque marking Kilometre Zero of the Trans-Canada Highway.

Centennial Square (11)
Surrounding the square are the renovated Old City Hall (1878), the McPherson Playhouse (1912), and an attractive shopping arcade.

Craigdarroch Castle (19)
Robert Dunsmuir, "coal king of Vancouver Island," built this stately pile of stone and

stained glass for his wife. It was completed after his death in 1889.

Craigflower Manor (2)
This estate was originally a farm established in 1853 by HBC bailiff Kenneth McKenzie. Now a museum, the restored manor displays 19th-century furniture and artifacts.

Craigflower School (1)
Western Canada's oldest standing schoolhouse (1855) is now a pioneer museum.

Empress Hotel (13)
With its vine-covered walls and formal gardens, this impressive hotel on Victoria's harborfront was built by the CPR in 1908.

Long Victoria's social center, the Empress has been restored to its original opulence.

Helmcken House (15)
Built in 1852 by Dr. J. S. Helmcken, who helped to negotiate British Columbia's entry into Confederation in 1871, this pioneer residence is now a provincial museum.

Maritime Museum of British Columbia (5)
Displays tracing Victoria's maritime history include ship models, figureheads, ships' tools, bells, naval uniforms and a cat-o'-nine-tails. The 11-metre *Tilikum* (1860), a dugout canoe modified to a three-masted schooner, sailed from Victoria to England in 1901-04.

Pacific Undersea Gardens (7)
A giant octopus, sharks, sea cucumbers and other sea life are viewed through windows below the surface of the inner harbor.

Parliament Buildings (9)
These imposing buildings house the British Columbia Legislative Assembly. Crowning the copper-covered dome of the main edifice (1898) is a statue of Capt. George Vancouver.

Across the street from the Parliament Buildings are the Royal British Columbia Museum (8) and the 62-bell Netherlands

Visitors can explore the late-19th-century interiors of imposing Craigdarroch Castle.

Centennial Carillon, a gift from Canadians of Dutch origin. The museum contains a collection of Emily Carr paintings, wildlife dioramas, and a replica of Captain Cook's HMS *Discovery*.

Point Ellice House Museum (3)
Victorian furnishings are displayed in this pioneer residence (1861), once owned by Peter O'Reilly, one of the founders of British Columbia, and his descendants.

Sealand of the Pacific (22)
A glassed-in observation gallery provides underwater views of seals, sea lions, eels, sea plumes and killer whales.

Thunderbird Park (14)
A collection of totem poles, most carved between 1850 and 1890, represents the styles of several Pacific coast tribes. The park has cedar dugout canoes and a replica of 19th-century Kwakiutl house. Visitors can watch woodcarvers working on totem poles that have been commissioned by international collectors.

Klee Wyck —Victoria's 'Crazy Old Millie Carr'

To the Indians of Vancouver Island she was *Klee Wyck*—the Laughing One. To the stolid citizens of her native Victoria she was "Crazy Old Millie Carr"—an eccentric painter who wheeled her pet monkey around in a baby carriage.

Influenced by the Impressionists and Canada's Group of Seven, Emily Carr evolved a bold style that captured the haunting mystery of deserted Indian villages and the wild grandeur of British Columbia's coast. Her paintings are characterized by sculptural forests and skies bursting with light and energy.

Despite early criticism of her work, Emily Carr produced about 1,000 major paintings and drawings before her death in 1945. Her book *Klee Wyck* won the 1941 Governor-General's Award for literature. Her painting *Big Raven* (*left*) adorns a stamp commemorating the centennial of her birth (1971). The restored Emily Carr House (10) is now a museum and art gallery.

Coach Roads and Hedges, and the Skylarks of England

Vancouver Island

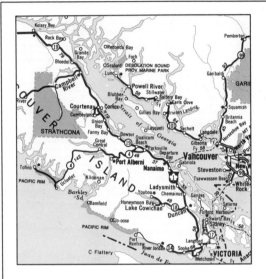

Low tide at Patricia Bay

PATRICIA BAY

The sandy sweep of Patricia Bay abounds in marine life. Each receding tide reveals goose barnacles clinging to drifting logs, shrimps digging in the sand, and a teeming multitude of other creatures—swimmers, drifters, crawlers and burrowers. Beachcombing enthusiasts watch for telltale squirts of water in the sand, then dig down on the seaward side to harvest littleneck and butter clams. Great numbers of shorebirds congregate on the beach and headlands in winter.

Secluded Islands in the Strait of Georgia

Gulf Islands car ferry

The tranquil Gulf Islands, lying north of the Saanich Peninsula in the Strait of Georgia, can be reached by car ferry from Swartz Bay. They consist of 15 relatively large islands and several dozen smaller ones, some of which are islets scarcely above water at high tide. Their rugged coastlines are molded by wind and sea; their hollows and caves are created by undercutting waters.

Saltspring Island was settled in the 1850s by California blacks—many of them former slaves—who built successful farming and lumbering operations. Later, lured by the Fraser River gold rush, other settlers arrived in the area. Many remained to establish fruit farms. Today there is no commercial fruit production, but the old fruit trees still stand.

Saltspring lamb, raised on the island's salty marshes and served as a traditional English roast with mint sauce, is a local delicacy. On sand and gravel beaches visitors can find butter and horse clams, rock and Dungeness crabs, and oysters.

BUTCHART GARDENS

In a vast bowl amphitheater of solid rock—a former quarry—thousands of flowering plants, trees and shrubs create a wonderland of color. Footpaths lead across emerald lawns past towering arborvitae trees to a lake banked with marigolds. From the far rim of the bowl, hung with ivy, a waterfall cascades into a fountained pool. The gardens, with several distinctive sections, are planned to bloom year round. The Italian topiary garden has trees and shrubs trimmed in ornamental shapes, Florentine arches and statuary, and a star-shaped lily pond flanked by beds of seasonal flowers. In the Japanese garden are bonsai (dwarf trees), rhododendrons, a secluded waterfall, lacquered bridges and lantern-lit summerhouses on stilts. Arched walkways wind through the English rose garden. The road to the gardens has been planted with more than 500 Japanese cherry trees. At night, the soft glow of hidden lamps illuminates the paths and gardens. Entertainment is offered daily from mid-May through September. Stage shows and fireworks displays are presented in July and August.

Butchart Gardens

0 5 1 1.5 2 2.5 Miles

0 1 2 3 4 Kilometres

Vancouver Island's Saanich Peninsula is a gentle place. Nothing dramatic, no great mountains or wild rivers, just the quiet pleasures of country life. There are beaches for clam digging and bird-watching, countless little meandering lanes, weathered churches and welcoming inns, fresh produce and old-fashioned hospitality.

Many of the peninsula's roads trace old stagecoach routes, now paved but still for the most part narrow, sinuous and hemmed in by thick hedges. Roadside gardens are bright with fragrant English violets, and here and there are gabled Tudor cottages. Beyond the old cemetery of Holy Trinity Church (1885), in the fields around Victoria Airport, short-eared owls and English skylarks soar. Though the skylark, buffy brown and little bigger than a sparrow, is difficult to see, its tireless torrent of melody is unmistakable.

Butchart Gardens, at the end of a winding road lined with flowering cherry trees, is a onetime limestone quarry transformed into a fabulous huge flower bowl. High on a rocky bluff nearby, the dome of the Dominion Astrophysical Observatory looms above gnarled Garry oaks like something from science fiction.

Scattered in the Strait of Georgia off the northern tip of the Saanich Peninsula is the archipelago of the Gulf Islands. Accessible by sea and air, they have a slow-paced existence of field, forest and seascape, happily oblivious to the world outside.

SIDNEY
Saanich Peninsula history is highlighted in the Sidney Historical Society Museum, housed in a former customs building (1912). Displays include an early edition of Capt. George Vancouver's *Journals* (1801), farm tools, Indian artifacts and a dugout cedar canoe. On Tuesdays, Thursdays and Saturdays, visitors can watch local craftspeople carve, quilt, spin and weave.
□ Sidney Spit Marine Provincial Park, on Sidney Island, is five kilometres by ship from town. There are several campsites and picnic areas.

Christmas holly

Garry oak

SAANICHTON
Western Canada's oldest agricultural fair has been held here each September since 1871. On the fairground are two museums of local history. The Pioneer Museum, in a log building (1932), displays pioneer artifacts from the Saanich Peninsula. The Centennial Museum has a collection of early farm machinery.

DOMINION ASTROPHYSICAL OBSERVATORY
Maintained by the National Research Council, the observatory is equipped with a 182-centimetre reflecting telescope, in operation since 1918. On display is the original mirror, used until 1974— a two-tonne piece of ordinary glass polished to within a tolerance of .000001 centimetre. On Saturday evenings visitors can watch the observatory in action as the dome roof slides back and the giant telescope swings around to focus on a particular star.

A quiet road on the Saanich Peninsula

Erythroniums

Skylarks and Holly, Only in the Saanich

The song of the skylark is heard in the Saanich Peninsula—the only place in North America where these birds are found. Homesick English settlers brought more than 100 pairs of skylarks to the peninsula in the early 1900s. The field-dwelling birds thrived throughout the farming country of the peninsula, whose mild climate is similar to that of England.

The name Saanich comes from an Indian word meaning "fertile soil." Japanese cherry trees and plum trees blossom here in February and daffodils—13 million a year are shipped from Saanichton alone—bloom in April. Loganberries are the major crop on the peninsula's many berry farms. The area also supports an industry unique in Canada—the growing of Christmas holly.

Wildflowers such as erythroniums and the rarer trillium grow along roadsides and among groves of elm, cedar, arbutus and fir.

English skylark

CORDOVA CHANNEL

17

20

6

ELK BEAVER LAKE PK

Elk Lake

CORDOVA BAY

DOMINION ASTROPHYSICAL OBSERVATORY

ospect
ke

14

Beaver Lake

3.5

Prospect Lake

Royal Oak

5

SAANICH

17

Lake Hill

CADBORO BAY

CATTLE PT

1

Trans-Canada Highway

1

VICTORIA
(see Road Unit 2)

Esquimalt

Oak Bay

PLUMPER

PASSAGE

In Dairy and Logging Country, the Famous Cowichan Sweaters

Vancouver Island

This part of Vancouver Island is known for its hand-knit sweaters, fine dairy herds and scenic logging roads.

Sweaters from Cowichan River valley sheep are renowned for their durability and distinctive patterns. Designs are derived from those on cedar bark and wild goat wool blankets once worn by Coast Salish Indians. Cowichan sweaters are made from undyed wool heavy with lanolin, a grease which makes them rain-resistant.

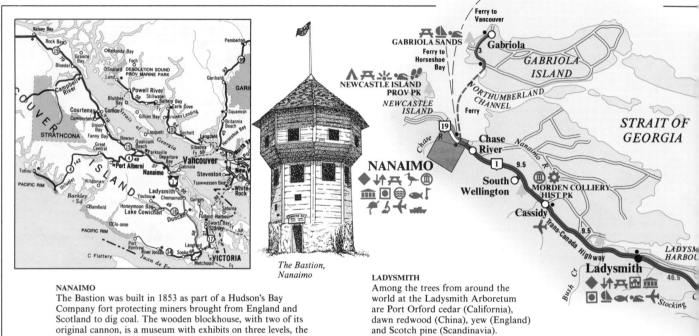

The Bastion, Nanaimo

NANAIMO
The Bastion was built in 1853 as part of a Hudson's Bay Company fort protecting miners brought from England and Scotland to dig coal. The wooden blockhouse, with two of its original cannon, is a museum with exhibits on three levels, the last reached by a ship's ladder.
□ The Nanaimo Centennial Museum in Piper Park has a replica of a coal mine, showing equipment and methods used from 1853 to 1968; a diorama depicting the life of the Coastal Salish Indians before European settlement; a Kwakiutl mask exhibit; and relics from the city's HBC period (1852-62).
□ Prehistoric rock carvings in Petroglyph Provincial Park represent humans, birds, wolves, lizards and sea monsters.
□ Nanaimo claims the title of "Bathtub Capital of the World." Powered bathtubs and other outlandish craft are navigated across the Strait of Georgia from Nanaimo to Vancouver in the Great International Bathtub Race each July.

LADYSMITH
Among the trees from around the world at the Ladysmith Arboretum are Port Orford cedar (California), dawn redwood (China), yew (England) and Scotch pine (Scandinavia).

DUNCAN
At the British Columbia Forest Museum, between May and September, a steam engine rumbles along 2.5 kilometres of narrow-gauge track through 16 hectares of forest, over a 92-metre trestle, and past donkey engines, a sawmill, a waterwheel and a cedar log three metres in diameter. Other exhibits at the museum include Little Jakey, a steam log-hauler (c. 1890), hand-pump cars, two gasoline-powered locomotives, and a slice from the base of a Douglas fir which dates from about A.D. 640. Along Forester's Walk are 25 species of trees, including 300-year-old Douglas firs 55 metres high.
□ Whippletree Junction, a recreated turn-of-the-century town, has a livery stable, a fire hall, a general store, a barber shop, a blacksmith-gunsmith shop and an ice-cream parlor.

LAKE COWICHAN
This community is at the eastern end of Cowichan Lake, a year-round source of giant cutthroat and rainbow trout. Roads girdling the 45-kilometre-long lake take visitors deep into fragrant mossy forests. The densest stands of fir on Vancouver Island are in Gordon Bay Provincial Park, west of Honeymoon Bay—a sawmill settlement named for a settler who left to bring a bride from England. He never returned, but the name stuck.

Great International Bathtub Race, Nanaimo to Vancouver

```
0   1   2   3   4   5 Miles
0     2     4     6   8 Kilometres
```

In the gentle climate of the Cowichan Valley (*Cowichan* is an Indian word meaning warmed by the sun), the small farms the pioneers wrested from the forests yielded abundant forage. It was ideal for raising cattle, so dairying thrived. Today the Holstein herds in the Cowichan Valley produce much of British Columbia's milk.

Dairy exhibits are featured at the annual post-Labor Day Cowichan Exhibition in Duncan. Special events include sheepdog trials and logger sports. For lumbering, too, is an important industry in this area. Logging roads weave through forests where camp and picnic sites have been developed by the lumber industry and the B.C. Forest Service. Because some logging roads are closed during working hours, visitors should check with the Forest Service before setting out to explore these backwoods. Travelers must yield to logging trucks, which travel at high speeds and often in convoys.

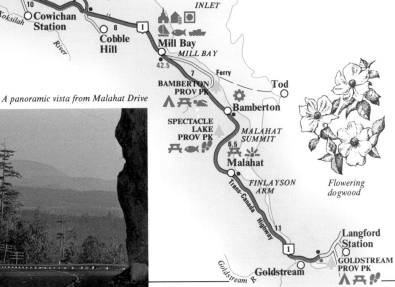

Galiano Galleries, Gabriola Island

GABRIOLA ISLAND
With one of the best climates in North America, Gabriola Island is green in winter, a garden of wildflowers in spring. This 50-square-kilometre haven, a short ferry ride from Nanaimo, is a fine place for beachcombing, clam digging and oyster gathering. The island is also known for its rock formations. Most famous are the 90-metre-long, 4-metre-high Galiano Galleries, which wind and waves have carved in sandstone at Malaspina Point in Gabriola Sands Provincial Park.
□ South of the galleries are stalactites which hang from a 30-metre-high cliff.

CHEMAINUS
Visitors can admire the 21 larger-than-life murals that have been painted by professional artists on the walls of buildings in this picturesque town. The murals depict different aspects of Chemainus's history—the life of local native peoples, the arrival of settlers in the early 1800s, and the heyday of the logging industry.

The "Butter Church," Cowichan Bay

COWICHAN BAY
A missionary priest, the Rev. Peter Rondeault, kept cows and sold butter, using the proceeds to build the "Butter Church" in 1870. Sandstone for the structure was quarried from nearby Comiaken Hill. The church, on a Cowichan Indian reserve, was restored in 1958.
□ Cowichan Bay is a favorite with coho salmon anglers.
□ Deep-sea ships load lumber at the harbor, which has five marinas.

MILL BAY
This community at the north end of the Malahat Drive, the coast road built in 1911, is said to enjoy the most temperate climate in Canada. There are ocean and lake fishing, hunting, boating, a golf course, tennis clubs, marinas, and a ferry service to Brentwood Bay, southwest on the Saanich Peninsula.

GOLDSTREAM PROVINCIAL PARK
Gold was discovered here in 1855 and old mining shafts and tunnels are still to be seen. Throughout the park are Douglas firs, some almost 600 years old. Arbutus, Canada's only broad-leafed evergreen, grows alongside flowering dogwood on the three-kilometre Arbutus Ridge Trail. Oregon grape, red huckleberry, salmonberry and thimbleberry are abundant. A variety of wildflowers includes trilliums, calypso bulbosa orchids and twinflowers.
□ Thousands of chum and coho salmon head up the shallow Goldstream River each November, bound for spawning grounds.

Flowering dogwood

A panoramic vista from Malahat Drive

STUART CHANNEL

emainus

1

emainus

○ Westholme

Stratfords Crossing

11

Somenos Lake

Quamichan Lake

VANCOUVER ISLAND

Maple Bay

COWICHAN BAY

MOUNT REVOST

4   3

Duncan   Koksilah

Cowichan Bay

10   5

Koksilah

illcrest

Cowichan Station

ahtlam

18

8   Cobble Hill

River

SAANICH

INLET

1

Mill Bay

MILL BAY

42.5

BAMBERTON PROV PK

7   Ferry

Tod

Bamberton

SPECTACLE LAKE PROV PK

MALAHAT SUMMIT

6.5

Malahat

FINLAYSON ARM

Trans-Canada Highway

11

Langford Station

1

GOLDSTREAM PROV PK

Goldstream R

Goldstream

Fine Fishing and Towering Firs in the Shadow of Mount Arrowsmith

Vancouver Island

Reaching halfway into Vancouver Island, Alberni Inlet is one of the major waterways of Canada's west coast. From this channel the island's forest products are shipped to countries around the rim of the Pacific. The inlet is also a fertile fishing ground where salmon are intercepted as they head for spawning rivers.

At the end of the inlet is Port Alberni, a community of about 20,000. The highway between here and Parksville lies in the shadow of Mount Arrowsmith and climbs

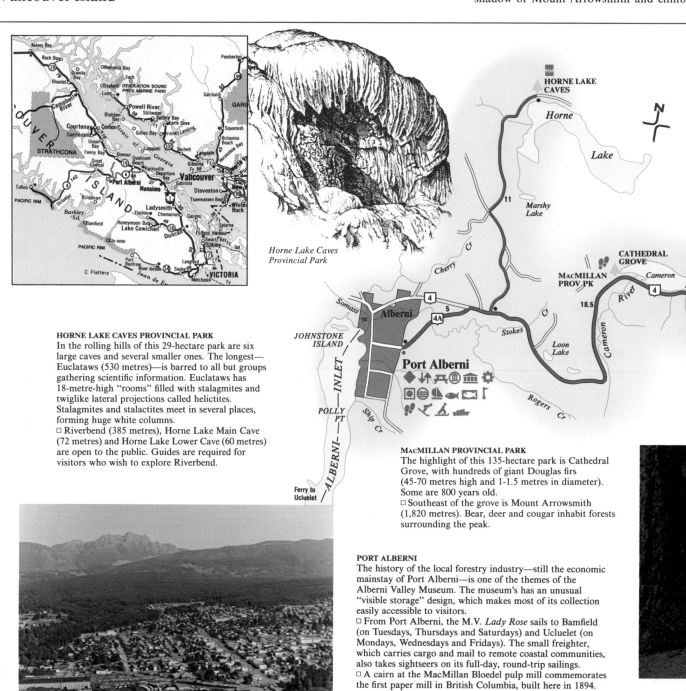

Horne Lake Caves
Provincial Park

HORNE LAKE CAVES PROVINCIAL PARK
In the rolling hills of this 29-hectare park are six large caves and several smaller ones. The longest—Euclataws (530 metres)—is barred to all but groups gathering scientific information. Euclataws has 18-metre-high "rooms" filled with stalagmites and twiglike lateral projections called helictites. Stalagmites and stalactites meet in several places, forming huge white columns.
□ Riverbend (385 metres), Horne Lake Main Cave (72 metres) and Horne Lake Lower Cave (60 metres) are open to the public. Guides are required for visitors who wish to explore Riverbend.

MacMILLAN PROVINCIAL PARK
The highlight of this 135-hectare park is Cathedral Grove, with hundreds of giant Douglas firs (45-70 metres high and 1-1.5 metres in diameter). Some are 800 years old.
□ Southeast of the grove is Mount Arrowsmith (1,820 metres). Bear, deer and cougar inhabit forests surrounding the peak.

PORT ALBERNI
The history of the local forestry industry—still the economic mainstay of Port Alberni—is one of the themes of the Alberni Valley Museum. The museum's has an unusual "visible storage" design, which makes most of its collection easily accessible to visitors.
□ From Port Alberni, the M.V. *Lady Rose* sails to Bamfield (on Tuesdays, Thursdays and Saturdays) and Ucluelet (on Mondays, Wednesdays and Fridays). The small freighter, which carries cargo and mail to remote coastal communities, also takes sightseers on its full-day, round-trip sailings.
□ A cairn at the MacMillan Bloedel pulp mill commemorates the first paper mill in British Columbia, built here in 1894. The monument incorporates grinding stones, all that remains of the mill.
□ A fish hatchery, about 20 kilometres northwest of Port Alberni, has facilities for incubating 3 million eggs of Chinook and coho salmon. Visitors can explore the hatchery. There is also sports fishing, except in March and April.

Port Alberni

0   1   2   3   4   5 Miles

0   2   4   6   8 Kilometres

Little Qualicum Falls

LITTLE QUALICUM FALLS PROVINCIAL PARK
Picturesque Little Qualicum Falls, plunging
[?] metres down three giant steps, is at the end of a
[?]5-kilometre trail that starts at the park entrance.
[T]he park covers four square kilometres and has 91
[ca]mpsites and scores of picnic tables. There are
[se]veral places for swimming, and the river area just
[ab]ove and below the park provides good trout fishing.
[S]cenic trails lead to nearby Mount Arrowsmith.

through Vancouver Island's highest road
pass (370 metres). Much of the forested terrain along this route was scarred by a fire
in 1967; the effects are still visible.

At Cathedral Grove in MacMillan Provincial Park are towering stands of Douglas
fir, trees that were seedlings when Cabot
sailed to North America in 1497. Nearby
forests have abundant wildlife, including
deer, bear, wolf and cougar. (Vancouver
Island's concentration of cougar is believed
the greatest in North America.)

Parksville is a popular vacation headquarters for visitors to this region. Situated on a
beautiful bay on the east coast of Vancouver
Island, the town is noted for its fine beaches,
excellent fishing and lovely parks. Local
annual events include Country Bluegrass
Festivals at Coombs (May and August), a
sand-castle competition
(July), and a salmon derby
and barbecue (August).

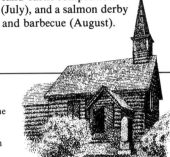
St. Ann's Church, French Creek

PARKSVILLE
A 1.5-kilometre beach on the Strait of Georgia, good
salmon and trout fishing, and two nearby parks—on the
Englishman River and the Little Qualicum River—
make Parksville a popular resort.
□ Craig Heritage Park, on Highway 19, displays Indian
and Inuit artifacts, firearms, early photographs and
music boxes.
□ At nearby French Creek is St. Ann's Church, one of
the oldest churches on Vancouver Island. The stone
church was built in 1894; its rectory dates from 1912.

RATHTREVOR BEACH PROVINCIAL PARK
A 1.5-kilometre beach skirts the park's
eastern edge. At low tide almost 200
hectares of flats are exposed. Among
42 species of birds found here is the
black brant, an endangered member of the
Canada goose family. This park covers 350
hectares—mostly flatland—and has several
nature trails.

Black brant

Mount Arrowsmith

Cathedral Grove, MacMillan Provincial Park

ENGLISHMAN RIVER FALLS PROVINCIAL PARK
This 100-hectare park, one of the most popular on
Vancouver Island, has 100 individual campsites and
37 picnic sites. The Englishman River descends from
snowfields high in the Beaufort Range and carries with
it Kamloops, steelhead, cutthroat and rainbow trout.
A wooden footbridge offers visitors a dramatic view
of 40-metre Englishman River Falls.

A Grove of Giant Trees

The world's biggest trees grow in the ancient rain forests
of the Pacific coast. As in every forest, these trees compete to reach sunlight essential for growth. But in the
rain forest, abundant water and a long growing season—
and the long life of Pacific coast conifers—enable trees to
soar to heights impossible in other forests.

In most parts of the world trees are tall at 30 metres. In
mature Pacific rain forests they average 60 metres, and
giants grow to more than 90 metres.
□ Logging has destroyed most rain forests, but the best
and most accessible in British Columbia is Cathedral
Grove in MacMillan Provincial Park. Here, huge Douglas firs, with some red cedars and Sitka spruces, grow in
dense stands on thick, wet moss cushions. Ferns, mosses
and lichens often grow high up the trees, whose upper
branches sometimes interlock. In the dense undergrowth
grow only shade-tolerant western hemlocks, which will
replace the firs centuries from now.

Western red cedar   *Sitka spruce*   *Western hemlock*

Whales and Sea Lions Off a Surf-Swept Shoreline

Vancouver Island

Pacific Rim National Park clings to Vancouver Island's rugged west coast where surf-swept beaches, rocky headlands and craggy islands are bathed by the Pacific—and battered by its fury.

The sea provides for every visitor: surfers ride waves off Long Beach, fishermen cast for lingcod in the sea pounding, clam diggers probe white sands for geoduck and razor clams, beachcombers search for the ocean's exotic castoffs.

Pacific Rim's Broken Group Islands—

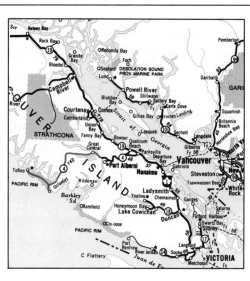

Tufted puffin

TOFINO
A salmon, herring and shrimp fleet docks at this harbor, which was named after Spanish admiral Vincente Tofino in 1792. The town is also a mining and logging center.
□ Eight kilometres north are the remains of Fort Defiance, established in 1791 by Capt. Robert Gray. Later Gray discovered the Columbia River and named it after his ship.
□ The Whale Center displays marine-life and whaling exhibits.
□ The West Coast Maritime Museum at Tofino displays cannonballs, harpoons and the remains of sunken ships.
□ An annual whale festival, held from mid-March to mid-April, celebrates the migration of the gray whale.

CLELAND ISLAND
Tufted puffins nest in rocky hollows on this treeless island. The puffin uses short wings and webbed feet to "fly" under water. It can carry as many as 10 fish in its red, blue and yellow beak. Rhinoceros auklets and more than 10,000 storm petrels are also found here.

LONG BEACH
This 11-kilometre crescent of hard-packed, nearly white sand in Pacific Rim National Park is often shrouded in fog. As the mists lift, strollers and clam diggers explore the steaming sands. Beachcombers browse for refuse cast up by the sea—weirdly twisted driftwood, colorful shells and glass fishing floats that winds and currents have pushed all the way from Japan.
□ On the vast tidal mud flats of Grice Bay eelgrass and algae provide food for migrating black brants, pintails and mallards. An estimated 10,000 Canada geese stop here during October and November.
□ Long Beach is backed by stands of Sitka spruce, which thrive in summer fog and winter salt spray, and by salal, salmonberry and black twinberry. Ryegrass grows on wind-whipped sand dunes.
□ Wickaninnish Centre (located on Wickaninnish Beach section of Long Beach) offers exhibits and films about the Pacific Ocean.

Pacific gray whale

Long Beach, Pacific Rim National Park

PACIFIC RIM NATIONAL PARK
The park extends 105 kilometres along the west coast of Vancouver Island and comprises three distinct sections—Long Beach, the Broken Group Islands and the West Coast Trail.
□ Tidal mud flats at Long Beach attract thousands of migrating waterfowl. The dense rain forests are backed by the 1,200-metre-high Mackenzie Range. A boat tour from Long Beach takes visitors to offshore rocks where Steller's sea lions often bask in the sun. At Radar Hill, near Highway 4 at the north end of Long Beach, there is a splendid view of Vancouver Island.
□ The Broken Group Islands—more than 100 islands in Barkley Sound—offer fine fishing for coho and Chinook salmon.
□ The West Coast Trail is a coastal wilderness area between Bamfield and Port Renfrew. The 77-kilometre trail skirts the Pacific shore, winding through stands of Sitka spruce and lush stream-eroded ravines. Only experienced hikers should consider attempting this rugged trail.

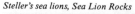

Steller's sea lions, Sea Lion Rocks

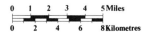

0   1   2   3   4   5 Miles

0   2   4   6   8 Kilometres

known as the "graveyard of the Pacific"—have claimed 50 vessels in the last 100 years. Scuba divers explore barnacle-encrusted wrecks.

West Coast Trail in the park once helped shipwrecked sailors reach safety. Other paths lead to sea caves, weathered rock arches, water-blasted blowholes, and tidal pools inhabited by barnacles, mussels, limpets and hermit crabs.

At Tofino and Ucluelet, bustling ports adjacent to the park, restaurants serve fresh- and saltwater fish, crabs, oysters and shrimps.

Sproat Lake and its tributary, the Taylor River, teem with trout and salmon during the spawning season. Giant Douglas fir and western red cedar flourish in dense stands on the blue-tinted Mackenzie Range.

Fishing boats, Tofino

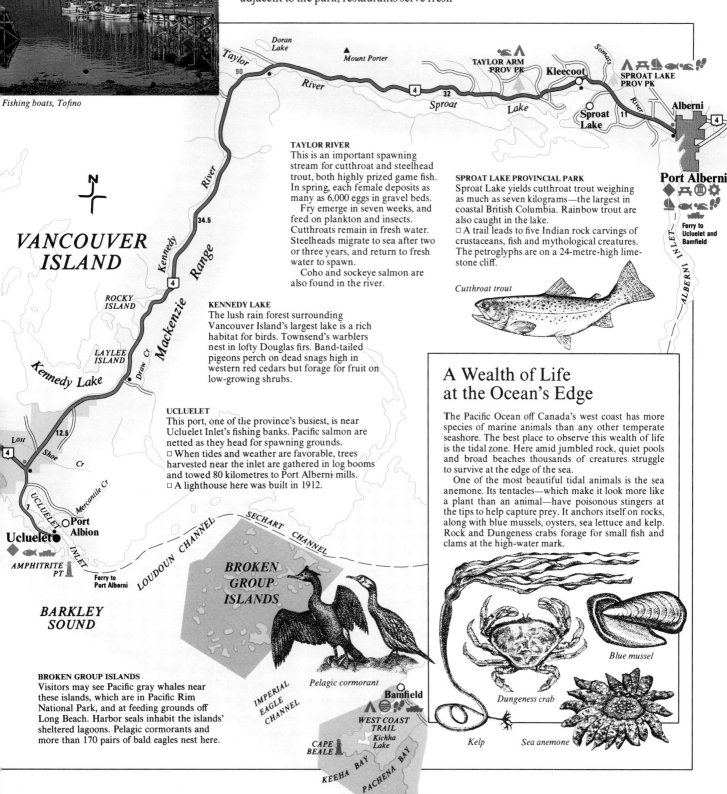

VANCOUVER ISLAND

TAYLOR RIVER
This is an important spawning stream for cutthroat and steelhead trout, both highly prized game fish. In spring, each female deposits as many as 6,000 eggs in gravel beds.
Fry emerge in seven weeks, and feed on plankton and insects. Cutthroats remain in fresh water. Steelheads migrate to sea after two or three years, and return to fresh water to spawn.
Coho and sockeye salmon are also found in the river.

KENNEDY LAKE
The lush rain forest surrounding Vancouver Island's largest lake is a rich habitat for birds. Townsend's warblers nest in lofty Douglas firs. Band-tailed pigeons perch on dead snags high in western red cedars but forage for fruit on low-growing shrubs.

UCLUELET
This port, one of the province's busiest, is near Ucluelet Inlet's fishing banks. Pacific salmon are netted as they head for spawning grounds.
□ When tides and weather are favorable, trees harvested near the inlet are gathered in log booms and towed 80 kilometres to Port Alberni mills.
□ A lighthouse here was built in 1912.

SPROAT LAKE PROVINCIAL PARK
Sproat Lake yields cutthroat trout weighing as much as seven kilograms—the largest in coastal British Columbia. Rainbow trout are also caught in the lake.
□ A trail leads to five Indian rock carvings of crustaceans, fish and mythological creatures. The petroglyphs are on a 24-metre-high limestone cliff.

Cutthroat trout

A Wealth of Life at the Ocean's Edge

The Pacific Ocean off Canada's west coast has more species of marine animals than any other temperate seashore. The best place to observe this wealth of life is the tidal zone. Here amid jumbled rock, quiet pools and broad beaches thousands of creatures struggle to survive at the edge of the sea.

One of the most beautiful tidal animals is the sea anemone. Its tentacles—which make it look more like a plant than an animal—have poisonous stingers at the tips to help capture prey. It anchors itself on rocks, along with blue mussels, oysters, sea lettuce and kelp. Rock and Dungeness crabs forage for small fish and clams at the high-water mark.

Pelagic cormorant

Dungeness crab

Blue mussel

Kelp

Sea anemone

BROKEN GROUP ISLANDS
Visitors may see Pacific gray whales near these islands, which are in Pacific Rim National Park, and at feeding grounds off Long Beach. Harbor seals inhabit the islands' sheltered lagoons. Pelagic cormorants and more than 170 pairs of bald eagles nest here.

Rich Farmland, Fighting Salmon and Indian Rock Carvings

Vancouver Island

Until the 1890s, only a trail led northward from the Comox Valley. Although a rough wagon road was built by 1904, the first paved road north to Kelsey Bay was built during the Second World War.

Today, Highway 19 leads from the flourishing farmland of the Comox Valley, where fresh fruits, vegetables and honey can be bought at roadside stands, to Campbell River and the forestry community of Kelsey Bay. Courtenay, on Vancouver Island's east coast, is at the southeast corner

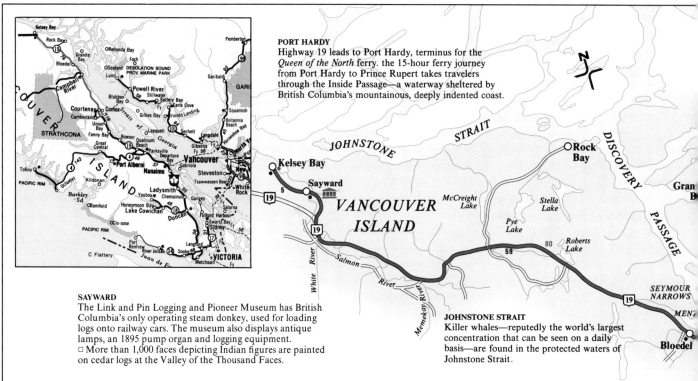

PORT HARDY
Highway 19 leads to Port Hardy, terminus for the *Queen of the North* ferry. the 15-hour ferry journey from Port Hardy to Prince Rupert takes travelers through the Inside Passage—a waterway sheltered by British Columbia's mountainous, deeply indented coast.

JOHNSTONE STRAIT
Killer whales—reputedly the world's largest concentration that can be seen on a daily basis—are found in the protected waters of Johnstone Strait.

SAYWARD
The Link and Pin Logging and Pioneer Museum has British Columbia's only operating steam donkey, used for loading logs onto railway cars. The museum also displays antique lamps, an 1895 pump organ and logging equipment.
□ More than 1,000 faces depicting Indian figures are painted on cedar logs at the Valley of the Thousand Faces.

Colorful Castoffs of the Pacific Coast

Purple shore crab

Red rock crab

Hairy horse crab

Pacific beaches are littered with colorful shells of crabs that thrive by the shore. A crab shell splits when it gets too tight—sometimes twice or three times a year. The animal climbs out with a soft, new shell. The crab fills its body with water until the shell expands to a comfortable size, then hardens. The kelp crab, which frequents beds of eel grass, covers its shell with a camouflage of seaweed and barnacles. It transfers its disguise to a new shell with each moult. Hermit crabs, with soft, shell-less abdomens, live in empty snail shells, and move into bigger homes as they grow. Pea crabs live inside the mantle cavity of horse clams, existing on some of the clam's food.

The two best-known species are purple and green shore crabs, which are found under rocks on most beaches. Red rock crabs, which live on gravel beaches, are brick red with black pincers. The edible crab, which usually burrows in sand, is larger than the red rock crab, and uniformly colored from light buff to reddish brown. The hairy horse crab has a yellow-orange shell and is covered with stiff, rusty-brown hairs.

CAMPBELL RIVER
This "salmon-fishing capital of the world," famous for its fighting Chinook salmon, is headquarters of the Tyee Club. Membership is awarded to fishermen who land trophy-sized Chinooks (more than 14 kilograms), called tyee.
□ A July salmon festival includes a parade, fishing derby, and war canoe races.
□ The town is a lumber and commercial fishing center. There are guided tours of a pulp and paper mill five kilometres north at Duncan Bay.
□ A five-metre-tall totem pole with bear designs stands outside Campbell River Centennial Museum. In the rotunda is a huge thunderbird. The museum's Indian artifacts are principally from the Kwakiutl and Nootka tribes, a few are Salishan. There are also collections of guns, logging and mining equipment and pioneer household articles.

Campbell River harbor

0   2   4   6   8   10 Miles

0   4   8   12   16 Kilometres

of the valley. The hiking and skiing area of Forbidden Plateau can be reached from a lodge 24 kilometres northwest of the town. A year-round car ferry links nearby Comox with Powell River on the mainland across the Strait of Georgia.

Miracle Beach Provincial Park, on the coast, has abundant marine life and a spectacular view of the Coast Mountains.

Where the Campbell River flows into the narrow, turbulent channel of Discovery Passage is the town of Campbell River, famous for towering trees in surrounding forests and trophy-sized salmon in nearby waters. Visitors can enjoy fishing, camping and hiking here, and cross by ferry to Quadra Island, with its ancient Indian rock carvings.

Highway 19 was extended north of Kelsey Bay in the late 1970s. Today, travelers can explore the scenic northern tip of Vancouver Island and the thriving fishing, lumbering and mining communities of Port McNeill and Port Hardy.

Quadra Island

QUADRA ISLAND

Quadra Island, nearly 24 kilometres long, is the largest island in the Discovery Passage.
□ Accessible by ferry from Campbell River, Quadra has an Indian village and authentic totem poles. Cape Mudge has the most important Indian rock carvings on the Pacific coast. Petroglyphs on 26 boulders include masks and mythological creatures.
□ A lighthouse was built on the cape in 1898 to guide ships through the narrow entrance of Discovery Passage.
□ Rebecca Spit Provincial Park has campsites, picnic sites and boat facilities. Gravel roads at the island's northern end lead to freshwater lakes, the old Finnish settlement site at Granite Bay, and the "Lucky Jim" gold and copper mine, discovered when workmen were laying a logging railway.
□ Visitors can hike, fish and beachcomb, and gather oysters and clams.

SEYMOUR NARROWS

Vertical rock walls, in places more than 60 metres high, line the deep, blue waters of Seymour Narrows. The cliffs on the west side of the narrows are part of Vancouver Island.
□ Until the late 1950s Ripple Rock was the graveyard of ships negotiating the treacherous currents and eddies of the narrows. In 1958 this navigational hazard was eliminated in Canada's biggest controlled explosion.

Glaucous-winged gull

MIRACLE BEACH PROVINCIAL PARK

Porpoises and hair seals can be seen near the mouth of Black Creek. Killer whales are often spotted in the Strait of Georgia. Several types of crabs and seabirds inhabit the shorelines and 195 plant species have been identified. Mammals in the park include black-tailed deer, raccoons and black bears.
□ A nature house has a herbarium and a saltwater aquarium showing the area's tidal pool life.
□ Self-guiding and conducted nature walks skirt the shore and wander through forests of hemlock and Douglas fir.

Indian rock carvings, Cape Mudge, Quadra Island

MITLENATCH ISLAND PROVINCIAL NATURE PARK

Mitlenatch is a Salish Indian word meaning "calm water all around." Harbor seals are common and sea lions are sometimes spotted off this small, craggy island. Colonies of red sea urchins blanket rocky shores, and garter snakes frequent tidal pools to feed on blennies, sculpins and clingfish. Purple and orange sea stars abound in rock crevices. Thousands of seabirds, including black oyster catchers, glaucous-winged gulls and pelagic cormorants, nest on rocky ledges. The prickly pear cactus, the only cactus found on the British Columbia coast, blooms here during hot, dry days in June.

QUADRA ISLAND *(map labels)*

SLAND

Heriot Bay REBECCA SPIT

REBECCA SPIT PROV PK

uncan ay

Campbell River

K FALLS ROV PK) e Road Unit 8)

CAPE MUDGE

19

23

MITLENATCH ISLAND PROV NATURE PK

MITLENATCH ISLAND

OYSTER BAY

STRAIT OF GEORGIA

VANCOUVER ISLAND

Oyster River

MIRACLE BEACH PROV PK

Black Creek

58

11.5

Merville

Tsolum River

12

KITTY COLEMAN BEACH

KIN BEACH

Comox

Ferry to Powell River

COMOX HARBOUR

Royston

5.5

Trent R.

6

19

Cumberland

COURTENAY

The Courtenay and District Historical Society Museum features artifacts from Cumberland's Chinatown, a pioneer kitchen and dairy, and a blacksmith shop and forge. Indian displays include baskets and fish traps. A fossil collection features a 70-million-year-old impression of a fern found in a Cumberland coal mine.
□ "1-Spot," a locomotive brought to Courtenay in 1909 by the Comox Logging and Railway Company, is displayed at a local tourist information center.

CUMBERLAND

Swayback buildings of an almost deserted Chinatown are reminders of Cumberland's days as a booming coal-mining center. During the 1890s, Cumberland's Chinatown was reputedly bigger than San Francisco's. When coal mining ended in 1966, the Chinese community all but disappeared. Cumberland is now a quiet resort village. Old buildings still in use include a hospital (1894) and a post office (1907).

The Pacific Wilderness
That Awed Captain Cook

Vancouver Island

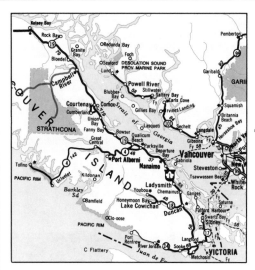

Life-jacketed canoeists and kayakers preparing
to run the Campbell River

Coast
deer

GOLD RIVER

Canada's first all-electric town, Gold River was built in six
months in 1965 to house employees of a pulp mill. It is in
the Gold River valley at the junction of the Gold and
Heber rivers, 14 kilometres from the Tahsis Company mill.
□ *Uchuck III*, a converted Second World War minesweeper, runs 56 kilometres between Gold River and
Zeballos farther north, three times a week, stopping at
coastal settlements with supplies and passengers. One stop
is Friendly Cove, where Capt. James Cook landed in 1778.

An Island Named for Rival Sea Captains

George Vancouver was a 20-year-old mid-
shipman on the 1778 James Cook expedition
when he first saw the island he later named.
   In 1789, after the Spanish seized British
trading vessels and a small battery in Nootka
Sound, Britain threatened war. Spain capitu-
lated, and Vancouver (now a commander)
was sent to secure the territory. In 1792, he
met with Capt. Juan Bodega y Quadra, sent
by Spain to negotiate the transfer. They became friends and the Englishman named
the island "Vancouver's and Quadra's Island." Quadra's name was eventually
dropped and given to a smaller island in the
Strait of Georgia. A stained-glass window
(*left*) commemorating the first meeting between the rival sea captains is in Friendly
Cove Catholic Church.

Hikers in Strathcona
Provincial Park

NOOTKA SOUND

Capt. James Cook, the first European to stand on Canada's
west coast, named his 1778 anchorage King George's Sound,
but later changed it to Nootka, under the mistaken impression
that this was its Indian name. Eleven years later, Spain seized
control of the sound. This act almost led to war between Spain
and England. In 1792 a British naval expedition under the
command of George Vancouver met the Spaniards at Friendly
Cove to take possession of the Nootka Sound territory.

The fog-shrouded landscape of Vancouver Island has changed little since Capt. James Cook anchored off Friendly Cove in 1778. Nowadays, visitors can call on Friendly Cove aboard *Uchuck III*, a converted minesweeper that supplies coastal settlements with everything from logging machinery to livestock.

Strathcona Provincial Park preserves a vast tract of the wilderness admired by Cook. Halfway between Campbell River and Gold River, a road skirts the eastern shore of Buttle Lake and provides access to the 2,240-square-kilometre park. Western red cedar and Douglas fir dominate the valleys, giving way to myriad wildflowers on higher slopes. To the west of Buttle Lake is 2,200-metre Golden Hinde, the highest peak on Vancouver Island. Wolverine, coast deer and the last remaining elk on Vancouver Island inhabit the park. From Great Central Lake, a 16-kilometre trail leads to Della Falls, a 440-metre ribbon of cascading water.

Fishermen marvel at the size and gameness of the Chinook salmon in the Campbell River. Salmon of 36 kilograms and more have been recorded here, and fishing is as much a way of life in this area as it was for the original Indian inhabitants.

Visitors here can comb wide beaches for clams, climb rugged mountain trails, and marvel—as did Captain Cook—at the spectacular scenery of Vancouver Island.

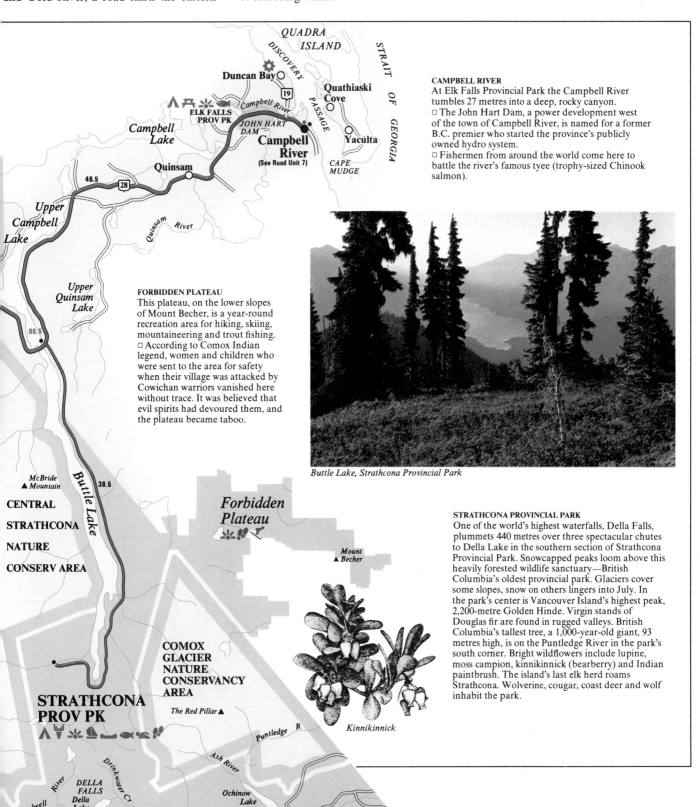

CAMPBELL RIVER
At Elk Falls Provincial Park the Campbell River tumbles 27 metres into a deep, rocky canyon.
□ The John Hart Dam, a power development west of the town of Campbell River, is named for a former B.C. premier who started the province's publicly owned hydro system.
□ Fishermen from around the world come here to battle the river's famous tyee (trophy-sized Chinook salmon).

FORBIDDEN PLATEAU
This plateau, on the lower slopes of Mount Becher, is a year-round recreation area for hiking, skiing, mountaineering and trout fishing.
□ According to Comox Indian legend, women and children who were sent to the area for safety when their village was attacked by Cowichan warriors vanished here without trace. It was believed that evil spirits had devoured them, and the plateau became taboo.

Buttle Lake, Strathcona Provincial Park

STRATHCONA PROVINCIAL PARK
One of the world's highest waterfalls, Della Falls, plummets 440 metres over three spectacular chutes to Della Lake in the southern section of Strathcona Provincial Park. Snowcapped peaks loom above this heavily forested wildlife sanctuary—British Columbia's oldest provincial park. Glaciers cover some slopes, snow on others lingers into July. In the park's center is Vancouver Island's highest peak, 2,200-metre Golden Hinde. Virgin stands of Douglas fir are found in rugged valleys. British Columbia's tallest tree, a 1,000-year-old giant, 93 metres high, is on the Puntledge River in the park's south corner. Bright wildflowers include lupine, moss campion, kinnikinnick (bearberry) and Indian paintbrush. The island's last elk herd roams Strathcona. Wolverine, cougar, coast deer and wolf inhabit the park.

Kinnikinnick

A Place in the Sun on a Mountainous Coast

Sunshine Coast

Highway 101 between Langdale and Lund follows British Columbia's Sunshine Coast, which promises visitors more sunny days than any other coastal area in the province. (Its annual precipitation is about 900 millimetres—some 170 less than rainy Vancouver.) Although this region is on the mainland, it has no road link with the rest of the province. Access is by ferry—across Howe Sound between Horseshoe Bay and Langdale, and across the Strait of Georgia between Comox on Vancouver Island and

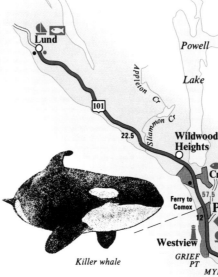

Killer whale

POWELL RIVER
The MacMillan Bloedel pulp and paper plant is one of the world's largest and produces mainly newsprint. A breakwater of ten ships, anchored place and chained together, creates a storage po for logs. There are plant tours from mid-May to the end of August.
□ Powell River is one of the main diving centers British Columbia. Experts and beginners explore the depths of the coastal waters for gorgonian corals, lingcod, wolf eels and octopuses.
□ At Cranberry Wildlife Sanctuary visitors can watch migratory birds common to this region.
□ A two-kilometre trail through stands of Dougl fir and hemlock leads to a 160,000-hectare tree farm and demonstration forest.

Carved Masks, Lavish Ceremonies

More than any other native Canadians, the Indians of Canada's west coast were blessed with natural wealth: salmon from the sea; game, roots and berries from the forests, and cedar wood for frame houses and dugout canoes. Among the native peoples who still live along this coast are the Haida (on the Queen Charlotte Islands), the Gitksan (in the Skeena River valley), and the Coast Salish (along the Strait of Georgia). Freed from the pressing needs of survival in the past,

these Indians developed rich, regional cultures. They expressed their art in totem poles, carved masks, and brightly colored weavings. Wealth determined social status. At a lavish potlatch ceremony a host would destroy his possessions and shower guests with gifts. Modern versions of this ceremony (*below*) are still part of the west coast Indian life. There has also been a renewal of traditional arts and skills among the Coast Salish Indians at Sechelt.

LUND
The small fishing village of Lund, the last stop on the Sunshine Coast, is roughly 150 kilometres north of Vancouver. It is also the northern terminus of Highway 101, one of the longest stretches of road on the North American continent. This famous highway, which begins at Mexico City, closely parallels the Pacific coast from San Ysidro, Calif., to Lund.
□ The Lund Hotel was built in 1905 by the community's first settlers, Frederick and Charles Thulin, who arrived in December 1899 and named the site after their birthplace in Sweden. In the early days, Lund was so inaccessible that the Thulin brothers had to use a rowboat to reach Vancouver.
□ North of Lund is Desolation Sound Provincial Park, which is rich in birds, marine life and shellfish. This marine park attracts sailors who enjoy exploring its sheltered channels and mountainous islands.

MADERIA PARK
The offshore waters of this area are a source of killer whales (properly known as *orcas*) for the world's famous aquariums. A visitor may spot the whales, which travel in "pods" of 100 or more, slicing the waves with their distinctive triangular dorsal fins.

| 0 | 2 | 4 | 6 | 8 | 10 Miles |
| 0 | 4 | 8 | 12 | | 16 Kilometres |

Powell River. (The upper and lower Sunshine Coast is also linked by ferry between Earls Cove and Saltery Bay.)

The Sunshine Coast has broad beaches, rugged headlands, quiet lagoons and lakes backed by heavily forested uplands—all set against the backdrop of the Coast Mountains to the east. The serene beauty of the land and the unhurried life-style of its people make this area an ideal outdoor retreat.

From Langdale, Highway 101 runs through Gibsons, the location of CBC-TV's *The Beachcombers.* The road continues north to Sechelt, situated on a narrow strip of land between Sechelt Inlet and the Strait of Georgia, then winds past the sheltered bay of Pender Harbour.

From Saltery Bay to Lund, there are opportunities for salmon fishing and scuba diving in the Malaspina Strait and the Strait of Georgia. Hiking is a popular activity and boat charters are available to take enthusiasts into remote and scenic areas such as Okeover Inlet and Desolation Sound.

Breakwater of anchored ships, Powell River

EGMONT
Skookumchuck Narrows, four kilometres southeast of Egmont, is a 400-metre-wide, rock-strewn tidal bore between Jervis and Sechelt inlets. Skookumchuck is Chinook (a Coast Salish dialect) for "turbulent water." Four times daily—twice during flood tide and twice during ebb tide—the waters of the Pacific Ocean rush through the narrow passage creating boiling rapids, eddies and whirlpools. Extreme tides, mostly in spring, may reach five metres in height and a speed of 20 kilometres per hour. The roar of churning waters can be heard for many kilometres. The tidal spectacle can be viewed from Roland and Narrows points, two lookouts within a provincial park along the western edge of the Narrows.
□ Nearby Sechelt Inlet is base for more than half of British Columbia's thriving fish farms.

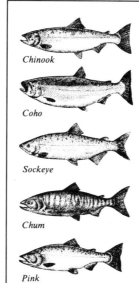

Five Superb Salmon of the Pacific Coast

Chinook

Coho

Sockeye

Chum

Pink

Five indigenous salmon species have made the tidal waters of the Sunshine Coast a fisherman's paradise. The fish are most abundant between June and August.

Chinook are the largest Pacific salmon, weighing up to 55 kilograms. They can be identified by a lightly spotted blue-green back and a black lower jaw.

Coho salmon weigh up to 10 kilograms. They are distinguished by a bright, silvery body with a metallic-blue stripe, and have a white lower jaw.

Sockeye salmon are the slimmest and most streamlined of the species. They weigh up to 3.5 kilograms and are a silvery blue.

Chum salmon resemble sockeye, but have faint, gridlike bars and black specks on their silvery sides. They weigh up to 5 kilograms.

Pink salmon are the smallest of the species, with a maximum weight of 2.5 kilograms. They have heavily spotted backs.

SECHELT
Coast Salish Indian craftsmen on a reserve about 1.5 kilometres east of Sechelt have kept alive the traditional weaving and carving skills of their ancestors. Examples of their work are on display in the reserve's administrative center. Exhibits include woven cedar bark baskets, wooden masks, a brightly colored carved desk, and jewelry made of shells and jade.

Gibsons

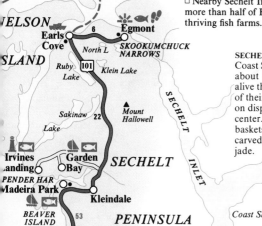

Coast Salish mask, Sechelt

ter clam

Moon snail

Horse clam

GIBSONS
Salmon Rock, near the entrance of Gibsons' harbor, is one of British Columbia's finest fishing areas. Chinook and coho salmon are present throughout the year. The Elphinstone Pioneer Museum documents the evolutionary development of mollusks and crustaceans in a 25,000-shell collection.
□ A cairn at Gower Point, some four kilometres southwest, marks where George Vancouver stopped in June 1792 while mapping the Pacific Coast of North America. Nearby is a campground.

A View of Howe Sound From a Cliff-Hugging Highway

Howe Sound/Garibaldi Provincial Park

North of Vancouver Highway 99 (known as the Sea-to-Sky Highway) weaves through some of the most spectacular coastal scenery in British Columbia. Blasted through granite on the east side of Howe Sound, the highway at places hugs near-vertical mountain slopes. On a twisting ribbon of track below the highway, the restored *Royal Hudson* steam-driven locomotive chugs along on summer days, bringing visitors from Vancouver to this rugged, scenic region.

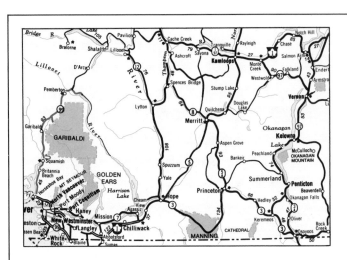

Fjords and Hanging Valleys on an Ice-Carved Coast

Some of Canada's most beautiful scenery is found among the tangle of islands, fjords and towering mountains of the Pacific coast. This dramatic landscape was created during the last ice age, when the coastline sagged under an immense burden of ice, and glaciers carved cliffs and riverbeds. Some 11,000 years ago the ice sheet began to melt. The ocean rose and flooded inland. Some river valleys, widened and deepened by glaciers, became fjords—arms of the sea (such as Howe Sound). Tributary valleys that had not been deepened by glacial erosion were stranded atop the fjords' steep walls. Waters that drain these "hanging valleys" often cascade hundreds of metres down the sides of fjords.

When the weight of the ice lifted, the land began to rise. For a time surf pounded on shores that are now mountainsides 300 metres above sea level.

Highway 99 by Howe Sound

WHISTLER

Located at the base of Whistler and Blackcomb mountains is Whistler Village, one of Canada's finest ski resorts. All its 117 ski runs are more than a kilometre in length; the longest is some 11 kilometres. Blackcomb Mountain has a vertical drop of more than 1,200 metres—the largest of any North American ski resort.
□ Whistler Village is also a base for helicopter expeditions onto nearby glaciers, where experienced skiers can enjoy fields of unbroken powdery snow.
□ In summer, Whistler Village offers hiking and windsurfing, as well as golfing on an 18-hole course designed by American champion Arnold Palmer.

Alpine skiing, Whistler Mountain

SQUAMISH

Squamish is a lumber center where huge log booms are assembled for towing to southern mills. Overlooking the village is Stawamus Chief, a 762-metre mountain resembling the head of an Indian. Three kilometres south is 198-metre-high Shannon Falls.
□ The *Royal Hudson,* a restored steam locomotive (1940), pulls a sight-seeing excursion train between Vancouver and Squamish during the summer.
□ Squamish Loggers Days, held in August, feature an international logging competition.

The Royal Hudson

BRITANNIA BEACH

At the British Columbia Museum of Mining, visitors put on hard hats before boarding a covered mining train for a ride through the murky depths of the old Britannia copper mine. (In 1930-35, the Britannia and several neighboring local mines were the largest producers of copper in the British Empire.) The guided underground tour includes mining demonstrations and equipment displays. The museum also exhibits artifacts and photographs relating to the history of the Britannia mines.

The lumber town of Squamish, where Highway 99 turns inland, is in an alpine setting of forest and mountains. Gazing down on the town is the granite visage of the 762-metre-high Stawamus Chief. Beyond, in a cloud of spray and mist, Shannon Falls cascades nearly 200 metres.

A paved road north of Squamish is the main access to Garibaldi Provincial Park. The pristine character of the park endures in a dramatic landscape of canyons, gulleys and glaciated peaks.

Snowcapped mountains surround the Indian village of Mount Currie and present a tranquil backdrop for square-timbered barns with moss roofs.

It was through this harsh but beautiful wilderness that fortune-seekers trekked to the Cariboo goldfields in the 1860s. The D'Arcy Road between Pemberton and Lillooet follows part of their trail, past abandoned cabins, forests and icy lakes.

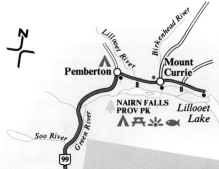

Black Tusk, Garibaldi Provincial Park

PEMBERTON

A choice of logging roads in the Pemberton area invites adventurous travelers to explore the surrounding wilderness. The 10.5-kilometre paved road from Pemberton to Mount Currie leads to the D'Arcy and the Duffey Lake roads.

□ In summer, drivers can take the challenging 93.5-kilometre Duffey Lake road leading from the rain forests of the valley where Pemberton is situated, over the Cayoosh Range, to the semiarid area around Lillooet. Before setting out, drivers should check road conditions with the local branch of the British Columbia Ministry of Transportation.

□ The first 48 kilometres of the road between Pemberton and D'Arcy are paved. From D'Arcy to Seton Portage, there is a 35-kilometre dirt road suitable only for 4-wheel drive vehicles.

□ The D'Arcy road is the northern part of the route (known as the Douglas Trail) from Fort Langley to Lillooet, which was used by gold miners of the early 1860s. The Douglas Trail was abandoned in 1864 when the Fraser Canyon was opened up.

□ The Pemberton Meadows road, leading north to Bradlorne, is paved for 24 kilometres. Beyond this point, there is a forest service road to Bradlorne, suitable for summer travel only.

GARIBALDI PROVINCIAL PARK

Volcanic rock formations are found throughout this 1,958-square-kilometre wilderness park, which is dominated by 2,678-metre Mount Garibaldi. Atop 2,315-metre Black Tusk Mountain is a basalt formation, the eroded remains of an ancient volcanic core. The Barrier, a lava flow 1.5 kilometres long, towers 457 metres above the west side of Garibaldi Lake. Erosion has sculpted The Gargoyles—strange rock formations reached by a trail from the park's southern entrance. Garibaldi Park is forested with fir, hemlock, balsam and red cedar, and alpine flowers bloom in meadows beneath sharp, glaciated peaks. Wildlife includes grizzly and black bears, mountain goats, deer, wolverines and martens.

Marbled murrelets

HORSESHOE BAY

For centuries, the coastal Salish Indians used dugout cedar canoes—almost as long as the vessels of the 17th-century European explorers—to sail the protected waters of Horseshoe Bay and the Strait of Georgia.

□ A plaque at Horseshoe Bay commemorates Capt. George Vancouver and the pioneer navigators who charted the intricate coastline of British Columbia.

□ From Horseshoe Bay, visitors can cross by ferry to Langdale to explore British Columbia's "Sunshine Coast."

A 'Shattered Climate' of Rain Forest and Semidesert

The coast of British Columbia has what meteorologists call a shattered climate. While some parts receive as much as 800 centimetres of rain and snow in a year, others get barely 50 centimetres. These extremes are caused by the rugged, intricate topography of the coast.

When warm, moisture-laden air from the Pacific Ocean reaches the coastal mountains of British Columbia, it is forced upward. The air cools as it rises, and its ability to retain moisture is greatly reduced. This results in heavy rainfall, which feeds lush coastal rain forests on the mountains' western slopes. Some fjords cause even greater precipitation in limited areas: their steep sides act as a funnel, compressing rain clouds, then driving them upward at the end of the fjord.

When air masses descend the eastern slopes of the mountains, they become warmer and retain more moisture. The result is often a dramatic reduction in rainfall within a few kilometres—a "rain shadow" effect that can create barren, semidesert conditions.

The Pacific for a Doorstep, Coastal Peaks for a Backyard

No single image can portray Vancouver. Cosmopolitan and small-townish, always changing, a city that grew from a mill town to a metropolis in less than a century.

The shantytown that sprang up around a Burrard Inlet sawmill in 1862 was incorporated as the City of Vancouver in April 1886. In June of that year a forest fire raced toward the waterfront and the ramshackle frame buildings. An hour later the town was a smoking ruin.

Within weeks, a fire engine was purchased, new streets were laid out, and brick and stone buildings were erected. By the end of 1886 Vancouver was a city of 5,000 looking confidently to the future.

During the last 30 years, the population of Greater Vancouver soared from 530,000 to nearly a million and a half people, while the city expanded into outlying Burnaby, Port Coquitlam, New Westminster, Delta and Surrey. European and Asian immigrants introduced their distinctive cultures and customs, transforming the city's traditionally British character.

Part of Vancouver's appeal is the sheer beauty of its setting. Behind the sweep of its beaches soar high-rise buildings, symbols of dynamic urban growth. The city's harbors and inlets are freckled with pleasure craft and oceangoing vessels from around the world. To the north of Vancouver are inviting mountain parks, such as Grouse Mountain and Mount Seymour; to the south and east are the fertile farmlands of the Fraser River valley.

B.C. Place Stadium (36)
Opened in 1983, this 60,000-seat stadium with its vast air-supported "big top" dome is the centerpiece of residential and commercial redevelopment at False Creek, the main Expo 86 site. Visitors can tour the stadium, which is used for concerts and trade shows as well as sporting events.
Burnaby Mountain Park (19)
A lookout on Burnaby Mountain offers a

Dominating Vancouver's waterfront, Canada Place (above top) symbolizes the city's growing importance as a financial, commercial, industrial and transportation center. Strung across Capilano Canyon, the world's longest footbridge (above bottom) has thrilled visitors since 1899. Papier-mâché dragon (left) in North America's second largest Chinatown is a reminder of Vancouver's rich ethnic mix.

sweeping view of Indian Arm inlet, the Strait of Georgia, the Fraser River delta and the distant mountains of Vancouver Island.

Canada Place (32)
Built as the Canadian Pavilion at Expo 86, this complex includes a 500-room hotel, a convention center and a cruise ship terminal. Its roof, 10 peaks that resemble a cluster of unfurled sails, dominates the waterfront.

Capilano Suspension Bridge (5)
Swaying 70 metres above the Capilano Canyon, this 135-metre footbridge (the world's longest) thrills visitors as it has since 1899.

Chinatown (38)
This is the largest Chinese community in North America after San Francisco's. Even the telephone booths have pagoda-style roofs in a three-block neighborhood of Oriental restaurants, shops, teahouses and social clubs.

George C. Reifel Bird Sanctuary (17)
More than 200 bird species have been sighted at this marshy refuge on Westham Island in the Fraser River estuary. Its 344 hectares support Canada's largest wintering waterfowl population and are a resting place for some 12,000 snow geese that fly between California and Siberia. There is a 3.2-kilometre nature walk in the sanctuary.

Granville Island (26)
Attractions at this 15-hectare redevelopment of former railway yards include a public market, an art school, theaters and restaurants.

Grouse Mountain (6)
Canada's largest aerial tramway takes visitors (up to 100 persons per car) to the summit of this 1,192-metre mountain, for spectacular views of Vancouver, its harbor and the surrounding mountains.

Harbor Centre (34)
Glass-enclosed exterior elevators whisk visitors to the revolving observation deck on the 40th floor of this business tower.

Hastings Mill Store Museum (4)
Built in 1865 by Capt. Edward Stamp, the store is Vancouver's oldest building, one of the few not destroyed in the 1886 fire.

Heritage Village (18)
This living museum re-creates life at the turn of the century. It has a blacksmith shop, an old general store and a one-room schoolhouse.

H.R. MacMillan Planetarium (24)
The planetarium's projection and sound systems simulate the night sky on a 19-metre dome.

Kitsilano Beach Park (22)
Engine 373, the locomotive that pulled the first passenger train from Montreal to Vancouver (1887), is displayed in the park.

Lighthouse Park (13)
Nature trails lead past giant Douglas fir and cedar trees, eagles' nests and rocky coves to Point Atkinson Lighthouse (1874).

Lynn Canyon Suspension Bridge (15)
This 80-metre-high footbridge spans Lynn Creek. There are picnic sites and trails.

Minoru Park (10)
This park contains the Aquatic Centre and a museum with exhibits tracing local history.

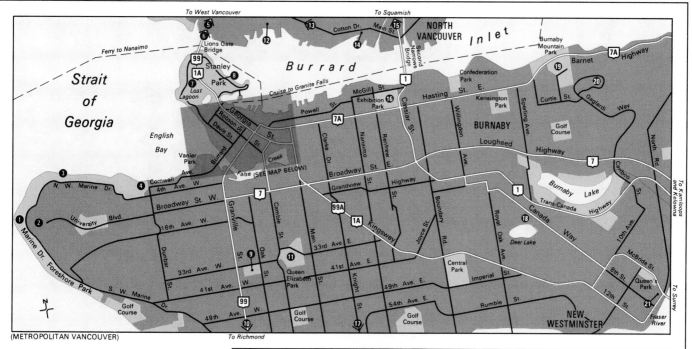

(METROPOLITAN VANCOUVER)

Vancouver

1 Nitobe Memorial Gardens
2 University of British Columbia
3 Spanish Banks Park
4 Hastings Mill Store Museum
5 Capilano Suspension Bridge
6 Grouse Mountain
7 Stanley Park
8 Vancouver Public Aquarium
9 Vandusen Botanical Display Garden
10 Minoru Park
11 Queen Elizabeth Park
12 *Royal Hudson* Terminus
13 Lighthouse Park
14 Park and Tilford Gardens
15 Lynn Canyon Suspension Bridge
16 Pacific National Exhibition Grounds
17 George C. Reifel Bird Sanctuary
18 Heritage Village
19 Burnaby Mountain Park
20 Simon Fraser University
21 New Westminster Museum and Irving House Historic Centre
22 Kitsilano Beach Park
23 Vancouver Maritime Museum
24 H.R. MacMillan Planetarium
25 Vancouver Museum
26 Granville Island
27 Robsonstrasse
28 Provincial Court House
29 Orpheum Theater
30 Tourist Information
31 Vancouver Art Gallery
32 Canada Place
33 Gastown
34 Harbor Centre
35 Queen Elizabeth Theatre
36 B.C. Place Stadium
37 Science World British Columbia
38 Chinatown

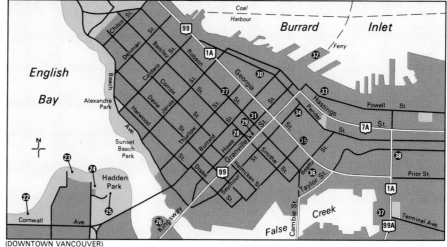

(DOWNTOWN VANCOUVER)

New Westminster Museum and Irving House Historic Centre (21)

The two-story frame William Irving House (1862-64) depicts the history of the New Westminster area. It has the original wallpaper, Wilton carpets imported from England in the 1860s, and period furniture.

Nitobe Memorial Gardens (1)

This traditional Japanese garden—one of the finest in North America—has an artificial mountain, and a pond filled with golden carp and spanned by five bridges.

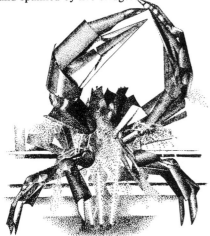

The Crab *sculpture outside MacMillan Planetarium*

Orpheum Theater (29)

Saved from the wrecker's ball in 1972, this ornate theater, built in 1927, is now home to the Vancouver Symphony Orchestra.

Pacific National Exhibition Grounds (16)

Year-round sporting events at this 70-hectare park include horse racing at the five-furlong track, lacrosse and hockey at the Pacific Coliseum (home of the Vancouver Canucks) and track-and-field events at the Empire Stadium. The Pacific National Exhibition, western Canada's largest fair, is held here in August. The B.C. Pavilion houses the provincial Sports Hall of Fame. It also has a 22- × 24-metre relief map of British Columbia, built over seven years from 968,842 pieces of plywood. Visitors can view the map from a gallery or a moving platform.

Park and Tilford Gardens (14)

There are year-round displays in rhododendron, rose, colonnade, nature woods, Oriental and flower gardens.

Provincial Court House (28)

This striking building is a highly acclaimed work of local architect Arthur Erikson.

Queen Elizabeth Park (11)

This flower lover's paradise sits on 150-metre Little Mountain, Vancouver's highest point. There are rose, sunken and quarry gardens, and an arboretum. The triodetic dome of the Bloedel Conservatory—15 metres high and 43 metres in diameter—encloses 400 tropical plants and 100 free-flying exotic birds.

Queen Elizabeth Theatre (35)

This 2,800-seat theater is set in a landscaped plaza. A small adjoining theater is the home of the Playhouse Theatre Company.

Vancouver's 144 parks range from pocket-size patches to 400-hectare Stanley Park (above), an escape from the big-city din mere minutes away. Polar bears frolic in the park's zoo (right). Its beauty doubled by a luminous reflection, MacMillan Planetarium (below right) is a showpiece of modern architecture.

Robsonstrasse (27)

Officially, it's Robson Street, but the concentration of ethnic shops and restaurants—particularly German—has earned this two-block area its popular name.

Royal Hudson **Terminus** (12)

At North Vancouver, the steam locomotive *Royal Hudson* departs for a scenic journey along Howe Sound to Squamish.

Science World British Columbia (37)

"Hands-on" exhibits here blend art, science and technology. Science World is served by Sky Train, Vancouver's rapid transit system.

Simon Fraser University (20)

Located atop 360-metre Burnaby Mountain, SFU commands breathtaking views of Vancouver, Burrard Inlet and Indian Arm. Founded in 1963, its architecturally outstanding campus was designed by Vancouver architect Arthur Erikson.

Spanish Banks Park (3)

Off this long, sandy beach on June 22, 1792, Capt. George Vancouver met the captains Galiano and Valdez and accepted Spain's surrender of the northwest coast. "It was dawn for Britain," reads a plaque on the cliffs, "but twilight for Spain."

Stanley Park (7)

Dedicated in 1899, this 400-hectare park on downtown Vancouver's doorstep was named for Lord Stanley, Canada's governor-general in 1888-93 and presenter of hockey's Stanley Cup. Some 35 kilometres of trails skirt Lost Lagoon, Beaver Lake, and stands of huge

Douglas fir, hemlock and cedar. The 10-kilometre seawall footpath passes Second and Third beaches and Siwash Rock—a young Indian turned to stone, according to the legend by poet Pauline Johnson (1861-1913).

A lookout at Prospect Point gives fine views of the North Shore mountains and Lions Gate Bridge, which spans the harbor entrance. A replica of the dragon figurehead of *Empress of Japan*, a liner that plied the Pacific from 1891 to 1922, is on the seawall path near Brockton Point Lighthouse. Nearby is a collection of totem poles. At Hallelujah Point, which honors the Salvation Army, the Nine O'Clock Gun booms out as it has each evening since 1894.

The Stanley Park Zoo houses more than 570 animal species, among them polar bears, otters, monkeys, seals, and one of the world's finest collections of king penguins.

University of British Columbia (2)
The wooded University Endowment Lands, the Strait of Georgia and Burrard Inlet provide a striking setting for the campus on Point Grey. Among more than 470 buildings on the 396-hectare site are the UBC Health Sciences Centre—a teaching and research hospital—and the main library, which houses more than 2.5 million books. The M.Y. Williams Museum of Geology has an extensive collection of fossils, minerals and gemstones. The Museum of Anthropology houses more than 20,000 artifacts, many relating to the history of the Northwest Coast Indian culture. The Great Hall of the museum exhibits 12- to 14-metre-high totem poles—some of the largest ever found. Both museums are open to visitors as are the 44-hectare UBC Botanical Gardens.

Vancouver Art Gallery (31)
The gallery, in a former courthouse, contains the largest collection of paintings by British Columbia artist Emily Carr (1871-1945) and presents contemporary art exhibitions.

Vancouver's Gastown Hums With New Life

Vancouver was founded as Gastown (34), a cluster of waterfront shanties near a lumber mill. The nearest drinking spot was in New Westminster until John "Gassy Jack" Deighton arrived in 1867 and set up his saloon. Deighton was a Yorkshireman who came to Canada in the 1860s and tried his hand at odd jobs before turning to pubkeeping. To build his saloon, he enlisted volunteer lumberjacks and fortified them with spirits. In just 24 hours, the Deighton House was open for business. As the settlement prospered, it became known as Gastown. Over the decades it declined into a slum but now hums with new life as buildings are restored and refurbished as boutiques, antique shops, pubs, cafés and art galleries.

While saner folk watch, some 200 bathers brave the chill waters of English Bay during the New Year's Day Polar Bear Swim (left), staying in anywhere from two seconds to two hours. Centerpiece of Queen Elizabeth Park is this former quarry (below) transformed into a lush sunken garden.

Vancouver Maritime Museum (23)
Built to celebrate B.C.'s 1971 centennial, the museum houses ship models, maps, photographs and artifacts illustrating the province's maritime history. The prize exhibit is the 30-metre RCMP schooner *St. Roch,* which battled Arctic ice in 1940-42 to become the first ship to navigate the Northwest Passage from west to east.

Vancouver Museum (25)
The museum depicts local history from fur-trading days to Victorian times. Exhibits include a car from the first CPR transcontinental train to reach Vancouver in 1887.

Vancouver Public Aquarium (8)
Killer and beluga whales, dolphins, Atlantic harp seals and rare sea otters are among more than 8,500 specimens and 650 species on view at this aquarium in Stanley Park. A two-million-litre pool has underwater whale-viewing areas and outdoor terraces.

Vandusen Botanical Display Garden (9)
This park, which has an impressive collection of ornamental plants, comprises more than 30 different gardens, man-made lakes, waterfalls and large stone sculptures.

A Landscape Like Holland ...
and the Legend of the Sasquatch

North Shore, Lower Fraser River Valley

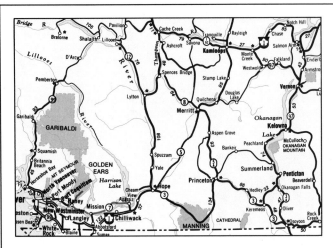

GOLDEN EARS PROVINCIAL PARK
The snow-crested twin peaks of 1,706-metre Golden Ears Mountain dominate 55,000-hectare Golden Ears Provincial Park, wedged between Pitt Lake to the west and the Mount Judge Howay Recreation Area to the east. At Alouette Lake are two campgrounds with swimming and boating facilities. Hiking trails lead through forests of Douglas fir, western red cedar, hemlock and balsam in the park's lower regions. Stands of alpine fir, yellow cedar and mountain hemlock thrive at higher elevations.

Golden Ears Mountain

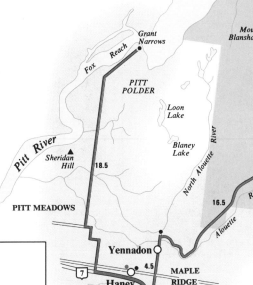

PITT LAKE
This lake, a widening of the Pitt River, stretches some 25 kilometres between the steep, forested slopes and glacier-capped peaks of the Coast Mountains at its northern reaches and bogs of sphagnum moss at its southern end. Near the lake's outlet are tangles of swamp laurel and huckleberry, where rare sandhill cranes nest each spring. The waters of Pitt Lake rise and fall with the tides of the Pacific Ocean.

A Dutch Polder in the Mountains

In Pitt Polder, on the east bank of the Pitt River and in the shadows of the Coast Mountains to the north and east, herds of Holstein and Guernsey dairy cattle browse in lush meadows. (Polder is Dutch for a tract of low-lying land reclaimed from a river or the sea.) Sheltered behind dikes and neatly segmented by a web of drainage channels, these pastures were once impassable marshes regularly flooded by the Pitt River. In 1948, Dutch immigrants acquired the area and used their native dike-building skills to turn it into a polder. Over paths on top of the dikes, hikers and bicyclists can explore this man-made farmland.

Meadows in the Pitt Polder

MAPLE RIDGE
Incorporated in 1984, the district municipality of Maple Ridge includes Haney and other former communities.
□ Visitors can view the fully restored 1878 Haney House (11612—224th Street), a historic site donated by the descendants of Thomas Haney who settled here in 1876.
□ St. John the Divine Anglican Church (21299 River Road) is B.C.'s oldest church. Built by military engineers in 1858 on the south shore of the Fraser River three kilometres upstream, the church was floated across the river, then moved to its present site in 1882.

0   1   2   3   4   5 Miles

0   2   4   6   8 Kilometres

The drive from Haney in the Maple Ridge district to Harrison Hot Springs passes through a verdant plain, flanked by the Fraser River to the south and the Coast Mountains to the north. Across the plain flow dozens of creeks, rivers, and narrow lakes. They carry mountain runoff into the silty waters of the Fraser, which flows sedately through this region on its way to the Pacific.

Dairy farming is one of the valley's agricultural mainstays. Along the Pitt River, a Fraser tributary, Dutch immigrants drained and diked the marshy flood plains to resemble the countryside of their native Holland.

In contrast with the valley's fertile pastures, the slopes of the Coast Mountains are densely forested with fir, cedar and hemlock. Some basalt peaks are almost 1,800 metres high; many are covered with snowfields and glaciers.

The legendary Sasquatch is believed by some to roam the wooded slopes of the Coast Mountains. Sasquatch Provincial Park is named after the apelike giant.

At Harrison Hot Springs are mineral springs said to have been discovered one chilly day in 1859, when a gold miner fell from his canoe into Harrison Lake and found the water unusually warm. The lake is today a popular vacation spot.

The Sasquatch: Man, Ape or Legend?

The mountain slopes around Harrison Lake are Sasquatch country. Reportedly seen dozens of times in British Columbia and the northwestern United States, the Sasquatch is usually described as an apelike creature, up to twice the size of a man, with a flattened nose, sloping forehead and long, swinging arms. Its footprint is said to be almost 45 centimetres long.

The strongest evidence that Sasquatches exist is a short color film, taken by an amateur photographer near Yakima, Wash., in the mid-1960s, that shows a large apelike creature loping across a clearing. Scientists disagree as to the film's authenticity.

Visitors to Sasquatch Provincial Park, 6.5 kilometres north of Harrison Hot Springs, are more likely to sight bald eagles, great blue herons and mallards than they are to spot the legendary monster.

Harrison Lake

HARRISON MILLS
The Kilby General Store Museum, built as a general store and post office in 1904, is a provincial historic site, where merchandise from the early 1900s—the collection of the store's original proprietor Acton Kilby—is displayed in antique showcases.

MISSION
The district municipality of Mission takes its name from St. Mary's Indian Mission, founded by Oblate Fathers in 1861.
□ On Mount Mary Ann, overlooking the Fraser Valley, is the Benedictine monastery, Westminster Abbey, with its 51-metre-high Pfitzer bell tower. It is open to the public on weekday and Sunday afternoons.
□ Among Mission's attractions is Storyland Trails (9134 Hayward St.), which offers nature walks and displays more than 400 storybook characters.

HARRISON HOT SPRINGS
Two mineral hot springs are the main attractions of this small vacation resort at the southern end of 65-kilometre-long Harrison Lake. Up to 20 litres per minute of the springs' sulphur- and potash-rich waters are cooled to 37°C (from their original 68°C and 72°C) and piped into one outdoor and two indoor public swimming pools and into the baths of a health spa.
□ The town has a sand beach dredged from the bed of Harrison Lake. Boaters can explore the lake's remote coves, beaches and islets.

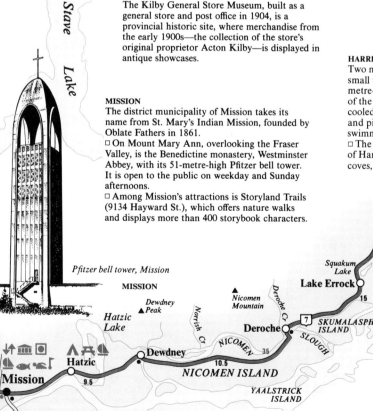

Pfitzer bell tower, Mission

AGASSIZ
On Mount Agassiz, north of this town, is a lookout over the Fraser Valley. A plaque tells that, during the past 50 million years, the Fraser River has built up a 1.5-kilometre-thick layer of silt on top of the valley's ancient floor.
□ On gravel bars upstream, rock hounds find agates deposited by the Fraser River.

Where the Fraser Turns Tame, a Garden for Vancouver

South Shore, Lower Fraser River Valley

Fort Langley

FORT LANGLEY NATIONAL HISTORIC PARK

At Fort Langley, a palisaded Hudson's Bay Company trading post on the banks of the Fraser River, the Crown Colony of British Columbia was inaugurated on Nov. 19, 1858. The ceremony took place in the Big House, which contained officers' quarters, guest rooms and a community hall. Furnished in 1850s style, the Big House is now reconstructed as the centerpiece of an eight-hectare national historic park. (The original Fort Langley was completed in 1841 and abandoned 45 years later.) Today staff in period costumes re-create life and work at Fort Langley during the 1840s and 50s. Other historic structures include an artisans' building, where craftsmen make a type of barrel once used to export salted salmon, and a bastion, which served as a lookout for armed sentries. An 1840 warehouse—Fort Langley's only original surviving structure—displays furs, traps, a balance scale, trade goods, provisions and a press used to bale furs into 50-kilogram packs. Visitors can attend a slide presentation about the fort's history.

Sentry in period costume at Fort Langley National Historic Park

SURREY

With 342 square kilometres, Surrey is British Columbia's largest district municipality in area. It comprises the communities of Cloverdale, Guildford, Newton, Sunnyside and Whalley.

□ The Canadian Museum of Flight and Transportation at Cloverdale displays 40 historic aircraft from the two world wars, as well as vintage cars.

□ Of the more than 60 parks in the Surrey area, Redwood is one of the most interesting. Some 26 varieties of trees are found in the park, including the largest stand of redwoods north of California.

□ The Serpentine Fen, a marshy area at the mouth of the Serpentine River, is a bird sanctuary for New Westminster's Douglas College. Part farm and part wildlife refuge, the fen is home to more than 100 species of birds as well as species of wild animals. Pheasants and wood ducks are raised for release in the wild. Visitors can explore the fen on marked trails.

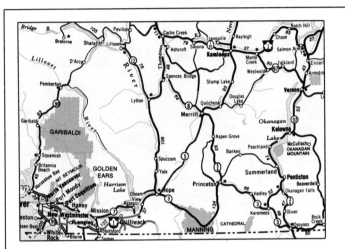

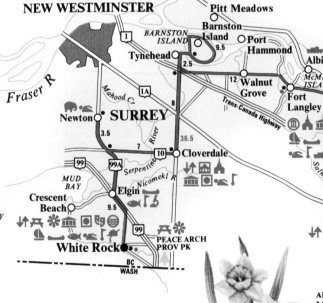

Rufous hummingbird

WHITE ROCK

This is the southwesternmost community on the Canadian mainland. A giant boulder lies on a sand beach at Semiahmoo Bay. Sailors used to paint it white as a navigation mark; hence the community's name.

□ The International Peace Arch straddles the Canadian-American border in a 20-hectare park jointly maintained by British Columbia and the state of Washington. It commemorates the peaceful relations that have existed between the United States and Canada since 1814.

Daffodil

ABBOTSFORD

Modern jets and vintage biplanes soar over this farming community at the annual Abbotsford International Air Show in August. Formation and stunt-flying are a spectacular part of a show that also displays the latest products from the aircraft and aerospace industry.

□ The Fraser Valley Trout Hatchery is open to visitors, who can view the facility by using the glassed-in walkways overlooking the trough room and rearing pond. Seven species of trout and char are displayed in the aquarium.

□ Nearby Bradner grows some 400 different kinds of daffodils. The community's flower show is held each Easter.

0	2	4	6	8	10 Miles
0	4	8	12		16 Kilometres

By the time the Fraser River reaches the broad flood plain stretching about 100 kilometres between Chilliwack and the Pacific Ocean, it is no longer the torrent that cut the Fraser Canyon into British Columbia's interior plateau. Instead it meanders sluggishly here, toward its wide delta at the sea. The Fraser Valley's 1,500-metre-thick layer of rich soil is silt which the river has gathered on the wild journey from its headwaters near 3,954-metre Mount Robson—the highest peak in the Canadian Rockies.

This 50-million-year accumulation, interrupted only by glaciation and mountain formation, has made the Fraser Valley British Columbia's most fertile farmland.

Dairy farms and market gardens support prosperous rural communities in the valley. Milk-processing plants, cheese factories, canneries, frozen-food plants, cattle- and poultry-feed industries and farm machinery sales and service outlets are the mainstays of Chilliwack, Abbotsford and Surrey, the valley's principal communities. Agricul-

tural fairs such as the Chilliwack Fall Exhibition and the Bradner Flower Show are showcases of the region's farm products. The Fraser Valley is the main source of food for the nearly 1.5 million people who live in Greater Vancouver.

CHILLIWACK

Chilliwack Museum is housed in the former city hall, which is a national historic site. Permanent exhibits illustrate the history of the Upper Fraser River valley.
□ Minter Gardens offers ten gardens featuring different floral themes, as well as three aviaries. There also is a petting zoo and play area for children.
□ The Canadian Military Engineering Museum, on the grounds of CFB Chilliwack at Vedder Crossing, displays memorabilia from the two world wars and conflicts such as the Zulu and the Boer wars. There is an extensive collection of badges, medals, uniforms and weapons—some dating from the 16th century.
□ Chilliwack Fall Exhibition is a major agricultural fair, which is held in mid-August. Other local celebrations include the Country Living Festival (May) and the Children's Festival (June).

BRIDAL VEIL FALLS PROVINCIAL PARK
At Bridal Veil Falls, a curtain of water descends 25 metres over a sheer cliff. A 15-minute walk, up a steep trail from the park's picnic site, brings visitors to a lookout by the falls. Adventurous—and experienced—climbers can reach the base of the falls, above the lookout, along a rocky incline.

Chilliwack Lake

CHILLIWACK LAKE
There is a campground, a boat-launching ramp and picnic sites on the north shore of Chilliwack Lake. On the opposite shore is Sapper Park, also a picnic site, which can be reached by a narrow logging road on the lake's east side. The park, built by the Royal Canadian Engineers, is on the site where a party of military engineers—"sappers"—camped while surveying the International Boundary in the 1850s.

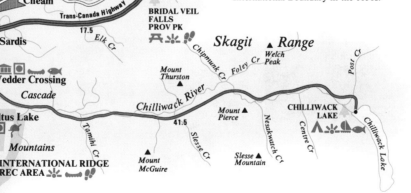

Narrow-capped morel

Cultus Lake Indian Festival

CULTUS LAKE
This inviting lake is set among the foothills of the Cascade Mountains. The 656-hectare Cultus Lake Provincial Park offers visitors 300 campgrounds, as well as a wide range of facilities for recreations, such as boating, swimming and wilderness hiking.
□ At the annual Cultus Lake Indian Festival in June, participants from British Columbia and neighboring Washington State stage a number of events, including a war-canoe race across the lake.

Grand, Wild and Beautiful:
Hells Gate and the Raging Fraser

Fraser and Thompson River Valleys

Two of Canada's most famous rivers, the Fraser and the Thompson, push through central British Columbia. At Lytton, where they converge, visitors can see the blue-green waters of the Thompson swallowed in the murky torrent of the Fraser—within less than 50 metres.

North of Lytton, along the banks of the Thompson, the terrain is hilly, bare of almost everything except sagebrush. Herds of beef cattle, tended by cowboys on horseback, graze on the expansive rangeland.

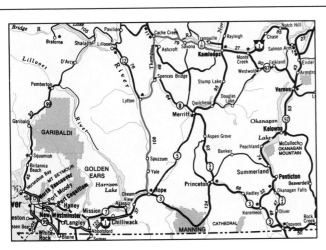

Hells Gate Airtram

LYTTON
Founded during the gold rush of 1858, Lytton was a staging post on the road to Cariboo Country. The town was named for Sir Edward Bulwer-Lytton, author of *The Last Days of Pompeii* and other novels, who was serving as British Colonial Secretary at this time.
□ Jackass Mountain, to the south, was named for the mules that carried miners' and ranchers' supplies. Because of its difficult terrain, the mountain was originally known as the Hill of Despair.
□ Rock hounds in this region seek not only what gold remains but also fine jade.
□ Anglers can fish for steelhead trout in the Fraser River here.

HELLS GATE
The Fraser Canyon is at its narrowest here, barely 30 metres across. The gorge is 180 metres deep and the Fraser River thunders through it at more than 7 metres a second.
□ A rockslide at Hells Gate in 1914 drastically constricted the channel, hindering the progress of salmon to their spawning grounds and causing huge losses to the fishing industry during the next 30 years. Fish ladders built since 1945 bypass the turbulent waters. The fish ladders can be seen from a suspension bridge.
□ The Hells Gate Airtram takes visitors across the gorge for a close-up look at the Fraser River.

ALEXANDRA BRIDGE
Three bridges have spanned the Fraser River here. The site was chosen by a Royal Engineers sergeant in 1861. The first bridge built in that year was named for Alexandra, Princess of Wales, who was later Edward VII's queen. The second bridge, of similar design and in the same place, still exists—upstream from a $14 million Trans-Canada Highway bridge erected in 1962. On this latest bridge a cairn commemorates the work of the Royal Engineers in constructing the Cariboo Wagon Road.

Johnson Peak landslide, near Hope

HOPE
Huge boulders strewn about a site 16 kilometres east of Hope on Highway 3 are remnants of the Hope Slide. In January 1965, the side of Johnson Peak plunged into the valley below, burying the highway in 45 metres of rubble. A plaque by the highway marks the site of the disaster.
□ Highway 3, which links Hope with Princeton and other communities in the lower B.C. mainland, was completed in 1949, opening Manning Provincial Park to cars. The highway is almost at sea level at Hope and reaches a summit of 1,370 metres at Allison Pass.
□ The four- to six-lane Coquihalla Highway (Highway 5), which is the largest road to the British Columbia interior, begins about seven kilometres east of Hope at the interchange with Highway 3. The Coquihalla Highway links Hope with Merritt and Kamloops.

YALE
The Anglican Church of St. John the Divine, the oldest house of worship in British Columbia on its original site, dates from 1859-60. It was built by miners who flocked here when gold was discovered in 1858 at nearby Hill's Bar. Once the richest of some 25 sandbars in a 50-kilometre stretch of the Fraser, Hill's Bar yielded gold worth $2 million.
□ A plaque commemorates Yale's founding in 1848 as a fur-trading post. Fifteen years later it became the southern terminus of the Cariboo Wagon Road. Later it was important during construction of the CPR.

Phacelia

Thompson River, near Lytton

South of Lytton is Hells Gate. The raging Fraser River and the grandeur of the surrounding mountains make this rugged gorge a photographer's delight. In 1808, when explorer Simon Fraser became the first white man to pass this way, he wrote: "I . . . have never seen anything like this country. We had to pass where no human should venture . . . ."

Today, travelers on the Trans-Canada Highway venture here—just to see the wildness and beauty. The spectacular Fraser Canyon remains much as it was when the explorer first journeyed down the river that now bears his name. Lookouts have been built on the route. Airtrams at Hells Gate and Boston Bar whisk sightseers across deep gorges of the Fraser.

This region was the domain of Indians and fur traders until 1858, when thousands of prospectors arrived in search of gold. Although this wealth was quickly depleted, many of the early settlements, such as Hope, Yale and Lytton, survived.

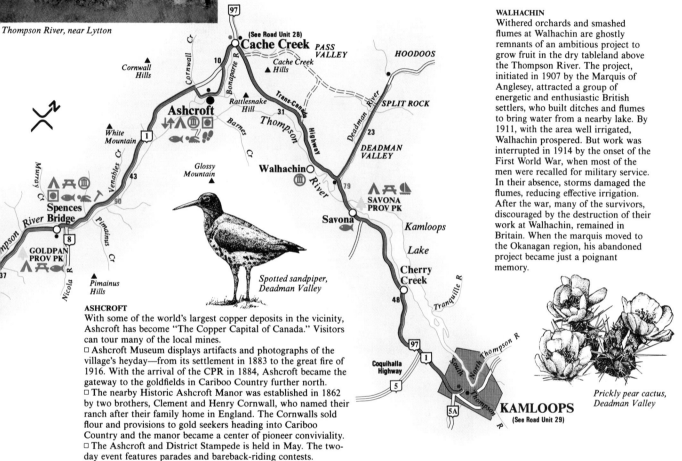

Spotted sandpiper, Deadman Valley

WALHACHIN

Withered orchards and smashed flumes at Walhachin are ghostly remnants of an ambitious project to grow fruit in the dry tableland above the Thompson River. The project, initiated in 1907 by the Marquis of Anglesey, attracted a group of energetic and enthusiastic British settlers, who built ditches and flumes to bring water from a nearby lake. By 1911, with the area well irrigated, Walhachin prospered. But work was interrupted in 1914 by the onset of the First World War, when most of the men were recalled for military service. In their absence, storms damaged the flumes, reducing effective irrigation. After the war, many of the survivors, discouraged by the destruction of their work at Walhachin, remained in Britain. When the marquis moved to the Okanagan region, his abandoned project became just a poignant memory.

Prickly pear cactus, Deadman Valley

ASHCROFT

With some of the world's largest copper deposits in the vicinity, Ashcroft has become "The Copper Capital of Canada." Visitors can tour many of the local mines.
□ Ashcroft Museum displays artifacts and photographs of the village's heyday—from its settlement in 1883 to the great fire of 1916. With the arrival of the CPR in 1884, Ashcroft became the gateway to the goldfields in Cariboo Country further north.
□ The nearby Historic Ashcroft Manor was established in 1862 by two brothers, Clement and Henry Cornwall, who named their ranch after their family home in England. The Cornwalls sold flour and provisions to gold seekers heading into Cariboo Country and the manor became a center of pioneer conviviality.
□ The Ashcroft and District Stampede is held in May. The two-day event features parades and bareback-riding contests.

St. John the Divine, Yale

High Cliffs and Hoodoos

Deadman Valley, one of the hottest and driest areas of British Columbia, was named about 1815 after a North West Company employee who was murdered here. Much of the area is desert, dotted with hardy scrub, sagebrush and prickly pear cactus. Other parts are surprisingly fertile.

A road leads north from the Trans-Canada Highway, through the Deadman Valley.

Along this road a multicolored cliff formation called Split Rock rises 60 metres from the Deadman River, Volcanic in origin, Split Rock is fretted with caves and fissures. Beyond Split Rock are five hoodoos, almost 12 metres high, that stand like sentinels near the northern end of the valley. These eroded pinnacles of rock and clay, each topped by an overhanging capstone, resemble giant mushrooms.

There are several lakes in the valley, and fishing for rainbow trout and kokanee salmon is good.

Hoodoos, Deadman Valley

Red Cedars in the Rain Forest, Prickly Pear Cactus in the Desert

Southwestern British Columbia

Few roads in Canada pass through a greater variety of vegetation, within such a short distance, than Highway 3 between Tashme and Osoyoos. At the western end there are dense rain forests; to the east is a desert where prickly pear cactus thrives.

In Manning Provincial Park, the highway climbs 1,350-metre Allison Pass through clumps of stunted alpine fir with an undergrowth of wild rhododendron. The eastern slope of the pass is covered by a thick blanket of Engelmann spruce which grad-

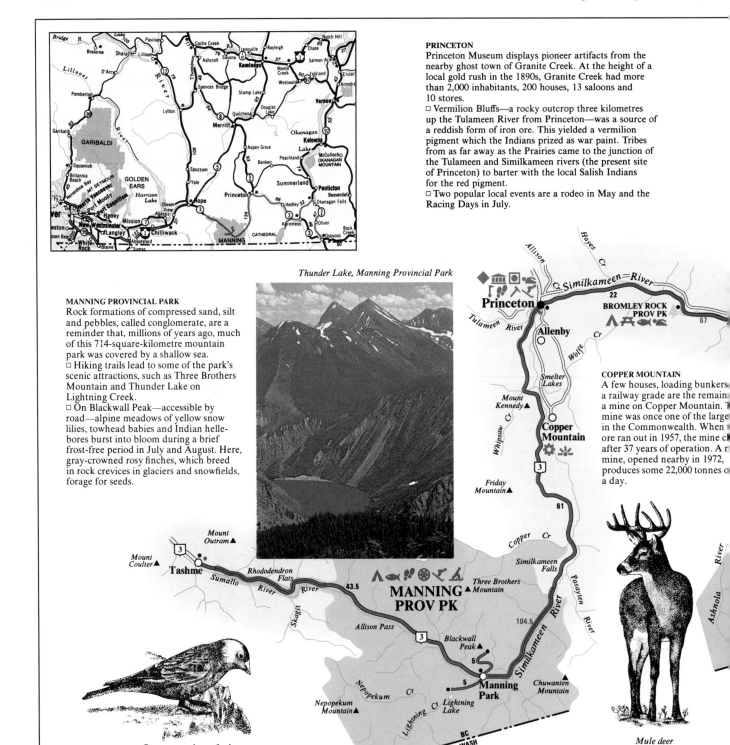

PRINCETON
Princeton Museum displays pioneer artifacts from the nearby ghost town of Granite Creek. At the height of a local gold rush in the 1890s, Granite Creek had more than 2,000 inhabitants, 200 houses, 13 saloons and 10 stores.
□ Vermilion Bluffs—a rocky outcrop three kilometres up the Tulameen River from Princeton—was a source of a reddish form of iron ore. This yielded a vermilion pigment which the Indians prized as war paint. Tribes from as far away as the Prairies came to the junction of the Tulameen and Similkameen rivers (the present site of Princeton) to barter with the local Salish Indians for the red pigment.
□ Two popular local events are a rodeo in May and the Racing Days in July.

Thunder Lake, Manning Provincial Park

MANNING PROVINCIAL PARK
Rock formations of compressed sand, silt and pebbles, called conglomerate, are a reminder that, millions of years ago, much of this 714-square-kilometre mountain park was covered by a shallow sea.
□ Hiking trails lead to some of the park's scenic attractions, such as Three Brothers Mountain and Thunder Lake on Lightning Creek.
□ On Blackwall Peak—accessible by road—alpine meadows of yellow snow lilies, towhead babies and Indian hellebores burst into bloom during a brief frost-free period in July and August. Here, gray-crowned rosy finches, which breed in rock crevices in glaciers and snowfields, forage for seeds.

COPPER MOUNTAIN
A few houses, loading bunkers a railway grade are the remain a mine on Copper Mountain. T mine was once one of the large in the Commonwealth. When ore ran out in 1957, the mine c after 37 years of operation. A r mine, opened nearby in 1972, produces some 22,000 tonnes o a day.

Gray-crowned rosy finch

Mule deer

0 2 4 6 8 10 Miles

0 4 8 12 16 Kilometres

ually gives way to aspen, juniper, lodge-pole pine and red cedar. Between Princeton and Keremeos, the scenery changes to rolling hills with sagebrush cover, where Herefords roam expansive ranges in search of nourishment, which is sparse. In the desert surrounding Osoyoos, irrigation has created lush orchards which produce some of Canada's earliest fruits each season.

Between Tashme and Manning Provincial Park, and between Princeton and Keremeos, the road follows the route of the old Dewdney Trail. This 468-kilometre former mule track, blazed by British engineer Edward Dewdney in the 1860s, connected Hope, on the Fraser River, with the goldfields of the Kootenay region.

Mountain road to Mascot and Nickel Plate mines, near Hedley

HEDLEY

The ruins of two mineheads, the Nickel Place and Mascot, are perched on Nickel Plate Mountain overlooking the town of Hedley. A precipitous switchback road, three kilometres east of Hedley, leads to the mines. For almost half a century, until they closed in 1955, the mines produced almost $1 million worth of gold, silver, copper and arsenic each year. The path of an aerial tramway, which cut through the forest and carried the ore to a mill at the base of the mountain, can still be seen.

VASEUX LAKE PROVINCIAL PARK

This park, on the shore of Vaseux Lake, is in one of Canada's few deserts. Annual precipitation here seldom exceeds 20 centimetres (less than one-fifth that of Vancouver). Bighorn sheep and mule and white-tailed deer graze among patches of antelope bush, mariposa lily, Oregon grape and prickly pear cactus. Rattlesnakes, painted turtles and jumping mice are common. On the lake, rare trumpeter swans stop during spring and fall migrations and Canada geese live here year round.

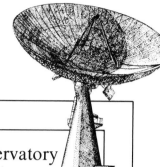

Kaleden's Observatory Listens to the Stars

Astronomers at the Dominion Radio Astrophysical Observatory near Kaleden listen to radio waves emitted by celestial bodies. Their "ears" are two types of radio telescopes: giant dish-shaped metal reflectors and large field arrays of antennas. These instruments receive radio waves of different lengths from space. For example, a small reflector at the Kaleden Observatory records the 11-centimetre radio waves from the sun. The 26-metre reflector (*above*) collects the 21-centimetre-long emissions from more distant sources. In a field near the Kaleden Observatory 624 antennas arranged in a giant T form a receiver that picks up waves 13.5 metres long. Radio telescopes have led to the discovery of remote galaxies too far away to be photographed by the largest optical telescopes. (The observatory may be visited on Sunday afternoons in summer.)

SPOTTED LAKE

This lake, some eight kilometres west of Osoyoos, has a higher concentration of minerals than almost any body of water in the world. The minerals include magnesium sulfate (Epsom salts), sodium sulfate, calcium sulfate, sodium chloride and sodium carbonate. Except in spring and after heavy rains, the lake is almost dry. Evaporation reduces it to mud pools covered by a few centimetres of water. The pools shimmer in hues of green and blue as sunlight is reflected by the dissolved minerals. At a nearby health spa, arthritic and rheumatic ailments are treated with warm packs of mud from the lake, and baths in heated lake water.

KEREMEOS COLUMNS PARK

The only access to this 20-hectare park is by a steep eight-kilometre logging road, which branches off Highway 3 about three kilometres north of Keremeos. The park is named for a 90-metre wide jumble of hexagonal rocks which rises 30 metres from the base of a lava escarpment outside the park boundary.

OSOYOOS

A narrow sand spit almost cuts Osoyoos Lake in two. It projects from the lake's west shore, creating a shallow ford—a *sooyoos* in Okanagan Indian dialect. Osoyoos, a version of the Indian word, became the name of the settlement which sprang up here in the mid-1800s.

□ Osoyoos has remodeled a number of its downtown buildings in the Spanish style.

□ A replica of a Dutch windmill, located just east of Osoyoos, is still used to grind grain into flour. Guided tours are available to the public.

CATHEDRAL PROVINCIAL PARK

Six lakes with trout (rainbow and cutthroat), five glacier-topped peaks about 2,500 metres high, and a campground on the Ashnola River are the focal points of 73-square-kilometre Cathedral Provincial Park. Hiking trails lead to eroded quartzite rocks resembling a cluster of buildings and to a towering granite cliff, 2,545 metres above sea level, which gives sweeping views of the park.

Spotted Lake

Bathtub Races, Torchlight Parades and Lush Orchards

Okanagan Valley

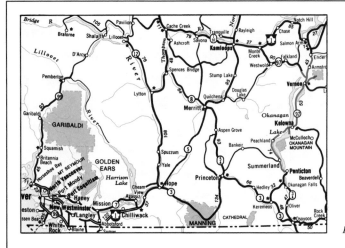

Floating bridge, Kelowna

KELOWNA

A third of all apples harvested in Canada are shipped from Kelowna.
□ The first white settlement in the Okanagan Valley was a mission, established in 1859 by the Rev. Charles Pandosy and members of his order. They planted fruit trees, and their farm and ranch (their brand was OM for Oblates of Mary) attracted other settlers.
□ A 1,400-metre-long floating bridge, built in 1958, links Kelowna with Westbank and is the longest of its kind in Canada.
□ The Kelowna International Regatta, held in July, is the city's biggest annual event. The 150 competitions and exhibitions include a water ballet, waterskiing and hydroplane tournaments.
□ The winter highlight of the year in Kelowna is the annual Snowfest, which includes a parade, casino, dances, and a snowmobile race.

Kelowna
International Regatta

Ogopogo— the Monster of Okanagan Lake

Long before white men came to the Okanagan Valley, Indians told of a lake monster they called *N'ha-a-tik*. The creature lived in a cave near present-day Kelowna at a place called Squally Point. Indians rarely canoed near here; when they did, they would throw an animal overboard as a sacrifice.

N'ha-a-tik received its modern name in 1924 when it was dubbed "Ogopogo." A small stone statue of Ogopogo (*below*) in a Kelowna park is all most people see of the monster, but there are occasional reports from persons who claim to have seen the real thing. Ogopogo is said to be between 9 and 21 metres long, a fast swimmer with a head shaped like that of a sheep, goat or horse.

SUMMERLAND

An Agriculture Canada Research Station, covering some 325 hectares near the southern entrance to Summerland, provides picnic sites for visitors in an attractive ornamental garden.
□ Visitors can tour the Summerland Trout Hatchery, which raises brook and rainbow trout used to stock provincial lakes.

PENTICTON

To the nomadic Salish Indians, *Pen-Tak-Tin* was a "place to stay forever." And so it was to Thomas Ellis, who arrived here from Ireland in 1866 and planted the first orchard in the Okanagan Valley. A plaque seven kilometres south honors Ellis, and a scale model of his homestead and some of his farm equipment are displayed at the Penticton Museum and Archives.
□ *Sicamous*, the last CPR stern-wheeler on Okanagan Lake (launched in 1914 and retired in 1951), is beached at Penticton and on view to the public.
□ Siberian tigers, rhinoceros, timber wolves and musk-oxen are among more than 650 animals at the Okanagan Game Farm, eight kilometres south of Penticton.
□ Local festivities include: the Blossom Festival (May), Peach Festival (midsummer) and the British Columbia Square Dance Jamboree in August.

Giraffe, Okanagan Game Farm

The Okanagan Valley abounds in spectacular mountain scenery, lush orchards and quiet roads lined with fruit stands. Its northern end is dotted with dairy farms and is famed for its cheese industry. More than three million tonnes of cheddar are produced here annually.

Most years the Okanagan has more than 2,000 hours of sunshine. The Penticton area claims 10 hours of sunshine a day in July and August—more, say locals, than Hawaii.

Summer fairs and festivals include the Interior Provincial Exhibition, one of the biggest agricultural festivals in British Columbia. Begun in 1899, the four-day event is held in early September at Armstrong.

Another popular event is the Kelowna Regatta, held on Okanagan Lake (home of the legendary lake monster Ogopogo). The regatta, held in July, features bathtub races, and swimming and diving competitions. Other attractions in the valley are the Okanagan Game Farm, south of Penticton, annually visited by more than 100,000 people, and the historic O'Keefe Ranch, which reflects the pioneer life-style of a century ago.

Winters of the Okanagan Valley are crisp. The climate encourages outdoor activities such as skiing and snowmobiling. Western Canada's biggest winter carnival is held at Vernon in February. The celebration includes torchlight parades, dogsled races and sleighrides.

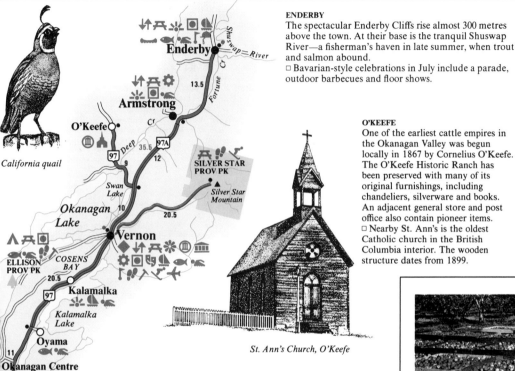

California quail

ENDERBY

The spectacular Enderby Cliffs rise almost 300 metres above the town. At their base is the tranquil Shuswap River—a fisherman's haven in late summer, when trout and salmon abound.
□ Bavarian-style celebrations in July include a parade, outdoor barbecues and floor shows.

O'KEEFE

One of the earliest cattle empires in the Okanagan Valley was begun locally in 1867 by Cornelius O'Keefe. The O'Keefe Historic Ranch has been preserved with many of its original furnishings, including chandeliers, silverware and books. An adjacent general store and post office also contain pioneer items.
□ Nearby St. Ann's is the oldest Catholic church in the British Columbia interior. The wooden structure dates from 1899.

ARMSTRONG

This proudly western town began as a ranching community, but today it is the trading center for the productive agricultural district of the Spallumcheen Valley. The Armstrong-Spallumcheen Museum preserves items of local historical interest.
□ An annual rodeo and the Interior Provincial Exhibition are among the local popular events here.

St. Ann's Church, O'Keefe

VERNON

Exhibits in the Greater Vernon Museum and Archives include Salish Indian artifacts, pioneer implements and such turn-of-the-century relics as a livery stable coach and a double-cutter sleigh. A natural history section displays local birds, animals and minerals. The museum is part of the Vernon Civic Center.
□ Polson Park has a replica of a Japanese teahouse, Japanese gardens and a nine-metre floral clock made of 3,500 plants. The clock is the only one of its kind in western Canada.

Japanese garden, Polson Park, Vernon

Apple harvest in the Okanagan Valley

A Cornucopia of Fruit From a Lush, Lovely Valley

Once only cactus and sagebrush grew on the dry slopes of the Okanagan Valley. But since the successful introduction of irrigation in the 1930s, the Okanagan Valley has been known as the "fruit basket of Canada." Orchards and vineyards flourish in the fertile soil and the year-round mild climate. Crops ripen earlier here than in any other fruit-growing area of Canada. In June, when fresh fruit become available, stands piled with produce for sale are set up along the roads.

About 30 to 40 percent of Canada's apples, cherries, peaches, pears and plums—and all its apricots—are grown in the Okanagan Valley. Local processing plants turn the cornucopia of fruit into juices, concentrates, nectars and pie fillings. Local grapes—combined with imported varieties—are used to produce wines. Wineries at Kelowna and Penticton are open for tours and tastings.

Long Lakes; Flocks of Birds; Berries, Peaches and Plums

Southeastern British Columbia

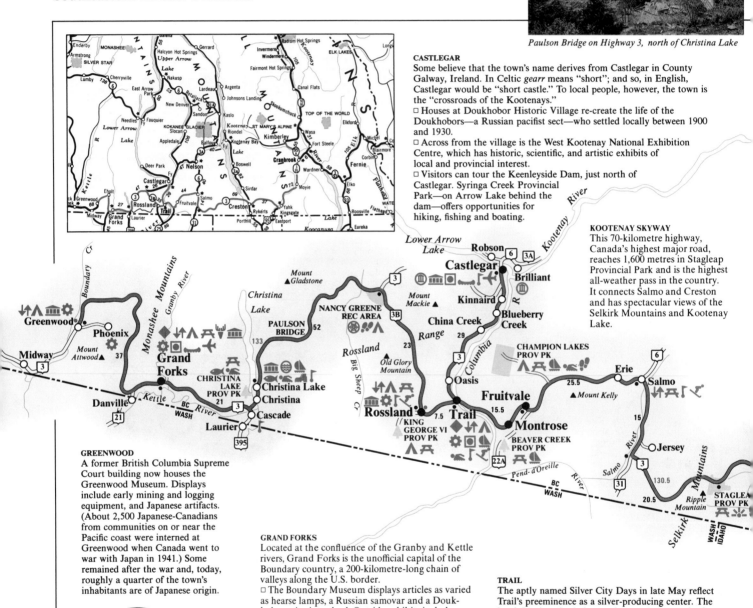

Paulson Bridge on Highway 3, north of Christina Lake

CASTLEGAR
Some believe that the town's name derives from Castlegar in County Galway, Ireland. In Celtic *gearr* means "short"; and so, in English, Castlegar would be "short castle." To local people, however, the town is the "crossroads of the Kootenays."
□ Houses at Doukhobor Historic Village re-create the life of the Doukhobors—a Russian pacifist sect—who settled locally between 1900 and 1930.
□ Across from the village is the West Kootenay National Exhibition Centre, which has historic, scientific, and artistic exhibits of local and provincial interest.
□ Visitors can tour the Keenleyside Dam, just north of Castlegar. Syringa Creek Provincial Park—on Arrow Lake behind the dam—offers opportunities for hiking, fishing and boating.

KOOTENAY SKYWAY
This 70-kilometre highway, Canada's highest major road, reaches 1,600 metres in Stagleap Provincial Park and is the highest all-weather pass in the country. It connects Salmo and Creston and has spectacular views of the Selkirk Mountains and Kootenay Lake.

GREENWOOD
A former British Columbia Supreme Court building now houses the Greenwood Museum. Displays include early mining and logging equipment, and Japanese artifacts. (About 2,500 Japanese-Canadians from communities on or near the Pacific coast were interned at Greenwood when Canada went to war with Japan in 1941.) Some remained after the war and, today, roughly a quarter of the town's inhabitants are of Japanese origin.

GRAND FORKS
Located at the confluence of the Granby and Kettle rivers, Grand Forks is the unofficial capital of the Boundary country, a 200-kilometre-long chain of valleys along the U.S. border.
□ The Boundary Museum displays articles as varied as hearse lamps, a Russian samovar and a Doukhobor spinning wheel. Outside exhibits include a stagecoach and an early fire engine (c.1897).
□ Christina Lake is one of the warmest and clearest lakes in British Columbia. The lake abounds in bass and rainbow trout.

Fire engine, Grand Forks

TRAIL
The aptly named Silver City Days in late May reflect Trail's preeminence as a silver-producing center. The local Cominco lead-zinc smelter produces much of Canada's silver—as a by-product of lead and zinc concentrate.
□ Another tribute to the town's mining history—the frieze *City of Lead and Zinc* that decorates a window a Trail city hall—is the work of Victoria-based artist George Norris.
□ In summer visitors can tour Cominco's 480,000-horsepower hydroelectric plant at Waneta.
□ The cairn marking the site of the Hudson's Bay Company post of Fort Shepherd (1856-70), at the junction of the Columbia and Pend d'Oreille rivers, was built with stones taken from the original structure.

0 2 4 6 8 10 Miles
0 4 8 12 16 Kilometres

Towering mountains and gentle valleys, sparkling lakes and inviting beaches—this is British Columbia's Kootenay region.

One of the most popular areas for tourists—particularly canoeists—is the Arrow lakes. Flanked by the Selkirk and Monashee mountains, the Upper and Lower Arrow lakes stretch for 185 kilometres but are seldom wider than 3 kilometres. Beaches and campgrounds line their shores.

The Kootenay River links the Arrow lakes with Kootenay Lake and the Creston Valley. Lush and lovely, nestled between the 2,000-metre peaks of the Selkirk and Purcell mountains, the valley is a cluster of neat towns, a patchwork of grainfields and orchards, an expanse of lakes and marshes—and a bird-watcher's delight. Thousands of geese, swans and ducks pass this way regularly.

Strawberries, raspberries, pears, cherries, peaches, plums and apples are cultivated here in abundance, and in July the town of Creston celebrates with a blossom festival. Another July festival, Bavarian-style, is held at nearby Kimberley. The event attracts thousands of visitors.

Much of the Kootenay country was shaped by gold-seekers who flocked here in the 1890s. Their presence can still be felt in museums, ghost towns and abandoned mine workings scattered throughout the region.

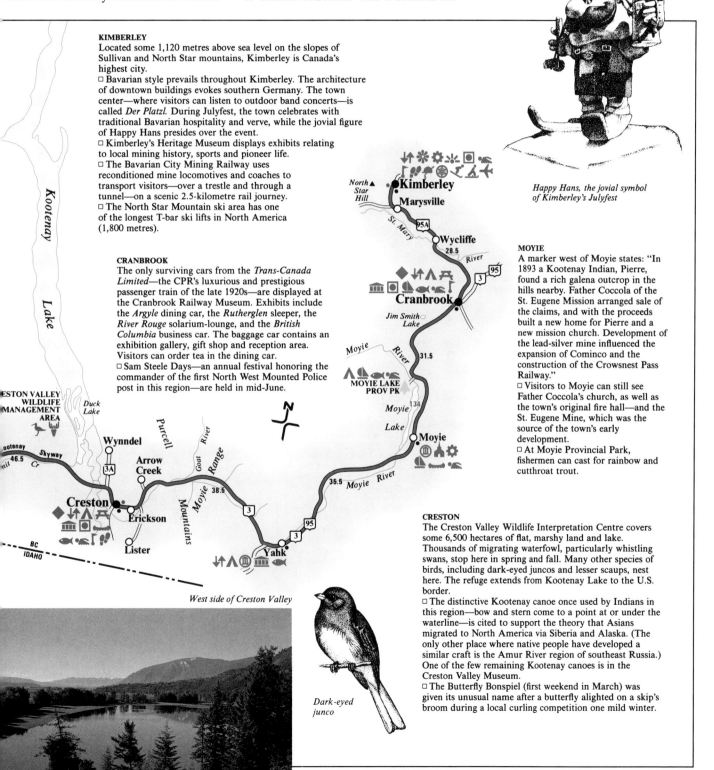

Happy Hans, the jovial symbol of Kimberley's Julyfest

KIMBERLEY

Located some 1,120 metres above sea level on the slopes of Sullivan and North Star mountains, Kimberley is Canada's highest city.

□ Bavarian style prevails throughout Kimberley. The architecture of downtown buildings evokes southern Germany. The town center—where visitors can listen to outdoor band concerts—is called *Der Platzl*. During Julyfest, the town celebrates with traditional Bavarian hospitality and verve, while the jovial figure of Happy Hans presides over the event.

□ Kimberley's Heritage Museum displays exhibits relating to local mining history, sports and pioneer life.

□ The Bavarian City Mining Railway uses reconditioned mine locomotives and coaches to transport visitors—over a trestle and through a tunnel—on a scenic 2.5-kilometre rail journey.

□ The North Star Mountain ski area has one of the longest T-bar ski lifts in North America (1,800 metres).

CRANBROOK

The only surviving cars from the *Trans-Canada Limited*—the CPR's luxurious and prestigious passenger train of the late 1920s—are displayed at the Cranbrook Railway Museum. Exhibits include the *Argyle* dining car, the *Rutherglen* sleeper, the *River Rouge* solarium-lounge, and the *British Columbia* business car. The baggage car contains an exhibition gallery, gift shop and reception area. Visitors can order tea in the dining car.

□ Sam Steele Days—an annual festival honoring the commander of the first North West Mounted Police post in this region—are held in mid-June.

MOYIE

A marker west of Moyie states: "In 1893 a Kootenay Indian, Pierre, found a rich galena outcrop in the hills nearby. Father Coccola of the St. Eugene Mission arranged sale of the claims, and with the proceeds built a new home for Pierre and a new mission church. Development of the lead-silver mine influenced the expansion of Cominco and the construction of the Crowsnest Pass Railway."

□ Visitors to Moyie can still see Father Coccola's church, as well as the town's original fire hall—and the St. Eugene Mine, which was the source of the town's early development.

□ At Moyie Provincial Park, fishermen can cast for rainbow and cutthroat trout.

CRESTON

The Creston Valley Wildlife Interpretation Centre covers some 6,500 hectares of flat, marshy land and lake. Thousands of migrating waterfowl, particularly whistling swans, stop here in spring and fall. Many other species of birds, including dark-eyed juncos and lesser scaups, nest here. The refuge extends from Kootenay Lake to the U.S. border.

□ The distinctive Kootenay canoe once used by Indians in this region—bow and stern come to a point at or under the waterline—is cited to support the theory that Asians migrated to North America via Siberia and Alaska. (The only other place where native people have developed a similar craft is the Amur River region of southeast Russia.) One of the few remaining Kootenay canoes is in the Creston Valley Museum.

□ The Butterfly Bonspiel (first weekend in March) was given its unusual name after a butterfly alighted on a skip's broom during a local curling competition one mild winter.

West side of Creston Valley

Dark-eyed junco

Kootenay Lake

CRESTON VALLEY WILDLIFE MANAGEMENT AREA

Duck Lake

North Star Hill

Kimberley

Marysville

St. Mary River

95A

Wycliffe
28.5

95

River

Cranbrook

Jim Smith Lake

Moyie River

31.5

MOYIE LAKE PROV PK

Moyie Lake

3

95

35.5 Moyie River

Moyie

134

Wynndel

3A

Arrow Creek

Purcell River

Goat River

Moyie Mountains

38.5

Creston

Erickson

Lister

Kootenay Skyway

46.5

Cr

BC IDAHO

Yahk

Where a Steep Trail Traces Slocan Valley's 'Silver Past'

Southeastern British Columbia

Fishing in clear lakes, exploring ghost towns and hiking through wilderness are among the many vacation activities that draw travelers to this region. The route between the communities of Nakusp and Howser passes by the snow-mantled peaks of the Valhalla, Slocan and Kokanee ranges, and skirts lakes abounding with rainbow trout (some of the world's biggest), Dolly Varden and kokanee salmon.

At New Denver a steep hiking trail leads to the top of 2,280-metre Idaho Peak. The

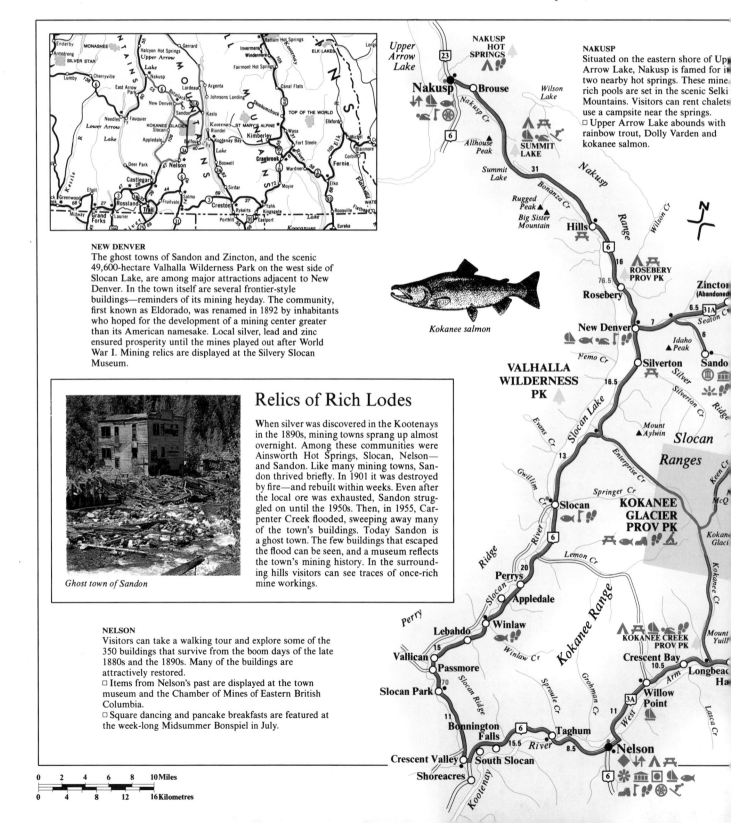

NEW DENVER

The ghost towns of Sandon and Zincton, and the scenic 49,600-hectare Valhalla Wilderness Park on the west side of Slocan Lake, are among major attractions adjacent to New Denver. In the town itself are several frontier-style buildings—reminders of its mining heyday. The community, first known as Eldorado, was renamed in 1892 by inhabitants who hoped for the development of a mining center greater than its American namesake. Local silver, lead and zinc ensured prosperity until the mines played out after World War I. Mining relics are displayed at the Silvery Slocan Museum.

Relics of Rich Lodes

When silver was discovered in the Kootenays in the 1890s, mining towns sprang up almost overnight. Among these communities were Ainsworth Hot Springs, Slocan, Nelson—and Sandon. Like many mining towns, Sandon thrived briefly. In 1901 it was destroyed by fire—and rebuilt within weeks. Even after the local ore was exhausted, Sandon struggled on until the 1950s. Then, in 1955, Carpenter Creek flooded, sweeping away many of the town's buildings. Today Sandon is a ghost town. The few buildings that escaped the flood can be seen, and a museum reflects the town's mining history. In the surrounding hills visitors can see traces of once-rich mine workings.

Ghost town of Sandon

NELSON

Visitors can take a walking tour and explore some of the 350 buildings that survive from the boom days of the late 1880s and the 1890s. Many of the buildings are attractively restored.
□ Items from Nelson's past are displayed at the town museum and the Chamber of Mines of Eastern British Columbia.
□ Square dancing and pancake breakfasts are featured at the week-long Midsummer Bonspiel in July.

NAKUSP

Situated on the eastern shore of Upper Arrow Lake, Nakusp is famed for its two nearby hot springs. These mineral rich pools are set in the scenic Selkirk Mountains. Visitors can rent chalets or use a campsite near the springs.
□ Upper Arrow Lake abounds with rainbow trout, Dolly Varden and kokanee salmon.

Kokanee salmon

0 2 4 6 8 10 Miles
0 4 8 12 16 Kilometres

way is lined with abandoned tunnels and mine dumps, ghosts of the 1890s when rich silver, lead and zinc deposits made the Slocan Valley famous. Near the summit of Idaho Peak is Sandon, once a silver boom town. The Idaho Lookout, a provincial fire tower, provides a spectacular panorama of the region.

At Nelson, jagged peaks tower to 2,750 metres above ice cliffs and alpine lakes in nearby Kokanee Glacier Provincial Park. The 20-metre Bonnington Falls and rapids

boil on the Kootenay River below some magnificent mountain scenery. Rocks in the area bear Indian paintings of undetermined age and origin.

At Ainsworth Hot Springs visitors can bathe in mineral-rich waters or explore the dark passageways of the Cody Caves. Farther north, at Kaslo, is the drydocked stern-wheeler *Moyie*, now a museum. South of Howser visitors can see the mammoth Duncan Dam, part of the multimillion-dollar Columbia River project.

Meadow Creek spawning channel, Howser

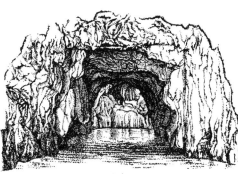

KASLO
S.S. *Moyie,* last of the Kootenay Lake stern-wheelers, now in drydock, is a museum and a monument to Kaslo's pioneers. The 50-metre vessel, built in 1897, was used for 60 years.
□ Big silver strikes in 1893 made Kaslo a thriving community. Today the village is a popular resort and distribution center for the Lardeau Valley.
□ The town's annual May Day Festival includes a parade, craft displays, and log-rolling and hang-gliding competitions.

Ainsworth Hot Springs

AINSWORTH HOT SPRINGS
Discovered in the 1880s by Henry Cody, a prospector searching for gold, the Cody Caves near Ainsworth Hot Springs received little publicity until 1966, when they were designated a provincial park. The biggest chamber is the Throne Room, a 38-square-metre limestone gallery of "soda straws" (hollow fingers of calcium), stalactites and stalagmites. Other chambers include an echo room, and a room with an underground creek that drops 11 metres over upper and lower Cody Falls.
□ Not far from the caves visitors can relax and bathe in the invigorating waters of the Ainsworth Hot Springs.

HOWSER
A swimming area and boat-launching ramp have been created at Howser as part of the Duncan Dam reservoir. A viewpoint overlooks the dam.
□ At nearby Meadow Creek is a three-kilometre-long spawning channel for kokanee salmon. The spawning season begins in mid-August.

Days of the Stern-Wheelers

Boat travel on Kootenay Lake peaked with the arrival of prospectors seeking silver, zinc and lead—and by the 1890s a fleet of stern-wheelers plied the lake. These steamships carried supplies for the mines, and passengers to lakeside settlements. But with the coming of the railway in the early 1900s, the need for water transportation was greatly reduced (although stern-wheelers continued to be made until the 1920s). The last stern-wheeler on the lake, the S.S. *Moyie*, was retired in 1957.

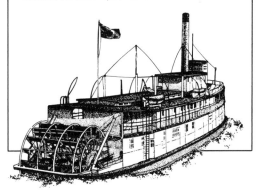

BALFOUR
This tiny community at the junction of the north, south and west arms of Kootenay Lake is the western terminus of the longest free ferry ride in North America. The 45-minute trip takes visitors across Kootenay Lake to Kootenay Bay.
□ Swimming, year-round fishing, boating, houseboating, and miniature golf are available in Balfour.

Kootenay Lake near Ainsworth Hot Springs

Gold in the Wild Horse River, Coal From the Rockies

Southeastern British Columbia

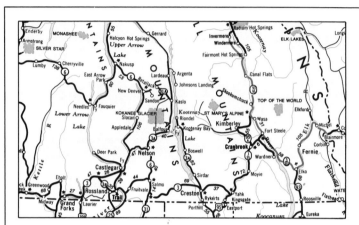

Looking for River Gold—With a Pan and a Little Luck

Visitors to Fort Steele Turn-of-the-Century Town can pan for gold in nearby Wild Horse River, scene of a gold rush in the 1860s. All you need to recover nuggets or flakes is a traditional shallow steel or plastic pan (15 to 40 centimetres in diameter) and a little luck.

Fill the pan three-quarters full with sand and gravel from the riverbed or from rock crevices flooded during spring run-off. Fill the rest of the pan with water and knead (1) to remove stones and pebbles. Now shake the pan from side to side so that heavy material (gold is the heaviest) sinks to the bottom. The lighter sands are then washed away by tilting the pan and rotating it gently in the river's current (2) until a coarse dark layer, called concentrate, remains. Gold nuggets and flakes show up against the concentrate and can be picked out.

Extracting gold dust from the concentrate is more complicated. Many early prospectors used a method called mercury amalgamation. A small amount of mercury (about 12 grams per kilogram of concentrate) was kneaded into the wet mixture. It absorbed the gold and worked its way to the top, where it was collected and squeezed through a cloth (to be reused)—leaving a paste which was mostly gold. The remaining mercury was evaporated by heating the paste over fire, leaving pure gold.

Commercial mines have adapted the mercury amalgamation method on a large scale. But it is not recommended for amateur prospectors because mercury fumes are extremely poisonous.

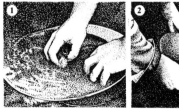

INVERMERE

Thirty-two kilometres west of Invermere is the 1,315-square-kilometre Purcell Wilderness Conservancy. A 61-kilometre-long hiking trail crosses the Purcell Mountains to Argenta on Kootenay Lake. The highest point on the trail is 2,256-metre-high Earl Grey Pass.
□ Panorama Mountains, on the way to the Purcell Wilderness Conservancy, offers downhill, cross-country and heliskiing from November to April.

PREMIER LAKE PROVINCIAL PARK

The 662-hectare park, at the south end of Premier Lake, is some 15 kilometres east of Skookumchuck. A campground has swimming beaches and boat-launching facilities. Visitors may see the white-tailed and mule deer and wapiti that come to the shore to drink. Fishermen can angle for rainbow and brook trout.

WASA LAKE PROVINCIAL PARK

The sharp nasal call of the common nighthawk can be heard at dusk, as it hunts insects in this park at the northern corner of 2.3-kilometre-long Wasa Lake. A campground with sandy beaches and a boat-launching ramp is backed by a mixed forest of ponderosa and lodgepole pine, Douglas fir and trembling aspen. Western chipmunks and Columbian ground squirrels are the park's most common mammals.

Common nighthawk

Bull thistle

Kootenay Trout Hatchery, Wardner

Much of the route between Invermere and Crowsnest Pass parallels the Columbia, the Kootenay and the Elk rivers. In this region, the Columbia heads northwest, while its nearby tributary, the Kootenay, flows in the opposite direction.

Invermere offers visitors skiing on the groomed slopes and trails of Panorama Mountain, and hiking through the silent majesty of the Purcell Mountains.

South of Invermere, past Windermere, Columbia (source of the Columbia River) and Wasa lakes, is Fort Steele Turn-of-the-Century Town. Originally named Galbraith's Ferry, Fort Steele sprang up in the 1860s after a gold discovery in nearby Wild Horse River. Within 20 years, the community became a prosperous center. Decline began after 1900 when it was bypassed by the railway.

As gold ran out, coal—discovered near Fernie in the 1870s—became the region's economic mainstay. The CPR used the coal for steam locomotives after the 1885 opening of the transcontinental line. Today the area between Fernie and Crowsnest Pass is one of the world's major soft coal strip-mining districts. Its coal fuels industries in western Canada, the United States and Japan.

Fort Steele Turn-of-the-Century Town

Waterwheel, Fort Steele Provincial Historic Park

SPARWOOD
Established in 1960, Sparwood sits atop the largest soft coal deposits in North America. Westar mining operation produces five million tonnes of coal here annually from the largest strip mine in Canada. Some is shipped directly to industries in western North America and Japan; the rest is turned into coke for smelters throughout Canada and the United States. The local chamber of commerce conducts tours of the vast mining complex.
□ The local Fall Fair in September is popular with visitors.

FORT STEELE TURN-OF-THE-CENTURY TOWN
Historic Fort Steele commemorates its exciting past. In the heady gold rush days of 1864, the town began as a ferry terminal—Galbraith's Ferry—on the Kootenay River. Within two decades, it had become an administrative center. The residents renamed the town for the legendary major (later major general) Sir Samuel Steele of the North West Mounted Police, who established a police post nearby in 1887.
□ Today visitors to Fort Steele can tour some of the 60 restored or reconstructed buildings—including the police post barracks, the 1864 ferry office, and the Prospector Printing Office, which produces an old-time newspaper on its own presses. Fort Steele also offers steam train and stagecoach rides. The Wildhorse Theatre presents Victorian music hall fare. In summer, visitors can watch wood stove baking, quilting and other skills from Fort Steele's past.

FERNIE
As the sun sets on 2,506-metre Mount Hosmer, some 15 kilometres northeast of Fernie, the shadow of a man on a galloping horse appears on the mountain wall. According to legend, the ghostly figure, cast by the jagged surface of the mountain, reminds the town that it was once cursed by a Kootenay Indian chief. In the 1880s, William Fernie, the town's founder, angered the Indians when he broke his engagement to the chief's daughter. The Indians lifted the curse in 1964.

ARDNER
ght kilometres north of Wardner,
ootenay Trout Hatchery—the second
rgest provincial hatchery in British
olumbia—raises roughly six million fish
om eggs collected in the wilderness. Species include
inbow, brook and cutthroat trout, and kokanee
lmon. A constant flow of fresh, cool water through
ant troughs and ponds simulates the fishes' natural
vironment. The hatchery consumes as much water as
town of 50,000. Visitors are welcome year-round.

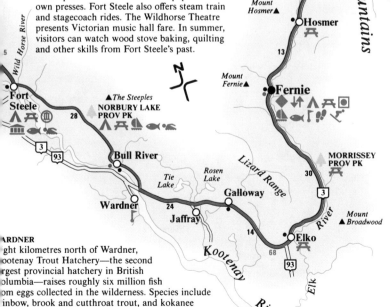

Mount Hosmer (right) and Elk River valley, near Fernie

Canada's Houseboat Capital ...
and Swarms of Sockeyes

South-Central British Columbia

The fur trade, a short-lived gold rush and the transcontinental railway, all lured fortune-seekers to "the Shuswap." In their wake, thousands of vacationers now throng to this gentle wilderness.

Protected anchorages, warm water and safe, sandy beaches have made Shuswap Lake a boater's paradise. Sicamous, one of several bustling towns ringing the lake, proudly bills itself as the "Houseboat Capital of Canada."

From Sicamous boaters have access to

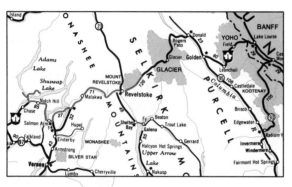

A Run of Salmon From Sea to River

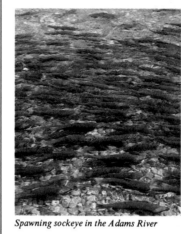

Spawning sockeye in the Adams River

Every year, for a three-week period in October, the Adams River is in crimson flood as up to two million sockeye salmon return here to spawn and die.

The salmon have a four-year life cycle. Hatched in the cold clear rivers, they spend a year in the calm depths of Shuswap Lake. The next spring, as fingerlings, they swim some 500 kilometres to the Pacific Ocean.

At the onset of sexual maturity in their fourth year, the salmon—guided mainly by a highly developed sense of smell—leave the ocean and make the run back to the stream of their birth.

For weeks the Fraser and Thompson rivers and the Kamloops and Little Shuswap lakes teem with fish, their bodies changed from silvery blue to brilliant red. The salmon travel up to 50 kilometres a day; many die of exhaustion, in rapids or in trying to leap waterfalls. At last, in the Adams River, each female digs a depression in the gravel bed and lays her eggs, and a male fertilizes them. Then both fish waste away and die within a few days. Only one in a thousand eggs will produce a salmon which will reach maturity.

ADAMS LAKE

Even in non-peak years, the October spawning run of sockeye salmon up the Adams River is a spectacular sight. A tract of land at the river's mouth has been set aside for spectators; a viewing platform here overlooks the Adams River.
□ Local lakes and rivers offer fishing for kokanee salmon, rainbow and lake trout, and Dolly Varden.

Shuswap Indian kekuli under construction, Shuswap Lake Provincial Park

SHUSWAP LAKE PROVINCIAL PARK

This park is on the west arm of Shuswap Lake, the site of placer-gold operations in the 1930s and '40s.
□ In the park is a replica of a Shuswap Indian *kekuli* (winter dwelling). A *kekuli* was built in a pit one to two metres deep and up to nine metres in diameter. Logs angled upward were set in the floor of the pit and on them was placed a framework of slim poles, then layers of grass, brush and bark. A thick layer of earth completed the structure.
□ At Scotch Lake travelers can board the stern-wheeler *Sorrento Queen* for a 45-minute expedition to Copper Lake.

SALMON ARM

Located in a rich farming belt, Salmon Arm is noted for its fruit, vegetables and dairy products.
□ On nearby Mount Ida, rock hounders hunt for blue-gray and banded agates, prase, crystalline geodes and amethyst.

SHUSWAP LAKE

A popular way of exploring Shuswap Lake is by houseboat. Visitors can rent boats from local operators and take advantage of several overnight anchorages with shore facilities.
□ On the map, Shuswap Lake has the shape of a huge distorted letter "H." At the point where the four arms of the lake meet is Cinnemousun Narrows Provincial Park, one of many attractive spots accessible only by boat.

SICAMOUS

Visitors can enjoy a day's excursion on the old-time stern-wheeler *Phoebe Ann* that travels between Sicamous and Seymour Arm.
□ At several places along the shores of Shuswap and Mara lakes near Sicamous are rock paintings of sticklike animals and birds, human faces and what may be a calendar. The rock paintings, which resemble similar work in Russia, may be the work of prehistoric people who crossed the Bering Strait to North America.

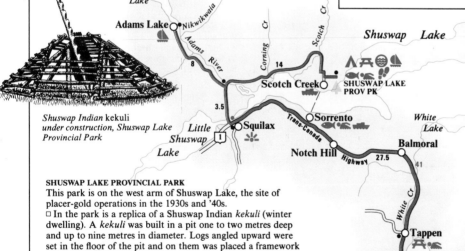

Houseboat, Shuswap Lake

0 1 2 3 4 5 Miles
0 2 4 6 8 Kilometres

two lakeside provincial parks and roughly 1,000 kilometres of an attractive shoreline dotted with marinas, campgrounds and fine swimming spots.

One of many natural attractions in the Shuswap is the sockeye salmon run in the Adams River. During a three-week period in October, as many as two million salmon in crimson spawning colors gather to bury their eggs in a short stretch of riverbed.

In contrast with placid Shuswap Lake is the high, rocky spine of Mount Revel- stoke National Park. Erosion and glaciers have relentlessly chipped and carved its landscape. Abundant rainfall in the park supports thick forests of giant cedar and hemlock in the valleys, and a kaleidoscope of alpine flowers on the peaks. Rising to the very top of 1,938-metre Mount Revel- stoke, Summit Road presents a spectacular transition from the park's dense lowland forest to alpine meadows.

Mount Revelstoke National Park

MOUNT REVELSTOKE NATIONAL PARK
Mount Revelstoke lies in the Columbia Mountains, a range of castellated mountains and broad valleys bordered on the east by the Rockies and on the west by the Interior Plateau.
□ The Mountain Meadows Trail, one of several in the park, leads past the "Icebox," a permanent patch of ice protected from melting by the rock walls around it. This trail and others cross mountain meadows sprinkled with Indian paintbrush, blue lupine, yellow arnica and white valerian.
□ The turquoise waters of Upper and Lower Jade lakes contrast with the glaciers on nearby mountain slopes. Eva Lake rests on a ledge—a few metres from its shore the land drops more than a hundred metres to a valley below.
□ A 26-kilometre Summit Road, begun in 1911, switchbacks to the summit of Mount Revelstoke (1,938 metres). There, at a lookout, arrows identify the surrounding peaks.

THREE VALLEY GAP
A three-story, 103-room hotel and a saloon with an ornately carved bar are among the 20 restored 19th-century buildings in this re-creation of an old-time mining town. The buildings have been moved to Three Valley Gap from different places throughout central British Columbia. Other historic buildings include a combination barbershop and dentist's office, a 12-pew church, a trapper's log hut, a log schoolhouse, a blacksmith's shop, a general store, a buggy shop, a jail and the Golden Wheel saloon.

REVELSTOKE DAM
Canada's highest concrete dam (175 metres) is about five kilometres north of Revelstoke. Visitors can tour the powerhouse. There is an interpretive center and a lookout.

REVELSTOKE
Situated on the Columbia River, Revelstoke was first called "The Eddy" for a powerful swirl in the river. It was renamed for the British banker Lord Revelstoke, who saved the CPR from financial ruin during the construction of the transcontinental line in the 1880s.
□ Revelstoke Museum's collection of early mining and railway equipment includes a chair used by an itinerant dentist on his journeys through local mining country in the early 1900s.

Where the Last Spike Was Hammered Home

Canada's most famous photograph (*left*) shows Donald Smith, a director of the CPR, driving the last spike in Canada's first transcontinental railway. The date was Nov. 7, 1885; the site, a siding named Craigellachie, in Eagle Pass. Smith hammered home an ordinary iron spike. There was a moment of silence, and then a cheer went up among the men who were gathered around. "All I can say is that the work has been well done in every way," summed up William Cornelius Van Horne, the stubborn, hard-driving CPR vice-president who had completed the railway in four years when everybody said it couldn't be done in ten. Today a cairn marks the spot where the last spike was driven. A plaque beside the nearby Trans-Canada Highway reads: "A nebulous dream was a reality: an iron ribbon crossed Canada from sea to sea. Often following the footsteps of early explorers, nearly 3,000 miles of steel rail pushed across vast prairies, cleft lofty mountain passes, twisted through canyons, and bridged a thousand streams."

Revelstoke

Snow-Mantled Peaks in a Mountain Playground

Southeastern British Columbia

The 8,000-kilometre Trans-Canada Highway encounters few regions as spectacular as the hot springs, ice fields and glaciers of the Purcell, Selkirk and Rocky mountains. Between Glacier and Yoho national parks, the Trans-Canada follows the Illecillewaet, Columbia and Kicking Horse rivers through a mountain playground resplendent with awe-inspiring beauty. For those who seek nature's solitude, the region has a vast network of trails along rocky slopes and through evergreen forests.

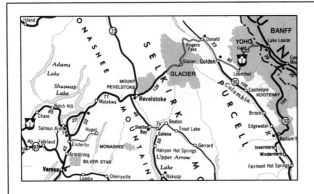

In Glacier National Park, one of the world's heaviest snowfalls creates huge avalanches that can strip mountains of trees and bury sections of road. Concrete snow sheds, one more than half a kilometre long, cover the Trans-Canada Highway at danger spots. Earth dams and barriers of rubble divert less severe slides. When scientists notice avalanche buildups, parts of the highway are closed and an artillery crew fires howitzer shells into unstable snow. This triggers an avalanche, but under controlled conditions, and prevents dangerous accumulations of snow.

Fighting Avalanches With Artillery

GLACIER NATIONAL PARK

Established in 1886, Glacier National Park was accessible only by railway for its first 70 years. Now it is traversed by 43 kilometres of the 147-kilometre Rogers Pass section of the Trans-Canada Highway. □ The ancient mountains of the Selkirk Range, formed millions of years before the Rockies, cradle more than 400 glaciers in this 1,350-square-kilometre park. The Illecillewaet and Asulkan glaciers near the slopes of Mount Sir Donald are reached by hiking trails from the Illecillewaet campground. More than 250 square kilometres of glaciers and *névé* (granular snow) provide superb skiing in the Asulkan Valley. The park's slow-moving rivers of ice spawn a glistening network of alpine lakes, rivers and waterfalls. Thick forests of western red cedar and western hemlock are home to ravens and Steller's jays. Grasses and mountain flowers such as alpine anemones and glacier lilies thrive in meadows above the tree line.

Alpine anemone

Glacier National Park

ROGERS PASS

One of the world's most beautiful mountain roads is the Rogers Pass section of the Trans-Canada Highway (between Golden and Revelstoke). It winds past rugged peaks, emerald lakes and immense ice fields, threads deep ravines and clings to precipitous cliffs. A 1.5-kilometre hiking trail at the summit of 1,320-metre Rogers Pass wanders east through the Selkirk Range.

Clark's nutcracker

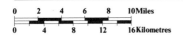

More than 400 glaciers mantle the peaks of the Purcell Mountains and Selkirk Range in Glacier National Park. Meltwater from the glaciers spawns hundreds of alpine lakes, rivers and waterfalls. Thick forests and meadows covered with lush grasses and vivid wildflowers are also part of the stunning scenery.

The glacier-fed Kicking Horse River (named for an ornery packhorse) courses through Yoho National Park. Yoho's peaks —30 of which are more than 3,000 metres— are interlaced with spectacular alpine waters.

Blue-green Emerald Lake and its collar of evergreens are surrounded by gargantuan ice-topped peaks. The Yoho River, milky gray with silt from Yoho Glacier, crashes into the clear Kicking Horse River at the Meeting of the Waters. The misty plume of Laughing Falls and the 254-metre-high Takakkaw Falls, one of Canada's highest waterfalls, are in the Yoho River valley.

Takakkaw Falls, Yoho National Park

TAKAKKAW FALLS
One of our highest waterfalls, the 254-metre-high Takakkaw plunges into the Yoho River in Yoho National Park. The stream that feeds the waterfall originates in Daly Glacier and courses through a U-shaped hanging valley.
□ At the nearby Meeting of the Waters, the Yoho River, laden with silt from Yoho Glacier, merges with the clear Kicking Horse River.

ERALD LAKE
vely Emerald Lake in Yoho National Park, ned for its deep green color, is surrounded a dozen snowcapped peaks. Two hiking ils—one of which passes through the 2,180-tre Burgess Pass—skirt the lake and lead to Wapta Icefield in the northern part of the k. Also at Emerald Lake is the refurbished herald Lake Lodge, one of a number of inns ce operated in the park by the CPR.

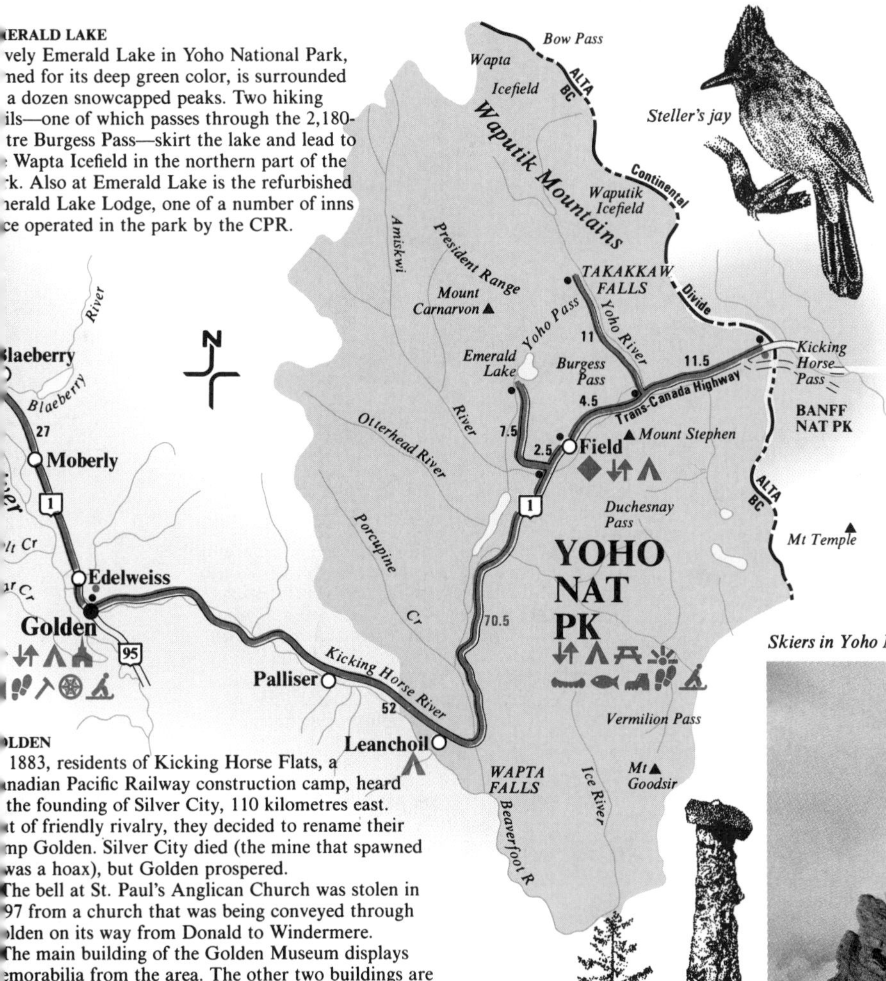

Bow Pass
Wapta
Icefield
ALTA
BC
Waputik Mountains
Continental
Divide
Waputik Icefield
Steller's jay
President Range
Amiskwi
Mount Carnarvon
TAKAKKAW FALLS
Yoho Pass
Yoho River
11
Emerald Lake
Burgess Pass
11.5
Kicking Horse Pass
Trans-Canada Highway
4.5
BANFF NAT PK
River
Blaeberry
Blaeberry
27
Moberly
Otterhead River
7.5
2.5
Field
Mount Stephen
1
Duchesnay Pass
Porcupine
Cr
YOHO NAT PK
Mt Temple
Edelweiss
Golden
95
70.5
Kicking Horse River
Palliser
52
Leanchoil
Vermilion Pass
WAPTA FALLS
Ice River
Mt Goodsir
Beaverfoot R

LDEN
1883, residents of Kicking Horse Flats, a nadian Pacific Railway construction camp, heard the founding of Silver City, 110 kilometres east. t of friendly rivalry, they decided to rename their mp Golden. Silver City died (the mine that spawned was a hoax), but Golden prospered.
The bell at St. Paul's Anglican Church was stolen in 97 from a church that was being conveyed through lden on its way from Donald to Windermere.
The main building of the Golden Museum displays morabilia from the area. The other two buildings are og school and a blacksmith shop and farm shed.

KICKING HORSE PASS
This gap in a jagged mountain wall is 1,625 metres above sea level. It is the eastern entrance to Yoho National Park and a passage through the Rockies for the Trans-Canada Highway and the Canadian Pacific Railway. The highway and railway follow the twisting Kicking Horse River across the park. The pass straddles the Continental Divide, a height of land which separates rivers and streams flowing to the Pacific, Arctic and Atlantic oceans.

YOHO NATIONAL PARK
This 1,313-square-kilometre park on the west slope of the Rockies richly deserves its Indian name: Yoho is an exclamation of awe and astonishment. The park, which was established in 1886, has its administrative center at Field. West of Field, the Kicking Horse River has carved a hole in a wall of sedimentary rock, leaving a 15-metre-long natural bridge. To the southwest, at Wapta Falls, the river is a 60-metre-wide sheet of water. Some 400 kilometres of trails lead to other geological features. In Hoodoo Valley are 15-metre-high pillars of glacial till capped by precariously balanced boulders. Wildlife includes wapiti, bears, moose, deer, mountain goats and 180 species of birds. Valleys are clothed with evergreens—lodgepole pine, Douglas fir and white spruce—and above the 2,133-metre tree line are colorful alpine flowers and bushes. The Trans-Canada Highway, which passes through the park, offers superb views of Yoho's peaks—30 of which are higher than 3,000 metres.
□ The Burgess Shale site, in the vicinity of Field, contains fossils of about 140 species of marine creatures that existed during the Cambrian period, 530 million years ago. The Burgess Shale site, discovered in 1909 by American geologist and paleontologist Charles Walcott (1850-1927), was declared a United Nations World Heritage Site in 1981. Visitors can make reservations with the park to tour the Walcott quarry—part of the Burgess Shale deposits—also near Field.
□ Just east of Field on the Trans-Canada Highway, a viewpoint for the world-famous spiral railway tunnels attracts as many as 300,000 visitors annually.

Skiers in Yoho National Park

Boulder-capped hoodoo, Yoho National Park

Primroses and Mountain Goats in a Park of Hanging Glaciers

Kootenay National Park

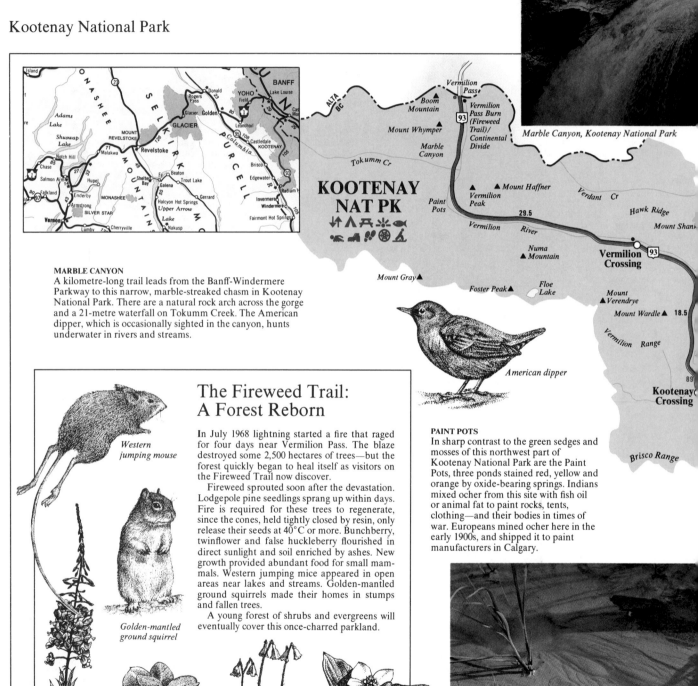

Marble Canyon, Kootenay National Park

American dipper

MARBLE CANYON

A kilometre-long trail leads from the Banff-Windermere Parkway to this narrow, marble-streaked chasm in Kootenay National Park. There are a natural rock arch across the gorge and a 21-metre waterfall on Tokumm Creek. The American dipper, which is occasionally sighted in the canyon, hunts underwater in rivers and streams.

The Fireweed Trail: A Forest Reborn

In July 1968 lightning started a fire that raged for four days near Vermilion Pass. The blaze destroyed some 2,500 hectares of trees—but the forest quickly began to heal itself as visitors on the Fireweed Trail now discover.

Fireweed sprouted soon after the devastation. Lodgepole pine seedlings sprang up within days. Fire is required for these trees to regenerate, since the cones, held tightly closed by resin, only release their seeds at 40°C or more. Bunchberry, twinflower and false huckleberry flourished in direct sunlight and soil enriched by ashes. New growth provided abundant food for small mammals. Western jumping mice appeared in open areas near lakes and streams. Golden-mantled ground squirrels made their homes in stumps and fallen trees.

A young forest of shrubs and evergreens will eventually cover this once-charred parkland.

Western jumping mouse

Golden-mantled ground squirrel

Fireweed

False huckleberry

Twinflower

Bunchberry

PAINT POTS

In sharp contrast to the green sedges and mosses of this northwest part of Kootenay National Park are the Paint Pots, three ponds stained red, yellow and orange by oxide-bearing springs. Indians mixed ocher from this site with fish oil or animal fat to paint rocks, tents, clothing—and their bodies in times of war. Europeans mined ocher here in the early 1900s, and shipped it to paint manufacturers in Calgary.

Paint Pots, Kootenay National Park

Blessed with magnificent mountain scenery, Kootenay National Park is a striking blend of hot springs and cold lakes, of deep canyons and of glaciers twisting down lofty summits. This 1,406-square-kilometre park lies on the western slopes of the Rocky Mountains, and borders Banff and Yoho national parks.

In summer, streams draining glaciers rush down mountain slopes and empty into the Vermilion, Kootenay and Columbia rivers. Some lakes nestle among mountains whose sheer rocky walls descend to the water's edge. Hundreds of pools, marshes and small lakes are cradled in glacial depressions known as kettles. An abundance of wildflowers—red and white heather, columbine, and paintbrush—cover the meadows near hanging glaciers and snowfields.

Western tanagers, pine siskins and Audubon's warblers are found in the forests. Mountain goats, grizzly bears and wapiti inhabit the park. Moose and deer are frequently seen at creekside "licks"—clay banks rich in minerals that animals find pleasant-tasting.

Landmarks along the Banff-Windermere Parkway (Highway 93) dividing the park are Radium Hot Springs, the Sinclair and Marble canyons, the Paint Pots and, at the northern entrance, 1,650-metre Vermilion Pass—the boundary between Alberta and British Columbia, and the summit of the Continental Divide. Rivers east of here drain to the Arctic Ocean or Hudson Bay. Waters to the west flow toward the Pacific.

KOOTENAY NATIONAL PARK

This park was established in 1920 to preserve canyons, mineral hot springs and waterfalls along the Banff-Windermere Parkway. The 105-kilometre highway provides dramatic views of snowcapped mountains. It passes through Sinclair Canyon, whose sheer walls rise some 61 metres above the road, over 1,485-metre Sinclair Pass, and skirts the Rock Wall, a vertical face of the Vermilion Valley.

□ The self-guiding Fireweed, Marble Canyon and Paint Pots trails begin along the parkway. The Fireweed Trail, near Vermilion Pass, loops through meadows of fireweed, harebell, yellow columbine, Labrador tea, and lodgepole pine.

□ Kootenay National Park is actually an ancient ocean floor that, some 75 million years ago, was compressed, folded and sculpted into the Rocky Mountains. Marble Canyon follows a fault in the limestone and marble bedrock, which has been eroded to depths of 37 metres by Tokumm Creek. A 21-metre waterfall at the head of the canyon is milky white from glacial meltwaters that feed it.

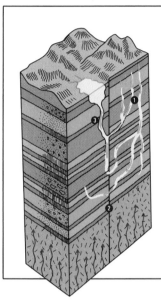

Spring-Fed Pools—Rich in Minerals, Bathwater Warm

Hot springs originate as surface water (1)—rain or melted snow—which seeps through cracks or faults until it is heated by molten rock (2) some five kilometres underground. Temperatures as high as 1,000°C turn the water to steam, which rises through cracks in the rocks, condenses into water as it cools, and bubbles from the ground (3) as warm as bathwater. Some two million litres of water gush from the ground each day at Radium Hot Springs.

Health spas and bathing pools are often built near hot springs because the mineral-rich water is reputed to relieve arthritis and other ailments. A trace of dissolved radium gives Radium Hot Springs its name—but the radioactivity is less than that of a watch's illuminated dial.

RADIUM HOT SPRINGS

The resort is situated about 3 kilometres from the southern entrance to Kootenay National Park. Winter or summer, visitors to Radium Hot Springs can soak or swim in two park-operated outdoor pools known as the Aquacourt. The temperature of the steamy, odorless mineral water averages about 35°C. Development of Radium Hot Springs—known as *kootemik* to local Indians—began in the late 19th century. Radium Hot Springs offers visitors a choice of accommodations—the private lodge beside the Aquacourt or the park campgrounds. A bus shuttle travels between the town and the hot springs.

□ The Kootenay Park information office is situated just south of the park entrance. From a campground at the base of the 2,156-metre Redstreak Mountain (behind the office), visitors can follow a hiking trail to the Aquacourt.

Mountain goats, Kootenay National Park

WINDERMERE

The original site of St. Peter's Anglican Church—sometimes called St. Peter's the Stolen by local people—was at Donald, some 160 kilometres north. When the CPR abandoned Donald in 1897, the church was granted to a neighboring congregation. But the parishioners who were moving to Windermere dismantled St. Peter's and transported the structure to their new hometown by rail and Columbia River barge.

□ A monument commemorates Kootenae House, established in 1807 by David Thompson as the first trading post on the Columbia River.

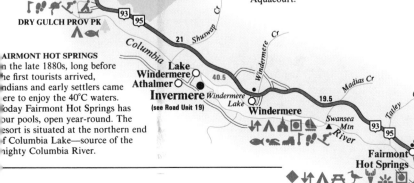

Mount
Mount
Daer Mount
Harkin ▲

Kootenay

93
Banff-Windermere Highway
41

River

▲ Mount Sinclair

Sinclair
Canyon

Stanford Range

Mount Berland ▲

Sinclair

Sinclair
Pass

Redstreak
▲ Mountain

Deer Cr

Radium Hot Springs ◯ •
◆ ∧ ⚓

93
95

DRY GULCH PROV PK
∧ ⚓

21 Shuswap Cr

Columbia

AIRMONT HOT SPRINGS
n the late 1880s, long before
the first tourists arrived,
ndians and early settlers came
ere to enjoy the 40°C waters.
oday Fairmont Hot Springs has
our pools, open year-round. The
esort is situated at the northern end
f Columbia Lake—source of the
ighty Columbia River.

**Lake
Windermere**
Athalmer ◯
Invermere ●
(see Road Unit 19)

40.5

Windermere Cr

Windermere
Lake

Madias Cr

19.5

Tatley Cr

Windermere

Swansea
▲ Mtn

River

93
95

**Fairmont
Hot Springs** ◯

*Fairmont
Mountain* ▲

◆

Columbia
Lake

A Sense of Mystery, Traces of a Haida Past

Queen Charlotte Islands

The rugged mountains and lush forests of the Queen Charlotte Islands are often shrouded in mist and rain, heightening a sense of mystery in the remote land that was once the domain of Haida Indians. Here and there in the silent forests are the remains of ancient Haida totem poles and dugout canoes. Along the coast are a number of abandoned whaling stations.

The Queen Charlottes are poised on the brink of the continental shelf. The islands'

McIntyre Bay

Robert Davidson's totem pole, Haida

HAIDA
In this village, a totem pole (erected in 1969) was carved by artist Robert Davidson in honor of his grandfather, a Haida chief.
□ Two more new totems are at a museum displaying Haida artifacts.

MASSET
The fishing industry is the economic mainstay of Masset, the largest settlement on Graham Island. Delkatla Inlet provides a harbor for the local fishing fleet.
□ During migration, Canada geese, sandhill cranes, trumpeter swans and other waterfowl stop over at the Delkatla Wildlife Sanctuary.

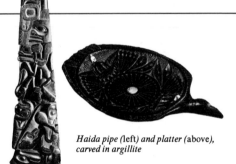

Haida pipe (left) and platter (above), carved in argillite

Beauty in Carved Stone

The Haida, whose domain was the lush Charlotte Islands, were expert hunters and fishermen, fearless warriors, and skilled wood-carvers. From cedar logs they built longhouses and seagoing dugout canoes, and carved totem poles.

After Europeans arrived in 1774, the Haida traded for goods and liquor. Sea otters and seals were slaughtered almost to extinction in only 40 years. The Haida, nearly annihilated by the white man's diseases, abandoned ancestral homes and settled in villages now called Skidegate Mission and Haida.

In the 1820s, with the discovery of argillite, a soft, slatelike stone found only at Slatechuck Mountain on Graham Island, the Haida used their wood-carving skills to make stone sculptures with designs based on their mythology. Beautiful argillite ornaments (*above*) made by modern craftsmen at Haida and Skidegate Mission attest to the survival of this unique art form.

The Golden Spruce, near Port Clements

PORT CLEMENTS
The local museum displays items from this Graham Island community's past, including its logging days.
□ On the Yakoun River, south of Port Clements, a trail leads into a rain forest, where one tall tree of gold looms from the dark green woods. The Golden Spruce, more than 300 years old and 50 metres tall, is a mystery to foresters. It produces only green-boughed seedlings.
□ Farther southwest another trail leads to an uncompleted Haida dugout canoe, dating from at least 1900. Other uncompleted canoes have been found in the bush, but this site (cleared by logging operation) is the only accessible one on the Queen Charlotte Islands. Signs mark the trail, and the canoe is protected by a shelter.

west coasts plummet almost 3,050 metres to the floor of the Pacific Ocean. But the seabed of Hecate Strait, which separates the islands from the British Columbia mainland, is part of the continental shelf and, in some places, only 15 metres deep.

Although the islands are at the same latitude as James Bay, winters are mild. The warm Japanese ocean current ensures an average 8°C temperature year-round.

The two main islands, Graham and Moresby, are separated by Skidegate Channel. Visitors can reach these islands by air from Vancouver or Prince Rupert, or by ferry from Prince Rupert. Sandspit Airport, on Moresby Island, has a bus and ferry link to Skidegate on Graham Island. Rental cars are available at Sandspit and on Graham Island. (Bus and boat tours are also available.)

The southern three-quarters of Moresby is a national park reserve. At Moresby's southern tip is Anthony Island—site of a major collection of Haida totem and mortuary poles. The island, with its abandoned village, Ninstints, is a United Nations World Heritage Site.

Naikoon Provincial Park

NAIKOON PROVINCIAL PARK
Naikoon ("long nose") was the Haida name for the sharp northeast tip of Graham Island that juts into Hecate Strait. Today the spike of land is part of Naikoon Provincial Park, which preserves some 707 square kilometres of pristine wilderness, including about 94 kilometres of unspoiled beach. From a picnic site at McIntyre Hill, visitors can climb to the top of 109-metre Tow Hill, which overlooks Dixon Entrance—the channel between the Queen Charlotte Islands and the distant Dall and Prince of Wales islands of Alaska.

High-Flying Eagles and Ancient Murrelets

The streamlined, powerful peregrine falcon (one of the fastest of all birds) is more abundant in the Queen Charlotte Islands than anywhere else in the world. Easily overtaking flying prey, this bird often kills in the air with a single blow from its large, taloned feet.

Bald eagles (*left*) nest in tall trees all over the islands. The adults' white heads and tail plumage contrast sharply with their brown, almost black bodies. The young are brown, mottled with white, until their fourth year. In late summer and early fall, bald eagles can be seen flocking to salmon-spawning streams.

Subspecies of the saw-whet owl, hairy woodpecker and Steller's jay are restricted to these islands, as are ancient murrelets (the Queen Charlottes are their only Canadian breeding ground).

SKIDEGATE
Queen Charlotte Islands Museum, situated on a wooded peninsula near Skidegate, emphasizes the culture of the local Haida Indians. The collection contains archaelogical finds, examples of Haida art, including totem poles, and items from the time of the fur trade and the pioneers.
□ A totem pole, carved by Haida artist Bill Reid, stands in front of the Skidegate Band Council office, which is constructed in the style of a traditional Haida longhouse.
□ Fishing and boating excursion are available at Skidegate and other island communities.
□ At nearby Skidegate Mission, Haida craftsmen fashion argillite ornaments, miniature totems, and jewelry in traditional designs.
□ On the shore north of Skidegate Mission is Balance Rock, a four-metre-high boulder perched on a narrow base.

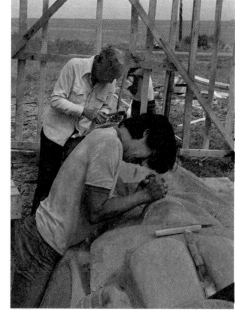

Indian sculptors, Skidegate

Balance Rock, north of Skidegate Mission

HECATE STRAIT

Oeanda River

Cape Ball

CAPE BALL

NAIKOON PROV PK

Mayer Lake

Mayer River

22

QUEEN CHARLOTTE ISLANDS

Tlell

Tlell River

18.5

LAWN PT

Lawnhill   HALIBUT BIGHT

DEAD TREE PT

51.5

18.5

SKIDEGATE INLET

BALANCE ROCK

Sandspit

Skidegate Mission

Skidegate

14.5   MORESBY ISLAND

Queen Charlotte

5

Ferry   Alliford Bay

LINA ISLAND

MAUDE ISLAND

KAGAN BAY

The 'River of Mists' in a Land of Totem Poles

Skeena River Valley

Called by Indians "the river of mists," the Skeena surges through rock-ribbed canyons and past sculpted mountains on its journey to the Pacific Ocean. Along the Yellowhead Highway, travelers can witness the river's final flourishes.

Its headwaters are icy, emerald pools in the Gunanoot Mountains. From there, the Skeena flows in a broad valley flanked by 1,800-metre peaks, then is joined by the muddy Bulkley River at Hazelton.

High above the junction of the rivers is

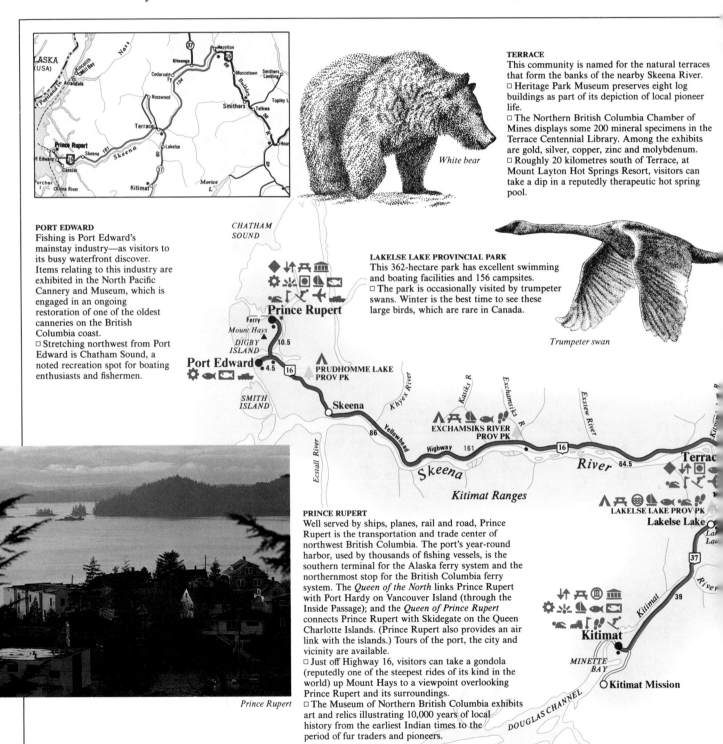

White bear

Trumpeter swan

Prince Rupert

TERRACE
This community is named for the natural terraces that form the banks of the nearby Skeena River.
□ Heritage Park Museum preserves eight log buildings as part of its depiction of local pioneer life.
□ The Northern British Columbia Chamber of Mines displays some 200 mineral specimens in the Terrace Centennial Library. Among the exhibits are gold, silver, copper, zinc and molybdenum.
□ Roughly 20 kilometres south of Terrace, at Mount Layton Hot Springs Resort, visitors can take a dip in a reputedly therapeutic hot spring pool.

LAKELSE LAKE PROVINCIAL PARK
This 362-hectare park has excellent swimming and boating facilities and 156 campsites.
□ The park is occasionally visited by trumpeter swans. Winter is the best time to see these large birds, which are rare in Canada.

PORT EDWARD
Fishing is Port Edward's mainstay industry—as visitors to its busy waterfront discover. Items relating to this industry are exhibited in the North Pacific Cannery and Museum, which is engaged in an ongoing restoration of one of the oldest canneries on the British Columbia coast.
□ Stretching northwest from Port Edward is Chatham Sound, a noted recreation spot for boating enthusiasts and fishermen.

PRINCE RUPERT
Well served by ships, planes, rail and road, Prince Rupert is the transportation and trade center of northwest British Columbia. The port's year-round harbor, used by thousands of fishing vessels, is the southern terminal for the Alaska ferry system and the northernmost stop for the British Columbia ferry system. The *Queen of the North* links Prince Rupert with Port Hardy on Vancouver Island (through the Inside Passage); and the *Queen of Prince Rupert* connects Prince Rupert with Skidegate on the Queen Charlotte Islands. (Prince Rupert also provides an air link with the islands.) Tours of the port, the city and vicinity are available.
□ Just off Highway 16, visitors can take a gondola (reputedly one of the steepest rides of its kind in the world) up Mount Hays to a viewpoint overlooking Prince Rupert and its surroundings.
□ The Museum of Northern British Columbia exhibits art and relics illustrating 10,000 years of local history from the earliest Indian times to the period of fur traders and pioneers.

| 0 | 4 | 8 | 12 | 16 | 20 Miles |
| 0 | 8 | 16 | 24 | 32 Kilometres |

Rocher Déboulé Mountain, a 2,438-metre peak furrowed by meltwater channels. Within 65 kilometres of the confluence are communities such as Kispiox, Kitwanga and Kitseguecla—and the greatest concentration of totem poles in Canada.

The Skeena bursts through the Coast Mountains at Kitselas, then empties into the Pacific at Prince Rupert, the province's second most important port (after Vancouver). Its harbor is a colorful mixture of fishing fleets and pleasure craft. Waterfront canneries process halibut, the port's main catch. Founded on Kaien Island at the turn of the century, Prince Rupert was established by the Grand Trunk Pacific Railway (later the CN) as a rival to CPR's Vancouver terminus. Its importance increases with the expansion of Canada's grain, coal and timber exports to the Pacific Rim countries.

Longhouses, 'Ksan Indian Village

SKEENA RIVER
The Skeena rises in northern British Columbia and winds through narrow canyons and broad valleys to the Pacific. The mouth of the Skeena is near Prince Rupert, a port city where pleasure craft, fishing boats, cruise ships and ferries dock. Tides push up the Skeena almost to the town of Terrace. North of Terrace the river separates the Nass and Bulkley ranges of the Hazelton Mountains; west of Terrace it enters the Coast Mountains.

KITWANGA
At the village of Kitwancool, just north of Kitwanga, visitors can see the world's largest standing totem pole—"Hole-through-the-Ice"—just one among many historic totems concentrated in this region.
From Kitwancool, Highway 37—known as the Cassiar-Stewart Highway—leads north to Upper Liard in the Yukon.

Indian canoe, 'Ksan Indian Village

HAZELTON
'Ksan Indian Village—a nearby historic reconstruction—occupies a site, at the junction of Bulkley and Skeena rivers, where a centuries-old Gitksan community stood in the 1870s, when the first settlers arrived. The newcomers renamed the Indian village, originally known as *Git-an-maks* ("the place where the people fish by torchlight"), Hazelton.
□ The heavily forested region within a 65-kilometre radius is sacred to the Gitksan. Among the village's reconstructions are six communal longhouses, all embellished with paintings and carved poles of traditional design. The Frog House of the Stone Age features early methods of making clothes and utensils from cedar bark. The Wolf or Feast House shows Gitksan life after white traders introduced blankets, iron kettles and muskets. The Treasure Room and Exhibition Centre displays costumes, handicrafts, carvings and other objects. Guided tours are available. Traditional dance performances are scheduled in summer.

KITIMAT
During the early 1950s the Aluminum Company of Canada built Kitimat—and its mighty smelter—in what was virtually wilderness. The site was chosen for its proximity to a deep-sea harbor and the abundant hydroelectric power at Kemano to the southeast. Level land at the proposed building site also influenced the choice. Another industry—the Ocelot methanol plant—has spurred the continuing development of the town.
□ Eight kilometres from Kitimat, Alcan's smelter—one of the largest in the world—can produce almost 300,000 tonnes annually. Such activity keeps the harbor busy receiving raw materials—alumina from Australia and Jamaica—and shipping finished ingots to customers abroad. Tours of the smelter and docks are available. Reservations are recommended.
□ The Kitimat Centennial Museum has natural history, pioneer and native history displays. The museum's gallery offers art exhibitions.
□ Nearby Douglas Channel has year-round saltwater fishing (lingcod, salmon and halibut). For much of the year, Kitimat River and its tributaries offer good freshwater fishing (salmon, trout and Dolly Varden).

A Totem in a Top Hat

The Gitksan Indians were hunters and fishermen who prospered in the mild Skeena River valley with its plentiful fish and wildlife. In their leisure time the Gitksan developed elaborate art forms—songs, dances, and totem poles carved in red cedar.

By the mid-19th century, with the arrival of white traders, metal tools replaced stone implements. Gitksan totem-pole carving enjoyed a brief "golden age." When the Gitksan were forced to work for European employers to obtain the white man's coveted trade goods, they lost the free time for their arts. Missionaries and government officials tore down totem poles, and banned rituals, ceremonies and dances as pagan observances.

Fears that the few remaining Gitksan treasures would be lost or destroyed led to the construction in 1970 of the 'Ksan Village. New artifacts were produced by local carvers, and ceremonial dancing and singing were revived. Of the five totem poles in the village, one with a top-hatted figure (*right*) was erected to mark the help of non-Indians in restoring the Gitksan way of life.

Steelhead Trout, Salmon and Stands of White Spruce

North-Central British Columbia

Highway 16 leads across a gently rolling plateau, bordered by the Coast Mountains to the west and by the high spine of the Rockies to the east. This region is freckled with lakes—from icy trout ponds to huge reservoirs teeming with arctic char.

In the clear waters of Tchesinkut Lake, trout are tantalizingly visible at depths of seven metres. Babine Lake, north of Topley, is an important spawning ground for sockeye salmon. Its shoreline is indented with secluded bays and inlets.

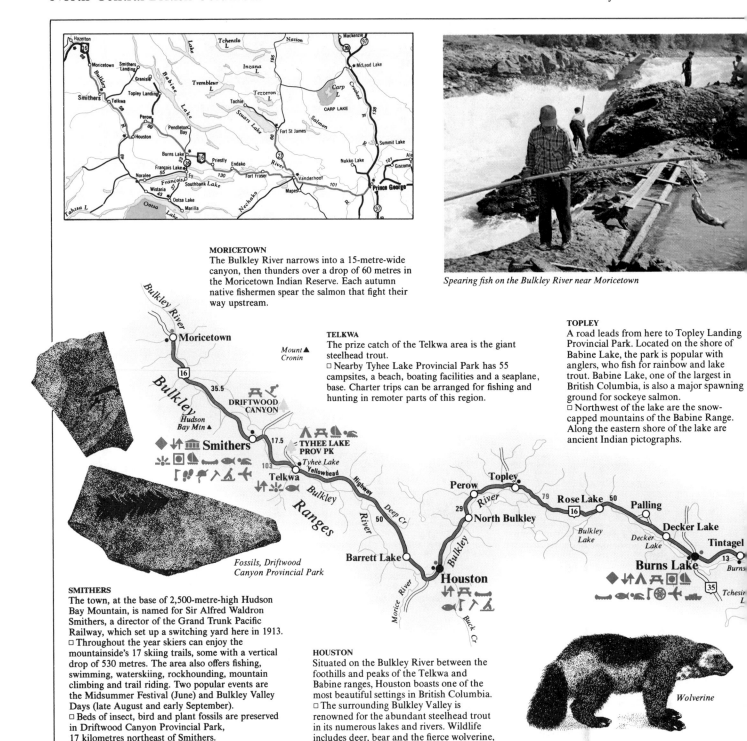

Spearing fish on the Bulkley River near Moricetown

MORICETOWN
The Bulkley River narrows into a 15-metre-wide canyon, then thunders over a drop of 60 metres in the Moricetown Indian Reserve. Each autumn native fishermen spear the salmon that fight their way upstream.

TELKWA
The prize catch of the Telkwa area is the giant steelhead trout.
□ Nearby Tyhee Lake Provincial Park has 55 campsites, a beach, boating facilities and a seaplane, base. Charter trips can be arranged for fishing and hunting in remoter parts of this region.

TOPLEY
A road leads from here to Topley Landing Provincial Park. Located on the shore of Babine Lake, the park is popular with anglers, who fish for rainbow and lake trout. Babine Lake, one of the largest in British Columbia, is also a major spawning ground for sockeye salmon.
□ Northwest of the lake are the snow-capped mountains of the Babine Range. Along the eastern shore of the lake are ancient Indian pictographs.

Fossils, Driftwood Canyon Provincial Park

SMITHERS
The town, at the base of 2,500-metre-high Hudson Bay Mountain, is named for Sir Alfred Waldron Smithers, a director of the Grand Trunk Pacific Railway, which set up a switching yard here in 1913.
□ Throughout the year skiers can enjoy the mountainside's 17 skiing trails, some with a vertical drop of 530 metres. The area also offers fishing, swimming, waterskiing, rockhounding, mountain climbing and trail riding. Two popular events are the Midsummer Festival (June) and Bulkley Valley Days (late August and early September).
□ Beds of insect, bird and plant fossils are preserved in Driftwood Canyon Provincial Park, 17 kilometres northeast of Smithers.

HOUSTON
Situated on the Bulkley River between the foothills and peaks of the Telkwa and Babine ranges, Houston boasts one of the most beautiful settings in British Columbia.
□ The surrounding Bulkley Valley is renowned for the abundant steelhead trout in its numerous lakes and rivers. Wildlife includes deer, bear and the fierce wolverine, which Indians call the "invulnerable beast."

Wolverine

0   4   8   12   16   20 Miles
0   8   16   24   32 Kilometres

Anglers can land steelhead trout where the Bulkley River passes the town of Telkwa. Nearby the river flows through a reserve where Indians spear salmon struggling upstream to spawn.

Farther north along the Bulkley River, the town of Smithers lies at the base of Hudson Bay Mountain. This 2,500-metre peak, with its three-kilometre-long icy blue Kathlyn Glacier, affords excellent downhill skiing. In summer its meadows are ablaze with alpine flowers.

Rivers lined with cottonwoods meander through farms and ranches in the Vanderhoof district. The horizon is broken by serrated peaks with summits wreathed in mist.

In 1807, Simon Fraser's men felled stands of white spruce near the junction of the Nechako and Fraser rivers to build Fort George (present-day Prince George). Pulp-and-paper-processing plants and sawmills have made this community the commercial capital of north-central British Columbia.

Sinkut Falls, near Vanderhoof

Fraser's Fort in New Caledonia

Fort St. James dates from 1806, when Simon Fraser and John Stuart built a North West Company fort here. When the company merged with the Hudson's Bay Company in 1821, the HBC made Fort St. James its chief post in New Caledonia, a vast area between the Rockies and the Coast Mountains. One of the old fur warehouses (*left*), a clerk's house (c. 1880) and a fish cache remain on the site, now a national historic park.

A Roman Catholic mission was founded here in 1843 and Our Lady of Good Hope Church (1870) is still used for services.

A Carrier Indian village—"Carrier" because widows once carried around their dead husbands' ashes—adjoins Fort St. James. In the village is the grave of Kwah, a Carrier chief who saved the life of James Douglas (governor of British Columbia between 1858 and 1864) in an Indian uprising. Douglas was an HBC assistant factor at Fort St. James in the late 1820s.

VANDERHOOF
This town is the geographical center of British Columbia. It was named after Herbert Vanderhoof, a Chicago publicity agent hired in 1908 by the Canadian government to launch a campaign to attract settlers to western Canada.
□ The town, in the Nechako Valley, is on a major Canada goose flyway. To the west is Fraser Lake, where Simon Fraser built a North West Company fort in 1806. There is a monument to the explorer.

FORT ST. JAMES
The village—British Columbia's oldest continuously inhabited community—preserves its past at the Fort St. James National Historic Site. The fort buildings have been restored to the 1890s—when the fur trade began to decline. The site is open from mid-May to mid-October.

FORT FRASER
A plaque, some 2 kilometres east of Fort Fraser, commemorates the place where the last spike of the Grand Trunk Pacific Railway (later the CNR) was driven on April 7, 1914.

BURNS LAKE
This community began as a tent town, founded in 1914 by a trapper named Barney Mulvaney. In 1917 Mulvaney had the townsite surveyed and sold in lots. A cabin which he operated as a gambling hall—nicknamed "The Bucket of Blood"—can still be seen. Next to it once stood Mulvaney's hotel. Near Burns Lake, on the road to Endako, a white picket fence surrounds the grave of "Bulldog" Kelly, shot and killed in a poker game argument in 1913. The grave is all that remains of the railway camp of Freeport.

PRINCE GEORGE
Situated at the junction of the Fraser and Nechako rivers, Prince George—after Vancouver and Victoria, British Columbia's third largest city—was founded as Fort George by Simon Fraser in 1807.
□ Exhibits in Fort George Regional Museum in Fort George Park illustrate the area's natural history, the city's history and the development of local lumbering and transportation. Near the museum—within a palisade—are historic buildings including a schoolhouse and an old-time railway station. The Fort George Railway invites passengers aboard a vintage locomotive that runs on a kilometre-long narrow-gauge track through the park.
□ Among Prince George's other attractions are art galleries, craft shops, and an 800-seat concert hall. A nearby wilderness area offers a wide range of outdoor recreational activities. The city celebrates Simon Fraser Days in August.

Prince George

Open Rangelands, Steep Canyons and Coastal Rain Forests

Central British Columbia

West of Williams Lake Highway 20 winds through open rangelands, wild sedge and grass meadows, and clumps of lodgepole pine. This is the expansive Chilcotin country, a section of British Columbia's interior plateau that lies between the Fraser River and the Coast Mountains. It is one of the province's main ranching

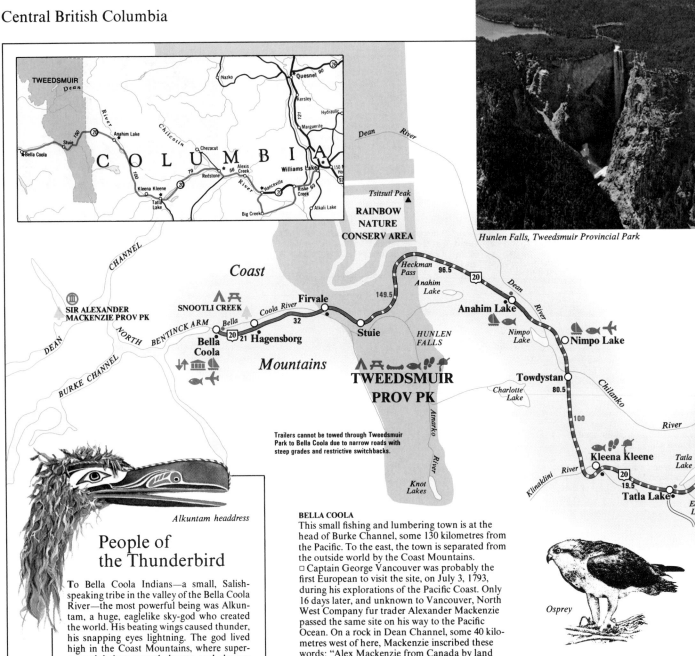

Hunlen Falls, Tweedsmuir Provincial Park

Alkuntam headdress

People of the Thunderbird

To Bella Coola Indians—a small, Salish-speaking tribe in the valley of the Bella Coola River—the most powerful being was Alkuntam, a huge, eaglelike sky-god who created the world. His beating wings caused thunder, his snapping eyes lightning. The god lived high in the Coast Mountains, where supernatural beings staged dances and dramas for his entertainment. His worshipers believed that after death the soul of a Bella Coola ascended to the benevolent Alkuntam.

The Bella Coola once numbered about 3,000. But diseases brought by traders decimated their numbers. Today there are about 600 living in the town of Bella Coola. Their ancient tribal dances still are reenacted at special private ceremonies in the winter.

BELLA COOLA
This small fishing and lumbering town is at the head of Burke Channel, some 130 kilometres from the Pacific. To the east, the town is separated from the outside world by the Coast Mountains.
□ Captain George Vancouver was probably the first European to visit the site, on July 3, 1793, during his explorations of the Pacific Coast. Only 16 days later, and unknown to Vancouver, North West Company fur trader Alexander Mackenzie passed the same site on his way to the Pacific Ocean. On a rock in Dean Channel, some 40 kilometres west of here, Mackenzie inscribed these words: "Alex Mackenzie from Canada by land 22ᵈ July 1793." Sir Alexander Mackenzie Provincial Park has been established around what is believed to be Mackenzie's Rock. The park is accessible only by boat.
□ Bella Coola was founded in 1894, by about 90 Norwegian-Americans escaping an economic depression in the United States. The Bella Coola Museum exhibits household articles, tools and fishing implements used by these pioneers.

Osprey

ANAHIM LAKE
A stampede is held at Anahim Lake during the second weekend of July.
□ At nearby Ulkatcho Indian Village are smokehouses where Indians dry salmon caught in the Atnarko River in Tweedsmuir Provincial Park.
□ There is fly-fishing for rainbow trout in the quiet waters of Anahim Lake.

Trailers cannot be towed through Tweedsmuir Park to Bella Coola due to narrow roads with steep grades and restrictive switchbacks.

0 4 8 12 16 20 Miles
0 8 16 24 32 Kilometres

areas, where herds roam freely, often grazing alongside the highway or ambling across it. (On Chilcotin roads the herds have the right-of-way!)

Between Hanceville and Redstone the drive is along the Chilcotin River, which flows through steep canyons—some more than 300 metres deep—marked by sandstone pillars and lava escarpments.

Leaving the river, the road meanders past quiet lakes such as Puntzi, Tatla, Nimpo and Anahim, where fly-fishing for rainbow trout is excellent. Nights in this area can be cold, even in summer. The village of Kleena Kleene, for instance, at 880 metres elevation, has only 30 frost-free days per year.

At Anahim Lake the road leaves the Chilcotin plateau and climbs over 1,500-metre Heckman Pass through the mountains of Tweedsmuir Provincial Park. (Because the narrow road has steep grades and precarious switchbacks, trailers cannot be used in the park and must be left at Anahim Lake.)

Beyond the park the highway twists for 20 breathtaking kilometres into the Bella Coola Valley, a region of coastal rain forests some 1,000 metres below, with tangles of salmonberry, thimbleberry, bearberry, maple and cedar. The road ends at Bella Coola on the tidal flats of North Bentinck Arm, an extension of Burke Channel, a fjord of the Pacific Coast.

TWEEDSMUIR PROVINCIAL PARK
Imposing snowcapped mountains, grassy basins, alpine meadows, glaciers, fast rivers, deep canyons, peaceful lakes, and thundering waterfalls make Tweedsmuir Provincial Park one of Canada's most varied wilderness areas.
□ This 9,600-square-kilometre park is bounded on the north by Ootsa and Whitesail lakes, on the west by the Coast Mountains, and on the east by British Columbia's interior plateau. Highway 20 cuts through the southern tip of the park; the northern portion has no road access.
□ A 16-kilometre hiking trail leads south between Atnarko River Campground and Hunlen Falls, whose 366-metre drop is the third highest in Canada. Nearby Lonesome Lake is the winter home for about 400 trumpeter swans, an estimated 20 percent of the world's population of this endangered species.
□ The Atnarko and Talchako rivers and their tributaries provide fishing for cutthroat, steelhead and rainbow trout, and coho and chinook salmon. In fall local Indians meet at pools on the rivers, as they have done for centuries, to spear and net fish to be smoked for winter use.

Williams Lake Stampede, Williams Lake

WILLIAMS LAKE
Williams Lake is the gateway to Chilcotin country, a cattle-grazing area to the west. Dubbed the "cowboy capital" of British Columbia, the town is the province's main livestock center. Its stockyards handle about 40,000 head of cattle annually.
□ Traditional cowboy skills are displayed at the Williams Lake Stampede, which is held each July. Rodeo performers from Canada and the United States compete for prizes in bronco riding, steer wrestling, calf roping, bull riding, wild-cow milking, and wild-horse racing. Apart from the competitions, there are cowboy breakfasts, barbecues and square dances.

RISKE CREEK
Almost 400 California bighorn sheep live in this triangular, 450-hectare provincial game preserve at the confluence of the Chilcotin and Fraser rivers, some 20 kilometres south of Riske Creek. California bighorns are one of only six species of wild sheep in the world. These stocky animals can be seen climbing the steep river banks.

Farwell Canyon, Chilcotin River

California bighorn sheep

Cowboy Country

The Chilcotin region is a 5,000-square-kilometre plateau of rangeland, where tens of thousands of beef cattle roam expanses of unfenced grassland. The herds are mostly Herefords, efficient grazers who are hardy and fast-maturing. Cowboys ride out in all weather to tend their animals. They round up the herds for sales or winter feeding, keep them from straying, and rope and brand young animals. Ranching has been the mainstay of the Chilcotin region since settlement began in the 1860s. The grasslands attracted stockmen who found a ready market for their beef in the gold camps of the Cariboo, east of the Fraser River. Now the cattle are sold at Williams Lake and sent to markets across Canada.

Gold-Rush Relics, Roadhouses and an El Dorado named Barkerville

Central British Columbia

The Williams Lake–Quesnel–Barkerville stretch of the modern Cariboo Highway follows parts of a wagon road, built in stages during the gold rush of the 1860s. Between Williams Lake and Kersley, Highway 97 leads through Cariboo country, a vast rolling plateau with scattered groves of aspen and lodgepole pine, and with sloughs and small, shallow lakes.

At Soda Creek Highway 97 passes the head of a canyon eight kilometres long. North of Kersley the highway crosses an

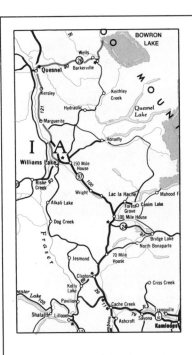

QUESNEL

Until the mid-1800s a Hudson's Bay Company store (now restored on Front Street) was the only building on the site of what is now Quesnel. But the Cariboo Gold Rush of the 1860s led to the development of a town here, where miners from the goldfields farther east brought supplies. Now the town, with a population of more than 8,000, is the largest in the Cariboo.
□ A Cornish waterwheel, used to pump water from mine shafts during gold rush days, is preserved on the east bank of the Fraser River. Quesnel and District Museum features exhibits that depict the development of local mining, logging, ranching and farming.
□ During Billy Barker Days in July, Quesnel commemorates its gold rush origins. Gold-pan-throwing contests, dances and raft races are some of the festivity highlights.

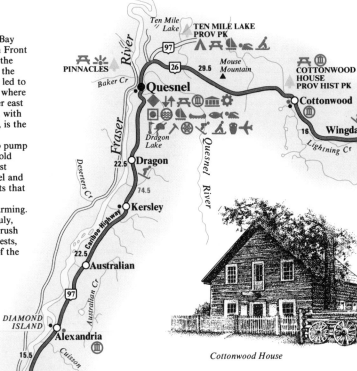

Rocky Point, Alexandria

ALEXANDRIA

A cairn marks the approximate site of Fort Alexandria, a North West Company fur trading post, built in 1821 and named for Alexander Mackenzie, the first man to cross the northern part of North America by land from coast to coast.
□ The modern Cariboo Highway passes west of a formation of basalt columns, known as Rocky Point.

Cottonwood House

COTTONWOOD HOUSE PROVINCIAL HISTORIC PARK

Here, in a 10-hectare provincial historic park, is Cottonwood House, the only complete surviving roadhouse from the 610-kilometre Cariboo Wagon Road between Yale and Barkerville. The building dates from 1864. It still contains its old furnishings brought to the Cariboo during the gold rush of the 1860s. Among the period pieces are desks, chests, a table, two reclining chairs, a barrel stove and a kitchen stove with two ovens.

SODA CREEK

This community is at the head of the eight-kilometre-long Soda Creek Canyon. During the Cariboo Gold Rush, steam engines, boilers and other ship parts were brought to Soda Creek, then assembled into stern-wheelers. The first vessel was built in 1863. Eventually a fleet of nine steamers were used to ferry miners and their supplies along the 90-kilometre stretch of the Fraser River between Soda Creek and Quesnel. From Quesnel, miners had to trek overland to the goldfields.
□ In 1921 the era of steam navigation on the upper Fraser ended when the last of the stern-wheelers smashed up near Prince George. About 18 kilometres north of Soda Creek, a plaque commemorates the contribution of the stern-wheelers to the development of the Cariboo.

Map labels: BOWRON LAKE, Wells, Quesnel, Barkerville, Kersley, Keithley Creek, Hydraulic, Quesnel Lake, Marguerite, Horsefly, Williams Lake, 150 Mile House, Riske Creek, Wright, Lac la Hache, Mahood L, Alkali Lake, Forest Grove, Canim Lake, Dog Creek, 100 Mile House, Jesmond, 70 Mile House, Bridge Lake, North Bonaparte, Clinton, Kelly Lake, Criss Creek, Center Lake, Pavilion, Cache Creek, Shalalth, Lillooet, Ashcroft, Savona, Tranquille, Kamloops, Fraser

Route map labels: Ten Mile Lake, TEN MILE LAKE PROV PK, PINNACLES, Baker Cr, Quesnel, Mouse Mountain, 29.5, COTTONWOOD HOUSE PROV HIST PK, Cottonwood, Wingda, Lightning Cr, Dragon Lake, Deserters Cr, Dragon, 22.5, 74.5, Kersley, Quesnel River, Cariboo Highway, 22.5, Australian, Australian Cr, DIAMOND ISLAND, Alexandria, Cuisson Cr, 15.5, Castle Rock, Tingley Cr, Marguerite, Macalister, 22, McLeese Lake, McLeese Lake, 70, Soda Creek, Hawks Cr, 33, Fraser River, Williams Lake River, Chimney Cr, Williams Lake, WILLIAMS LAKE (see Road Unit 26)

Scale:
0 2 4 6 8 10 Miles
0 4 8 12 16 Kilometres

area thick with Engelmann spruce and alpine fire. A maze of creeks and streams draining the Cariboo Mountains has cut gullies and canyons into the land. Precipitation is high, usually more than 120 centimetres annually (about 20 centimetres more than Vancouver).

Here nature has placed one of the strongest lures known to man: gold. Among cracks in the rocks of the Cariboo Mountains are threaded thick veins of it. Erosion and ice age glaciers wore away much of the metal.

It was deposited in the form of powder, flakes or nuggets in the sand and gravel beds of Cariboo rivers and streams.

In the early 1800s, Indians sold chunks of gold to the Hudson's Bay Company. When the company exchanged the metal for money at the San Francisco mint, in February 1858, the rumors of untold riches in the Cariboo flew out and a gold rush began.

Almost all settlements along the Cariboo Highway owe their origins to the influx of gold-seekers during the following decade. These men built stopping places along their transportation routes, supply centers and mining towns. When the gold ran out, in the 1870s and '80s, many fortune seekers drifted away, but others stayed. They had discovered the Cariboo's other treasures: its timber, its ranchland and its great outdoors.

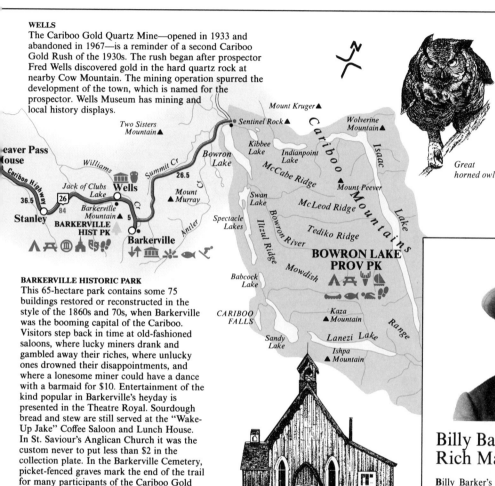

WELLS
The Cariboo Gold Quartz Mine—opened in 1933 and abandoned in 1967—is a reminder of a second Cariboo Gold Rush of the 1930s. The rush began after prospector Fred Wells discovered gold in the hard quartz rock at nearby Cow Mountain. The mining operation spurred the development of the town, which is named for the prospector. Wells Museum has mining and local history displays.

Great horned owl

BOWRON LAKE PROVINCIAL PARK
Set against the backdrop of the snow-capped 2,100-metre peaks of the Cariboo Mountains, this 1,216-square-kilometre park has six major lakes and connecting waterways that form a 116-kilometre-long circular canoe route. Moose and deer feed in marshes along the Bowron River. Caribou, mountain goats and grizzly bears frequent higher elevations. The lakes and streams abound with steelhead trout, Dolly Varden, and kokanee salmon. A campground with a canoe-launching facility is on the north shore of Bowron Lake.

BARKERVILLE HISTORIC PARK
This 65-hectare park contains some 75 buildings restored or reconstructed in the style of the 1860s and 70s, when Barkerville was the booming capital of the Cariboo. Visitors step back in time at old-fashioned saloons, where lucky miners drank and gambled away their riches, where unlucky ones drowned their disappointments, and where a lonesome miner could have a dance with a barmaid for $10. Entertainment of the kind popular in Barkerville's heyday is presented in the Theatre Royal. Sourdough bread and stew are still served at the "Wake-Up Jake" Coffee Saloon and Lunch House. In St. Saviour's Anglican Church it was the custom never to put less than $2 in the collection plate. In the Barkerville Cemetery, picket-fenced graves mark the end of the trail for many participants of the Cariboo Gold Rush.

St. Saviour's Anglican Church, Barkerville

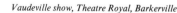

Vaudeville show, Theatre Royal, Barkerville

Billy Barker— Rich Man, Poor Man

Billy Barker's Shaft (now restored), at the south end of Barkerville, is where it all started on Aug. 21, 1862. Barker (*above*), a 42-year-old Cornish sailor, reached Williams Creek in the summer of 1862, four years after the first gold strike in the Cariboo. On Aug. 13, Billy and six companions staked a claim in one of the few easily accessible spots still available. Others had panned and sluiced there before and found nothing. To the jibes of old-timers the seven men began digging down into the gravel. Eight days later, at a depth of 16 metres, they hit pay dirt: 30 centimetres yielded $1,000; within four years the claim would relinquish over $600,000 in gold. The jokes about crazy Billy stopped and other prospectors rushed to stake claims near his. In his honor the collection of stores, cabins and saloons that grew up around his shaft was named Barkerville. In 1863 Billy married a widow from Victoria with a taste for high living. She helped him spend his gold as fast as it came out of the ground and then left him. Poor Billy died penniless in a Victoria old men's home, on July 11, 1894, and was laid to rest in a pauper's grave.

Steep Canyons and Sagebrush on the Road to Caribou Country

Central British Columbia

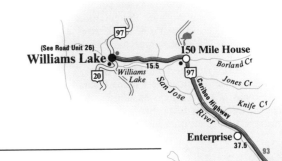

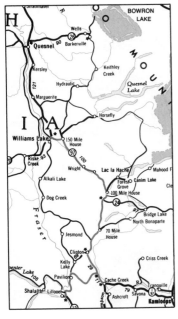

100 MILE HOUSE

Established as a stagecoach stop on the Cariboo Wagon Road in the gold rush days of the 1860s, 100 Mile House was named for its distance from the start of the road at Lillooet. Today this thriving lumber and ranch community of more than 2,000 still has reminders of its past: an 1860s stagecoach (in front of the Red Coach Inn) and a pioneer carpenter shop, which serves as a chapel.
□ Annual events include the 42-kilometre Cariboo Cross-Country Ski Marathon from Lac La Hache to 100 Mile House (February), the Little Britches Rodeo (May) and the Great Cariboo Ride—a horseback ride through the Cariboo region—in August. Winter visitors can enjoy ice fishing. In summer, a sports fishing derby is a major local attraction.

Stagecoach, 100 Mile House

Balsamroot

An Arduous Expedition Down the Fraser

Where Highway 12 now permits easy travel through the Fraser Canyon between Lillooet and Pavilion, two dozen adventurers spent several days in early June 1808, covering the same distance, moving slowly along narrow ledges and slippery rocks over the churning waters.

Led by North West Company fur trader Simon Fraser, the men were on their way from Fort George (now Prince George) to the Pacific Ocean. They were the first Europeans to travel the river—which they believed to be the Columbia and a trade route to the sea. Their goal was to secure it for British North America against rival claims from the United States.

After 35 days the expedition reached the river's delta, near present-day New Westminster. Fraser concluded this was neither the Columbia nor a trade route. Though he considered his journey a commercial failure, he had saved one of the major rivers west of the Rockies from the American grasp. The river and canyon now bear his name.

Simon Fraser in the Canyon,
a painting by John Innis

Fraser Canyon between Lillooet and Pavilion

LILLOOET

Lillooet's wide main street dates from the 1860s. It was laid out so that two 10-tonne freight wagons, hitched together and hauled by up to 10 spans of oxen, mules or horses, could turn in it. In 1863-64, during Lillooet's brief boom period as the southern terminus of the Cariboo Wagon Road, these large wagons left here with supplies for the Cariboo goldfields. The town declined after 1865, when it was bypassed by a new branch of the Wagon Road which started farther south at Yale.
□ The Lillooet and District Museum exhibits memorabilia from the town's pioneer and gold rush past. Opposite the museum is a stone cairn marking "Mile 0" of the original Cariboo Wagon Road. The road's construction is commemorated by a plaque on the east bank of the Fraser River, facing the town.
□ Visitors are invited to dress up as gold seekers during Lillooet Days in June, when the town celebrates its past.

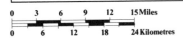

0	3	6	9	12	15 Miles
0	6		12	18	24 Kilometres

The road between Lillooet and Williams Lake leads through parts of British Columbia's interior plateau, a region scoured by glaciers during the last ice age and broken up by deposits of rock and gravel, and by gorges formed by meltwater.

North of Lillooet the road hugs the steep east wall of the Fraser River for almost 60 kilometres. Then it skirts 1,665-metre Mount Pavilion and turns northeast passing through level sagebrush country. At Clinton it joins the Cariboo Highway, which leads north past stands of lodgepole pine and expansive ranches.

The drive between Lillooet and 150 Mile House is over part of British Columbia's oldest mainland road, the Cariboo Wagon Road. Built in 1861-63, between Lillooet and Soda Creek (47 kilometres north of 150 Mile House), it was the main supply route to the goldfields of the Cariboo. Roadside stations, usually 25 kilometres apart, were built to serve construction crews and, later, travelers. Called "Mile Houses" they were named for their distances from Lillooet, "Mile 0." At milepost 100, for instance, was 100 Mile House, from which sprang the present town of the same name.

Within a decade the wagon road was extended by a southern branch between Yale and Clinton, and by a northern addition between Soda Creek and Barkerville in the heart of the gold country. For more than a century the road and its successors have served those who followed the original gold miners—ranchers, loggers and tourists.

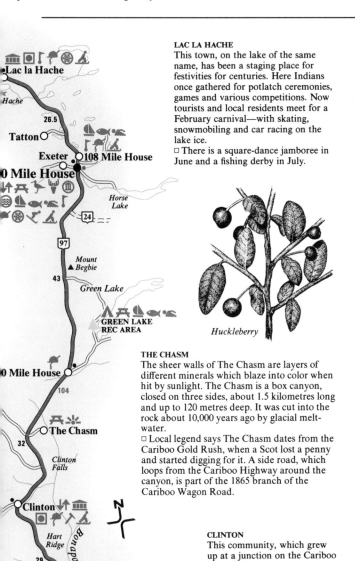

LAC LA HACHE
This town, on the lake of the same name, has been a staging place for festivities for centuries. Here Indians once gathered for potlatch ceremonies, games and various competitions. Now tourists and local residents meet for a February carnival—with skating, snowmobiling and car racing on the lake ice.
□ There is a square-dance jamboree in June and a fishing derby in July.

Huckleberry

THE CHASM
The sheer walls of The Chasm are layers of different minerals which blaze into color when hit by sunlight. The Chasm is a box canyon, closed on three sides, about 1.5 kilometres long and up to 120 metres deep. It was cut into the rock about 10,000 years ago by glacial meltwater.
□ Local legend says The Chasm dates from the Cariboo Gold Rush, when a Scot lost a penny and started digging for it. A side road, which loops from the Cariboo Highway around the canyon, is part of the 1865 branch of the Cariboo Wagon Road.

CLINTON
This community, which grew up at a junction on the Cariboo Wagon Road, has held an annual May Ball and Rodeo— possibly the oldest social event of its kind in British Columbia—since 1868. During the first May balls, people from hundreds of kilometres away came to dance, drink and gamble at the Clinton Hotel. Although the hotel burned down in 1958, some mementos—including wine decanters from the hotel bar— survive among displays at the local South Cariboo Historical Society Museum.

Fences by the Roadside— the Snake Rail and the Russell

Log fences line much of the Cariboo Highway as it winds through the rangeland of British Columbia's interior. The fences are practical and cheap. They require no post holes, which would be difficult to dig into the rocky Cariboo soil. Nor do they need nails or wire. They are made entirely of lodgepole pine, the most abundant timber in the Cariboo.

Fence styles vary depending on terrain. The two most popular designs are the snake rail and the Russell. The snake rail is a wide-angled zigzag fence of equally long sections. It is four to five logs high and the logs are notched where they join. The Russell fence (*above*) is straight and held upright by teepee-like structures at the section joints.

On the road to the summit of Mount Pavilion

CACHE CREEK
The town had its beginnings in the 1860s as a stopping place on the Yale-Clinton branch of the Cariboo Wagon Road. In 1874 the British Columbia government chose Cache Creek as the site for the first boarding school in the interior of the province. The school, which provided instruction to about 50 youngsters from the Cariboo region, no longer exists.
□ On an Indian reserve is Bonaparte Church, built in 1894 and named after the nearby Bonaparte River. Its original log walls are now covered with boards.

Bonaparte Church, Cache Creek

Silent Volcanoes, Echoing Waterfalls and the Rockies' Highest Peak

Wells Gray and Mount Robson Provincial Parks

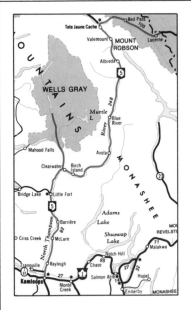

Helmcken Falls, Wells Gray Provincial Park

WELLS GRAY PROVINCIAL PARK

Among a dozen large waterfalls in the park are 135-metre-high Helmcken Falls and Dawson Falls, 90 metres wide and 18 metres high. In the Murtle River is the Mush Bowl, a series of riverbed craters carved by raging waters. A 240-metre-high extinct volcano rises from the north shore of Kostal Lake. On the rim of its cone, 1,500 metres above sea level, is a stand of Douglas fir, a tree which normally grows at lower elevations. A round-trip canoe route winds for 102 kilometres between the Clearwater Lake campground and Azure Lake. Experienced canoeists can fish for rainbow trout downstream from 14-metre-high Rainbow Falls. There are more than 100 icy mineral springs in the park. Golden eagles and rufous hummingbirds are occasionally sighted—particularly at abandoned Ray Farm. The 19-kilometre Battle Mountain Trail leads through subalpine forest to Caribou Meadows, a grassy expanse laced with streams and marshes and dotted with colorful wildflowers.

CLEARWATER

The nearby Yellowhead Museum presents exhibits of Indian and pioneer life. Many displays are in log buildings on the museum grounds, one of the original homesteads in the Clearwater region.
□ Local businesses offer whitewater rafting expeditions on the Clearwater River.
□ Two of the most popular local events are the May Day Parade and the Strawberry Festival in July.

SPAHATS CREEK PROVINCIAL PARK

Spahats Creek has carved a 120-metre-deep gorge through an ancient lava flow in the park. The canyon ends at Spahats Creek Falls, where the creek cascades 60 metres into the Clearwater River. An observation deck overlooks the falls.

KAMLOOPS

The city began as a fur trading post in 1812. The site—at the confluence of the North and South Thompson rivers—was known to local Indians as *cume-loups*, a term for "the meeting of the waters" or simply "meeting place." Kamloops became a depot for the gold seekers of the 1860s, and a regional CPR center with the railway's arrival in the 1880s. A century later, it has become one of the most important tourist centers in the British Columbia interior, largely because of improved access through the Coquihalla Highway.
□ A Hudson's Bay Company trading post—a replica of an 1821 log structure—has been assembled on the grounds of the Kamloops Museum. Other displays include Salish Indian basketry and carvings, a furnished Victorian drawing room, medical equipment used in an early Kamloops hospital and—from Kamloops jail—an invitation to an 1899 hanging.
□ A stern-wheeler—built in the 1970s—offers two-hour cruises on the South Thompson River.
□ Tod Mountain has 18 square kilometres of ski slopes and a 2,786-metre-long double chair lift—the longest in North America.
□ Important local events include Wonder Weekend on Tod Mountain (May) and a country music festival and Kamloops Sunfest, both in July.

Fort Kamloops

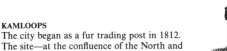

0   4   8   12   16   20 Miles

0   8   16   24   32 Kilometres

Lava and water have shaped the broad valley of the North Thompson River. In the not-too-distant geological past, volcanoes created and changed the landscape with each eruption. Penned in or diverted, rivers widened into lakes, scoured deep gorges and funneled into plummeting waterfalls.

At Spahats Creek Provincial Park, the volcanic origins of the area are still visible. Here, Spahats Creek crashes through a steep-walled gorge whose exposed rock layers represent past volcanic upheavals.

Near the entrance to Wells Gray Provincial Park, Helmcken Falls roars its welcome as it plunges 135 metres over the brink of a lava-layered precipice. The vast wilderness park echoes everywhere with the rumbling of falling water, but there is more: silent volcanoes, mineral springs, serene mountain-edged lakes and vast ice fields.

Farther east, in Mount Robson Provincial Park, are the highest peak in the Canadian Rockies and the deepest cave in Canada. Clear, cold lakes teem with kokanee salmon and brook, rainbow, steelhead and Kamloops trout.

The breathtaking Yellowhead Highway winds past these parks and the small towns strewn along the North Thompson. The highway traces the route of the Overlanders of 1862, fortune-seekers who risked their lives to reach Cariboo gold. Many of these pioneers remained, cleared homesteads, and built rough-hewn log homes, snake fences and wagon bridges that still stand.

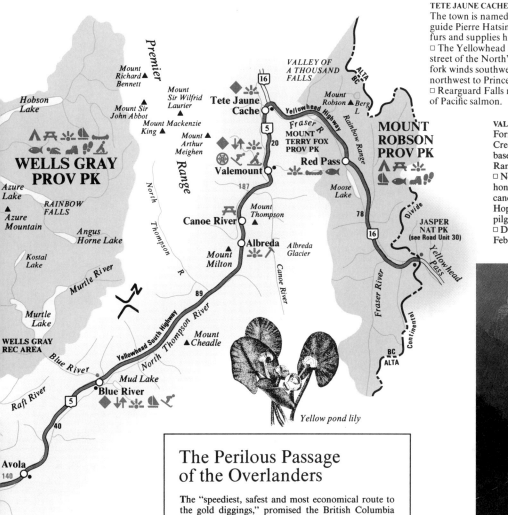

Yellow pond lily

Overlander Days Raft Race,
North Thompson River

The Perilous Passage of the Overlanders

The "speediest, safest and most economical route to the gold diggings," promised the British Columbia Overland Transit Company in 1862. More than 200 men and one pregnant woman with three children bought tickets and set out in May from Quebec and Ontario to seek gold in the Cariboo Country.

The Overlanders expected a leisurely trip. Instead they traveled by creaking Red River carts across the Prairies, then struggled on foot through the Rockies. At the turbulent Fraser River, the Overlanders split into two groups. One group built dugout canoes and rafts to run the river and, in the attempt, several were drowned. By September 10, the survivors reached Fort George—present-day Prince George.

The 36 others made their way down the North Thompson River. They were near starvation on September 13 when they reached Fort Kamloops. (The next day Mrs. August Schubert gave birth to the first white child born in the B.C. interior.) Sadly, after this arduous ordeal, only one Overlander found gold.

TETE JAUNE CACHE
The town is named for fair-haired Indian trapper and guide Pierre Hatsinaton ("Tête Jaune"), who stored his furs and supplies here in the early 1800s.
□ The Yellowhead Highway—the 2,976-kilometre "main street of the North"—splits at Tete Jaune Cache. One fork winds southwest to Kamloops, the other angles northwest to Prince Rupert.
□ Rearguard Falls marks the farthest inland migration of Pacific salmon.

VALEMOUNT
Formerly a logging camp known as "Swift Creek Spur 2," Valemount now serves as a base for heliskiing expeditions to the Premier Range.
□ Nearby Mount Terry Fox Provincial Park honors the one-legged runner, who died from cancer before completing his "Marathon of Hope." Valemount holds a Mount Terry Fox pilgrimage in August.
□ Dogsled races highlight a winter festival in February.

Mount Robson

MOUNT ROBSON PROVINCIAL PARK
Bordered on the east by the Continental Divide and Jasper National Park, Mount Robson preserves more than 200,000 hectares of snowcapped mountains, forested valleys, precipitous canyons, glacier-fed lakes and wild rivers. The 22-kilometre Berg Lake Trail runs from the Yellowhead Highway through the Valley of a Thousand Falls to Berg Lake at the base of 3,953-metre Mount Robson. Some 15 glaciers are seen along the trail, among them Berg Glacier, 1,800 metres thick and nearly a kilometre wide. Berg Lake is often dotted with ice slabs that have broken away from the glacier. At the southern tip of the park are the headwaters of the Fraser River. Arctomys Cave, surveyed to a depth of 522 metres, lies in a valley east of Mount Robson. The 2,400-metre-long passage to the bottom is difficult even for experienced cavers.

An Alpine Wilderness Filled with Wildlife

Jasper National Park

Gray jay

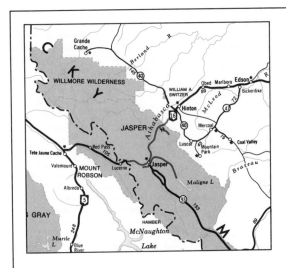

A view of Jasper from The Whistlers

JASPER

In the last century Jasper was a way station for wilderness travelers—trappers, missionaries, geologists, surveyors, naturalists and prospectors. The first facility for park visitors was established in 1915 in the form of a tent camp on Lac Beauvert. Today the town is a year-round recreation center with facilities ranging from the primitive to the plush.

□ Located near the confluence of the Athabasca and Miette rivers, Old Fort Point is the site of Henry House (1811), an early fur-trade post. Nearby grassy slopes are a grazing area for mule deer and bighorn sheep.

□ Pyramid Lake Drive winds for eight kilometres north to 2,763-metre Pyramid Mountain and a pair of sparkling glacial lakes.

□ The totem pole outside the railway station was carved by Haida Indians of the Queen Charlotte Islands.

□ A cairn near the mouth of the Rocky River commemorates Jasper House, built by the North West Company in the early 1800s.

Black bear

YELLOWHEAD HIGHWAY

The 2,987-kilometre highway is named for Tête Jaune (Yellow Head), a fair-haired Indian trapper and guide whose real name was Pierre Bostonnais. It extends from Portage la Prairie, Man., into British Columbia, splitting at Tête Jaune Cache. One branch leads southwest to Kamloops, the other west to Prince Rupert.

Entering Jasper National Park from the east, the highway follows the Athabasca River through a low, arid valley. West of Jasper townsite the scenery changes dramatically as the highway climbs through the narrow, densely forested Miette Valley—the route of 19th-century fur brigades traveling west to New Caledonia (central British Columbia).

□ Yellowhead Pass, 1,131 metres above sea level, is one of the lowest gaps along the entire Continental Divide. Waters east of the divide flow to the Arctic Ocean via the Miette, Athabasca and Mackenzie rivers. West of the divide, runoff feeds the Fraser River flowing into the Pacific.

THE WHISTLERS

The long, shrill whistle of the hoary marmot, a member of the woodchuck family, gives the mountain its name.

□ From an altitude of 1,257 metres, skytrams whisk passengers at 420 metres a minute to the 2,250-metre level, providing spectacular views of Jasper townsite and the ring of mountains that surrounds it. Some 40 lakes dot the broad valley of the Athabasca River—remnants of one large lake which once covered the area. Across the valley are the reddish quartzite cliffs of Pyramid Mountain.

Skytram, The Whistlers

Jasper National Park is a sweeping expanse of scenic beauty—of awesome mountain peaks and centuries-old glacial ice, of flower-carpeted meadows and mirrorlike lakes.

In the early 1800s the need for a fur-trade route across the Continental Divide brought the first white men to this alpine wilderness. Three log buildings were built for weary voyageurs traveling over the Yellowhead and Athabasca passes. The ramshackle settlement was named Jasper House after North West Company clerk Jasper Hawes. In 1907 the coming of the railway through Yellowhead Pass prompted the federal government to preserve the area as a national park.

Today, Jasper covers more than 10,800 square kilometres, of which only 800 square kilometres are flat valley bottoms. Grassy meadows carpet the lower slopes, where rainfall is scant. Higher up, a moister climate has produced bands of forest on the mountain flanks. Above the timberline—about 2,100 metres—a subarctic climate stunts even tenacious alpine vegetation.

Mule deer graze among the poplar and lodgepole pine stands of the Miette and Athabasca valleys. Bighorn sheep share their lofty range with mountain goats, but are left far behind when the goats climb to narrow ledges shared only with eagles. Rarest of all sights in the park are the mountain caribou that range throughout the park.

Roche
▲ a Perdrix

Fiddle River

Ashlar Ridge

16

Miette Range

Miette
Hot Springs

PUNCHBOWL FALLS
The falls, where Mountain Creek plummets over a limestone cliff, have cut a narrow cleft into the stone. Below, the falls have eroded a picturesque pool. The pebbly bedrock was formed in the bed of a fast-moving stream about 130 million years ago.
□ A dark seam of low-grade coal, 30 centimetres thick, is visible nearby.

Miette Hot Springs

Lofty Peaks From a Primeval Sea

A vast sea covered the land where the Rockies now tower. For 500 million years, the seafloor was pressed downward by heavy layers of sediment (sand, silt and remains of marine life). Since new layers built up as fast as the seafloor sank, the sea remained shallow. Eventually, pressure turned the sediment to rock.

Great geological forces beneath the earth's crust pushed the rock layers eastward, causing them to fold and buckle. In places the layers cracked along fault lines, and some of the oldest rocks were thrust upward to overlap younger rock. Erosion continued to shape the land; rivers carried debris east from the highlands and deposited it on broad plains and swamps.

The great plains continued to rise, and as river gradients became steeper the effects of erosion were more pronounced. Water carved broad valleys and left behind jutting peaks of resistant rock. Ice-age glaciers helped sculpt the ridges and glacial meltwater later formed deep mountain lakes. Millions of years from now further erosion will have reduced the Rockies to rolling plains.

150 MILLION YEARS AGO

50 MILLION YEARS AGO

2 MILLION YEARS AGO

Range

46

Maligne

Medicine Lake

Queen Elizabeth Ranges

River

MIETTE HOT SPRINGS
The hottest spring water in the Canadian Rockies—54°C—is piped into a swimming pool here and cooled to 39°C. The waters are believed to originate as rain and melted snow which have seeped into bedrock fissures. This runoff is heated at depths of several thousand metres, then percolates back to the surface at the rate of a million litres a day.

MEDICINE LAKE
For most of the year Medicine Lake is a dry gravel bed. In summer, runoff and glacial meltwater transform it into a lake eight kilometres long and up to 18 metres deep. The lake has no apparent outlet except in times of high water. It drains into subsurface channels, emerging in the Maligne River farther downstream.

Medicine Lake

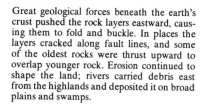

Maligne
Lake

Mountain caribou

Maligne
Mtn ▲

SAMSON
NARROWS

SKYLINE TRAIL
This hiking trail parallels the Maligne River for 43 kilometres—more than 25 of them above the timberline. The trail passes the Snowbowl, a lovely subalpine meadow sprinkled with wildflowers, and Wabasso Lake—a stark, rocky pond set in a steep-walled cirque. From The Notch can be seen a panorama of summits including distant Mount Robson (3,954 metres), the highest peak in the Canadian Rockies.

MALIGNE LAKE
Emerald-green Maligne Lake is set among the snow-mantled peaks of the Front Range and stretches for nearly 22 kilometres. Some 11,000 years ago, a massive tongue of ice advanced down the valley, gouging out the deep basin that today contains Maligne Lake.
□ At the Samson Narrows, a brook flowing from Maligne Mountain has deposited debris and sediment that nearly cut the lake in half.

Big Game and Abandoned Mines in the Faraway Foothills

West-Central Alberta

This foothills region is ideal vacation country for anglers, nature lovers, big-game hunters, and those who would explore the wilderness.

In 4,597-square-kilometre Willmore Wilderness Park—Alberta's largest wilderness area—visitors can hike or canoe for a few days (or a few weeks) without meeting or seeing others. There are no permanent residents and, except for a few Forest Service cabins and some fire lookouts, no buildings in this wilderness. Motor vehicles are prohib-

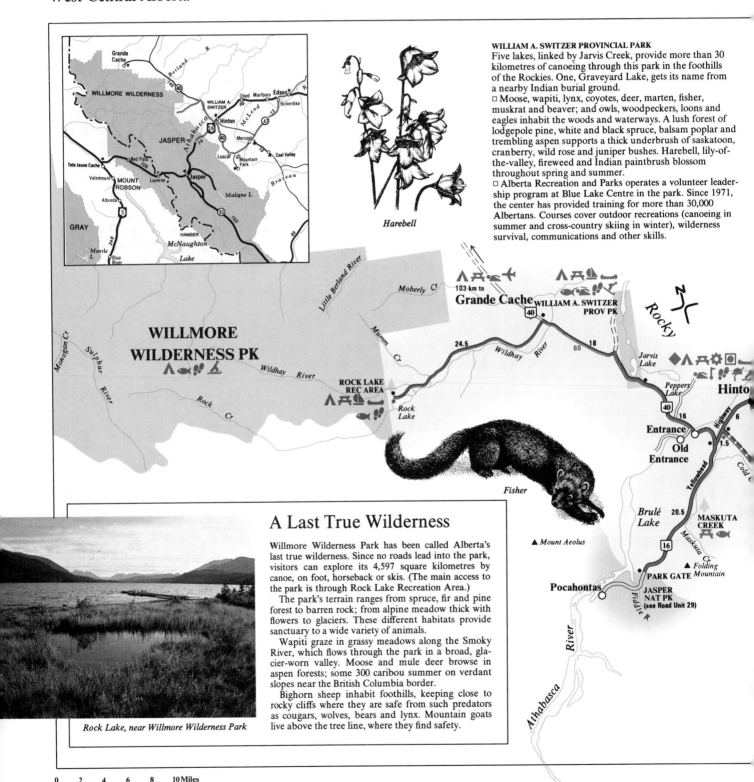

Harebell

Fisher

Rock Lake, near Willmore Wilderness Park

WILLIAM A. SWITZER PROVINCIAL PARK

Five lakes, linked by Jarvis Creek, provide more than 30 kilometres of canoeing through this park in the foothills of the Rockies. One, Graveyard Lake, gets its name from a nearby Indian burial ground.

□ Moose, wapiti, lynx, coyotes, deer, marten, fisher, muskrat and beaver; and owls, woodpeckers, loons and eagles inhabit the woods and waterways. A lush forest of lodgepole pine, white and black spruce, balsam poplar and trembling aspen supports a thick underbrush of saskatoon, cranberry, wild rose and juniper bushes. Harebell, lily-of-the-valley, fireweed and Indian paintbrush blossom throughout spring and summer.

□ Alberta Recreation and Parks operates a volunteer leadership program at Blue Lake Centre in the park. Since 1971, the center has provided training for more than 30,000 Albertans. Courses cover outdoor recreations (canoeing in summer and cross-country skiing in winter), wilderness survival, communications and other skills.

A Last True Wilderness

Willmore Wilderness Park has been called Alberta's last true wilderness. Since no roads lead into the park, visitors can explore its 4,597 square kilometres by canoe, on foot, horseback or skis. (The main access to the park is through Rock Lake Recreation Area.)

The park's terrain ranges from spruce, fir and pine forest to barren rock; from alpine meadow thick with flowers to glaciers. These different habitats provide sanctuary to a wide variety of animals.

Wapiti graze in grassy meadows along the Smoky River, which flows through the park in a broad, glacier-worn valley. Moose and mule deer browse in aspen forests; some 300 caribou summer on verdant slopes near the British Columbia border.

Bighorn sheep inhabit foothills, keeping close to rocky cliffs where they are safe from such predators as cougars, wolves, bears and lynx. Mountain goats live above the tree line, where they find safety.

ited. Local commercial outfitters take families horseback riding along trails in summer, and guide hunters in the fall.

Bear, deer, moose, mountain sheep and wapiti, abundant in the park, are found throughout the region. Hunters regard this as one of the finest big-game areas in the world, and flock to Edson and Hinton in the autumn.

Within easy reach of these towns are abandoned mines—ghostly reminders of the heyday of the "Coal Branch." This once thriving area of coal-mining towns prospered from 1910 to the 1930s, revived during the Second World War, but slumped again in the late 1940s, when the railways introduced diesel-powered engines.

Tourism is now the area's most important industry—but old ties are strong. Among the thousands camping and fishing here on weekends there are usually some former residents of these once-thriving, close-knit communities.

Sailing at Blue Lake Centre, William A. Switzer Provincial Park

HINTON
Visitors here may tour the tree nursery of Weldwood of Canada.
□ Hikers and horseback riders can explore a 20-kilometre restored section of the Bighorn Trail, an early pack trail that extended some 140 kilometres along the Bighorn Ridge between Hinton and Nordegg. There are two wilderness campsites on the trail.

FOLDING MOUNTAIN
This mountain, typical of the eastern ranges of the Rockies, is clearly visible from Highway 16, about 18 kilometres west of Hinton. Its layers of rock, once horizontal, folded when the Rocky Mountains were formed. The layer of gray rock (mainly limestone) was deposited by a warm shallow sea which covered North America more than 300 million years ago. Above it is brown siltstone laid down by another sea 100 million years later.

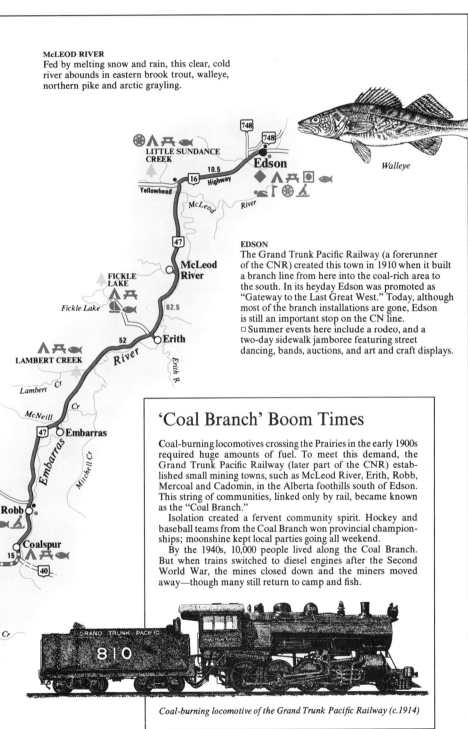

McLEOD RIVER
Fed by melting snow and rain, this clear, cold river abounds in eastern brook trout, walleye, northern pike and arctic grayling.

Walleye

EDSON
The Grand Trunk Pacific Railway (a forerunner of the CNR) created this town in 1910 when it built a branch line from here into the coal-rich area to the south. In its heyday Edson was promoted as "Gateway to the Last Great West." Today, although most of the branch installations are gone, Edson is still an important stop on the CN line.
□ Summer events here include a rodeo, and a two-day sidewalk jamboree featuring street dancing, bands, auctions, and art and craft displays.

'Coal Branch' Boom Times

Coal-burning locomotives crossing the Prairies in the early 1900s required huge amounts of fuel. To meet this demand, the Grand Trunk Pacific Railway (later part of the CNR) established small mining towns, such as McLeod River, Erith, Robb, Mercoal and Cadomin, in the Alberta foothills south of Edson. This string of communities, linked only by rail, became known as the "Coal Branch."

Isolation created a fervent community spirit. Hockey and baseball teams from the Coal Branch won provincial championships; moonshine kept local parties going all weekend.

By the 1940s, 10,000 people lived along the Coal Branch. But when trains switched to diesel engines after the Second World War, the mines closed down and the miners moved away—though many still return to camp and fish.

Coal-burning locomotive of the Grand Trunk Pacific Railway (c.1914)

A Land of Glaciers Along the Continental Divide

Jasper National Park

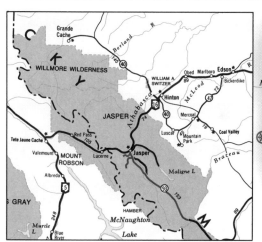

Athabasca Falls

ATHABASCA FALLS

In a cloud of spray and mist, the Athabasca River plu[nges] 22 metres over a ragged cliff of Precambrian quartzite at Athabasca Falls. Below the falls the river roars thro[ugh] a narrow gorge and emerges at a line of cliffs a few hundred metres beyond. Near the falls, old channels [and] potholes indicate that the river has changed its course several times in the past. A fine sediment gives the riv[er] a milky appearance.

Crawling Glaciers That Break into a Gallop

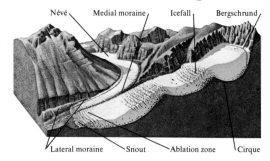

High in the Rocky Mountains lie vast permanent ice fields that spawn glaciers—rivers of ice. Unlike the frozen water of a lake or pond, glacial ice forms from snow that remains from winter to winter. The granular snow that survives each year is called *névé* or *firn*. It accumulates in a firn field, often a sheltered mountain slope which weathering and ice erode into giant steep-walled depressions called *cirques*.

After many years, pressure changes the ice crystals (which were once snow crystals) into glacier ice. This mass begins to flow under the pressure of its own weight, usually a few centimetres a day.

A *bergschrund* is the deep crevasse that appears when the flowing ice breaks away from a mountain wall. *Icefalls*, massive blocks of jagged ice, form when brittle surface ice cracks as it moves down a steep descent.

Rock debris, deposited by the glacier as it creeps over the land, creates *lateral moraines* (visible as dark strips at a glacier's edges); when two glaciers flow together the lateral moraines merge to become a *medial moraine* (a dark strip down the center). The lower part of the glacier is in the *ablation zone* (area of melting).

MOUNT EDITH CAVELL

This majestic peak (3,361 metres) is named for a British nurse executed by a German firing squad during the First World War.
□ Angel Glacier lies in a saddle on the flank of the mountain and a tongue of the glacier licks into the valley.
□ Glacier-fed Cavell Lake nestles in a rock-walled amphitheater. Reflected in the lake's turquoise water is the sheer northeastern face of Mount Edith Cavell.
□ A trail into the valley bottom opposite Angel Glacier passes over a mass of boulders, cobbles, sand and rock flour ground and scattered by glacial action.

Athabasca Glacier, Columbia Icefield

COLUMBIA ICEFIELD

Once part of the vast ice sheet that covered most of Canada for more than a million years, the Columbia Icefield is the largest accumulation of ice in the Rocky Mountains. It blankets an area of nearly 325 square kilometres to depths of 300 metres.
□ The most accessible of the many glaciers that jut from the main body of the icefield is the Athabasca Glacier, which can be reached from the Icefields Parkway. Snowcoach tours on the glacier give visitors a close look at mill holes (deep, circular depressions) and crevasses (long, nearly vertical fissures). Athabasca Glacier is receding at about seven metres a year.

Adjoining Banff National Park at the Columbia Icefield, Jasper National Park sweeps northwest along the Continental Divide. It is a ragged rectangle some 200 kilometres long and close to 90 kilometres across at its widest.

From east to west, gradually loftier ranges rear up from the foothills of Alberta. These mountains once formed a prehistoric ocean floor. Geologic forces created the present landscape of ice-capped peaks.

Each of three entrances to the park is guarded by sentinel mountains. The most spectacular gateway is Sunwapta Pass on the Icefields Parkway. At the summit, a flower-carpeted meadow provides a view of 3,435-metre Mount Athabasca.

Leaving the Icefields Chalet at 2,100 metres, the parkway winds down to the valley of the Sunwapta River 450 metres below. At Summit Viewpoint, forested ridges frame the hanging glaciers of Mount Kitchener (3,450 metres) and the Stutfield Glacier. The breathtaking scenery is often enhanced by the sight of a black bear or a bighorn ram foraging beside the road. Jasper's abundant wildlife is a main park attraction, to be seen and photographed but not fed.

Hikers and trail riders take to the backcountry for days or weeks at a time on more than 900 kilometres of trails traversing this wilderness of mountains, glaciers, lakes and wild rivers.

ICEFIELDS PARKWAY
The 230-kilometre Icefields Parkway ranks among the great highroads of the world and commands some of the most majestic scenery in the Canadian Rockies. It runs between Lake Louise and Jasper townsite, follo ving in turn the Bow, Mistaya, North Saskatchewan, Sunwapta and Athabasca rivers, crossing the Bow and Sunwapta passes and presenting a panorama of peaks, glaciers, waterfalls and canyons. Some landmarks bear the names of early guides and explorers—Wilcox, Stanley, Nigel; others have descriptive names such as Tangle Ridge and Whirlpool River, or Indian names such as Sunwapta (turbulent river).

SUNWAPTA RIVER
From its headwaters at the foot of the Athabasca Glacier, the Sunwapta courses through a deep valley carved by eons of erosion. In places the river flows in several intertwining channels across a broad riverbed choked with silt and gravel—a braided pattern typical of glacier-fed rivers.
□ Some 56 kilometres south of Jasper, the green Sunwapta is divided by a small, pine-clad island. Swiftly the arms are reunited in a headlong plunge through the two canyons of Sunwapta Falls. A kilometre downstream the river adds its volume to the mighty Athabasca and 20 kilometres farther the combined waters hurtle over Athabasca Falls.

Sunwapta River

JONAS CREEK
Quartzite boulders litter both sides of the Icefields Parkway where rockslides have swept down here from the mountain slopes to the east. Above the boulder field, near the top of the ridge, is a distinct pink scar where part of the rock sheared away. The Sunwapta River now breaks in rapids over the foot of the slide area. The rock itself has been used extensively as building stone in Jasper National Park.
□ To the southeast of Jonas Creek loom Tangle Ridge and 3,315-metre Sunwapta Peak. In the opposite direction Endless Chain Ridge stretches to the northwest.

Audubon's warbler

TANGLE RIDGE
Carved and scoured by glacial action, the mass of Tangle Ridge (2,953 metres) rises dramatically to the east of the Icefields Parkway. Boulders and rock faces bear striations—lines and furrows gouged by glacial debris.
□ Beauty Creek is a fast-flowing mountain stream which rises above Tangle Ridge, then cascades to the Sunwapta River through a deep canyon and over a series of limestone cliffs.

NIGEL PEAK
Named for 19th-century guide Nigel Vavasour, the 3,160-metre peak rises like a giant layer cake from the valley floor. The mountain's alternating layers of limestone and shaly rock are bent into a U-shaped fold called a syncline.
□ A trail winds from the highway to 2,167-metre Nigel Pass with sweeping views of the surrounding mountains.

Bighorn ram

SUNWAPTA PASS
Jasper and Banff national parks border one another here, along the divide between the headwaters of the Sunwapta and North Saskatchewan rivers. Waters flowing north from this divide eventually reach the Arctic Ocean via the Mackenzie River, while those flowing south cross the Prairies via the Saskatchewan River to Hudson Bay.
□ The Icefields Parkway crosses the divide at 2,035 metres above sea level. At this elevation snowbanks remain in sheltered areas throughout the summer. Like many high valleys near timberline, the bottomland near Sunwapta Pass is virtually treeless.

Rocky Mountain goats

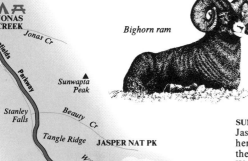

Iridescent Lakes and Trails Alive with Color

Banff National Park

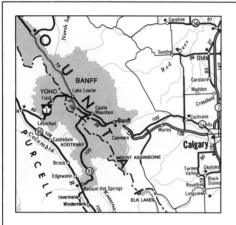

SASKATCHEWAN RIVER CROSSING

The crossing is part of the historic route to Howse Pass followed by explorer David Thompson in 1807.
□ To the south, Mount Murchison (3,333 metres) rises more than a thousand metres from the valley floor. Indians believed the mountain to be the highest in the Rockies.
□ The North Saskatchewan River is born in the gravel-strewn tongue of the Saskatchewan Glacier, just off the Icefields Parkway.

HOWSE RIVER

In 1807, the North West Company sent David Thompson up the North Saskatchewan River from Rocky Mountain House to establish a trading post west of the Rockies. Traveling by horse and canoe, Thompson crossed Howse Pass (southwest of Howse Peak) in June, blazing the earliest trade route across the Rockies. The pass, peak and river were later named for Joseph Howse, a trader with the rival Hudson's Bay Company who followed Thompson's trail in 1810.

WATERFOWL LAKES

Upper and Lower Waterfowl Lakes are two in a series of lakes through which the Mistaya River flows on its 32-kilometre journey to the North Saskatchewan River. The low, marshy lakes attract a variety of wildlife, including moose.

□ Here, as at few other points along its length, the Continental Divide appears as a sheer barrier of rock. So wall-like is the divide here that it is difficult to distinguish where one mountain ends and the next begins. Two peaks that dominate the scene are ice-covered Howse Peak (3,291 metres) and the leaning, pyramid-shaped Mount Chephren (3,266 metres).
□ From the Waterfowl Lakes Campground, a trail leads to the rock amphitheaters containing Cirque and Chephren lakes.

Lower Waterfowl Lake

Mistaya Canyon

MISTAYA RIVER

Gathering its waters from glaciers and streams along the Continental Divide, the Mistaya River snakes past majestic, snow-mantled peaks. Ice-age glaciers gouged the wide Mistaya Valley.
□ A short nature trail drops down from a roadside pull-off to Mistaya Canyon. Here the rushing waters of the river have cut deeply into the limestone bedrock to form a narrow, twisting gorge with vertical walls. Swirling rocks and boulders have ground rounded potholes into the base of the canyon walls.
□ A footbridge spans the gorge, and trails lead to Sarbach Lookout (five kilometres) and Howse Pass (27 kilometres).

BARBETTE GLACIER

This alpine glacier is set within a deep cirque on the southwest flank of Mount Patterson (3,197 metres). The glacier's meltwaters drop 300 metres into Mistaya Lake. Although the three-kilometre-long lake is one of the largest in the Mistaya River Valley, it is so well hidden by the surrounding forest that few visitors have ever seen it. Only a kilometre from the highway, the lake can be reached by a steep trail.

PEYTO LAKE

Between Lake Louise and Saskatchewan Crossing, the Icefields Parkway passes a series of large lakes formed by glacier-fed streams. Off the highway at Bow Pass, a viewpoint overlooks Peyto Lake, named for Bill Peyto, a turn-of-the-century mountain man and respected guide who later became a park warden at Banff. The lake is fed by the meltwaters of Peyto Glacier, a tongue of the extensive Wapta Icefield.

0	1	2	3	4	5 Miles

0	2	4	6	8 Kilometres

Banff National Park was created by an Act of Parliament in 1887, but the real story of the park begins much earlier.

Once covered by a vast inland sea, the area underwent dramatic geologic changes some 70 million years ago. Like folds in a crinkling blanket, mountains emerged from the ancient sea floor. Over the centuries the erosive forces of wind, water and ice carved them to their present shapes.

The mountains of Banff are a geologist's delight. Layer upon layer of sedimentary rock can be distinguished in the peaks that flank the road, and geological oddities range from potholes to hanging valleys.

The most visible—and striking—of the forces that have shaped Banff are the glaciers that cling to the mountains and poke their icy tongues into the valleys. Emerald-green Lake Louise, like many of the park's lakes, owes its iridescent color to glacial sediment.

Although the park is dominated by rock and ice, nature enlivens even the harshest scene. Mountain roads and trails are alive with color—magenta fireweed, blue clematis and yellow columbine.

Banff's fauna is no less diverse than its flora. Sixty species of mammals and 225 species of birds make their homes in the park. The grizzly, Banff's most formidable resident, and the black bear frequent campgrounds and garbage dumps in search of food. A sharp eye will sight moose, elk, deer, beavers, marmots, pikas and, perhaps, Rocky Mountain sheep.

BOW PASS

This summit serves as the watershed for the North and South Saskatchewan River systems. Waters that drain from this divide meet again in central Saskatchewan. There, the two branches join and flow to Hudson Bay.
□ A trail from the Bow Pass Viewpoint follows a fire road to the Bow Fire Lookout some two kilometres away. In late summer the meadows are colored with heather, mountain avens, globeflowers, western anemones and alpine forget-me-nots. Hoary marmots are often seen lumbering across the alpine tundra or sunbathing on rocks. The elusive pika, another high-country resident, is recognized by its sharp, clipped cry of warning.

HECTOR LAKE

Blue-green Hector Lake is named for Dr. James Hector, geologist with the Palliser Expedition and the first white man to pass through this valley, in the autumn of 1858. Surrounding the lake is the Waputik ("white goat") Range.
□ Rising above the south end of the lake is Pulpit Peak (2,724 metres). On its slopes grow some of the most northerly stands of alpine larch in the Rockies. In the fall, their needles turn from pale green to gold, splashing the slopes with color.
□ Avalanche scars can be seen fingering down from the upper ridges of Pulpit Peak into the forest below. A hanging valley on the northwest slope contains tiny Turquoise Lake.

KICKING HORSE PASS

The pass straddles the Continental Divide at an elevation of 1,624 metres. While exploring the pass in 1858, geologist James Hector was kicked by a packhorse and, while unconscious, was almost buried by his grieving Stoney Indian guides.
□ Early locomotives traveled so slowly up Kicking Horse Pass that seats were attached to the front of the engines so that passengers could savor the scenery.

Hector Lake

LAKE LOUISE

The scene first surveyed in 1882 by a CPR workman named Tom Wilson is today one of the most familiar mountain vistas in the world.
□ The impressive Chateau Lake Louise stands atop a giant glacial moraine that dams the lake, whose waters are a milky green color due to suspended sediments.
□ The 6.5-kilometre Plain-of-the-Six-Glaciers Trail leads to a spectacular view of the Victoria Glacier. Almost 150 metres thick in places, the glacier covers more than two square kilometres.

□ Lake Louise Gondola takes visitors about 400 metres up Mount Whitehorn to a vantage point overlooking the mountainous area around the lake.

MORAINE LAKE

Emerald-green Moraine Lake, somewhat smaller than Lake Louise, is set before the spectacular backdrop of the Wenkchemna Peaks. Great cones of glacial debris, pried loose by the freezing and thawing of ice, flank the lake's southeast shore. The gigantic rock pile that dams the lake is believed by geologists to be the remains of two massive rock slides from the 2,314-metre Tower of Babel above.
□ A lodge at the lake offers accommodation and meals throughout the summer. Canoe rentals are also available.

VALLEY OF THE TEN PEAKS

Cradling Moraine Lake are the sharp, glaciated Wenkchemna (an Indian word for ten) Peaks. Quartzites lend a reddish-orange hue to the mountains' lower slopes. Steep gray limestone cliffs comprise the summits.
□ A trail from Moraine Lake Lodge climbs steadily for 2.4 kilometres to open, subalpine meadows at the foot of Sentinel Pass (2,610 metres). The meadows are laced with stands of stunted Engelmann spruce, alpine fir and alpine larch, and dotted with several small lakes (known as the Minnestimma, which is an Indian expression for sleeping waters).

Map labels

rvation
76
Bow Lake
Icefields
93
Parkway
Rocky
Crowfoot Glacier
24
MOSQUITO CREEK
Bow Peak
St. Nicholas Pk
ALTA BC
N
Hector Lake
Bow
Mt Balfour
Waputik
River
Mount Hector
Continental
Waputik Pk
Range
Mountains
Divide
Bath
Pipestone River
17
ALTA BC
Cr
Kicking Horse Pass
7.5
93
Stephen
1
Pika
5
Lake Louise
Mount St. Piran
Lake Louise
2
The Beehive
Mount Whyte
Fairview Mountain
1A
1
Mt Aberdeen
18
Trans-Canada Highway
Paradise Cr
13
Mount Temple
93
Moraine Cr
Valley of the Ten Peaks
Sentinel Pass
Eiffel Peak
Pinnacle Mtn
Tower of Babel
Moraine L
Mount Babel
ALTA BC
Allen Mount

Western anemone

High Peaks and Hot Springs in Canada's First Park

Banff National Park

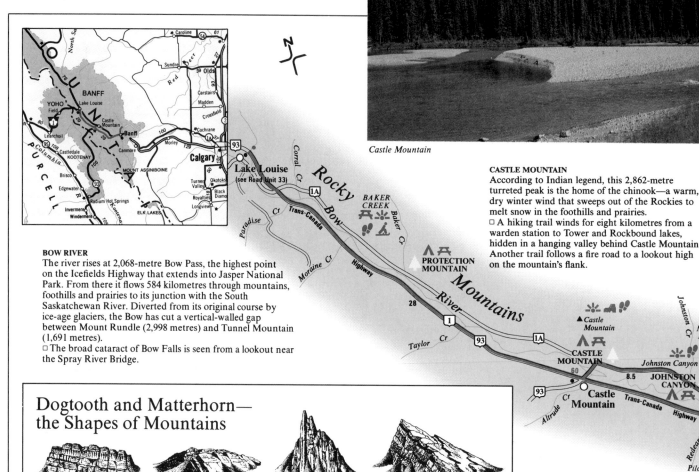

Castle Mountain

CASTLE MOUNTAIN

According to Indian legend, this 2,862-metre turreted peak is the home of the chinook—a warm, dry winter wind that sweeps out of the Rockies to melt snow in the foothills and prairies.
□ A hiking trail winds for eight kilometres from a warden station to Tower and Rockbound lakes, hidden in a hanging valley behind Castle Mountain. Another trail follows a fire road to a lookout high on the mountain's flank.

BOW RIVER

The river rises at 2,068-metre Bow Pass, the highest point on the Icefields Highway that extends into Jasper National Park. From there it flows 584 kilometres through mountains, foothills and prairies to its junction with the South Saskatchewan River. Diverted from its original course by ice-age glaciers, the Bow has cut a vertical-walled gap between Mount Rundle (2,998 metres) and Tunnel Mountain (1,691 metres).
□ The broad cataract of Bow Falls is seen from a lookout near the Spray River Bridge.

Dogtooth and Matterhorn— the Shapes of Mountains

Castellate mountain

Anticlinal mountain

Dogtooth mountain

Dipping layered mountain

Synclinal mountain

Sawtooth mountains

Matterhorn mountain

Complex mountain

Visitors to Banff have long noted the distinctive shapes of individual mountains.

Castellate mountains (such as Castle Mountain) are made from alternating layers of sedimentary rock. As softer layers erode, the harder rock is undermined and breaks off, forming steep slopes and cliffs.

One side of a *dipping layered* mountain (Mount Rundle) is usually a smooth slope from peak to base, following the angle of a single layer of rock.

A jagged *dogtooth* mountain (Mount Louis) results when erosion leaves behind a near-vertical core of resistant rock. Long ridges of such peaks are called *sawtooth* mountains (Sawback Range).

The folding of sedimentary rock layers creates arched *anticlinal* mountains (Fairholme Range) and trough-shaped *synclinal* mountains (Cirrus Mountain). A mountain with both anticlines and synclines is said to be *complex* (Palliser Range). A *matterhorn* mountain is formed when glaciers carve depressions in the sides of a peak creating a pyramidal summit.

JOHNSTON CANYON

Johnston Creek has carved a deep canyon from soft underlying rock here, and plummets over Upper and Lower Falls farther downstream.
□ Among the canyon's wildlife is the dipper or water ouzel, a bird which lives at the very edge of turbulent mountain streams. In feeding, the dipper will wade, swim, dive, even walk underwater on the streambed.
□ The Ink Pots are a group of seven springs located in a meadow beyond the canyon. Two of the pools are noted for their murky, blue-green color—a hue created by suspended sediments.
□ To the west, open meadows mark the site of Silver City, a mining boom town. During its heyday (1883-85), the town boasted a population of 2,000, four general stores and several hotels. The mines failed to meet expectations, however, and a disputed claim helped to speed the town's demise.

The first and most famous of Canada's national parks is an incomparable combination of towering peaks and high meadows, emerald lakes and keen mountain air. These—and sulphur hot springs—have made Banff National Park one of North America's most spectacular scenic and recreation areas.

In the winter of 1883, CPR workmen noticed wisps of steam rising from a fissure on the south side of the Bow Valley. A candle lowered down the hole on a string revealed a cavern with a pool of steaming, sulphurous water. The upshot, in June 1887, was an Act of Parliament designating 673 square kilometres around the springs as "Rocky Mountains Park."

As befits Canada's oldest park—now 6,640 square kilometres and spanning the Continental Divide for 240 kilometres—Banff offers a wide variety of ways to enjoy its natural splendors. One starting point is Banff townsite, a bright and bustling community of some 4,600 permanent residents who, thanks to a skiing boom, serve a year-round tourist population. Split by the Bow River, the town is surrounded by a stunning mountain landscape crisscrossed by more than 1,500 kilometres of hiking trails.

Near the Bow River Bridge stands the Banff Springs Hotel. Far below, the glinting blue of the river winds through a green valley past the limestone walls of Tunnel Mountain (1,690 metres) and Mount Rundle (2,949 metres).

MOUNT NORQUAY
From Banff townsite, a 5.7-kilometre road climbs to a lookout 300 metres above the valley floor with expansive views of the major mountains and valleys to the south and east. Dominating the peaks is the sloping, layer-cake summit of Mount Rundle (2,998 metres).
□ Known locally as the Green Spot, an open meadow adjacent to the viewpoint is fringed with huge Douglas fir trees.

LAKE MINNEWANKA
Sightseeing launches ply this 19-kilometre-long lake near Banff. It is the largest in the park and the only lake on which motors are permitted. The mountains along the north shore comprise the southern terminus of the Palliser Range. The massive cliffs of Mount Inglismaldie (2,964 metres) contain the lake to the south.
□ The foundations of the small resort town of Minnewanka lie beneath the cold waters of the lake. The resort flourished during the early 1900s but was abandoned with construction of a dam in 1912. The lake's level was raised 4 metres in 1912 and another 19 metres in 1941.

Banff townsite

VERMILION LAKES
A nine-kilometre drive skirts the shores of the three Vermilion Lakes. The surrounding wetland, a marshy area of the Bow River, is rich in plant and animal life. Sedges, rushes and swamp horsetail provide a habitat for beaver and muskrat. On slightly drier ground grow willows, black currants and bracted honeysuckle. Beyond the wetland are groves of white spruce sprinkled with poplars. Ringing the lakes are Sulphur Mountain, Mount Rundle and the peaks of the Sundance Range.

BANFF
The townsite of Banff is the park's headquarters and a year-round recreation center for tourists, horseback riders, skiers, hikers and mountain climbers.
□ The Archives of the Canadian Rockies house a community library and research center for the history of the region.
□ Specimens of wildlife native to Banff National Park are displayed in the Banff Natural History Museum.
□ Indian lore and customs are shown in dioramas at the Luxton Museum, built to resemble a 19th-century fur-trade post.
□ The Banff Center is one of North America's foremost schools of visual and performing arts. The center's program of concerts, drama and ballet is highlighted by the Festival of the Arts in late summer.

SULPHUR MOUNTAIN
One of Banff's most popular attractions is the Sulphur Mountain lift. Four-passenger gondolas rise 690 metres in eight minutes to the summit ridge (2,348 metres) and a sweeping panorama of mountains and valleys.
□ At Upper Hot Springs, an outdoor swimming pool (37°–42°C) is open to the public year-round.

CAVE AND BASIN CENTENNIAL CENTRE
This is the birthplace of Banff National Park. In the early days, bathers descended into the cave by means of a ladder through a hole in the cavern ceiling. Since then a tunnel has been burrowed into the chamber so that visitors can view the historic site. Inside the grotto, jagged rock walls arch above steaming Cave Pool, fed by sulphur springs flowing at 675 litres a minute.

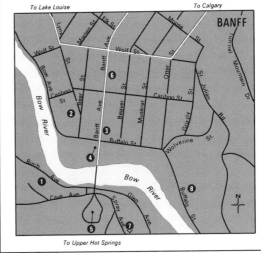

1 Luxton Museum
2 The Whyte Museum of the Canadian Rockies
3 Banff Natural History Museum
4 Banff National Parks Museum
5 Parks Canada Administration Building
6 Tourist Information
7 Banff Springs Hotel
8 Banff Centre

Mount Rundle

Where Mountain Meets Prairie in the Kananaskis Region

Southwestern Alberta

Horse packing in the Stoney Wilderness Centre

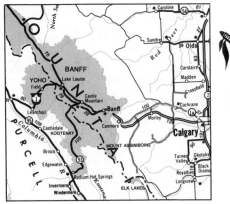

Stoney Indian emblem

STONEY WILDERNESS CENTRE
In a unique outdoor education program sponsored by the Stoney Indians, teenagers from across Canada spend two weeks of their summer holiday sleeping in tepees, baking bannock over a campfire and riding horseback through the foothills near Morley. The students are taught camping and traditional Indian skills by native instructors and learn to "tread the delicate face of this land in harmony with nature."

CANMORE
The triple peaks of The Three Sisters near Canmore are made of molten rock, solidified beneath the earth's surface, then thrust up among older peaks.
□ Canmore Nordic Centre, a site of the 1988 Winter Olympics, offers cross-country skiers more than 56 kilometres of trails.

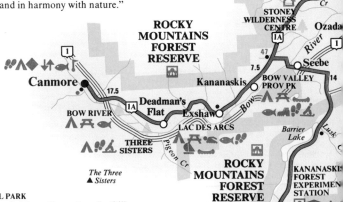

The Three ▲ Sisters

The Three Sisters, near Canmore

BOW VALLEY PROVINCIAL PARK
When the last glacier receded from the eastern foothills some 10,000 years ago, it left behind a number of glacial remnants that are visible in this park. Eskers (serpentine ridges) and moraines are landforms composed of glacial debris. Where blocks of trapped glacial ice melted and the ground above sank, kettles and potholes were formed.
□ The meeting of three major vegetation zones—mountain, forest and grassland—is responsible for the diverse flora of the Bow Valley.

KANANASKIS FOREST EXPERIMENT STATION
Established in 1934, the station serves as a living laboratory for forest management. Also located at the station is the University of Calgary's Environmental Sciences Center.
□ An early administration building called the Colonel's Cabin (1936) is made of lodgepole pine logs.
□ The 2.5-kilometre self-guiding Resource Management Trail winds through a portion of the 6,070-hectare experimental forest. The first loop leads to an observation deck and shows forest vegetation, the role of fire in forest ecology, wildlife habitat and climate. A second loop focuses on forest management techniques including logging and reforestation.

Hoary marmot

PETER LOUGHEED PROVINCIAL PARK
The rugged wilderness of Alberta's first and largest mountain provincial park has been a camping area for at least 5,000 years. Several ancient campsites have been unearthed here, and early Indians may have hunted mammoths as well as bison in this area. Outstanding scenery includes six large lakes, ice caps, remnant valley glaciers, alpine tundra, waterfalls and canyons. The lowest elevation in the park is 1,737 metres.

Upper Kananaskis Lake

0 1 2 3 4 5 Miles

0 2 4 6 8 Kilometres

The Kananaskis region has changed little since explorer John Palliser came here in 1858. It remains a land of cobalt-blue lakes, lush meadows, thundering cataracts and sheer mountain flanks.

Because it embraces both prairie and mountain, the Kananaskis region is alive with fascinating plants and animals. In summer the lowlands are sprinkled with pasqueflowers, wild roses, moss phlox and geraniums of brilliant pinks and purples.

White-tailed deer, wary of cougars and coyotes, move stealthily across open meadows. Higher up, the grasses give way to a dense carpet of lichens and mosses, and the lodgepole pine forests to Engelmann spruce, alpine fir and larch. Above the timberline, marmots, pikas and mountain goats forage among hardy perennials and stunted alpine shrubs.

Many rivers have their chill births here as glacial trickles threading down the slopes of the Kananaskis and Opal ranges. Cutthroat, rainbow, brook and brown trout rise and strike fiercely in these translucent streams.

A pattern of trunk roads winds through the Kananaskis bush, affording access for fire fighters and foresters protecting a vital watershed area. These roads also enable campers and fishermen to explore a great wilderness.

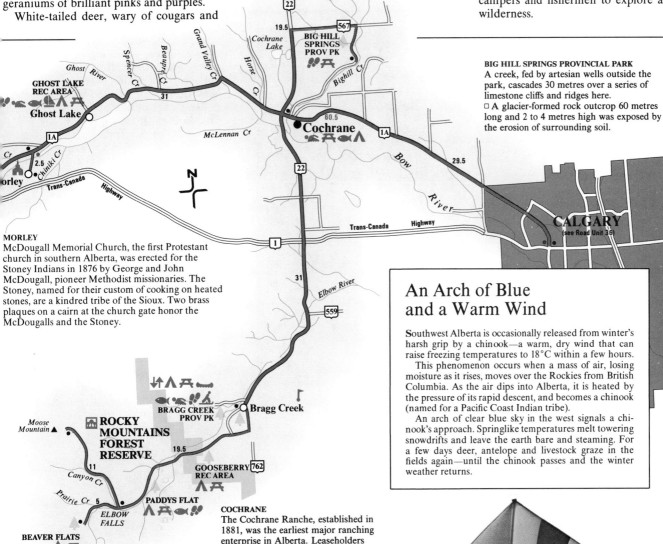

BIG HILL SPRINGS PROVINCIAL PARK
A creek, fed by artesian wells outside the park, cascades 30 metres over a series of limestone cliffs and ridges here.
□ A glacier-formed rock outcrop 60 metres long and 2 to 4 metres high was exposed by the erosion of surrounding soil.

MORLEY
McDougall Memorial Church, the first Protestant church in southern Alberta, was erected for the Stoney Indians in 1876 by George and John McDougall, pioneer Methodist missionaries. The Stoney, named for their custom of cooking on heated stones, are a kindred tribe of the Sioux. Two brass plaques on a cairn at the church gate honor the McDougalls and the Stoney.

An Arch of Blue and a Warm Wind

Southwest Alberta is occasionally released from winter's harsh grip by a chinook—a warm, dry wind that can raise freezing temperatures to 18°C within a few hours.

This phenomenon occurs when a mass of air, losing moisture as it rises, moves over the Rockies from British Columbia. As the air dips into Alberta, it is heated by the pressure of its rapid descent, and becomes a chinook (named for a Pacific Coast Indian tribe).

An arch of clear blue sky in the west signals a chinook's approach. Springlike temperatures melt towering snowdrifts and leave the earth bare and steaming. For a few days deer, antelope and livestock graze in the fields again—until the chinook passes and the winter weather returns.

Hang glider, Cochrane

BRAGG CREEK PROVINCIAL PARK
Winding through this small park is the fast-flowing Elbow River, its shale-littered banks rising 10 metres in places. When water levels are high, experienced canoeists and kayakers challenge the river's powerful current and numerous rapids.

KANANASKIS COUNTRY
This 5,200-square-kilometre region has been set aside by the Alberta government as an area for outdoor recreation and nature conservation. It includes three provincial parks: Peter Lougheed, Bragg Creek and Bow Valley. The region offers facilities for picnicking, camping (particularly at Bow Valley Provincial Park), hiking and horseback riding. During the Winter Olympics of 1988, the Nakiska Ski Area at Mount Allen was the site of the alpine ski events. Highway 40 leads visitors through the heart of this spectacularly scenic region of Alberta.

COCHRANE
The Cochrane Ranche, established in 1881, was the earliest major ranching enterprise in Alberta. Leaseholders originally paid one cent per acre per year. In 1906, almost the entire block was sold to the Mormon Church for $6 million—the largest land deal in Alberta to that time.
□ Colorful hang gliders soar and wheel above Cochrane Hill. Air currents and thermals (rising columns of warm air) along the ridge enable skilled pilots to keep their manned kites aloft. Novice hang-glider pilots must receive 15 hours of instruction before they are permitted to fly here.

ELBOW FALLS
After a series of rapids, the Elbow River drops seven metres over a limestone cliff in Elbow Falls. Part of the water then flows into an underground cavern, and reappears some 30 metres downstream. Small fissures and potholes flank the falls.

Cowboys, Oil and Skyscrapers in Alberta's 'Sandstone City'

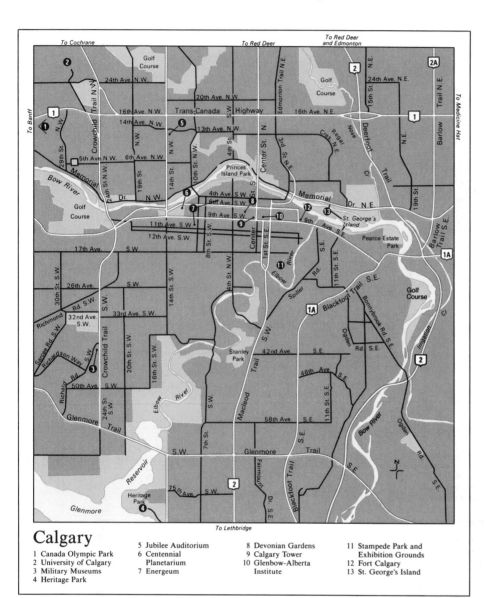

Calgary

1 Canada Olympic Park
2 University of Calgary
3 Military Museums
4 Heritage Park
5 Jubilee Auditorium
6 Centennial Planetarium
7 Energeum
8 Devonian Gardens
9 Calgary Tower
10 Glenbow-Alberta Institute
11 Stampede Park and Exhibition Grounds
12 Fort Calgary
13 St. George's Island

Valley) and richer finds elsewhere in the province after World War II launched Calgary from a quiet prairie city to its present eminence as an oil capital and site of corporate headquarters. Hundreds of local companies are involved in supplying or financing Alberta's oil industry and, among Canadian cities, only Toronto and Montreal have more head offices.

Calgary Tower (9)
The revolving observation deck (and restaurant) at the top of the 190-metre Calgary Tower offers a 96-kilometre view of the city, the surrounding prairie and the Rockies. The tower—part of the VIA Rail complex—is linked by enclosed walkways with the Glenbow-Alberta Institute, the city's convention center, and other downtown attractions.

Canada Olympic Park (1)
This park on the Trans-Canada Highway, just west of Calgary, was built for the ski jumping, bobsled races, and luge runs of the 1988 Winter Olympics. The world-class facility is now a popular public ski area and an athletic sports training center. (Year-round tours of the facility are available.) The Olympic Hall of Fame gives the history of the win-

The Saddledome (above) is one of many innovative structures that have changed the face of Calgary. Olympic Plaza (right) and other public spaces provide havens from the growing city's hectic pace.

ter games since their inception in 1924 at Chamonix, France.

Centennial Planetarium (6)
At the 255-seat Star Theater visitors can scan images of planets and stars projected onto a 20-metre-wide, domed screen.

Devonian Gardens (8)
The glassed-in Devonian Gardens, on the 4th floor of the Toronto-Dominion Centre, contain more than 1,600 subtropical plants and trees in a 1-hectare oasis of fountains,

Soaring symbol of oil-fueled progress, Calgary's skyline continually climbs against the horizon, rimmed 100 kilometres to the west by the Rocky Mountains. Blessed with a dry, bracing climate and warmed by winter chinook winds, Calgary has grown from a muddy garrison to a major center in less than a century. But the white-collar city reverts to jeans each summer during its famous Calgary Stampede, when cowboys—real and drugstore—join in street dances, rodeos and parades.

The city started as Fort Calgary, a North West Mounted Police post built in 1875. The settlement that grew around the fort became a local trading center. With the completion of the Canadian Pacific Railway in 1883 came the first influx of homesteaders and ranchers. A year later, Calgary was incorporated as a city.

Pioneer Calgary was a place of wood construction until fire gutted 14 houses in 1886. Afterward the city decreed that all buildings be of yellow sandstone from local quarries. Many fine old sandstone structures remain. The Grain Exchange, the turreted Bank of Montreal, the Alberta Hotel and the old City Hall all survive from days when Calgary was known as "The Sandstone City."

Oil discoveries nearby in 1914 (at Turner

pools and waterfalls. The gardens provide an exhibition space for work by local artists.

Energeum (7)
Visitors can learn about the development of Alberta's energy through models, videos and displays at the Energeum.

Fort Calgary (12)
Wooden posts and gateways in this 8-hectare park outline the North West Mounted Police (NWMP) fort built here in 1875. The history of the fort and the NWMP's role in the development of western Canada are described in audiovisual presentations at the interpretive center.

Glenbow-Alberta Institute (10)
One of the largest institutes of its kind in Canada, the Glenbow consists of a museum, an art gallery, a library and archives. Originally a private foundation (established in 1954), it was donated to Alberta in 1966.

The museum depicts the Plains Indian as hunter, nomad and trader, displays Indian, Inuit and pioneer artifacts, and has an outstanding collection of minerals in their natural form.

Indian, Inuit and many of Canada's early artists (Paul Kane, for example) are represented in the art gallery. *Aurora Borealis*, a four-story, acrylic sculpture by James Houston, dominates the stairwell.

The library and archives contain documents, tape recordings, movies, diaries, microfilm copies of western Canadian newspapers, 100,000 photographs, and 30,000 books and pamphlets.

Heritage Park (4)
Visitors to this 25.6-hectare park step back into a pre-1914 prairie community. Situated on a peninsula that juts into the Glenmore Reservoir, it has more than 100 buildings, including a hotel with a two-story outhouse (1906), a general store (1905), a ranch house (1904), a working grain elevator (1909) and a log "opera" house from the 1890s. The park offers rides on an old-time steam railway and stern-wheeler cruises on the reservoir.

Jubilee Auditorium (5)
The 2,750-seat Southern Alberta Jubilee Auditorium—built in 1955 to commemorate Alberta's 50th anniversary—is the twin of Edmonton's Northern Alberta Jubilee Auditorium.

Military Museums (3)
Two museums at the Canadian Forces Base recount the history of Princess Patricia's Canadian Light Infantry and Lord Strathcona's (Royal Canadian) Regiment. The museums display regimental weapons, uniforms and mementos, including a flag designed and sewn by Princess Patricia for the division which bears her name.

St. George's Island (13)
Located only a few minutes from downtown Calgary, St. George's Island is the site of Calgary Zoo (the second largest in Canada), the Botanical Gardens, and Prehistoric Park. Among more than 1,400 animals at the zoo are a Himalayan snow leopard and Canada's only breeding pair of South American spectacled bears. There is also a children's zoo, a tropical aviary and a conservatory with some 11,000 tropical plants. In the adjoining Prehistoric Park are some 20 huge replicas of dinosaurs and other creatures that roamed Alberta 230 million years ago.

University of Calgary (2)
Originally a branch of the University of Alberta, this institution became autonomous in 1964 and took its present name two years later. The McMahon Stadium and the Nickle Arts Museum, which offers changing exhibitions in its four galleries, are both nearby.

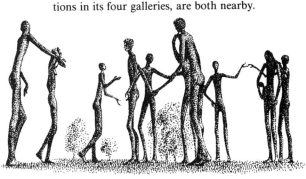

Ceremonial headdress (left) once worn by Sioux chief Sitting Eagle is displayed at Glenbow Center. Family of Man by Mario Armengol (above), seen at Expo 67, is at Calgary's Education Centre.

Calgary's Wild and Woolly Stampede Days

Wranglers calm a feisty bronco.

Dancing in the streets, Indians in colorful regalia, the thunder of hooves, the creak of harness and chuck wagon . . . for 10 days in July it's one of the biggest and most famous shows in the world—the Calgary Stampede at Stampede Park (11).

There's saddle and bareback broncobusting, Brahma bull and buffalo riding, a wildhorse race, calf wrestling and wild-cow milking as cowboys scramble for big money prizes. The most hair-raising event was invented in Alberta—races in which four chuck wagons, 20 riders and 32 horses all dash for a single point on the track.

There are fireworks, grandstand shows, a midway, a frontier casino, livestock exhibits, thoroughbred horse racing and a village with Sarcee, Stony, Peigan, Blood and Blackfoot tepees. Fancy livestock are brought to town and prettied up like beauty contestants to compete for blue ribbons and money. The fun includes a parade of cowboys, Indians and Mounties—and flapjacks at curbside.

Foothills, Ranches, and Rumors of Gold

Southwestern Alberta

This is part of Alberta's renowned foot hills country, the land of the chinook where the flat of the prairie gives way to the gentle roll of the Porcupine Hills and their upward march to the Rocky Mountains. Here is some of the finest grazing land in Canada. Grasses cure on the stalk, producing a natural hay, and in winter the chinook—a warm, dry wind from the west—sweeps down from the Rockies and melts the snow, enabling livestock to feed freely on the exposed vegetation.

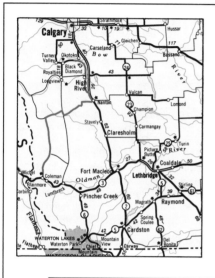

THE HUMP
Men still search these parts for a lost gold mine—and settle, not unhappily, for views such as seen (*right*) from The Hump, a 1,996-metre elevation off the Forestry Trunk Road. Prospectors named Blackjack and Lemon are said to have found gold near here in the 1880s, but they quarreled and Lemon killed Blackjack with an ax. Two Indians witnessed the slaying and (so the legend goes) their chief put a curse on the place and removed all evidence of gold. When Lemon returned he went insane. Nearly a century later there are those who insist there *is*—somewhere—a Lost Lemon Gold Mine.

View from The Hump

Lodgepole Pine, a Tree Born of Fire

The lodgepole pine is the commonest tree in the Alberta foothills. It grows to 30 metres and has thin, scaly, yellow-brown bark and bright yellow-green needles. Indians used the straight, strong trunks as tepee poles; they boiled the soft inner bark for food. Today the lodgepole pine's moderately hard wood is used for railway ties, mine props and pulp.

This tree's cones release seeds only at 40°C or higher—temperatures that occur in the forest only during a fire. The seeds germinate within days and the seedlings develop rapidly on the mineral-rich, fire-prepared ground. Lodgepole pines frequently form dense stands of timber, sometimes merging with jack pine.

The lodgepole pine is also common on the west coast. The coastal variety is often scrubby and cracked and has thick, furrowed reddish brown bark. It is used locally for firewood.

Cattle grazing near Mount Livingstone

MOUNT LIVINGSTONE
The white-crowned sparrow, common in the Mount Livingstone area and throughout this part of Alberta, is found from low valleys to mountain meadows. Larger than most sparrows (17 to 19 centimetres long), it has a gray, black-and-white-striped head, a gray, brown-streaked back, a white throat patch and two white bars on each wing. Its underside is gray, its tail, dark brown.

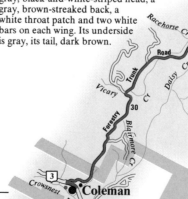

LIVINGSTONE FALLS

LIVINGSTON FALLS

ROCKY

MOUNTAIN

FOREST

RESERVE

OLDMAN RIVER

DUTCH CREEK

RACE HORSE CREEK

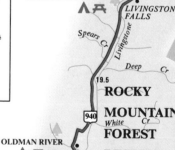

White-crowned sparrow

Crowsnest R. **Coleman**

| 0 | 2 | 4 | 6 | 8 | 10 Miles |
| 0 | 4 | 8 | 12 | 16 Kilometres |

Ranching began soon after the arrival of the North West Mounted Police in 1874. The Mounties introduced law and order to the region. Before long the ranchers began to prosper as the demand for beef cattle and sheep grew. One of the first herds of cattle was brought across the mountains from British Columbia where ranching had flourished since the gold rush days of the 1860s. Subsequent herds were brought from Montana and eastern Canada.

Many pioneer ranchers were ex-Mounties who developed a society here reminiscent of their former way of life but with a distinctive western flavor. It was a sports-oriented society where cricket, polo, horse racing and hunting were popular. Balls were held in conjunction with sports gatherings, and musical evenings and theatrical events were common.

The life of the foothills ranching community remained relatively unchanged until 1914, when many men went to war. The area remained ranch country—and some of its institutions such as race meets survived—but it never recaptured the old-world gentility of its past.

BIG ROCK
This giant boulder, 40 metres by 18 metres by 9 metres and estimated to weigh 18,000 tonnes, is the biggest among thousands in a 644-kilometre chain called the Foothills Erratics Train. One theory is that the train was created by a rock slide onto a moving glacier; as the glacier melted, the rocks dropped in its wake. Although this train is at least 10,000 years old, it is slowly losing its distinctive identity. Weathering and erosion have split Big Rock.

Big Rock near Okotoks

OLD WOMAN'S BUFFALO JUMP
A flash flood here in 1952 exposed a blanket of bones and a buffalo kill apparently 1,500 years old. Sandstone cliffs over which Indians stampeded the animals were presumably much higher than now (seven metres). There are traces of ritual cairns and medicine wheels (boulders placed in circles). Blackfoot ceramics 300 years old have been unearthed.

HIGH RIVER
A restored 1950 passenger and freight train, as well as replicas of a barbershop and a blacksmith shop of the sort the homesteaders knew, is in the Museum of the Highwood. Settlers' and ranchers' tools and effects and prehistoric Indian artifacts are exhibited. There is also a collection of lamps. One display records the geological history of this area with rocks, fossils, petrified wood, the tooth of a mammoth and parts of a dinosaur skeleton arranged in time sequence. The art of saddle making can be seen at two harness shops in town.

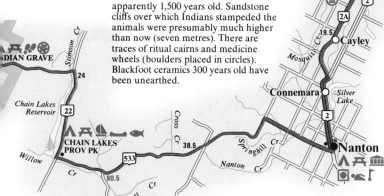
Brand marks on the wall of the blacksmith shop, Museum of the Highwood, High River

NANTON
Nanton's famous spring water is piped from the Porcupine Hills, 11 kilometres west of town.
□ A replica of the Mosquito Creek Crossing Post of the Royal Northwest Mounted Police is situated in Centennial Park, and houses a tourist information office. Also in the park there is a World War II Lancaster; a plaque explains the history of this famous class of four-engine bombers.

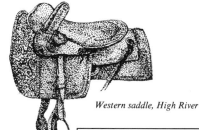
Western saddle, High River

CHAIN LAKES PROVINCIAL PARK
This four-square-kilometre park is noted for outstanding scenery and good fishing. Rimmed by the Rocky Mountains and the Porcupine Hills, it contains one of Alberta's most heavily stocked trout lakes, the 11-kilometre-long Chain Lakes Reservoir. This reservoir was formed in the mid-1960s out of three small lakes. It forms part of Willow Creek, which links up with the Oldman River. A pleasant canoe route follows these rivers through the foothills where deer, elk, moose, black bear and coyote roam.

Bar-U and Lazy-S... Brands of the West

Branding—the marking of livestock to denote ownership—may have originated some 4,000 years ago in Egypt. The practice was brought to the Americas by the Spanish and was adopted in western Canada in the late 1870s. Initially brands were simple, often a single letter. But as more brands were registered, variations were introduced. (An important consideration was to choose a brand that could not easily be altered by rustlers.) Cattle were sometimes branded on the ribs or hip, occasionally on the shoulder, jaw or neck.

 Brands are read from the left, from the top down or the outside in. This brand is the Bar-U.

 Letters joined together were called "running." The running MP was the brand of the North West Mounted Police.

 Any letter lying on its side was called lazy—in this case the Lazy-S.

 Any letter with a curved line below was called "rocking": the Rocking-P.

 A letter with its upper ends extending outward was called "flying." This is the Flying-U.

Fair Winds and a Great Slide on a Famous Mountain Route

Southwestern Alberta

Scenery is excitingly varied in southwestern Alberta. From this stretch of road are to be seen rolling ranch country, the foothills, the towering majesty of the Rockies—and the scars of long-ago calamities, chief among them the great Frank Slide of 1903. Seventy lives were lost in that disaster when a landslide on Turtle Mountain hit part of the town of Frank, covering the nearby road and railway. Today this classified historical site is one of the most photographed landmarks in the Crowsnest region.

The Town That Awoke to a Nightmare

Scattered rocks up to 50 metres deep cover three square kilometres of the valley of the Crowsnest River in gruesome testimony to the Frank Slide of April 29, 1903. That day at 4:10 a.m. a wedge of limestone 915 metres wide, 640 metres high and 150 metres thick hurtled down the side of Turtle Mountain toward the sleeping town of Frank. After only 100 seconds some 82 million tonnes of rock were strewn across the valley floor, 70 persons were dead, and part of the town—including a mine plant and a railway siding—had disappeared.

Geologists believe that the weak internal structure of Turtle Mountain made the Frank Slide inevitable. Local mining may have caused it to occur prematurely.

Frank Slide Interpretive Centre highlights the settlement of the region and early railway and coal-mining development industry. An award-winning audiovisual presentation is shown daily.

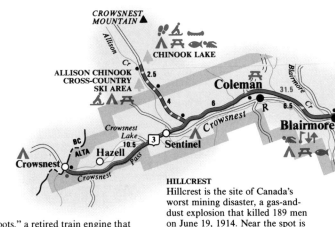

The Frank Slide

CROWSNEST PASS

Magnificent Crowsnest Mountain guards the north side of this famous pass. According to legend, the mountain was named for the birds that nested below its peak.

□ Discovered in 1873, the Crowsnest Pass is one of the lowest routes through the Rockies (1,357 metres above sea level).

□ The municipality of Crowsnest Pass was formed in 1979, by the amalgamation of all the towns, villages and hamlets in the Alberta portion of the Crowsnest Valley. Occupying an area of some 148 square kilometres, the community is the third largest urban land region in the province.

COLEMAN

"Ten Ton Toots," a retired train engine that residents hail as "the biggest piggy bank in the world," is here. The locomotive is used as a receptacle for charitable donations. Another locomotive—complete with boxcars and caboose—lies at the bottom of Crowsnest Lake where it came to rest in the early 1900s. The train was carrying illicit whiskey during prohibition; it left the track after the driver had sampled his cargo. The whiskey was never recovered.

COLEMAN VOLCANIC DEPOSITS

A plaque just west of Coleman records that the rocks here are 93 million years old. It also marks the only significant occurrence of volcanic deposits in Alberta. Many of the large blocks of ash and cinder are similar to pumice bombs ejected by active volcanoes. The absence of lava also suggests volcanoes in this region once erupted explosively.

HILLCREST

Hillcrest is the site of Canada's worst mining disaster, a gas-and-dust explosion that killed 189 men on June 19, 1914. Near the spot is their mass grave, unmarked but for a picket fence.

BLAIRMORE

A crow nesting in a tree is the symbol of Blairmore, which was the first settlement in the Crowsnest Pass. The town became an important bituminous coal-mining center. It displays a life-size statue of a coal miner, sculpted from a 350-year-old tree, and a 1914 locomotive that was used in the Hillcrest collieries, about seven kilometres east of town. (Blairmore and the former towns of Bellevue, Coleman, Frank and Hillcrest have been part of the Municipality of Crowsnest Pass since 1979.)

Statue of a coal miner, Blairmore

Crowsnest Mountain

But there is more to photograph: rivers and coulees, Lundbreck Falls, Bow-Crow Forest Reserve, Beaver Mines Lake, with a superb view of 2,163-metre-high Gladstone Mountain to the south, and such routes as the Adanac Road—between Lynx Creek and Hillcrest Mines—through a spectacular forest of lodgepole, limber and white pines, mixed with Douglas and subalpine firs.

On this route there are several former townsites. Some reached their peak supplying railways ties as the CPR pushed through the Crowsnest in 1897-98. Others such as Passburg, near Bellevue, were planned as coal-mining centers. But they were abandoned when schemes to transform local coal into coke for industrial purposes failed. Some coal is still dug in the pass, and oil and gas have been discovered.

The wind in the Crowsnest Pass sometimes reaches 160 kilometres an hour and has been known to push boxcars as much as 24 kilometres. Old-timers tell of a wind-measuring device that was made up of a steel ball suspended by a chain from a high pole. When the ball and chain pointed straight out, residents figured there was a "fair wind."

Lundbreck Falls

BELLEVUE
Pioneers were impressed by the *belle vue* (beautiful view) from this town's setting high in the Crowsnest Pass. It was the first of many southern Alberta coal towns that supplied the railways in the steam era. Two old mine buildings can be seen at nearby Police Flats, and interpretive displays of early coal mining are featured at the Leitch Collieries Provincial Historic Site, nine kilometres east of town. The Back to God Chapel at the edge of town holds only eight persons at a time but attracts as many as 20,000 visitors annually.

LUNDBRECK FALLS
The east end of the Crowsnest Pass has an impressive beginning here as the Crowsnest River plunges 18 metres to form Lundbreck Falls. (There are campgrounds nearby.) The road follows the Crowsnest River part of the way, past trees often photographed for their gnarled and weather-beaten ruggedness.
□ Members of the Christian Community of Universal Brotherhood came here from British Columbia in 1915 and established Alberta's first Doukhobor settlement near Lundbreck Falls. Many of their descendants still live here.

COWLEY
A steady stream of air from the Rockies ("standing mountain waves") makes for excellent gliding conditions at Cowley. Gliding enthusiasts, who gather here in summer and fall, ride the mountain waves to heights of more than 9,000 metres.
□ A highway sign at Massacre Butte, north of Cowley, recalls the 1867 slaying of some 12 immigrants by a Blood Indian war party.

Abandoned mine buildings at Police Flats

Gliding at Cowley

PINCHER CREEK
Kootenai Brown Historical Park was named in memory of John George "Kootenai" Brown, a local pioneer who became the first superintendent of Waterton Lakes National Park. Early farm machinery is displayed in the park.
□ The architectural style of the Timothee Lebel Mansion (1919) reflects French-Canadian and New Orleans influences. The restored mansion houses a local arts center.

Glacier lily

BEAUVAIS LAKE PROVINCIAL PARK
This park in the shadow of the Rockies has some of the richest diversity of plant life in Alberta. Spruce and poplar thrive throughout and in early spring the yellow flower of the glacier lily brightens hillsides still white with the last of winter's melting snow. Beauvais Lake, 1,337 metres above sea level, offers fishermen an abundance of rainbow trout.

BEAVER MINES LAKE RECREATION AREA
This popular recreation area at the foot of Gladstone Mountain has picnic and camp facilities and a boat launch. In spring the landscape is ablaze with flowers. One of the commonest is the western spring beauty, a white or pink flower that grows at the edge of woodlands. The flower, its leaves and stem make a delicious salad.

Western spring beauty

Where Shining Peaks Rise Sheer from the Prairies

Southwestern Alberta

Few places in Canada can equal the dramatic contrast of landscapes in Waterton Lakes National Park. Snowcapped peaks rise abruptly from low, rolling grasslands. The proximity of prairie and mountain offers visitors a stunning variety of scenery and wildlife.

A narrow strip of foothills parallels the Rockies in the northeast corner of the park, and supports luxuriant grasslands carpeted with prickly rose, many-flowered aster and wild geranium.

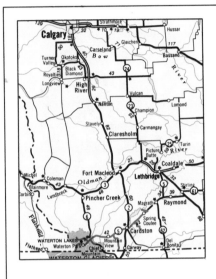

WATERTON LAKES NATIONAL PARK
In 1931 Waterton Lakes National Park was linked with Glacier National Park in Montana to form the world's first international peace park.
□ The three Waterton lakes, connected by Bosporus and Dardanelles straits, separate the Lewis and Clark mountain ranges. The lakes lie in a valley that was formed by a river but was deepened and sculpted by glaciation. The park is noted for its geological formations—U-shaped valleys, hanging valleys and canyons.
□ More than 160 kilometres of hiking trails meander through the park, linking such features as Red Rock Canyon and Cameron Falls. The cruise ship *International* travels the length of Upper Waterton Lake. A herd of 20 bison grazes in a paddock near the northern entrance to the park.

RED ROCK CANYON
A self-guiding hiking trail in Waterton Lakes National Park follows the brightly colored canyon of Blakiston Creek. The 20-metre-high canyon walls were streaked red, purple, green and yellow by chemical changes of minerals in the rocks. Ripples in cliffs and fossils of algae are evidence that an ancient sea once covered this area.

In recent geological time (about a million years ago), glaciers carried boulders here from surrounding mountains.

Looming above the canyon is Mount Blakiston (2,940 metres), the highest peak in the park.

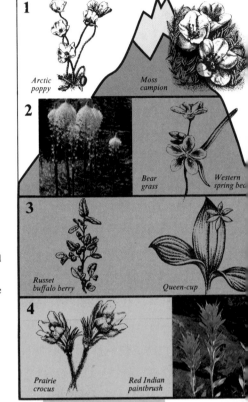

1 Arctic poppy / Moss campion
2 Bear grass / Western spring bea[uty]
3 Russet buffalo berry / Queen-cup
4 Prairie crocus / Red Indian paintbrush

Waterton Lakes National Park

CAMERON LAKE
A hiking trail in the southwest corner of Waterton Lakes National Park passes waterfalls, canyons and towering cliffs, then crosses a steep rise. Below is Cameron Lake, a blue gem set in a bowl-shaped valley at the foot of Mount Custer.

DISCOVERY WELL
The site of western Canada's first oil well is marked by a cairn in Waterton Lakes National Park. For centuries Kutenai Indians had used oil from seepage pools along Cameron Creek to help heal wounds. Settlers had used it to lubricate wagons. In 1902, a prosperous rancher named John Lineham sank a well that produced up to 300 barrels of oil a day. Four years later the flow ebbed and the well was shut down.

Discovery Well,
Waterton Lakes National Park

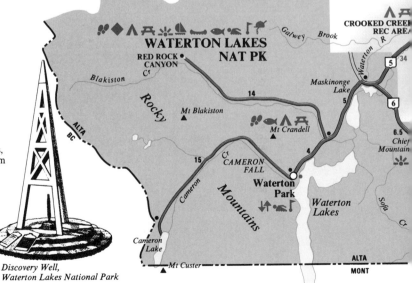

WATERTON LAKES NAT PK
RED ROCK CANYON
Blakiston Cr
Galwey Brook
CROOKED CREEK REC AREA
Maskinonge Lake
Mt Blakiston
Mt Crandell
Rocky
CAMERON FALL
Waterton Park
Waterton Lakes
Cameron
Mountains
Cameron Lake
Mt Custer
Chief Mountain
Sofa Cr
ALTA BC
ALTA MONT

0 1 2 3 4 5 Miles
0 2 4 6 8 Kilometres

Towering above the prairie is a "land of shining mountains," once the floor of an immense inland sea. Movements of the earth's crust uplifted layers of sediment, and subsequent glaciation sculpted the landscape.

Mount Blakiston (2,940 metres) is the highest peak in the park, but many others soar to 2,500 metres. Some mountains are streaked red, green, gray and purple by chemicals. Others, such as Chief Mountain, are isolated and castlelike.

One of the oldest geological formations in the Rockies—more than a billion years old—is along Cameron Creek near the town of Waterton Park. Cameron Lake, like many others in the park, is in a cirque, a steep-walled basin carved by glaciers. The clear lake waters are fed by snowfields high in the mountains.

St. Mary River Dam

Life Zones of a Park

From icy peaks to dry prairie, Waterton Lakes National Park abounds with plant life. Botanists have classified vegetation in zones according to elevation.

1 Arctic/Alpine Zone (2,225-2,375 metres to peaks): Above the tree line is tundra. Arctic poppy and moss campion huddle close to the ground, out of the wind.
2 Hudsonian Zone (1,830 to 2,225-2,375 metres): Evergreens flourish in the cold, dry air, though often stunted by high winds. Flowers such as western spring beauty and bear grass also grow at this elevation.
3 Canadian Zone (1,370 to 1,830 metres): Douglas maple, white spruce and lodgepole pine comprise this heavily forested region. Russet buffalo berry, silvery lupine and queen-cup are also found here.
4 Prairie and Parkland zones (1,280 to 1,370 metres): Rough fescue and blue grama grasses predominate. Prairie crocus and Red Indian paintbrush thrive amid aspen groves.

Rough fescue

ST. MARY RIVER DAM
This earth-fill dam and its 27-kilometre-long St. Mary Reservoir have transformed the surrounding semiarid prairie—once considered unsuitable for agriculture—into a prosperous farming region.

Irrigation makes possible the cultivation of sugar beets, potatoes, peas, beans, corn, carrots and other vegetables.

In 1897 Mormons from Utah dug more than 100 kilometres of canals and tapped the St. Mary River for Canada's first major irrigation project. But the canals usually ran dry in midsummer when water was most needed. In 1946, the St. Mary River was dammed to create a reservoir that would provide a reliable source of water for irrigation.

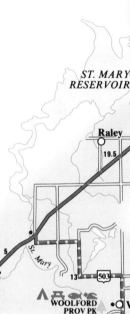

ST. MARY RIVER DAM

ST. MARY RESERVOIR

Spring Coulee

Raley

Cardston

WOOLFORD PROV PK   Woolford

Leavitt

Mountain View

Beazer

CHIEF MOUNTAIN
This castle-shaped mountain in Waterton Lakes National Park is a prominent landmark. It is a klippe—a peak separated from its mountain range by erosion.

Chief Mountain is "upside down." Old rocks overrode younger rocks when this peak was being formed.

Belly River

Paine Lake

Outpost Lake

POLICE OUTPOST PROV PK
ALTA
MONT

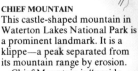

A Temple on the Plains

Canada's only Mormon temple is in Cardston. A white granite edifice, it was built in 1913-23 by Mormons who had come to Alberta from Utah. The granite was quarried in British Columbia's Kootenay Valley; each stone was hand shaped. Visitors may tour the grounds.

Cardston was named for Charles Ora Card, a son-in-law of Brigham Young and leader of 40 Mormon families who immigrated here in 1887. He was the town's first mayor, and built a gristmill, a sawmill and a cheese factory. His restored and refurnished log cabin (1887) is now a museum. The Card family Bible is displayed along with hand-carved furniture.

Sunshine, Sugar Beets and Old Whiskey Forts

Southwestern Alberta

Whiskey forts—riotous trading posts where liquor was sold illegally to Indians—flourished in the late 19th century in this region of southern Alberta. The liquor contained anything from red peppers to red ink. Yet a cupful was worth a fine buffalo robe; a quart, a fast horse.

A letter from one of these posts reflects

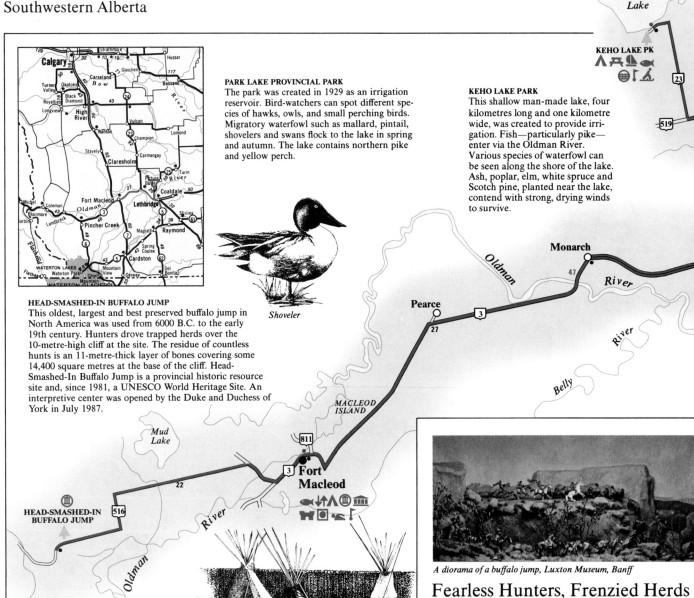

PARK LAKE PROVINCIAL PARK
The park was created in 1929 as an irrigation reservoir. Bird-watchers can spot different species of hawks, owls, and small perching birds. Migratory waterfowl such as mallard, pintail, shovelers and swans flock to the lake in spring and autumn. The lake contains northern pike and yellow perch.

Shoveler

KEHO LAKE PARK
This shallow man-made lake, four kilometres long and one kilometre wide, was created to provide irrigation. Fish—particularly pike—enter via the Oldman River. Various species of waterfowl can be seen along the shore of the lake. Ash, poplar, elm, white spruce and Scotch pine, planted near the lake, contend with strong, drying winds to survive.

HEAD-SMASHED-IN BUFFALO JUMP
This oldest, largest and best preserved buffalo jump in North America was used from 6000 B.C. to the early 19th century. Hunters drove trapped herds over the 10-metre-high cliff at the site. The residue of countless hunts is an 11-metre-thick layer of bones covering some 14,400 square metres at the base of the cliff. Head-Smashed-In Buffalo Jump is a provincial historic resource site and, since 1981, a UNESCO World Heritage Site. An interpretive center was opened by the Duke and Duchess of York in July 1987.

A diorama of a buffalo jump, Luxton Museum, Banff

Fearless Hunters, Frenzied Herds

Before the advent of firearms, Indians killed bison by driving thundering herds over steep cliffs known as buffalo jumps. The oldest site of this kind in Canada is at Head-Smashed-In.

In preparation for the kill, the Indians built drive lines—two rows of piled stones that converged at the buffalo jump. (The drive lines at Head-Smashed-In start about 11 kilometres from the cliff edge.) Hunters stampeded the bison between the drive lines, and the frenzied animals rushed over the cliff edge.

Bison provided the Indians with most of their necessities. Introduction of firearms to Alberta (c.1850) led to thoughtless slaughter of the bison by Indians and whites. Within 30 years, the huge herds had disappeared from the plains—and the simple economy of the Indians collapsed.

Tepees, Fort Macleod

FORT MACLEOD
A replica of the first North West Mounted Police fort stands at the edge of town. The original fort, built in 1874, was on a nearby island in the Oldman River. Buildings in the reconstructed fort include a museum with early NWMP weapons and uniforms, and artifacts from the original fort. There are a law office, blacksmith shop, chapel and medical-dental center. Displays in the center include a foot-pedal drill and a primitive X-ray machine (c.1910). Within the fort's palisade are Indian tepees and covered wagons.

the lawlessness that prevailed: "My partner Will Geary got to putting on airs and I shot him and he is dead. The potatoes is looking good . . ."

Law and order finally came in the 1870s when the North West Mounted Police arrived—led by legendary scout Jerry Potts, a bandy-legged half-breed who drank excessively and trimmed mustaches with his six-shooter. (Potts's grave is near Fort Macleod.)

Today some of Alberta's finest grain farms are found on this now tranquil prairie. Sugar beets are an important crop. The landscape undulates, giving unexpected, often spectacular views of deep-cut coulees and eroded banks along the Oldman River. Trees are few, planted mainly as windbreaks by farmers. Solitary grain elevators stand like sentinels, guarding the rich patchwork of gold, beige and brown fields.

Lethbridge, Alberta's third largest city, is a major meat-packing and grain-distribu-

tion center. Originally called Coalbanks, Lethbridge was built on coal in the 1870s. But coal now is secondary to livestock, grain and sugar beets, and the oil and gas that spring from the surrounding land. The city boasts that it receives more hours of sunshine annually than any other place in Canada. But the semiarid climate makes irrigation essential. Some 400,000 hectares of land surrounding the city are watered by reservoirs, canals and sprinkler systems.

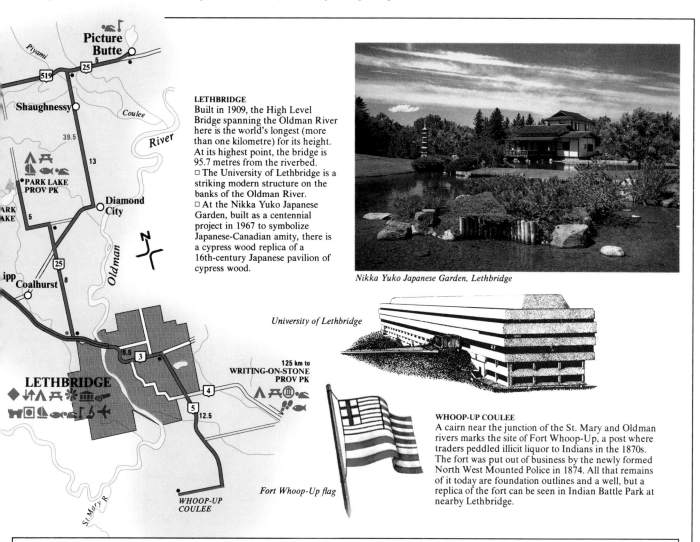

LETHBRIDGE
Built in 1909, the High Level Bridge spanning the Oldman River here is the world's longest (more than one kilometre) for its height. At its highest point, the bridge is 95.7 metres from the riverbed.
□ The University of Lethbridge is a striking modern structure on the banks of the Oldman River.
□ At the Nikka Yuko Japanese Garden, built as a centennial project in 1967 to symbolize Japanese-Canadian amity, there is a cypress wood replica of a 16th-century Japanese pavilion of cypress wood.

Nikka Yuko Japanese Garden, Lethbridge

University of Lethbridge

125 km to WRITING-ON-STONE PROV PK

Fort Whoop-Up flag

WHOOP-UP COULEE
A cairn near the junction of the St. Mary and Oldman rivers marks the site of Fort Whoop-Up, a post where traders peddled illicit liquor to Indians in the 1870s. The fort was put out of business by the newly formed North West Mounted Police in 1874. All that remains of it today are foundation outlines and a well, but a replica of the fort can be seen in Indian Battle Park at nearby Lethbridge.

'Writings' on Sandstone

An Indian drawing of a battle between dozens of armed mounted warriors (*right*) is carved on the sandstone cliffs of Writing-on-Stone Provincial Park (125 kilometres southeast of Lethbridge). Other "writings" depict a buffalo hunt, mountain goats, wapiti and deer. The petroglyphs were carved over a 300-year period.

The park's sandstone has been shaped by wind and water: bizarre rock towers (hoodoos) line the Milk River, and once led Indians to believe spirits lived in this valley.

In 1899 a North West Mounted Police outpost was established here to curb whiskey smuggling. Some of the post's buildings have been reconstructed.

Writing-on-Stone Provincial Park

Weird Hoodoos, Ancient Bones and Strange Mechanical Scarecrows

East-Central Alberta

HORSESHOE CANYON
Horseshoe Canyon covers almost 200 hectares of badlands and is more than 1.5 kilometres at its widest. On the canyon floor are petrified shells and wood, and dinosaur bones. Vegetation includes sagebrush, saskatoon and chokecherry.

DRUMHELLER
The Drumheller Exhibition and Stampede, in July, features arts and crafts displays, parades, rodeo events, canoe races, dances and barbecues.
□ Just outside the town is the Homestead Antique Museum. Its collections include restored farm tractors (1915-25), a barbershop (c. 1915), dolls and toys from the 1890s, and Indian relics.

DINOSAUR TRAIL
The Dinosaur Trail leads west from Drumheller to a 1.6 kilometre-wide valley nearly 120 metres deep—a vast prehistoric graveyard where whole skeletons of dinosaurs have been found. This "Valley of the Dinosaurs" is part of Alberta's Badlands, a long, dry stretch of terrain dotted with cacti and mushroom-shaped columns of clay and rocks called hoodoos.
□ Along this 48-kilometre drive is the "Biggest Little Church in the World," a tiny pink and white structure with a bright brass bell shining in its belfry. The church seats 20,000 people a year—six at a time.
□ The trail climbs to a lookout at the edge of Horse Thief Canyon, drops again, then skirts oil and wheat country before winding back toward Drumheller. The Bleriot Ferry transports cars to the west side of the Red Deer River.
□ Near the end of the Dinosaur Trail is Prehistoric Park, where life-size dinosaur models are displayed.

Plains prickly pear cactus

ROSEDALE
A 115-metre-long suspension footbridge, with a wooden walkway and high wire sides, offers visitors a dizzying view of the Red Deer River. Local miners built the bridge in the 1930s. A sign at one end records the structure's history. Another bridge to the west is wide enough to accommodate cars.

EAST COULEE
The first coal mine was opened he[re] in 1924, by J. N. Murray. Four ye[ars] later the railway arrived, facilitati[ng] transportation and encouraging industrial growth. East Coulee experienced its greatest expansion between 1928 and 1955, when the population reached some 3,500 (mostly mining families) and coal output peaked. During one period coal mines operated full time in th[e] area. Only the Atlas Mine is left today. Surface tours are available.

A Fossil Repository Older than the Rockies

Hoodoos, Red Deer Valley

The sunbaked, multilayered walls of the Red Deer River valley are a record of eons of land building. Silts and sands were carried here millions of years ago by streams flowing into the Mowry Sea, which once covered the North American plains. Each layer of sediment became a storehouse for the dead plant, animal and marine life of its age. In time this primordial mud turned to rock, and fossils were formed.

Some 70 million years ago enormous underground pressures began to thrust the Rocky Mountains out of the plains. The Red Deer River and its tributaries were shifted eastward, cutting a deep valley and exposing ancient rock layers and fossil remains. Furrowed gullies and strangely shaped hoodoos (rock pillars) are evidence of continuing erosion by the elements.

CLUNY
A metal cross near here marks the grave of Crowfoot, chief of the Blackfoot. A simple inscription on the cross reads: "Father of His People." Raised as a warrior—he was only 13 when he took part in his first raid—he fought in 19 battles and was wounded six times. But he realized the futility of intertribal warfare and became a man of peace. In 1877, at Blackfoot Crossing, five kilometres south of Cluny, he signed Treaty Seven with the British Crown, surrendering almost 130,000 square kilometres of Indian land.
□ A century later, on July 6, 1977, His Royal Highness Prince Charles and seven Blackfoot chiefs took part in a reenactment of the signing of the historic treaty at Blackfoot Crossing.
□ Near the treaty site is a boulder effigy of Young Medicine Man, a Blood Indian killed in 1872 by a Blackfoot avenging the death of a fellow tribesman at the hands of Young Medicine Man's band.

0   2   4   6   8   10 Miles

0   4   8   12   16 Kilometres

Alberta's Red Deer Badlands, millions of years ago the domain of the dinosaur, is a wild and windswept expanse of eroded hoodoos, weathered bluffs and steep-sided gullies. Awed by its rough magnificence, artist A. Y. Jackson described this area as "the most paintable valley in western Canada."

The best-preserved badlands are in Dinosaur Provincial Park. From a vantage point near the park entrance, visitors can look out over some 9,000 hectares of this eerie, sandstone landscape—and see, perhaps, the ghosts of Tyrannosaurus Rex and other prehistoric giants.

Near Drumheller, the scenery changes. Wheat grows waist-high on gently rolling prairie, and here and there oil pumps dot the fields like strange mechanical scarecrows. Antelope, deer, duck, partridge and pheasant in abundance make this area popular with sportsmen. Fish caught here include pike, walleye and trout.

Drumheller—named after Sam Drumheller who, in 1911, began the first coal-mining operation here—is a popular base for tourists exploring the Red Deer Badlands. The 50-kilometre Dinosaur Trail gives travelers a fascinating tour through an area rich in fossils.

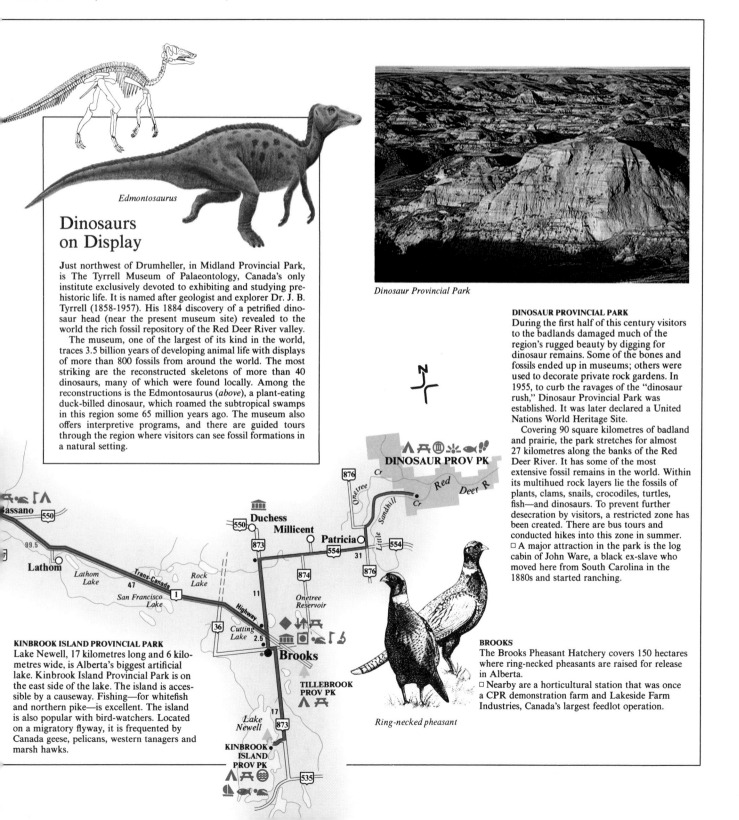

Edmontosaurus

Dinosaurs on Display

Just northwest of Drumheller, in Midland Provincial Park, is The Tyrrell Museum of Palaeontology, Canada's only institute exclusively devoted to exhibiting and studying prehistoric life. It is named after geologist and explorer Dr. J. B. Tyrrell (1858-1957). His 1884 discovery of a petrified dinosaur head (near the present museum site) revealed to the world the rich fossil repository of the Red Deer River valley.

The museum, one of the largest of its kind in the world, traces 3.5 billion years of developing animal life with displays of more than 800 fossils from around the world. The most striking are the reconstructed skeletons of more than 40 dinosaurs, many of which were found locally. Among the reconstructions is the Edmontosaurus (*above*), a plant-eating duck-billed dinosaur, which roamed the subtropical swamps in this region some 65 million years ago. The museum also offers interpretive programs, and there are guided tours through the region where visitors can see fossil formations in a natural setting.

Dinosaur Provincial Park

DINOSAUR PROVINCIAL PARK
During the first half of this century visitors to the badlands damaged much of the region's rugged beauty by digging for dinosaur remains. Some of the bones and fossils ended up in museums; others were used to decorate private rock gardens. In 1955, to curb the ravages of the "dinosaur rush," Dinosaur Provincial Park was established. It was later declared a United Nations World Heritage Site.

Covering 90 square kilometres of badland and prairie, the park stretches for almost 27 kilometres along the banks of the Red Deer River. It has some of the most extensive fossil remains in the world. Within its multihued rock layers lie the fossils of plants, clams, snails, crocodiles, turtles, fish—and dinosaurs. To prevent further desecration by visitors, a restricted zone has been created. There are bus tours and conducted hikes into this zone in summer.
□ A major attraction in the park is the log cabin of John Ware, a black ex-slave who moved here from South Carolina in the 1880s and started ranching.

KINBROOK ISLAND PROVINCIAL PARK
Lake Newell, 17 kilometres long and 6 kilometres wide, is Alberta's biggest artificial lake. Kinbrook Island Provincial Park is on the east side of the lake. The island is accessible by a causeway. Fishing—for whitefish and northern pike—is excellent. The island is also popular with bird-watchers. Located on a migratory flyway, it is frequented by Canada geese, pelicans, western tanagers and marsh hawks.

BROOKS
The Brooks Pheasant Hatchery covers 150 hectares where ring-necked pheasants are raised for release in Alberta.
□ Nearby are a horticultural station that was once a CPR demonstration farm and Lakeside Farm Industries, Canada's largest feedlot operation.

Ring-necked pheasant

Climbing Above the Prairies...
'The Hills That Shouldn't Be'

Southeastern Alberta

Gentle valleys, forested hillsides, grassy meadows, a rolling belt of brilliant green that breaks a treeless prairie—these are Alberta's Cypress Hills.

High elevation (1,372 metres above sea level) spared the western part of the hills from glaciation that scoured the surrounding prairie some 10,000 years ago. The hills were the only part of western Canada left uncovered by a kilometre-thick sheet of ice between the Rockies and the Laurentians.

Centuries ago the hills were a natural

Medicine Hat

The Day the Medicine Man Lost His Hat

The citizens of Medicine Hat are often asked to explain the origin of their town's unusual name. Stories abound, but perhaps the most popular is of a fierce battle between Cree and Blackfoot warriors beside a southern Alberta river. The Cree fought bravely until their medicine man fled across the river. In midstream he lost his headdress, which the Cree believed to be a bad omen. They lost heart and were slaughtered. The battle site was called *Saamis* (Blackfoot for "medicine man's hat"). The name was given to the settlement that sprang up nearby in 1882.

MEDICINE HAT
The three-day Medicine Hat Exhibition and Stampede in July attracts circuit cowboys from all over North America and crowds of more than 80,000. Activities include parades, flapjack breakfasts, chuck wagon races and an agricultural exhibition with livestock and horse shows.
□ A walking tour of historic Medicine Hat leads visitors to turn-of-the-century buildings in the downtown area.
□ Beneath Medicine Hat is an aquifer—a buried, preglacial river—that provides Medicine Hat with unlimited cool water. Natural gas from an underground reserve lights the city's lamps.
□ At nearby Redcliff the public is welcome to the former site of Medalta Potteries, now a provincial and national historic site. Interpretive programs are available in the summer.
□ Also open to the public are Redcliff's greenhouses, whose owners produce flowers for distribution throughout Alberta and western Canada.

Looking south to the Sweetgrass Hills of Montana, from Head of the Mountain, Cypress Hills Provincial Park

HEAD OF THE MOUNTAIN
This is the highest elevation (1,500 metres) between the Rocky Mountains and Labrador. Unlike the rest of western Canada, this summit was never covered by ice-age glaciers. From here visitors can see as far south as the Sweetgrass Hills of Montana. To the south and east Head of the Mountain slopes gently to the prairie, but to the north and west are nearly vertical cliffs. The high Cypress Hills are moister and cooler than the surrounding prairie. Lodgepole pine, common to the Rockies, grows on upper reaches. Forests of white spruce and trembling aspen thrive at lower elevations.

barrier separating Plains Indian tribes such as the Blackfoot, Assiniboine and Cree, each of which was eager to control this rich hunting ground.

In 1859 John Palliser led a British survey team into the region, then owned by the Hudson's Bay Company. He recorded that much of the land was desert or semidesert, unsuitable for settlement. But he called the hills "an island in a sea of grass."

Settlers soon arrived in the region—attracted by the fertility and bountiful wildlife of the hills. But construction of roads and dams, cattle grazing and clearing of land for farms destroyed much of the region's natural beauty.

Today the most attractive area of Alberta's Cypress Hills (the range extends into Saskatchewan) has been preserved in 200-square-kilometre Cypress Hills Provincial Park. Here, visitors can still enjoy the scenic wilderness that Blackfoot Indians called *Ketewius Netumoo*—"the hills that shouldn't be."

In contrast to this tranquil park is the busy city of Medicine Hat. Vast natural gas reserves here—today more than 20 billion cubic metres—prompted Rudyard Kipling, in 1907, to describe this as a place with "all hell for a basement."

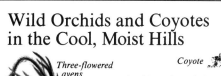

Wild Orchids and Coyotes in the Cool, Moist Hills

Three-flowered avens

Coyote

A wide variety of plants thrives in the cool, moist air of the Cypress Hills. An annual rainfall of 46 centimetres—only 18 centimetres fall on the plains—feeds fescue grasslands and stands of lodgepole pine, white spruce and trembling aspen.

Mountain flowers such as silvery lupine and shooting star grow here. Among 14 orchid types are the calypso bulbosa, the green-flowered bog orchid and a rare striped variety of round-leafed orchid. Gaillardia, golden bean and three-flowered aven brighten grassy meadows.

Some 200 bird species have been sighted in the hills: red-breasted nuthatches, mourning doves, MacGillivray's warblers and trumpeter swans (once close to extinction). Red-tailed hawks and great horned owls soar over grasslands.

Bobcats, red foxes and coyotes prey on shrews, mice, voles and ground squirrels. Wapiti and moose have been successfully introduced to the area. Pronghorn antelope and white-tailed and mule deer also roam the hills.

Gaillardias

Shooting stars

CYPRESS HILLS PROVINCIAL PARK
Visitors discover a wide variety of plants and animal life in Alberta's second largest provincial park. Hiking trails wind through wildflower meadows, tranquil valleys and cool forests of white spruce and lodgepole pine. Guided automobile tours lead to points of interest throughout the park. Most routes lie along the grassy plateau that caps the hills. In spring and summer this height of land is a garden of wildflowers—crocus, phlox, daisy and harebell. A lookout near Reesor Lake affords a view of the glacier-scarred prairie surrounding the hills. Ice-age meltwaters eroded the plateau's steep north and west slopes.
□ Northern pike and rainbow and brook trout are landed in Spruce Coulee Reservoir and Elkwater and Reesor lakes.
□ Winter activities include ice fishing, snowshoeing and cross-country and downhill skiing.

BATTLE CREEK
The broad shelf of rock that caps the Cypress Hills is best seen at the headwaters of this creek. Forty million years ago this plateau was the bed of a stream that carried quartz pebbles and stones east from the Rocky Mountains. The gravel hardened into a concretelike conglomerate that protects the hills from erosion.

ELKWATER LAKE
On this spring-fed lake, noted for its cool, clear water, is one of Alberta's oldest resorts. A park established in 1938 on the lake's southern shore is now part of Cypress Hills Provincial Park. A swallow colony nests in cliffs along the north shore. Wild turkeys can be seen near the Elkwater campground. This large brown bird, an ancestor of the domestic turkey, was introduced into the hills in 1962, and is now found throughout the park.

Elkwater Lake, Cypress Hills Provincial Park

REESOR LAKE
Great blue herons, kingfishers, cormorants and red-necked grebes fish in this tranquil lake. Stands of trembling aspen and white spruce south of the lake are home to wapiti and white-tailed and mule deer. Ruffed and sharp-tailed grouse forage in grasslands and aspen groves to the north.

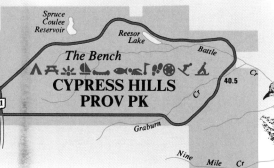

Mourning dove

Elkwater Lake

Spruce Coulee Reservoir

Reesor Lake

Battle

The Bench
CYPRESS HILLS PROV PK

Elkwater

4.5

9.5

41

ead of the Mountain

Graburn

Nine Mile Cr

40.5

34

41

515

88.5

A Rugged Region
Where Wild Horses Roam

West-Central Alberta

This vast scenic wilderness was explored in the early 1800s by David Thompson who earned a reputation as one of the finest geographers in history. Thompson's records and maps were so accurate that many of them are used today. He charted the Great Lakes, the 49th parallel, and the Saskatchewan, Athabasca and Columbia river basins.

This rugged, spectacular region is steeped in the history of the fur trade. Thompson's North West Company headquarters, Rocky

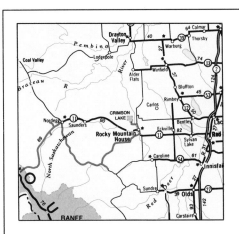

NORDEGG
This abandoned town was named after Martin Nordegg, a German immigrant who came to Canada in 1906. He helped establish the Canadian Northern Western Railway and the Brazeau Collieries here. Development of the mine was carried on as the railway was being constructed, and in 1914 some 544 tonnes of coal were being mined daily. Disaster struck the mine in 1941 when an explosion took the lives of 29 men. In 1955 the mine closed down, and with it the town.

CRESCENT FALLS
These spectacular falls on the Bighorn River are near the David Thompson Highway. A scenic hike leads to a lookout onto the Bighorn Canyon.

Abraham Lake

BIG HORN DAM
Visitors to this 91-metre-high dam, begun in 1969 by Calgary Power Ltd. and completed in 1972, will see Alberta's longest man-made lake—a 48-kilometre-long reservoir named Abraham Lake. Water from the dam is channeled through a 335-metre tunnel to a hydroelectric plant which houses two generators with a total capacity of 120,000 kilowatts. The powerhouse may be toured by appointment. Abraham Lake, named after a family of Stoney Indians who lived in the area for many years, is stocked with Dolly Varden and brook trout.

KOOTENAY PLAINS
This is one of the few natural grasslands in this mountainous region. Its climate is mild, and snow is rare.

FORESTRY TRUNK ROAD
This 998-kilometre gravel road is the only continuous north-south route through Alberta's western forests. Linking Grande Prairie in the north with the Crowsnest Pass in the south, it was built over 15 years, beginning in 1948. Service stations, grocery stores and lunch counters are at points along the road, and campgrounds are located at regular intervals. In the adjacent Rocky Mountains Forest Reserve are mountain sheep and goats, and wapiti, moose, deer and bears. Travelers should check the road and weather conditions before setting off.
□ One of the highlights of the Forestry Trunk Road is Ram River Falls, where white water plunges spectacularly into a deep, dark ravine. The falls can best be viewed from a nearby lookout. A recreation area here has picnicking and camping facilities.

SIFFLEUR WILDERNESS AREA
Valleys, streams and rugged mountain terrain characterize the 412-square-kilometre Siffleur Wilderness Area, a remote sanctuary where visitors may travel only on foot. Wapiti and mountain goats are common here, and grizzly bears are occasionally seen.

Siffleur Canyon, Siffleur Wilderness Area

0	2	4	6	8	10 Miles
0	4		8	12	16 Kilometres

Mountain House, was at the heart of the richest fur-producing area in northwestern Canada. Annually it shipped great bales of otter, sable, cross fox and other furs. During its stormy history the fort was burned to the ground by Indians three times. But it was rebuilt by dogged traders each time until the decline of furs forced abandonment of the post in 1869. Upriver from Rocky Mountain House is a cliff over which Indians stampeded thousands of bison to their deaths.

Hunting has been greatly curbed since the days of the fur trade and many fur-bearing animals can be seen in their natural habitat in wilderness areas set aside by the Alberta government. Here, too, small herds of wild horses may be glimpsed.

Trail trips into the Rockies are increasingly popular as visitors discover the thrill of exploring by horseback. Some of the best fishing in western Canada is found in this region. Trout, perch, pike, goldeye and Dolly Varden are common. Splendid waterfalls—such as those on the Ram River—also attract visitors.

Still only moderately populated, this area was first settled about 1900. The newcomers established industries that took advantage of the wealth of local timber—producing mine props, railway ties, fence posts and telegraph poles. Oil, mining and mixed farming also contribute to the area's economy.

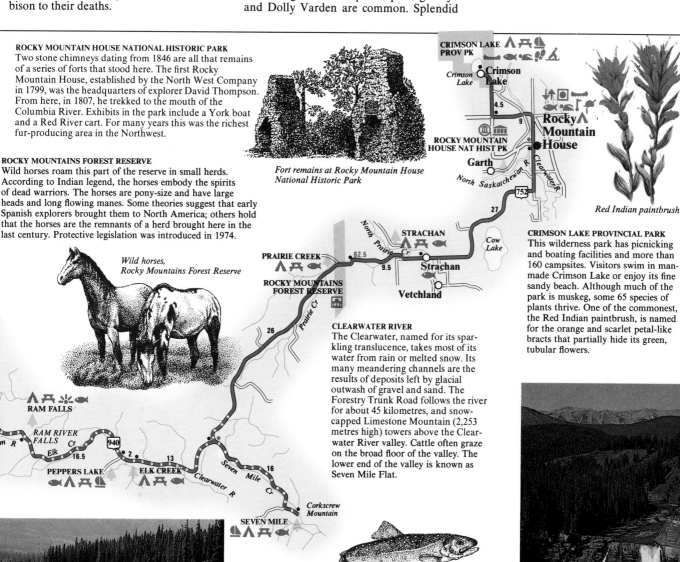

ROCKY MOUNTAIN HOUSE NATIONAL HISTORIC PARK
Two stone chimneys dating from 1846 are all that remains of a series of forts that stood here. The first Rocky Mountain House, established by the North West Company in 1799, was the headquarters of explorer David Thompson. From here, in 1807, he trekked to the mouth of the Columbia River. Exhibits in the park include a York boat and a Red River cart. For many years this was the richest fur-producing area in the Northwest.

ROCKY MOUNTAINS FOREST RESERVE
Wild horses roam this part of the reserve in small herds. According to Indian legend, the horses embody the spirits of dead warriors. The horses are pony-size and have large heads and long flowing manes. Some theories suggest that early Spanish explorers brought them to North America; others hold that the horses are the remnants of a herd brought here in the last century. Protective legislation was introduced in 1974.

Fort remains at Rocky Mountain House National Historic Park

Wild horses, Rocky Mountains Forest Reserve

Red Indian paintbrush

CRIMSON LAKE PROVINCIAL PARK
This wilderness park has picnicking and boating facilities and more than 160 campsites. Visitors swim in man-made Crimson Lake or enjoy its fine sandy beach. Although much of the park is muskeg, some 65 species of plants thrive. One of the commonest, the Red Indian paintbrush, is named for the orange and scarlet petal-like bracts that partially hide its green, tubular flowers.

CLEARWATER RIVER
The Clearwater, named for its sparkling translucence, takes most of its water from rain or melted snow. Its many meandering channels are the results of deposits left by glacial outwash of gravel and sand. The Forestry Trunk Road follows the river for about 45 kilometres, and snow-capped Limestone Mountain (2,253 metres high) towers above the Clearwater River valley. Cattle often graze on the broad floor of the valley. The lower end of the valley is known as Seven Mile Flat.

Dolly Varden, Ram River

RAM RIVER
Many of the rivers that flow from the Rocky Mountains into Alberta's foothills pass through valleys that were deepened and widened millions of years ago by glaciers. Two such waterways, Elk Creek and the Ram River, are breeding grounds for an imaginatively titled species of fish, the Dolly Varden—named after Miss Dolly Varden, a character in Charles Dickens's *Barnaby Rudge* who wore a pink polka-dot dress. This orange- or red-spotted char weighs as much as 14 kilograms. It matures at six years and can live to 18 or more. A fall spawner, it favors cold, clear, gravel-bottomed streams, which it enters between September and November. It usually winters in lakes.

Ram River Falls

Wild Roses by the Roadside, White Sand by a Prairie Lake

Central Alberta

Between Pigeon and Buck lakes, Highway 13 passes through rolling parkland. At each crest of the road, there are sweeping views of gentle hills and scattered groves of trembling aspen. In fields west of Buck Lake, donkey-head pumps nodding with a hypnotic rhythm tap the Pembina Oil Field, one of the world's largest.

The landscape changes as the traveler turns south on Highway 12. The road parallels the Blindman River and cuts through the lush, green farmland of its valley. This

MISSION BEACH

The Rev. Robert T. Rundle, the first resident missionary (1840) in what is now Alberta, founded a Methodist agricultural mission here in 1847. Near a two-story log and stone retreat house is a stone altar on a concrete platform. Flanking the altar are two 10-metre-high stylized arms with symbols of Indian culture, Christianity and agriculture carved in relief.

Log church,
Pas-Ka-Poo Historical Park,
Rimbey

RIMBEY

In Pas-Ka-Poo Historical Park, a restored church (1908) contains an 1873 Bible and the original pews and altar. A restored log schoolhouse (1903) has original blackboards and desks. Other buildings include the former Rimbey town office, a general store and a trapper's cabin. Also on the grounds are a threshing machine (1915) and a steam engine (1910). Flower gardens border a pond in the park.
□ Chuck wagon racing is the main attraction at the annual rodeo.

MEDICINE LODGE HILLS

These hills, 22 kilometres south of Rimbey, were once the site of Indian rituals celebrating the arrival of spring. Today, downhill ski runs and snowmobile trails wind through the hills' forests of trembling aspen and white spruce—forests frequented by mule and white-tailed deer.
□ Aspen Beach Provincial Park, east of the hills, has a broad beach on warm, shallow Gull Lake.

SUNDRE

In a campground alongside the Red Deer River are a reconstructed log cabin (1913), furnished with pioneer artifacts, and a 1908 schoolhouse.
□ A 60-kilometre stretch of the Red Deer River between Sundre and Mountain Aire Lodge is dotted with rapids and falls. Only experienced white water canoeists should attempt this route.

Below Rich Farmland, 'Pools' of Oil in Spongelike Rock

Although oil men speak of pools or fields, oil does not lie underground in vast liquid-filled caverns. Instead, deposits are held—like water in a sponge—in porous rock such as limestone and sandstone.

One of the world's largest oil fields—the 3,200-square-kilometre Pembina field west of Buck Lake in central Alberta—lies below rich farmland. Reserves may total 7.5 billion barrels of oil, but less than two billion barrels can be extracted. Some wells are more than 1.5 kilometres deep.

Pembina oil is in a stratigraphic trap: a porous oil-bearing layer of rock below nonporous rock. Some deposits in the Alberta foothills are in fault traps: rock layers that have cracked and shifted out of alignment, sealing off porous oil reservoirs.

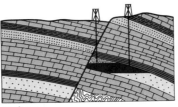

Fault trap

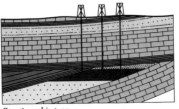

Stratigraphic trap

region produces most of Alberta's oats and barley, and half of its cattle. Wheat and rapeseed thrive in its rich, black soil. The roadside in summer is ablaze with wild roses, bluebells and fireweed.

Along this route the faint outline of the Rockies—illusive as a mirage—can be glimpsed. The first unmistakable view of the mountains is at Sundre, where Highway 27 dips down into the Red Deer River valley. From this point, travelers may venture westward to the vacation playgrounds of the Rocky Mountain Forest Reserve and Banff National Park.

But recreation is as attractive in this area as it is farther west. Four provincial parks —Aspen Beach, Ma-Me-O-Beach, Pigeon Lake and Red Lodge—offer water sports in the "dry" central Alberta plain. Sailing competitions are held at Sylvan Lake Provincial Park, which is noted for its beaches of fine, white sand. At Buck Lake, pike, yellow perch and walleye can be landed in a June fishing derby.

Interior of "The Spruces," Innisfail Historical Museum

INNISFAIL
In a historical park are 10 buildings transported from the surrounding countryside to recreate a typical pioneer village. In summer, tea is served each Friday in the dining room of "The Spruces," a log roadhouse built in 1886 on the Calgary-Edmonton wagon trail. Other buildings include a railway station (1904) and a blacksmith shop (1915).
□ A plaque in a campground commemorates Anthony Henday of the Hudson's Bay Company, the first European in this area. In 1754 he explored the Prairies to persuade Indians to trade furs at Hudson Bay.

Icelandic Legacies: Alberta's First Library and a Leading Poet

In 1888-89, a hundred almost penniless Icelanders took homesteads along Alberta's Medicine River, after an unsuccessful attempt to settle in North Dakota. Their first years in Canada were difficult: the Icelanders knew little about farming, and the heavy soil was hard to work. They lived in sod huts and ate fish, game and berries. Markerville became the center of their close-knit community—with a post office and, in 1891, probably the first library in Alberta. A butter and cheese factory provided steady incomes.

One of these early pioneers, Stephen G. Stephansson, has been called Canada's leading poet. But few Canadians have read his works: all his poems are in Icelandic. Stephansson died in 1927 and was buried near his home in Markerville. The poet's house (*left*) is now a provincial historic site.

BOWDEN
The Royal Canadian Mounted Police training kennels, five kilometres north of Bowden, are open to the public during the week. In 1929 Sgt. John N. Cawsey of the provincial police purchased a German shepherd named Dale to help him patrol central Alberta. The dog proved invaluable in tracking suspects. Sergeant Cawsey and Dale joined the Mounties in 1932. Five years later the force established a training school for men and dogs. The canine corps originally included Riesenschnauzers, Doberman pinschers—even mongrels. The force finally selected German shepherds, a strong, courageous and hardy breed. Today, about 15 dogs teamed with masters undergo 14 weeks of training. The animals learn basic obedience, then progress to agility courses and search-and-rescue training.

German shepherd

RED LODGE PROVINCIAL PARK
This park's abundant beaver live in burrows along the Little Red Deer River (most beaver inhabit lodges). Their dams form quiet pools where northern pike and brook trout may be landed. Several pairs of sandhill cranes that nest nearby are occasionally sighted here. These tall, brown birds, noted for their buglelike mating call, feed on insects, berries and grain. Moose and white-tailed deer winter in the park's white spruce forests.

OLDS
Olds College, founded in 1913, is an agricultural school with 850 students. It emphasizes business aspects of farming.
□ Mountain View Museum has turn-of-the-century photographs that tell of the area's pioneers and early history.

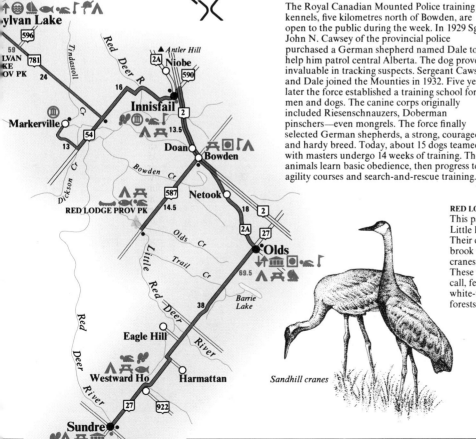

Sandhill cranes

A Moonscape of Fluted Bluffs and Stark Spires

Central Alberta

Eerie but exquisite are the ravines and rock formations of the Red Deer Badlands. West of the city of Red Deer, this two-kilometre-wide, deep-cut section of the Red Deer River winds 320 kilometres southeast to Brooks. This great, eroded gash is perhaps most dramatic when approached from the west near Dry Island Buffalo Jump Provincial Park.

Fields of rapeseed and wheat grow right to the canyon rim. Then greens and golds of crops give way to gorges devoid of vege-

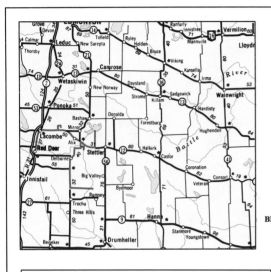

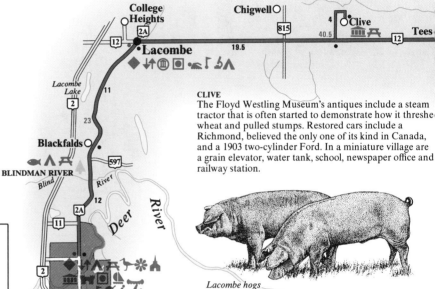

A Swirling Structure

"I don't design boxes," said Edmonton architect Douglas Cardinal, a Métis born and raised in Red Deer. One of Cardinal's outstanding achievements, St. Mary's Church in Red Deer, was completed in 1968, after he returned to Alberta following his graduation from the architectural school at the University of Texas. The swirling brick structure reflects a distinctive style that Cardinal has applied to other major commissions, notably the Canadian Museum of Civilization, which opened in 1989 in Hull, Qué.

The exterior of St. Mary's Church curves shell-like around a semicircular interior. The altar is the focus: aisles radiate from it like spokes. Natural light from an immense concrete tube suspended from the ceiling illuminates the altar.

St. Mary's Church, Red Deer

CLIVE
The Floyd Westling Museum's antiques include a steam tractor that is often started to demonstrate how it threshe wheat and pulled stumps. Restored cars include a Richmond, believed the only one of its kind in Canada, and a 1903 two-cylinder Ford. In a miniature village are a grain elevator, water tank, school, newspaper office and railway station.

Lacombe hogs

LACOMBE
This town is named for Father Albert Lacombe (1827-1916), an Oblate missionary in the Northwest.
□ Visitors may walk or drive through gardens at an experimental farm operated by the federal government. The Lacombe hog was developed here.
□ The 11-room, sandstone Hardwick House has a second-story "walk" or gallery that is reminiscent of the architecture of the Maritimes. Built about 1910, this private residence has ornate woodwork and leaded windows.

RED DEER
Chinese painting, Scottish glass cutting, and Ukrainian silversmithing are among crafts demonstrated by some 15 ethnic groups at an International Folk Festival in July. Other annual events include five rodeos (one at the six-day Red Deer Exhibition in mid-July) and the Highland Games in June.
□ The city hall, a massive structure of exposed concrete columns and beams, was the winning entry in a Canada-wide design competition in 1961. The building is in a large park containing some 40,000 plants.
□ A 1902 Holsman Autobuggy, a 1918 Kissel Kar Speedster and a 1922 Ford Firewagon (a Model T used as fire engine) are among 21 vehicles in the C. R. Parker collection.
□ Fort Normandeau, built in 1885 during the Northwest Rebellion, was a North West Mounted Police post in 1886-93. It has been restored near its original location and is now a historic site.

Ukrainian dancers at the International Folk Festival, Red Deer

0 1 2 3 4 5 Miles

0 2 4 6 8 Kilometres

tation save for stubborn cactus and lichen. Roads twist to the valley floor some 122 metres below. At the bottom is the muddy Red Deer River, contrasting with the pinks, yellows and greens of rock walls layered like a giant cake.

These layers record eons of land building. Once this was a swampy delta at the edge of an inland sea. Rivers and streams flowing east from the still-forming Rockies dumped billions of tonnes of sediment into this marshy region. The primordial mud even-

tually turned to rock, then was eroded by glaciers, wind and water into a stark moon-scape of steep, isolated hills called buttes, and pillars of erosion-resistant clay, sand and gravel called hoodoos.

The multicolored valley walls contain not only dinosaur remains but also the fossils of crocodiles, turtles, fish, oyster shells and of trees that once flourished here—redwood, swamp cypress, plane tree and sub-tropical gingko.

Scoured by ancient glaciers, Buffalo Lake

is the largest in the Badlands. According to Indian legend, the 19-kilometre-long lake was formed by water pouring from a young bull killed by two Sarcee warriors. The legend tells that many of the hunters' tribe drowned here the following spring when the lake ice broke beneath them. The barking of dogs and the laughter of children are said to come from the bottom of the lake.

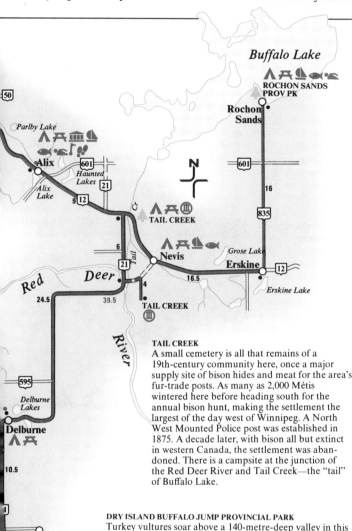

ROCHON SANDS PROVINCIAL PARK
Several sandy beaches on Buffalo Lake are in Rochon Sands Provincial Park, a small area with aspen groves and saskatoon and chokecherry shrubs. Baltimore orioles inhabit the park and great blue herons are seen in the vicinity. This is a favorite spot for bird-watchers, fishermen, swimmers, water-skiers and windsurfers. Many campers and picnickers use this sheltered park.

Power and Water From Prairie Windmills

Most Alberta farmers used oil lamps as recently as the mid-1950s, when only a fifth of the province's farms had electricity. A few farmers generated small amounts of electricity with "wind chargers"—windmills connected to storage batteries. Old wooden windmills can still be seen in some areas.

A few farmers in central Alberta still rely on the wind. Modern windmills on steel towers drive pumps that supply water for homes and livestock. The windmills are a cheap and practical source of power in Alberta's parkland, where winds average 15 kilometres an hour.

TAIL CREEK
A small cemetery is all that remains of a 19th-century community here, once a major supply site of bison hides and meat for the area's fur-trade posts. As many as 2,000 Métis wintered here before heading south for the annual bison hunt, making the settlement the largest of the day west of Winnipeg. A North West Mounted Police post was established in 1875. A decade later, with bison all but extinct in western Canada, the settlement was abandoned. There is a campsite at the junction of the Red Deer River and Tail Creek—the "tail" of Buffalo Lake.

DRY ISLAND BUFFALO JUMP PROVINCIAL PARK
Turkey vultures soar above a 140-metre-deep valley in this scenic park beside the Red Deer River. Plants and animals characteristic of the prairies, badlands and northern forest regions, and a tremendous variety of landforms are among the park's diverse natural features.

The park is named for a mesa, or island of isolated, water-eroded rock. Gullies, round-topped hills called buttes, and pillars of rock called hoodoos are typical of badlands. Yellow umbrella plant, salt sage, winter fat, prickly pear cactus, thorny buffalo berry, sagebrush and long-leafed sage not found in the surrounding uplands grow here.

Trees in a massive landslide area include aspen, paper birch and balsam poplar. Juniper, saskatoon, pin cherry, chokecherry and wild rose shrubs form a thick ground cover.

Bones near the base of a cliff mark the site of a buffalo jump. Indians once stampeded the animals over this precipice.

Dry Island Buffalo Jump Provincial Park

'Donkey Heads' Bob Quietly Where 'Black Gold' Gushed

Central Alberta

In the rippling grain fields near Leduc, pumps, known as "donkey heads," bob up and down to a slow, steady rhythm. From the earth beneath rich farmland, the pumps draw oil that has been stored there for millions of years.

The Leduc field has been yielding oil since the late 1940s. Until that time, Canada's oil sources (notably the Turner Valley, south of Calgary) provided less than 10 percent of the nation's needs. Years of exploration yielded no significant new supplies.

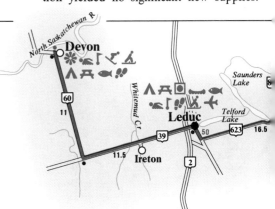

DEVON
Cacti, yucca plants, gladioli and peonies grow amid sand dunes and ponds at the University of Alberta Devonian Botanic Garden—North America's most northerly botanic garden. Every known Alberta plant is among some 26,000 species exhibited. A plaque at the entrance notes that part of the Leduc oil field lies 1.5 kilometres underground.

LEDUC
The site of Imperial Leduc No. 1—the well that on Feb. 13, 1947, tapped the 300-million-barrel Leduc oil field—is marked by a plaque 17 kilometres northwest. Imperial Oil had drilled 133 dry holes before striking oil at 1,771 metres here. Nearby is the site of Atlantic No. 3, a well that went wild in March 1947, spewing oil for almost six months before catching fire.

"Donkey head" oil pump near Leduc

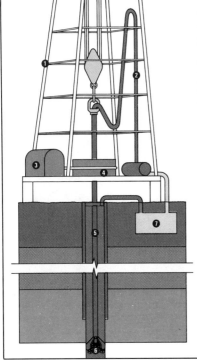

Roughnecks and Rock Cuttings

Oil exploration in the late 1800s was simple, and usually successful: prospectors drilled wherever they found oil or gas seeping out of the ground. Today, as oil becomes scarce, companies looking for new sources use more sophisticated methods. Scientists study the land for clues to what lies underground. Oil is usually found in porous sedimentary rock (such as sandstone) covered by dense, nonporous rock. Seismologists locate such structures by setting off small explosions and analyzing the shock waves that rebound to the surface. Other clues to underground oil deposits are provided by aerial photographs, and by gravimeters and magnetometers, which measure differences in the earth's gravity and magnetism.

Once a spot has been discovered, the drilling crew (called "roughnecks") set up the derrick (1) that supports the drill pipe and hose (2). An engine (3) powers the rotary table (4) that drives the drill pipe downward. Inside the pipe is the stem (5) which has a hard-toothed bit (6) at the end. As the stem turns, the bit cuts through rock layers. Specially formulated mud (7) is pumped through the hose to lubricate the bit and bring rock cuttings to the surface. The mud also fills the hole to prevent gushers, which occur when oil under high pressure rushes out of the ground.

Provincial building, Ponoka

PONOKA
A four-story, enclosed atrium with a year-round tropical garden is part of Ponoka's impressive provincial building, which houses eight government departments and a courthouse. The curvilinear brick structure was built in 1977 as part of a government decentralization program. Ponoka, which was incorporated in 1904, derived its name from the Blackfoot word for elk.
□ A midsummer stampede features calf roping, steer wrestling, and saddle and bareback riding.
□ Fort Ostell, now a museum, was established by Capt. J. Ostell in 1885 to protect settlers during the Riel Rebellion. Native and pioneer artifacts and photographs are displayed.

0	2	4	6	8	10 Miles
0	4	8	12		16 Kilometres

All that changed on Feb. 13, 1947, the day "black gold" gushed from the Imperial Leduc No.1 well.

Within a year, 61 derricks—some as high as 15-story buildings—were drilling on the prairies near Leduc. But the discovery brought its dangers. Atlantic No. 3, a little to the northwest of the discovery well, went out of control in March 1947. After spewing oil over the prairie for six months, the rogue well burst into flames. (To seal the well,

oilmen used 20,000 bags of cement, 16,000 bags of sawdust, 1,000 sacks of cottonwood hulls, eight railway carloads of wood fiber, and two carloads of turkey feathers.)

The awesome fire made the public aware that Alberta was a major oil-producing area. There was further investment, and intensive exploration of other gas and oil fields. As the oil poured out, new wealth flooded in.

The derricks have long since gone from Leduc, as oilmen seek new sources under-

ground or in oil-rich tar sands. (The high steel tower which was used to drill the discovery well has been moved to a site on the southern outskirts of Edmonton.) Pumping and storing oil is the business of Leduc today, with farming a second source of wealth.

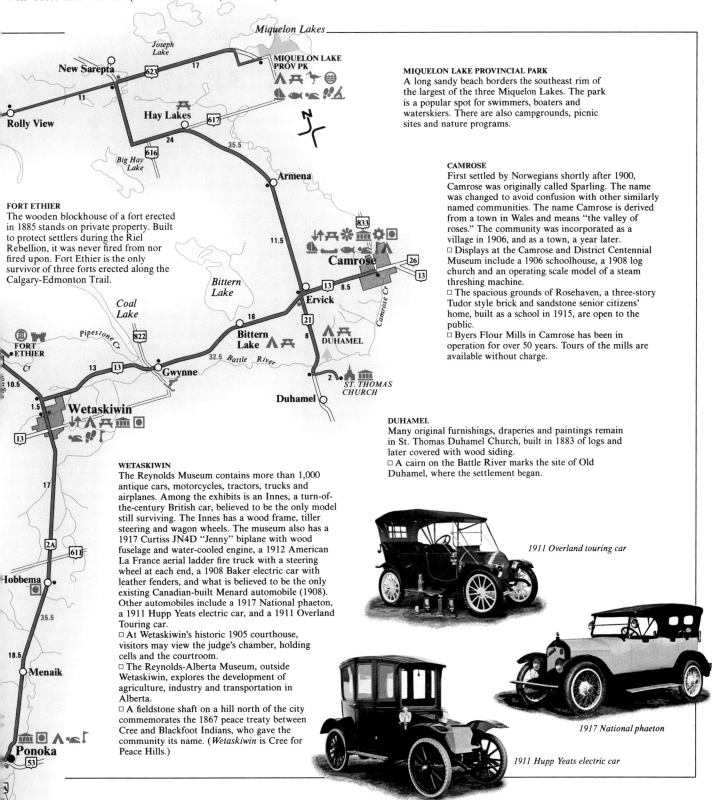

MIQUELON LAKE PROVINCIAL PARK
A long sandy beach borders the southeast rim of the largest of the three Miquelon Lakes. The park is a popular spot for swimmers, boaters and waterskiers. There are also campgrounds, picnic sites and nature programs.

CAMROSE
First settled by Norwegians shortly after 1900, Camrose was originally called Sparling. The name was changed to avoid confusion with other similarly named communities. The name Camrose is derived from a town in Wales and means "the valley of roses." The community was incorporated as a village in 1906, and as a town, a year later.
□ Displays at the Camrose and District Centennial Museum include a 1906 schoolhouse, a 1908 log church and an operating scale model of a steam threshing machine.
□ The spacious grounds of Rosehaven, a three-story Tudor style brick and sandstone senior citizens' home, built as a school in 1915, are open to the public.
□ Byers Flour Mills in Camrose has been in operation for over 50 years. Tours of the mills are available without charge.

FORT ETHIER
The wooden blockhouse of a fort erected in 1885 stands on private property. Built to protect settlers during the Riel Rebellion, it was never fired from nor fired upon. Fort Ethier is the only survivor of three forts erected along the Calgary-Edmonton Trail.

DUHAMEL
Many original furnishings, draperies and paintings remain in St. Thomas Duhamel Church, built in 1883 of logs and later covered with wood siding.
□ A cairn on the Battle River marks the site of Old Duhamel, where the settlement began.

WETASKIWIN
The Reynolds Museum contains more than 1,000 antique cars, motorcycles, tractors, trucks and airplanes. Among the exhibits is an Innes, a turn-of-the-century British car, believed to be the only model still surviving. The Innes has a wood frame, tiller steering and wagon wheels. The museum also has a 1917 Curtiss JN4D "Jenny" biplane with wood fuselage and water-cooled engine, a 1912 American La France aerial ladder fire truck with a steering wheel at each end, a 1908 Baker electric car with leather fenders, and what is believed to be the only existing Canadian-built Menard automobile (1908). Other automobiles include a 1917 National phaeton, a 1911 Hupp Yeats electric car, and a 1911 Overland Touring car.
□ At Wetaskiwin's historic 1905 courthouse, visitors may view the judge's chamber, holding cells and the courtroom.
□ The Reynolds-Alberta Museum, outside Wetaskiwin, explores the development of agriculture, industry and transportation in Alberta.
□ A fieldstone shaft on a hill north of the city commemorates the 1867 peace treaty between Cree and Blackfoot Indians, who gave the community its name. (*Wetaskiwin* is Cree for Peace Hills.)

1911 Overland touring car

1917 National phaeton

1911 Hupp Yeats electric car

A Pastoral Refuge for a Pacifist People

Central Alberta

A Hutterite family of Alberta

Coal-oil lamps, Donalda

Where Salt Grass Grows by Prairie Lakes

Barren, salt-crusted shores characterize the thousands of alkaline lakes, marshes and sloughs throughout the parkland of central Alberta. Natural salts, concentrated by evaporation, make these waters deadly to fish and most aquatic plants. Only salt-loving plants known as halophytes, such as sea blite, salt grass (*above*), and samphire, grow near these shores.

At the end of the last ice age, receding glaciers left shallow depressions in this region. Runoff, containing dissolved salts from surrounding alkali soils, has filled the depressions creating alkaline (often lifeless) bodies of water.

The numerous freshwater lakes and ponds in central Alberta, however, teem with plants and animals. Willows and aspens commonly grow to lake edges here. Pintails, mallards and other ducks nest in the dense bulrushes and cattails that surround prairie sloughs. Insects and grain from nearby fields provide a reliable food supply for these birds.

Buffalo Lake

BUFFALO LAKE REC AREA

DONALDA

Antique lamps once lit by whale oil, lard and tallow are among a collection of more than 600 at the Donalda and District Museum. Also on display are miniature kerosene lamps, peg lamps (so called because they fitted into candle holders) and sparking lamps—the timepieces of old-time courtships. Parents lit the sparking lamps when a suitor came to call on their daughter. The lamp contained enough oil to last about an hour. It was the rule that, when the lamp went out, the suitor had to leave.
□ Because of the museum's lamp collection, Donalda is known as Canada's Lamp Capital. Open year-round, the museum has many other pioneer artifacts including an Edison Gem Gramophone with cylinder records, and a mouseproof kitchen cabinet brought to Donalda by wagon in 1903.
□ In scenic Meeting Creek valley east of town are some of Alberta's most fascinating badlands. Hills and coulees here are a natural playground for skiers, tobogganers and snowmobilers. A snowmobile rally is held here in February.

STETLER

Among objects in the museum building at the Stettler Town and Country Museum are some 20 different makes of butter churns. Historic buildings on the museum grounds include Stettler's first schoolhouse, an old courthouse, a 1908 church, a 1911 station, and a harness shop.
□ At Stettler visitors can board *The Province,* an old-fashioned steam-powered train, for a nostalgic ride through the surrounding farmland.

Century-old barrel churn, Stettler

0 1 2 3 4 5 Miles
0 2 4 6 8 Kilometres

Much of this region is farmed by Hutterites, members of a religious sect founded in Europe in the 16th century. Persecuted for rejecting infant baptism and refusing to bear arms, Hutterites migrated frequently before settling in western Canada during the First World War. Some 6,000 are in central Alberta.

The Hutterites hold property in common and perform work collectively. Each communal settlement has about 100 residents —some 10 families. Offshoot colonies are formed when the population nears 150. Jobs are rotated frequently by the elected *wirt*, or household boss. The head of the colony is an elected lay preacher.

Families occupy simple, almost identical apartments. Meals are eaten in a communal dining hall, where men and women, grouped according to age, sit at separate tables. The Hutterites reject old age pensions, unemployment insurance, welfare, the rights to vote and to hold public office. Infants, from 18 weeks, are cared for in nurseries. From age two, they spend six hours a day in *klein-schul* or nursery school.

The Hutterites speak a German dialect, and German is the language of their church services. Most trace their families back to the 1500s—and wear clothes reminiscent of that era. The men wear dark suits, broad-brimmed hats and, if married, beards. Women wear ankle-length dresses in plaids and prints and polka-dot kerchiefs.

FORESTBURG

Guided tours are available weekdays at Forestburg Collieries Ltd., which operates one of the world's largest power shovels. The 30-metre-high giant, on four crawler tracks, can move more than 900 cubic metres of earth an hour. It took 38 railway cars to transport the machine here in 1949, when strip mining replaced the underground techniques in use since 1907.
□ Coal mining is a major industry in this part of Alberta, a province with more than half Canada's coal reserves and the nation's second largest coal producer (after Nova Scotia). When the coal is extracted, the mined area is reclaimed by replacing topsoil and reseeding the area with grass and trees.
□ This area has good cross-country skiing and pike fishing.

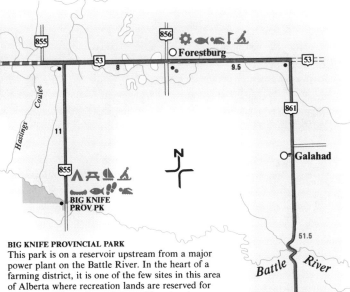

BIG KNIFE PROVINCIAL PARK

This park is on a reservoir upstream from a major power plant on the Battle River. In the heart of a farming district, it is one of the few sites in this area of Alberta where recreation lands are reserved for public use. The park, a mixture of forest and grassland, contains dense stands of poplar, birch and white spruce. There are facilities for camping, picnicking, canoeing and boat launching, and there is good fishing for northern pike.
□ The park commemorates two Indian warriors— Big Man, a Cree, and Knife, a Blackfoot—who fought and killed each other beside Big Knife Creek more than 200 years ago. A plaque marks the site.

Battle River near Big Knife Provincial Park

Animal Life of Alberta's Parkland Belt

White-tailed deer

Meadowlark

Varying hare

The area around Stettler and Castor is part of the Alberta parkland. This broad belt of aspen groves and grasslands between northern forest and open prairie is home to a wide variety of animals.

Varying hare (named for their coats: gray brown in summer, white in winter) and white-tailed deer feed on the bark of young aspens in winter, often killing the trees. In summer deer venture into grasslands to browse on twigs and plants.

Burrowing rodents common in the grasslands are badgers, Richardson's ground squirrels (or gophers) and 13-lined ground squirrels. Earth moved by their burrowing helps to spread shrubs and aspens: seeds germinate easily in the loose soil.

Insects attract many birds to aspen groves; downy and hairy woodpeckers, least flycatchers and yellow warblers nest here. Other birds, such as horned larks and meadowlarks, live only in the grasslands. Birds of prey, such as red-tailed hawks, nest in aspen groves and hunt over the grasslands.

CASTOR

The center for some of the finest duck, geese and deer hunting in Alberta, this community has two airstrips, a stock car track, golf course and heated swimming pool. There is boating, swimming and free camping on Castor Creek, fishing at the Huber Dam (rainbow trout) and the Canadian Utilities Dam (pike and pickerel), and waterskiing on the Tarr Reservoir.
□ Each January, Castor hosts a winter festival, which is highlighted by ice sculpture displays throughout the town.

Golden Fields, Salty Sloughs and Silver-Green Valleys

East-Central Alberta

Hillsides veined with gullies and dotted with groves of trees; fields golden with ripening rapeseed; sloughs rimmed with salt; valleys silver green with wolf willow—such are the vistas of this undulating countryside.

At the turn of the century, colorful government posters portrayed the Prairies as "Canada West—The Last Best West," and told of its ranching and farming potential. A quarter-section (160 acres) could be bought for $10. Farmers' sons from Ontario

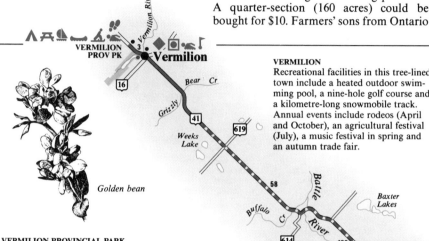

Golden bean

VERMILION PROVINCIAL PARK
Plants seldom found this far north—puccoon, bladderpod, purple prairie clover, buffalo bean and the poisonous golden bean—grow here. White-tailed deer and coyotes roam through aspen groves. Canada geese, herons and swans feed in marshes. □ The park has camp and picnic sites, hiking and cross-country trails, fishing (northern pike, yellow perch and walleye), boating and swimming.

VERMILION
Recreational facilities in this tree-lined town include a heated outdoor swimming pool, a nine-hole golf course and a kilometre-long snowmobile track. Annual events include rodeos (April and October), an agricultural festival (July), a music festival in spring and an autumn trade fair.

Ribstones

RIBSTONES HISTORICAL SITE
Two quartzite rocks important in Cree Indian hunting rituals are here. On each rock is a centimetre-deep relief of a bison's backbone and ribs, painstakingly engraved with pebbles and sand some 1,000 years ago. One rock (about 130 by 90 centimetres) represents a bull bison; the other (130 by 40 centimetres), a cow.

Indians could survey their hunting grounds from this site and watch the bison migrate. Bison were sacrificed on the stones to ensure a successful hunt. When settlers arrived here in the early 1900s, Indians were still leaving beads, tobacco and meat at the stones.

A Swift and Graceful Bird Saved From Extinction

All birds of prey—hawks, falcons, eagles, owls—are in danger of extinction. They are at the end of a food chain that progresses from plant-eaters to insect-eaters to flesh-eaters. Pesticides, which become more concentrated at each link in the chain, accumulate at dangerously high levels in birds of prey.

Only two wild peregrine falcons were known to exist in Alberta in 1970. The peregrine, one of the swiftest birds of prey, can dive faster than 320 kilometres an hour. But its speed and power—distinct advantages in nature—do not protect it from man's poisons.

In 1970 the Canadian Wildlife Service established a center at Camp Wainwright to breed peregrines in captivity, and introduce them to the wild. There are now about 100 peregrines at the center. Naturalists use closed-circuit television to monitor the birds.

Peregrine falcon

0 2 4 6 8 10 Miles

0 4 8 12 16 Kilometres

and the Maritimes, adventuresome Britons, oppressed Mennonites and Ukrainians and Americans whose own West was filling up flocked here. They planted crops and built homes—and endured droughts, dust storms, hailstorms, grass fires, grasshopper plagues, and frosts that blighted a season's hopes.

Many a homesteader kept body and soul together by gathering bison bones in the wedge-shaped Nose Hills north of Veteran. The bones were piled in the hills from the days when Indians stampeded bison over bluffs. For years a major export to the United States, where they were used in fertilizer and for refining sugar, the bones netted $10 to $16 a ton.

Homesteaders unsuited to the harsh life soon left. Those who measured up to the land and the climate remained, and found a good and prosperous life. Some of the giant tractors with which they broke the prairie sod still throb to life at Wraight's Tractor Museum near Veteran. Other links with these hardy pioneers are a reconstructed kitchen and parlor at the Wainwright District Museum, and exhibits in the Pioneer Panorama Museum at Czar.

Alberta wheat harvest

WAINWRIGHT

A reconstructed post office with furniture and equipment from the early 1900s, old milking equipment and a wooden cradle churn are features of the Wainwright District Museum.
□ The stone clock tower is dedicated to local men who fought and died in World War I.
□ Oil and gas, discovered here in 1921, are piped from some 400 wells. An early rig is among oil-drilling exhibits in Petroleum Park.
□ British army units train at CFB Camp Wainwright, formerly Buffalo National Park. Bison, wapiti and deer roamed these grounds in 1908-41. A fiberglass statue of a bison, the town symbol, stands at one of the entrances to Wainwright.

Memorial clock tower, Wainwright

CZAR

Despite its Russian name, this area was settled mainly by Scandinavians. The Prairie Panorama Museum has pioneer household items, books, costumes and toys, and displays that illustrate the natural and archaeological history of the Prairies. Prized exhibits are some 1,100 pairs of salt and pepper shakers, in designs ranging from mallard ducks to praying hands.
□ On Shorncliffe Lake are municipally operated camping and picnic grounds, and beach and boating facilities.

NEUTRAL HILLS

For centuries Plains Indians kept the Neutral Hills as a hunting preserve where no fighting or raiding was allowed. Their folklore tells how the hills were raised by the Great Spirit to keep two warring tribes apart. The Indians then held a great council and made peace.
   A cairn of stones at the highest point in the hills marks what is said to have been the meeting spot.
□ Archaeologists have discovered many Indian ceremonial sites in the hills, including tepee rings, and boulder outlines of bison and turtles.

Silverberry

GOOSEBERRY LAKE PROVINCIAL PARK

Because of its high alkaline content Gooseberry Lake has no fish. But it provides the only swimming spot in the area. The park has camping, picnicking and boat-launching facilities and a golf course.
   Aspen, lance-leaf, poplar, silverberry, wild rose and willow grow in moist areas of the park and on the lakeshore. Windbreaks of pine, spruce and caragana have been planted but require a great deal of care to survive in the dry, sandy soil. Coyotes, Richardson's ground squirrels and meadowlarks are among the park's fauna.

VETERAN

Wraight's Tractor Museum, north of Veteran, displays an oil-cooled 1910 Rumely with a 15-horsepower motor, a 1928 Hart-Parr, and a 1929 John Deere. All the museum's 46 tractors, used in Alberta and Saskatchewan in the early 1900s, are in working order. Other exhibits are threshing machines and stationary engines used to power feed grinders and washing machines. Visits to the museum are by appointment.

Rumely tractor (1910), Veteran

CRONATION
is community, settled in 1897, was med for the coronation of George n 1911. Streets and avenues are med Windsor, Mary, Queen, King, yal and George.
On the migration route of the large nada goose, the Coronation district ers some of the best goose hunting Alberta.
Annual events include a rodeo in ne and an agricultural fair and exhiion in August.

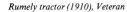

Where the Sun Sets Late on Farmland, Lake and Forest

Lesser Slave Lake

The summer sun sets late in this region of farmland, lake and forest. (At eleven o'clock, it is still light enough to fish, golf, or pitch a tent.) The area was once the preserve of the Slavey Indians, for whom many of its sites are named. (It was the warlike Cree who, contemptuous of their peaceful kin, called them slaves, or Slavey.)

Northern Alberta's Indians surrendered vast tracts of land to the Canadian government in 1899. The treaty was signed near Grouard, the oldest settlement (1872) in

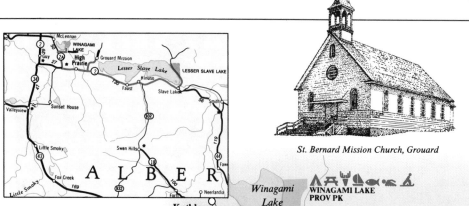

St. Bernard Mission Church, Grouard

GROUARD
This hamlet, once a bustling town on the overland route to the Klondike from Edmonton, is named for Bishop Emile Jean Baptiste Grouard (1840-1931), an Oblate missionary to the Indians, and translator and publisher of hymnals and prayer books in the languages of various tribes. A painting behind the altar in the 1½-story, wood frame St. Bernard Mission Church is by Bishop Grouard. He is buried in the adjoining cemetery.

WINAGAMI LAKE PROVINCIAL PARK
A woodland setting (aspen, balsam and poplar) and a long sandy beach have made the park popular with campers, picnickers and swimmers. There is good fishing (northern pike, walleye, and yellow perch) and boating.
□ Bald eagles, greater yellowlegs, rusty blackbirds, Franklin's gulls, and 15 species of woodpeckers are among some 150 bird species sighted here. Black bears, moose, deer and red foxes roam through an underbrush of cranberries and wild roses. Northern green orchids and marsh cinquefoil are abundant in swampy areas.

A Great Man of Prayer

In 1863 a young Roman Catholic missionary, Father Emile Jean Baptiste Grouard, arrived in the remote Peace River district of northern Alberta. For 68 years—until his death at age 91—he worked with the Cree and Beaver Indians of the Northwest.

Many Indians blamed missionaries for sickness and famine; but Father Grouard, who learned to speak eight Indian dialects, became their trusted friend. *Kitchi-Aya-miheiviyiniw* (Great Man of Prayer), they called him. He set up the first press in the Peace River district, and translated and printed hymns and prayer books. He was an accomplished artist; one of his paintings still hangs in the St. Bernard Mission Church in Grouard—the town named after him.

Grouard, who was named archbishop in 1930, died in 1931. His grave can be seen in the mission cemetery in Grouard.

HIGH PRAIRIE
A sword and a 3,000-year-old adze (an ancient cutting tool) are among curiosities in the High Prairie and District Museum. The sword, possibly made in the early 1800s, was plowed up about a mile from here in 1923. How it got there is a mystery. The adze, made of metamorphic stone of a type not native to this area, was found near where the sword was unearthed. An extensive collection of pioneer furniture includes washing machines made of wood by pioneers about 1900, and a brass bed with posts some 10 centimetres in diameter.
□ There are an outdoor swimming pool, a golf course and, just east of town, a campground. A stampede is held in August.

FAUST
A piece of stained glass, salvaged during the Second World War from the bombed St. Paul's Cathedral in London, has been placed in a window at St. Paul's Anglican Church here. The glass has a rosette pattern.
□ This hamlet on Giroux Bay of Lesser Slave Lake is a center for commercial fishing, lumbering and mink ranching. The Swan Hills oil fields are to the south.

Myrtle warbler

0   2   4   6   8   10 Miles

0   4   8   12   16 Kilometres

this area. At the turn of the century, Grouard boasted banks, restaurants, a hotel, a newspaper and 4,000 souls. (In 1905 it vied with the smaller and less busy Edmonton to become the provincial capital.)

Grouard's growth began when gold was discovered in the Klondike in 1896. The town was on the overland, all-Canadian route from Edmonton to the Yukon. The town grew as long as settlers ventured northward. Supplies to the fast-growing northern communities were hauled across frozen Lesser Slave Lake by horse-drawn sleds in winter, by steamboats in summer.

The eastern terminus of the lake traffic was the town of Slave Lake, known then as Sawridge. The community was settled in 1898 by would-be prospectors who decided to stay rather than face the arduous journey to the Yukon. With five boats in regular service, Sawridge proudly called itself the steamboat capital of Canada. The boats were withdrawn when the railway came through in 1914. Both Grouard and Sawridge sank into obscurity.

Fifty years later the town of Slave Lake enjoyed a new importance when oil was discovered in the area. From some 500 persons in the 1960s, the population has grown to about 5,600 today.

Lesser Slave Lake

LESSER SLAVE LAKE

Dunes up to six metres high are in a five-kilometre-long belt at the southern tip of 1,195-square-kilometre Lesser Slave Lake, one of the largest of the readily accessible bodies of water in Alberta. (The term "Lesser" was added to the name of the lake to distinguish it from Great Slave Lake in the N.W.T.)

□ Bald eagles and ospreys inhabit Lesser Slave Lake Provincial Park. Moose, deer, wolves and bears, including some grizzlies, roam the poplar-, spruce- and birch-clad hills.

□ Swimming, fishing (walleye and northern pike), boating and canoeing are excellent in the park. There are boat-launching facilities on Lesser Slave Lake and three large campgrounds—North Shore, Lily Creek and Marten Creek. Hikers have a panoramic view of the lake and rolling countryside from the top of 915-metre Marten Mountain.

Bay-breasted warbler

The Magnificent Grizzly

The grizzly bear ranks with the shark as an object of terror for man. But in fact the grizzly avoids man, and an attack is usually the result of a sudden meeting at close range.

These magnificent bears once roamed as far east as the Red River. Because of man's encroachment, grizzlies are found only in parts of the Yukon and Northwest Territories, the Rocky Mountains, and the Swan Hills, south of Lesser Slave Lake.

The grizzly is a massive, heavy-limbed animal ranging from creamy yellow to black. In spite of its reputation as a cattle killer, it usually eats fish, rodents, insects, roots and berries.

SLAVE LAKE

The area around this town was once an Indian hunting ground and was a stopping place on a land and water route used by war parties, early explorers, traders, Klondike prospectors and Peace River pioneers. The Hudson's Bay Company had two trading posts here when frustrated gold-seekers settled the district in 1898. By the 1900s the area was a transportation and trading center for settlers moving northward. Four cargo ships and one passenger boat made regular stops here at the height of riverboat traffic. This fell off in 1914 when the railway arrived.

The town was first known as Sawridge for its saw-edged sand ridges. The name was changed to Slave Lake in 1923.

Water rose to more than a metre's depth on main street during a 1935 flood. The following year the town's buildings were loaded on sleds and moved over the ice to high ground some four kilometres from the original site.

□ Fireworks, logging contests and a fastball tournament are featured at a July and August carnival called Riverboat Daze.

In Fertile Farming Country, Echoes of a Missionary Past

Central Alberta

Churches and museums at St. Albert, Morinville and other communities in this rich agricultural region evoke the era of the 19th-century missionaries who ministered to the Plains Indians and helped prepare for the coming of the settlers. One of the most famous of these missionaries was the Rev. Albert Lacombe, who came to this area in 1852 and served in the west for 67 years. An Oblate priest, Father Lacombe was loved and respected as a peacemaker between Cree and Blackfoot.

PEMBINA RIVER

Adventurers on their way to British Columbia's Cariboo goldfields in 1862 were mystified by smoke that wafted from the ground near the Pembina River. What they took to be a volcano was coal, set afire by natural causes. Today, the fires have died, and coal near here is mined to fuel power plants on Wabamun Lake.

□ Pembina River Provincial Park, set in a deep valley, provides a rich habitat for yellow warblers, downy woodpeckers and white-throated sparrows.

A Water Garden in Wabamun Lake

So many plants grow in nutrient-rich Wabamun Lake that its warm, shallow waters are always clouded.

Waves prevent plants from growing on its sometimes sandy, sometimes rocky shores, but protected bays are crowded with bulrushes, cattails, water horsetails and towering reed grass. Thousands of birds nest along these marshy shores. Moose and beaver eat the long, spongy stems of yellow water lilies whose blossoms brighten the lake in spring and summer. Crustaceans, insect larvae and minnows feed on the lake's abundant algae.

Masses of duckweed, a brilliant green, floating plant, cover parts of the lake in summer. From Wabamun's silty bottom, pondweed, hornwort and water milfoil reach toward the surface.

Water horsetails

LAC STE. ANNE

As many as 20,000 persons visit a shrine here on July 26, the feast day of Saint Anne.

□ The first Roman Catholic parish in Alberta was established here in 1844 when the Rev. Jean-Baptiste Thibault, an Oblate priest, founded a mission to the Indians and Métis. At that time, the lake was called Devil's Lake. The priest blessed it, and renamed it for Saint Anne—and built a shrine to her. It became a place of pilgrimage in 1889, when rain fell following prayers at the shrine to end a drought.

Yellowstone — Gunn

Lac Ste. Anne — Castle Island

Sunset Point

Alberta Beach

ALBERT BEAC

ALBERTA BEACH

In the Alberta Beach Museum, claimed to be the world's smallest stone church, are about 100 Bibles, some dating from 1814. Other exhibits include a 210-year-old Scottish melodeon and more than 100 antique guns. Indian artifacts and geological specimens are displayed outdoors.

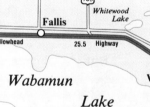

Isle Lake

Lobstick R.

Evansburg

Magnolia

Magnolia Bridge

Whitewood Lake

Fallis

Langford Park

Smithfield

Entwistle

PEMBINA RIVER PROV. PK

Gainford

Yellowhead 25.5 Highway

Lakeview

Wabamun

WABAMUN LAKE PROV. PK

Wabamun

Point Alison

Lake

Pembina River

Wabamun Lake Provincial Park

WABAMUN LAKE PROVINCIAL PARK

At sunset the peaceful waters of the lake (*Wabamun* is Cree for mirror) attract canoeists, especially to Moonlight Bay. During the day the bay is busy with sailors and anglers, some heading out into the 20-kilometre-long lake to troll for northern pike, yellow perch and lake whitefish.

□ Located on the Yellowhead Highway 64 kilometres west of Edmonton, Wabamun Lake is one of Alberta's most popular day-use parks. Sandy beaches draw swimmers and sunbathers, and there are picnic and boat-launching facilities. Bird-watchers can spot such birds of prey as red-tailed, marsh and sparrow hawks, and merlins, which hunt rabbits, mice and shrews. Moose, white-tailed deer and beaver frequent the park.

0 1 2 3 4 5 Miles

0 2 4 6 8 Kilometres

Today, a statue of Father Lacombe looks down on the city of St. Albert, where he established a mission in 1861. In that year, using hand-hewn timbers, ropes, horses, and every able-bodied man in the parish, Father Lacombe erected the first bridge in western Canada. Although the bridge no longer stands, the original log mission has been preserved as the Father Lacombe Museum. A model of the bridge carved from one of its beams is displayed there. Other exhibits include some of the missionary's books in Cree and Blackfoot, and his snowshoes, presumably worn on his long winter treks to remote Indian camps.

Morinville was also founded by a missionary, the Rev. Jean-Baptiste Morin, like Lacombe Quebec-born. The town's ornate church and its Notre Dame convent are part of an historical and cultural center.

The first wave of immigrants to this area arrived in 1885, when the CPR was completed. They transformed the empty prairie into a rich farmland that yields abundant and varied crops. Visitors can sample a cornucopia of local produce at the Saturday market in Stony Plain.

Farmers' market, Stony Plain

MORINVILLE
Ornate St. Jean-Baptiste Roman Catholic Church was built in 1907 and restored in 1973. Triple spires, arched doorways and circular windows reflect traditional Quebec church design. Murals depicting biblical scenes embellish the walls and ceiling above the altar. The church, part of which was built of logs in 1895, is a provincial historic site.

GLORY HILLS
North of Stony Plain the road dips and climbs through the rugged Glory Hills. Each summit offers a panoramic view of the countryside. Clear blue lakes bordered by tall spruce trees provide cool, secluded picnic areas.

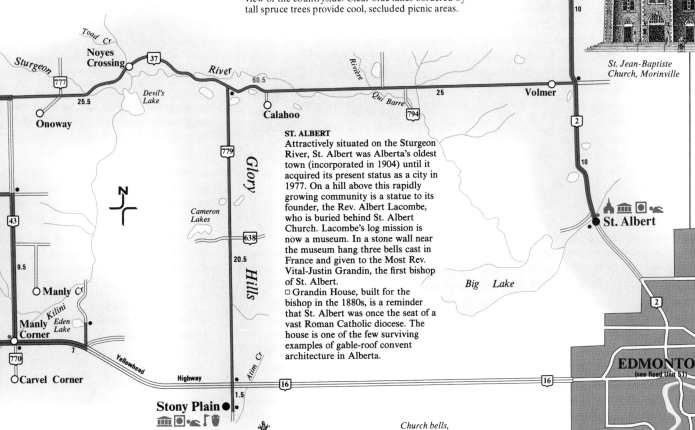

St. Jean-Baptiste Church, Morinville

ST. ALBERT
Attractively situated on the Sturgeon River, St. Albert was Alberta's oldest town (incorporated in 1904) until it acquired its present status as a city in 1977. On a hill above this rapidly growing community is a statue to its founder, the Rev. Albert Lacombe, who is buried behind St. Albert Church. Lacombe's log mission is now a museum. In a stone wall near the museum hang three bells cast in France and given to the Most Rev. Vital-Justin Grandin, the first bishop of St. Albert.
□ Grandin House, built for the bishop in the 1880s, is a reminder that St. Albert was once the seat of a vast Roman Catholic diocese. The house is one of the few surviving examples of gable-roof convent architecture in Alberta.

STONY PLAIN
Visitors sample ethnic fare prepared in a homesteader's kitchen at the Multicultural Heritage Centre: Ukrainian *pirogi* (dumplings) and *holupchi* (cabbage rolls) and Russian borscht. Pioneer skills are demonstrated in a recreated settler's cabin. Townsfolk make soap, butter and ice cream, and card and weave wool. Old books and photographs in a library tell the history of Stony Plain.
□ A statue of a horse and rider by Don Bednar was erected in 1974 to commemorate the centennial of the North West Mounted Police in Alberta.

Father Lacombe Museum, St. Albert

Church bells, Father Lacombe Museum, St. Albert

A Booming, Growing Capital City and the Gateway to Canada's North

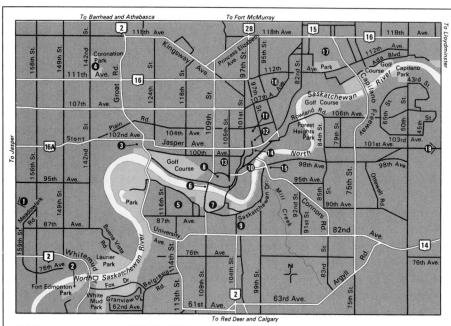

Edmonton

1 West Edmonton Mall
2 Fort Edmonton Park
3 Provincial Museum of Alberta
4 Space Sciences Centre
5 University of Alberta

6 High Level Bridge
7 Capital City Recreation Park
8 Alberta Legislature
9 Old Strathcona Historic Area
10 AGT Vista 33 View Gallery and Museum

11 Edmonton Art Gallery
12 Citadel Theatre
13 Edmonton Police Museum
14 Convention Centre/ Canada's Aviation Hall of Fame

15 Muttart Conservatory
16 Commonwealth Stadium
17 Edmonton Northlands
18 Refinery Row

Edmonton, Alberta's capital and Canada's most northerly major city, is a thriving metropolis astride the North Saskatchewan River. It was this vast river that initially brought traders in the 1790s to Fort Edmonton, the Hudson's Bay Company post that was the start of the present-day city. In the next century the Calgary–Edmonton Trail was carved out of the wilderness by freight wagons and oxcarts.

A supply base to the Klondike Gold Rush of the late 1890s, Edmonton expanded even more dramatically in 1905 with the arrival of a transcontinental railway and new status as provincial capital.

The advent of commercial aviation in the 1920s made it "The Gateway to the North." (Its three airports are still essential links to remote regions.) But it was the 1947 Leduc oil field discovery that first spurred Edmonton's decades of sustained expansion.

AGT Vista 33 View Gallery and Museum (10)
The gallery at the top of the Alberta Telephone Tower provides a stunning view of Edmonton. The museum displays antique phones and the latest telecommunication devices.

Alberta Legislature (8)
Overlooking the North Saskatchewan River, the high-domed 1912 Legislature—built with Quebec, Pennsylvania and Italian marble—is an imposing presence among the towers of downtown Edmonton. Tours are available.

Capital City Recreation Park (7)
This vast expanse of parkland straddling the North Saskatchewan River has 22.5 kilometres of cycling and hiking trails.

Citadel Theatre (12)
This glass-and-wood complex, built in 1976 and enlarged in 1984, houses five theaters, rehearsal rooms, workshops, offices and a reference library.

Commonwealth Stadium (16)
The 60,217-seat stadium was built for the 1978 Commonwealth Games and expanded for the 1983 World University Games. Other recreational facilities, which were also built for the 1978 games but designed for post-game use, are the Argyll Velodrome, the Coronation Bowling Greens, the Strathcona Range and the Kinsmen Aquatic Center.

Convention Centre (14)
Built into the bluffs above the North Saskatchewan River, the Convention Centre

houses a visitors information bureau and Canada's Aviation Hall of Fame. Displays of aeronautical artifacts and model aircraft and a photographic panorama depicting the story of Canadian aviation give Hall of Fame visitors a glimpse of the past.

Edmonton Art Gallery (11)
Alberta's largest gallery features works by the Group of Seven and modern artists.

Edmonton Northlands (17)
This complex comprises the Northland Coli-

Rowand House, built in the 1840s, is one of many historic buildings at Fort Edmonton.

seum (home of the Edmonton Oilers), a racetrack, and exhibition space for trade and agricultural shows. Major annual events here include the Superodeo (March), Klondike Days (July), and the Canadian Finals Rodeo—Canada's biggest indoor rodeo—in November.

Edmonton Police Museum (13)
Displays at the museum are devoted to the history of law enforcement in Alberta.

Fort Edmonton Park (2)
This outdoor museum beside the North Saskatchewan River has three small-town streets that re-create the period between 1885 and 1905. Among the more than 50 pioneer buildings are a reconstruction of Fort Edmonton and the original 1878 office of the *Edmonton Bulletin,* western Canada's first newspaper.

The park's George McDougall Church is named for the Methodist missionary who built it in 1872. Restored in the 1940s and 1950s and now a museum, it displays McDougall's bibles and prayer books.

The John Janzen Nature Centre, which offers natural history exhibits, has more than 4 kilometres of trails within the park.

High Level Bridge (6)
This Edmonton landmark was constructed in 1910-13. The top deck carries trains; motor traffic is on a lower level. Nearby is the man-made Great Divide Waterfall, built for Edmonton's 75th birthday celebrations.

Muttart Conservatory (15)
Four glass-walled pyramids dominate this

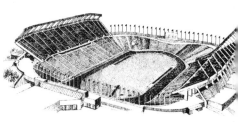

Edmonton's 60,217-seat stadium was opened in 1978 when the city was host for the Commonwealth games.

complex. Three of the pyramids contain plants from three different climatic regions; the fourth is a show house with a display of ornamentals.

Old Strathcona Historic Area (9)
Several buildings dating from the early 1900s can be seen in this old commercial section of Edmonton. Preserved structures include the Old Firehall, the Strathcona Hotel and the Princess Cinema. There is a walking tour of the area.

Provincial Museum of Alberta (3)
This large building, Alberta's 1967 centennial project, is on the grounds of old Government House (once the lieutenant governor's residence).

An 11-piece bronze frieze in an orientation gallery gives an overview of the museum exhibits. There are four main exhibit galleries: Indian, habitat, historical and natural history. Artifacts, dioramas, specimens and photographs are used to tell Alberta's story in terms of its zoology, geology, Indians, fur traders and pioneers.

Refinery Row (18)
Located east of the city, Refinery Row includes a polyethylene plant, giant storage tanks and pipeline pumping stations.

Space Sciences Centre (4)
One of the features of this multipurpose facility is the Margaret Zeidler Star Theatre, which offers planetarium shows.

University of Alberta (5)
Founded in 1906, the university overlooks the North Saskatchewan River. Among its showpieces are a medical sciences complex and the Hub, a solar-heated student residence.

West Edmonton Mall (1)
Some 800 shops and services, the world's largest indoor amusement park, two indoor lakes (one large enough for surfing, and the other deep enough for submarine rides and scuba diving), an NHL-size skating rink, an 18-hole miniature golf course and a host of other features (spread over an area of 45 hectares) have made this one of Edmonton's major tourist attractions. The *Guinness World Book of Records* has called the mall "the eighth wonder of the world."

The towers of downtown Edmonton's constantly changing skyline provide a striking contrast to the stately old Hotel Macdonald (above left). Edmonton's Convention Centre (above right) has been built into the bluffs of the North Saskatchewan River. West Edmonton Mall (right), a city-within-a-city, offers a wide range of shopping, entertainment and recreational pleasures.

A Blackfoot Thunder Shield (above), dating from about 1870, is from the collection of the Provincial Museum of Alberta.

Klondike Days — Reliving the Rollicking '90s

During Klondike Days, a 10-day jamboree held in Edmonton each July, the city relives the excitement of the gold rush of '98. Modern stores don false fronts and fancy-lettered signs. Pubs and lounges become saloons, where piano players wear straw hats and old songs are sung. Downtown streets are closed to traffic for the Sunday Promenade so Edmontonians can stroll about in their Klondike finery.

Contests ranging from rock lifting to log chopping are held; the winner is crowned the King of the Klondike. More than a hundred rafts compete in the World Championship Sourdough Raft Race on a 16-kilometre stretch of the North Saskatchewan River.

Highlights of the Klondike Days Exposition at Edmonton Northlands are the Silver Slipper Gambling Saloon (legal gambling) and a daily prize in gold. (The winner rides downtown by stagecoach to trade it for cash.) Northland's 13-metre-high Chilkoot Mountain—built of lumber, wire mesh and plaster—has a waterfall and a meandering stream, where visitors can pan for gold nuggets.

Sourdough Raft Race during Klondike Days

An "Island" of Unspoiled Nature Amid Pastures and Grainfields

Central Alberta

Situated in the northern section of the Beaver Hills, Elk Island National Park takes its name from the large herds of elk (wapiti) that once roamed the area. Trapping, hunting and settlement had all but wiped out the elk in 1906 when the federal government first set aside part of the present park as a wildlife refuge. Later the refuge was upgraded to the status of a national park and further expansions took place through the years.

Elk Island is not encircled by water; it

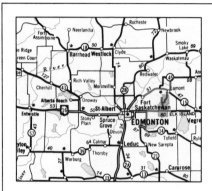

FORT SASKATCHEWAN
A three-by-two-metre mural in the Fort Saskatchewan Museum tells the town's story from the days of Anthony Henday, the first white man to explore this part of Alberta. A Hudson's Bay Company trader-explorer, Henday traveled into Blackfoot country south of here in 1754-55.

The museum has collections of photographs and Indian and pioneer relics. One artifact is a copying machine (c.1908) in which wet linen and sheets of tin were used for duplicating. A two-story, red brick courthouse (1909), a two-story log farmhouse (c.1900), the Soda Lake Anglican Church (c.1911), and a schoolhouse (c.1905) are among restored buildings in a small park. Horse-drawn harvesting machinery and steam-engine threshing machines are displayed. A cairn is formed of stones from the original RCMP fort (1875).

Log schoolhouse, Fort Saskatchewan Museum

UKRAINIAN CULTURAL HERITAGE VILLAGE
Domed churches and other pioneer buildings are in the Ukrainian Cultural Heritage Village, just outside the east gate of Elk Island National Park. The buildings were relocated here from original sites in surrounding communities □ A farmers' market is held on weekends and there is a harvest festival in September.

POLAR PARK
Visitors to this 6.27-square-kilometre zoo can see more than 100 different wildlife species from Canada, the Soviet Union, northern China, and other cold-climate countries. There are also a few warm-climate species, such as cheetahs, lions and rhinoceros, as well as a pair of endangered mountain gorillas. Altogether more than 1,000 animals are found within the park. Unpaved roads connect the areas where the animals are exhibited to visitors.

Hayrides are available in summer; sleigh rides, in winter. The park has picnicking grounds and a restaurant. During winter, cross-country skiers can explore 32 kilometres of trails within the park.

Siberian tigers, Polar Park

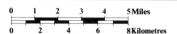

is a chunk of unspoiled nature amid surroundings cultivated by man. Its hills set it apart from the prairies. Relics of its geologic past—hollows, knobs and gullies—emphasize its separateness even further. Such terrain is vastly different from the pastures and grainfields along the park's perimeter. There are also differences in climate. In summer the hills are cooler than the surrounding sunbaked plains; in winter they deflect the vicious winds that rip across the prairies.

Elk Island National Park remains a refuge for elk and other endangered species—plains and wood bison, and trumpeter swans. Also found here are beavers, coyotes, mink, moose and mule deer. Elk Island's many small lakes and sloughs teem with more than 200 species of waterfowl—some nesting, others stopping over during spring and autumn migrations.

Trees of Elk Island include trembling aspen, birch, poplar and spruce. Marsh marigolds and wild sarsaparilla—plants that have disappeared from the area outside the park—grow here.

But Elk Island National Park has become more than a refuge for wildlife. Within easy access of Edmonton, which is a mere 48 kilometres to the west, it is also a welcoming, year-round playground for campers, canoeists, golfers, hikers and skiers.

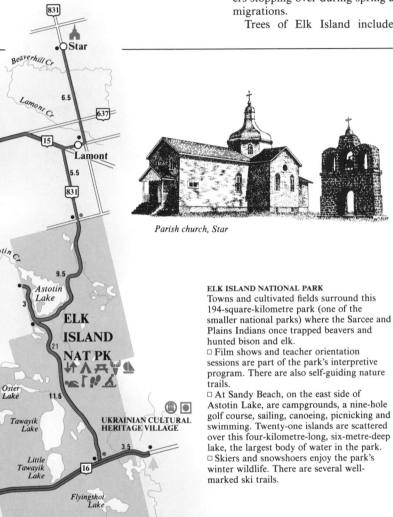

Parish church, Star

ELK ISLAND NATIONAL PARK
Towns and cultivated fields surround this 194-square-kilometre park (one of the smaller national parks) where the Sarcee and Plains Indians once trapped beavers and hunted bison and elk.
□ Film shows and teacher orientation sessions are part of the park's interpretive program. There are also self-guiding nature trails.
□ At Sandy Beach, on the east side of Astotin Lake, are campgrounds, a nine-hole golf course, sailing, canoeing, picnicking and swimming. Twenty-one islands are scattered over this four-kilometre-long, six-metre-deep lake, the largest body of water in the park.
□ Skiers and snowshoers enjoy the park's winter wildlife. There are several well-marked ski trails.

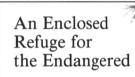

UKRAINIAN CULTURAL HERITAGE VILLAGE

Astotin Lake, Elk Island National Park

STAR
The oldest Ukrainian Catholic parish in Canada is here, where the first Ukrainian immigrants settled in 1892-94. (At that time, the community was called Edna.) The present church, the third since the parish was founded in 1897, was built in 1926-27. In it, saved from a fire that destroyed the second church in 1922, are enameled paintings of Christ, the Virgin and the four Evangelists.

BEAVER HILLS
Rising some 30 to 60 metres above the surrounding prairie are Alberta's Beaver Hills, a series of ridges, bogs and shallow lakes, all formed by retreating glaciers.
□ The bedrock of the hills was formed some 100 million years ago, when a melting ice sheet deposited sand, gravel and mud in an ancient seabed. The present rolling landscape, known as "dead-ice moraine," was created when boulders from the Canadian Shield were laid on this bedrock by a glacier retreating slowly toward the northeast between one million and 10,000 years ago. Bogs, lakes and ponds formed in depressions in this glacial debris.

An Enclosed Refuge for the Endangered

A two-metre-high fence around Elk Island National Park excludes wolves and other predators thus keeping its endangered wildlife population intact. Within the park's enclosed environment, naturalists must control mammal population and monitor potentially damaging natural happenings. Rapidly multiplying deer can deplete the food supply, for example, and dams built by the park's 2,500 beavers can cause extensive flooding.

Plains and wood bison are among the rare species successfully protected in Elk Island National Park. Some 450 plains bison roam north of Highway 16, which cuts through the park. More than 200 wood bison are kept in an area south of the highway. Survival of the bison at Elk Island has resulted in their release in areas that they once inhabited.

Great horned owls and black-capped chickadees (*above*) are among the more than 200 species of birds that fly over the park's undulating terrain. Common loons, pintail ducks and white-winged scoters nest in sloughs and marshes.

Church Domes and a Giant Egg Gleaming in the Sunshine

Central Alberta

People of Ukrainian origin, the largest ethnic group in this region, arrived here between 1898 and 1910. Deeply religious, hardy and self-reliant, these settlers cleared two to four hectares of land a year. The men bought animals and implements by working in mines or lumber camps, or by laying railway track.

The settlers' first habitations, known as *boordays*, were humble affairs consisting of dugouts roofed with boughs and sod. As their farms prospered, the settlers built

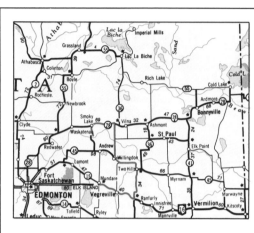

Prickly rose

VICTORIA TRAIL
Bushes of prickly rose, Alberta's floral emblem, flank this historic route along the North Saskatchewan River. The Victoria Trail dates from the 1870s. It was part of the route followed by Red River carts hauling supplies between Winnipeg and Edmonton. Today the trail to the west of Victoria Settlement offers a panorama of lush valley and steep, wooded riverbanks.

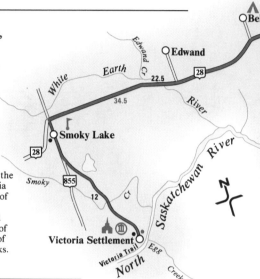

VICTORIA SETTLEMENT
Southwest of Smoky Lake is Victoria Settlement, which has been the site of Fort Victoria (a Hudson's Bay Company post), a Methodist mission and an early settlement. The clerk's quarters of Fort Victoria, the oldest building (1864) still on its original site in Alberta, have been restored. The Pakan Methodist Church, the other historic building here, presents a slide-show describing the early settlement of the site. Tour guides in period costume take visitors through the buildings and around the site.

Thatched Roofs, Blue and Yellow Trim

Most early Ukrainian settlers in Alberta made their first homes in simple dugout huts called *boordays*: metre-deep pits lined with logs and roofed with aspen boughs and sod. Two dark cramped rooms often sheltered several families while they built sturdy log cabins, some of which are preserved at the Shandro Historical Living Village and Pioneer Museum, and in other areas of central Alberta.

Such two-room cabins were usually made of poplar or aspen logs plastered with mud. Whitewash protected the walls from rain. The cabins reflected traditional Ukrainian design—thatched roofs, bright blue and yellow trim on doors and windows, and ornately carved eaves. As soon as their homes were completed the settlers built a church—a simple log structure topped with a distinctive pear-shaped dome.

Thatched log house, Shandro Historical Living Village and Pioneer Museum

Miraculous icon, Mundare

A Boorday, the First House, a painting by William Kurelek

Ukrainian Orthodox Church, Shandro Historical Living Village and Pioneer Museum

log cabins in a style echoing the architecture of their homeland. Carefully preserved examples of both types of dwellings can be seen today at the Shandro Historical Living Village and Pioneer Museum.

The religious values of the Ukrainians were expressed in their churches, whose domes still gleam in the sunlit prairie air. What were symbols of faith to these pioneers remain as memorials to their fortitude.

Ukrainian traditions have survived, too. Descendants of the settlers keep alive the folk songs and dances, the handicraft skills of embroidery and Easter-egg decoration, and the fine culinary arts. A showcase for this rich cultural heritage is the Ukrainian Pysanka Festival, held in early July at Vegreville. A striking attraction of this community is its giant Pysanka (Easter egg), built to honor the early pioneers. Its design symbolizes prosperity, good harvests and security—all of which the first settlers found here.

Sunset on the North Saskatchewan River, near Wasel

SHANDRO
The Historical Living Village and Pioneer Museum recreates life in an early Ukrainian immigrant community. Among 18 buildings are the 1902 thatched log home of the first settler, Nikon Shandro, a 1926 granary, and one of the province's oldest Orthodox churches—built near Chipman by Russian missionaries in 1904. Other buildings include a blacksmith shop, a wind-driven gristmill, and a replica of a *boorday*—the pioneers' first shelter.

BOIAN
Attracted by the fertile land, Roumanians arrived here in 1899, and named their settlement after a village in their native province, Bukovina. Perched on a hill is St. Mary's Roumanian Orthodox Church (1903), believed to be the oldest Roumanian church still in use in North America. The log structure is sheathed in wood. Nearby are an old stone schoolhouse (now a community hall) and a cemetery—the only remains of the early community. Many families have left the area in recent years for industrial centers in Ontario and Quebec.

St. Mary's Roumanian
Orthodox Church, Boian

HAIRY HILL
This village is named for a hill where buffalo shed their hair in spring. The Thompson Canoe Co. annually builds some 50 canoes similar to those made in eastern Canada in the 1880s. The 5-to-5.5-metre-long canoes are made of sitka spruce, oak and maple, and covered with canvas.

TWO HILLS
Natural gas gathering systems and processing plants surround this community west of which runs the main Alberta Gas Trunk Line.
□ A baseball tournament, an indoor rodeo and an agricultural fair are held in August.

VEGREVILLE
A seven-by-six-metre, 2,270-kilogram aluminum Pysanka (Ukrainian Easter egg) in Heritage Park honors the area's pioneers and the Mounties who protected them. The bronze, gold and silver-patterned egg rotates on a steel and concrete base. Designs of stars, equilateral triangles, six-vane windmills and wolves' teeth symbolize prosperity, good harvests and security.
□ Three days of music, dancing, ethnic food, cultural displays and talent contests highlight the Ukrainian Pysanka Festival in early July. A parade, nightly grandstand shows and a fly-in breakfast for guests arriving at Vegreville Airport are features of a three-day agricultural exhibition in late July.
□ Our Lady of the Highway Shrine, east of town, has a two-metre-high statue of Mary, sculpted in Italy of Carrara marble.

MUNDARE
An unusual collection of East European art, church relics, and Ukrainian artifacts is in a museum at the Basilian Fathers Monastery. Included are a 12th-century gospel handwritten in Old Slavic, four 14th-century icons, copies of the first printed Latin Bible (1520) and the first printed French Bible (1558). Also displayed are a 17th-century altar cloth embroidered in silver and an Italian violin (1723).
□ Stained-glass windows in the monastery's St. Peter and St. Paul Church depict the life of Christ and the history of Mundare and the Ukrainian people. In a chapel-like nook in the vestibule is an enlarged reproduction of an icon (of the Mother of God) at Pochayev in the western Ukraine. (The original icon was investigated by a church commission in 1770 and accredited with 539 miracles.) The church, an octagonal brick building, with a wooden dome, is crowned by eight semi-arches and an aluminum cross.

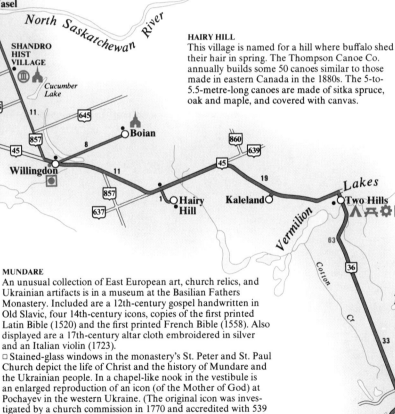

Giant Easter egg,
Vegreville

Northern Pike and Grayling from Clear, Island-Dotted Lakes

East-Central Alberta

North of Long Lake Provincial Park, flat, open farmland gives way to rolling, forested countryside. Because this area is thinly populated, many species of birds flourish—white pelicans, blue herons, western grebes, loons, bald eagles, ospreys, hawks, sandhill cranes and owls. Blueberries, cranberries, raspberries and saskatoons carpet the roadsides. (Early settlers dried the berries on blankets in the sun, before storing them for winter's needs.)

In the forested hills are scores of glis-

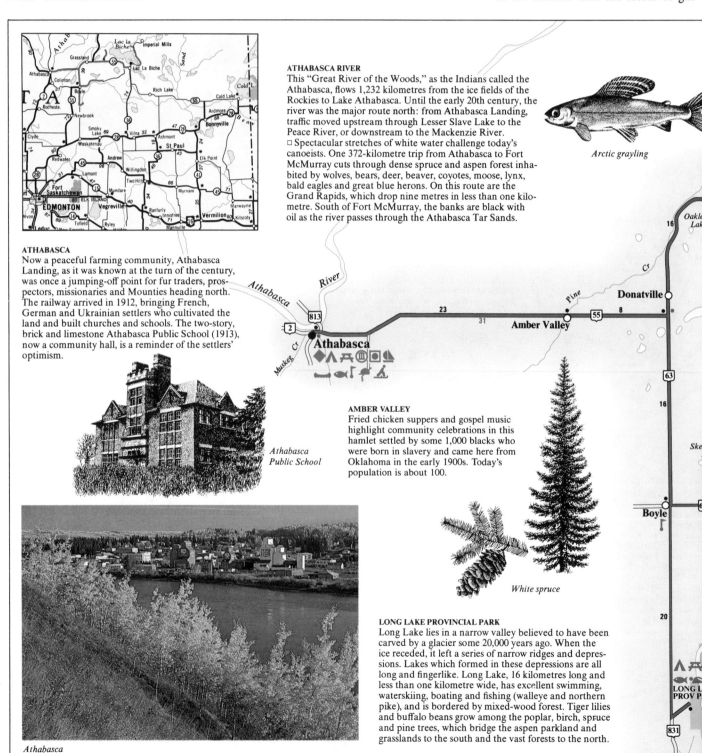

ATHABASCA RIVER
This "Great River of the Woods," as the Indians called the Athabasca, flows 1,232 kilometres from the ice fields of the Rockies to Lake Athabasca. Until the early 20th century, the river was the major route north: from Athabasca Landing, traffic moved upstream through Lesser Slave Lake to the Peace River, or downstream to the Mackenzie River.
□ Spectacular stretches of white water challenge today's canoeists. One 372-kilometre trip from Athabasca to Fort McMurray cuts through dense spruce and aspen forest inhabited by wolves, bears, deer, beaver, coyotes, moose, lynx, bald eagles and great blue herons. On this route are the Grand Rapids, which drop nine metres in less than one kilometre. South of Fort McMurray, the banks are black with oil as the river passes through the Athabasca Tar Sands.

Arctic grayling

ATHABASCA
Now a peaceful farming community, Athabasca Landing, as it was known at the turn of the century, was once a jumping-off point for fur traders, prospectors, missionaries and Mounties heading north. The railway arrived in 1912, bringing French, German and Ukrainian settlers who cultivated the land and built churches and schools. The two-story, brick and limestone Athabasca Public School (1913), now a community hall, is a reminder of the settlers' optimism.

Athabasca Public School

AMBER VALLEY
Fried chicken suppers and gospel music highlight community celebrations in this hamlet settled by some 1,000 blacks who were born in slavery and came here from Oklahoma in the early 1900s. Today's population is about 100.

White spruce

LONG LAKE PROVINCIAL PARK
Long Lake lies in a narrow valley believed to have been carved by a glacier some 20,000 years ago. When the ice receded, it left a series of narrow ridges and depressions. Lakes which formed in these depressions are all long and fingerlike. Long Lake, 16 kilometres long and less than one kilometre wide, has excellent swimming, waterskiing, boating and fishing (walleye and northern pike), and is bordered by mixed-wood forest. Tiger lilies and buffalo beans grow among the poplar, birch, spruce and pine trees, which bridge the aspen parkland and grasslands to the south and the vast forests to the north.

Athabasca

0 1 2 3 4 5 Miles
0 2 4 6 8 Kilometres

tening lakes. (There are some 50 of these within a 100-kilometre radius of Lac La Biche.) Most are typical north-country lakes—clear, studded with small wooded islands, and surrounded by splendid, sandy beaches.

Boating, canoeing, sailing, swimming and fishing are excellent. Northern pike, walleye and perch are the principal catch. Pike are present in enormous quantities and sizes—many in the 9-to-13-kilogram range are taken every year. Some of the best arctic grayling fishing in Canada is found in the area around Lac La Biche.

A brief wave of tourism swept this area in 1916, when visitors from Edmonton flocked to the imposing, railway-owned Lac La Biche Inn. During that summer a boating accident claimed the lives of several sportsmen who, ignoring the warnings of Indian fishermen on the shore, had ventured onto Lac La Biche during a squall. The tragedy killed the tourist trade and, except for quarters occupied by the station-master, the inn was abandoned for decades.

Tourists have recently rediscovered the area's scenic beauty and fine fishing, hunting, boating and camping. But the inn is no longer available to them. Converted to hospital use in 1937, it remains part of St. Catherine's Hospital.

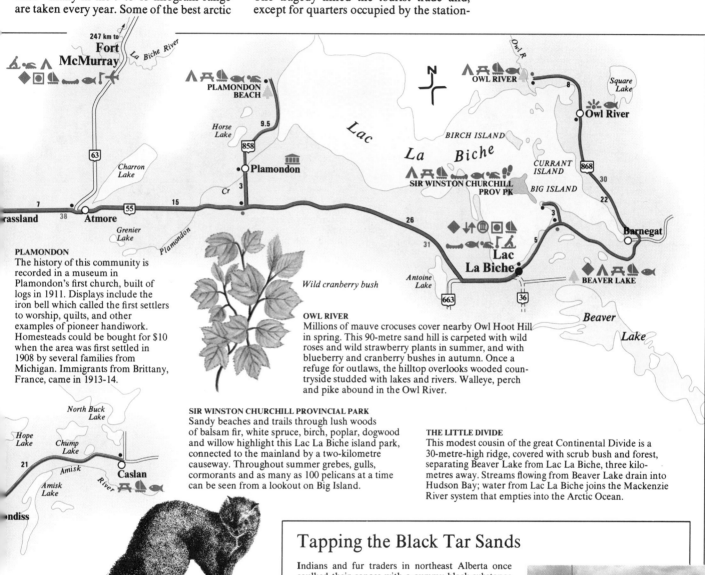

PLAMONDON
The history of this community is recorded in a museum in Plamondon's first church, built of logs in 1911. Displays include the iron bell which called the first settlers to worship, quilts, and other examples of pioneer handiwork. Homesteads could be bought for $10 when the area was first settled in 1908 by several families from Michigan. Immigrants from Brittany, France, came in 1913-14.

Wild cranberry bush

OWL RIVER
Millions of mauve crocuses cover nearby Owl Hoot Hill in spring. This 90-metre sand hill is carpeted with wild roses and wild strawberry plants in summer, and with blueberry and cranberry bushes in autumn. Once a refuge for outlaws, the hilltop overlooks wooded countryside studded with lakes and rivers. Walleye, perch and pike abound in the Owl River.

SIR WINSTON CHURCHILL PROVINCIAL PARK
Sandy beaches and trails through lush woods of balsam fir, white spruce, birch, poplar, dogwood and willow highlight this Lac La Biche island park, connected to the mainland by a two-kilometre causeway. Throughout summer grebes, gulls, cormorants and as many as 100 pelicans at a time can be seen from a lookout on Big Island.

THE LITTLE DIVIDE
This modest cousin of the great Continental Divide is a 30-metre-high ridge, covered with scrub bush and forest, separating Beaver Lake from Lac La Biche, three kilometres away. Streams flowing from Beaver Lake drain into Hudson Bay; water from Lac La Biche joins the Mackenzie River system that empties into the Arctic Ocean.

Mink

LAC LA BICHE
Powwows that Cree Indians held here until the arrival of white settlers are revived in August in conjunction with the Blue Feather Fish Derby. Twice a year, Indians and Métis from a vast area used to gather on the shores of Lac La Biche for dances and games, and to ask the Manitou's blessing. Today's four-day celebration features a parade, native contests, dancing and baseball.
□ Enormous quantities of beaver, fox, lynx, bear, and coyote were trapped and sold here until the late 1800s. Trapping controls were enforced, fur farming developed and mink farming was a major industry here by the 1940s. Only a few mink farms survive but the area is still known for its fine pelts.

Tapping the Black Tar Sands

Indians and fur traders in northeast Alberta once caulked their canoes with a gummy black substance that oozed from the banks of the Athabasca River. Today, engineers at the Syncrude Plant in Fort McMurray have developed techniques for extracting oil from the Athabasca tar sands—possibly the world's largest oil reserve.

Conveyor belts move mountains of asphaltlike tar sand, mined in open pits, to the extraction plant. Raw bitumen is withdrawn by dropping an oily slush of steaming sand into hot water. As the sand sinks, the oil is skimmed off the top. Intense heat turns the bitumen into synthetic crude oil, ready for further refining.

Daily output at the Syncrude Plant can reach 160,000 barrels of synthetic crude oil. The Oil Sands Interpretative Center, open year-round, offers hands-on exhibits and equipment displays.

Syncrude mine at Fort McMurray

Grainfields and Sailboats
Where Cree and Blackfoot Once Traded

East-Central Alberta

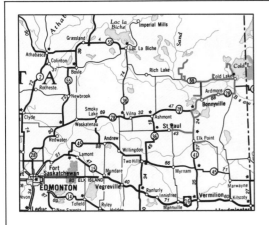

MOOSE LAKE PROVINCIAL PARK

The land that now comprises the park was initially known as "Anshaw," after Angus Shaw, a North West Company fur trader who established the area's first trading post in 1789. It was Shaw who gave the lake its name, calling it *l'orignal,* French for moose.

□ Hiking trails along Deadman's Point lead to a mature forest of white spruce underlain with Indian pipe, wintergreen and feather mosses. This is the only portion of the original forest to survive fires in 1927 and 1942. Today jack pine covers much of the rest of this park on the north shore of Moose Lake.

□ Among the birds that have been sighted here are terns, hermit thrushes, spotted sandpipers, ospreys, broad-winged hawks and pelicans.

Jack pine

Handcrafted weavings, Kehiwin Indian Reserve

KEHIWIN INDIAN RESERVE

Descendants of Chiefs Big Bear and Poundmaker are among some 500 Indians on this reserve named for another Plains Cree warrior, Kehiwin. Visitors may tour the plants of Kehiwin Steel Industries Ltd., and Kehiwin Cree-ations Ltd. A shop sells blankets, rugs, wall hangings, shawls, vests and shoulder bags woven in the Cree-ations plant and depicting the ancient symbols and geometric patterns favored by the Plains Indians.

□ Kehiwin Lake, southwest of the reserve, and Muriel Lake to the northeast are stocked with perch, walleye and northern pike. Both have picnicking, camping and boat-launching sites, and Muriel Lake has a sandy beach.

UFO landing pad, St. Paul

ST. PAUL

Before the white man's arrival, this was the territory of the Cree Indians, especially Wood Cree who roamed north of the North Saskatchewan River away from the fierce Blackfoot Indians to the south. The nearby Thérien lakes—then a wilderness haven for waterfowl—were known as Manawan, meaning egg gathering place.

□ The world's first and only flying saucer landing pad was built here in 1967 as a Centennial project. The raised, 12-metre-wide, circular platform displays provincial and territorial flags. The landing pad contains letters to be opened June 3, 2067.

ELK POINT

Rum-barrel hoops, belt buckles, locks, hinges and cast-iron tools in the Fort George Museum date from the 1790s, when the North West and Hudson's Bay companies had rival fur trade posts in the area—Fort George and Buckingham House, both built in 1792. Other exhibits are musket balls, old pistols, flintlock parts and trinkets, rings and factory-made metal arrowheads traded with the Indians for furs.

Indian artifacts, Fort George Museum, Elk Point

0	2	4	6	8	10 Miles
0	4	8	12		16 Kilometres

Clear and moderately warm, the lakes of east-central Alberta are favored by fishermen for their trout, pike, yellow perch, walleye and whitefish. Sandy beaches and good camping facilities further enhance the lakeland region east, west and north of Elk Point.

Some two centuries ago, this was the major fur-trading center on the North Saskatchewan River. Mounds, charred timbers and archaeological digs near Elk Point mark where the Hudson's Bay Company's Buckingham House and the North West Company's Fort George were built in 1792. Canoes and York boats lined the riverbank and teepees dotted the meadows when Cree traded furs and Blackfoot bartered dried buffalo meat here. When the area was depleted of fur-bearing animals, both posts were abandoned. The wilderness remained undisturbed until the early 1900s, when Europeans returned—to fish, trap, log and eventually homestead.

Today roads dip and curve through fields of grain and wooded parkland. North of Moose Lake the countryside is dotted with sloughs, breeding ground for wildfowl that make this a hunter's paradise. Beaches, such as those at Moose Lake and Cold Lake, are characterized by fine sand extending far into the clear water. Cold Lake—at 352 square kilometres one of Alberta's largest lakes—is easily accessible. Sailing, water-skiing, and guided fishing tours are among the activities available here.

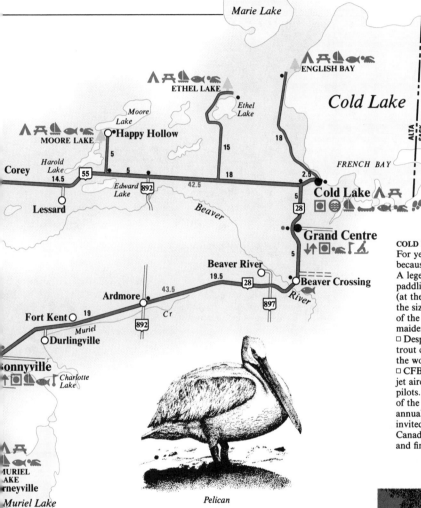

Pelican

Lake trout

COLD LAKE

For years no Indians dared cross 352-square-kilometre Cold Lake because of Kinosoo—a monster said to lurk in its 113-metre depth. A legend tells of a young Wood Cree Indian brave who was paddling across the lake to see his betrothed. Near French Bay (at the southern end of the lake), a white, humpbacked creature the size of a whale grabbed the canoe in its powerful mouth. Pieces of the craft were found floating in the lake the next day; the Indian maiden never saw her brave again.
□ Despite Kinosoo, Cold Lake is a popular fishing resort. Lake trout caught here, weighing as much as 18 kilograms, are among the world's tastiest. Northern pike and walleye are abundant.
□ CFB Cold Lake is the largest and most active Canadian Forces jet aircraft base. It is responsible for training all Canadian fighter pilots. The base's satellite tracking unit and radar station form part of the North American Air Defense Command. CFB stages an annual Armed Forces Day (usually in June) to which the public is invited. The activities include an air show, an exhibit of many Canadian and American military aircraft, and displays of rescue and fire-fighting equipment.

BONNYVILLE

Since 1907, when it was first settled by French Canadians, this mixed-farming region has been an expanding multicultural community. The recent establishment of several oil plants within a 40-kilometre radius of Bonnyville has added to its economic growth.
□ This area has an airstrip, a nine-hole golf course, and good boating and fishing. There are also modern facilities for winter and summer sports. The major annual activities include a winter carnival in March, the Trade Fair and Fish Derby in June, and a rodeo in August.

LINDBERGH

Up to 345 tonnes of salt are produced daily at the Canadian Salt Co. plant. Discovered in the 1940s, a salt bed 300 metres thick and several kilometres long contains enough salt to supply Canada's needs for the next 2,000 years. Forty-one grades of salt are refined and packed at the plant. Tours are available.

Cold Lake

Echoes of '85 and Indian Unrest

Northwestern Saskatchewan

FLOTTEN LAKE
The lake has large colonies of ring-billed and California gulls, common terns and western grebes. On the eastern shore are kames—mounds of sand and gravel deposited by glacial meltwater.

MEADOW LAKE PROVINCIAL PARK
Within this 157,000-hectare park—one of the largest in Saskatchewan—are deep forests, meadows and marshes. Its most striking feature is the chain of lakes that stretches more than 110 kilometres from Cold Lake on the Alberta-Saskatchewan border to Waterhen Lake. Hiking trails and canoe routes encourage exploration of every corner.

Western grebe

STEELE NARROWS PROVINCIAL HISTORIC PARK
The last battle in the Northwest Rebellion was fought here June 3, 1885, between the Cree led by Big Bear and militia led by NWMP Maj. Sam Steele. Big Bear subsequently surrendered, was imprisoned and died Jan. 17, 1888. Plaques in this park describe the battle and the lives of Steele and Big Bear.

Historic plaque overlooking Steele Narrows

FORT PITT PROVINCIAL HISTORIC PARK
From 1829 to 1890, Fort Pitt was a Hudson's Bay Company fur trading post. During the Northwest Rebellion of 1885, it was manned briefly by North West Mounted Police led by Insp. Francis Dickens (son of author Charles Dickens). Besieged and outnumbered by the Cree, the NWMP was forced to withdraw: the Cree lifted their siege to permit the departure. Interpretive panels outline events of the rebellion and the local history of the fur trade.
□ Nearby Frenchman Butte National Historic Site marks where the Cree later fought the militia (May 28, 1885). Signposts indicate the preserved gun pits and the battle positions of both sides.

LLOYMINSTER
This city of 17,400 is situated in Alberta *and* Saskatchewan: the main north-south street—50th or Meridian Avenue—is both the provincial border and the 110th meridian of longitude. The provincial split occurred in 1905, when the two provinces were established. Roughly 60 percent of the population lives in Alberta.
□ Lloydminster was founded in 1903 by a group of English settlers whose first leader was Rev. Isaac Barr. There was dissension in the group en route to Canada and many of the immigrants deserted Barr's scheme. Barr was dismissed at Saskatoon, and the remaining settlers traveled here with Rev. George Lloyd and set up the community that now bears his name.
□ Colony Heritage Cultural Centre contains the Barr Colony Antique Museum, the Fuchs' Wildlife Display and the Imhoff Art Gallery. The gallery has more than 70 works by German-born Count Berthold von Imhoff (1866-1939), who lived in this area from 1913 until his death. Imhoff decorated more than 90 churches in Canada and the United States. Eighteen Imhoff panels can be seen in a church at nearby Paradise Hill.

CUT KNIFE
Tepee poles on a lonely hill mark the grave of Poundmaker who in 1876 signed Treaty Six for his band of Cree. Nine years later, during the Northwest Rebellion, the Cree led by Poundmaker repulsed some 300 policemen and soldiers. But after the battle, the Cree chief kept his warriors from slaughtering the white men. A nearby cairn commemorates the battle site. When the rebellion ended, Poundmaker surrendered, and was sentenced to a year in penitentiary. He died in 1886.

0	4	8	12	16	20 Miles

0	8	16	24	32 Kilometres

Memories of Big Bear and Poundmaker, desperate men who made war because they saw their people starving, haunt this part of northwestern Saskatchewan where much of the Northwest Rebellion was fought in 1885. Although today this pleasant land contains lakes and parks, prosperous farms and bustling prairie communities—notably, Lloydminster and North Battleford—there are still echoes of the '85 rebellion lingering at the old forts and battle sites that are also part of the local landscape.

By 1880 most Prairie Indians were on reserves, some farming, most subsisting on welfare. Rations were cut in 1883 and many Indians died. In March 1885, after the Métis attacked a North West Mounted Police post, Poundmaker's Cree warriors marched on Battleford and burned the settlement. A month later, not far away at Cut Knife Hill, they defeated a force of 300 soldiers and policemen. Big Bear's Cree massacred nine whites at Frog Lake, Alta., and pillaged Fort Pitt (near Lloydminster). A militia force engaged Big Bear's warriors at Frenchman Butte and pursued them to Loon Lake, only to have them escape across Steele Narrows and into the forest of what now is Meadow Lake Provincial Park.

The dream of a Métis-Indian nation ended May 12 when Louis Riel was defeated at Batoche. Soon after that, near present-day Goodsoil, Big Bear released his white prisoners. He and Poundmaker were jailed and lived only briefly after their release.

Von Imhoff murals, Roman Catholic church, Paradise Hill

COCHIN

The village is named for the Rev. Louis Cochin, a missionary who had a moderating influence on Poundmaker's band in the Northwest Rebellion.
□ A plaque marks a trail which connected the Cochin mission with a Hudson's Bay Company post on Green Lake, 110 kilometres north. The trail was used by troops pursuing Big Bear in 1885.

Fort Battleford — Settlers' Refuge in the Rebellion

Fort Battleford, established in 1876 as NWMP district headquarters and now restored, was a refuge for 400 settlers who fled their homes as the Cree looted nearby settlements in 1885. The Cree chief Poundmaker surrendered here after the Métis were defeated at Batoche. Eight Indians convicted of murder in the Frog Lake Massacre were hanged at Fort Battleford in Canada's last public execution. In the commanding officer's residence (1877) are original parlor and dining chairs. In the officers' quarters (1886) is the speaker's chair from the Territorial Legislative Assembly (1883-1905) in Regina. In an interpretive center are Poundmaker's war club and Winchester rifle and a 10-barrel Gatling gun used in the rebellion.

Gatling gun, Battleford National Historic Park

NORTH BATTLEFORD

This city of 15,000 began when the CNR decided in 1905 to build its line through here, bypassing Battleford. Residents from the older community, realizing greater growth and opportunity lay on the other side of the North Saskatchewan River, moved to North Battleford. Within five years, the new community had become a city.
□ At the Western Development Museum, visitors can explore a small 1925 Saskatchewan village, which has a bank, a barbershop, and a drugstore. Also at the museum are pioneer farmhouses, churches, an 1890 NWMP post, and old-time railway and agricultural equipment. Demonstrations of 1920s farming methods are featured at Those Were the Days celebrations in August.
□ The George Hooey Wildlife Exhibit across from the Western Development Museum displays more than 400 animals, birds and fish, all mounted by the late George Hooey.

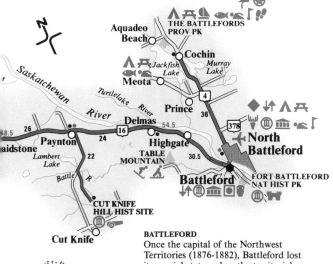

Poundmaker's grave, Cut Knife

BATTLEFORD

Once the capital of the Northwest Territories (1876-1882), Battleford lost its special status when the territorial government was shifted to Regina. Government House, the Northwest Territories council chamber (1878), is now one of the community's most prized historic buildings. Other important buildings from that period are at Fort Battleford National Historic Site. The town also preserves the Gardiner Church (1886), a post office, a courthouse and a land title office (all built in 1911) and the town hall (1912).

Western Development Museum, North Battleford

Once a Temperance Town, Now a Flourishing City

Central Saskatchewan

The only reminder of Saskatoon's sober origins is Temperance Street. In 1882 John Lake was sent to the Northwest Territories (of which Saskatchewan was then part) by an Ontario temperance society to establish a colony. He chose a site overlooking the South Saskatchewan River and named it Saskatoon—the Cree word for a purplish berry that thrives there.

A year later 35 teetotalers arrived from Ontario. The society had sold them homesteads for $320. The buyers were not told

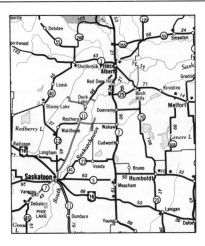

VANSCOY
Mine galleries under Vanscoy honeycomb the world's largest deposit of potash. The salts, evaporation residue of ancient seas, lie in a 180-metre-thick band across Saskatchewan. Discovered by oil drillers in 1943, the potash deposits are processed for fertilizer.

Derby car, Western Development Museum, Saskatoon

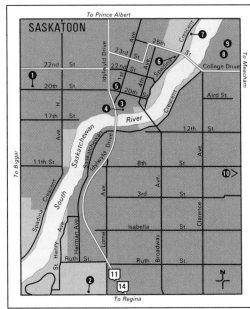

1 Museum of Ukrainian Culture
2 Western Development Museum
3 Saskatoon Visitors and Convention Bureau
4 Meewasin Valley Centre
5 Centennial Auditorium
6 Ukrainian Museum of Canada
7 Mendel Art Gallery and Conservatory
8 University of Saskatchewan
9 The Right Honourable John G. Diefenbaker Centre

Looking across the South Saskatchewan River, Saskatoon

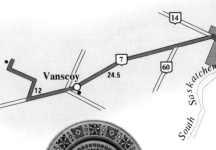

SASKATOON
A fast-growing center of business, industry and education, Saskatoon offers a wide range of cultural and recreational activities. In the heart of the city visitors can explore the parkland along the South Saskatchewan.
□ The Museum of Ukrainian Culture displays some 2,000 items—ceramics, tapestries and pioneer implements—that explain Ukrainian history and traditions. Of special interest are collections of costumed dolls and religious articles.
□ The Saskatoon branch of the Western Development Museum encloses a 1910 "Boom Town." A collection of agricultural machinery and antique automobiles includes the Derby, an automobile built in Saskatoon during the 1920s.
□ Visitors to the Ukrainian Museum of Canada can examine decorative objects and see displays about Ukrainian immigration.
□ The Mendel Art Gallery includes works by Lawren Harris and A. Y. Jackson in its permanent collection.
□ On the University of Saskatchewan campus is Saskatoon's first school and oldest building—the Little Stone School House. A costumed "school mistress" describes its history to visitors. The Right Hon. John G. Diefenbaker Centre, an archive and museum devoted to preserving materials relating to the former Prime Minister, is also on campus.

Wood inlaid plate and box, Ukrainian Museum of Canada, Saskatoon

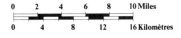

| 0 | 2 | 4 | 6 | 8 | 10 Miles |
| 0 | 4 | 8 | 12 | 16 Kilomètres |

the territories were "dry" anyway and homesteads could be purchased from the government for $10. By 1906 the settlement had become a city—but the temperance ideal had withered as Saskatoon flourished.

Today it is the province's largest city (pop. 185,000), a manufacturing and distribution center, and home of the University of Saskatchewan.

A picturesque view of the city can be seen from the high east riverbank, near a cairn marking John Lake's campsite. Reflected in the river, bordered here with parks, are church steeples, six bridges, and the turreted Bessborough Hotel. Saskatoon's natural setting is enhanced by broad, tree-lined streets and numerous parks.

Fort Carlton

FORT CARLTON PROVINCIAL HISTORIC PARK

The most important fur trade fort between the Red River and the Rockies has been reconstructed here. Fort Carlton, built in 1810, was headquarters of the Hudson's Bay Company's Northern Council and a halfway house between Winnipeg and Edmonton.

□ Fort Carlton's reconstructed stockade and bastions evoke the prosperous fur trading era of the 1860s. The stockade encloses a fur and provisions store, clerk's quarters and a trading shop, all of which have period furnishing and supplies. Interpretive staff show how traders baled and graded fur.

DUCK LAKE

In 1895 a Cree Indian named Almighty Voice shot a stray cow for his wedding feast. He was imprisoned in the North West Mounted Police jail here. He escaped, and one week later shot an NWMP sergeant. After a 19-month manhunt he was killed in a battle with Mounties northeast of Batoche. At the Duck Lake Historical Museum is the restored jail. The museum also has Gabriel Dumont's cane and gold watch, and Louis Riel's shotgun.

ROSTHERN

A plaque six kilometres east identifies the farm where Seager Wheeler grew wheat that won five world championships between 1910 and 1918. For years his 10-B Marquis wheat was the Prairies' most common variety.

BATOCHE NATIONAL HISTORIC SITE

At the Battle of Batoche (May 12, 1885), the North West Field, an 850-man militia force from eastern Canada, overwhelmed fewer than 300 Métis, who were making their final stand in the Northwest Rebellion. Visitors can still see the remains of Batoche Village, and trenches and rifle pits. An interpretive center explains the conflict.

□ The nearby Church of Saint-Antoine-de-Padoue (1884) and its rectory are the only remains of the Métis "capital." A museum in the bullet-scarred rectory contains some of Louis Riel's personal effects, and Gabriel Dumont's .44 revolver and his bridle of horsehair and leather. Dumont is buried in the church cemetery.

Church of Saint-Antoine-de-Padoue, Batoche

FISH CREEK

A road leads six kilometres south along the South Saskatchewan River to a peaceful meadow where militia battled Métis on April 24, 1885, during the Northwest Rebellion. The national historic site is marked by a cairn. A headstone marks the graves of some of the militiamen killed in action.

An 850-man force led by Maj. Gen. Frederick Middleton advanced in the nearby Fish Creek ravine and was ambushed by Gabriel Dumont and 150 Métis on higher ground (depressions used by the sharpshooters can still be seen). Even artillery failed to dislodge the snipers who suffered four casualties (10 soldiers were killed). Before reinforcements arrived the Métis slipped away, ending the Battle of Fish Creek.

Louis Riel

Gabriel Dumont

A Leader of Rebels and the 'Prince of the Plains'

The dream of a Métis state on the prairies ended on May 12, 1885, at the Battle of Batoche. The Métis—offspring of Indian mothers and white fathers—hunted dwindling buffalo herds and farmed in the South Saskatchewan River valley. Batoche became their unofficial capital. In 1884, their leader Louis Riel sent a petition to Ottawa requesting land rights. When it was ignored, Riel formed a provisional government with Gabriel Dumont as his commander in chief.

Some 850 militiamen from Ontario and Quebec were led west by Maj. Gen. Frederick Middleton to put down the insurrection. Although Dumont engineered several brilliant victories, Middleton captured Batoche in a four-day siege.

Riel was tried for treason, and was hanged in Regina. Dumont escaped and joined William "Buffalo Bill" Cody's Wild West Show as the sharpshooting "Prince of the Plains." Granted amnesty, he returned to Batoche where he died in 1906.

Fishing Lakes and a Wilderness River in an Unchanging Northland

North-Central Saskatchewan

A cairn near Montreal Lake marks the geographic center of Saskatchewan. To the west, in Prince Albert National Park, boreal forest gives way to aspen parkland and it, in turn, yields to the prairie that is the familiar face of the province.

North of Montreal Lake is the unknown half of Saskatchewan—a majestic wilderness little changed since it was penetrated by fur traders during the 1700s. The only signs of man's presence are the highway itself and the lakeshore campsites.

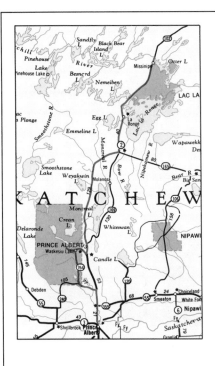

Waskesiu Lake, Prince Albert National Park

Labrador tea

BOUNDARY BOG NATURE TRAIL
This self-guiding trail in Prince Albert National Park skirts muskeg, a sphagnum bog typified by cranberry and Labrador tea (its leaves can be steeped to make a Vitamin-C-rich brew). Insect-eating plants such as round-leaved sundew, bladderwort and pitcher plant thrive in the bog.

WASKESIU LAKE
Prince Albert National Park's only townsite has a golf course, riding stables and an interpretive center with displays of the park's flora, fauna and geological formations. In summer a paddle-wheeler offers daily cruises on Waskesiu Lake.

Beside an Empty Cabin, Grey Owl's Lonely Grave

A hiking trail in Prince Albert National Park leads to the cabin and grave of the woodsman, author and conservationist Grey Owl (1888-1938), who claimed to be the son of an Apache father and a Scots mother. After his death, however, journalists discovered that he was an Englishman—Archibald Stansfeld Belaney. In 1906, at age 17, he came to Canada and settled in northern Ontario, where he learned the language and lore of the Ojibway. Dressed in buckskins and moccasins, the lean, dark-skinned Grey Owl spent much of his time campaigning against the unnecessary killing of animals. At the height of his fame, he lectured in the United States and Great Britain (where he addressed George VI at Buckingham Palace). Grey Owl set up a beaver colony in Prince Albert National Park, where he spent his last years. Several of his books, such as *The Adventures of Sajo and Her Beaver People* and *Tales of an Empty Cabin*, are classics.

Dogsled races, Prince Albert

PRINCE ALBERT
Located on the North Saskatchewan River, Prince Albert (with a population of roughly 34,000) is one of the main centers of Saskatchewan's forest industry and the jumping-off point for travelers to the province's northern regions.
□ A major attraction is the Diefenbaker House, where displays commemorate the political career of Prime Minister John Diefenbaker (1895-1979), who represented Prince Albert from 1953 until his death. (Two other prime ministers—Wilfrid Laurier and Mackenzie King—also represented Prince Albert.)
□ The Prince Albert Historical Museum tells the story of the city with photos, documents and historical objects.
□ The Nisbet Church, at Kinsman Park, dates from 1866, when Prince Albert was founded.
□ Local events include National Forestry Week (May), High Noon Optimist Founder's Day (June) and the Prince Albert Exhibition (July/August).

| 0 | 4 | 8 | 12 | 16 | 20 Miles |
| 0 | 8 | 16 | 24 | | 32 Kilometres |

Lac La Ronge Provincial Park, the province's largest, has outfitters and guides who take adventurous visitors to the park's renowned canoe routes and fishing lakes.

The Churchill River, a maze of lakes connected by raging white water and treacherous rapids, cuts across the park's northern border. This is the only great wilderness river in Canada that can be easily reached by the average traveler.

Lining the river are great banks of pink granite, black basalt and gray metamorphic rock formed two billion years ago. Among the birds found here are gulls, terns, mallards and flocks of white pelicans.

One of the great beauty spots in the Canadian Shield is at Otter Rapids, the only place where the main stem of the Churchill is bridged. Here the river, which drains thousands of square kilometres of northern Saskatchewan, pours through a rocky gorge into the placid waters of Otter Lake.

Fly-in fishing, Otter Lake

LAC LA RONGE PROVINCIAL PARK
With almost 100 freshwater lakes (including Lac La Ronge), Saskatchewan's largest provincial park (344,500 hectares) is noted for outstanding walleye, northern pike and lake trout.

LA RONGE
Local outfitters fly fishermen to camps in Lac La Ronge Provincial Park and to even more remote northern lakes. La Ronge—as well as many other communities in this region—has a craft shop offering native wares and souvenirs.
□ The history of the surrounding area is the theme of La Ronge Regional Museum. Mistasinihk Place Interpretive Centre explains northern life-styles and features local art.

STANLEY MISSION
Holy Trinity Church, Saskatchewan's first Anglican church, is this community's oldest building. The church was constructed between 1854 and 1860 from hardwood logs cut by local Indians and stained glass imported from Britain. Visitors to Stanley Mission must take a gravel road through Lac La Ronge Provincial Park and then a ferry across the Churchill River.

Handcrafted moccasins, La Ronge

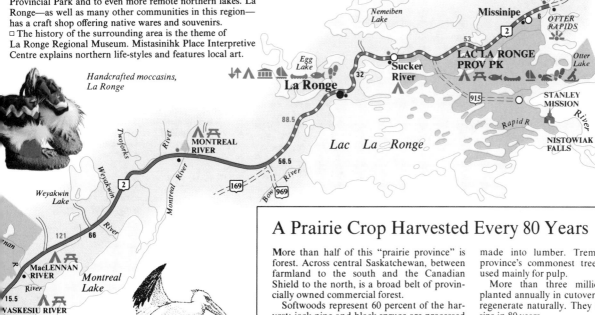

Bald eagle

White pelican

PRINCE ALBERT NATIONAL PARK
Three distinct vegetation zones are found in this park. Badgers inhabit a prairie region typified by meadow rue and prickly rose. Wapiti roam aspen parkland—an area abundant with highbush cranberry and wild sarsaparilla—and woodland caribou range boreal forests. Among 200 bird species found in the park are white pelicans (a rookery of 4,500 is found at Lavallée Lake) and rare bald eagles. There is a small herd of bison.
□ A self-guiding driving tour along the southern shore of Waskesiu Lake passes a beaver pond (a boardwalk leads to the lodge) and ridges left by glaciers. Lobsticks—trees from which Indians and trappers lopped the lower branches when blazing trails—mark some of the park's 140 kilometres of hiking paths.

A Prairie Crop Harvested Every 80 Years

More than half of this "prairie province" is forest. Across central Saskatchewan, between farmland to the south and the Canadian Shield to the north, is a broad belt of provincially owned commercial forest.

Softwoods represent 60 percent of the harvest: jack pine and black spruce are processed into railway ties, fence posts, plywood, and pulp for making newsprint. White spruce is made into lumber. Trembling aspen—the province's commonest tree—is a hardwood used mainly for pulp.

More than three million seedlings are planted annually in cutover areas that cannot regenerate naturally. They reach harvestable size in 80 years.

In summer visitors to the mill near Prince Albert can see softwoods processed into pulp.

Logging operations in Saskatchewan's commercial forest

Lush Lowlands, Blue Ridges...
and Trophy–Sized Trout

Northern Saskatchewan and Manitoba

Until recently the pathless forests of northern Saskatchewan and Manitoba looked much as they did in 1690 to Henry Kelsey, the first European to visit this area.

Now scenic highways such as the Kelsey Trail and the Hanson Lake Road beckon visitors to wilderness fishing, hiking and camping.

The Kelsey Trail skirts the Pasquia Hills, whose rugged ridges can only be explored on foot. Rivers such as the Rice, Pasquia and Waskwei teem with brook trout.

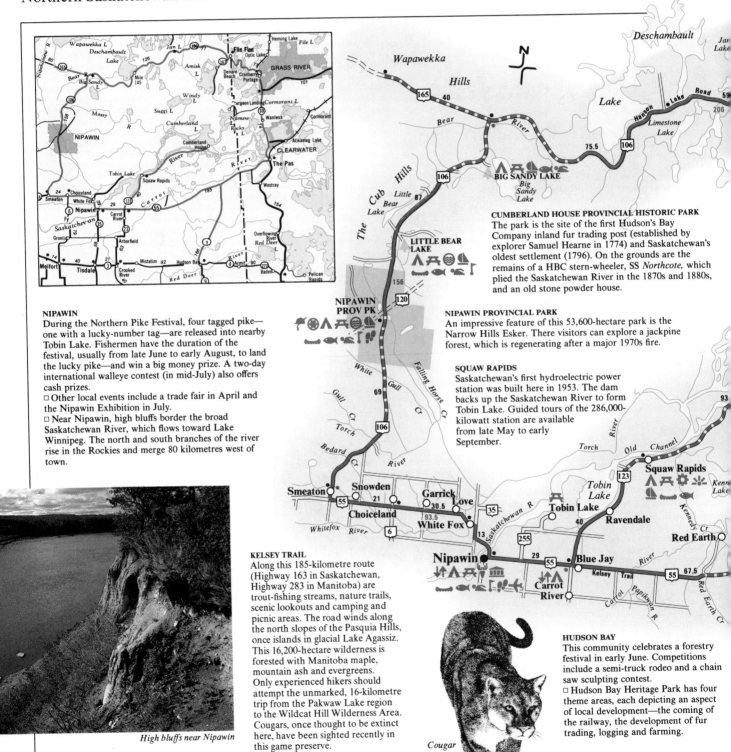

NIPAWIN
During the Northern Pike Festival, four tagged pike—one with a lucky-number tag—are released into nearby Tobin Lake. Fishermen have the duration of the festival, usually from late June to early August, to land the lucky pike—and win a big money prize. A two-day international walleye contest (in mid-July) also offers cash prizes.
□ Other local events include a trade fair in April and the Nipawin Exhibition in July.
□ Near Nipawin, high bluffs border the broad Saskatchewan River, which flows toward Lake Winnipeg. The north and south branches of the river rise in the Rockies and merge 80 kilometres west of town.

CUMBERLAND HOUSE PROVINCIAL HISTORIC PARK
The park is the site of the first Hudson's Bay Company inland fur trading post (established by explorer Samuel Hearne in 1774) and Saskatchewan's oldest settlement (1796). On the grounds are the remains of a HBC stern-wheeler, SS *Northcote*, which plied the Saskatchewan River in the 1870s and 1880s, and an old stone powder house.

NIPAWIN PROVINCIAL PARK
An impressive feature of this 53,600-hectare park is the Narrow Hills Esker. There visitors can explore a jackpine forest, which is regenerating after a major 1970s fire.

SQUAW RAPIDS
Saskatchewan's first hydroelectric power station was built here in 1953. The dam backs up the Saskatchewan River to form Tobin Lake. Guided tours of the 286,000-kilowatt station are available from late May to early September.

KELSEY TRAIL
Along this 185-kilometre route (Highway 163 in Saskatchewan, Highway 283 in Manitoba) are trout-fishing streams, nature trails, scenic lookouts and camping and picnic areas. The road winds along the north slopes of the Pasquia Hills, once islands in glacial Lake Agassiz. This 16,200-hectare wilderness is forested with Manitoba maple, mountain ash and evergreens. Only experienced hikers should attempt the unmarked, 16-kilometre trip from the Pakwaw Lake region to the Wildcat Hill Wilderness Area. Cougars, once thought to be extinct here, have been sighted recently in this game preserve.

High bluffs near Nipawin

HUDSON BAY
This community celebrates a forestry festival in early June. Competitions include a semi-truck rodeo and a chain saw sculpting contest.
□ Hudson Bay Heritage Park has four theme areas, each depicting an aspect of local development—the coming of the railway, the development of fur trading, logging and farming.

Cougar

0   4   8   12   16   20 Miles

0   8   16   24   32 Kilometres

Perhaps the most sweeping panorama in northern Saskatchewan is at the junction of the Kelsey Trail and Highway 9. A lookout at the eastern edge of the Pasquia Hills affords a view of the Cumberland Delta, a lush lowland choked with marsh grass and alive with ducks and geese.

The Hanson Lake Road pushes through dense coniferous forests and skirts muskeg and renowned fishing lakes such as Deschambault, Jan and Little Bear. Northwest of Nipawin Provincial Park and Big Sandy Lake the highway passes the lofty blue ridges of the Wapawekka Hills.

Flin Flon Trout Festival

This region's lively communities love celebrations. Many festivals have fishing themes —not surprising in an area where lakes yield trophy-size catches. At Flin Flon, fishing-derby contestants at the June Trout Festival sometimes land winners weighing as much as 18 kilograms. At Nipawin, which calls itself "the northern pike capital of the world," the fishing festival (usually held from late June to early August) offers awards for biggest catch of the day and the week as well as the largest catch of the festival.

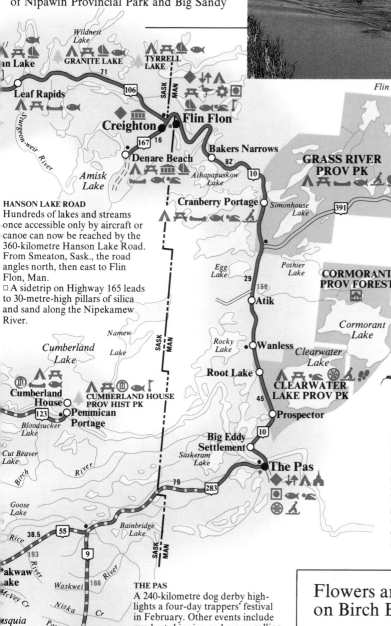

HANSON LAKE ROAD
Hundreds of lakes and streams once accessible only by aircraft or canoe can now be reached by the 360-kilometre Hanson Lake Road. From Smeaton, Sask., the road angles north, then east to Flin Flon, Man.
□ A sidetrip on Highway 165 leads to 30-metre-high pillars of silica and sand along the Nipekamew River.

THE PAS
A 240-kilometre dog derby highlights a four-day trappers' festival in February. Other events include muskrat skinning and moose calling.
□ Opasquia Indian Days in August feature native dances and hatchet- and spear-throwing contests.
□ Christ Church (1896) in Devon Park has decorations from an earlier structure. They were carved in 1848 by a rescue party en route to the Arctic to search for Sir John Franklin's missing expedition.
□ The Little Northern Museum displays Inuit miniature ivory carvings.

FLIN FLON
A six-metre fiberglass statue by cartoonist Al Capp immortalizes this mining town's namesake. In J. E. Preston-Muddock's novel *The Sunless City* (1905), Josiah Flintabbatey Flonatin descends a bottomless lake and reaches a golden city at the center of the earth. Prospector Tom Creighton found a battered copy of the novel on a Churchill River portage in 1908. When he discovered minerals here six years later, he decided this was where "old Flin Flon" had found his golden city.
□ The Hudson Bay Mining and Smelting Co., which offers tours, refines gold, silver, copper, cadmium and zinc.
□ Much of Flin Flon is built on solid rock. Sewer and water pipes are in aboveground wooden conduits which double as sidewalks.
□ Willowvale Wildlife Park has pheasants, peacocks and guinea fowl.

GRASS RIVER PROVINCIAL PARK
A 130-kilometre stretch of the Grass River Canoe Route links 24 of the park's 154 lakes. Rapids and falls are scattered along the way. Kettle holes eroded in rock by swirling pebbles can be seen in the riverbank. This route, traveled by explorer Samuel Hearne in 1774, cuts through *le pays du rat*, a region where muskrats were once abundant.

Josiah Flintabbatey Flonatin statue by Al Capp

CLEARWATER LAKE PROVINCIAL PARK
Spring-fed Clearwater Lake is noted for its remarkably clear blue water. Dissolved limestone particles in the lake reflect light; cold water and a lack of nutrients discourage the growth of plants and plankton. A hiking trail leads to crevices in a 15-metre-high limestone cliff along the lake's southern shore.
□ A small herd of caribou winters in the northern part of adjacent Cormorant Provincial Forest, where moose, wolves and black bears are common.

Flowers and Birds on Birch Bark

Birch-bark biting—an ancient and little-known Indian craft—is still practiced by a few Cree women in northern Manitoba and Saskatchewan. The women fold thin bark into a wedge shape, then bite and rub it with their teeth to produce delicate flower, insect, bird and snowflake designs. Such marks were once used as patterns for beadwork.

The Denare Beach Museum displays and sells birch bark decorated by biting.

High, Green Hills
in a Hot, Dry Plain

Southwestern Saskatchewan

The fascinating, often bizarre Cypress Hills are one of nature's freaks. Surrounded by a sea of shortgrass prairie—sparse, hot and dry—they form a lofty oasis of forests, lakes and verdant pastures.

The hills rise like a narrow wedge above the plains. The thin edge, 1,067 metres above sea level, is near Eastend. The hills extend westward for 100 kilometres and are 1,463 metres above sea level in southeastern Alberta. Two-thirds of their length is in Saskatchewan.

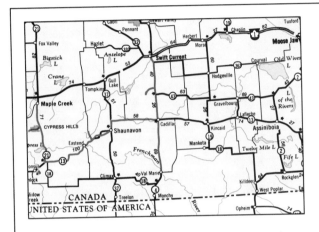

MAPLE CREEK
The "Old Cow Town" is in the heart of the province's ranching country. Northwest of Maple Creek on Highway 1 is a plaque commemorating the "76" Ranch. Organized in 1888, it was one of the largest spreads in the West in the days of the open range. It was broken up in 1921. The office building from ranch headquarters is at the Antique Tractor Museum and Frontier Village south of Maple Creek.
□ Maple Creek's Old Timers' Museum has antique guns, Indian artifacts and an 1890 hand-pumped fire engine.

Hand-pumped fire engine (1890), Maple Creek

CYPRESS HILLS PROVINCIAL PARK
The Gap—a 16-kilometre-wide valley—separates the two sections of Saskatchewan's Cypress Hills Provincial Park. The park's 57-square-kilometre eastern section includes Loch Leven, an artificial lake stocked with brook, brown and rainbow trout. The 148-square-kilometre western section is a provincial forest and wilderness area.
□ At Bald Butte, near Loch Leven, is a view of The Gap. This valley is dotted with knobs (rock and earth pushed into mounds by glaciers) and kettles (depressions formed by melting glacial ice). Near Adams Lake, in the western section, the route passes cliffs of naturally cemented gravel.

FARWELL'S TRADING POST
Abe Farwell's trading post (near Fort Walsh) has been recreated. A warehouse is stocked with furs, tobacco, whiskey kegs and patent medicines, and is staffed by guides in 1870s dress.
□ Assiniboine Indians were killed near here in May 1873 by American wolf hunters. What became known as the Cypress Hills Massacre prompted formation of the North West Mounted Police.

Fort Walsh

FORT WALSH NATIONAL HISTORIC PARK
Two years after the 1873 Cypress Hills Massacre, the North West Mounted Police established Fort Walsh to end the whiskey trade, which fed bad liquor to the Indians and cheated them of their furs.

Named for NWMP Insp. James Walsh, the fort was essential in keeping the peace among Sitting Bull's Sioux. Some 4,000 Sioux escaped into the Cypress Hills in 1876-77 after defeating the U.S. cavalry in the Battle of the Little Big Horn in Montana.

Abandoned in 1883, then burned, Fort Walsh was rebuilt in 1944. For some years the RCMP bred horses there.
□ Reconstructed buildings in Fort Walsh National Historic Park include workshops, a barracks, stable, commanding officer's residence, powder magazine and guardroom. An interpretive center describes a buffalo hunt, the fur and whiskey trades, a policeman's life at Fort Walsh, and the history of the Plains Indians.

Farwell's Trading Post

0	3	6	9	12	15 Miles
0	6	12	18	24 Kilometres	

A broad plateau that caps the hills supports luxuriant grasslands of rough fescue, timber oat grass, bluegrass and bearded wheat grass. In July the plateau is brightened by yellow shrubby cinquefoils, violet silvery lupines and smooth blue beardtongues. Lodgepole pine grows at the highest elevations. French explorers mistook it for jack pine (*cyprès*) and called the hills *Montagne du Cyprès*. This was translated badly into Cypress Hills—although no cypress trees grow here.

Forty million years ago the plateau was a streambed of quartz pebbles and boulders that have since been cemented into a hard, erosion-resistant cap. Narrow north-south valleys cut the plateau into a series of hills. Glaciers have ground the north face of the plateau into steep slopes. Low, rolling hills on the southern face of the plateau merge with the plains.

A lookout near Loch Leven affords a view of surrounding arid flatlands, and of the Great Sand Hills to the north of Maple Creek. These rippled dunes are home to pronghorn antelope, kangaroo rats and western spadefoot toads.

Soaring Storehouses

Clinging to railway lines that crisscross the West, some 4,500 grain elevators give prairie towns their distinctive (and only) skylines. First used in Canada in 1881 at Gretna, Man., elevators replaced low storage sheds. Vertical warehouses take advantage of grain's flow qualities. Gravity, not shoveling, loads railway cars.

Operated by individuals, dealers and co-operatives, elevators have changed little since the early 20th century.

Farmers bring grain to the elevators in trucks. The grain is weighed, graded and dumped into the pit (1). A conveyor (2) carries the grain to one of 20 storage bins (3). For shipment, grain is released into the pit, conveyed to the top, then loaded by chute (4) into a boxcar.

SWIFT CURRENT
One of Saskatchewan's biggest rodeos takes place during Swift Current's Frontier Days Celebration, usually held in late June and early July.
□ Since 1921, the local Agriculture Canada Research Station has been developing forage crops and cereal grains suitable for the semiarid conditions in this region. Tours of the station can be arranged.
□ The Swift Current Museum is principally a natural history museum with habitat displays of local wildlife. It also exhibits pioneer and Indian artifacts.
□ Canada's only helium plant, 12 kilometres north of town, can be toured.
□ The Wright Historical Museum, 6.5 kilometres north of Swift Current, displays pioneer items and a large collection of Third Reich artifacts.

PINE CREE REGIONAL PARK
This campground and picnic area is hidden in a deep ravine. A plaque commemorates John Macoun (1831-1920), a botanist with Sandford Fleming's 1872 expedition, which surveyed possible railways routes across the prairies. One of Canada's leading botanists for 50 years, Macoun made excursions to almost every part of the country to gather botanical and other scientific data.

EASTEND
This town nestles in the Frenchman River valley, here 1.5 kilometres wide.
□ The High School Museum displays a lower jawbone of a double-horned titanothere, the only remains recovered of this prehistoric creature. Similar to a rhinoceros, the titanothere grazed on grasslands 40 million years ago.

Frenchman River valley near Eastend

Black-tailed prairie dog

VAL MARIE
A colony of black-tailed prairie dogs east of Val Marie is protected by the Saskatchewan Natural History Society. Enormous "dog towns" were among the wonders of nature. But man decimated prairie dogs, seeing them as a threat to ranching. Today there are only an estimated 6,000, restricted to a few areas in southern Saskatchewan.

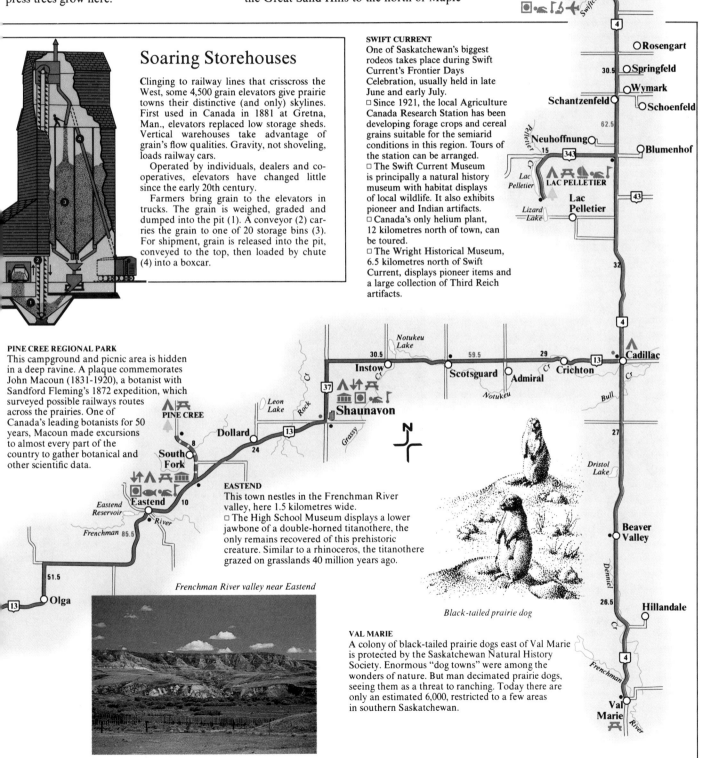

Memories of Desperadoes in the Big Muddy Badlands

South-Central Saskatchewan

Turn-of-the-century outlaws found the Big Muddy Badlands a convenient refuge from the law. The Big Muddy's hoodoos, buttes and secluded coulees were ideal places for losing a posse or hiding stolen livestock.

When drought in 1883 bankrupted many large cattle outfits, some unemployed cowpunchers formed outlaw gangs. Dutch Henry, a rustler, smuggler and horse thief, was chased out of Dodge City, Kans., in the late 1880s. He drifted to Montana and,

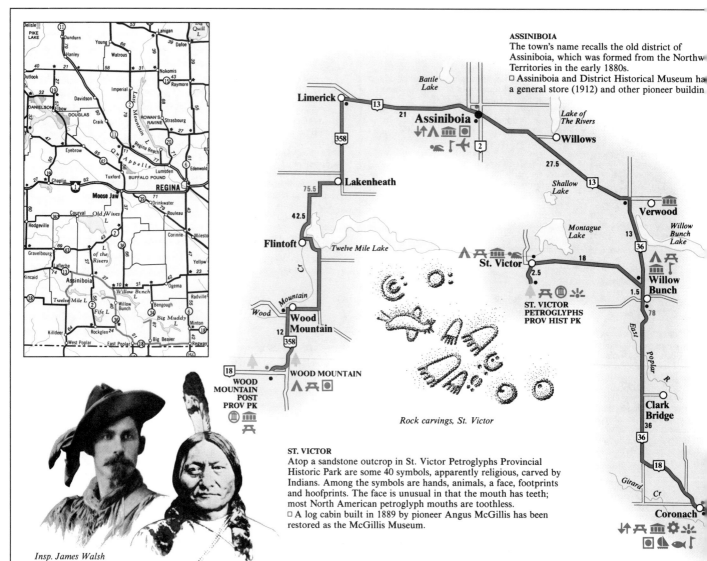

ASSINIBOIA
The town's name recalls the old district of Assiniboia, which was formed from the Northwe Territories in the early 1880s.
□ Assiniboia and District Historical Museum ha a general store (1912) and other pioneer buildin

Rock carvings, St. Victor

Insp. James Walsh and Sitting Bull

ST. VICTOR
Atop a sandstone outcrop in St. Victor Petroglyphs Provincial Historic Park are some 40 symbols, apparently religious, carved by Indians. Among the symbols are hands, animals, a face, footprints and hoofprints. The face is unusual in that the mouth has teeth; most North American petroglyph mouths are toothless.
□ A log cabin built in 1889 by pioneer Angus McGillis has been restored as the McGillis Museum.

WOOD MOUNTAIN POST PROVINCIAL PARK
A barracks and mess hall of a North West Mounted Police post from which Mounties controlled Sitting Bull and his Sioux have been re-created here. After the Battle of the Little Big Horn in 1876, some 4,000 Sioux Indians fled to southwestern Saskatchewan from Montana. Peace was maintained by a handful of Mounties led by Insp. James Walsh, commander of Fort Walsh in the Cypress Hills and of the Wood Mountain outpost. Walsh described the Indian Chief Sitting Bull as "the shrewdest and most intelligent living Indian . . . brave to a fault." In 1881 the Sioux surrendered to American authorities.
□ In the re-created buildings are displays about the life of NWMP and the Sioux at Wood Mountain.

WOOD MOUNTAIN UPLANDS
This plateau is a height of land dividing the drainage systems of the Saskatchewan River, flowing northeast to Hudson Bay, and the Missouri River, flowing south to the Gulf of Mexico. Headwaters of the rivers have eroded deep ravines in the uplands' flanks. Wooded with trembling aspen and pussy willow, these gullies are frequented by sage grouse foraging for seeds and berries. In spring pronghorn antelope and mule deer graze on upland grasses such as blue grama, spear, wheatgrass and wild oat.
□ In the Killdeer Badlands, 32 kilometres southwest, are dobbies—eroded, isolated clay hills that support no vegetation. Some are 90 metres high.
□ The Wood Mountain Stampede is held over two days in July at Wood Mountain Regional Park. The event, first held in 1912, is Canada's oldest continuous rodeo.

```
0    2    4    6    8   10 Miles
0    4    8    12      16 Kilometres
```

between rustling raids, rested in the Big Muddy, just a gallop across the border. He and partner Tom Owens carved two caves—one large enough for horses, the other for men. Nearby was a year-round source of water and, from Peaked Butte, an uninterrupted view of the approaches to their hideout. Henry and Owens were joined here by several other notorious outlaws, including Bloody Knife and Pigeon Toed Kid.

In 1903 Henry and his men joined the Nelson-Jones gang, part of the West's largest and most feared outlaw band—the Wild Bunch. The gangs terrorized ranchers on both sides of the border. In one raid, 200 horses were stolen and herded into Canada. They were sold, stolen again, and resold in Montana. After the gang rustled 140 cattle from the Diamond Ranch Company, a $1,200 reward was offered for the ringleaders.

In 1906 Dutch Henry was shot dead in a gunfight in Roseau, Minn. Bloody Knife was killed in a drunken brawl, Pigeon Toed Kid was shot by a posse and Jones was shot by a U.S. sheriff. Nelson (alias Sam Kelly) was acquitted of murder, in the United States. He died in North Battleford, Sask., in 1954—in bed with his boots on.

WILLOW BUNCH
A life-size papier-mâché model of Edouard Beaupré, an eight-foot three-inch giant born here in 1881, is in Willow Bunch Museum. His clothes, ring and bed are also displayed. Beaupré, 6.4 kilograms at birth, joined P.T. Barnum's circus at age 17. He died six years later.
□ In a regional park southwest of Willow Bunch is a cairn honoring Jean-Louis Légaré, a rancher and trader who supplied food to Sitting Bull's Sioux during their exile in Canada (1876-81).

CASTLE BUTTE
Rising like a fortress from the rolling prairie, this 60-metre-high mound of compressed clay marks the northern extent of the Big Muddy Badlands. Thousands of years ago glacial meltwater eroded soft shale surrounding the butte, leaving an erosion-resistant, flat-topped hill with almost vertical sides.

Big Muddy Badlands

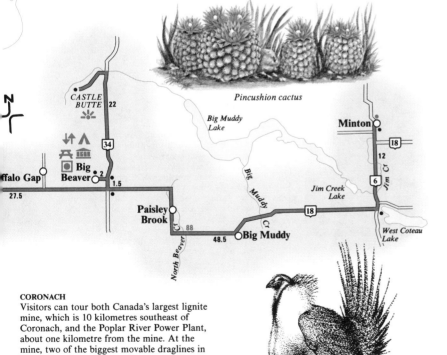

Pincushion cactus

Sage grouse

CORONACH
Visitors can tour both Canada's largest lignite mine, which is 10 kilometres southeast of Coronach, and the Poplar River Power Plant, about one kilometre from the mine. At the mine, two of the biggest movable draglines in North America strip topsoil to expose the seams of soft, brown coal, which fuels the power plant.

BIG MUDDY BADLANDS
This three-kilometre-wide valley of eroded earth and sandstone winds southeast from Willow Bunch to Big Muddy Lake. The region features hoodoos (isolated pillars of rocks), buttes (flat-topped hills with vertical sides), and coulees (stream-eroded ravines). Also seen are the Sam Kelly outlaw caves, the site of a 1902 North West Mounted Police post, and prehistoric Indian buffalo and turtle effigies (outlines made of stones).
□ About a million years ago, the area was a slight depression in the plains. Then glaciers gouged the valley. Meltwater streams such as Big Muddy Creek (today a rivulet) excavated the weird rock formations.
□ Spring comes to the badlands in a rush of color. On dry south-facing slopes, the yellow and purple flowers of prickly pear and pincushion cacti bloom amid white patches of moss phlox. Mixed-grass prairie on western and northern slopes blaze with the western red lily and early yellow locoweed.
□ Soaring above the valley are such bird species as the ferruginous hawk and golden eagle. Mallard, American coot and blue-winged teal nest on Big Muddy Lake in spring.

A Man-Made Prairie Lake and Oases for Recreation

Giant on the South Saskatchewan

Sod house, Elbow

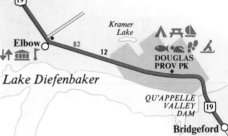

Furnished interior of the sod house, Elbow

ELBOW
Many of the West's early settlers built the walls and roofs of their first dwellings from the most abundant building material available, the deep-rooted sod of the seemingly endless prairie. A replica of a sod house, adjoining the Elbow Museum, was built in 1965. It shows how comfortable the interior (*above*) could be. Furnishings include a hand-cranked record player, a wrought-iron stove, and a butter churn.
□ The Elbow Museum is in a 1908 schoolhouse and contains the original blackboard, desk and organ, and several early bone grinders and coffee grinders.

DOUGLAS PROVINCIAL PARK
Visitors to this park on the eastern shore of Lake Diefenbaker can enjoy camping and picnicking facilities and supervised swimming. Fishing is excellent, for the lake is well stocked with sturgeon, trout, northern pike, perch and walleye. Almost a tenth of the park consists of sand dunes. Some are stabilized by scrub brush, but many are constantly shifting. Other areas of the park are patchily forested with trembling aspen and black poplar.
□ On the road north from the park to Elbow is a small fragment of a 362-tonne rock, venerated by Cree Indians, that could not be saved when Lake Diefenbaker was formed by the construction of the Gardiner Dam. The original boulder was thought to have been moved some 322 kilometres by ice age glaciers. The Cree, believing the rock to be the petrified remains of a buffalo dropped by an eagle, named it Mistusinne and made it a shrine. Archaeologists tried in vain to have the rock moved to higher ground to save it from being flooded. The salvaged piece overlooks the lake that hides the rest of Mistusinne.

Giant on the South Saskatchewan

Gardiner Dam

The earth-fill Gardiner Dam, five kilometres long and 64 metres high, is the largest of its kind in Canada. Begun in 1959 and completed eight years later, it has changed the semiarid face of the South Saskatchewan River valley. Lake Diefenbaker, the 225-kilometre-long reservoir behind the dam, is used for recreation and irrigation.

Visitors to the Gardiner Dam can tour the Coteau Creek hydroelectric station, designed to produce 800 million kilowatt-hours of energy a year. The self-guiding tour includes a view of the huge generating units, an exhibit on the development of electricity, and displays that explain the workings of the station.

A secondary dam, the Qu'Appelle, was constructed in the 1960s at the southeastern end of Lake Diefenbaker to make possible the release of water into the Qu'Appelle Valley.

0	2	4	6	8	10 Miles

0	4	8	12	16 Kilometres

Centuries before the arrival of whites, Indians used the South Saskatchewan River as a prairie highway. They called it Kisiskatchewan—swift-flowing—and so it must have seemed to them as they launched their frail birchbarks upon its wide waters.

Fur traders used the river and its many tributaries to ship pelts eastward in canoes, later in York boats and stern-wheelers.

The idea of damming the South Saskatchewan originated in 1858 when an expedition surveyed the river and proposed that some of its flow might be diverted to form a commercial water route via the Qu'Appelle and Assiniboine rivers. But when the railway arrived in 1885, the need for a water route was no longer important.

During the dry years of the 1930s, the Prairie Farm Rehabilitation Administration was formed to conserve Saskatchewan's land and water resources. The PFRA was the forerunner of the South Saskatchewan River Project, which developed the river for power, irrigation and recreation.

Control of the South Saskatchewan was achieved with the completion of the Gardiner Dam in 1967. Today a hydroelectric station at the dam provides power. Lake Diefenbaker, the man-made reservoir formed by the dam, supplies water for irrigation. Along the lakeshore are Douglas Provincial Park, Coldwell Recreation Area, and Danielson Provincial Park—three recreational oases in a semiarid region.

BUFFALO POUND PROVINCIAL PARK
A stable here provides horses and Shetland ponies for visitors to explore the Big Valley Nature Trail. Along the trail are a ravine where sage and cactus grow, and the Pound Cliff over which Indians stampeded bison to their death to provide food and clothing for the tribe. Some 25 species of birds—including red-tailed hawks and yellow-shafted flickers—can be seen along the trail.

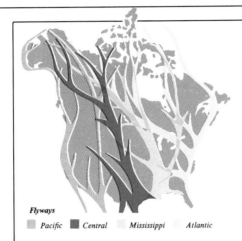

Flyways Over the Continent

The birds that gather by Saskatchewan's lakes and marshes (such as Nicolle Flats) travel the Central flyway—one of four major North American routes used by migratory birds. In spring some 2 million ducks and geese follow the Central flyway to northern nesting grounds. In autumn the birds return to southeastern Texas along the same route.

North America's three other main flyways are the Pacific, Mississippi and Atlantic. Birds on the Pacific route winter mainlay in California. The floodplains of the Mississippi River and the marshes of Louisiana are the principal wintering grounds on the Mississippi flyway. Birds that migrate along the Atlantic coast winter in Florida and the Caribbean. The four flyways intersect over the Peace-Athabasca Delta in northeastern Alberta.

Flyways
■ *Pacific* ■ *Central* ■ *Mississippi* ■ *Atlantic*

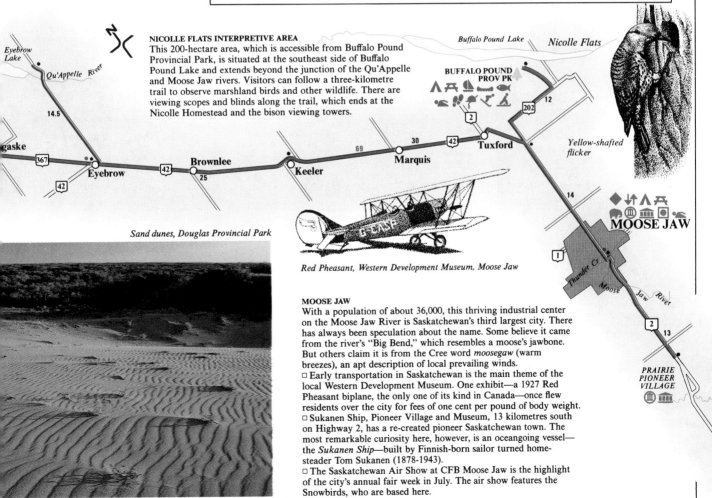

NICOLLE FLATS INTERPRETIVE AREA
This 200-hectare area, which is accessible from Buffalo Pound Provincial Park, is situated at the southeast side of Buffalo Pound Lake and extends beyond the junction of the Qu'Appelle and Moose Jaw rivers. Visitors can follow a three-kilometre trail to observe marshland birds and other wildlife. There are viewing scopes and blinds along the trail, which ends at the Nicolle Homestead and the bison viewing towers.

Eyebrow Lake

Qu'Appelle River

14.5

gaske

367

Eyebrow

42

42

25

Brownlee

Keeler

69

Marquis

30

42

Tuxford

Buffalo Pound Lake   *Nicolle Flats*

BUFFALO POUND PROV PK

2

202

12

14

Yellow-shafted flicker

Sand dunes, Douglas Provincial Park

Red Pheasant, Western Development Museum, Moose Jaw

MOOSE JAW

1

Thunder Cr.

Moose Jaw River

2   **13**

PRAIRIE PIONEER VILLAGE

MOOSE JAW
With a population of about 36,000, this thriving industrial center on the Moose Jaw River is Saskatchewan's third largest city. There has always been speculation about the name. Some believe it came from the river's "Big Bend," which resembles a moose's jawbone. But others claim it is from the Cree word *moosegaw* (warm breezes), an apt description of local prevailing winds.
□ Early transportation in Saskatchewan is the main theme of the local Western Development Museum. One exhibit—a 1927 Red Pheasant biplane, the only one of its kind in Canada—once flew residents over the city for fees of one cent per pound of body weight.
□ Sukanen Ship, Pioneer Village and Museum, 13 kilometres south on Highway 2, has a re-created pioneer Saskatchewan town. The most remarkable curiosity here, however, is an oceangoing vessel—the *Sukanen Ship*—built by Finnish-born sailor turned homesteader Tom Sukanen (1878-1943).
□ The Saskatchewan Air Show at CFB Moose Jaw is the highlight of the city's annual fair week in July. The air show features the Snowbirds, who are based here.

A Little Wood and Water— and a Prairie City Blooms

Central Saskatchewan

For generations Indian hunters heaped buffalo bones near a creek they called Wascana (Pile of Bones). In 1882 the site was chosen the capital of what was then the Northwest Territories and renamed Regina in honor of Queen Victoria.

The "Queen City of the Plains" did not have a regal setting. Sir John A. Macdonald

MANITOU BEACH
Swimmers can float with ease on the buoyant waters of Little Manitou Lake, which is three times saltier than the ocean. Mineral-rich underground streams feed the 19-kilometre body of water. But with no outlet, constant evaporation increases the salt content year by year. This was hallowed ground to the Plains Indians who attributed curative properties to this "Lake of the Healing Waters."
□ Between the world wars, Little Lake Manitou was a popular vacation spot—known as the "Karlsbad of Canada," a reference to a European spa of the day. The main attraction, the Chalet Pool, was eventually destroyed by fire. Today, however, the new Manitou Spring Mineral Pool is reviving the old popularity.

Lewis' wild flax

LAST MOUNTAIN LAKE BIRD SANCTUARY
Established in 1887, this 10-square-kilometre preserve at the north end of Last Mountain Lake is the oldest bird sanctuary in North America. In mid-September it attracts as many as 10,000 double-crested cormorants and 20,000 sandhill cranes. Migrating Ross's geese and whooping cranes stop here. White pelicans and white-winged scoters nest on islands in the lake.
□ Grasslands bordered by trembling aspen and willow here are brightened in June and July by many-flowered aster, goldenrod and harebell.

ROWAN'S RAVINE PROVINCIAL PARK
This 270-hectare recreational park has a ravine seven metres deep and more than one kilometre long.
□ Last Mountain Lake—a narrow, 97-kilometre-long stretch of water—has excellent fishing for northern pike, yellow perch and walleye.

Master's House, Last Mountain House Provincial Historic Park

LAST MOUNTAIN HOUSE PROVINCIAL HISTORIC PARK
Established in 1869, Last Mountain House was a small Hudson's Bay Company post that traded in buffalo meat and hides. Three post buildings—the master's house, the men's quarters and an underground icehouse—have been restored. Interpretive staff guide visitors through the site.

Sunset near Last Mountain Lake Bird Sanctuary

noted in 1886: "If you had a little more wood, and a little more water, and a hill here and there, I think the prospect would be improved."

Farsighted city fathers took Macdonald's advice: when Regina was named the capital of newly formed Saskatchewan in 1905, they decided to make the desolate prairie bloom. A park was established alongside a lake formed by damming Wascana Creek.

Today the park, a verdant playground in the heart of the city, is called Wascana Center. Cycling paths and scenic drives encircle a lake busy with sailboats and canoes. Visitors feed waterfowl in a bird sanctuary. Between the Legislative Building, enhanced with formal gardens and fountains, the University of Regina and a natural history museum, are trees, lawns and picnic areas.

Regina was once dependent on agriculture. But the city's economy has been expanded by the addition of new industries, such as Co-Upgrader, Canada's first heavy oil upgrading plant.

The city's history is interwoven with that of the Royal Canadian Mounted Police. Once headquarters for the force (1882-1920), Regina still has Depot Division, a recruit-training center.

Fountain from Trafalgar Square and Legislative Building, Regina

REGINA

A center of government, business and education, Saskatchewan's capital, population 180,000, is renowned as the home of the Mounties: the force maintains its only training school here.

□ The Dunlop Art Gallery (at the Regina Public Library) presents changing art exhibitions and other programs year-round. Also at the library is the Prairie History Room, which preserves collections of old photographs, newspaper clippings and other records of local history.

□ The Globe Theatre (at the Old Post Office) is the home of Regina's professional acting company.

□ Government House Historic Property features performances of the *Trial of Louis Riel* during summer. Visitors can explore Government House—once the residence of Saskatchewan's lieutenant governors and now restored to turn-of-the-century elegance.

□ Regina Plains Museum (at the Old Post Office) tells the history of the Plains Indians.

□ A monument at Victoria Park marks where Saskatchewan's elevation to provincial status was proclaimed on Sept. 4, 1905.

□ Popular local events include Buffalo Days, a celebration of frontier life (late July/early August), and the Canadian Western Agribition, Canada's largest agricultural show (late November/early December).

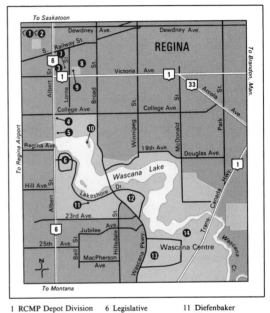

1 RCMP Depot Division	6 Legislative Building	11 Diefenbaker Homestead
2 Government House Historic Property	7 Dunlop Art Gallery	12 Saskatchewan Centre of the Arts
3 Tourist Information	8 The Old Post Office	13 University of Regina
4 Saskatchewan Museum of Natural History	9 Victoria Park	14 Wascana Centre
5 Speaker's Corner	10 Wascana Waterfowl Park	

RCMP "DEPOT" DIVISION

The RCMP Centennial Museum chronicles the history of the force with displays of weapons, uniforms, historic documents and photographs.

□ The Little Chapel on the Square—Regina's oldest building (1883)—has a baptismal fount dedicated to a Mountie killed during the 1885 Northwest Rebellion.

□ At Sleigh Square, there are monuments commemorating the RCMP's centenary (1973), Mounties who died in the line of duty, and the RCMP arctic patrol ship *St. Roch*.

RCMP crest

WASCANA CENTRE

Man-made Wascana Lake is the focal point of 930-hectare Wascana Centre, site of the Legislative Building (1912) and other government and cultural institutions. The center's recreational facilities include bicycle paths and a marina.

□ The boyhood home of former Prime Minister John G. Diefenbaker (1895-1979) was moved here from Borden, Sask., in 1967. The restored three-room frame dwelling (1906) contains Diefenbaker memorabilia.

□ In the Legislative Building, three galleries display portraits of Saskatchewan's prominent historical and political figures. In the gardens surrounding the building is a fountain from London's Trafalgar Square.

□ The Saskatchewan Centre of the Arts is the home of the Regina Symphony—Canada's oldest continuously operating symphony orchestra. The center contains two theaters and a convention hall. Tours are available in summer.

□ The Saskatchewan Museum of Natural History has more than 100 showcase-displays on geology, archeology, history and other subjects. One of the museum's most outstanding features is the dioramas showing mounted wildlife in natural settings.

□ Saskatchewan Science Centre (1989) has, among other themes, "hands-on" exhibits on the living planet and the human body.

□ The Mackenzie Art Gallery (at the University of Regina) exhibits ancient Egyptian sculpture, Renaissance works and contemporary art.

Saskatchewan Center for the Arts

A Tale of Two Settlements Where Coal Is King

Southeastern Saskatchewan

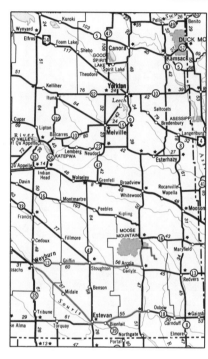

WEYBURN

Mosaic panels set between the spokes of the brass-rimmed mahogany Wheel of Progress at Weyburn's City Hall depict local history.
□ In the Soo Line Historical Museum are Indian artifacts dating from 5,000 years ago. On display are arrowheads, tomahawks, and coupsticks from which scalps were hung.
□ Weyburn is the home of W. O. Mitchell, author of *Who Has Seen the Wind?*, and politician T. C. Douglas, who was Saskatchewan's premier from 1944 to 1961.

Weyburn's Wheel of Progress

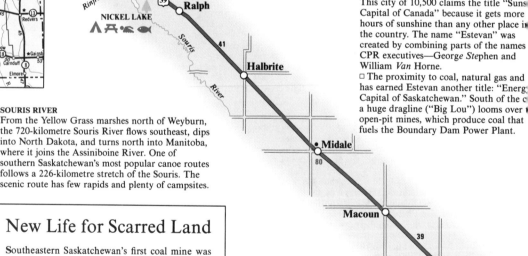

ESTEVAN

This city of 10,500 claims the title "Suns Capital of Canada" because it gets more hours of sunshine than any other place in the country. The name "Estevan" was created by combining parts of the names CPR executives—George *Ste*phen and William *Van* Horne.
□ The proximity to coal, natural gas and has earned Estevan another title: "Energ Capital of Saskatchewan." South of the c a huge dragline ("Big Lou") looms over open-pit mines, which produce coal that fuels the Boundary Dam Power Plant.

SOURIS RIVER

From the Yellow Grass marshes north of Weyburn, the 720-kilometre Souris River flows southeast, dips into North Dakota, and turns north into Manitoba, where it joins the Assiniboine River. One of southern Saskatchewan's most popular canoe routes follows a 226-kilometre stretch of the Souris. The scenic route has few rapids and plenty of campsites.

Open-pit coal mining, near Estevan

New Life for Scarred Land

Southeastern Saskatchewan's first coal mine was a small pick-and-shovel operation begun by a Roche Percée homesteader in 1895. From this developed a network of underground mines. Then in 1930 a safer and more efficient process—strip mining—was introduced. Instead of tunneling and obtaining only 60 percent of the available coal, miners stripped away the earth above a coal seam to reach more than 85 percent of the mineral.

But strip mining gouged the land, destroying the vegetative cover. Soil and rock were left in massive, unsightly piles. To heal these scars a reclamation program was initiated in the early 1970s.

Reclamation is accomplished in three stages. First the spill piles are bulldozed flat. Then the soil is cleaned of rocks, plowed and fertilized. Finally grass seeds are sown and trees are planted. Many reclaimed areas in Saskatchewan are now pastures or wildlife reserves.

BOUNDARY DAM RESERVOIR

Named because its reservoir extends to the United States border, the Boundary Dam has a generating capacity of 882 megawatts—more than any other dam in the province. Its power station houses the largest lignite-burning plant in Canada and has a ready supply of fuel from southeastern Saskatchewan's vast coal reserves. The lignite is used for firing the boilers to create steam and drive the dam's generators. Tours of the dam are available, and swimming and boating are allowed on Boundary Dam Lake.

0	2	4	6	8	10 Miles
0	4	8	12		16 Kilometres

Two sites in this region—Cannington Manor and Hirsch—tell contrasting stories of pioneer days. At Cannington Manor, English aristocrats tried to bring their way of life to the prairie. Persecuted Jews from Europe came to Hirsch in 1892 in search of religious freedom. The two settlements failed—each for different reasons.

Harsh winters and rainless summers doomed the Jewish settlement. By 1894 all but seven of 47 original families had abandoned Hirsch.

The Cannington Manor colony—a "little England on the prairie"—was founded in 1882 by Edward Michell Pierce, a retired British army captain. Here he and his peers lived as English gentry, recreating the grand style of Victorian England. But the settlement failed within a generation. In the late 1890s many of the residents headed for Klondike goldfields, others for battlefields of South Africa to fight in the Boer War. The final blow occurred in 1900 when the CPR bypassed Cannington Manor.

The railway gave rise to new towns and new industries. Coal from underground mines provided fuel for the railway and for domestic heating. In the 1920s, outside competition threatened the local coal industry. But in 1930 the introduction of strip mining—more efficient than underground mining—revitalized the economy of southeastern Saskatchewan.

Bufflehead duck

MOOSE MOUNTAIN PROVINCIAL PARK

Set in splendid isolation above the prairie grasslands, this 400-square-kilometre park is located atop an aspen-forested plateau. The park's hundreds of small lakes and marshes attract blue-winged teal, buffleheads, turkey vultures, white-tailed deer and beaver. A hiking trail and a self-guiding nature trail lead through some of the most scenic areas of the park. Visitors can enjoy swimming, horseback riding, and excellent fishing for pike and perch.

KENOSEE LAKE

This lake, one of the most popular in Moose Mountain Provincial Park, has excellent fishing and swimming, and facilities for canoeing and camping.
□ Among the numerous species of plants found in this area is the western red lily, Saskatchewan's floral emblem. Its flame red flowers, dotted with black, highlight open woodlands and moist meadows in June and July. Each plant bears up to five blossoms, which are so attractive that this lily has suffered badly from overpicking.

Western red lily

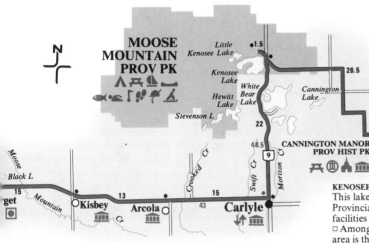

Roche Percée

ROCHE PERCÉE

Sandstone outcroppings here have been eroded by the elements and mutilated by the knives and axes of autographers. The 7.5-metre-high Roche Percée was venerated by generations of Indians who covered it with petroglyphs. In July 1874 Mounties on their march west camped here for four days and carved their initials in the rock. A cairn records that they held religious services here.

CANNINGTON MANOR PROVINCIAL HISTORIC PARK

In the late 19th century, English country life was lived to the full here with horse racing, cricket and tennis matches, billiards and a hunt club. All that remains of Cannington Manor, the colony established here in 1882 by English aristocrats, are Maltby and Hewlett houses, a carpenter's shop and a bachelor's shack.
□ All Saints, a log Anglican church (1884), has been restored. Its collection of antique silverware includes a chalice once used as a racing trophy.
□ In the museum are watercolor sketches dating from 1870, a muzzle-loading walking stick for shooting pigeons and a scale model of Cannington Manor in its heyday.

HIRSCH

This tiny community was one of the first Jewish settlements in western Canada. It was founded by Eastern European Jews who came to Canada in the 1890s in search of religious freedom. Their colony was sponsored by the German philanthropist, Baron de Hirsch. A plaque three kilometres west of the town marks the site of the settlers' cemetery.

All Saints Anglican Church, Cannington Manor Provincial Historic Park

Maltby House, Cannington Manor

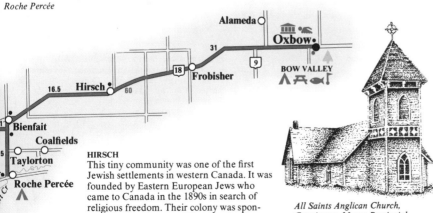

In a Tranquil Valley, Echoes of an Indian Legend

Qu'Appelle Valley

FORT QU'APPELLE
Visitors to the Hansen-Ross Pottery see craftsmen shape Cypress Hills clay into distinctive stoneware. Items displayed are for sale.
□ A cabin used by Maj. Gen. Frederick Middleton during the Northwest Rebellion of 1885 now is part of the Fort Qu'Appelle Museum. The cellars of an NWMP post can be seen on the town's golf course. A plaque nearby records that Fort Qu'Appelle was built in 1875 to protect settlers.
□ At Motherwell Homestead National Historic Park, which is eight kilometres south of Highway 10 at Abernathy, visitors can explore the gracious 1912 homestead of W. R. Motherwell (1860-1943), Saskatchewan's first agricultural minister (1905) and federal agricultural minister in the 1920s.

Hansen-Ross Pottery, Fort Qu'Appelle

LEBRET
Stations of the Cross lead to a hillside chapel overlooking the town, Sacred Heart Church, and Mission Lake. An illuminated cross stands where a wooden cross was placed in 1865 to mark a Roman Catholic mission site.
□ A statue on the grounds of an Indian industrial school commemorates the Rev. Joseph Hugonard, the first principal of one of Canada's oldest Indian residential schools.

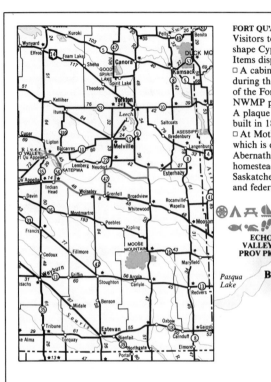

Sacred Heart Church, Lebret

ECHO VALLEY PROVINCIAL PARK
The park is between Pasqua and Echo lakes. Two nature trails enter ravines wooded with maple, poplar, elm and birch.
□ Nearby Katepwa Point Provincial Park offers programs in crafts and organized sports.

From Experiment to Bumper Crop

Through the years, research at Canada's experimental farms, such as the one at Indian Head, has developed crops that give bumper yields. Hard red spring wheat, Saskatchewan's commonest grain, is ideal for bread flour. This variety, high in protein and rich in color, is the major source of income for Saskatchewan farmers.

Durum, the province's second most common wheat, is excellent for making pasta. It is usually grown in central and southern Saskatchewan.

Flax is processed into linseed oil for use in paints. Second only to cotton as a source of commercial fibers, its by-products are used as livestock feed.

Fall rye is used in flour, whiskey distillation and as livestock feed. It is planted also as a cover crop to prevent soil erosion.

Hard red spring wheat   *Durum wheat*   *Flax*   *Fall rye*

INDIAN HEAD
The Prairie Farm Rehabilitation Administration has given farmers millions of trees for shelterbelts since the federal government established the Shelterbelt Centre here in 1902. Visitors can picnic on the grounds, which are planted with flowers and ornamental shrubs. Groups can arrange tours of the greenhouses and arboretum.
□ A round stone stable three kilometres north of Indian Head is on the site of the Bell Farm, established in 1882. The farm was named after Maj. W. R. Bell who managed 100 tenants for the Qu'Appelle Valley Farming Company.
□ In 1887, part of the company's land was sold to the Indian Head Experimental Farm, the first of its kind in what was then the Northwest Territories. Landscaped with trees, shrubs and lawns, and open to visitors, the farm studies crop rotation, weed control and the use of fertilizers.
□ A cairn commemorates the Territorial Grain Growers' Association, founded in Indian Head in 1902. It was the first cooperative established by farmers to improve the shipping and marketing of grain.

The Qu'Appelle River extends across two-thirds of southern Saskatchewan. It meanders eastward from Lake Diefenbaker to join the Assiniboine in Manitoba. The broad and tranquil valley of the Qu'Appelle is best known as a verdant farmland and a well-endowed recreation area.

At Fort Qu'Appelle, the river widens into a chain of sparkling lakes bordered by provincial parks. In this part of the valley, visitors can enjoy swimming and boating. Cottages line The Fishing Lakes—Pasqua, Echo, Mission and Katepwa.

The Qu'Appelle Valley is famous for its poignant legend. The story, told on a marker near Lebret (and in a poem by Pauline Johnson), is of an Indian on his way to see his bride-to-be. The brave was crossing one of the valley lakes when he heard someone call his name. "Qu'appelle?" (Who calls?) he shouted—but only his echo answered. When he reached the camp where his sweetheart lived, he was told that she had fallen ill and died moments earlier. He realized that she had called his name an instant beyond dying. "When the moonrise tips the distant hill," Pauline Johnson wrote in *The Legend of Qu'Appelle Valley,* one seems to hear the echo of the heartbroken brave:

I listen heartsick, while the hunters tell
Why white men named the valley The
Qu'Appelle.

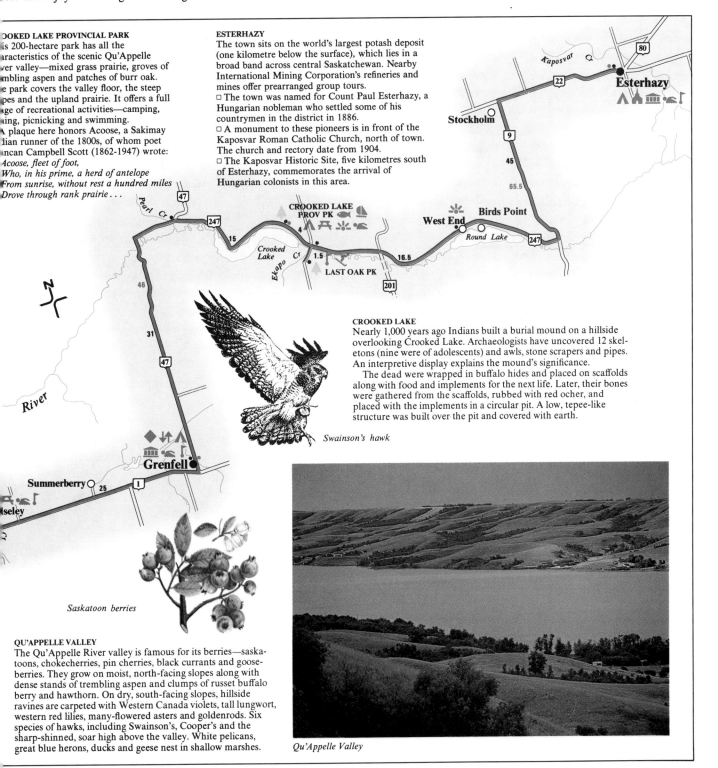

CROOKED LAKE PROVINCIAL PARK
This 200-hectare park has all the characteristics of the scenic Qu'Appelle River valley—mixed grass prairie, groves of trembling aspen and patches of burr oak. The park covers the valley floor, the steep slopes and the upland prairie. It offers a full range of recreational activities—camping, hiking, picnicking and swimming.

A plaque here honors Acoose, a Sakimay Indian runner of the 1800s, of whom poet Duncan Campbell Scott (1862-1947) wrote:

Acoose, fleet of foot,
Who, in his prime, a herd of antelope
From sunrise, without rest a hundred miles
Drove through rank prairie . . .

ESTERHAZY
The town sits on the world's largest potash deposit (one kilometre below the surface), which lies in a broad band across central Saskatchewan. Nearby International Mining Corporation's refineries and mines offer prearranged group tours.
□ The town was named for Count Paul Esterhazy, a Hungarian nobleman who settled some of his countrymen in the district in 1886.
□ A monument to these pioneers is in front of the Kaposvar Roman Catholic Church, north of town. The church and rectory date from 1904.
□ The Kaposvar Historic Site, five kilometres south of Esterhazy, commemorates the arrival of Hungarian colonists in this area.

Swainson's hawk

CROOKED LAKE
Nearly 1,000 years ago Indians built a burial mound on a hillside overlooking Crooked Lake. Archaeologists have uncovered 12 skeletons (nine were of adolescents) and awls, stone scrapers and pipes. An interpretive display explains the mound's significance.

The dead were wrapped in buffalo hides and placed on scaffolds along with food and implements for the next life. Later, their bones were gathered from the scaffolds, rubbed with red ocher, and placed with the implements in a circular pit. A low, tepee-like structure was built over the pit and covered with earth.

Saskatoon berries

QU'APPELLE VALLEY
The Qu'Appelle River valley is famous for its berries—saskatoons, chokecherries, pin cherries, black currants and gooseberries. They grow on moist, north-facing slopes along with dense stands of trembling aspen and clumps of russet buffalo berry and hawthorn. On dry, south-facing slopes, hillside ravines are carpeted with Western Canada violets, tall lungwort, western red lilies, many-flowered asters and goldenrods. Six species of hawks, including Swainson's, Cooper's and the sharp-shinned, soar high above the valley. White pelicans, great blue herons, ducks and geese nest in shallow marshes.

Qu'Appelle Valley

A Rich Farmland That Lured 'Spirit-Wrestlers' from Russia

East-Central Saskatchewan

Settlement in this area of Saskatchewan started in the late 19th century. Each community has woven its own thread into the ethnic tapestry of the province: Russians at Veregin; Germans at Gorlitz; Scots at Kylemore. Evidence of these early settlers is still apparent. In Kamsack and Yorkton, the silver domes of Ukrainian churches gleam like beacons above rooftops. Lively troupes in ethnic costumes perform traditional songs and dances at a fair

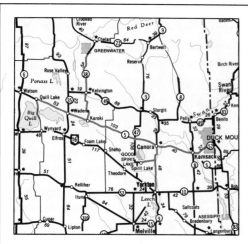

GREENWATER LAKE PROVINCIAL PARK
Birds in this park include great blue herons, which nest on an island in Marean Lake. This tall wading bird, once hunted for its long slender head plumes, now is protected by law. White pelicans, bald eagles, ospreys and several pairs of turkey vultures also nest here. Moose, elk, deer and black bears may be seen throughout the park.

A nature trail follows a creek into highland timber country. Stuffed animals and pioneer artifacts are displayed in a nature center. A plaque honors Henry Kelsey of the Hudson's Bay Company, the first European in this area (1690-92).

Sandhill cranes

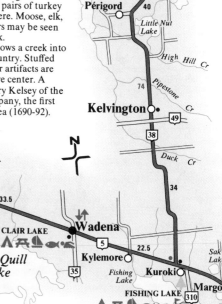

Big Quill Lake

QUILL LAKES
These shallow lakes are fed by streams laden with mineral salt. There are no outlets, and constant evaporation increases the salt content year by year. Although once fished commercially, Big Quill has not yielded a catch since 1934. Little Quill, half as salty as Big Quill, was fished until the mid-1940s.

In summer much of their water evaporates, leaving dazzling white salt flats whose infertile soil supports only the hardiest rushes and sedges, and a few aspen groves.

Sandhill cranes and thousands of ducks and geese on the continental flyway stop here. Indians once gathered goose feathers from around the lakes and traded them for goods at Hudson's Bay Company posts. The quills were then made into pens—hence the lakes' name.

Silverweed

Star-flowered Solomon's seal

Red-osier dogwood

Plants of the Dunes—Roots That Bind the Sand

Few plants survive on the narrow beach along the southern shore of Good Spirit Lake, where sand is tumbled by waves. Fast-growing willows, poplars and grasses take root in sand dunes backing the beach. Yellow-flowered silverweed flourishes in this moist but nutrient-poor soil.

Farther from the beach, red-osier dogwood grows sparsely, poison ivy abundantly. Star-flowered Solomon's seal thrives in steep-sided hollows where moisture and nutrients are concentrated. A blanket of moss protects the sand from wind erosion; its roots bind the soil.

Dense brush on the sheltered back slopes of the dunes gives way to stands of trembling aspen and balsam poplar, and moist sedge meadows.

0   4   8   12   16   20 Miles

0   8   16   24   32 Kilometres

in Yorkton each July. This city's Western Development Museum has rooms furnished in different pioneer styles—an English parlor, a German dining room, a Swedish bedroom.

North of Yorkton, near the site of what was once York City, a plaque tells that in 1882 a colonization company bought large tracts of land for $1 an acre and sold it to about 200 settlers from Ontario. York City was their trading post. In 1890, when the railway was built five kilometres south, the settlement was moved and renamed Yorkton. Millstones near the plaque are from the colony's gristmill.

Doukhobors—members of a Russian religious sect whose name means "spirit-wrestlers"—perhaps fought harder than any other group to retain their heritage. And to little avail. In 1899 some 7,400 Doukhobors, financed in part by Russian writer Leo Tolstoy, emigrated from their homeland. Canada had promised them religious freedom and exemption from military service. Yet Doukhobors resented any interference in their way of life. In 1903 some protested in Yorkton against government regulations that would break up their communal farms into individual homesteads. Some members of the sect eventually complied with the demands. Others sought greater freedom in British Columbia.

Women Pulled Plows in Solemn, Painful Toil

Most Doukhobors who emigrated from Russia to Canada in 1899 arrived penniless. Men from this pacifist religious sect worked at railway construction to earn money. For lack of draft animals, women harnessed themselves to plows. A Russian playwright, Leopold Soulerzhitsky, observed this toil: "There was something solemn and deeply gripping in these womanly figures as they pulled the heavy plow. Thick sticks, tied to the towline, cut sharply into their stomachs, while their sunburnt hands strove to cushion the pain." Some 60 communities flourished briefly around Yorkton. Doukhobors eventually established individual farms and the settlements disappeared.

A Doukhobor prayerhouse in Veregin (*left*) is still used for services. A second-floor museum has a model of a Doukhobor village.

DUCK MOUNTAIN PROVINCIAL PARK
This rolling, lake-dotted upland marks the southern limit of mixed forest in Saskatchewan. Trembling aspen and balsam poplar grow in the park's sandy soil, white birch beside its lakes and streams, and black spruce and tamarack near marshy areas.
□ Rare turkey vultures, which soar gracefully on long, broad wings, are often seen above Madge Lake. White pelicans, bald eagles and great horned owls also inhabit the park.
□ In a nature center are artifacts from Fort Pelly, a Hudson's Bay Company post built in 1824 on the Assiniboine River. A mushroom display includes a seven-kilogram giant puffball.
□ The park's ski area has four downhill runs. About 80 kilometres of scenic roads skirt Madge Lake and lead to fine beaches.

KAMSACK
In town are the onion-shaped domes of Ukrainian Orthodox and Catholic churches, and a Russian-style meeting hall—evidence of settlers who came here at the turn of the century. An abandoned meeting hall, five kilometres south of Kamsack, is all that remains of Voskrissenie, a turn-of-the-century Doukhobor communal settlement.
□ A marker tells of several fur-trade posts built at the Assiniboine Elbow, a pronounced bend in the Assiniboine River about 24 kilometres northwest of Kamsack. The first post was built in 1793; by 1912 all had been abandoned. North of the Assiniboine Elbow was Fort Livingstone, headquarters of the North West Mounted Police in 1874-75.

Turkey vulture

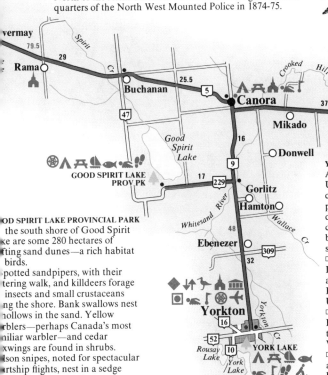

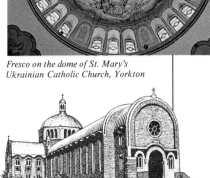

Fresco on the dome of St. Mary's Ukrainian Catholic Church, Yorkton

GOOD SPIRIT LAKE PROVINCIAL PARK
[On] the south shore of Good Spirit [La]ke are some 280 hectares of [shif]ting sand dunes—a rich habitat [for] birds.
[S]potted sandpipers, with their [tee]tering walk, and killdeers forage [for] insects and small crustaceans [alo]ng the shore. Bank swallows nest [in h]ollows in the sand. Yellow [wa]rblers—perhaps Canada's most [fam]iliar warbler—and cedar [wa]xwings are found in shrubs. [Wil]son snipes, noted for spectacular [cou]rtship flights, nest in a sedge [me]adow backing the dunes.

YORKTON
A fresco on the dome of St. Mary's Ukrainian Catholic Church depicts the crowning of the Virgin Mary in heaven. The painting, with a diameter of 19 metres, was done by Stephen Meush in 1939-41. The church (1914) has an icon painted in 1964 by Igor Suhacev, who also designed the sanctuary woodwork.
□ The Yorkton branch of the Western Development Museum has a collection of agricultural implements and vintage cars. Rooms furnished in pioneer style include a Ukrainian kitchen with inlaid cedar chests.
□ A Thresherman's Reunion and Seniors Festival, which has been held annually since the 1890s, takes place on the grounds of the Western Development Museum in mid-August.
□ In late May, the prestigious Yorkton Short Film and Video Festival—the longest running event of its kind in North America—attracts worldwide entries.

St. Mary's Ukrainian Catholic Church, Yorkton

Two 'Mountain' Peaks Overlooking the Prairie

West-Central Manitoba

Great blue herons

DUCK MOUNTAIN PROVINCIAL PARK

Baldy Mountain (831 metres), Manitoba's highest elevation, is one-seventh as high as the Yukon's Mount Logan, Canada's highest peak. A lookout at Baldy's summit offers a panorama of the Manitoba Escarpment to the north and Dauphin Lake to the southeast.

□ Within Duck Mountain Provincial Park, much of it untouched wilderness, are more than 70 small lakes. Six colonies of great blue herons nest in more than 150 sites.

□ Two plaques and a sundial near Wellman Lake honor Polish astronomer Nicolaus Copernicus (1473-1543).

LAKE OF THE PRAIRIES

This artificial lake flooded 72 kilometres of the broad Assiniboine River valley. Asessippi Provincial Park, at the southern end of the lake, contains several eskers—ridges of gravel and sand deposited by subglacial streams.

□ A plaque near the park commemorates the Shell River Mill, built at the townsite of Asessippi. When the railway was built farther south some 50 Ontario homesteaders, who had settled the area in 1883, left and Asessippi became a ghost town.

GRANDVIEW

The Watson Crossley Community Museum displays pioneer artifacts, antique cars and early agricultural equipment. Exhibits include an undated, anonymous book of home remedies with the intriguing title, *Egyptian Secrets.*

Riding Mountain National Park

RIDING MOUNTAIN NATIONAL PARK

Riding Mountain, the focal point of Manitoba's only national park, is part of the Manitoba Escarpment. The park's sharply defined northern and eastern boundaries are some 450 metres above the surrounding farmland. The park's 3,000 square kilometres encompass boreal and deciduous forest, aspen parkland, open grassland and meadow.

□ Near Lake Audy, a herd of bison graze in a 530-hectare enclosure of wood and pasture. An interpretive center describes the bison's role in the development of Plains Indian culture.

Prairie buttercups

ERICKSON

A federal aquaculture field station here seeks to improve a new prairie crop—rainbow trout. The Prairies are dotted with hundreds of thousands of small, water-filled glacial depressions formed some 10,000 years ago. Until recently these potholes were only used, if at all, for watering livestock. The shallow lakes had no permanent fish because of oxygen shortages in the water during winter. In the late 1960s researchers discovered that some potholes could support rainbow trout. In spring farmers and ranchers stock large potholes with fingerlings, which feed all summer on freshwater shrimp, insect larvae and microscopic plankton. In late autumn the fish, then meal-size, are harvested with gill nets, dressed, and sold to local consumers and restaurants. Some 1,500 prairie farmers and ranchers raise rainbow trout, another foodstuff from the breadbasket of the world.

Pothole fishing, Erickson

A great valley separates the low blue ridge of Riding Mountain from the bold outline of Duck Mountain to the north. These "mountains" are part of the Manitoba Escarpment—a series of uplands that angle northwest through Manitoba and into Saskatchewan.

Riding Mountain National Park's varied terrain supports an unusual range of plant life—almost 500 species thrive in meadows, aspen groves and evergreen forests.

The park is believed to be the dividing line of the satyrid butterfly's range. In even-numbered years these insects are seen only east of the park, but in odd-numbered years they are found only west of here—a phenomenon not understood.

More than 160 kilometres of hiking trails lead to remote areas of the park where naturalists conduct wolf-howl sessions on summer nights. Visitors' howls are met with authentic, spine-tingling responses.

Large herds of wapiti and mule deer roam Duck Mountain Provincial Park. The park is also a major nesting ground for great blue herons, turkey vultures and white pelicans.

Manitoba's highest point, Baldy Mountain (831 metres), is in the park's southeast corner. A platform on Baldy's summit affords a view of the great valley to the south, checkered with fields of wheat and sunflowers.

Ukrainian costumes, Dauphin

Traditional Ukrainian Easter basket

DAUPHIN
During Canada's National Ukrainian Festival here in early August, as many as 40,000 visitors attend the *Selo Ukraina* ("Ukrainian Village") about 10 kilometres southwest of town. Professional entertainers perform folk songs and dances in a 5,000-seat outdoor amphitheater. The festival is also an occasion for parading and dressing up in colorful national costumes, and sampling such culinary delights as traditional Easter baskets of *paska* and *babka* (special breads), ham, cheese, and *pysanky*—intricately painted Easter eggs.
□ A bastion and wooden palisade typical of a fur trading post surround the Fort Dauphin Museum. Artifacts include a lamp, pieces of musket barrels, and an ax head from the site of the original Fort Dauphin—a North West Company post on the western shore of Dauphin Lake.

Greatest extent of Lake Agassiz

The World's Largest Lake Left the Prairies' Richest Soil

The world's largest freshwater lake, larger than the present-day Great Lakes, once covered much of southern Manitoba. Lake Agassiz is no more but its legacy includes lakes Winnipeg, Manitoba, Winnipegosis, Dauphin and Lake of the Woods.

During the past 13,500 years Lake Agassiz formed four times as glaciers advanced and retreated. The first two lakes drained to the Mississippi River; the third flowed to Lake Nipigon; the fourth drained into Hudson Bay. Lake Agassiz dried up 8,000 years ago leaving a thick deposit of silt and clay that now is fertile prairie farmland.

Bison, Lake Audy

MINNEDOSA
Nestled in a broad, pastoral valley, Minnedosa has several times been chosen Manitoba's most beautiful town. A dam on the Minnedosa River forms a lake which attracts boaters, swimmers and water-skiers.
□ Summer events include the Country Fun Fair and the local agricultural fair (on the first and third weekends of July) and the Minnedosa rodeo, which includes chuck wagon, chariot and Ben Hur races (on the second weekend of August).

NEEPAWA
At the Manitoba Holiday Festival of the Arts in early July, professional instructors give courses in the visual, literary and performing arts. The works of students and teachers are presented to the public in concerts and art exhibitions.
□ Visitors can learn the town's history on a self-guiding walking tour. The sites that attract most attention are the Beautiful Plains County Court Building—the oldest operating courthouse on the prairies and Manitoba's second oldest public building—and the childhood home of writer Margaret Laurence (1926-1987).

GLADSTONE
A plaque commemorates the Pioneer Trail (also called the Saskatchewan Trail) which crossed the Whitemud River near here. (There are also plaques on the former trail in Neepawa and Minnedosa.) A network of trails crisscrossing the Prairies was used until the early 20th century by Indians, fur traders, surveyors and settlers.
□ Williams Park offers camping and recreational facilities. A nearby pioneer museum is housed in the CNR building.

Secluded Valleys and Sparkling Lakes in a Prairie Setting

Southwestern Manitoba

Visitors to southwestern Manitoba may expect to see prairie stretching to an unbroken horizon. But this region has another face—secluded river valleys, gently undulating farmland, and wooded hills.

Steep, oak-covered slopes of the Pembina River valley in places plunge deep below surrounding prairie. Eroded in bedrock by glacial meltwater, the broad, 160-kilo-

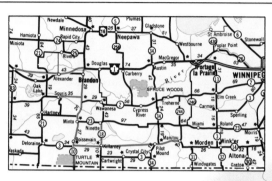

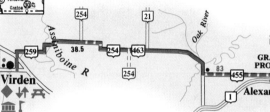

Bronco riding, Brandon

VIRDEN
Discoveries in the 1950s made this the main oil-producing area in Manitoba. Some of the wells are in town.
□ A Victorian residence built in 1888 houses the Pioneer Home Museum. Made of local brick, like many homes in town, the museum is furnished with Limoges china, brass beds, 10-piece ironstone washstand sets, buffalo- and musk-ox-hide rugs, and an 1865 rosewood piano. In an upstairs alcove are two 1880 bridal gowns, items of handmade lace and a nursery containing china dolls.

ASSINIBOINE RIVER VALLEY
Just east of Brandon is a cairn at the former townsite of Grand Valley, a docking place for the "prairie navy"— a fleet of seven stern-wheelers that from 1876 to 1885 sailed the Assiniboine River between Winnipeg and Fort Ellice near the Saskatchewan border. Riverboat traffic declined after the railway reached the area in the early 1880s.

GRAND VALLEY PROVINCIAL RECREATION AREA
Archaeologists have uncovered the remains of a 1,200-year-old Indian village here whose Algonkian-speaking inhabitants were the first Indians known to have migrated from northern forests to the prairies.

SOURIS
One of Canada's longest suspension footbridges (177 metres) is a replica of the original built in 1904 by William Sowden, founder of Souris. Sowden's mansion is now the Hillcrest Museum.
□ Rock hounds can find agates, epidote, dendrite, jasper and other treasures at the Souris Agate Pit, which has North America's largest variety of semiprecious stones. Rockhounding fees are paid in advance at the Rock Shop in Souris.

BOISSEVAIN
Some 100 turtles race in the local Canadian Turtle Derby each July. The contestants must "dash"—in any direction—from the center of a circle to its circumference, 15 metres away.
□ Boissevain has two museums: Moncur Gallery of Prehistory, which contains native artifacts dating back 10,000 years, and the Beckoning Hills Museum, which has pioneer artifacts.
□ Turtle Mountain Provincial Park south of town has 400 lakes and marshes, where migratory birds and western painted turtles (for which the park is named) thrive. Several of the park lakes—for example, Max and Adam lakes—are well stocked with northern pike, rainbow and brown trout. There are campsites, hiking trails, and canoe routes.

Assiniboine River valley

INTERNATIONAL PEACE GARDEN
Opened in 1932, this garden is dedicated to peace between Canada and the United States. It straddles the Manitoba–North Dakota border at a point midway between the Atlantic and the Pacific oceans. Its most notable landmarks are the Peace Chapel, the Errick F. Willis Pavilion (a meeting hall and exhibition area), the 35-metre Peace Tower and the flower clock.
□ The garden, with its sunken pools and profusions of flowers, is the setting for the International Music Camp (June and July) and The Royal Canadian Legion Athletic Camps (July and August).

| 0 | 3 | 6 | 9 | 12 | 15 Miles |
| 0 | 6 | 12 | 18 | 24 Kilometres |

metre-long valley glitters with a chain of lakes—Pelican, Lorne, Louise and Rock—connected by the Pembina River. These lakes attract large colonies of pelicans in summer. A checkerboard of fields borders the meandering river.

The valley winds through the Pembina Hills, part of the Manitoba Escarpment—a series of uplands extending from North Dakota through Manitoba and into Saskatchewan. Fields of oats, wheat and barley in the Pembina Hills are strewn with stones,

remnants of an ancient glacial beach. Bedrock breaks to the surface here to form whaleback ridges, such as the one at Pilot Mound. The hills flatten into a plateau west of the Pembina River valley. Southeast of the plateau is Turtle Mountain whose rolling hills rise to 245 metres above the lowlands. Amongst the hills is a maze of ponds and marshes left by the last ice sheet.

North of Turtle Mountain is the Assiniboine River valley, broadest of the river valleys that cut through the Manitoba Es-

carpment. More than 100 kilometres wide east of Brandon, the Assiniboine River valley has low hills interspersed with broad, flat plains where wheat and rye are grown. The fields are dotted with potholes—circular water-filled depressions—surrounded by reeds, cattails, willows and trembling aspens.

BRANDON

Manitoba's second largest city—its population is close to 40,000—is also the oldest prairie city west of Winnipeg. It was founded in 1882, when the CPR crossed the Assiniboine River.
□ Outstanding among the city's heritage buildings are Brandon Court House (1884), the Paterson-Matheson House (1895), and the Brandon Normal School (1913).
□ At Brandon University, the B.J. Hales Museum of Natural History exhibits mounted birds and animals, Indian artifacts and items relating to pioneer farm life.
□ Guided tours of the local Agriculture Canada Research Station can be arranged.
□ The Commonwealth Air Training Plan Museum commemorates the aircrew training program, which was one of Canada's notable contributions to World War II. The museum (at Brandon Airport) displays historic aircraft.
□ Brandon Allied Arts Council Inc. has an art gallery and a performing art space.
□ Brandon's major annual events are the Provincial Ex (June), the Royal Manitoba Winter Fair (April), and Ag-Ex Manitoba, held at Keystone Centre with the Manitoba Rodeo Championship (late October).

Manitoba's Prehistoric Potters

The Indians who made the 1,200-year old Blackduck pottery unearthed in Grand Valley Recreation Area belonged to a trade network stretching across North America. (In southwestern Manitoba have been found shells from the Gulf of Mexico and the Pacific, and copper from north of Lake Superior.) The influence of far-flung tribes that were part of this network can be seen in the pottery created by prehistoric Manitoba Indians. The commonest kinds of Blackduck containers were large, thin-walled, conical or globular pots used

for cooking or food storage. Bowls, platters, lamps and ceremonial vessels have also been discovered.

The pottery was made from riverbank clay. Sand, crushed rocks or shells were added to reduce cracking during drying and firing. Many Blackduck pots were shaped by lining cloth molds with the clay. (Fabric impressions on the pots tell archaeologists much about prehistoric weaving techniques.) Cord-wrapped sticks were used to decorate the soft clay pots with patterns. The pottery was dried, and then fired in a pit of coals.

Blackduck vessel

Prehistoric Indian arrowheads excavated at Grand Valley Recreation Area

KILLARNEY

Nestled at the foot of a hill wooded with maple and oak is Killarney Lake, once described as "a gem set in jade." Four parks enhance southwestern Manitoba's largest town. In Erin Park is a replica of the Blarney Stone and a shamrock-shaped fountain with a statue of a leprechaun astride a turtle. The old town bell on a cairn honors district pioneers. Erin Park has a beach and public dock.
□ The J.A. Victor David Museum contains pioneer artifacts, stuffed wildlife specimens and an art gallery.

PILOT MOUND

The mound after which this town is named is a 35-metre-high whaleback ridge of bedrock. A plaque records that excavations in 1908 uncovered an Indian burial mound on top of the ridge. In the 1850s Sioux Indians and Métis buffalo hunters battled on the ridge, and Indians once held ceremonial dances there.

ARCHIBALD HISTORICAL MUSEUM

The 1878 log cabin in which suffragette Nellie McClung boarded while teaching at a nearby rural school in 1890-91 is at this museum northwest of Manitou. Refurbished according to the description of it in her book *Clearing in the West,* the cabin has autographed copies of McClung's books.

McClung was a fiery orator. Her motto: "Never retract, never explain, never apologize—get the thing done and let them howl." She led parades, buttonholed premiers and formed the Political Equality League. In 1916, largely through her efforts, Manitoba became the first province to give women the vote. She was the first woman on the CBC Board of Governors (1936-42) and the only woman in the 1938 Canadian delegation to the League of Nations. Despite her active public life, she raised five children and published 17 books.

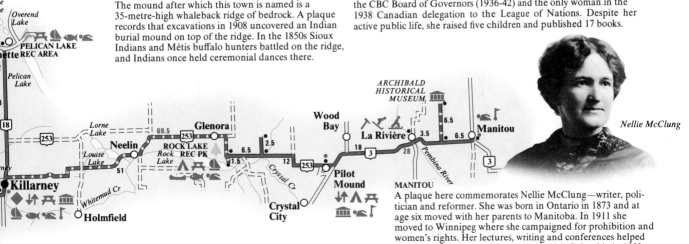

Nellie McClung

MANITOU

A plaque here commemorates Nellie McClung—writer, politician and reformer. She was born in Ontario in 1873 and at age six moved with her parents to Manitoba. In 1911 she moved to Winnipeg where she campaigned for prohibition and women's rights. Her lectures, writing and conferences helped to enfranchise women. She died in British Columbia in 1953.

A Tract of Sand Dunes in the Heart of the Plains

South-Central Manitoba

Between the prosperous prairie communities of Portage La Prairie and Brandon, the Trans-Canada Highway passes through a region of rolling prairie and forest. The contrast with the rich farming plains to the east and west is striking. This region has fewer farms and more open, untamed tracts of land than other parts of southern Manitoba. The terrain was formed more than 10,000 years ago, when the region was the delta of a one-kilometre-wide river that flowed eastward from a retreating ice cap into Lake Agassiz.

Hognose Snakes and Skinks, Creatures of the Dunes

Lizards called northern prairie skinks are found in Canada only in Spruce Woods Provincial Heritage Park and the adjoining provincial forest. The alert little creatures are rarely seen. They winter in deep burrows and seldom venture into the open during summer. Occasionally, however, their tracks can be seen on the dunes of the Spirit Sands—a miniature desert set within a stand of spruce trees. The boldly striped skinks are thought to be a colony separated from the main range of the species, which extends from Texas to North Dakota.

Another unusual resident of the sandhills is the western hognose snake, named for its upturned nose, which it uses to burrow for toads. The hognose's defense when threatened is to hiss angrily (but harmlessly) or, if that fails, to play dead. The nocturnal serenade of coyotes is often heard in the sandhills, especially in June when pups are taught to howl.

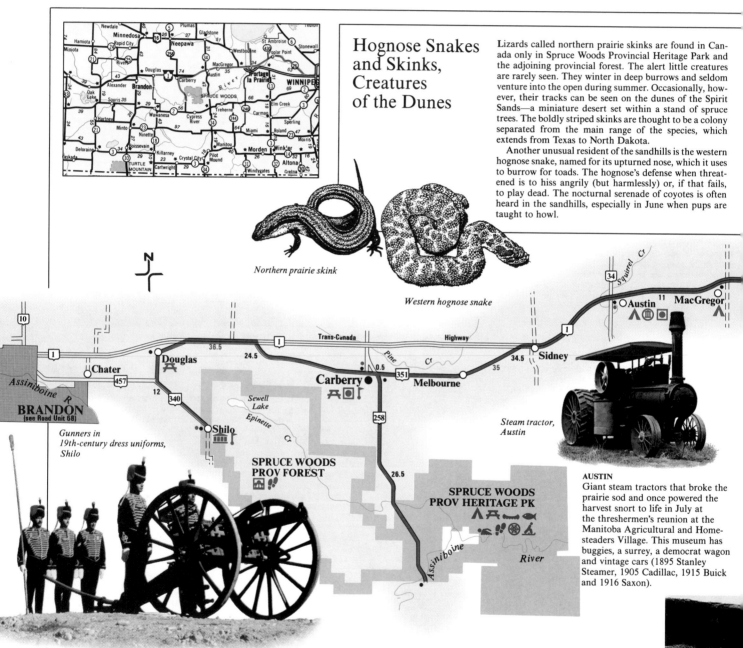

Northern prairie skink

Western hognose snake

Gunners in 19th-century dress uniforms, Shilo

Steam tractor, Austin

AUSTIN
Giant steam tractors that broke the prairie sod and once powered the harvest snort to life in July at the threshermen's reunion at the Manitoba Agricultural and Homesteaders Village. This museum has buggies, a surrey, a democrat wagon and vintage cars (1895 Stanley Steamer, 1905 Cadillac, 1915 Buick and 1916 Saxon).

SHILO
A six-pounder perhaps used by the Selkirk settlers at the time of the Seven Oaks Massacre in 1816 is one of 60 guns in the Royal Regiment of Canadian Artillery Museum at CFB Shilo. Also displayed are the gun carriage used to transport the body of Queen Victoria for burial in 1901, and the plate with which *Punch* first printed John McCrae's *In Flanders Fields*.

SPRUCE WOODS PROVINCIAL HERITAGE PARK
The Spruce Woods area was virtually inaccessible until the park was opened in the mid-1960s. Today the road from Carberry leads to this popular park's outdoor games area, campgrounds, canoe routes and hiking trails. Visitors can take a self-guiding trail through the Spirit Sands to a sunken pit—the Devil's Punch Bowl—which was created by an underground stream. Horse-drawn covered wagon rides through the dunes are available.

| 0 | 2 | 4 | 6 | 8 | 10 Miles |
| 0 | 4 | 8 | 12 | 16 Kilometres |

From a bird's-eye view, the region has a fan-like shape, which extends from Neepawa southeast to Portage La Prairie and south to Spruce Woods Provincial Heritage Park.

The essence of this Manitoban region is preserved in Spruce Woods Provincial Heritage Park, which is about 30 kilometres south of the Trans-Canada Highway. The park's rolling hills are dotted with stands of spruce and basswood, oxbow lakes and blue-green springs. But its most notable feature is a 25-square-kilometre tract of sand dunes—the

Spirit Sands—where cacti grow and lizards lurk. There is no other place like this in Manitoba and indeed few such areas elsewhere in Canada.

After the homesteaders of the 1890s failed in an attempt to farm the region now occupied by the park, the federal government set it aside as a forest reserve, which was acquired by Manitoba in 1930. Spruce Woods Provincial Park—as it was first known—was created from the eastern section of the forest reserve in the 1960s.

Today the park that was once inhospitable to the homesteader has become a welcoming spot for the vacationer. Its rolling hills and sand dunes remain relatively unchanged since the 1880s and 90s, when the British-born author and naturalist Ernest Thompson Seton (1860-1946) first blazed trails here. Seton, working at the time as a naturalist for the Manitoba government, described the locale in his book, *The Trail of a Sandhill Stag* (1899).

Lake Manitoba

DELTA MARSH
A long ridge of sand separates Lake Manitoba from the Delta Marsh, a vast bed of tall, yellow reedlike grasses broken by a maze of shallow bays, sloughs and channels. This 18,000-hectare sanctuary and nesting ground is a haven for mallards, pelicans, Canada geese, and trumpeter swans—and the site of the privately operated Delta Waterfowl Research and Wetlands Research Station. The station is not open to the public.

POPLAR POINT
St. Anne's, an Anglican church here built of logs in 1859, is still in use. Today's worshipers occupy the pews of the first parishioners, Red River settlers who had moved west from what now is Winnipeg. St. Anne's has the original organ, pulpit and chancel and a bell, cast in 1871, that once tolled the hour at York Factory, Man., on Hudson Bay. The log walls are lathed with willow and plastered with lime.

KE MANITOBA
covered in 1738 by Pierre La Vérendrye, Lake nitoba is 40 kilometres wide s southern end and narrows t stretches north. Originally ed Lac des Prairies, its sent name is derived from anitou bau"—or Strait of God—after the narrows t separate it from Lake nnipegosis to the north. Waters he 190-kilometre-long lake in into Lake Winnipeg the Dauphin River.

PORTAGE LA PRAIRIE
Situated in the heart of rich farmland, this city of 13,000 is a prosperous food processing center with a rich history. Its origins go back to 1738, when explorer and fur trader Pierre de La Vérendrye built Fort La Reine here. For 15 years, he used the fort as headquarters while exploring the prairies.
□ Cairns near Portage La Prairie mark the fort site—and the spot where, in 1872, Scottish farmer John Sutherland Sanderson turned the sod of the first western Canadian homestead.
□ The Fort La Reine Museum and Pioneer Village, on the outskirts of Portage La Prairie, has a replica of La Vérendrye's fort, the "Farm of the Century" home (1890), a country church and a schoolhouse of the 1880s.
□ Portage La Prairie's Island Park, which is set in Cresent Lake, has a deer and waterfowl sanctuary, recreational facilities and picnic sites.

Spruce Woods Provincial Heritage Park

Fort la Reine Museum and Pioneer Village

ST. FRANÇOIS XAVIER
A statue of a white horse *(below)* commemorates an Indian legend that such a creature once roamed the plain here. A Sioux and a Cree both sought the hand of an Assiniboine maiden but, with the gift of a rare white horse, the Cree outbid his rival and took the woman as his bride. The Sioux chased and killed both but the horse escaped. The legend grew that, with the woman's spirit in its body, the great beast would inhabit the White Horse Plain forever.
□ The plain in the 1800s was a gathering place for Métis buffalo hunters who supplied pemmican to the fur brigades.

A Comic-Opera Republic

Newly minted silver coins of the Republic of Manitobah, legal tender in Portage la Prairie during Republic Days each May, are like a glitter out of the province's frontier past. The comic-opera republic they commemorate was proclaimed in 1867 by one Thomas Spence (who decided to be president, with his capital at Portage la Prairie). When a shoemaker named McPherson refused to pay taxes—claiming Spence and his council used tax money for liquor—Spence had him arrested for treason. There was a scuffle but McPherson went free and that was pretty well the end of the republic. Belatedly came word from the British Colonial Office that the whole thing had been illegal anyway.

WINNIPEG
(see Road Unit 71)

Where Festivals and Fairs Seem to Be a Way of Life

South-Central Manitoba

Although a new church now serves the community of Gardenton, special services are still held in nearby St. Michael's, the first Ukrainian Orthodox Church to be built in Canada. Twice a year the bells of the old church summon worshipers—a reminder that once this tiny community had no priest and there were services only at Christmas and Easter. Gardenton, like many southern Manitoba settlements, is proud of its ethnic heritage and preserves its past in ritual and celebration.

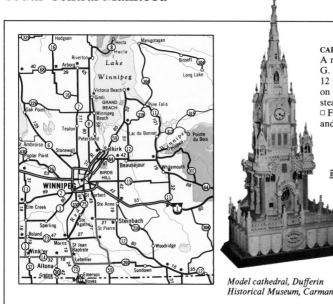

CARMAN
A miniature cathedral, built of balsa wood by handicapped craftsman G. M. Strachan, is in the Dufferin Historical Museum. Strachan took 12 years to carve and assemble the cathedral's 4,514 separate pieces. Also on display is a collection of 24 watercolors by Arthur Brooke, a homesteader of the 1890s, whose work depicts pioneer life.
□ Fiddlers from across Canada and the United States compete for trophies and other prizes during Carman's Fiddle Festival each August.

Model cathedral, Dufferin Historical Museum, Carman

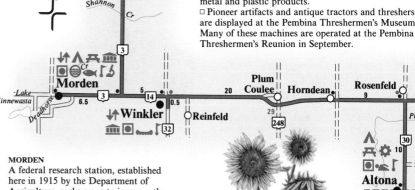

Arthur Brooke watercolor, Dufferin Historical Museum, Carman

Eggs, Skulls and Skins of Mighty Dinosaurs

Dinosaurs thrived here in prehistoric times when this area was covered by a shallow inland sea. They became extinct some 63 million years ago—but their remains, preserved in the shale and sandstone bedrock of southern Manitoba, are frequently unearthed. The first discovery of dinosaur fossils on the prairies was by the Palliser expedition in 1857-60. Since then dinosaur skulls, backbones, eggs and even skins have been found, and more than a hundred skeletons have been removed to museums. The Morden District Museum, which displays bones of birds and reptiles taken from local fossil beds, has among its exhibits the almost complete skeletons of a mosasaur (the largest of these was some 12 metres long) and a plesiosaur, a turtlelike creature with a long neck.

WINKLER
This agricultural town in the heart of the rich Pembina Triangle has developed as a manufacturing center. Its output includes motor homes, recreational vehicles, metal and plastic products.
□ Pioneer artifacts and antique tractors and threshers are displayed at the Pembina Threshermen's Museum. Many of these machines are operated at the Pembina Threshermen's Reunion in September.

Sunflowers

MORDEN
A federal research station, established here in 1915 by the Department of Agriculture, seeks ways to improve the size, quality and disease resistance of local crops. Visitors will see laboratories, an arboretum and more than 3,000 species of plants on the landscaped grounds.
□ In May, Morden celebrates the winter's end with a Blossom Week. Free corn and cider are the ingredients of another Morden celebration—the Corn and Apple Festival in August.

ALTONA
Sunflower seeds, a major crop here, are processed into vegetable oil at the C.S.P. Foods plant (which may be toured). The Manitoba Sunflower Festival in July features soap and sausage making, parades and agricultural exhibits. Traditional Mennonite dishes are served at the festival.

Festivals and rural fairs seem to be a way of life in this region. Winkler's threshermen's reunion, Morris's stampede and Altona's sunflower festival reflect cultural and commercial diversity. The reconstructed Mennonite village at Steinbach reveals the religious way of life of early settlers.

French Canadians, the first settlers in this region, arrived in the 1870s and established such communities as St. Malo and St. Pierre. Immigrants from central and eastern Europe followed soon after, attracted by the promise of religious freedom and the availability of inexpensive farmland.

The land west of the Red River—southern Manitoba's Pembina Triangle—is among the most fertile in North America. Sheltered by the Pembina Hills, it has more frost-free days than anywhere else in the province. Crops that are usually found farther south—potatoes, corn, sugar beets, sunflowers and apples—thrive here.

Farm vacations in this area (and elsewhere in southern Manitoba) are popular with summer visitors. The Manitoba Farm Vacations Association, with some 60 host farms throughout the province, offers holidayers of all ages a taste of country life. Some visitors "live in" with a host family, helping with traditional farm chores and enjoying home-cooked meals. Others camp on farm property. Many farm vacations offer fishing, swimming and riding.

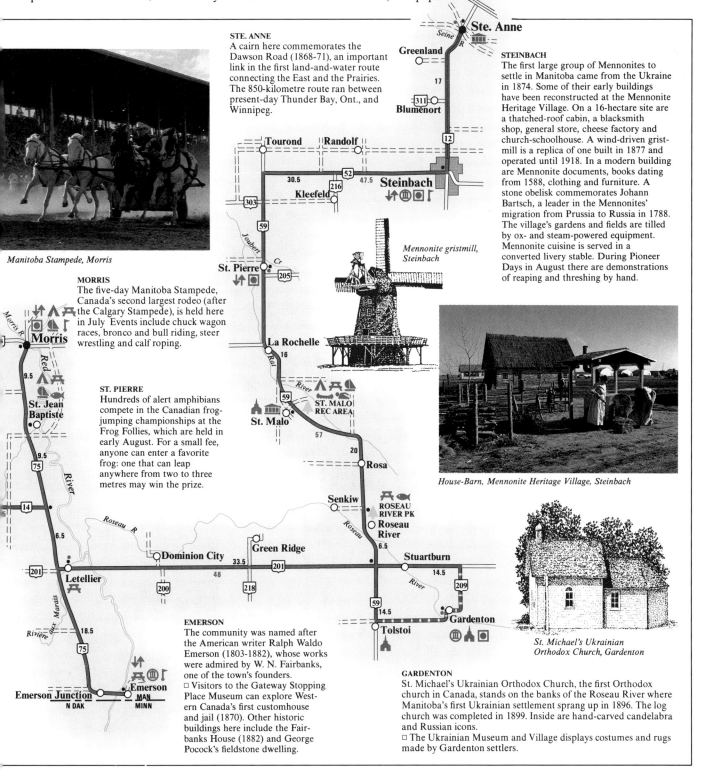

Manitoba Stampede, Morris

STE. ANNE
A cairn here commemorates the Dawson Road (1868-71), an important link in the first land-and-water route connecting the East and the Prairies. The 850-kilometre route ran between present-day Thunder Bay, Ont., and Winnipeg.

MORRIS
The five-day Manitoba Stampede, Canada's second largest rodeo (after the Calgary Stampede), is held here in July. Events include chuck wagon races, bronco and bull riding, steer wrestling and calf roping.

ST. PIERRE
Hundreds of alert amphibians compete in the Canadian frog-jumping championships at the Frog Follies, which are held in early August. For a small fee, anyone can enter a favorite frog: one that can leap anywhere from two to three metres may win the prize.

Mennonite gristmill, Steinbach

STEINBACH
The first large group of Mennonites to settle in Manitoba came from the Ukraine in 1874. Some of their early buildings have been reconstructed at the Mennonite Heritage Village. On a 16-hectare site are a thatched-roof cabin, a blacksmith shop, general store, cheese factory and church-schoolhouse. A wind-driven gristmill is a replica of one built in 1877 and operated until 1918. In a modern building are Mennonite documents, books dating from 1588, clothing and furniture. A stone obelisk commemorates Johann Bartsch, a leader in the Mennonites' migration from Prussia to Russia in 1788. The village's gardens and fields are tilled by ox- and steam-powered equipment. Mennonite cuisine is served in a converted livery stable. During Pioneer Days in August there are demonstrations of reaping and threshing by hand.

House-Barn, Mennonite Heritage Village, Steinbach

St. Michael's Ukrainian Orthodox Church, Gardenton

EMERSON
The community was named after the American writer Ralph Waldo Emerson (1803-1882), whose works were admired by W. N. Fairbanks, one of the town's founders.
□ Visitors to the Gateway Stopping Place Museum can explore Western Canada's first customhouse and jail (1870). Other historic buildings here include the Fairbanks House (1882) and George Pocock's fieldstone dwelling.

GARDENTON
St. Michael's Ukrainian Orthodox Church, the first Orthodox church in Canada, stands on the banks of the Roseau River where Manitoba's first Ukrainian settlement sprang up in 1896. The log church was completed in 1899. Inside are hand-carved candelabra and Russian icons.
□ The Ukrainian Museum and Village displays costumes and rugs made by Gardenton settlers.

Where the West Begins…
a Bustling, Cosmopolitan City

Winnipeg is situated at the "forks" of the Red and Assiniboine rivers—once the meeting place of Indians, explorers, fur traders and settlers. The city's development accelerated with the arrival of the Canadian Pacific Railway in 1885. Within 30 years, Winnipeg grew from a small prairie outpost to a metropolis, an expansion almost unparalleled in Canadian history. The downtown exchange district preserves a cluster of turn-of-the-century skyscrapers—unique in North America—which recall that boom time. The railway brought immigrants seeking opportunities in the wide open spaces of western Canada. Winnipeg was not just a stop on the way out West, it was also the place where many decided to stay. Their legacy is a city enriched by ethnic diversity.

Today Winnipeg is a thriving, friendly provincial capital, home to about 650,000—more than half Manitoba's population. The city's economic strengths are commerce, manufacturing and transportation. Its cultural achievements include first-class ballet, music, and theatre.

Assiniboine Park (3)
In this 152-hectare park, visitors can stroll through the English Gardens and a conservatory with some 8,000 tropical trees and shrubs. Assiniboine Park Zoo has more than 135 bird species and 80 animal species including such rarities as the snow leopard and the Irkutsk lynx. The Tropical House—a miniature jungle of ferns and vines—displays monkeys, reptiles and free-flying exotic birds. The Kinsman Discovery Centre houses a children's zoo.

Centennial Centre (20)
This complex includes the Manitoba Museum of Man and Nature (21) and the Centennial Concert Hall, which is the home of Winnipeg's world-famous Royal Winnipeg Ballet, the Winnipeg Symphony and the Manitoba Opera Association. The Manitoba Theatre Centre (22) is located nearby.

Dalnvert (14)
This restored Victorian house (1895) was the residence of Sir Hugh Macdonald (1850-1929), ninth premier of Manitoba and son of Canada's first prime minister. Costumed guides escort visitors through this provincial historic site.

The Forks National Historic Site (24)
The site commemorates the significance of "the forks"—the junction of the Red and Assiniboine rivers—in western Canada's development. Riverside promenades provide views of this historic and scenic site.

Fort Garry Gate (23)
A small park contains Fort Garry Gate—the last remnant of Upper Fort Garry, built by the Hudson's Bay Company in 1836. A tablet commemorates this fort and others built in the area: Fort Rouge (1738), Fort Gibraltar (1804) and the first Fort Garry (1821).

Fort Whyte Centre
for Environmental Education (6)
Open year-round, the 80-hectare Fort Whyte Centre encompasses lakes, marshes and forest. Two self-guiding nature trails—on boardwalks built over the marshes—provide glimpses of local animals and waterfowl. An interpretive center features wildlife exhibits. The Aquarium of the Prairies displays Manitoba's freshwater fish.

Grant's Mill (2)
In 1829, Métis leader Cuthbert Grant (1793-1853) built the first mill west of the Great Lakes. This working replica of that mill grinds flour for sale or sampling.

Kildonan Park (16)
The best-known attraction in this 40-hectare park is the 2,342-seat outdoor Rainbow Stage, which presents musicals and plays in summer.

Legislative Building (10)
The neoclassic Legislative Building, opened in 1921, was built with Manitoba's Tyndall stone and imported Italian marble. Atop the building's dome soars *Golden Boy,* the famous 4-metre-high gilt figure. Statues of Queen Victoria and other notable figures, as well as a monument to Métis leader Louis Riel (1844-85), stand in the surrounding gardens. The residence (1883) of Manitoba's lieutenant governor is also on the grounds.

Living Prairie Museum (1)
The "museum" preserves a 20-hectare nature reserve of uncultivated tallgrass prairie that once covered much of southern Manitoba. An interpretive center displays wildlife exhibits and offers audiovisual presentations. Guided tours are available in summer.

Manitoba Museum of Man
and Nature (21)
This museum contains seven galleries, which use dioramas, reconstructions and sight-and-sound presentations to depict human life in specific natural settings. The *Nonsuch* gallery has a full-size replica of the first trading vessel to enter Hudson Bay in 1688. The mu-

Broad Portage Avenue (above) is Winnipeg's busiest thoroughfare. More than half the province's total population lives within the city limits. Bronze bison (below) guard the lobby of the Manitoba Legislative Building.

seum's planetarium has a 280-seat Star Theatre, which presents multimedia shows about the nature of the universe.

Manitoba Theatre Centre (22)
Established in 1958, the Manitoba Theatre

Gleaming walls of the Royal Canadian Mint (above) house a coin museum and display of ancient minting tools. Destroyed by fire in 1968, the Roman Catholic St. Boniface Basilica (right) was rebuilt behind the façade of the old (1908) building.

Centre is a recognized leader in Canadian regional theatre.

Pan Am Pool (7)
This sports facility, built for the 1967 Pan Am Games, houses the Aquatic Hall of Fame and Museum of Canada, which exhibits the world's largest sports stamp collections and models of 19th-century ships.

Portage Place (12)
Winnipeg's largest building project (covering three city blocks), Portage Place is a lively downtown shopping complex.

Prairie Dog Central Steam Train (5)
The 1882 steam engine, pulling old-time passenger coaches, makes a two-hour, 58-kilometre round-trip from Winnipeg to Grosse Ile every Sunday, June through September.

Visitors can catch the Prairie Dog Central at the CNR St. James station.

Riel House National Historic Site (25)
The home of Louis Riel's mother has been transformed into a memorial to the Métis leader. The small log house (1880) displays antiques and family possessions.

Ross House (18)
This restored log house—western Canada's first post office (1854)—contains the desk and chair of postmaster William Ross. A cairn in front of Ross House marks the site of Fort Douglas, built in 1813 by the Hudson's Bay Company.

Royal Canadian Mint (28)
This branch of the Royal Canadian Mint (the only one outside Ottawa) produces Canadian and foreign coins. An audiovisual show describes coin production, and a museum displays ancient minting tools.

St. Boniface Basilica (27)
The facade and walls of the 1908 St. Boniface Basilica—gutted by fire in 1968—enclose a 1972 structure. (The original was built in 1818 and replaced several times.) The grave of Louis Riel is in the basilica cemetery.

St. Boniface Museum (26)
Once a Gray Nuns convent, the St. Boniface Museum, Winnipeg's oldest building (1846), displays Franco-Manitoban memorabilia. A nearby monument on the grounds of St. Boniface Hospital honors Pierre de La Vérendrye (1685-1749) and his sons.

Seven Oaks House (17)
Built by merchant John Inkster in 1851-53, the restored Seven Oaks House—Manitoba's oldest residence—contains some of its original furnishings. Inkster's store—next to Seven Oaks House—displays period merchandise.

**Ukrainian Cultural
and Educational Centre** (19)
This organization—comprising a museum, an art gallery, a library and archives—has one of the largest collections of Ukrainian artifacts and books in North America.

University of Manitoba (11)
Founded in 1877, the University of Manitoba is western Canada's oldest university.

University of Winnipeg (8)
Formerly known as United College, this downtown university was created in 1967.

Western Canada Aviation Museum (4)
Canada's second largest aviation museum exhibits a Tiger Moth, Junkers JU52 and a Bristol Freighter.

Winnipeg Art Gallery (9)
This wedge-shaped building contains nine galleries and a 300-seat auditorium. The permanent collection includes contemporary works by Canadians (with an emphasis on Manitoban artists) and many fine examples of contemporary Inuit art.

Winnipeg Commodity Exchange (15)
Established in 1887, the Winnipeg Commodity Exchange—the only commodity and futures market in Canada—deals in agricultural products, gold, silver, and interest rates. A visitors' gallery provides a view of the trading floor.

Winnipeg

1 Living Prairie Museum
2 Grant's Mill
3 Assiniboine Park
4 Western Canada Aviation Museum
5 Prairie Dog Central
6 Fort Whyte Centre
7 Pan Am Pool
8 University of Winnipeg
9 Winnipeg Art Gallery
10 Legislative Building
11 University of Manitoba
12 Portage Place
13 Winnipeg Convention Centre/Tourist Information
14 Dalnvert
15 Winnipeg Commodity Exchange
16 Kildonan Park
17 Seven Oaks House
18 Ross House
19 Ukrainian Cultural and Educational Centre
20 Centennial Centre
21 Manitoba Museum of Man and Nature
22 Manitoba Theatre Centre
23 Fort Garry Gate
24 The Forks
25 Riel House
26 St. Boniface Museum
27 St. Boniface Basilica
28 Royal Canadian Mint

On the Shores of a Vast Lake, a 'Home of the Gods'

Southwestern Shore, Lake Winnipeg

The first sighting of 24,400-square-kilometre Lake Winnipeg may have been by English explorer Henry Kelsey in 1690. Today, Canada's sixth largest freshwater lake presents contrasting shores. The eastern shore—still relatively remote—has the granite promontories and sandy bays of the Canadian Shield; the easily accessible western prairie shore offers holiday beaches and homes, and marshes teeming with bird life.

In the mid-1870s, some 1,500 Icelanders settled at Gimli—the name means "home of

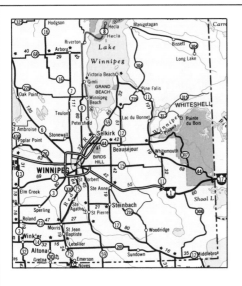

Stefansson Memorial Park, Arnes

ARNES

Vilhjalmur Stefansson, born here in 1879, demonstrated that Arctic explorers could live off the land as the Inuit did. In a memorial park is a statue of Stefansson and a representation of an Inukshuk (an Inuit landmark built of rocks in the form of a man). A quote from his autobiography—"I know what I have experienced, and I know what it has meant to me"—is inscribed on the Inukshuk.

Traditional Icelandic dress, Gimli

GIMLI

The largest Icelandic community outside Iceland, Gimli hosts *Islendingadagurinn* (Icelandic Day) in early August. The *Fjallkona* (Maid of the Mountains) presides over toasts and tributes to Iceland and Canada. Descendants of pioneers wear traditional dress during the festival, which includes drama, poetry, music and athletic competitions.
□ The Gimli Historical Museum displays jiggers for setting nets under ice and a 12-metre whitefish boat, typical of the Lake Winnipeg commercial fishing fleet. Other displays include pioneer household artifacts and the reconstructed log cabin of Alafur Johannsson, the first child born in Gimli.

SELKIRK

A concrete-and-wood replica of a Red River cart in Selkirk Park stands seven metres high (three times actual size). Usually made entirely of wood, the two-wheeled oxcart was the main form of land transportation until railways reached the West.
□ Manitoba's oldest surviving steamship, MS *Keenora* (1897), and CGS *Bradbury* (1915), the only icebreaker to sail Lake Winnipeg, are kept in dry dock at the Marine Museum.

York Boats and Steamboats, Successors to Birchbark Canoes

The York boat was heavier and slower than the sleek birchbark canoe of the voyageurs, but by the 1820s the more cumbersome craft had become the main form of transportation in the West. Unlike birchbarks, York boats were durable—and did not require skilled paddlers. They were propelled by six to nine oarsmen and, on large lakes, by a square canvas sail. Too heavy to carry over portages, York boats were dragged or winched overland on rollers to avoid rocks, rapids and falls. There is an authentic York boat at Lower Fort Garry National Historic Park.

York boats were replaced by steamboats on major western rivers in the 1870s. Steamboats brought freight and passengers down the Red River from the railhead in Minnesota, and then into Lake Winnipeg.

Rocks and rapids in rivers and sudden squalls on the lake made navigation treacherous. The SS *City of Winnipeg,* which offered passengers the luxury of a piano and chandeliers, sank in an 1881 gale.

Steamboat traffic declined on Manitoba's rivers after the railway reached Winnipeg in the 1880s. Today, summer visitors can recapture the excitement of the old-time vessels on the sightseeing ships that sail on the Red and Assiniboine rivers through the heart of Winnipeg. The cruise ships MS *Lady Winnipeg* and MS *Paddlewheel Princess* offer voyages to historic Lower Fort Garry.

A modern stern-wheeler on the Red River

York boat

World's largest Red River cart, Selkirk

the gods"—and on Hecla Island on Lake Winnipeg's western shore. Life at the outset was as hard as it had been in Iceland. Many died of scurvy and smallpox during the first years. Others left after repeated crop failures. The colony that remained enjoyed a brief independence (1878-1881): then Manitoba extended its boundaries north and encompassed the Icelandic settlements.

Eventually, the Icelanders built proudly self-sufficient communities, whose prosperity was based on farms, forest and fish.

They remained relatively remote until the late 1940s when the arrival of road, rail and ferry service ended their isolation.

Summer "colonists" began coming to Lake Winnipeg's southwestern shore as early as the 1890s. The first resort—at Winnipeg Beach—opened in 1903. Today, the Lake Winnipeg holiday area of weekend cottages and campgrounds extends as far as Hecla Provincial Park.

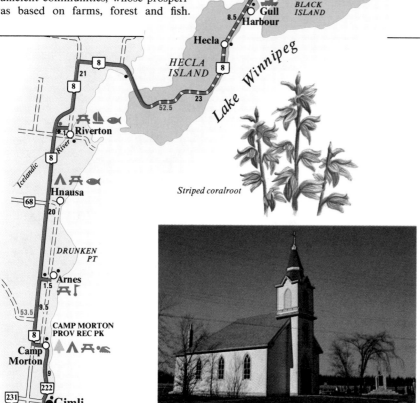

Striped coralroot

HECLA PROVINCIAL PARK
This provincial park consists of islands strewn like stepping stones across Lake Winnipeg. Hecla Island, the park's largest island, has stands of red pine, unusual in northern Manitoba. Trembling aspen, jack pine, birch, tamarack and black spruce are found on the western part of the island. Striped coralroot, a vivid lavender orchid, grows in pastures on the eastern shore, where Icelandic farmers once cut hay. At the southern end of Hecla, marshes support Canada, blue and snow geese, whistling swans, bald eagles, and some 15 species of ducks.
□ Hecla Island is linked to the mainland by a causeway. A ferry runs between Gull Harbour on Hecla Island and nearby Black Island. The park's other islands are accessible by boat.
□ The Gull Harbour Resort and Conference Centre has walking trails, campgrounds, tennis courts and a golf course.
□ The restored Hecla Icelandic Fishing Village—on the road to Gull Harbour—includes a Lutheran church, built in 1922, and other reminders of local Icelandic settlement and tradition.

Restored Lutheran church, Hecla Island

LOWER FORT GARRY NATIONAL HISTORIC PARK
The hustle and bustle of the fur trade is recaptured at Lower Fort Garry National Historic Park, a reconstruction of the Hudson's Bay Company district headquarters from 1831 to 1837.

Costumed personnel bake hardtack, scones and bannock, spin and card wool, and make soap and candles. The sales shop is stocked with the kinds of goods offered to farmers, trappers and housewives a century ago—sugar, tea, traps, rum, guns and Hudson's Bay blankets, and such luxuries as perfumes and spices. In the shop's third-floor loft are a fur-baling press and hundreds of muskrat, beaver, wolf and fox pelts. The Big House was built of local limestone in 1832 for HBC Governor George Simpson. Its fine china, monogrammed silverware and a piano—reputedly the first in the Red River valley—reflect the gracious way of life of company officials.

Southwest bastion, Lower Fort Garry

Storage area, fur loft building, Lower Fort Garry

A Fisherman's Paradise on the Edge of the Shield

Red River Valley/Winnipeg River

Dark and brooding, an endless repetition of rocks, trees and water, the Canadian Shield dips beneath the prairie in southeastern Manitoba. But between prairie and Shield is a vast area of sandy soil that supports jack pine, elm, birch and trembling aspen. A discontinuous chain of provincial forest reserves—Sandilands, Agassiz and Belair—stretches north from the Manitoba-Minnesota border to Lake Winnipeg. Lumber and pulpwood are harvested here for mills on the Winnipeg River,

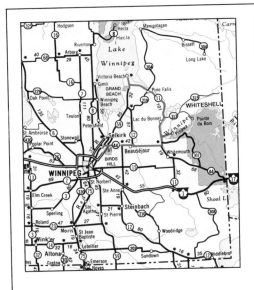

LOCKPORT
The only lock on the Prairies was opened here in 1910. It bypasses St. Andrews rapids on the Red River near St. Andrews and gives access to Winnipeg and Lake Winnipeg. Above the lock is the Red River Floodway. After winters of heavy snowfall, sudden spring thaws often caused the Red River to flood, turning the flat basin around Winnipeg into a vast lake. In 1950, when the river rose 10 metres above normal, Winnipeg suffered a major flood. Today the Red River Floodway diverts floodwaters around the city. Opened in 1968, the channel is 47 kilometres long and is almost as wide as the Red River is at Winnipeg.
□ Also upstream from the lock is the former home of Arctic explorer Capt. William Kennedy (1814-90). The fieldstone and Tyndall limestone house (1866) is now a museum. Kennedy is buried in the graveyard at St. Andrew's Anglican Church.

Tyndall stone quarries, Garson

GARSON
Tyndall limestone, quarried here since 1895 from one of the world's oldest sedimentary rock formations, has been used in many important Canadian buildings, including the Parliament Buildings in Ottawa and the Manitoba Legislative Building in Winnipeg. The grayish limestone contains the fossils of marine animals that lived in warm seas that covered much of North America 400 million years ago.

ST. ANDREWS
St. Andrew's Anglican Church (1849) is the oldest stone church in western Canada continuously used for worship. It has original pews and buffalo-hide kneeling pads. Above the altar is a stained-glass window dedicated to the Rev. William Cockran, missionary and founder of the St. Andrews parish. He is buried in the adjoining graveyard.

St. Andrew's Anglican Church, St. Andrews

Prairie crocuses

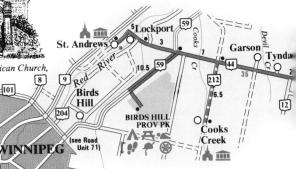

BIRDS HILL PROVINCIAL PARK
Birds Hill is an esker—a long, narrow ridge of sand and gravel deposited by a glacial stream. Settlers took refuge on Birds Hill to escape Red River floods. Today the esker is the centerpiece of a provincial park, an attractive summer setting for picnics, hikes, and horseback rides. In July the park hosts the Winnipeg Folk Festival, one of the biggest events of its kind in North America.
□ The prairie crocus, Manitoba's floral emblem, grows on much of the park's uncultivated prairie. In late summer, grasslands here are dotted with many-flowered asters, goldenrods and blazing stars.

COOKS CREEK
Two buildings here are one man's expression of religious faith—the Grotto of Our Lady of Lourdes and the Grotto-Church of the Immaculate Conception. The Rev. Phillip Ruh, Oblate pastor of the Cooks Creek parish for 32 years, supervised their design and construction in the early 1950s. The grotto, the site of an annual August pilgrimage, commemorates the reported 1858 apparition of the Virgin Mary at Lourdes, France.
□ The adjacent grotto-church has a cluster of ornate Byzantine cupolas.

Grotto-Church of the Immaculate Conception, Cooks Creek

0 2 4 6 8 10 Miles
0 4 8 12 16 Kilometres

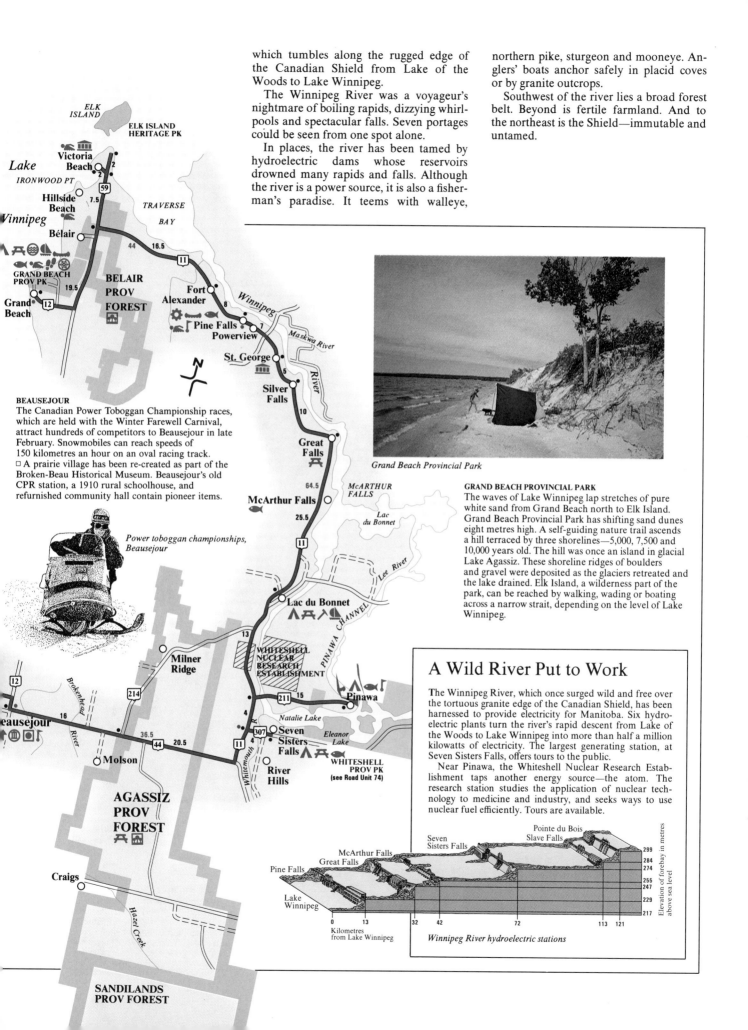

which tumbles along the rugged edge of the Canadian Shield from Lake of the Woods to Lake Winnipeg.

The Winnipeg River was a voyageur's nightmare of boiling rapids, dizzying whirlpools and spectacular falls. Seven portages could be seen from one spot alone.

In places, the river has been tamed by hydroelectric dams whose reservoirs drowned many rapids and falls. Although the river is a power source, it is also a fisherman's paradise. It teems with walleye,

northern pike, sturgeon and mooneye. Anglers' boats anchor safely in placid coves or by granite outcrops.

Southwest of the river lies a broad forest belt. Beyond is fertile farmland. And to the northeast is the Shield—immutable and untamed.

BEAUSEJOUR

The Canadian Power Toboggan Championship races, which are held with the Winter Farewell Carnival, attract hundreds of competitors to Beausejour in late February. Snowmobiles can reach speeds of 150 kilometres an hour on an oval racing track.
□ A prairie village has been re-created as part of the Broken-Beau Historical Museum. Beausejour's old CPR station, a 1910 rural schoolhouse, and refurnished community hall contain pioneer items.

Power toboggan championships, Beausejour

Grand Beach Provincial Park

GRAND BEACH PROVINCIAL PARK

The waves of Lake Winnipeg lap stretches of pure white sand from Grand Beach north to Elk Island. Grand Beach Provincial Park has shifting sand dunes eight metres high. A self-guiding nature trail ascends a hill terraced by three shorelines—5,000, 7,500 and 10,000 years old. The hill was once an island in glacial Lake Agassiz. These shoreline ridges of boulders and gravel were deposited as the glaciers retreated and the lake drained. Elk Island, a wilderness part of the park, can be reached by walking, wading or boating across a narrow strait, depending on the level of Lake Winnipeg.

A Wild River Put to Work

The Winnipeg River, which once surged wild and free over the tortuous granite edge of the Canadian Shield, has been harnessed to provide electricity for Manitoba. Six hydroelectric plants turn the river's rapid descent from Lake of the Woods to Lake Winnipeg into more than half a million kilowatts of electricity. The largest generating station, at Seven Sisters Falls, offers tours to the public.

Near Pinawa, the Whiteshell Nuclear Research Establishment taps another energy source—the atom. The research station studies the application of nuclear technology to medicine and industry, and seeks ways to use nuclear fuel efficiently. Tours are available.

Winnipeg River hydroelectric stations

A Harvest of Wild Rice
in Glacier-Carved Lakes

Whiteshell Provincial Park

Some of the world's oldest rocks, an estimated 2½ billion years old, are along the Winnipeg River in Whiteshell Provincial Park. They are the remains of mountains formed millions of years before the Rockies. Repeated glaciation wore down the mountains' soft rock, exposing the ancient outcrops and shaping the low, rolling hills of the Canadian Shield.

Ten thousand years ago glaciers scraped the rock clean of vegetation. First lichen grew on the rock, and then plant seeds from

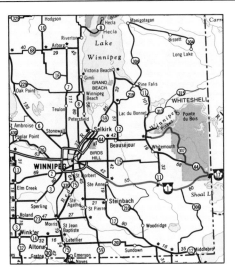

NUTIMIK LAKE
The Nutimik Lake Natural History Museum displays stuffed animals native to the park. Other exhibits include minerals of the Canadian Shield, and Indian artifacts—rock and bone spearheads and arrowheads, stone axes and shell tools. The Pine Point Hiking Trail passes a series of rapids and falls on the Whiteshell River.

Boulder effigies, Betula Lake

BETULA LAKE
A trail near this lake leads to boulder outlines of birds, turtles, fish and snakes made nearly 1,000 years ago by Algonkian-speaking Indians. The boulder effigies are on a broad, barren granite shelf—an ancient Indian ceremonial medicine ground—alongside the Whiteshell River. The largest outline, 7.5 metres long, is of a turtle.

SANDILANDS PROVINCIAL FOREST
Within this forest reserve the Trans-Canada Highway crosses seven sandridges, former shorelines of glacial Lake Agassiz. Tamarack and cedar swamps between the ridges abound with deer, moose, beaver, lynx, wolves and bears. There are hiking, cross-country skiing and snowshoeing trails, and picnic sites along the highway. Hunting is permitted in the reserve and there is fishing in the Whitemouth River for walleye and northern pike.

Sandilands Provincial Forest was established in 1923 to protect ecologically fragile areas. The forest reserve would erode quickly were it cleared for farmland or logged indiscriminately. Controlled logging of mature trees combined with reforestation helps to preserve the area.

RENNIE
As many as 1,000 geese can be seen here in September and October at the Alf Hole Wild Goose Sanctuary, on the Mississippi flyway migration route. An interpretive center has migratory route maps, stuffed geese and an audiovisual presentation. In 1939 outdoorsman Alfred Hole nurtured four abandoned goslings. Their descendants are part of the sanctuary's resident flock.

Canada geese

Black spruce (left) and trembling aspen

SANDILANDS FOREST CENTRE
Near Hadashville, 2.5 kilometres south of the junction of the Trans-Canada and Highway 11, visitors can explore different forest environments—black spruce bogs, eastern deciduous and jackpine forests—at the 120-hectare Sandilands Forest Centre. Other attractions include the Beaven Suspension Bridge across the Whitemouth River, a fire tower, a tree-planting "car," and a museum with displays about local wildlife, logging and forest conservation.

PINELAND PROVINCIAL FOREST NURSERY
Spruce and pine grown here replenish Manitoba forests. Visitors to this nursery, on the Trans-Canada Highway about one kilometre east of the junction with Highway 11, can tour greenhouses and fields. The seedlings nurtured here for three years are planted in burned or cutover areas. The nursery has a picnic area on the Whitemouth River.

unglaciated areas were scattered on the bleak landscape by winds. Ferns such as rusty woodsia cling precariously to crevices. Along streams boiling over jumbled rock grow eastern white cedar, black ash and mountain maple. Tamarack and black spruce border bogs that cover vast areas of the Shield.

Forests of trembling aspen, jack pine and balsam fir are dotted with some 200 lakes. All but West Hawk Lake—formed by a meteor—are glacial depressions. The lakes attract waterfowl that migrate along the Mississippi flyway. Wild rice is abundant in many of the lakes. At harvest time, Indians bend the tall stalks over canoes and flail the rice with sticks.

Prehistoric Indians used boulders to form outlines of animals and humans on the bare granite near Betula Lake, a ceremonial medicine ground.

The pristine lakes were sought by vacationers at the turn of the century when the area could only be reached by rail. Now several highways, including the Trans-Canada Highway, skirt Manitoba's first provincial park, created in 1962. Still much of the park's wilderness interior is only accessible by air or by water.

WHITESHELL PROV FOREST

Pointe du Bois

Eaglenest Lake

WHITESHELL PROV PK

River
Winnipeg
George Lake
umao Lake
Turtle Lake
Crowduck Lake
Betula Lake
Whiteshell Lake
20.5
Molloy Lake
RAINBOW FALLS 2
Little Whiteshell Lake
White Lake
Jessica Lake
Lone Island Lake
21.5
Whiteshell
Rennie River
307
Brereton Lake
Sailing Lake
St. Claire Lake
River
Rennie
2.5
44
Bear Lake
South Cross Lake
20
39.5
THE LILY POND
Caddy Lake
8 312
Star Lake
West Hawk Lake

West Hawk Lake
11.5
Barren Lake
301
17
Falcon Beach
Falcon Lake
FALCON LAKE SKI RESORT
Falcon River
23.5 1
45
st Boggy River
aintree

An Indian Dish, a Gourmet's Delight

It is known by many names but there is no mistaking its nutlike taste. Wild rice—also known as wild oats, crazy oats and weed of the wheatfields—grows in shallow lakes, marshes and slow streams in Manitoba's Whiteshell Park. In late August or early September Indians in canoes harvest up to 200 kilograms of wild rice a day. Long a staple of the Indian diet, wild rice has become a delicacy popular with gourmets.

Hunter's Casserole

INGREDIENTS:

1 cup wild rice	*1 box mushrooms*
6 pork chops	*1 can mushroom*
3 teaspoons fat	*soup*
1 cup chopped celery	*1 cup milk*
1 large chopped onion	*½ teaspoon salt*
1 chopped green	*½ teaspoon oregano*
pepper	*Pepper to taste*

Soak the wild rice in water overnight. Rinse the rice well, using several waters. Using four cups of water to one of rice, boil the rice for five minutes. Drain, rinse, then boil the rice again for 15 to 20 minutes. Drain and rinse again. Put in a casserole. Brown the meat, vegetables and mushrooms until tender. Add seasonings, mushrooms and mushroom soup thinned with milk. Heat well and pour over the rice. Bake for 30 minutes at 350°F.

LILY POND
Named for its myriad fragrant water lilies, Lily Pond (near West Hawk Lake) was carved thousands of years ago by glaciers. One of Canada's sweetest-smelling flowers, the fragrant water lily blooms from June to September. Its white and yellow blossoms open early in the morning and close shortly after noon.

WEST HAWK LAKE
Formed by a meteor some 150 million years ago, this 110-metre-deep lake is Manitoba's deepest. It is stocked with rainbow trout.

Lily Pond, Whiteshell Provincial Park

FALCON BEACH
This town, the focal point of Whiteshell Provincial Park, has riding stables, tennis courts, camping and a golf course. Nearby is a ski resort. Falcon Lake offers boating, waterskiing, swimming and fishing.

EAST BRAINTREE
Eastern white cedar and white and red pine—rare this far north—grow in Northwest Angle Provincial Forest, 40 kilometres south of this town. Granite outcrops rise above the forest's black spruce bogs, where moose often feed. Visitors may camp in the forest reserve.

WHITESHELL PROVINCIAL PARK
Manitoba's first provincial park, Whiteshell is also, at 2,590 square kilometres, one of the province's largest and most inaccessible. Although the Trans-Canada Highway and several provincial highways cross the park, many of its 200 lakes can be reached only by canoe, or by plane from Winnipeg, Lac du Bonnet or Pine Falls.
□ The French explorer Pierre de La Vérendrye passed through this region on his 1733 expedition to the Red River. Today the circular Whiteshell Canoe Route follows part of his journey.
□ Hiking and interpretive trails enable visitors to explore Whiteshell's black spruce swamps and other natural features.

A Boundary of Lakes and a Thundering Waterfall

Northwestern Ontario

Northwestern Ontario offers two contrasting wilderness areas, the Lake of the Woods and Quetico Provincial Park. The former lake has more than 14,600 islands and a 104,000-kilometre shoreline. Ontario, Manitoba and Minnesota share the lake's 4,350-square-kilometre expanse. (At least three quarters of the lake is Canadian.) But only the Ontario portion offers the profusion of islands and the beauty of rocky shores and cliffs; the lakeshore in Manitoba and Minnesota is sandy and low-lying.

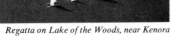

Regatta on Lake of the Woods, near Kenora

RUSHING RIVER PROVINCIAL PARK
The rapids and falls of the Rushing River tumble through this attractive 160-hectare park on the rocky shores of Dogtooth Lake. Thousands of years ago glaciers covered this region. Evidence of glaciation—grooves and scratches, which point in a southerly direction—appears on some surfaces of the park's Precambrian bedrock.
□ Rushing River Provincial Park has canoe routes, hiking trails, and sandy beaches, as well as a visitors' center and nearly 200 campsites.

KENORA
Holiday headquarters for the Lake of the Woods, this pulp-and-paper town overflows with recreational opportunities including boating and sailing, fishing and hunting.
□ Husky the Muskie—a 13-metre-high, 2½-tonne, wood, steel and fiberglass statue of a muskie—dominates Kenora's McLeod Park. This symbol of the Lake of the Woods honors one of its prize catches.
□ The Lake of the Woods Museum features Indian and pioneer exhibits that evoke the region's history.
□ The seven-day Lake of the Woods International Sailing Regatta (in late July and early August) begins and ends at Kenora. The around-the-lake race attracts sailors from all over North America and Britain.

EMO
This farming and resort community claims it has one of the world's smallest churches—the Norland Chapel, which was built in 1973. It can hold only eight people at a time.
□ Rainy River District Museum, organized by the Women's Institute, displays pioneer artifacts. The museum is open from late May to early October.

LAKE OF THE WOODS PROVINCIAL PARK
The discovery that this park was once an Indian stopover and campground was made—fittingly—when the park's Aspen campground was created. The park offers fine fishing and boating opportunities. A natural sand beach, some 100 metres long, is ideal for swimming and sunbathing.
□ Three vegetation zones overlap in the park, an unusual feature of the park. There are hardwoods, such as ash, elm and basswood, usually found in the Great Lakes region; prairie trees, such as Manitoba maple; and spruce and jack pine, typical of northern forests.
□ The park's flat and somewhat sandy terrain is a reminder that, thousands of years ago, this area was covered by the vast glacial Lake Agassiz. Lake of the Woods was the remnant left when Lake Agassiz drained away.

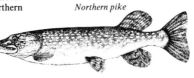

Northern pike

FORT FRANCES
This pulp-and-paper community (pop. 8,870), the gateway to a prime vacation area, is linked by bridge to International Falls, Minn., across the Rainy River. The local Boise Cascade specialty paper plant is open to visitors (reservations are required). Fort Frances Museum exhibits Indian, fur-trading and pioneer artifacts.
□ Pithers Point Park—overlooking Rainy Lake, just east of Fort Frances—contains the reconstructed Fort St. Pierre (the original was built in 1731), *The Hallett* (a restored logging tug) and the Look Tower Museum.

| 0 | 8 | 16 | 24 | 32 | 40 Miles |
| 0 | 16 | 32 | 48 | 64 Kilometres |

Each summer the Lake of the Woods offers ten of thousands of vacationers and cottagers an exceptional choice of recreational pleasures—boating, sailing, fishing, and swimming. The region's resort centers include Kenora and other smaller communities, such as Nestor Falls. Lakeside provincial parks—at Sioux Narrows, for example—invite visitors to delight in this easily accessible wilderness.

The first explorers of this region were the French Jacques de Noyan in 1688 and Pierre de La Vérendrye in the late 1730s. From 1780 until roughly 1840, the Lake of the Woods was part of the chain of waterways, stretching from Thunder Bay to Lake Winnipeg, that served as the main canoe route for fur traders.

Today Quetico Provincial Park preserves the pristine lakes, rivers and forest where the fur traders once traveled. Stands of red and white pine, some believed to be at least 200 years old, still survive here. The park contains the largest concentration of Indian rock paintings in eastern North America. These paintings of men, animals and abstract shapes—whose meaning is as yet unclear—are found at some 30 park sites.

Unlike the Lake of the Woods, Quetico Provincial Park is less accessible to casual visitors. Only one road, just off the Trans-Canada Highway, leads to campgrounds inside the park. From this point, visitors must venture on their own—by canoe or on foot—into Quetico's remote interior.

SIOUX NARROWS PROVINCIAL PARK
Situated on Long Point Island in Lake of the Woods, Sioux Narrows Provincial Park provides the setting for a full range of outdoor activities, including fishing, sailing, canoeing, swimming and waterskiing.
□ Rusty red and orange Indian pictographs—whose meaning mystifies experts—decorate the rocks along the lake.
□ The park and the nearby resort community were named for the narrows. Site of a battle between Ojibway and Sioux in the mid-1700s, the narrows are now bridged by Highway 11.

Mink

NESTOR FALLS
This small resort community offers fishing and water sports. Its 12-metre-high falls can be seen from a lookout on Highway 71.
□ Nearby Caliper Lake Provincial Park preserves one of the few remaining stands of big red and white pine, which were brought to this region by lumbermen from Quebec.

KAKABEKA FALLS PROVINCIAL PARK
Known as the "Niagara of the North," 39-metre-high Kakabeka Falls is the magnificent centerpiece of this 387-hectare provincial park. The park, situated just west of the village named for this waterfall, offers a visitors' center, camping and picnic facilities, and a beach. Lookouts provide views of the falls.
□ Below the falls, rapids are hemmed in by towering black rock walls, and the wind moans eerily through the narrow entrance of this "Cave of the Winds."

ATIKOKAN
This community developed when the rich iron deposits at nearby Steep Rock Lake began to be mined in the 1940s. Today Atikokan's economy is based on light industry and tourism. It is an outfitting center for visitors to nearby Quetico Provincial Park.
□ Local attractions include the Centennial Museum, which is part of the Civic Centre, and the Historical Park, which displays logging and mining equipment.

Round-lobed hepatica

Kakabeka Falls

Quetico Provincial Park

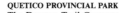

Osprey

QUETICO PROVINCIAL PARK
The Dawson Trail Campgrounds—Chippewa and Ojibwa—are the only sites accessible by car in this 4,662-square-kilometre park. They are located on French Lake several kilometres from the park entrance on the Trans-Canada Highway. An information pavilion at the entrance has displays about the history of the park and its trees, mosses, lichens and wildlife. Three interpretative trails near the campgrounds—each ramble for roughly 2½ kilometres long.
□ Experienced staff will help visitors who wish to venture—on their own—into the park's remote wilderness and to explore its canoe routes (altogether 1,500 kilometres in length) and portages.

Gold-Rush Relics
in a Land of Perfect Peace

Northwestern Ontario

The Canadian Pacific Railway pushed its line through this part of northwestern Ontario in 1879. Gold lured thousands of miners and prospectors here in the 1890s and later, in 1925-26. The gold seekers faced a challenging wilderness, where the tiny pioneer communities often consisted of a collection of humble buildings at a portage or by a railway siding.

Sometimes the existence of these settlements was as brief as the mining boom that had created them. At Gold Rock, near Dry-

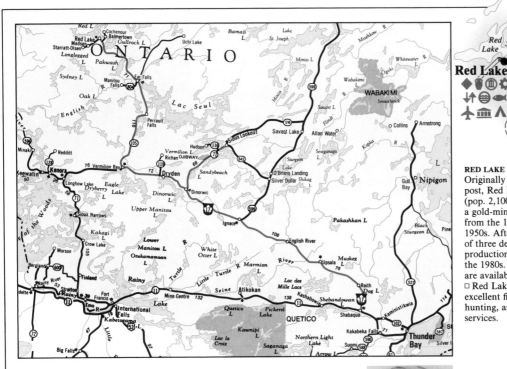

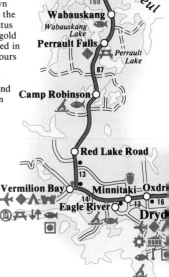

RED LAKE
Originally a fur trade post, Red Lake (pop. 2,100) was a gold-mining town from the 1920s to the 1950s. After a hiatus of three decades, gold production resumed in the 1980s. Mine tours are available.
□ Red Lake offers excellent fishing and hunting, and fly-in services.

A Castle in the Wilderness

At White Otter Lake, some 48 kilometres south of Ignace, a decaying, deserted three-story log castle (with a four-story tower) rises in the midst of the wilderness (*right*). The castle was completed just before 1914 by Scotsman Jimmy McQuat (*top right*), who arrived here as a gold prospector in 1903, but became a frontiersman who earned a living from trapping and fishing. McQuat's motive for building the castle has always been a puzzle. According to one story, the castle was designed for a sweetheart, reputedly a Scottish lady of noble birth. Whatever the motive, the self-reliant Scot built the castle with his own hands. The small, wiry man, who was in his fifties, felled the logs through the bush, squared the sides and dovetailed the ends for a near fit, and then raised the walls and roof. Some claim McQuat carried the heavy imported windows by canoe over 15 portages. McQuat's feat attracted the attention of a writer named Hodson, who described it in a book, *The Hermit of White Otter Lake*. (Contrary to the title, McQuat was a gregarious and hospitable man.) Sadly, McQuat repeatedly failed to obtain the title to the land the castle stood on. To the government, McQuat was just a squatter. The title question was never resolved. In October 1918 Jimmy

McQuat tangled in his own fish nets and drowned. Friends buried him near his log castle.

For more than 70 years, his castle was an empty, decaying shell. In the 1980s, townsfolk from Ignace and Atitkokan campaigned to save the site. Ignace adopted the castle as a civic symbol. Today, adventurous travelers can reach the castle in a day by logging road and canoe, and still wonder at this monument to one man's extravagant dream.

DRYDEN
Founded in 1894, Dryden (pop. 5,500) was named for John Dryden, then provincial minister of Agriculture. Successive provincial governments tried to promote the region's farming potential. But the town's economy is based on lumber products, pulp, paper, printing and tourism. The local pulp-and-paper mill is open for tours.
□ Dryden offers fishing and hunting. "Max the Moose," a 6-metre-high statue, beside Dryden's tourist bureau, honors local big game hunting.
□ South of Dryden, just off Highway 502, an old six-kilometre wagon road leads to the ghost town of Gold Rock, whose collection of rickety structures evokes memories of a mining boom of the early 1900s.

0	8	16	24	32	40 Miles
0	16	32		48	64 Kilometres

Ear Falls Generating Plant

den, an overgrown but well-preserved mining community stands deserted—a testament to the boom-and-bust cycle of the old gold rush days.

Other communities, such as Red Lake, Ear Falls and Dryden, escaped this fate. In 1948, the building of the road to Red Lake opened up a region that had been accessible only by the Lac Seul–English River waterway system. But it was lumber—this region's other major resource—rather than gold that became the local economic mainstay.

Tourism also became important to these communities. Today local outfitters operate fly-in services to fishing and hunting camps on remote lakes of this region, where the call of a loon and the splash of a leaping fish are the only sounds to disturb the perfect peace of a glorious evening.

EAR FALLS

This community came into existence in 1929 when a hydroelectric plant was built on the English River. The town's museum describes the history of local lumbering, mining and transport. Ear Falls is a vacation center for fishing and hunting resorts on Lac Seul and English River. During the 1920s, neighboring Goldpines was a stopover for tugs carrying supplies across Lac Seul for the gold-mining region around Red Lake.
□ Ear Falls is known as "The Bald Eagle Capital of the World." The majestic birds sometimes nest along nearby lakes.

Bald Eagle

Fly-in vacation services, northwestern Ontario

SIOUX LOOKOUT

This community is situated on Pelican Lake, part of the English River–Lac Seul waterway system. It is said that the town's name originated with the Ojibwa who used the local mountain as a lookout to ambush Sioux raiders. Today Sioux Lookout is a service center for communities as far north as Hudson Bay. Forestry is a major local industry.
□ Hunting and fishing are big tourist attractions. The area has plenty of moose and black bear, while the lakes offer walleye, pike, bass, lake trout, and muskellonge.
□ A reconstructed CNR locomotive is displayed in Centennial Park.

IGNACE

This community began as a railway town in 1879. It is named for Ignace Mentour, the guide for the survey team that mapped the CPR route in the early 1870s. The gold rush of the 1890s brought prospectors to the region. Today a revived mining industry (copper, lead and zinc) and forest products contribute to the local economy.
□ Ignace is a fly-in base for fishing and hunting in the vast region to the north. But travelers can also use nearby Highway 599 to reach remote resorts and camps at Savant, Pickle and Central Patricia lakes. No other highway in Ontario goes farther north.
□ Ignace celebrates White Otter Days in August. The town has adopted McQuat's log castle on White Otter Lake as its civic symbol.

SANDBAR LAKE PROVINCIAL PARK

This provincial park, just off Highway 509, has a kilometre-long beach left by a receding glacier thousands of years ago. The shallow waters of Sandbar Lake are ideal for swimming. All kind of boats can use the lake, and small sailboats are popular. There is fishing for northern pike and yellow perch.
□ Hikers can follow the two-kilometre Rock Cliff Trail to a spectacular lookout, which consists of several huge boulders (known as erratic blocks) deposited haphazardly by the glacier.
□ Red bunchberry and bluebead lily grow in the park's woods.

Red bunchberry

Bluebead lily

A Sleeping Giant on the World's Largest Lake

North Shore, Lake Superior

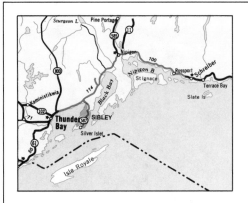

THUNDER BAY

Formed by the amalgamation of the cities of Port Arthur and Fort William in 1970, Thunder Bay is now the third largest port in Canada. This western terminus for ocean-going vessels on the St. Lawrence Seaway handles cargoes of prairie grain, iron ore, coal, potash and sulfur, and forest products. Its 15 terminal elevators can hold more than 2 million tonnes of grain. (Some elevators can be toured.) Thunder Bay is also a center for pulp-and-paper production (mill tours are available) and wood-processing industries.
□ Thunder Bay abounds with parks and lookouts. Centennial Park contains the Bluffs Lookout, which offers a view of the city and the Sleeping Giant. Other superb lookouts are at Hillcrest Park and at 183-metre-high Mount McKay, just south of the city.
□ Old Fort William, southwest of Thunder Bay off Highway 61, re-creates the days when Fort William was the hub of the North West Company's fur-trading empire. Another reconstructed site is the 1910 logging camp and museum at Centennial Park.
□ The Terry Fox monument, east of the city on Highway 11/17, marks the point where cancer forced the runner to abandon his "Marathon of Hope" on Sept. 1, 1980.

Grain elevators, Thunder Bay

LOON

Visitors to the open-pit mine of the Thunder Bay Amethyst Mine Panorama at Eagle Lake can dig their own samples of this semiprecious stone. Amethyst, a variety of crystallized quartz, is used in jewelry. Large pieces of granite faced with amethyst are used as decorative buiding stone.

1 Old Fort William
2 Mount McKay
3 Boulevard Lake Park
4 Centennial Park
5 Terry Fox Monument
6 Chippewa Park
7 Centennial Conservatory
8 Lakehead University
9 Vickers Park
10 Thunder Bay Museum
11 Tourist Information
12 Hillcrest Park
13 Tourist Information

Fort of the 'Great Rendezvous'

From 1803 until 1821, Fort William was the inland headquarters of the North West Company. Every summer thousands of company agents, Indians, voyageurs and trappers gathered at the fort to exchange furs for trade goods during the Great Rendezvous. For the voyageurs who traveled in fur-laden canoes from points as remote as Fort Chipewyan on Athabasca Lake (northeastern Alberta), the Great Rendezvous was a time for revelry. Today the Rendezvous pageant and other special events are reenacted at Old Fort William, the largest historic reconstruction of its kind, just outside Thunder Bay. The 50-hectare site on the Kaministiquia River, roughly 14 kilometres upriver from the original Fort William, is open year-round. The palisades enclose 42 buildings, including the Council House (where company officials conducted business), shops, sheds, jail, farm and hospital. A costumed staff brings to life the fort's bygone heyday.

Piping visitors into Fort William Historical Park

SILVER ISLET

This dot of rock, some 24 metres in diameter and never more than 2.5 metres above the water, became Canada's first major source of silver when a vertical vein was discovered in 1868. More than $3,000,000 worth of ore was mined before 1884, when the shaft reached a depth of 450 metres and it became impossible to keep the water out of it.

| 0 | 2 | 4 | 6 | 8 | 10 | Miles |
| 0 | 4 | 8 | 12 | 16 | Kilometres |

The high rocky cliffs of the Canadian Shield rim the north shore of Lake Superior, the world's largest freshwater lake. Roughly a third of its 82,000 square kilometres lies in Canada.

From the late 17th century, the canoe route of voyageurs and fur traders hugged the northern shoreline of Lake Superior. At the western end of the lake the adventurers paused at Kaministiquia—later Fort William and now Thunder Bay. With the opening of the ship canal at Sault Ste. Marie

in 1855, steamers with huge cargoes of grain and iron ore began to ply the open waters of this vast and often restless sea.

Today the Trans-Canada Highway skirts the north shore of Lake Superior. From vantage points along the road, visitors can gaze at the grandeur of the lake and its surroundings, and perhaps glimpse the oceangoing vessels—successors to yesterday's steamers—skimming its surface.

The Trans-Canada connects Thunder Bay and its lively urban features with the recrea-

tional opportunities of Lake Superior's north shore. It also leads to the region's natural attractions—dense forests, swift rivers, silvery cascades and majestic outcrops of the world's oldest rocks. Two of the most remarkable of these attractions are the Sleeping Giant—a range of high cliffs whose distant outline resembles a reclining figure—and the mysterious five-kilometre-long Ouimet Canyon, which may be a crack in the earth's crust or a creation of ancient glaciers.

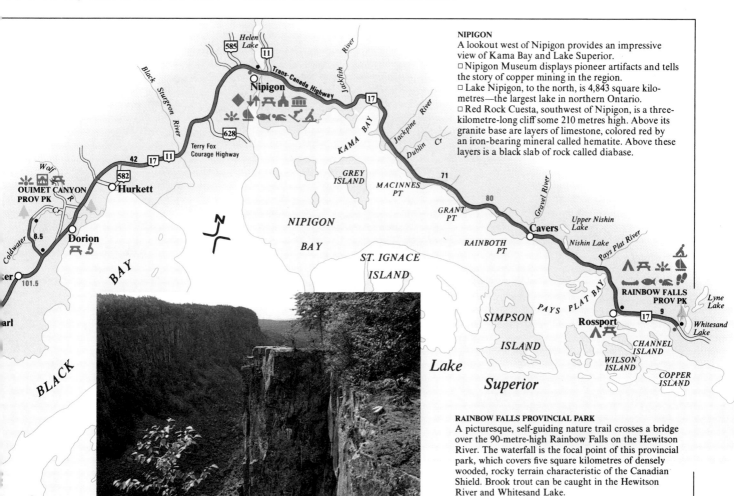

Ouimet Canyon

NIPIGON
A lookout west of Nipigon provides an impressive view of Kama Bay and Lake Superior.
□ Nipigon Museum displays pioneer artifacts and tells the story of copper mining in the region.
□ Lake Nipigon, to the north, is 4,843 square kilometres—the largest lake in northern Ontario.
□ Red Rock Cuesta, southwest of Nipigon, is a three-kilometre-long cliff some 210 metres high. Above its granite base are layers of limestone, colored red by an iron-bearing mineral called hematite. Above these layers is a black slab of rock called diabase.

RAINBOW FALLS PROVINCIAL PARK
A picturesque, self-guiding nature trail crosses a bridge over the 90-metre-high Rainbow Falls on the Hewitson River. The waterfall is the focal point of this provincial park, which covers five square kilometres of densely wooded, rocky terrain characteristic of the Canadian Shield. Brook trout can be caught in the Hewitson River and Whitesand Lake.
□ There are camp sites for tents and trailers in the park and at nearby Rossport Provincial Campground.

[SL]EEPING GIANT PROVINCIAL PARK
[Th]is 243-square-kilometre park occupies most of Sibley [Pe]ninsula. At the southwest corner of the park lies the [Sl]eeping Giant, whose mesas rise to more than 300 metres. [Fr]om Thunder Bay, 25 kilometres away, the mesas [re]semble a huge reclining figure.) Atop the Giant's chest, [th]ere is a view of Lake Superior and Sibley [Pe]ninsula.
[ ] Each of the park's six nature [tr]ails offers some special [att]raction. The Pineywood Hills [tr]ail, for example, has a moose-[wa]tching site above Joeboy Lake.
[Of] the park's nine blazed hiking [tr]ails, the Kabeyun offers a one-[da]y trek along the west coast [of] Sibley Peninsula.

Flying squirrel

OUIMET CANYON PROVINCIAL PARK
This park preserves Ouimet Canyon, a spectacular tree-lined gorge whose sheer cliffs plunge more than 100 metres to rock piles at the floor of the canyon. Several plant species usually found only in the Arctic grow on the canyon floor, which is kept cold by winter ice that persists into summer. Arctic wintergreen and several species of northern liverwort grow among thick carpets of moss. Pussy willows, normally upright, grow horizontally. Stunted cedar and birch trees are also found along the canyon floor. Gnarled jack pine and spruce protrude from the canyon's rim. Looming out of the base of the gorge near the west wall is a high rock pinnacle named Indian Head for its resemblance to a human profile.
□ Ouimet Canyon is 150 metres wide and nearly five kilometres long. There are no camping facilities in the eight-square-kilometre park. A kilometre-long trail leads from a parking lot to the rim of the canyon. Signs warn visitors to explore with caution: there are no fences along the rim and trails that skirt it are often slippery.

Common raven

Furs and Rails in a
Vast Northern Wilderness

North Shore, Lake Superior

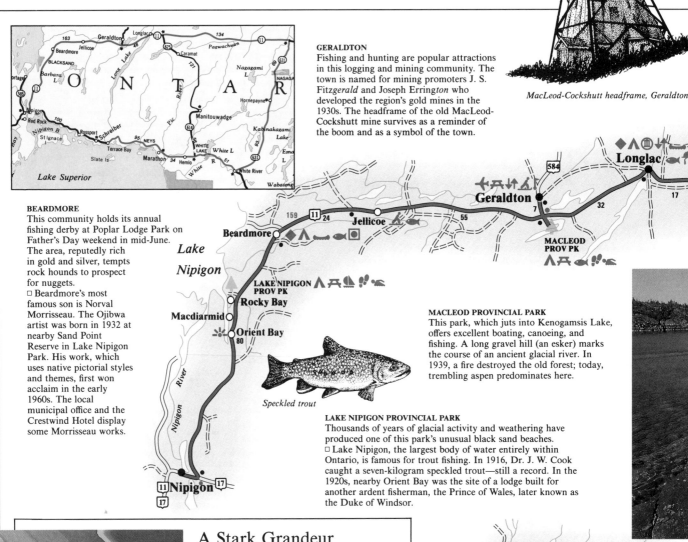

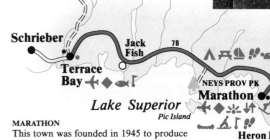

MacLeod-Cockshutt headframe, Geraldton

GERALDTON
Fishing and hunting are popular attractions in this logging and mining community. The town is named for mining promoters J. S. Fitz*gerald* and Joseph Erring*ton* who developed the region's gold mines in the 1930s. The headframe of the old MacLeod-Cockshutt mine survives as a reminder of the boom and as a symbol of the town.

BEARDMORE
This community holds its annual fishing derby at Poplar Lodge Park on Father's Day weekend in mid-June. The area, reputedly rich in gold and silver, tempts rock hounds to prospect for nuggets.
□ Beardmore's most famous son is Norval Morrisseau. The Ojibwa artist was born in 1932 at nearby Sand Point Reserve in Lake Nipigon Park. His work, which uses native pictorial styles and themes, first won acclaim in the early 1960s. The local municipal office and the Crestwind Hotel display some Morrisseau works.

Speckled trout

MACLEOD PROVINCIAL PARK
This park, which juts into Kenogamsis Lake, offers excellent boating, canoeing, and fishing. A long gravel hill (an esker) marks the course of an ancient glacial river. In 1939, a fire destroyed the old forest; today, trembling aspen predominates here.

LAKE NIPIGON PROVINCIAL PARK
Thousands of years of glacial activity and weathering have produced one of this park's unusual black sand beaches.
□ Lake Nipigon, the largest body of water entirely within Ontario, is famous for trout fishing. In 1916, Dr. J. W. Cook caught a seven-kilogram speckled trout—still a record. In the 1920s, nearby Orient Bay was the site of a lodge built for another ardent fisherman, the Prince of Wales, later known as the Duke of Windsor.

A Stark Grandeur That Inspired Painters

Situated on Coldwell Peninsula, Neys Provincial Park preserves a pristine stretch of the North Shore of Lake Superior that once inspired Lawren Harris, A. Y. Jackson and other painters of the Toronto-based Group of Seven. Harris and Jackson visited Schrieber and Rossport for the first time while on a sketching trip in the fall of 1921. Harris was so profoundly impressed by what he saw that he returned to the Coldwell Peninsula area on several occasions between 1922 and 1924. His bold vision of this rugged region, exemplified by the 1926 painting *North Shore, Lake Superior* (*left*) and other monumental canvases, has imprinted its image of stark grandeur on the Canadian imagination.

MARATHON
This town was founded in 1945 to produce pulp and paper. During the 1980s, the dormant economy revived when the original mill was modernized and gold was discovered locally.
□ Marathon is the gateway to Pukaskwa National Park, south on Highway 627, and Neys Provincial Park, east on the Trans-Canada Highway.

| 0 | 4 | 8 | 12 | 16 | 20 Miles |
| 0 | 8 | 16 | 24 | 32 Kilometres |

This route from Nipigon to Hornepayne passes through a region that developed only in this century. Until the arrival of the railway, the Lake Superior hinterland was a realm of explorers and fur traders. From the early 1760s until the 1820s, the interests of the Montreal-based North West Company and the Hudson's Bay Company overlapped here. (The Hudson Bay watershed begins north of Lake Nipigon, Longlac and Hornepayne). The two companies built rival trading posts—at Longlac, for example—where Cree and Ojibwa Indians exchanged pelts for beads, blades, knives and pots.

The National Transcontinental Railway (later the Canadian National Railway), built in the decade before the First World War, brought enormous change. Old trading communities, such as Longlac, were linked to new railway settlements, such as Geraldton and Hornepayne. The railway created an "upper" tier of settlement in northern Ontario; the "lower" tier, along Lake Superior, had been developed by the Canadian Pacific Railway. Gold mining, lumbering and tourism subsequently figured in the 20th-century development of these communities.

South of Hornepayne, the route returns to Marathon on the North Shore of Lake Superior. Nearby Neys Provincial Park perpetuates the rocky wilderness that profoundly influenced Group of Seven painter Lawren Harris (1885-1970), who visited here in the early 1920s.

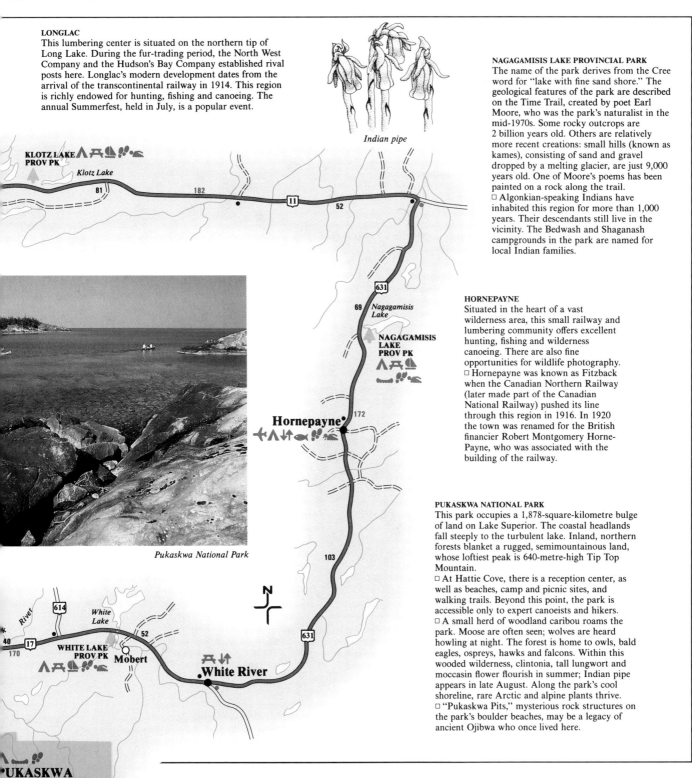

LONGLAC
This lumbering center is situated on the northern tip of Long Lake. During the fur-trading period, the North West Company and the Hudson's Bay Company established rival posts here. Longlac's modern development dates from the arrival of the transcontinental railway in 1914. This region is richly endowed for hunting, fishing and canoeing. The annual Summerfest, held in July, is a popular event.

Indian pipe

KLOTZ LAKE PROV PK
Klotz Lake

Pukaskwa National Park

Hornepayne

NAGAGAMISIS LAKE PROV PK
Nagagamisis Lake

White Lake

WHITE LAKE PROV PK

Mobert

White River

PUKASKWA NATIONAL PK

NAGAGAMISIS LAKE PROVINCIAL PARK
The name of the park derives from the Cree word for "lake with fine sand shore." The geological features of the park are described on the Time Trail, created by poet Earl Moore, who was the park's naturalist in the mid-1970s. Some rocky outcrops are 2 billion years old. Others are relatively more recent creations: small hills (known as kames), consisting of sand and gravel dropped by a melting glacier, are just 9,000 years old. One of Moore's poems has been painted on a rock along the trail.
□ Algonkian-speaking Indians have inhabited this region for more than 1,000 years. Their descendants still live in the vicinity. The Bedwash and Shaganash campgrounds in the park are named for local Indian families.

HORNEPAYNE
Situated in the heart of a vast wilderness area, this small railway and lumbering community offers excellent hunting, fishing and wilderness canoeing. There are also fine opportunities for wildlife photography.
□ Hornepayne was known as Fitzback when the Canadian Northern Railway (later made part of the Canadian National Railway) pushed its line through this region in 1916. In 1920 the town was renamed for the British financier Robert Montgomery Horne-Payne, who was associated with the building of the railway.

PUKASKWA NATIONAL PARK
This park occupies a 1,878-square-kilometre bulge of land on Lake Superior. The coastal headlands fall steeply to the turbulent lake. Inland, northern forests blanket a rugged, semimountainous land, whose loftiest peak is 640-metre-high Tip Top Mountain.
□ At Hattie Cove, there is a reception center, as well as beaches, camp and picnic sites, and walking trails. Beyond this point, the park is accessible only to expert canoeists and hikers.
□ A small herd of woodland caribou roams the park. Moose are often seen; wolves are heard howling at night. The forest is home to owls, bald eagles, ospreys, hawks and falcons. Within this wooded wilderness, clintonia, tall lungwort and moccasin flower flourish in summer; Indian pipe appears in late August. Along the park's cool shoreline, rare Arctic and alpine plants thrive.
□ "Pukaskwa Pits," mysterious rock structures on the park's boulder beaches, may be a legacy of ancient Ojibwa who once lived here.

Where Spectacular Surf Batters Earth's Oldest Rocks

Eastern Shore, Lake Superior

Between Sault Ste. Marie and Wawa, the Trans-Canada Highway passes its halfway point near Batchawana Bay. A cairn at Chippewa Falls marks the spot. The highway cuts through the Canadian Shield, which was formed billions of years ago. This resource-rich region occupies about two-thirds of Ontario. Deep within the Shield lies a treasure trove of prized minerals, and on its rugged surface, a mantle of productive forests.

Until the Trans-Canada Highway reached

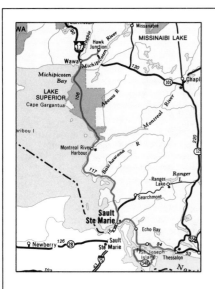

WAWA
Gold is part of Wawa's history. The 10-kilometre Surluga Loop Road, just east of the town, winds through a deserted goldfield. A narrow, unpaved road leads to nine abandoned mines, which produced several million dollars worth of nuggets and ore during the gold rush of 1897-1903. Today iron mining and tourism—not gold—are Wawa's economic mainstays.
□ A nine-metre steel sculpture of a goose—*wawa* is Ojibway for the wild goose—stands at a highway junction just south of here. In spring and fall thousands of migrating Canada geese can be seen flying in V formations over the town.
□ South of Wawa, five kilometres off Highway 17, is a 23-metre-high falls on the Magpie River.

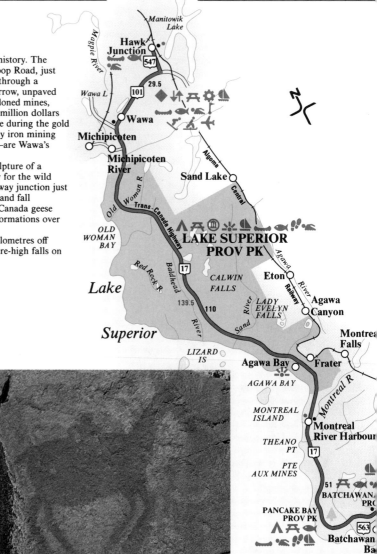

LAKE SUPERIOR PROVINCIAL PARK
This 1,554-square-kilometre park contains towering granite headlands along Lake Superior and dense inland forests of maple, birch, poplar and spruce. Through the ages, earthquakes, volcanoes and glaciers have shaped the park's lofty hills and steep valleys. The lava rock at Cape Gargantua is an example of such ancient upheaval.
□ The park's outstanding scenic areas include the Lake Superior shoreline, Agawa Valley, Sand River and the Mijinemungshing Lake area. Campgrounds are located at Crescent Lake and Agawa Bay (in the park's southern part) and Rabbit Blanket Lake (in the northern part). Visitors can explore the park by canoe or on foot. There are seven canoe routes, as well as trails for novice and experienced hikers.
□ The largest mammal in the park is the moose, which sometimes strays onto Highway 17. Black bears, timber wolves, beavers, muskrat, mink, marten, skunks and weasels are also found here. More than 250 bird species, including the Canada goose and the sandhill crane, have been recorded in the park.
□ The park's inland lakes and rivers are well stocked with brook and lake trout. The coastal rivers and Lake Superior contain lake trout, whitefish, and rainbow trout, as well as some salmon and brown trout.

Muskrat

Indian rock painting, Agawa Bay,
Lake Superior Provincial Park

PANCAKE BAY PROVINCIAL PARK
The name of the park harks back to the voyageurs who stopped here on their way east from Fort Williams. At this point food often ran low, and the voyageurs used up their remaining flour to make pancakes, knowing they could get more provisions at Sault Ste. Marie the following day.
□ This 467-hectare provincial park has a 3.2-kilometre-long beach, one of the best on Lake Superior. Apart from swimming and sunbathing, there are opportunities for boating and fishing (rainbow and lake trout abound). The park contains more than 335 campsites.

Wawa in 1960, much of this region was accessible to travelers only by train, floatplane and canoe. Huge tracts of this northland are still as unspoiled as they were when the first explorers passed through here more than 300 years ago.

Brooding mountains, foaming rivers, spring-fed lakes and rock-studded bays give Lake Superior's eastern shore a character that is unique among the Great Lakes. Spectacular surf usually batters much of the lakeshore. Here and there broad avenues of white sand curl around sheltered coves and bays. In the fall a belt of dense hardwoods, stretching for almost 145 kilometres north and east of Sault Ste. Marie, provides a dazzling array of colors.

'Snow train' to Agawa Canyon

AGAWA BAY
More than two centuries ago an Ojibway chief led a war party across Lake Superior and recorded his victory in rock paintings on a cliff face in Agawa Bay. In 1851 Henry Schoolcraft, an Indian agent at Sault Ste. Marie, Mich., found the paintings and carefully described them, but neglected to say where they were located. In the late 1950s, Canadian art researcher Selwyn Dewdney spent 14 months following clues that led to the discovery of the paintings at Agawa Rock, just north of Agawa Bay. Today the pictographs are among the outstanding attractions at Lake Superior Provincial Park.

AGAWA CANYON
This scenic canyon can be reached by the Algoma Central Railway's daily excursion train from Sault Ste. Marie (early June to mid-October). During a two-hour stopover at Agawa Canyon, passengers can picnic, hike, climb, fish or simply relax amid the breathtaking scenery.
□ A "snow train" excursion is available on weekends from January to March.

International bridge, Sault Ste. Marie

Ermatinger House, Sault Ste. Marie

SAULT STE. MARIE
Popularly known as "The Soo," this city of roughly 80,000 is Canada's second largest steel-producing center (after Hamilton). Its twin city sits on the American side of the St. Mary's River, which links Lake Huron and Lake Superior. The locks on the Canadian and American sides, which bypass the river's rapids (*sault* in French), are among the world's busiest. Through the locks pass lake and oceangoing vessels with cargoes of iron ore and grain. (Lock tours are available.).
□ Sault Ste. Marie Museum recounts the city's history from prehistoric times to the present. The 55-metre-long MS *Norgama*—the last ship built for passenger travel on the Great Lakes—has been converted into a museum of marine history.
□ Ermatinger House, a two-story Georgian-style house, was built in 1814 by fur trader Charles Ermatinger for his wife, an Ojibway princess. It is now a national historic site and a museum.
□ Great Lakes Forestry Centre—the largest research institute of its kind in Canada—offers tours.
□ A three-kilometre international bridge links the Ontario city with its Michigan twin.

THESSALON
The lumber town of Thessalon is the access point for a large recreation area to the north. Local tourism facilities include a government wharf and marina.

ST. JOSEPH ISLAND
A bridge off Highway 17 links St. Joseph Island with the mainland. The island (30 kilometres long and 24 kilometres wide) lies in the North Channel between Lake Huron and Lake Superior. The island provides quiet spots for swimming and fishing. The Ojibway Indians named the island *anipich,* which means the place of the hardwoods. Although hardwood forests remain, farmland predominates today.
□ The ruins of the most westerly military post in Upper Canada are preserved in Fort St. Joseph National Historic Park. The fort, built in 1796, was an important trading station and British military post in the War of 1812. An interpretive center tells the history of the fort.
□ At the St. Joseph Island Museum, local pioneer artifacts are displayed in a restored church, barn, schoolhouse and log cabin.

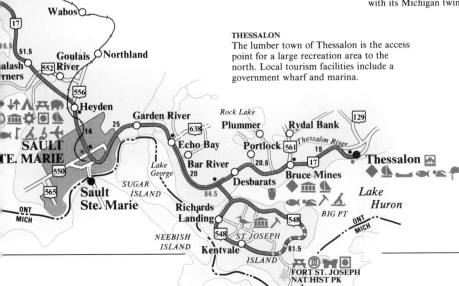

On a Record-Sized Island,
the Sanctuary of the Good Spirit

Manitoulin Island

Manitoulin Island, at about 2,700 square kilometres, is the world's largest island in a freshwater lake. The island's deeply indented shoreline is roughly 1,600 kilometres long. Its south and east sides face the open waters of Lake Huron and Georgian Bay. Its north side hems in the North Channel, which leads to the St. Mary's River and Sault Ste. Marie.

Bridges and causeways over the North Channel link Manitoulin Island to the mainland. A car ferry connects South Baymouth

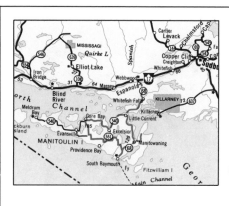

Gore Bay Museum

BIRCH ISLAND

Dreamer's Rock, on nearby Little Cloche Island, affords a fine view of the North Channel, Bay of Islands and La Cloche Mountains. A plaque tells that Indian youths were once required to fast here for many days before entering manhood. Through dreams, the youths would receive guidance from a "guardian spirit."
□ A stone monument on this island northeast of Manitoulin Island commemorates a visit by President Franklin D. Roosevelt in 1943.

KAGAWONG

Lake Kagawong, almost at the center of Manitoulin Island, is drained by the Kagawong River which drops over Bridal Veil Falls. A picnic park here has nature trails and, at the brink of the falls, a lookout.
□ St. John's Anglican Church, a small clapboard structure beside the village dock, has a pulpit fashioned from the bow of an old ship. Floats from fishing nets decorate the pews.

GORE BAY

This small, attractive community is the government center for Manitoulin Island.
□ Gore Bay Museum is housed in a former courthouse and jail. The cells are now converted into display rooms. There are relics from an ancient Sheguiandah Indian settlement, old coins and pioneer articles, and objects from a wreck believed to be La Salle's *Griffon,* the first ship to sail the upper Great Lakes. (The vessel may have sunk in a storm in Mississagi Strait at the west end of Manitoulin Island in 1679.)
□ The East Bluff Lookout near here gives a view of the surrounding hills, the clear water of Gore Bay and the North Channel of Lake Huron.

Lighthouse, South Baymouth

SOUTH BAYMOUTH

Two ferries—MS *Chi-cheemaun* (the big canoe) and MS *Nindawayma*—transport people and cars between this tiny community and Tobermory on the Bruce Peninsula. The ferry service runs from early April to late October, with four crossings a day in July and August. (A one-way trip takes 1¾ hours.)
□ The restored 19th-century Little Red Schoolhouse stands just north of the ferry terminal. A nearby museum displays pioneer objects and handicrafts.

| 0 | 2 | 4 | 6 | 8 | 10 Miles |
| 0 | 4 | 8 | 12 | 16 Kilometres |

on the island's south shore and Tobermory at the tip of the Bruce Peninsula.

Some 800 kilometres of road skirt the island's irregular shoreline and pass beside its clear lakes, sparkling streams and waterfalls. Smallmouth bass, northern pike, muskellunge, walleye and speckled lake trout can be caught in many of the island's more than 100 lakes. The island has fine sand beaches and the offshore waters attract enthusiastic sailors. The small community of Little Current is a summer base for divers who wish to search Manitoulin's offshore waters for shipwrecks.

The influence of the Ojibway and Ottawa Indians endures on Manitoulin Island. In the past, the island was thought to be the sanctuary of the good spirit Gitchi-Manitou and his evil adversary Matchi-Manitou. At Sheguiandah and other sites, archaeologists have unearthed evidence of Indian cultures that thrived on the island thousands of years ago. (Relics from these past cultures are displayed at museums in Gore Bay and elsewhere.) Today six Indian reservations are located here. Many local events, such as the annual powwows at Wikwemikong, strive to keep traditional arts and customs alive.

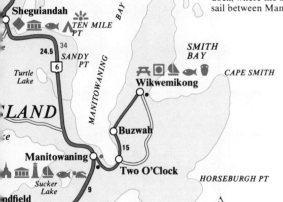

Woodcock

ESPANOLA
This tourism center just north of Manitoulin Island is the largest community in the region. Espanola was virtually abandoned during the 1930s, but revived with the construction of a pulp mill in the mid-1940s. Local recreational facilities include a golf course and an Olympic-size swimming pool.

MANITOWANING
Indians believed that this area was the home of the Great Spirit. Gitchi-Manitou. Manitowaning means "den of the Great Spirit."
□ St. Paul's Anglican Church, a white wooden building completed by Indians in 1849, is the oldest church on Manitoulin Island.
□ The Assiginack Museum includes a 19th-century stone jail, a log barn, smithy and one-room schoolhouse. Exhibits detailing the life of Indians and settlers in the region include a beaded wampum belt worn by Chief Assiginack, an Ottawa Indian who sided with the British during the War of 1812.
□ A playground and a beach are near the community dock, where the S.S. *Norisle*—the first car ferry to sail between Manitoulin and Tobermory—is moored.

LITTLE CURRENT
The Little Current-Howland Centennial Museum, 10 kilometres south at Sheguiandah, includes three two-story log houses, a two-story log granary and a blacksmith shop. The museum displays Indian and pioneer artifacts. There are picnic facilities on the museum's wooded, parklike grounds.
□ Little Current's annual Haweater Festival, held the first weekend in August, features a horse show and riding competitions, handicraft displays, dancing and a midway. The town's September cattle auction is one of North America's largest single-day sales.
□ A plaque on the R.H. Ripley House describes the Hudson's Bay Company's attempt to set up a post at Little Current in 1856. Opposition from local natives and missionaries forced the post's closure. Ripley House was later built on the site of the post, whose stone base forms part of the foundation.
□ Near Little Current are the remains of a Jesuit mission operated in 1648-50 by the Rev. Joseph Poncet, the first known European resident of the island.

Thunderbird, *a painting by Francis Kagige*

WIKWEMIKONG
This town (and several other small communities) is part of the Manitoulin Island Indian Reservation. Local handicrafts are available at the crafts center.
□ In spring and summer, Wikwemikong is the site of a powwow that attracts native dancers from all over North America.
□ The local school displays 30 paintings of Canadian wildlife by native artist and illustrator Francis Kagige. The school is open to the public throughout the summer.

Where a Pot of Gold Is a Basin of Nickel and Copper

Northeastern Shore, Georgian Bay

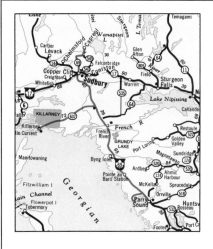

The Big Nickel, Sudbury

Steam locomotive, Capreol

CAPREOL
Visitors to this town in the Sudbury Basin can see the computer heart of the Canadian National Railways freight system in operation.
□ A railway handcar, a caboose and a steam locomotive are displayed in Precott Park. Also in the park is a 12-tonne fragment of an enormous meteorite that plummeted to earth near here in 1911 or 1912.
□ Near Capreol there is good fishing for walleye and northern pike in Burwash, Ferris and Takko lakes, and in the Groundhog and Vermilion rivers.

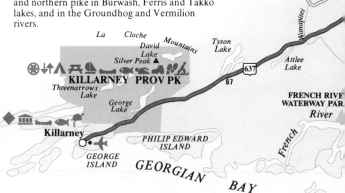

KILLARNEY PROVINCIAL PARK
This park, sometimes called the "crown jewel" of the Ontario park system, preserves roughly 345 square kilometres of prime wilderness. Located on the southern edge of the Canadian Shield, the park contains rock formations more than 2 billion years old and has a few of the remaining stands of sugar maple and yellow birch in Ontario. Its rugged beauty inspired paintings by four members of the Group of Seven—A. Y. Jackson, Frank Carmichael, Arthur Lismer and A. J. Casson. It was through Jackson's effort that this area became a park.
□ The park has visitors' services programs and a campground at Lake George with tent and trailer sites. The park is also popular with hikers and canoeists. A 32-kilometre trail through the La Cloche Mountains leads to the summit of Silver Peak. There are also trails to Cranberry Bog and Baie Fine.

FRENCH RIVER
Most rivers create their own beds by erosion, but the island-dotted French River follows a complex of natural faults and fissures on its course from Lake Nipissing to Georgian Bay. The voyageurs plied the river's maze of channels and secluded bays, and portaged rapids and falls. Its swift waters still challenge the skills of today's canoeists. Among its features are the Indian rock paintings at Keso Point. There is good fishing for walleye, muskellunge, bass and northern pike.

POINTE AU BARIL
In the late 1800s, a lantern set on a barrel guided fishing boats into this sheltered harbor—thus the name Pointe au Baril (Barrel Point). A wooden lighthouse, still in use, replaced the makeshift marker in 1889.
□ About five kilometres north of Pointe au Baril is Sturgeon Bay Provincial Park, which has a sand beach (an unusual feature in this area) and 82 campsites for tents and trailers. The bay provides a sheltered spot for small craft boating and sailing.

KILLBEAR PROVINCIAL PARK
There are some four kilometres of sand beach and 6.5 kilometres of hiking trails in this 11.7-square-kilometre park. Three rocky headlands provide impressive views of some of the Thirty Thousand Islands. Some of the islands are bare, craggy rocks; others are heavily wooded and up to eight kilometres long.

Killarney Provincial Park

0 2 4 6 8 10 Miles
0 4 8 12 16 Kilometres

This route offers four outstanding attractions—the industrial and mining city of Sudbury, the rugged landscape of Killarney Provincial Park, the historic French River and the scenic Thirty Thousand Islands.

Sudbury is situated in a large geological basin, possibly created either by the impact of a meteorite or by volcanic eruption. Whatever the cause, it endowed the Sudbury region with a wealth of minerals: gold, silver, cobalt, platinum, and the world's largest known deposit of nickel. In contrast to its intense mining activity, Sudbury can also offer parks, lakes and forests, and a lively cityscape with galleries, museums, and theaters.

Southwest of Sudbury, Killarney Provincial Park contains the rugged landscape that inspired the painter A. Y. Jackson and other members of the Group of Seven in the 1920s, and the renowned wildlife artist Robert Bateman in recent times. Among the park's scenic wonders are the white hills and ridges of the La Cloche Mountains.

The wide, swift French River, once part of the historic fur trade route from Montreal to Lake Superior, still attracts canoeists. It is also favored by fishermen for its large and abundant walleye and northern pike.

The Thirty Thousands Islands hug the eastern shore of Georgian Bay. Boats from Parry Sound cruise through this popular vacation land.

Slag pouring, Sudbury

SUDBURY

Two symbols of Sudbury's importance as a mining center are Inco's 380-metre-high Copper Cliff smokestack (the world's tallest) and the Big Nickel (a 9-metre-high 1951 Canadian commemorative coin).
□ When the mines are operating, the molten slag—the residue of the mining process—is poured on waste heaps. This fiery spectacle, which sometimes lights up the night sky, can be seen on Highway 144, west of Sudbury.
□ Within the Sudbury area, 30 lakes and some 2,500 hectares of forest provide opportunities for swimming and boating in summer, and skiing in winter. Bell Park on Ramsey Lake has an open-air amphitheater for concerts and theater.
□ Sudbury's museums and arts centers include Galerie du Nouvel-Ontario (specializing in Franco-Ontarian art), Flour Mill Museum, Copper Cliff Museum and the outstanding Science North. The city's bilingual Laurentian University also has an arts center and museum.

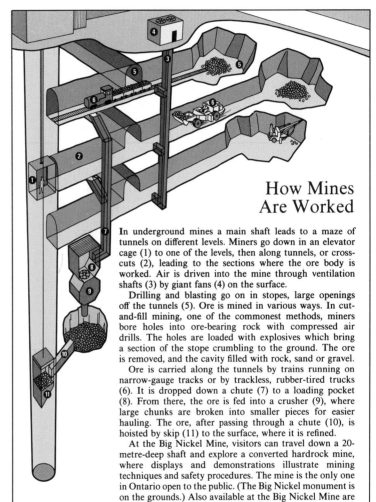

How Mines Are Worked

In underground mines a main shaft leads to a maze of tunnels on different levels. Miners go down in an elevator cage (1) to one of the levels, then along tunnels, or crosscuts (2), leading to the sections where the ore body is worked. Air is driven into the mine through ventilation shafts (3) by giant fans (4) on the surface.

Drilling and blasting go on in stopes, large openings off the tunnels (5). Ore is mined in various ways. In cut-and-fill mining, one of the commonest methods, miners bore holes into ore-bearing rock with compressed air drills. The holes are loaded with explosives which bring a section of the stope crumbling to the ground. The ore is removed, and the cavity filled with rock, sand or gravel.

Ore is carried along the tunnels by trains running on narrow-gauge tracks or by trackless, rubber-tired trucks (6). It is dropped down a chute (7) to a loading pocket (8). From there, the ore is fed into a crusher (9), where large chunks are broken into smaller pieces for easier hauling. The ore, after passing through a chute (10), is hoisted by skip (11) to the surface, where it is refined.

At the Big Nickel Mine, visitors can travel down a 20-metre-deep shaft and explore a converted hardrock mine, where displays and demonstrations illustrate mining techniques and safety procedures. The mine is the only one in Ontario open to the public. (The Big Nickel monument is on the grounds.) Also available at the Big Nickel Mine are 2½-hour bus tours of the Sudbury Basin.

Mourning warbler

Grass pink

PARRY SOUND

This community on Georgian Bay is named for Sir William Edward Parry, the 19th-century English explorer of the Arctic. Parry Sound is the center of a summer resort area, which has good boating facilities. Scuba diving among the vessels wrecked offshore is a popular pastime. Local rivers and streams teem with rainbow and brook trout, bass, splake and walleye.
□ A triple-deck cruise boat, *Island Queen*, offers three-hour trips through the Thirty Thousand Islands.
□ Visitors can climb a 24-metre-high tower on a hill just outside the town. The observation deck provides a splendid view of Georgian Bay and the surrounding region. Built in the 1920s, the tower was once used to spot forest fires.
□ The West Parry Sound District Museum traces the history of lumbering, shipping and other activities in this region.

Map labels

Alban 64
607
French River
07A
17 GRUNDY LAKE PROV PK
Pakesley
522
Little Key R
69
526 37
Still River
Britt
g Inlet 645
Giroux R
Trans-Canada Highway
529
Naiscoot R
Bayfield Inlet 529A
STURGEON BAY PROV PK 2
TE AU ARIL
Pointe au Baril Station
644 79
Shawanaga River
Shawanaga 28
529 69 Waubamik
Shebeshekong River
559
24.5 Nobel 12
124
Snug Harbour
Mill Lake
KILLBEAR PROV PK
PARRY SOUND
Parry Sound
Depot Harbour
PARRY ISLAND
GEORGIAN BAY
ISLANDS

Strongholds of the Past
in a Year-Round Playground

Southeastern Shore, Georgian Bay

On the southeastern shore of Georgian Bay are resorts, marinas and ski hills. But this year-round recreation playground has rich associations with the past. Two sites in this area—Sainte-Marie among the Hurons, and the Royal Navy and Military Establishments—recall events of early Canadian history.

Sainte-Marie among the Hurons, the first European settlement in Ontario, has been reconstructed beside the Wye River east of Midland. From a palisaded stronghold

MEAFORD
This community, like neighboring Thornbury, is situated at the heart of an apple-growing area. Meaford's recreational attractions include a marina, beaches and ski hills. The town was named for an English estate—Meaford Hall—when the settlement was laid out in the 1840s. Meaford Museum recounts local history.
□ The canine hero of *Beautiful Joe,* the classic novel by Canadian author Margaret Marshall Saunders (1861-1947), is buried in a park on the Big Head River. During a visit to Meaford, Saunders heard the story of a dog rescued from a brutal master, which inspired her to write the novel. Published in 1894, it was the first Canadian book to sell more than 1 million copies. In 1934 Saunders was made a C.B.E. (Commander of the British Empire) for her humanitarian efforts.

THORNBURY
Nearby Beaver Valley has ski hills, orchards and sparkling rivers that harbor rainbow trout. South of town, Eugenia Falls, on the Beaver River, cascades 24 metres over the Niagara Escarpment. The falls, named in 1854 by a former French officer for the Empress Eugénie, was the scene of an 1853 gold rush that yielded worthless pyrites but led to the area's development.

Rainbow trout

CRAIGLEITH PROVINCIAL PARK
Fossilized creatures from a sea that covered the area 375 million years ago are embedded in the limestone terraces of Craigleith Provincial Park on Nottawasaga Bay. A visitor center, overlooking Nottawasaga Bay, tells how these extinct invertebrates were turned to stone some 200 million years ago.

OWEN SOUND
Indians called it *Wad-i-need-i-ton* (beautiful valley) long before Capt. William Owen sailed into this harbor and named it Owen Sound. Pioneer memorabilia, demonstrations of pioneer crafts and a half-scale model of an Ojibway Indian encampment are features of the County of Grey-Owen Sound Museum.
□ The Tom Thomson Memorial Gallery and Museum of Fine Art commemorates the famous landscape artist who grew up in nearby Leith.

INGLIS FALLS CONSERVATION AREA
The Sydenham River tumbles over the Niagara Escarpment and into a picturesque gorge in this Owen Sound conservation area. Visitors enjoy picnicking, swimming, fishing, boating and hiking, and in winter, snowshoeing and cross-country skiing.

BLUE MOUNTAINS
The scenic caves in the Blue Mountains near Collingwood date from a time when a warm, shallow sea covered Ontario. Although some of the crevices are more than 25 metres deep, handrails allow safe access. A ladder descends to one deep cave where there is year-round ice and snow. Appropriately named for its narrow opening is Fat Man's Misery. The Indian Council Chamber is a reminder that the Hurons lived and worshiped among these rocks. Hart's-tongue, walking and maidenhair ferns are found in Fern Cavern. The pinnacle Ekarenniondi—"where the rock stands out"—was a landmark for the Petun tribes of the Huron nation.

Maidenhair fern

Inglis Falls near Owen Sound

Ekarenniondi, Blue Mountains

0   1   2   3   4   5 Miles
0   2   4   6   8 Kilometres

on this site, a group of French Jesuits directed their Huronia mission from 1639 to 1649. Here lived Saint Jean de Brébeuf and five other martyred saints.

Indian wars brought the Jesuits' efforts to an early end. Sainte-Marie, though never attacked, became isolated amid deserted Huron villages and increasingly hostile Iroquois. Fearing attack, the Jesuits abandoned their mission, and returned to Quebec. For 300 years, Sainte-Marie among the Hurons—the first bold step into the Ca-

nadian interior—remained a memory. Its recent reconstruction is a tribute to the faith and heroism of its founders.

North of Midland are the Historic Navy and Military Establishments at Penetanguishene. Built by the British after the War of 1812, the Establishments—part dockyard, part army camp—operated until the 1850s.

A lively settlement of French Canadian fur traders and British soldiers grew up around the bases. The town of Penetanguishene retains its bilingual character to this day. The bases have been renovated and reconstructed—symbols of the days of British power on the Great Lakes.

Sainte-Marie among the Hurons, with the Martyrs' Shrine in the background

A Lone Outpost and Huron Longhouses

Sainte-Marie among the Hurons at Midland was painstakingly reconstructed in the 1960s. Visitors enter through a lobby lined with C. W. Jeffreys' illustrations of events in Huronia history, then view a film on life in 17th-century New France. Inside the palisade are residences, a hospital, forge, cookhouse, stables and stockades. A chapel contains the grave of Saint Jean de Brébeuf. The site also preserves the Church of St. Joseph, the oldest Christian shrine in Canada. Overlooking the restoration stands the Martyrs' Shrine, commemorating the Jesuit Fathers.

One of the Huron villages that first drew the missionaries here has been reconstructed in Midland's Little Lake Park. Roots, dried corn and herbs hang from bunk-lined longhouses. Outside are food storage pits and a sweat bath.

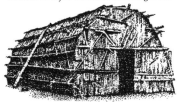

Huron longhouse, Midland

PENETANGUISHENE
Historic Naval and Military Establishments, the only combined military base to operate in Canada (1817-1856), contain 15 reconstructed buildings, such as offices and barracks. The 19th-century schooner *Bee* is docked at the wharf. Costumed guides are on the site.
□ The garrison church of St. James-on-the-Lines, built in 1836-38, has wooden pews carved by soldiers once based here and an aisle wide enough for four men to walk abreast.

Penetanguishene

Midland

WYE MARSH WILDLIFE CENTRE

MIDLAND
Three sites at Midland—Sainte-Marie among the Hurons, the Martyrs' Shrine and the Wye Marsh Wildlife Centre—perpetuate the historical, religious and natural heritage of this region.
□ A reconstructed 16th-century Huron Indian village is located beside the Huronia Museum and Gallery of Historic Huronia in Midland's Little Lake Park. The museum displays Huron artifacts and models of Great Lakes ships.
□ Midland and Penetanguischene provide access to Georgian Bay Islands National Park, which can be reached only by boat. This offshore park comprises 59 islands or parts of islands.

Cawaja Beach
Perkinsfield
Balm Beach
Ossossane Beach
Wymbolwood Beach
Wendake Beach
Bluewater Beach
Deanlea Beach
Woodland Beach
Allenwood Beach
Allenwood
New Wasaga Beach
Wasaga Beach

WASAGA BEACH PROVINCIAL PARK
This park offers 14 kilometres of white-sand beaches on Georgian Bay. It is reputedly the world's longest and safest freshwater beachfront.
□ The park's dune area, across the Nottawasaga River, is a protected place where visitors can fish, hike and canoe.
□ Nancy Island Historic Site is on an island in the Nottawasaga River that separates the beach and dune areas of Wasaga Beach Provincial Park. The island formed as sand and silt collected around the hull of the schooner *Nancy*, which sank here in 1814. A museum and a theater present diplays and a sight-and-sound show describing the role of the ship during the War of 1812.

Blue Mountain Pottery, Collingwood

COLLINGWOOD
A Great Lakes shipping center for almost a century, Collingwood is now a prosperous year-round resort town. Blue Mountain pottery, developed here in the 1940s, is made with red clay from local creeks. Visitors can watch potters at work.

East Black Bass Bay
PIGEON PT
Mair Mills
Collingwood
Batteaux
WASAGA BEACH PROV PK
Brocks Beach
Oakview Beach
Springhurst Beach

Ship's figurehead, Museum of the Upper Lakes, Wasaga Beach

Bold Headlands, Sheltered Bays, Clear Waters—and Tireless Winds

Bruce Peninsula

Within a few hours' drive of Toronto is an alluring yet accessible wilderness peninsula. Known locally as "the Bruce" this triangle of land jutting into Lake Huron is part of the Niagara Escarpment—a rocky spine arcing northwest from Lake Ontario to Manitoulin Island.

The bold landscape characteristic of the Bruce begins at Wiarton, where Colpoys Bay almost pinches the peninsula into an island. The east coast, on Georgian Bay, is sheer limestone cliffs, pounded and

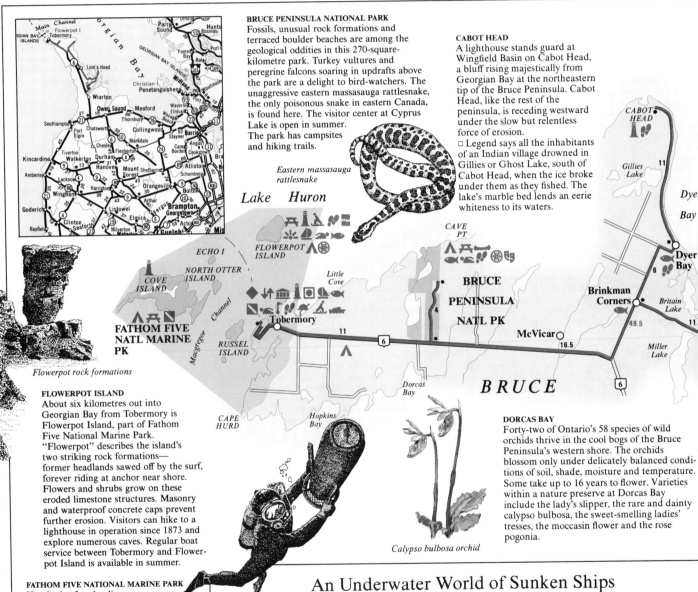

BRUCE PENINSULA NATIONAL PARK
Fossils, unusual rock formations and terraced boulder beaches are among the geological oddities in this 270-square-kilometre park. Turkey vultures and peregrine falcons soaring in updrafts above the park are a delight to bird-watchers. The unaggressive eastern massasauga rattlesnake, the only poisonous snake in eastern Canada, is found here. The visitor center at Cyprus Lake is open in summer. The park has campsites and hiking trails.

Eastern massasauga rattlesnake

CABOT HEAD
A lighthouse stands guard at Wingfield Basin on Cabot Head, a bluff rising majestically from Georgian Bay at the northeastern tip of the Bruce Peninsula. Cabot Head, like the rest of the peninsula, is receding westward under the slow but relentless force of erosion.
□ Legend says all the inhabitants of an Indian village drowned in Gillies or Ghost Lake, south of Cabot Head, when the ice broke under them as they fished. The lake's marble bed lends an eerie whiteness to its waters.

Flowerpot rock formations

DORCAS BAY
Forty-two of Ontario's 58 species of wild orchids thrive in the cool bogs of the Bruce Peninsula's western shore. The orchids blossom only under delicately balanced conditions of soil, shade, moisture and temperature. Some take up to 16 years to flower. Varieties within a nature preserve at Dorcas Bay include the lady's slipper, the rare and dainty calypso bulbosa, the sweet-smelling ladies' tresses, the moccasin flower and the rose pogonia.

Calypso bulbosa orchid

FLOWERPOT ISLAND
About six kilometres out into Georgian Bay from Tobermory is Flowerpot Island, part of Fathom Five National Marine Park. "Flowerpot" describes the island's two striking rock formations—former headlands sawed off by the surf, forever riding at anchor near shore. Flowers and shrubs grow on these eroded limestone structures. Masonry and waterproof concrete caps prevent further erosion. Visitors can hike to a lighthouse in operation since 1873 and explore numerous caves. Regular boat service between Tobermory and Flowerpot Island is available in summer.

FATHOM FIVE NATIONAL MARINE PARK
Hundreds of scuba divers converge each summer on Canada's first underwater park to see shipwrecks that include old sailing vessels and early tugs. The 19 wrecks in this 130-square-kilometre park have been explored and identified. An interpretive center at Tobermory pinpoints charted wrecks, some of which are visible from the surface.
□ Glass-bottom boats tour the islands and provide fine views of some of the underwater wrecks. Diving equipment and boats can be rented at Tobermory.

An Underwater World of Sunken Ships

Scores of broken hulls—victims of fierce nor'easters and treacherous shoals—lie beneath the clear waters of Georgian Bay. More than 70 wrecks, ranging from tugs and wooden-hulled schooners to propeller-driven steamers, have been charted near the Bruce Peninsula.

Easiest to locate are the *Sweepstakes,* a schooner lost in 1896, and the *City of Grand Rapids,* which burned in 1907. They are among four hulls lying at depths of three to nine metres in Tobermory's harbor.

The hull of the *China,* a schooner smashed in 1883 on what is now called China Reef, can be seen from the surface between Wreck Point and China Cove. In 1900 the *Marion L. Breck* went down southwest of Bears Rump. The lighthouse keeper on Flowerpot Island rescued her crew. Capt. John O'Grady of the schooner *Philo Scoville* was not so lucky. He was crushed between his vessel and the rocks during a winter gale in 1889.

In 1901, while towing the schooners *King* and *Brunette,* the steamer *Wetmore* ran aground off Russel Island. All three ships sank. When the water is low, the *Wetmore*'s boiler can be seen just above the surface.

chipped by wind and water, and scoured by ancient glaciers. Caves, shoals and rugged rock formations punctuate the ragged shoreline.

Everywhere along the bluff is a view across a bay to distant headlands or offshore islands. Towns and villages surround sheltered bays. Inland are small lakes and, particularly in the north, dense woodlands.

The west side of the peninsula slides into Lake Huron in a series of marshy cedar swamps and shallow inlets. Sand dunes and glacier-scarred ridges parallel the gently sloping shoreline.

One of North America's finest displays of rare wildflowers, ferns and orchids lends a wild beauty to the peninsula. Bears, deer, grouse and coyotes frequent game trails, and eagles are occasionally sighted. Blazed foot trails, including a 145-kilometre section of the famous Bruce Trail, invite visitors off the beaten path to explore ravines, caves, beaches and forest.

The clean, clear waters surrounding the peninsula belie its treacherous reefs and sudden storms. Scores of shipwrecks have been discovered in Georgian Bay and eastern Lake Huron.

A ferry connects Tobermory, at the northern tip of the peninsula, and South Baymouth on Manitoulin Island. In Tobermory, known locally as "the Tub," is a museum displaying pioneer relics and Indian artifacts. The bustling harbor serves as a jumping-off point for visits to Fathom Five National Marine Park.

A Long Trail That Leads Up Into the Clouds

The 720-kilometre Bruce Trail follows the Niagara Escarpment between Queenston in southern Ontario and Tobermory at the tip of Bruce Peninsula. Weaving through dense cedar and birch forest on the peninsula, the trail passes caves and sheer shale bluffs, and dips down to scenic shoreline villages. Low-lying clouds often envelop hikers at Cabot Head, where the trail traverses some of the highest land in Ontario.

On the Bruce Peninsula, the trail can be entered at Tobermory, Dyer Bay, Cabot Head, Hope Bay, Lion's Head, Cape Croker and Wiarton. A two-kilometre stretch near Halfway Rock Point makes a fine day hike.

A 50-kilometre section between Dunk's Bay and Cabot Head is a tough three-day trek for seasoned backpackers. Hikers are advised to carry canteens: the clean, pure drinking water of Georgian Bay, in full view along much of the Bruce Trail, is often out of reach.

CAPE CROKER
Ojibway Indians have turned the beautiful Cape Croker Indian Reserve into a park. Visitors camp on wooded bluffs overlooking Sydney Bay, or at the water's edge. Nature trails and 24 kilometres of the Bruce Trail run through the park. There are hidden coves, a sandy beach, a playground, picnic areas and good boating and fishing along the rugged coastline. A store near the park entrance offers Indian handicrafts. A lighthouse, reconstructed in 1905, includes part of the original structure erected in the early 1800s to guide ships past the cape's rocky shores.

Limestone cliffs, Bruce Peninsula

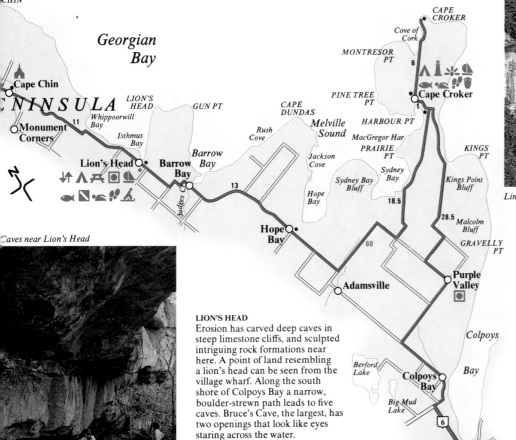

Caves near Lion's Head

LION'S HEAD
Erosion has carved deep caves in steep limestone cliffs, and sculpted intriguing rock formations near here. A point of land resembling a lion's head can be seen from the village wharf. Along the south shore of Colpoys Bay a narrow, boulder-strewn path leads to five caves. Bruce's Cave, the largest, has two openings that look like eyes staring across the water.

WIARTON
A provincial fish hatchery in Wiarton raises three million fish (coho, salmon and species of trout) annually. Visitors see the roe in incubator trays and young fish in holding trays. The hatchery's stocking program has made nearby Colpoys Bay an excellent place to catch rainbow trout. Northern pike inhabit Mountain, Miller and Isaac lakes. Splake (a hybrid trout developed by Canadian biologists) are abundant in the waters off Lion's Head. Lake Huron provides good bass, perch and pike fishing. Bass are found in inland lakes such as Chesley, Gould, Miller, Cyprus, Berford, Cameron and Gillies.

Georgian Bay

Cape Chin
CAPE CHIN
PENINSULA
LION'S HEAD
Monument Corners
11
Whippoorwill Bay
Isthmus Bay
GUN PT
Lion's Head
Barrow Bay
Barrow Bay
Judges
13
Rush Cove
CAPE DUNDAS
Melville Sound
Jackson Cove
Hope Bay
Sydney Bay Bluff
MONTRESOR PT
Cove of Cork
CAPE CROKER
PINE TREE PT
6
Cape Croker
1
HARBOUR PT
MacGregor Har
PRAIRIE PT
Sydney Bay
KINGS PT
Kings Point Bluff
18.5
28.5
Malcolm Bluff
GRAVELLY PT
Hope Bay
Hope Bay
60
Adamsville
Purple Valley
Colpoys Bay
Berford Lake
Colpoys Bay
Big Mud Lake
6
Wiarton

Through Fertile Farmland to the Shores of a "Sweet Sea"

Western Ontario

This route is a blend of tranquil farmland and sparkling lakeshore. From Milverton to Goderich, the road winds through gently rolling farmland, where aluminum silos stand like gleaming sentinels in summer fields of corn, flax, soybeans and sunflowers. Friendly communities, such as Listowel, Wingham and Clinton, recall the unhurried rural Ontario of bygone days.

At Goderich, the distinctive "cartwheel" street plan was designed by one of the city's ambitious cofounders, the Scotsman

MacGREGOR POINT PROVINCIAL PARK
This 1,204-hectare park encompasses woods, wetlands, sandy beaches and windswept shores. A bluff visible from the road leading to the park marks the ancient shoreline of Lake Algonquin, which covered this region 12,000 years ago.
□ A trail and boardwalk lead through the park's extensive wetlands. Many amphibians and reptiles, including the spotted turtle, thrive here. More than 200 bird species have been sighted in the park.

Spotted turtle

BRUCE NUCLEAR POWER DEVELOPMENT
This nuclear plant, one of the world's largest, provides a third of Ontario's power. A film, displays and a bus tour show how the plant works.

KINCARDINE
This community (named for the Earl of Elgin and Kincardine) was settled largely by Scots in the mid-1800s. One Scottish tradition that survives to delight townsfolk and visitors is the skirl of bagpipes that fills the air as the local pipe band parades through town on Saturday nights in summer.

BLYTH
This small community (pop. 900) is home to first-class summer theater. Since 1975, the Blyth Festival has earned a national reputation for its successful presentation of new Canadian plays. From June to September, the festival gives roughly 100 performances in a 490-seat theater, once the community hall. The festival usually offers realistic plays about country people and rural issues; its playwrights include Carol Bolt, Anne Chislett, Colleen Curran, Gordon Pinsent, Lister Sinclair and Michel Tremblay.

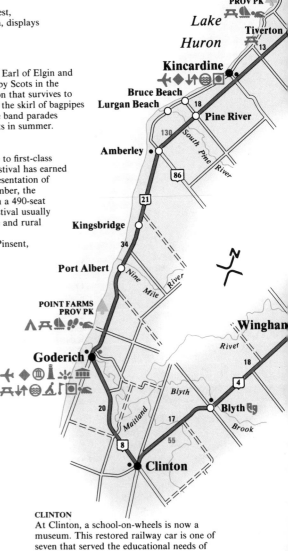

Court House Square, Goderich

Town Hall, Goderich

GODERICH
Queen Elizabeth II once called Goderich "the prettiest town in Canada." Situated on a bluff overlooking Lake Huron, Goderich (pronounced *god-rich*) has the largest harbor on the Canadian side of Lake Huron. Goderich is famous for its rock salt, an economic asset since its 1866 discovery.
□ One of Goderich's distinctive features is Court House Square, an octagonal (eight-sided) park at the heart of town, laid out in 1829 by Dr. William "Tiger" Dunlop, cofounder (with John Galt) of Goderich. Eight wide, tree-lined streets radiate from the park like spokes on a cartwheel.
□ The Huron County Pioneer Museum, housed in a 19th-century school building and a modern annex, offers a look at Goderich's history. Other local museums are the imposing Huron Historic Gaol (1839-42) and the Marine Museum, which is in the wheelhouse of a Great Lakes freighter.

CLINTON
At Clinton, a school-on-wheels is now a museum. This restored railway car is one of seven that served the educational needs of railside settlements in northern Ontario between 1926 and the late 1960s.

| 0 | 3 | 6 | 9 | 12 | 15 Miles |
| 0 | 6 | 12 | 18 | 24 Kilometres |

Dr. William "Tiger" Dunlop (1792-1848). Between the 1820s and the 1840s, Dunlop and his partner, John Galt (1779-1839), opened up this region for settlement.

From Goderich, Highway 21 runs parallel to the shore of Lake Huron and offers glimpses of bright blue lake waters. At roughly 37,000 square kilometres, Lake Huron is the second largest of the Great Lakes. (The Canadian portion is slightly more than 22,000 square kilometres.)

To the early 17th-century French explorers, Lake Huron was *la Mer douce* (the sweet sea). And sweet it must have seemed to the first vacationers who discovered its charms in the late 1800s. Point Farms Provincial Park was once the site of a grand hotel that attracted the rich and fashionable few from Toronto and the United States. Today the lakeside resort towns of Kincardine, Port Elgin and Southampton welcome thousands of summer vacationers eager to enjoy swimming, fishing, and windsurfing.

At Southampton, the route returns to farm country. In this particular region, Hanover and Durham carry on traditions of fine furniture making. Flesherton is noted for its antiques. Orangeville preserves a heritage of Victorian architecture. In autumn, the surrounding country—the scenic Hockley Valley near Orangeville, for example—puts on dazzling displays of color.

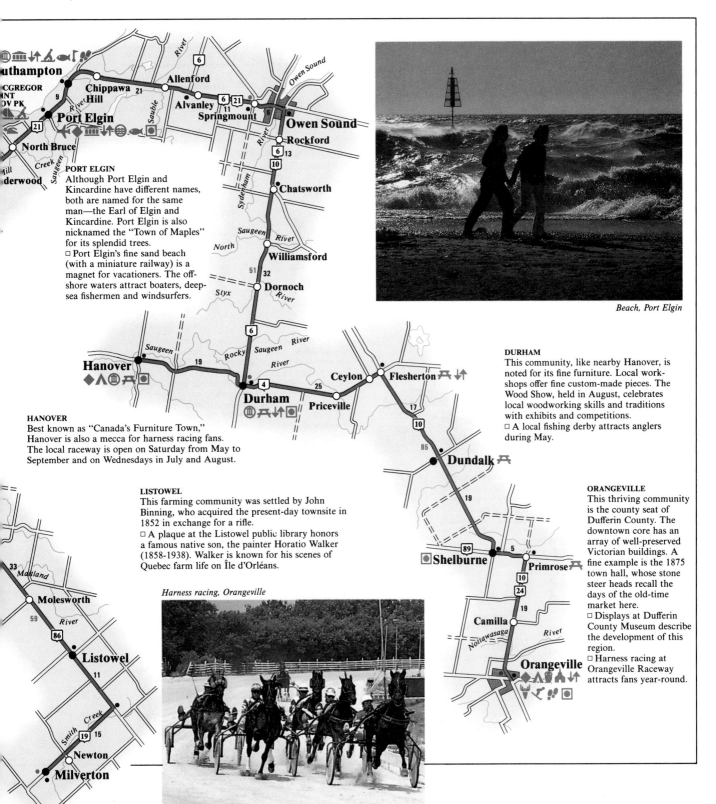

Beach, Port Elgin

PORT ELGIN
Although Port Elgin and Kincardine have different names, both are named for the same man—the Earl of Elgin and Kincardine. Port Elgin is also nicknamed the "Town of Maples" for its splendid trees.
□ Port Elgin's fine sand beach (with a miniature railway) is a magnet for vacationers. The offshore waters attract boaters, deepsea fishermen and windsurfers.

DURHAM
This community, like nearby Hanover, is noted for its fine furniture. Local workshops offer fine custom-made pieces. The Wood Show, held in August, celebrates local woodworking skills and traditions with exhibits and competitions.
□ A local fishing derby attracts anglers during May.

HANOVER
Best known as "Canada's Furniture Town," Hanover is also a mecca for harness racing fans. The local raceway is open on Saturday from May to September and on Wednesdays in July and August.

LISTOWEL
This farming community was settled by John Binning, who acquired the present-day townsite in 1852 in exchange for a rifle.
□ A plaque at the Listowel public library honors a famous native son, the painter Horatio Walker (1858-1938). Walker is known for his scenes of Quebec farm life on Île d'Orléans.

Harness racing, Orangeville

ORANGEVILLE
This thriving community is the county seat of Dufferin County. The downtown core has an array of well-preserved Victorian buildings. A fine example is the 1875 town hall, whose stone steer heads recall the days of the old-time market here.
□ Displays at Dufferin County Museum describe the development of this region.
□ Harness racing at Orangeville Raceway attracts fans year-round.

Where Lucky Prospectors Found a 'Golden Stairway' and Fabled Mines

Northeastern Ontario

Thousands of prospectors flocked to this rugged, mineral-rich region in the early 1900s. Many failed to find the fortunes they were seeking, while others let wealth slip through their hands. In 1903 two lumbermen, scouting for timber in the forest near Cobalt (about 130 kilometres south of Kirkland Lake), uncovered glittering sulphide ore. Samples sent to Montreal for analysis revealed high-grade silver. Cobalt was transformed into a boom town.

A few lucky prospectors stumbled on rich

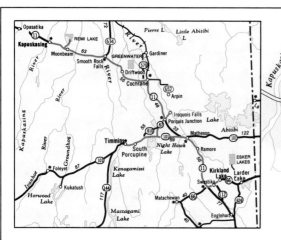

KAPUSKASING
A steam locomotive and two railway coaches house th[e] Ron Morel Memorial Museum. One coach contains railway memorabilia; the other, furniture and other items from Kapuskasing's settlement in the early 1900[s.] □ Heritage River Boat Tours offers a 4-hour round-trip to scenic Beaver Falls, with a 1½-hour stopover for picnicking, fishing or simply relaxing.

Lynx

TIMMINS
This mining and industrial center, which covers roughly 3,210 square kilometres, is the largest city in area in Canada. Within the city limits, Timmins (pop. 46,600) contains major mines and forest-related industries. The Kidd Creek Mine is the world's largest producer of silver and zinc. Other mines produce copper, gold, lead, nickel and tin. In summer, the Timmins Chamber of Commerce arranges mine and plant tours.
□ Timmins began to develop after gold was discovered in 1909, and it remained the leading gold producer until the 1960s. The city is named for one of its founders, mining executive Noah Timmins (1867-1936). The Timmins Museum and Exhibition Centre contains local history and mineral exhibits. The Porcupine Outdoor Mining Museum (just outside the Timmins Museum) displays early mining equipment.

RENÉ BRUNELLE PROVINCIAL PARK
This park is situated in the Great Clay Belt, which stretches between Cochrane and Hearst. The belt is a fertile oasis in the heart of the rocky Canadian Shield. At the end of the last ice age, melting glaciers formed a huge lake here. As the lake drained away, it left the thick layer of silt and clay sediments that still covers this area. The clay soil and cold temperatures favor the growth of black spruce, which thrives abundantly at René Brunelle and gives the park a distinctive appearance.

All Aboard— for a Journey 'Down North'

Travelers in search of Canada's more remote reaches can go "down north" from Cochrane to Moosonee, near James Bay, on the Polar Bear Express. The express, on the Ontario Northland Railway, winds through more than 300 kilometres of scrub brush and muskeg. Completed in 1932, the railway follows an old Indian canoe route. One-day summer excursions take up to 600 passengers for a five-hour visit to Moosonee.

The railway arranges with Indian guides to take adventuresome passengers the last few kilometres by canoe to Moose Factory—Ontario's oldest fur-trading post—on an island in the Moose River opposite Moosonee. Established in 1673 as a Hudson's Bay Company post, Moose Factory was the first English settlement in what is now Ontario. On the island, the home of Cree Indians, is St. Thomas' Anglican Church (1864), furnished with moosehide altar cloths and Cree hymn books. Moose Factory Museum Park has a restored gunpowder magazine, a log fort and a 1740 blacksmith shop.

Kidd Creek Mine near Timmins

```
0    4    8    12   16    20 Miles
0      8      16      24      32 Kilometres
```

lodes of silver and gold. In 1903 Harry Preston found a "golden stairway" of yellow-spattered quartz when his boot heel slipped on a mossy knoll. The find became the fabled Dome Mine. A Kirkland Lake claim filed in 1912 by Harry Oakes (later Sir Harry) became the famous Lake Shore Mine, one of the biggest gold producers in Ontario.

Others were less fortunate. One Scots prospector, in need of money for drink, sold his claim in one-eighth shares for as little as $25 apiece. He was Alexander McIntyre—and the McIntyre Porcupine Mine went on to produce gold worth $230 million.

Until the turn of the century lakes and rivers were the main transportation routes here. The Ontario Northland Railway was built in the early 1900s, following rich mineral finds in the Timmins, Porcupine, Cobalt and Kirkland Lake areas. Today, the railway links North Bay and Moosonee near James Bay. (A modern highway parallels the rails as far as Fraserdale, about 115 kilometres north of the town of Cochrane.)

Although rivers here have been dammed, forests hewed and mountains mined, this region still has countless tranquil lakes and vast areas of virgin forest. Between Cochrane and Moosonee civilization has barely touched the fringes of the wilderness.

COCHRANE
This tourist community is the departure point for the Polar Bear Express, which winds through the untouched wilderness of northern Ontario on its way to Moosonee on James Bay. A railway and pioneer museum, just across from Cochrane station, traces the history of the James Bay region.
□ Northwest of Cochrane is Greenwater Provincial Park, whose 26 vivid green lakes contain some of Ontario's purest water and finest trout fishing.

Polar bear statue, Cochrane

IROQUOIS FALLS
Abitibi-Price's Iroquois Falls Mill offers three daily tours in July and August. Visitors can see how logs are transformed into pulp and paper.
□ The local pioneer museum, housed in the old railway station, describes the development of the pulp-and-paper mill and the history of the early settlers.

SHALLOW RIVER WATERWAY PK

MATHESON
When "The Great Fire of 1916" swept through here, it destroyed more than 2,000 square kilometres of forest and the settlements of Porquis Junction, Iroquois Falls and Matheson. A plaque south of Matheson describes the disaster, which claimed 223 lives.
□ Pioneer artifacts, farm implements and pieces of early mining equipment are displayed in the Black River-Matheson Municipal Museum. One exhibit shows the interior of an early one-room schoolhouse.

The Mining 'King' of Kirkland Lake

One of the leading figures in Ontario mining history became the victim in a sensational unsolved murder case. American-born Harry Oakes (later Sir Harry) was a drifter and prospector who eventually became a millionaire. He traveled the mining camps of Australia, South Africa, Colorado and the Yukon, and arrived in the virgin bush area around Kirkland Lake in 1911 to prospect for gold. His second claim, in 1912, became the famous Lake Shore Mine, one of 12 mines along Kirkland Lake's Golden Mile.

Oakes married an Australian girl, built a 37-room mansion in Niagara Falls, and left Canada for the Bahamas in the mid-1930s to avoid taxes. In 1943 he was found brutally murdered in his Nassau home. His son-in-law was charged with the killing, but was acquitted, and the case was never closed.

Kenogami Lake near Kirkland Lake

Tunis

Nellie Lake

Iroquois Falls

Val Gagné

KETTLE LAKES PROV PK

Shillington Matheson

Night Hawk Lake

Ranmore

Bourkes

Common goldeneye

KETTLE LAKES PROVINCIAL PARK
The two-kilometre Kettle Trail passes several of the more than 20 kettle lakes that give this park its name. These spring-fed, usually circular bodies of water are depressions created at the end of the last ice age by huge blocks of glacial ice.
Because kettle lakes have no natural fish populations, the park's largest lakes are stocked annually with brook and rainbow trout.

Sesekinika
Sesekinika Lake

Kirkland Lake
Swastika Chaput Hughes

Kenogami Lake

Kenogami Lake

KIRKLAND LAKE
In 1912, Harry Oakes staked a claim that became the famous Lake Shore Mine. The discovery of this mine and a number of others sparked the rapid development of the mining community of Kirkland Lake. Today one mine still produces about a fifth of Canada's gold. Another mine produces iron. Mine tours are available.
□ Kirkland Lake's Museum of Northern History contains pioneer artifacts and early mining equipment.

Grey Owl's 'Lonely Land'—
an Accessible Wilderness

Northeastern Ontario

High Falls, Kap-Kig-Iwan Provincial Park, near Englehart

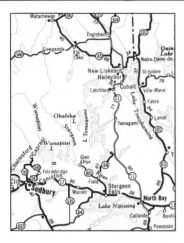

NEW LISKEARD
Between this farming community and Englehart, there is a strip of rich farmland. This agricultural region, known as the Little Clay Belt, is surrounded by the rugged Canadian Shield. A lookout south of New Liskeard offers a view of the nearby rolling farmland and the distant forests and hills of the Shield.
□ Boats tours of Lake Timiskaming are available.

HAILEYBURY
This community is situated on the hills that sweep down to 313-square-kilometre Lake Timiskaming. The town's scenic lakeside has beaches and marinas. The lake offers good fishing for bass, pike and pickerel.
□ Haileybury Fire Museum recalls the devastating fire of 1922, which almost destroyed the town and devastated the surrounding region.
□ Shaefer's Model Railroad features 100 model trains, which run through a miniature European landscape.

Jackleg mining competition, Cobalt Miners' Festival

Abandoned mine, Cobalt

COBALT
This is "the town that silver built." According to popular legend, the man who made the discovery in September 1903 was the blacksmith Fred La Rose, who threw a hammer at a fox's glimmering eyes (so he thought) and hit the world's richest silver vein. (In fact, two lumbermen working for a railway construction team made the initial discovery a month earlier.) During its boom years, Cobalt had 100 operating mines, and its population reached a peak of 10,000. (The present population is more than 2,000 inhabitants.) But Cobalt's fortunes faltered in the 1930s (when the mines closed) and revived in the 1950s and 1960s, when cobalt (for which the town is named) was mined for medical and other purposes. In all, Cobalt's mines yielded half a billion ounces of silver.
□ Cobalt's Northern Ontario Mining Museum exhibits one of the world's finest collection of native silver specimens. Visitors can explore mines, mills and lookouts on a six-kilometre self-driving tour.
□ The five-day Cobalt Miners' Festival, held in early August, offers mining competitions, concerts, dances and other events.

LATCHFORD
This tiny community claims the world's smallest covered bridge, which crosses Latchford Creek. Latchford enjoyed a brief mining boom in the early 1900s and then became a lumbering town until the 1960s. The Latchford House of Memories evokes the community's early days. Today, Latchford is a jumping-off point for canoeists, fishermen and hunters.

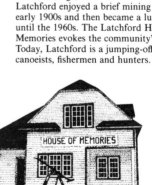

House of Memories Museum, Latchford

TEMAGAMI
Originally an Indian settlement, Temagami began to attract campers in the 1890s and became a tourist center (which it remains) after the arrival of the railway in 1903. There is good fishing, hiking, and hunting. Sightseeing flights over this region are available from local floatplane bases.
□ A plaque in nearby Finlayson Point Provincial Park honors the writer and pioneer conservationist Archibald Stansfeld Belaney, known as Grey Owl, who lived here from 1906 to 1910.

0   4   8   12   16   20 Miles

0   8   16   24   32 Kilometres

Ontario's "Near North" is an accessible wilderness within 500 kilometres of Toronto and other major cities. Lumbering, mining and tourism have encouraged the growth of such cities as North Bay. But much of this northern region is still as naturalist and writer Grey Owl described it in the early 1900s: "a great, lonely land of forest, lake and river where moose, deer, bears and wolves roam free."

Sportsmen come here in spring and summer to fish; in fall to hunt ducks, partridge, moose and deer; in winter to fish through the ice, to ski, and to drive snowmobiles on woodland trails.

Lake Nipissing—830 square kilometres of sheltered bays, sweeping beaches, open water and island-dotted shallows—is famous for its walleye. The deep, cold waters of Lake Temagami produce trophy-sized lake trout. Northern pike, muskellunge, sturgeon, whitefish, brook and rainbow trout are among 40 varieties of fishes in the lakes and rivers of the Near North.

Other attractions include a fall fair in New Liskeard and a summer miners' festival in Cobalt. Visitors to Cobalt can also tour a mine, and see the world's largest display of raw silver. Museums in Marten River tell of the area's oldest industries—trapping and logging. In North Bay, vacationers can cruise Lake Nipissing on the *Chief Commanda II*, or simply bask in the sun on the city's beaches.

ENGLEHART
This town at the northern end of the Little Clay Belt is a lumbering and farming community. Englehart's museum commemorates local pioneer life and railway development. The surrounding region offers opportunities for hunting and fishing.
□ Nearby Kap-Kig-Iwan Provincial Park has a series of falls and rapids on the Englehart River. (*Kap-Kig-Iwan* are Ojibway Indian words meaning "the high falls.") The park offers campgrounds, picnic sites and scenic lookouts. The Englehart River is too swift for swimming, but it is fine for fishing. There are four hiking trails in the park.

MARTEN RIVER
The Northern Ontario Trapper's Museum here has a trapper's cabin, a beaver house, pelts and trapping gear. An audiovisual display tells the history of trapping in this area.
□ Nearby Marten River Provincial Park preserves the pine forest that once attracted loggers to this region. A replica of a lumber camp in the park contains old-time logging equipment, including a Crazy Wheel or Barenger Brake—an arrangement of pulleys and rope used to slow log slides. A five-kilometre nature trail passes huge 300-year-old white pines. The Marten River has bass, walleye and northern pike.

The Famous Quints of Callander

Dionne quintuplets with their physician, Dr. A. R. Dafoe (1938)

The Dionne quintuplets were born in a Callander farmhouse on May 28, 1934. Their birth was unique, their survival a miracle. There had been only two other cases in all medical history of identical quintuplets—and no quintuplet had ever lived more than a few weeks. The Dionne babies, at least two months premature, were each small enough to be held in the palm of a hand.

Yvonne, Annette, Marie, Émilie and Cécile soon became the biggest domestic news item in North America. Two Chicago promoters persuaded their father to sign a contract to exhibit them at the Chicago Century of Progress Exposition. There was a public outcry and the Ontario government removed the quints from their parents' control and placed them under a board of guardians. They were moved to a specially built hospital, and in 1936 a horseshoe-shaped playground with a public observation gallery was opened. In ten years almost 3 million persons came to see the quints.

In 1943, after a long legal fight, the family was reunited in a new house provided by the Ontario government. Their birthplace is now a museum at North Bay.

NORTH BAY
Known as the Gateway to the North, this city of 50,000 began in 1882 when the CPR chose the flat shores of the north bay of Lake Nipissing as the site for railway yards. (The North Bay Area Museum recalls early settlement, lake shipping and railway building.) Today, North Bay is a distribution and industrial center, and a year-round hub for a large vacation area. The city's parks, beaches and marinas are ideal for swimming, boating and fishing.
□ From mid-May to Labor Day, the cruiser *Chief Commanda II* offers three- and six-hour trips on Lake Nipissing.
□ The Dionne Homestead Museum, beside the North Bay Regional Tourist Information Center, was the birthplace of the famous Dionne quintuplets. The small farmhouse, moved from its original site at nearby Callander, is restored and contains memorabilia, such as the basket where the quints were placed after birth.
□ At Callander, the North Himsworth Museum preserves other Dionne artifacts. The museum was once the home of Dr. Dafoe, the quints' physician.

Trout Lake, North Bay

LAKE NIPISSING
This lake—the Indian name means "little water"—was part of the historic route of the early explorers and fur traders heading westward. It provided a link between the Ottawa River valley and the French River, which flows into Georgian Bay.
□ Lake Nipissing is famous for its walleye fishing. In winter, "villages" of ice-fishing huts dot the surface of the lake.

Pine marten

Marten River
Kaotisinimigo Lake
Marten Lake
MARTEN RIVER PROV PK
99
11
23.5
Tilden Lake
Trans-Canada
Tomiko Lake
Little Sturgeon River
Tomiko River
37
Cooks Mills
Lake Talon
Trout Lake
123
63
Mattawa R
17
94
NORTH BAY
13
Nipissing Junction
Callander
CALLANDER BAY
Lake Nipissing
11

Hell's Gate and a Monster's Cave Along a Waterway to the West

Upper Ottawa River Valley

Ottawa River near Mattawa

MATTAWA
This community is situated at the junction of the Ottawa and Mattawa rivers—an historic crossroads of Canadian exploration and fur trading. (The Mattawa River was designated a Canadian Heritage River in 1988.) From the 17th century, explorers, missionaries, voyageurs and fur traders passed this way. In the early 1800s, loggers, farmers and settlers began to open up this region.
□ The Mattawa and District Museum recounts the life of the early settlers.

Echoes of Explorers on the Wild Mattawa

The wild Mattawa River—a historic link in the canoe route between the St. Lawrence River and the West—flows through Mattawa River and Samuel de Champlain provincial parks.
For more than 200 years explorers, missionaries and fur traders traveled the Ottawa and Mattawa rivers to Lake Nipissing, then the French River to Georgian Bay. Etienne Brûlé was the first white man to pass this way (in 1611). Later came Champlain, the Jesuit missionaries to Huronia, Radisson and Groseilliers, the La Vérendryes and Alexander Mackenzie. Samuel de Champlain Provincial Park on the Mattawa has a reconstruction of a *canot du maître*, a voyageur freight canoe of birch bark and spruce roots. A heritage center at Samuel de Champlain Provincial Park explains the life of voyageurs through film and exhibits.

Canot du maître *replica,*
Samuel de Champlain Provincial Park Museum

Barred owl

DRIFTWOOD PROVINCIAL PARK
The Des Joachims Dam, completed in 1950, flooded this stretch of the Ottawa River and formed Driftwood Bay. The provincial park on the bay was named for the great quantities of decorative driftwood that washed ashore after the flooding. Even today visitors can discover beautifully sculpted wood on the shoreline. A lookout in the park offers a view of the Ottawa River and the distant Laurentians on its opposite shore. Barred owls, kingfishers, great blue herons, osprey and, occasionally, a bald eagle can be spotted here. The park's trees include aspen, white birch, maple, and red and jack pine.

ROLPHTON
The Peter A. Nichol Driftwood Museum has hundreds of pieces of weirdly shaped driftwood from nearby Driftwood Provincial Park.
□ The 360,000-kilowatt Des Joachims Dam has the largest hydroelectric plant on the Ottawa River.

EGANVILLE
This picturesque community is named for John Egan, an early settler who came here in the 1820s. Fur traders plied the Bonnechere River, which divides Eganville.
□ There are guided tours of the Bonnechere Caves, eight kilometres southeast of Eganville. The limestone caves and twisting passages, formed by water erosion, contain the fossils of creatures that lived here 500 million years ago.
□ The Bonnechere River valley, between the communities of Eganville and Renfrew, is home to white-tailed deer, black bear and gray partridge.

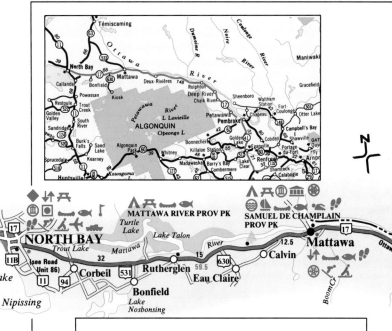

The Ottawa and Mattawa rivers were part of Canada's great waterway to the West—a highway used by explorers, missionaries and fur traders for nearly two centuries. Today, travelers can trace the same route along Highway 17.

The Ottawa River, which forms more than half the 1,120-kilometre Ontario-Quebec border, separates rich farmland to the south and an endless expanse of Laurentian hills, lakes and forests to the north.

Near the Chalk River atomic energy plant is long, sandy Pointe au Baptême, where North West Company brigades bound for Fort William stopped to "baptize" new voyageurs. After their initiation, novices treated old-timers to brandy.

The Mattawa River courses through some of the region's most rugged country. In places it slashes between towering granite walls. In cliff faces are weathered rock formations resembling castles.

A plaque in Mattawa River Provincial Park (half the river's 72-kilometre length is in the park) identifies a swift section as Porte de l'Enfer (Hell's Gate). Also in the park, near Portage de la Cave, is a steep-walled corridor darkened by overhanging cedar, spruce and pine. This brooding passage stirred the imaginations of voyageurs, who swore that a man-eating monster dwelt in the black depths of a cave on the north shore of the Mattawa River.

DEEP RIVER
This town was established in 1945 as the residential community for the employees of the nearby Chalk River nuclear facility. It was designed to preserve the natural beauty of its setting. The name of the community is taken from the journals of the 18th-century explorer Alexander Henry, who described the Ottawa River as "la rivière creuse" (the deep river). Swimming, golf and fishing are popular local summer activities.

PETAWAWA NATIONAL FORESTRY INSTITUTE
Established in 1918, the forestry institute is the oldest in Canada. There is a visitors' center and an outdoor exhibition of different local trees and related man-made wood products. The institute offers self-guided walking, driving, or water tours through its 98 hectares of forest. Bunchberry, red trillium and jack-in-the-pulpit are among the wildflowers that thrive here. There are facilities for boating, picnicking and swimming on the grounds.

CHALK RIVER
The name of the town may derive from the old-time loggers' custom of marking timber with chalk. Originally a 19th-century lumbering community, and later a farming and railway center, Chalk River became famous in 1945 when the first nuclear reactor outside the United States went into operation here. Today the Chalk River facility is one of the most advanced in the world. It is open to the public from late June to Labor Day. Tours begin at the information center, where visitors learn about nuclear energy through films, exhibits and models. The tours include a bus trip to one of the research reactors and a 3½-hour walk around the research area.

PETAWAWA
The local Canadian Forces base, originally set up in 1905, has two museums. One describes the development of the base; the other, the history of Canadian airborne forces since the Second World War.

Chalk River Nuclear Laboratories

PEMBROKE
The 19th-century lumber trade in the Ottawa River valley dominated Pembroke's early history. The community was the first in Canada to use electrical street lighting. Visitors to Pembroke's Riverside Park can see Ontario's largest totem pole. Beside the town's marina, there is the Swallows Roost, where swallows and other migratory birds gather every July before flying off to South America.
□ The pioneer buildings at Champlain Trail Museum include Pembroke's first schoolhouse (1838), a two-story 1872 log cabin (with period furnishings), a smokehouse and an outdoor bake oven. The museum has equipment from the great days of the 19th-century lumber trade. Among the items on display are a stump puller, a stone lifter, and timber-stamping hammers, used to stamp logs with the owner's mark.

RENFREW
Scottish pioneers named this bustling community after the ancestral home of the Scottish kings.
□ McDougall Mill Museum, housed in a stone gristmill (1855) on the Bonnechere River in O'Brien Park, contains pioneer artifacts from 19th-century Ottawa River valley farms. There is a suspension footbridge located next to the museum.
□ Storyland, a 16-hectare park, displays 200 fairy-tale characters in natural settings. The park also contains the 122-metre-high Champlain Lookout, which provides a superb view of the Ottawa Valley.
□ Logos Land, a 100-hectare Bible and recreation theme park, has a replica of Noah's Ark.

Bunchberry

White-tailed deer

McDougall Mill Museum, Renfrew

DACRE
Ontario's only "magnetic" hill is about one kilometre south of the junction of Highways 132 and 41. Visitors can observe an optical illusion—automobiles appear to roll up a downhill section of road.

Deep River
Chalk River
PETAWAWA NATIONAL FORESTRY INSTITUTE
Petawawa
C.F.B. PETAWAWA
Pembroke
Shady Nook
Locksley
Rankin
Lake Doré
Griersford
Eganville
Renfrew
Ferguslea
Perrault
Balaclava
Shamrock
Esmonde
Dacre
Mount St. Patrick
Alumette Lake
Indian River
Mud Lake
Lake Doré
Snake River
Mink Lake
Bonnechere R
Constant Lake
Constant
Petawawa R
Trans-Canada Highway

Beaches, Forest and History:
Links Between the Lakes

Southwestern Ontario

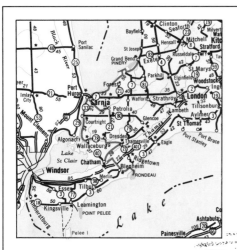

GRAND BEND
A wide sandy beach, where the Ausable River angles into Lake Huron, draws thousands of summer visitors to Grand Bend (winter population, 700). The community was originally named Brewster after the owner of a local mill. But the mill dam caused floods, and angry settlers burned the mill and renamed the town in 1860.

PINERY PROVINCIAL PARK
Sand dune ridges so high they are used as ski hills in winter rise three kilometres inland from the beach of this 22-square-kilometre park. The ridges, up to 27 metres high and 6,000 years old, were formed as sandbars when the area was a shallow bay. Well in from the lake is the northern fringe of the Carolinian forest; its trees include eight species of native oak. In the sand near the shore only small, hardy plants such as yellow puccoon are able to survive.

Yellow puccoon

KETTLE POINT
Spheres called kettles, 275 million years old, protrude from black shale on the shore of the Kettle Point Indian Reserve. Averaging 60 centimetres in diameter, the calcium carbonate kettles were exposed as the softer shale eroded. An outcropping of chert (a flintlike mineral) in nearby Ipperwash Provincial Park was a source of Indian weapons and utensils for 2,000 years.

Kettlelike rocks,
Kettle Point Indian Reserve

SARNIA
Vertical tanks like great fingers of steel, laced with tubing and ladders and railings, twinkling like fairy castles at night, identify Sarnia and the Chemical Valley south of it as the hub of Canada's oil refining and petrochemical industries. Here are the operations of Esso Petroleum, Sunoco, Shell, Dow, the NOVA Corporation and its Polysar Rubber Division, and other industry giants, such as DuPont, ICI, BASF, Akzo and Fiberglas.
□ Ships sailing the St. Clair River past Sarnia go under the Bluewater International Bridge (which links the city with Port Huron, Mich.) and over the St. Clair Tunnel (a 1,837-metre cast-iron tube built by the Grand Trunk Railway in 1889-91).

CHATHAM
The First Baptist Church is where American abolitionist John Brown and his followers in 1858 plotted a raid on an arsenal at Harper's Ferry, W.Va., as part of their campaign to end slavery in the United States. (Brown was captured as a result of the raid, tried for treason, and hanged.) Chatham was a major terminus of the Underground Railroad used by escaping slaves. Possessions of Brown's are in the Chatham-Kent Museum. Other museum exhibits include Indian and pioneer relics, an Egyptian mummy and Chatham's first steam fire engine—an 1870 Hyslop-Ronald.
□ Canoe races on the Thames highlight River Days in midsummer.

Oil refinery, Sarnia

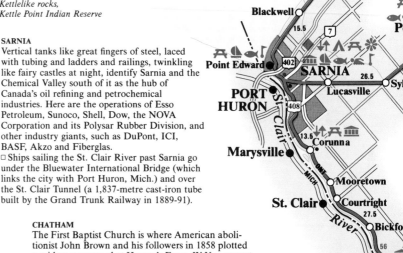

0   2   4   6   8   10 Miles

0   4   8   12   16 Kilometres

Between the sandy beaches of Lake Huron and Lake Erie is a lush farming region, the northernmost extension of the once great Carolinian forest, some fascinating glimpses of Canadian history, and, at Sarnia, the Chemical Valley that is one of Canada's great industrial areas. All this plus three of Ontario's finest provincial parks—Pinery and Ipperwash on Lake Huron, Rondeau on Lake Erie.

For more than a century vacationers have flocked to this part of southwestern Ontario. Others have come to drill for oil and to make synthetic rubber. But despite human encroachment much of the region remains pastoral and unspoiled. A few kilometres from the popular resort of Grand Bend are forests where deer still roam.

Many groups have found this a welcoming land. United Empire Loyalists established communities here after the American War of Independence. Indians found haven here, settling Moraviantown, about eight kilometres east of Thamesville, in 1792; in the Chatham-Kent Museum at Chatham are a powder horn and war club of Tecumseh, the Shawnee chief who died near Moraviantown in a battle with American invaders in the War of 1812. And it was a refuge for escaped slaves prior to the American Civil War in the 1860s. Chatham was one terminus of the Underground Railroad. Dresden was another. At Dresden is the restored home of the Rev. Josiah Henson, an escaped slave on whom Uncle Tom of *Uncle Tom's Cabin* was based.

Uncle Tom's Historic Site, Dresden

DRESDEN

The two-story house of the Rev. Josiah Henson, after whom Harriet Beecher Stowe modeled the hero of *Uncle Tom's Cabin,* is among seven buildings at the Uncle Tom's Historic Site. Henson, born a slave in Maryland in 1789, was ordained in the Methodist Episcopal Church in 1828 and escaped to Upper Canada with his wife and four children two years later. In 1841 he and a group of abolitionists bought property in this area and established the British American Institute, a refuge and vocational school for fugitive slaves. Henson's house, built soon after, still contains some of his furnishings. Other surviving buildings include a house where escaped slaves ate and slept, and a church with a pulpit from which Henson preached. A museum displays a ball and chain, whips, handcuffs, and a club used on slaves. Henson died in 1883 and is buried near his house.

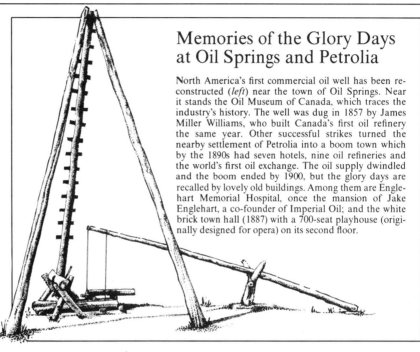

Memories of the Glory Days at Oil Springs and Petrolia

North America's first commercial oil well has been reconstructed (*left*) near the town of Oil Springs. Near it stands the Oil Museum of Canada, which traces the industry's history. The well was dug in 1857 by James Miller Williams, who built Canada's first oil refinery the same year. Other successful strikes turned the nearby settlement of Petrolia into a boom town which by the 1890s had seven hotels, nine oil refineries and the world's first oil exchange. The oil supply dwindled and the boom ended by 1900, but the glory days are recalled by lovely old buildings. Among them are Englehart Memorial Hospital, once the mansion of Jake Englehart, a co-founder of Imperial Oil; and the white brick town hall (1887) with a 700-seat playhouse (originally designed for opera) on its second floor.

THAMESVILLE

Markers and a gravel road 6.5 kilometres east identify the site of Fairfield, established in 1792 by Moravian missionaries and Delaware Indians who had fled the United States. Sacked during the War of 1812, the village was reestablished across the Thames River in 1815 as New Fairfield. The Mission Church, which still stands there, was built in 1848. The Fairfield Museum, at the 1792 site, tells the settlement's story.

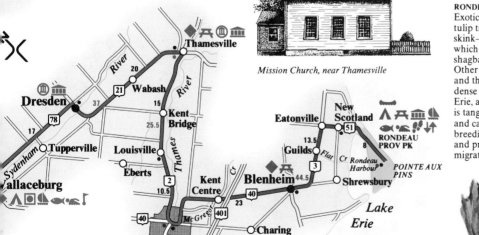

Mission Church, near Thamesville

RONDEAU PROVINCIAL PARK

Exotic plants and wildlife—from the lofty, flowering tulip tree to Ontario's only lizard, the blue-tailed skink—are to be seen in this lush park. Other trees which normally grow much farther south include shagbark hickory, black walnut, sassafras and sycamore. Other reptiles found here include the hog-nosed snake and the spiny soft-shelled turtle. The area includes dense forest, a big marsh, a warm, shallow bay of Lake Erie, and eight kilometres of sandy beach. The forest is tangled with Virginia creeper and wild grape vines, and carpeted with maidenhair fern. This is the main breeding ground in Canada for Acadian flycatchers and prothonotary warblers, and a resting place for migratory birds.

Prothonotary warbler

Giant Industries in a Garden Peninsula

Southwestern Ontario

Rosewood melodeon and chair, Hiram Walker Historical Museum, Windsor

International Peace Fountain, Windsor

WINDSOR

This major industrial center is Canada's most southerly city and busiest point of entry. The local economy is closely tied to Detroit and its automobile industry. The two cities are linked by the Ambassador Bridge (the world's longest international suspension bridge) and the Detroit-Canada tunnel.

□ Windsor and Detroit celebrate a joint International Freedom Festival—a week of parades, concerts, sporting events and fireworks—which coincides with Canada's Dominion Day (July 1) and the U.S. Independence Day (July 4).

□ Windsor's Coventry Gardens contains another symbol of Canadian-U.S. friendship—the International Peace Fountain. This spectacular floating fountain is located just offshore in the Detroit River.

□ The Hiram Walker Historical Museum, a two-story Georgian house built in 1811 by Col. François Bâby, is the oldest brick house west of Niagara. The house was used as headquarters by invading Americans in 1812, and the Battle of Windsor was fought on its grounds in 1838. The museum's furniture collection includes a rosewood melodeon made in New York in the 1840s.

□ The Art Gallery of Windsor exhibits a collection of Canadian art, including Inuit prints and carvings, a bronze by Marc-Aurèle de Foy Suzor-Côté, and works by Emily Carr, Cornelius Krieghoff and Arthur Lismer.

Military Pensioners Cottage, Fort Malden

AMHERSTBURG

Few military sites in Canada have been as strategically important as Fort Malden, now a national historic park here. Built by the British in 1796, the fort was a base in the War of 1812. When the Americans won the Battle of Lake Erie in 1813 the British pulled out of Fort Malden. Recovered from the Americans in 1815 under provisions of the Treaty of Ghent, the fort withstood four attacks by supporters of William Lyon Mackenzie during the Rebellion of 1837.

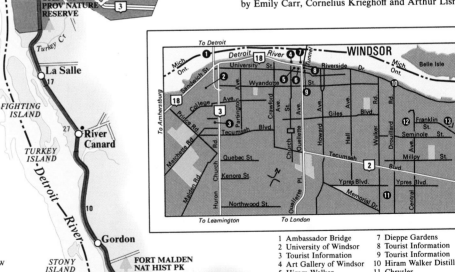

1 Ambassador Bridge
2 University of Windsor
3 Tourist Information
4 Art Gallery of Windsor
5 Hiram Walker Historical Museum
6 Cleary Auditorium
7 Dieppe Gardens
8 Tourist Information
9 Tourist Information
10 Hiram Walker Distillery
11 Chrysler
12 Ford of Canada
13 General Motors

0 1 2 3 4 5 Miles
0 2 4 6 8 Kilometres

Essex County is one of Canada's most industrialized areas. Its major city, Windsor, has an annual manufacturing output that exceeds that of many Canadian provinces. Yet Essex is essentially rural— a great garden peninsula of orchards and farmland, a place for nature study, bird-watching and lolling on sandy shores.

Bounded by Lake St. Clair to the north and Lake Erie to the south, the county has the warmest year-round climate in eastern Canada. Roadside stands here offer fruit and vegetables weeks before produce in other areas is ready for market. Ninety percent of Canada's greenhouse cucumbers, tomatoes and flowers are grown here.

In 1749 farmers from Quebec established Ontario's first permanent agricultural settlement in what is now Windsor. (Some streets follow old farm boundaries.)

Today Windsor, the largest Canadian city on the Canada–United States border, is Ontario's third biggest industrial center (after Toronto and Hamilton). It has large chemical, drug and textile industries, and produces about 25 percent of Canada's motor vehicles and parts. Two companies mine vast deposits of salt under the city.

Windsor's riverfront parks, Centennial and Dieppe, provide a fine view of the Detroit skyline. Thousands of Detroiters cross the border to enjoy Windsor's horse racing and nightclubs. In July, when the two cities host the International Freedom Festival, thousands line both sides of the Detroit River for a grand display of fireworks.

JACK MINER BIRD SANCTUARY
Daily in the migratory season tens of thousands of wild geese and ducks find rest, food and protection in the Jack Miner Bird Sanctuary near Kingsville. Established by the great naturalist in 1904, the sanctuary is open every day, except Sunday, from Oct. 1 to April 15.
□ The best time to see the migrating geese and ducks is late afternoons the last 10 days of October and the first two weeks of November, and the last 10 days of March and the first 10 of April.
□ Guides demonstrate banding and feeding and answer questions on wildlife and conservation.

Pink-flowered swamp rose mallow

A Park of Rare Plants, Birds and Butterflies

Point Pelee National Park has many plants usually associated with more southerly areas. Lake Erie moderates the seasonal changes and gives the park one of the longest frost-free growing periods in Canada.

Plant growth is rapid until late June and there is a spectacular succession of abundant flowers. The pink-flowered swamp rose mallow, Canada's only wild hibiscus, grows among marsh ferns and water lilies. During the hot, dry spells in early summer, the prickly pear cactus produces brilliant yellow flowers. The park has such rare shrubs as hop tree, spicebush and fragrant sumac.

The park's biggest attraction is its birds. Two major flyways intersect here and the spring and fall migrations are impressive. At the height of the warbler migration in May, more than 100 species can be seen and the dawn chorus is un-forgettable. Hawks, eagles, blue jays, blackbirds, ducks, geese, herons and terns all stop here. Of 300 species of birds that have been seen in the park, 90 stay to nest, including the great blue heron, saw-whet owl, great horned owl and least bittern.

In autumn thousands of monarch butterflies pause in the park on their way to southern wintering grounds.

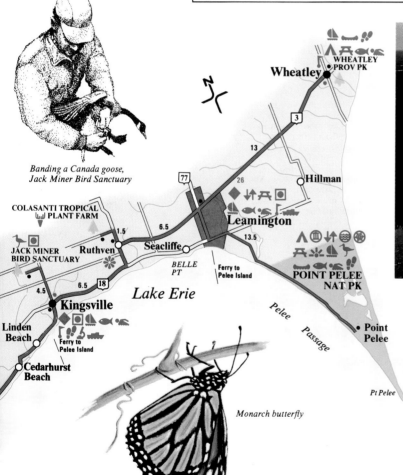

Banding a Canada goose, Jack Miner Bird Sanctuary

Monarch butterfly

Boardwalk, Point Pelee National Park

POINT PELEE NATIONAL PARK
Point Pelee is the southernmost part of the Canadian mainland, at the same latitude as northern California. The national park at the tip of this 18-kilometre-long sandy peninsula constantly struggles to maintain its triangular form against the buffeting of Lake Erie. The eastern shore is eroded by as much as half a metre a year in places but waves deposit sand and gravel on the wooded western shore. The park has one of Canada's few remaining stands of Carolinian forest. Hackberry, balck walnut, chestnut oak, cottonwood, shagbark hickory and white sassafras grow here.
□ An interpretive center identifies many of the park's animals, birds, flowers and insects. There is a nature trail through the forest. A boardwalk leads to an observation tower in the park's marsh.

A 'New London' and a Famous Festival

Southwestern Ontario

London was christened by Lieutenant Governor John Graves Simcoe on a 1792 visit to the Thames Valley. He named the site "New London" in the expectation that it would become the capital of Upper Canada. His high hopes were dashed a year later when the capital went to York (Toronto). But London grew into a prosperous industrial and commercial center where streets bear such names as Pall Mall and Piccadilly, reminders of its British namesake.

View of London from the Thames River

LUCAN
In a shaded corner of St. Patrick's Cemetery is a granite stone whose grim repetition of one date is like the sound of a bell tolling for five dead Donnellys. They were slain Feb. 4, 1880, in the bloody climax to one of Canada's most notorious feuds. It started in Ireland in the 1840s and festered for 40 years until the night vigilantes massacred James and Johannah, John, Thomas and Bridget Donnelly. The six men charged with the murders were acquitted. The stone was erected in the 1960s.

LONDON
This busy, growing city (pop. 270,000) is the center for a farming and industrial region. Its lively cultural scene encompasses an art gallery, a symphony orchestra and a professional theater company at the Grand Theatre. Academic quality and scenic beauty are combined on the campus of the University of Western Ontario. In September, the city hosts the Western Fair, one of the largest in Canada.
□ Examples of London's early-19th-century architecture include Eldon House (1834) and the fortresslike old courthouse and jail (1831). The Lawson Museum is housed in the Gothic Revival Grosvenor Lodge (1853). London's past is relived in Fanshawe Pioneer Village, a reconstructed crossroad village of the prerailroad era. Labatt's Pioneer Brewery is a replica of the original 1847 structure.
□ Among the museums worth touring are the Guy Lombardo Museum (where visitors can listen to the "sweetest music this side of heaven," while browsing through mementos of the famous bandleader's career), the Museum of Indian Archaeology and the Royal Canadian Regiment Museum.
□ London glories in its green spaces. Roughly a sixth of the city is parkland. The largest park, the 78-hectare Springbank Park on the Thames River, has a bird sanctuary, flower gardens, a zoo and Storybook Gardens, a fairyland of animals and nursery tale characters and scenes.

ST. MARYS
Overlooking the town is St. Marys District Museum in a large, old stone house (1850) built of the local limestone that characterizes many of the town's buildings, including the town hall. The museum displays pioneer objects from the region. The town also has a Gothic Revival opera house.

ST. THOMAS
Victorian elegance prevails—from the stone towers of City Hall to the Gothic-style shingled beehouse (c. 1826) on the grounds of the Elgin County Pioneer Museum. In the museum building (1848), the personal effects of Col. Thomas Talbot evoke the city's days as the "capital" of the vast Talbot Settlement.
□ Just opposite the museum, a life-size statue recalls the circus elephant "Jumbo," killed here in an 1885 railroad accident.

Gothic-style beehouse, Elgin County Pioneer Museum

HAWK CLIFF
In late September more than 20,000 migrating broad-winged hawks a day may fly over this Lake Erie vantage point. Between August and December nighthawks, peregrine falcons, bald eagles, loons and Canada geese are seen. In early October blue jays may pass at the rate of 500 a minute.

Broad-winged hawk

Middlesex County Courthouse, London

Labatt's Pioneer Brewery, London

Lucan
Prospect Hill
Elginfield   45.5   22.5
Birr   17.5
Arva
Fanshawe
Fanshawe Lake
SIFTON BOG NATURAL AREA
Thames River
LONDON
Lambeth   11.5
Scottsville
Tempo
Talbotville Royal
ST. THOMAS   10.5
Union
HAWK CLIFF
Port Stanley
Lake Erie

0   2   4   6   8   10 Miles
0   4   8   12   16 Kilometres

Simcoe's dream of settlement was realized by his former secretary, Col. Thomas Talbot, who acquired a vast tract of land north of Lake Erie in 1803. A cantankerous, hard-drinking military man, Talbot was an efficient administrator. A Talbot settler had to clear the roadway in front of his property before receiving the title to his land. Talbot's stipulation helped to create the best roads in Upper Canada.

Because of his despotic ways, Talbot was called the "Baron of Lake Erie." He lost control of his lands in the 1830s, but his imprint on this area is indelible. Many of the towns, including Talbot's "capital" of St. Thomas, owe their origins to his pioneering efforts. The fortresslike courthouse at London was modeled on Malahide Castle, Talbot's ancestral home in Ireland.

About the time Talbot opened up his tract, the land north of London was being settled by other hardworking settlers. Their values and learning came from the Bible and Shakespeare. Adherence to these traditional sources of wisdom may have influenced their decision to name one of their new towns, Stratford, and its river, the Avon.

More than a century later the pioneer dream of transplanting the best of the Old World into the New was fulfilled. In 1953 playgoers came to Stratford for the first Shakespearean festival. This enterprise thrived and has become a world-famous annual theatrical event.

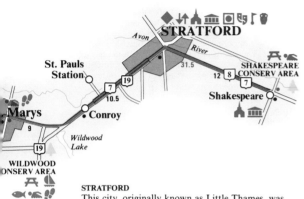

SHAKESPEARE
Sebastian Fryfogel, a Swiss immigrant, was the first settler in this area. He followed road-builders here in 1828 and built a log inn to receive the colonists who were pushing into the wilderness. In 1844-45 Fryfogel replaced the log building with a graceful brick-and-beam structure and adorned the interior with murals. The Fryfogel Inn, 2.5 kilometres east of Shakespeare, has been restored as a museum.

Fryfogel Inn, Shakespeare

STRATFORD
This city, originally known as Little Thames, was named for Shakespeare's birthplace after settlers arrived in 1831. (The Avon River had already been named by the Canada Company, which had organized the settlement of this region.) From the 1870s until the 1950s, Stratford's thriving economy was based on the railways that intersected here. Just as the railways began to decline, Stratford found its future as the site of the Stratford Festival. Today, the city's riverside parks provide a charming setting for this widely acclaimed annual theatrical event.

Stratford Stages: Past and Present

In 1951, Stratford businessman Tom Patterson had an idea—to found a Shakespearean summer festival in his hometown. The following year, the British director Tyrone Guthrie joined the Stratford venture and launched the first season in a tent theater.

On July 13, 1953, *Richard III,* with Alec Guinness and Irene Worth in the starring roles, played to a packed audience. This opening production set the pace for an exciting six weeks of theater, and established a standard that has attracted international acclaim and audiences ever since.

By 1957 the tent was replaced by the present 2,262-seat Festival Theatre. The theater was the work of Canadian architect Robert Fairfield, but its apron stage was created by British designer Tanya Moiseiwitsch, who was closely associated with Guthrie during the festival's early years. The stage thrusts into the auditorium and gives playgoers a close, unrestricted view of the performance. Other festival theaters include the 1,102-seat Avon and the smaller Third Stage, which is used for experimental productions and as a training ground for younger actors.

The Stratford festival gives roughly 500 performances during a six-month season (late April to mid-November). Its acting company numbers about 100 actors. The repertoire has been expanded to encompass classic works by Chekhov, Molière, Racine, Sophocles and other world renowned dramatists, as well as plays by top-notch contemporary Canadian playwrights, such as John Murrell, Sharon Pollock, and Michel Tremblay. Concerts, films and art exhibits also figure prominently on the festival's list of offerings.

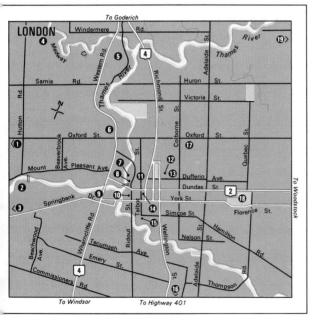

Apron stage, Festival Theatre, Stratford

1 Sifton Bog Natural Area
2 Guy Lombardo Museum
3 Springback Park
4 Museum of Indian Archaeology
5 University of Western Ontario
6 Lawson Museum
7 Eldon House
8 London Regional Art and Historic Museums
9 London Regional Children's Museum
10 Old Courthouse and Jail
11 The Grand Theatre
12 Centennial Hall
13 Tourist Information
14 Covent Garden Market
15 Labatt's Pioneer Brewery
16 Tourist Information
17 Royal Canadian Regiment Museum
18 Western Fairgrounds
19 Fanshawe Pioneer Village

Where the Faithful Drive Old-Fashioned Buggies

South-Central Ontario

Horse-drawn buggies and their somberly attired passengers remind visitors that the area surrounding the twin cities of Kitchener and Waterloo was settled by Mennonites. Some members of this faith still reject automobiles, electricity, telephones and tractors; will not accept family allowances, medicare and old-age pensions; will not vote, hold public office, or go to war.

Mennonites speak Pennsylvania Dutch, a mixture of German and English. The dia-

Mennonite horse-drawn buggy, Waterloo Region

ELMIRA
In late March or early April this market town's main street becomes a mall where pancakes, fresh maple syrup, sausages, sauerkraut, pies, cakes and apple fritter are sold during the annual Maple Syrup Festival. Thousands of residents and visitors see weaving, quilting, spinning and rug-hooking demonstrations. Visitors can tour a working maple sugar grove in horse- or tractor-drawn sleighs.

ST. JACOBS
One attraction of this community is The Meeting Place, a museum designed to help visitors understand Mennonite history, life-style and beliefs.
□ The Maple Syrup Museum of Ontario, housed in a 19th-century shoe factory, presents displays about this natural confection and demonstrations of syrup making.

WOODSIDE NATIONAL HISTORIC PARK
A driveway curves through treed grounds to Woodside, the 10-room boyhood home of Prime Minister Mackenzie King. The impressive Victorian house was built in 1853 and leased by Mackenzie King's father in 1886-93. The comfortably furnished house has the look of a home, not a museum. Among the highlights are a marble-topped table, an old kitchen cookstove, a brass bed, a square grand piano and distinctive pieces of Victoriana.
□ A contemporary exhibit portrays the family background and political life of Mackenzie King. Slide and film shows complement the display.

1 Doon Heritage Crossroads
2 Doon School of Fine Arts
3 Kitchener Farmers' Market
4 Pioneer Memorial Tower
5 Rockway Gardens
6 Joseph Schneider Haus
7 Waterloo Park
8 Wilfrid Laurier University
9 University of Waterloo

Oktoberfest parade, Kitchener

KITCHENER
With its twin city, Waterloo, Kitchener forms one of Canada's leading industrial communities. (The combined population is about 225,000.) Kitchener was founded in 1799 by Mennonites from Pennsylvania. With the arrival of settlers from Germany in 1833 the village was called Berlin. That name was dropped during the First World War.
□ The famous Kitchener Farmers' Market enlivens the city on Saturday mornings. Offered for sale are sausages, cheeses, and such Mennonite dishes as shoofly (molasses) pie.
□ The biggest annual celebration is Oktoberfest, nine days of German food and drink, oompah bands and dancing.
□ Doon Heritage Crossroads, a re-created 1860s settlement, has a collection of 23 historic buildings, including a school, church, store and station, and a museum. Joseph Schneider Haus is a restored house that reflects the life of the Mennonite pioneers during the 1850s.
□ The stone Pioneer Memorial Tower (1926), overlooking the Grand River, commemorates Menonnite settlers.
□ A plaque at the Doon School of Fine Arts marks the birthplace of Canadian landscape painter Homer Watson (1855-1936).

Pioneer Memorial Tower, Kitchener

lect evolved among their ancestors, who fled from Switzerland to Germany in the mid-1500s and, 100 years later, to Pennsylvania. In 1784, after the American Revolution, the first group came north to the Waterloo area.

The Amish, another Mennonite sect, came here from Europe after 1822. These and the Old Order Mennonites are the most conservative of more than a dozen sects in the region.

Amish men's garb lacks buttons, collars and pockets, a style originally designed to contrast with military uniforms. The Amish bury their dead in rows according to age and marital status, and grave markers bear only the initials of the deceased.

Women of the Old Order wear no jewelry, not even wedding rings. Most Old Order homes have no indoor plumbing, curtains, pictures or wallpaper.

In sickness or hard times, Mennonites take care of each other. If a barn burns, neighbors replace it within a month. Barn raisings, usually completed in one day, are triumphs of teamwork.

But members of the Old Order have made some concessions to the 20th century: their buggies now display triangular safety reflectors, as required by law. A few drive black, chromeless cars, and transact business by phones—installed in their barns.

ELORA

As the Grand River winds through Elora Gorge Conservation Area, it tumbles over The Cascade, then splits where Islet Rock perches in the middle of another waterfall. It passes Hole-in-the-Rock, a cave leading to the bottom of the gorge, and Hidden Valley, a crevice screened by trees.
□ A museum, antique and gift shops occupy restored turn-of-the-century buildings on Elora's Mill Street. Drimmies Mill, on the Grand River, has been converted into a country inn.

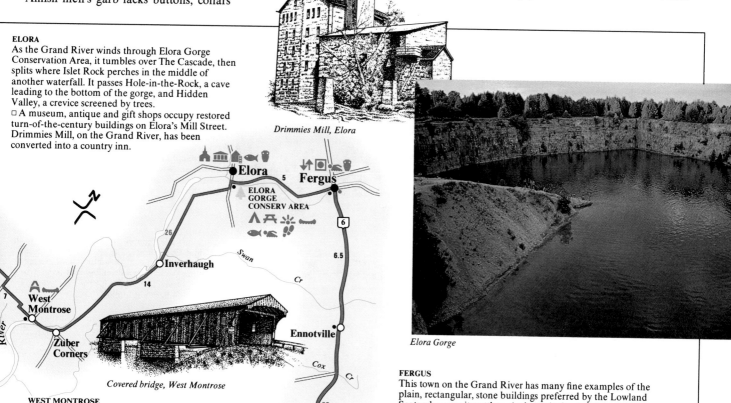

Drimmies Mill, Elora

Elora Gorge

Covered bridge, West Montrose

WEST MONTROSE

On the Grand River in this tiny community is the last of seven covered bridges that spanned Ontario rivers at the turn of the century. Built in 1881, the bridge was lit by coal-oil lamps until electric lights were installed in 1950. This reminder of the past was preserved as a historic site when the highway was rerouted over an upstream bridge in 1955.

WATERLOO

The oldest schoolhouse in the Waterloo region, a log cabin built in 1820, is in Waterloo Park. The park also has a lake, a swimming pool, a small zoo, picnic areas, tennis courts, playgrounds, and Sunday band concerts in summer. A plaque commemorates Abraham Erb, the city's founder.
□ At the University of Waterloo are Canada's largest engineering school and colleges affiliated with Anglican, Mennonite, Roman Catholic and United churches. The university's art collection includes William Kurelek's *Haying in Ontario*, and paintings, sculptures, ceramics and tapestries from 20 countries.
□ A plaque at Wilfrid Laurier University commemorates its beginnings (in 1911) as the Evangelical Lutheran Seminary of Canada.
□ The Seagram Museum describes the history of wine and spirits. Joseph Seagram (1841-1919) became sole owner of a Waterloo distillery in 1883. Seagram's VO was first blended here in 1907.

FERGUS

This town on the Grand River has many fine examples of the plain, rectangular, stone buildings preferred by the Lowland Scots who were its settlers. A plaque in front of the public library commemorates Adam Fergusson and James Webster, the town's founders.
□ In August visitors flock to the Fergus Highland Games—an annual spectacle of marching pipe bands, drum competitions, caber throws and sword dances. In September, the town hosts Ontario's oldest fall fair.

Hooded merganser, Kortright Waterfowl Park, Guelph

GUELPH

This city is characterized by fine limestone buildings such as the city hall, an excellent example of classic architecture.
□ The John McCrae House, birthplace of the author of *In Flanders Fields* (1915), contains his personal belongings.
□ Kortright Waterfowl Park, about four kilometres south of Guelph, is sanctuary for some 90 species of birds. This wildlife park and waterfowl research station also has picnic sites and a nature trail leading to an observation tower.

Through Tobacco Country
to a City Named for an Indian Chief

South-Central Ontario

Almost 50 percent of Ontario's tobacco is grown on the plains of Norfolk County near Simcoe. The combination of flat, well-drained land and sandy soil is well suited to the cultivation of tobacco. Harvesttime begins about mid-August. But before the tobacco crop is shipped to market, the leaves must be dried in the long, red or green curing sheds that are conspicuous features of the Norfolk County landscape.

Visitors to this area are struck by the fine homes and the big barns. But these signs

Heritage Inn Dining Room, Mount Pleasant

CAMBRIDGE
This city of some 80,000 was created in 1973 from the communities of Galt, Hespeler and Preston, and parts of Waterloo and North Dumfries townships. (The city was named after Cambridge Mills, which later became Preston.) During the early 19th century, all these communities used the Grand and Speed rivers to power their factories. Mill Race Park evokes this area's industrial past; some of the old riverside factories are now shopping outlets.
□ Local green spaces include Forbes Park and Riverside Park, which has picnic sites and a petting zoo. Shade's Mills Conservation Area is a popular year-round recreation spot.
□ Each summer Cambridge holds its Highland Games to honor this area's Scottish pioneers and traditions.

MOUNT PLEASANT
Eight-sided houses enjoyed a brief vogue in the mid-19th century. The style developed in the United States and spread to Ontario, where some 30 octagonal dwellings still stand. One of the surviving octagons is now the Heritage Inn Dining Room at Mount Pleasant.

A Bird-Watcher's Paradise

Within easy reach of the farming and resort community of Port Rowan is Long Point, which juts out into Lake Erie. For bird-watchers, this 40-kilometre-long peninsula of sand and marsh is a paradise. More than 350 species of birds have been recorded at Long Point; roughly a third of these nest there. Although much of Long Point is inaccessible to the public, the provincial park at the neck of the peninsula offers fine viewing, particularly during the spring migration. Nearby Long Point Bird Observatory, where staff band birds and study seasonal migration patterns, also welcomes bird-watchers.

Just north of Port Rowan is another outstanding attraction, the Backus Heritage Conservation Area, which contains 20 historic buildings, including the water-powered Backhouse Mill (1798), the oldest continuously operating gristmill in Ontario.

St. Williams Forestry Station, Ontario's first tree nursery, raises more than 7 million seedlings each year. The station, near St. Williams, can be toured.

PARIS
The Paris Plains Church (1845) is a fine example of cobblestone construction, rare in Canada. Another early structure is Penmarvian (formerly The Stone House), built in 1845-48 in Greek Revival style by Hiram "King" Capron, the town's founder. Capron arrived from Vermont in 1822. Due to his efforts the local gypsum deposits were developed and plaster of Paris made, giving the town its name.

Tobacco plant

Paris Plains Church

SIMCOE
The Eva Brook Donly Museum exhibits pioneer lamps, farm implements and paintings by Norfolk County artists.
□ A cairn in Lynnwood Park commemorates Gen. John Graves Simcoe, first lieutenant governor of Upper Canada, for whom the town is named.

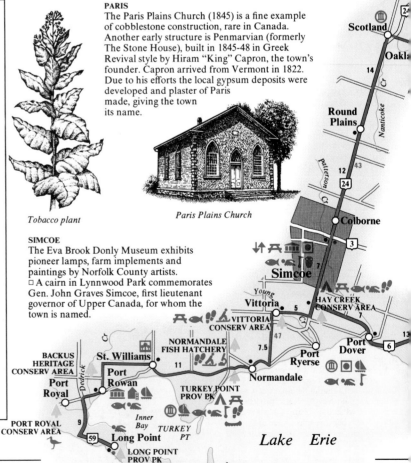

Whistling swans, Long Point

0   2   4   6   8   10 Miles

0   4   8   12   16 Kilometres

of well-being were not always present, nor was the land as open as it is now. When the first settlers arrived, there were vast stands of white and red pine. The trees were cut down to create farmland. The settlers grew grain, vegetables and fruit in the light soil. Lacking the binding of deep-rooted trees, the hard-won farmland eroded. Fertile fields were transformed into drifting sand, and many farms were abandoned. Fortunes were reversed in the 1920s, when local farmers began growing the tobacco crop that has turned their land into some of the most valuable in Ontario.

To the north of Norfolk County is Brantford. The city owes its name to Joseph Brant, a Mohawk chief, and its renown to the inventor, Alexander Graham Bell. Brant led the Indians of the Six Nations here in 1784 when their allegiance to the British during the American War of Independence cost them their land in upper New York State. Less than a hundred years later, Bell conceived the idea for the telephone here.

Sassafras tree

CAMBRIDGE

SHADE'S MILLS CONSERV AREA

Wrigley Corners

F.W.R. DICKSON WILDERNESS AREA
Sassafras trees reach the northern limit of their range in this wilderness area of marsh and meadows, tamarack swamp and hardwood forest. A nature trail passes through the wilderness on an elevated boardwalk through the swamp and close to fox dens in the forest. Feeding stations attract cardinals, woodpeckers and juncos.

Wyndham Hills

BRANTFORD

TUTELA HEIGHTS

Ohsweken

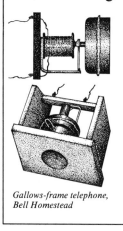
Chapel of the Mohawks, Brantford

When 'Long Distance' Called Mr. Bell

Gallows-frame telephone, Bell Homestead

In the summer of 1874, while visiting his parents' home in Tutela Heights near Brantford, Alexander Graham Bell had an idea that became the basis of the telephone. Returning to Boston where he worked as a speech therapist, Bell took two years to build his first, experimental apparatus. On Aug. 3, 1876, Bell tested his invention at the Dominion Telegraph Company office in Mount Pleasant. He heard his uncle, who was in Brantford, recite Shakespeare's "To be or not to be." This was the first intelligible telephone transmission from one building to another. One week later the first long-distance call was made—from Brantford to Paris, 13 kilometres away. The Bell Telephone Company came into being and by November 1877 it had four subscribers. The fifth request for the new device came from Prime Minister Alexander Mackenzie, who wanted a telephone link between his Ottawa office and the governor-general's residence. The company supplied it—and predated the prime minister's application to make him officially the first subscriber.

OHSWEKEN (SIX NATIONS RESERVE)
Iroquois Indians reenact their history at an August pageant in an open-air theater on the Six Nations Reserve.
□ The Haldimand Grant, which assigned the reserve to the Six Nations in 1784, is displayed in the original Band Council House (1863).
□ Exhibits at Chiefswood, the restored birthplace of Métis poet Emily Pauline Johnson (1861-1913), include her writing desk and several of her original manuscripts. Built in 1835 by her father, Chief G. H. M. Johnson, the mansion is furnished in the 1870s style.
□ A plaque commemorates Joseph Brant's son, John, the first Indian elected to the Upper Canada legislative assembly (in 1832).

Joseph Brant Monument, Victoria Park, Brantford

NANTICOKE
The Ontario Hydro Thermal Electric Power Plant (the world's largest), the blast furnaces of a giant steel processor, and other factories have transformed this Lake Erie city of some 20,200 inhabitants into an industrial center. Tours of the power plant and other facilities can be arranged.

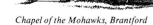
Bell Homestead, Brantford

BRANTFORD
A monument in Victoria Park honors Joseph Brant, the Mohawk chief, who gave this city its name. An inscribed sundial in Lorne Park marks the site where Brant and his Indian followers took up land given them by the British Crown in 1784.
□ The Bell Memorial on West Street commemorates Alexander Graham Bell's invention of the telephone at the family homestead in Tutela Heights.
□ The Bell Homestead, overlooking the Grand River, contains replicas of early telephones and many of the family's original furnishings. Canada's first telephone business office and switchboard (1877)—the Rev. Thomas Henderson's house—are on the grounds.
□ St. Paul's, Her Majesty's Chapel of the Mohawks, was the first Protestant church (1785) built in what is now Ontario. In the churchyard is Brant's tomb.
□ The Brant County Museum has a collection of Indian artifacts, antique weapons and period furniture.
□ The Glenhyrst Art Gallery of Brant, housed in an 11-room mansion, has paintings by Canadian artists Homer Watson and David Milne.

The Steel Capital of Canada in a Land of Blossoms and Wine

Niagara Peninsula

Hamilton is the steel-making capital of Canada. But it is free from the urban blight that afflicts many industrial centers. Older districts in the heart of the city, such as Hess Village, have been lovingly restored. Handsome modern buildings, such as Hamilton Place, an imposing cultural center, reflect vitality and confidence.

There are some 45 parks in the Hamilton area. At the Royal Botanical Gardens, abandoned gravel pits have been transformed into formal rock gardens and floral displays.

Steel mill, Hamilton

DUNDURN CASTLE
Hamilton's restored and refurnished Dundurn Castle reflects the elegant life-style of Sir Allan Napier MacNab, a lawyer, promoter, financier and politician, who built it in 1832-34. □ Among 35 rooms open to the public are a black walnut-paneled library from which MacNab practiced law and a dining room with an elegant mahogany table seating 20. □ The Hamilton Military Museum, on the Dundurn Castle grounds, is housed in The Battery Lodge, which was built in the 1830s.

HAMILTON
One of Canada's leading industrial cities, Hamilton (pop. 425,000) is situated on Burlington Bay on Lake Ontario. A shipping canal cuts through a sandspit at the mouth of the bay. Hamilton Harbour, one of the best on the Great Lakes, handles the third largest volume of shipping in Canada. A 90-metre-high embankment, known as the "mountain," rises above the city and, until recently, hemmed in the city southward expansion. The city is well endowed with parks and the famous Royal Botanical Gardens.
□ Hamilton Place is the cultural heart of the city. The nearby Art Gallery of Hamilton displays a fine collection of paintings, including works by Canadian painters William Kurelek, Cornelius Krieghoff and Marc-Aurèle de Foy Suzor-Côté. McMaster University is the home of one of the country's first nuclear reactors. The Museum of Steam and Technology, the Warplane Heritage Museum and a military museum at Dundurn Castle are worth visiting.
□ Whitehern, a handsome limestone house built in the 1840s, has been preserved in the heart of the city.

CANADIAN FOOTBALL HALL OF FAME
The shrine room of the Hall of Fame has busts of football's builders and great players, a computer that answers questions about Canadian Football League records, and a theater featuring Grey Cup films. Four stages of the game's evolution—1900, 1920, 1950 and the present—are depicted in a stained-glass mural.

Dundurn Castle, Hamilton

Stained-glass mural, Canadian Football Hall of Fame

ROYAL BOTANICAL GARDENS
The Royal Botanical Gardens have an arboretum and herbarium, a teahouse and a children's garden. The vast property includes the famous Rock Garden at the northwest tip of Hamilton; the Spring Garden (in Burlington), with June displays of irises, lilies and peonies, and the game preserve of Cootes Paradise. Walkways and nature trails crisscross the gardens which are open every day of the year.

1 Royal Botanical Gardens
2 McMaster University
3 Dundurn Castle and Military Museum
4 Hess Village
5 Art Gallery of Hamilton
6 Canadian Football Hall of Fame
7 Hamilton Place
8 Whitehern
9 Tourist Information
10 Sam Lawrence Park
11 Canadian Warplane Heritage Museum
12 Steel Company of Canada
13 James N. Allen Sky Bridge
14 Confederation Park
15 Hamilton Museum of Steam and Technolo

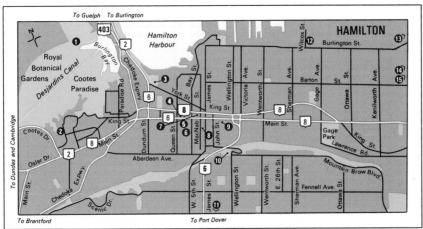

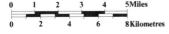

Trails from the gardens lead to nearby Sam Lawrence Park, on the top of Hamilton Mountain. Here visitors can view the city's steel mills, the harbor (one of the busiest on the Great Lakes), the James N. Allen Skyway Bridge and Lake Ontario.

East of Hamilton is the Niagara Peninsula, Canada's fruit belt and major wine-producing region. Most Canadian wine is pressed from grapes grown in its rich soil and mild climate. The scenery here is especially striking in May, when the cherry, peach and apple trees burst into blossom.

The area was settled by Loyalists, Mennonites, Quakers, Huguenots and at least 20 other groups that followed in their wake. The diverse cultural heritages are honored during a week-long Folk Arts Festival each spring in St. Catharines. The event begins a time of festivals, open-air markets and county fairs. The Niagara Grape and Wine Festival in September celebrates the bountiful harvest with a colorful parade in the streets of St. Catharines.

Lighthouse at Port Dalhousie near St. Catharines

STONEY CREEK
A battle on June 6, 1813, in which 700 British regulars routed 2,000 American troops, is commemorated in Battlefield Memorial Park. Battlefield House, which served as American headquarters, is a museum with displays relating to the battle and furnishings dating to 1790.

VINELAND
At Vineland, the Horticultural Institute, part of the Ontario Ministry of Agriculture and Foods, is a research facility open to the public. On the grounds, there are flower gardens and greenhouses where vegetables are grown in experimental conditions.

ST. CATHARINES
Situated on the Welland Canal just south of Lake Ontario, St. Catharines (pop. 124,000) is in the heart of the Niagara fruit-growing and wine-making area.
□ Remains of the first three Welland canals (1829, 1845 and 1887) still survive here. (The present—and fourth—canal dates from 1932.) St. Catharines Historical Museum has displays and exhibits that describe the building of the canal. A viewing center is open at Lock 3.
□ St. Catharines hosts the Royal Canadian Henley Regatta (early August), the Blossom and the Folk Arts Festival in May, and the biggest bash of all—the Niagara Grape and Wine Festival—in September.
□ Morningstar Mill-Mountains Mills Museum is a fine old gristmill (1872) at De Cew Falls. A nearby plaque marks the site of De Cew House. On June 22, 1813, Laura Secord came to the house (about a mile from Beaver Dams) to warn the British of an impending American attack.

Battlefield Monument, Stoney Creek

Lake Ontario

STONEY CREEK
Fruitland
DEVIL'S PUNCH BOWL CONSERV AREA
Winona
FIFTY POINT CONSERV AREA
BEAMER MEMORIAL CONSERV AREA
Grimsby Beach
Grimsby
Forty Mile Cr
Beamsville
Vineland
Jordan
BALL'S FALLS CONSERV AREA
Twenty Mile Cr
Sixteen Mile Cr
Twelve Mile Cr
Martindale Pond
Port Dalhousie
ST. CATHARINES
Welland Canal
QEW

JORDAN
The Jordan Historical Museum of the Twenty consists of the Vintage (c. 1840) and Jacob Fry (1815) houses, a stone schoolhouse (1859) and churchyard whose headstones mark the graves of Mennonite settlers. A rare, giant cider press on the grounds is a pioneer version of European fruit presses. Lowered by a three-metre screw carved from solid black walnut, the huge press beam exerted a force of 18 tonnes.

Marlatt Tavern door, Grimsby Museum

GRIMSBY
This thriving community was originally called "The Forty" because it was located on Forty Mile Creek. In 1816 it was renamed after Grimsby in England.
□ A Windsor side chair belonging to Col. Robert Nelles, a Loyalist settler in this region, is one of the items in the collection of the Grimsby Museum. The elaborate front door of the museum was once the entrance to the local Marlatt Tavern (1855-73).

Fruit press, Jordan Historical Museum of the Twenty

Parades and Grape Stomping Contests

For ten days in September, during the Niagara Grape and Wine Festival, St. Catharines lets go in a carnival overflowing with parades, marching bands and floats. The yearly celebration includes a grape-stomping contest between local mayors, and the crowning of a Royal Family to reign over the festival.

Ninety per cent of the wine produced in Canada comes from the Niagara Peninsula. Until the mid-1940s the grapes grown in this area were suitable only for the production of sherry and port. But with the introduction of new grape varieties in the 1970s, Ontario's wines have acquired a subtler flavor and are gaining international recognition. (Barnes Wines Ltd., Canada's oldest winery (1873), and Jordan Wines, both in St. Catharines, and Andrés Wines, in Winona, offer tours by appointment.)

A Mighty Cascade That Has Been 'Conquered,' Tamed and Saved

Niagara Peninsula

A "vast and prodigious Cadence of Water": that was Niagara Falls as described by Jean-Louis Hennepin in 1678. The Belgian-born missionary-explorer was the first eyewitness to write about the two mighty cataracts on the Niagara River—Canada's Horseshoe Falls (670 metres wide,

Remembering 1812

During the War of 1812, the Niagara Peninsula resounded with the clash of American and British arms. Two British strongholds of this time—Old Fort Erie (built in 1764) and Fort George (1797-99) at Niagara-on-the-Lake—still survive. By the end of the war, the two forts had passed from the British to the Americans and then back to the British, who abandoned them as strategic liabilities. Today, Old Fort Erie and Fort George National Historic Park help visitors recall the conflict.

Two legendary figures—military commander Sir Isaac Brock (1769-1812) and Laura Secord (1775-1868)—are also remembered here. At Queenston Heights, Brock routed American forces, but died in battle. Shields and other symbols of war (*right*) decorate the 64-metre-high Brock Monument (built in 1854) at Queenston Heights Park. Just below the monument, the Laura Secord Homestead honors the famous Canadian heroine. Her famous 30-kilometre walk from Queenston to Beaver Dams in 1813 saved the British from American attack.

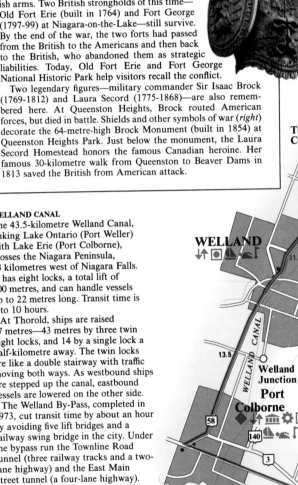

Ring-billed gull, Navy Island

WELLAND CANAL

The 43.5-kilometre Welland Canal, linking Lake Ontario (Port Weller) with Lake Erie (Port Colborne), crosses the Niagara Peninsula, 13 kilometres west of Niagara Falls. It has eight locks, a total lift of 100 metres, and can handle vessels up to 22 metres long. Transit time is 8 to 10 hours.

□ At Thorold, ships are raised 57 metres—43 metres by three twin flight locks, and 14 by a single lock a half-kilometre away. The twin locks are like a double stairway with traffic moving both ways. As westbound ships are stepped up the canal, eastbound vessels are lowered on the other side.

□ The Welland By-Pass, completed in 1973, cut transit time by about an hour by avoiding five lift bridges and a railway swing bridge in the city. Under the bypass run the Townline Road tunnel (three railway tracks and a two-lane highway) and the East Main Street tunnel (a four-lane highway).

□ The first Welland Canal (1824-29) was replaced by those built in 1845-86, in 1887-1931, and the present channel, 1913-32.

FORT ERIE

Situated on the Niagara River opposi[te] Buffalo, Fort Erie is linked to the United States by the Peace Bridge. It one of the busiest points of entry into this country. The scenic 56-kilometre Niagara River Parkway extends from Fort Erie to Niagara-on-the-Lake. Local attractions include the Mildred M. Mahoney Dolls' House Gallery an[d] Fort Erie Historical Railroad Museu[m]

PORT COLBORNE

Port Colborne is the site of Lock 8, reputedly the largest single lock in the world. Visitors can see the 421-metre-long lock from Fountain View Park.

□ This flour-milling center offers boat-launching facilities and sandy beaches. The Historical and Marine Museum—a complex of six buildings—exhibits relics of the region's pioneer and naval past.

Welland Canal

0 1 2 3 4 5 Miles
0 2 4 6 8 Kilometres

54 metres high), and the American Falls (305 metres wide, 56 metres high).

The cascade Hennepin saw has been greatly tamed. Power developments on both sides of the border divert waters that would otherwise flow over the falls.

Millions visit the falls every year. The tourist trade at Niagara developed in the early 1800s. With the tourists came daredevils, who defied the falls in barrels, boats and rubber balls. The most celebrated stunter was a French acrobat, the Great Blondin, who walked a tightrope across the Niagara Gorge in 1859. Stunting brought brief fame to some, but others died in their attempts to "conquer" the falls. Stunting was outlawed in 1912.

This legislation was one more attempt to prevent the scenic wonder from becoming a hucksters' paradise. Alarmed that entrepreneurs were grabbing land near the falls, Ontario created Queen Victoria Falls Park (Canada's first provincial park) in 1887, for public enjoyment of the area's beauty. Today, the Niagara Parks Commission maintains all land adjacent to the river and the Niagara River Parkway. Along this scenic route, visitors can discover enduring reminders of the War of 1812 at Fort Erie, Queenston and Niagara-on-the-Lake.

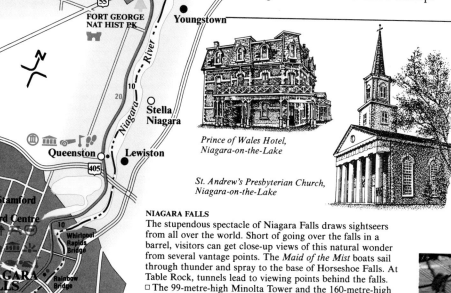

Prince of Wales Hotel, Niagara-on-the-Lake

St. Andrew's Presbyterian Church, Niagara-on-the-Lake

NIAGARA-ON-THE-LAKE

Originally known as Newark, Niagara-on-the-Lake was Upper Canada's first capital (1791-96) and a thriving port until the opening of the Welland Canal in 1829 reduced its shipping trade. Today Niagara-on-the-Lake is everyone's dream of what an early 19th-century town should be. On the main street are the Niagara Apothecary Museum (1866) and the elegant Prince of Wales Hotel. The town is remarkable for its well-preserved 19th-century residences, such as the Kirby (1815) and McFarlane (1800) houses. St. Andrew's Presbyterian Church (1831) is a fine Greek Revival structure.

□ The Shaw Festival (early April to mid-October) attracts 250,000 visitors. Its repertoire comprises plays by George Bernard Shaw and his contemporaries.

NIAGARA FALLS

The stupendous spectacle of Niagara Falls draws sightseers from all over the world. Short of going over the falls in a barrel, visitors can get close-up views of this natural wonder from several vantage points. The *Maid of the Mist* boats sail through thunder and spray to the base of Horseshoe Falls. At Table Rock, tunnels lead to viewing points behind the falls.

□ The 99-metre-high Minolta Tower and the 160-metre-high Skylon Tower, which overlook the falls, are topped by revolving restaurants. Helicopter flights over the falls are also available.

□ Some three kilometres below the falls, an aerocar travels on a 549-metre-long cable over the Niagara Gorge. Just north of the Whirlpool Rapids Bridge, an elevator takes visitors to walkways along the rapids of the Niagara River.

□ Quite apart from the falls, the city of Niagara Falls offers entertaining attractions for all tastes—marvels, midways, menageries and wax museums.

□ Navy Island in the Niagara River is sanctuary for ring-billed gulls and some 20 species of duck.

□ Niagara Glen, below the Whirlpool Rapids, has tulip trees and other plants rare in Canada.

Aerocar over the gorge at Niagara Falls

Leaves and bud of the tulip tree, Niagara Glen

A Cataract in Retreat

Some 12,500 years ago, as the last ice age was ending, old lakes were reborn. One was Lake Erie, which first drained southwest into the Mississippi River system.

As the great thaw continued, the lake found a new, lower outlet—north through the channel of the Niagara River into Lake Iroquois, the forerunner of Lake Ontario. When the water plunged some 60 metres over the edge of the Niagara Escarpment, Niagara Falls was born. At that moment, the mighty cataract began retreating some 1.2 metres a year. Already it is some 11 kilometres south of its birthplace at Queenston.

The rapid recession is due to the sedimentary rock structure of the escarpment—soft shale and limestone overlaid by harder limestone and dolomite. Shale at the base erodes quickly, leaving the upper, more resistant ledges jutting out. These, unable to support their own weight, break off and topple into the pool below.

Freshly Painted Gingerbread Trim and Cedar Rail Fences

Central Ontario

This is rural, small-town Ontario caught up in a fling with nostalgia. The pioneer village, the historical plaque, the museum and the restoration have all taken hold and flourished here. The gingerbread trim on brick, story-and-a-half farmhouses is freshly painted. Cedar rail fences, split and erected a hundred years ago by settlers, snake along roads and across fields. In the river towns, restored mansions stand grandly in view on the main streets. Old bank

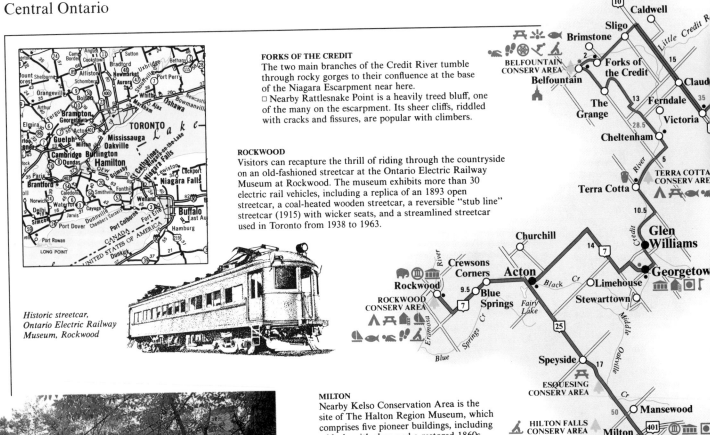

FORKS OF THE CREDIT
The two main branches of the Credit River tumble through rocky gorges to their confluence at the base of the Niagara Escarpment near here.
□ Nearby Rattlesnake Point is a heavily treed bluff, one of the many on the escarpment. Its sheer cliffs, riddled with cracks and fissures, are popular with climbers.

ROCKWOOD
Visitors can recapture the thrill of riding through the countryside on an old-fashioned streetcar at the Ontario Electric Railway Museum at Rockwood. The museum exhibits more than 30 electric rail vehicles, including a replica of an 1893 open streetcar, a coal-heated wooden streetcar, a reversible "stub line" streetcar (1915) with wicker seats, and a streamlined streetcar used in Toronto from 1938 to 1963.

Historic streetcar, Ontario Electric Railway Museum, Rockwood

MILTON
Nearby Kelso Conservation Area is the site of The Halton Region Museum, which comprises five pioneer buildings, including a blacksmith shop and a restored 1860s barn. The carriage house displays a collection of 19th-century horse-drawn vehicles. A display center describes local history.

BURLINGTON
A silver gorget (a decorative pendant), George III's gift to Joseph Brant, is displayed in the museum here that honors the memory of the Mohawk chief. The building is a replica of a cedar house built by Brant around 1800. Brant was granted much of the surrounding land as a reward for his loyalty during the American Revolution. He died here in 1807.

Joseph Brant Museum, Burlington

Falls on the Credit River, near Belfountain

DUNDAS
Dundas calls itself "The Cactus Capital of Canada." Local greenhouses display cacti and succulents in profusion, and a cactus festival is held here every August.
□ The town hall is one of the finest examples of pre-1850 Roman Classic architecture to be found in the province.

Tall bearded iris

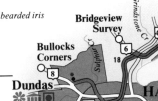

0 1 2 3 4 5 Miles
0 2 4 6 8 Kilometres

barns house the herds of holsteins for which the region is famous, and steam-era machinery is preserved in odd corners of farms.

The Credit Valley is a gently rolling landscape of stony pastures, limestone faults and deep woods crossed by rushing streams. Old dams, still evident on the rivers, once backed up water to run mill wheels geared to saws and grindstones, and later propelled turbines for electric power. It was here in 1883 that the Smith farm became the first electrified house in Ontario, and the old agricultural way of life began to change. Today, exhibits at the Ontario Agricultural Museum near Milton recount the history of farming in the province.

Sunday drivers and antique collectors have helped to preserve the character of the Credit Valley. Onetime general stores, hay-lofts, blacksmith shops and inns are now antique shops, artists' studios, galleries and restaurants. The Black Creek Pioneer Village re-creates rural life of a century ago. The stone and rough-hewn timber galleries of the McMichael Canadian Collection in Kleinburg display the works of the Group of Seven, many of whom lived in this area. These attractions, set in a rich, rolling farmland, give visitors an opportunity to experience the best of the past and present in rural southern Ontario.

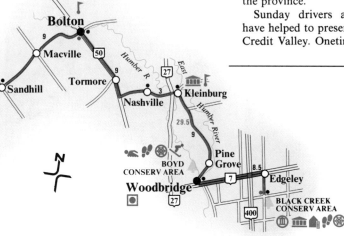

Gristmill, Black Creek Pioneer Village

BLACK CREEK CONSERVATION AREA
This is the site of Black Creek Pioneer Village, which depicts 19th-century life prior to 1867. The nucleus of the village is the Daniel Strong farm of five log farm buildings, all still standing where they were originally built.
□ Some 25 other buildings here, including a general store, gristmill, weaver's and shoemaker's shops, were brought from elsewhere and reconstructed on their present sites.
□ Burwick House, built in 1844, has early Ontario furnishings, antique rugs and tapestries. The Daziel Barn Museum, a huge cantilever barn (1809), contains the largest collection of 19th-century toys in Canada.
□ On educational tours of the village, students dip candles, churn butter, card wool, hook rugs, and bake bread in a wood-burning oven.

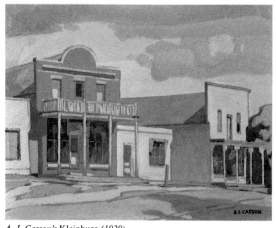

A. J. Casson's Kleinburg *(1929)*

A Home for the Group of Seven

One of Canada's largest collections of paintings by the Group of Seven is at Kleinburg in the McMichael Canadian Collection. Formed in 1920, the Group included Frank Carmichael, Lawren Harris, A.Y. Jackson, Frank Johnson, Arthur Lismer, J. E. H. MacDonald and F.H. Varley. Tom Thomson, who drowned in Algonquin Park in 1917, was one of the major influences on the Group. Works by these artists, and by later members of the Group such as A.J. Casson, are displayed at Kleinburg.

The collection was begun as a hobby by Robert and Signe McMichael in a six-room, stone-and-timber house they called *Tapawingo* (an Indian word meaning "place of joy"). In 1965 the McMichaels turned the collection over to the Province of Ontario. The gallery also houses Indian and Inuit art. The shack where Tom Thomson painted when he lived in Toronto is on the grounds.

OAKVILLE
More than two dozen 19th-century buildings in "Old Oakville" date from an era when shipbuilding flourished here. Oakville Museum comprises three buildings: the Thomas House (1829), the Old Post Office (1835) and the Custom House (1855). All contain historic exhibits and can be visited. Other old buildings include St. Andrew's Church (1840), the stone Romain and MacDougald Granary (1854) and St. Jude's Church (1883).

Old Post Office Museum, Oakville

BRONTE CREEK PROVINCIAL PARK
The deep ravine of Bronte Creek winds through this year-round provincial park. One of the park's features is Spring Lane Farm, a turn-of-the-century homestead, whose displays depict pioneer farm life. A separate children's farm has animals to see and touch, and a barn playloft full of hay, ropes and slides.

Eastern bluebird

Lake

Ontario

Canada's Major Metropolis, Still a 'People City'

Toronto's SkyDome, CN Tower, Harbourfront and skyscrapers (left), symbols of dynamic growth, light up the sky. The 41-story gold-glass tower of the Royal Bank Plaza (top) epitomizes the burgeoning Bay Street financial district. Casa Loma (above) is an extravagant vestige of the city's past.

In recent times, few cities in North America have changed as rapidly as Toronto. Explosive progress has turned this city of 3.6 million into a world-beater without inflicting major social ills. By and large, Canada's major metropolis is safe, civilized and orderly. Its success is a source of envy and wonder.

Toronto earned an early reputation as a livable, if dull, place. Originally a British garrison town, Toronto was a port, a seat of government and a regional center of 9,000 when it became a city in 1834. For more than a century, Toronto extended its economic influence, but remained resolutely a bastion of Anglo-Saxon rectitude. The postwar influx of immigrants from widely different cultures eventually transformed "Toronto the Good" into a cosmopolitan "People City." Today, Toronto fulfills a destiny implicit in its Huron name, which means a "place of meeting," and enriches its citizens' lives with an exciting array of museums, theaters and recreation areas.

Toronto's wealth stems from its role as Canada's business and manufacturing center. The Toronto Stock Exchange, the seventh largest in the world and the largest in Canada, is the heart of Bay Street, the site of bank and business headquarters. Toronto's central cluster of skyscrapers—the 54-story Toronto-Dominion Centre, the 57-story Commerce Court and the 74-story First Canadian Place—is an impressive endowment to what is essentially a city of small, diverse neighborhoods. Within its complex urban setting, Toronto also maintains a generous allotment of green space, as well as treasured vestiges of its past, such as Osgoode Hall, The Grange and Casa Loma.

Art Gallery of Ontario (12)
Major paintings include Rubens' *The Elevation of the Cross* and Gainsborough's *The Harvest Waggon*. The Canadian Collection features paintings by Krieghoff, Kane, Borduas, Carr, Thomson and the Group of Seven. The gallery houses the world's largest public collection of works by the British sculptor Henry Moore (1898-1986). Adjacent to the gallery is The Grange (1817-20), a restored manor of the 1830s and the original home of the Art Gallery of Ontario.

Campbell House (13)
The 1822 Georgian mansion of Sir William Campbell, chief justice of Upper Canada (1825-29), has been restored.

Canada's Wonderland (37)
This world-class theme park has 150 hectares of everything from roller coasters and wet-water rides to cartoon characters come to life and aquatic shows featuring dolphins and sea lions.

Canadian National Exhibition (1)
The largest annual exhibition in the world and a yearly event since 1878, the Canadian National Exhibition has 120 hectares of midway, grandstand shows, sports events and flower displays. There are science, education and fashion exhibits, and an agricultural display that features the latest computer technology of a working farm. Other popular attractions are the Canadian International Air Show and Kid's World, with face painting, pony rides and stage shows.

Casa Loma (41)
North America's largest castle was built by industrialist Sir Henry Pellatt in 1911-14. The 98-room building has hidden panels and long passageways, and a 210-metre tunnel leading to stables finished in Spanish mahogany.

Chinatown (6)
One of the largest Chinatowns in North America fills several city blocks from Bathurst to Bay streets. There are Chinese restaurants and foods markets, bookstalls and movie theaters, and Oriental shops that sell ivory, jade and silks.

Enoch Turner Schoolhouse (33)
Toronto's first free school, built by brewer Enoch Turner in 1848, is restored and contains displays about 19th-century Toronto.

Fort York (4)
Costumed guides conduct tours of the restored blockhouses, barracks and officers'

quarters within this walled garrison (1793, rebuilt 1813-15).

Gibson House (39)

This red brick Georgian house, built in 1849-51, was once the home of David Gibson, who supported William Lyon Mackenzie during the rebellion of 1837. The house, restored to its original elegance, offers pioneer craft and cooking demonstrations.

Harbourfront (18)

This 40-hectare renovated waterfront development attracts more than 3 million visitors every year. Its attractions include marinas, restaurants, shops, contemporary art galleries, craft studios and Canada's largest antique market. Harbourfront is also the site of concerts and cultural events.

High Park (38)

Nature trails in 141-hectare High Park wind past rock gardens, floral displays, a small zoo and Grenadier Pond. Much of the park was bequeathed to the city by John G. Howard (1803-90), one of Toronto's first surveyors and engineers. Howard's house, Colborne Lodge (1837), is now a museum in High Park containing a collection of his own watercolors and other belongings.

Kensington Market (5)

Not far from downtown skyscrapers, this colorful street market shares space with a cluster of ethnic restaurants.

Mackenzie House (29)

This two-story stone building (1857) was the home of William Lyon Mackenzie, Toronto's first mayor (1834), and leader of the rebellion of 1837.

Marine Museum of Upper Canada (2)

The museum is in the onetime officers' quarters of Stanley Barracks (1841). Preserved in drydock is the tugboat *Ned Hanlan* (1932).

Massey Hall (26)

Built in 1894, this Canadian musical landmark still hosts concerts and other events.

Metropolitan Toronto Zoo (45)

This 287-hectare world-class zoo is set in the rolling countryside of the Rouge River valley. More than 4,000 animals live in glass-roofed pavilions and outdoor settings designed to simulate their natural environments. Visitors can ride the Monorail or Zoomobile, or follow color-coded trails to view exotic animals grouped according to where they live in the wild.

Montgomery's Inn (36)

This stone inn, built about 1830 by Irish-born innkeeper Thomas Montgomery, is an example of Loyalist or late Georgian architecture. The interior has been restored in the style of the 1830-55 period; costumed staff re-create the atmosphere of its bygone days.

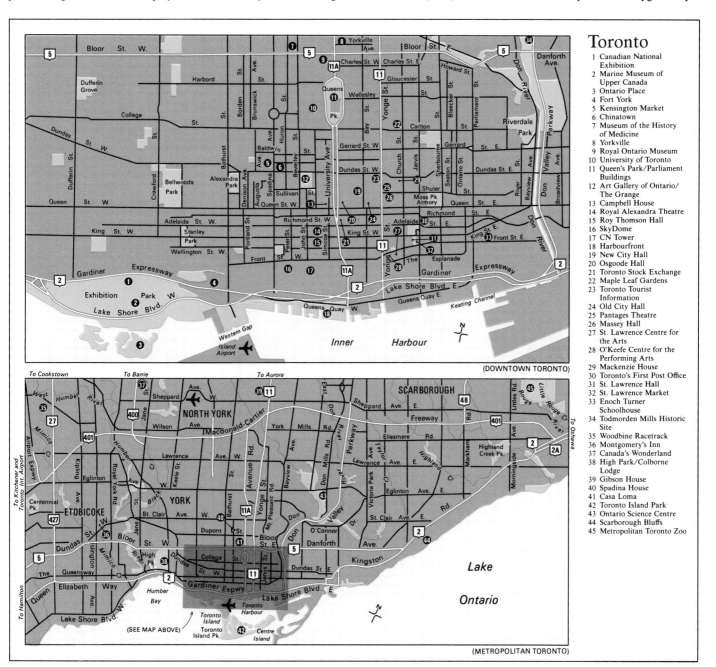

Toronto

1 Canadian National Exhibition
2 Marine Museum of Upper Canada
3 Ontario Place
4 Fort York
5 Kensington Market
6 Chinatown
7 Museum of the History of Medicine
8 Yorkville
9 Royal Ontario Museum
10 University of Toronto
11 Queen's Park/Parliament Buildings
12 Art Gallery of Ontario/ The Grange
13 Campbell House
14 Royal Alexandra Theatre
15 Roy Thomson Hall
16 SkyDome
17 CN Tower
18 Harbourfront
19 New City Hall
20 Osgoode Hall
21 Toronto Stock Exchange
22 Maple Leaf Gardens
23 Toronto Tourist Information
24 Old City Hall
25 Pantages Theatre
26 Massey Hall
27 St. Lawrence Centre for the Arts
28 O'Keefe Centre for the Performing Arts
29 Mackenzie House
30 Toronto's First Post Office
31 St. Lawrence Hall
32 St. Lawrence Market
33 Enoch Turner Schoolhouse
34 Todmorden Mills Historic Site
35 Woodbine Racetrack
36 Montgomery's Inn
37 Canada's Wonderland
38 High Park/Colborne Lodge
39 Gibson House
40 Spadina House
41 Casa Loma
42 Toronto Island Park
43 Ontario Science Centre
44 Scarborough Bluffs
45 Metropolitan Toronto Zoo

(DOWNTOWN TORONTO)

(METROPOLITAN TORONTO)

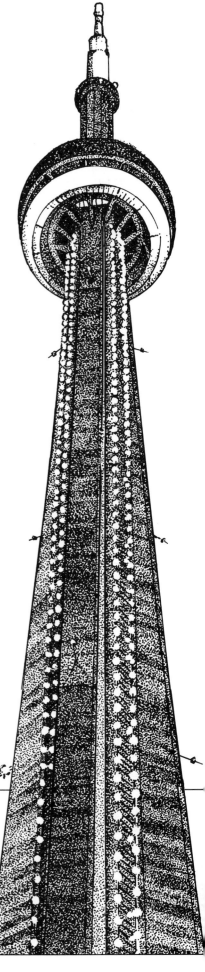

Museum of the History of Medicine (7)
The exhibits in this museum, housed in the Academy of Medicine, depict 5,000 years of health care and medical treatment.

New City Hall (19)
This architecturally striking structure was completed in 1965. Its curved twin towers of 27 and 19 stories flank the three-story "flying saucer" that contains the city council chamber. The forecourt, Nathan Phillips Square, is a lively, year-round gathering place for Torontonians. In winter the reflecting pool is converted into a skating rink.

O'Keefe Centre
for the Performing Arts (28)
Canada's largest proscenium theater seats 3,200 for Broadway musicals, concerts and a variety of shows. The center is also home to the National Ballet of Canada and the Canadian Opera Company.

Old City Hall (24)
A 90-metre clock tower is an imposing feature of this landmark structure (1891-99).

Ontario Place (3)
This 39-hectare entertainment and exhibition complex on Lake Ontario comprises islands and futuristic structures linked by walkways. Visitors can enjoy restaurants and shops, a marina, the Cinesphere, the Canadian Baseball Hall of Fame and the Forum, which offers outdoor music and dance programs. The Children's Village has a punching bag forest and a climbing hill. The

Toronto's multipurpose SkyDome stadium (below), located at the base of the CN Tower, can hold more than 53,000 baseball fans. Seating capacity can be increased to 55,000 for football games and 67,500 for rock concerts. With its fully retractable roof shut, the stadium could enclose a 31-story building.

destroyer HMS *Haida* is permanently berthed at Ontario Place.

Ontario Science Centre (43)
Built to commemorate Canada's Centennial in 1967, the Ontario Science Centre is set in the hillside and valley of a large ravine. Visitors are invited to participate and learn at this hands-on museum, whose exhibits include a simulated spaceship landing and computers that play tic-tac-toe.

Osgoode Hall (20)
This famous Toronto landmark is the headquarters for the Supreme Court of Ontario and the Law Society of Upper Canada, which built the hall in 1829-32.

Pantages Theatre (25)
This magnificently restored 1920 vaudeville theater and movie palace reopened in the autumn of 1989 with an extended run of Andrew Lloyd Webber's musical, *The Phantom of the Opera*. The 2,000-seat theater is a showcase for Broadway-style productions. The lights of the Elgin and the Winter Garden, two other downtown Toronto theaters of the same vintage as the Pantages, have also been rekindled for live entertainment.

Queen's Park (11)
The Romanesque-style Ontario Parliament in Queen's Park was built between 1886 and 1892. Guided tours are available.

Roy Thomson Hall (15)
This 2,800-seat concert hall has been acclaimed for its striking architectural design and its acoustical qualities. Built in 1982, it replaced Massey Hall as the home of the Toronto Symphony Orchestra.

Royal Alexandra Theatre (14)
The "Royal Alex" has been a leading Toronto theater since 1907.

Toronto's Towering Landmark

The 553.33-metre CN Tower (17), completed in 1976, is the tallest freestanding structure in the world. It has the world's highest elevator ride (447 metres) and the longest staircase (2,570 steps), and weighs more than 23,200 large elephants. Thousands of tonnes of reinforced concrete were used to form the tapering column. The structure, which serves as a communications tower, is the city's most conspicuous landmark. During construction, the 100-metre transmission mast was lowered on the top of the tower by helicopter. According to engineers, the CN tower can withstand fire, lightning,

high winds, earthquakes and other natural calamities, as well as the impact of planes.

Four elevators whisk visitors to the seven-story Sky Pod, 346 metres above the ground, which houses observation decks, a revolving restaurant and night club, and communications equipment. A fifth elevator rises to the 447-metre-high Space Deck, the world's highest public observation gallery, with its spectacular panoramic view of the Toronto area. The Tour of the Universe, at the tower's base, takes visitors on a simulated space flight to Jupiter.

Royal Ontario Museum (9)

Opened in 1914, the Royal Ontario Museum (ROM) is Canada's largest museum and one of the largest in North America. Its collections, which include 6 million artifacts, encompass the arts, archaeology, geology and mineralogy, zoology and paleontology. The impressive exhibitions in the main building range from world-famous Chinese art to dinosaur fossils.

At the McLaughlin Planetarium, next to the main building, the Theater of the Stars depicts man's knowledge of the universe. The George R. Gardiner Museum of Ceramic Art, opposite the main building, displays English and Continental porcelain. The Sigmund Samuel Building, a few blocks south of the main building, exhibits early Canadian furniture, paintings, glass and silver.

St. Lawrence Centre for the Arts (27)

The center offers drama, music, dance and film in its two theaters. It also presents public forums on topics of local concern.

St. Lawrence Hall (31)

The restored third floor of this Renaissance-style building (1850) is now used for public functions. The remainder of the building is home to the National Ballet of Canada.

St. Lawrence Market (32)

Toronto's first city hall (1844-99) was located in this restored building, which today houses a public marketplace.

Scarborough Bluffs (44)

The bluffs rise 90 metres from Lake Ontario in layers of clay and sand that provide a geologic record of the last ice age.

SkyDome (16)

The world's first multipurpose stadium with a fully retractable roof is home to baseball's Toronto Blue Jays, football's Toronto Argonauts and the world's largest video display board (three stories high by nine stories wide). Rock concerts, exhibitions and a variety of musical events are also presented, while the entire complex includes a hotel, health club, movie, restaurants and bars.

Spadina House (40)

This 1866 house next to Casa Loma is noted for its original furnishings and art, and its Victorian garden.

Todmorden Mills Historic Site (34)

This important 19th-century millsite includes two pre-Confederation dwellings, a former brewery (now a display area) and the Old Don railway station.

Toronto Island Park (42)

Ferries link Toronto with the three main islands of the park, which offers nature trails, beaches and lagoons, bike and boat rentals. There is an amusement park and petting farm on Centre Island.

Toronto Stock Exchange (21)

Canada's largest stock exchange, one of the most technically advanced in the world, has a visitor center and a public gallery overlooking the trading floor.

Toronto's First Post Office (30)

The 1833 post office, now a national historic site, is still operating. Costumed staff recreate the postal service of the past.

University of Toronto (10)

Founded as King's College in 1827, the university has more than 250 buildings on three campuses. Some 50,000 students attend this institution.

Woodbine Racetrack (35)

Woodbine is the site of the continent's oldest regularly run horse race. The first Queen's Plate was held in 1860.

Yorkville (8)

Several blocks of Victorian houses have been converted to elegant art galleries, boutiques and restaurants.

The opulent Pantages Theatre (above) proclaims Toronto's importance as a center for the performing arts. The hectic pace of the city slows to a stroll along the fashionable shopping lanes of Yorkville (right). Ontario Place (far right) packs a 39-hectare recreation world on a group of man-made islands and elevated futuristic pavilions. The twin-towered City Hall (below right) rises behind Nathan Phillips Square, alive with people, music and art shows year-round.

Small Towns and Temples on a Road Between Two Lakes

Central Ontario

BEAVERTON

The neoclassic St. Andrew's Presbyterian Church at Beaverton was built by the congregation between 1840 and 1853.
□ Just north of Beaverton, the Trent-Severn Waterway enters Lake Simcoe at the Gamebridge Lock.
□ McRae Point Provincial Park occupies a small three-pronged peninsula that juts out into Lake Simcoe. A 1.2-kilometre-long trail and boardwalk leads through a swamp rich in wildlife and birds. Fishing and boating here are excellent.

SIBBALD POINT PROVINCIAL PARK

This 200-hectare park was once the estate of the pioneer Sibbald family. Mrs. Susan Sibbald, the family matriarch, purchased the property in 1835, settled here with her four sons in the following year, and named the estate after her childhood home, Eildon Hall in Scotland. Her descendants remained here until 1951. The family house is now a museum.
□ St. George's Anglican Church (1877), built by Mrs. Sibbald's sons to honor their mother's memory, is on a point of land overlooking Lake Simcoe. Two famous Canadian literary figures are buried on the grounds: Stephen Leacock (1869-1944) and Mazo de la Roche (1879-1961), the prolific author of the *Jalna* novels.

SHARON

The three-story, white-frame Sharon Temple evokes memories of a 19th-century religious sect. In 1801, an American Quaker, David Willson, settled in this region. Willson broke with his coreligionists to form the Children of Peace, also known as the "Davidites." Willson's followers built the temple in 1830. Every part of the structure has symbolic meaning: the three stories represent the Trinity; the 12 pillars, the apostles. The square shape of the temple was intended to show that the Davidites "meant to deal on the square with all people." Although Willson was considered a fanatic, his traveling temple band enjoyed great popularity in small-town Ontario. Today, the Davidites no longer exist, but their graceful temple survives as a museum.

Sharon Temple

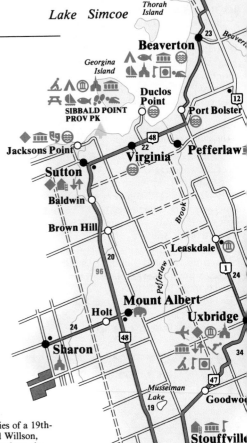

Thomas Foster Memorial Temple, Uxbridge

UXBRIDGE

The town was first settled by Scots, Germans and the Pennsylvania Dutch in the early 1800s.
□ The Byzantine-style Thomas Foster Memorial Temple (1935-36), just north of Uxbridge, was built by "Honest Tom" Foster, a Toronto mayor (1925-28) who was raised in Uxbridge. The mausoleum was reputedly inspired by the Taj Mahal in India.
□ The Uxbridge-Scott Museum comprises six pioneer buildings: the Hilson Carriage Shed, the Nesbitt Tool Shed, the Quaker Hill School, the Victoria Corners Lodge Hall, an implement shed, and the Fifth Line Church, built in the 1870s, which is still used for weddings. Several former Uxbridge residents are the subjects of permanent exhibits: author Lucy Maud Montgomery; painter David Milne (1882-1953) and pianist Glen Gould (1932-82).

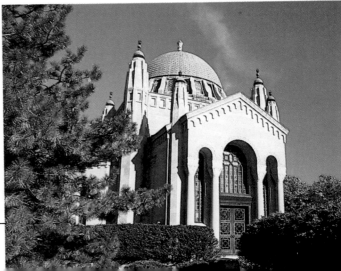

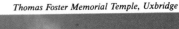

This route skirts the fringes of metropolitan Toronto and links Lake Ontario to Lake Simcoe. The region includes vast industrial workshops, recreational playgrounds and a number of historic curiosities.

The thriving cluster of cities from Oshawa to Pickering is the eastern edge of Ontario's "Golden Horseshoe," the largest conurbation in Canada, stretching as far as St. Catharines. Virtually all these lakeside cities began as ports and later became rail and industrial centers.

Although rapid development has often blurred the character of these places, efforts were made to preserve many century-old buildings and streets. One of the most successful of such endeavors has been mounted at Port Hope, where citizens rallied to keep intact the charms of an almost perfect mid-19th-century lakeside community.

The sights and sounds of small-town Ontario also survive in the farm country north of Lake Ontario and at communities such as Port Perry, Uxbridge, and Leaksdale, which

are increasingly popular getaway spots for busy Torontonians. Local historic and architectural delights include the old Tyrone Mill, the Thomas Foster Memorial Temple, the Sharon Temple, and Eildon Hall at Sibbald Provincial Park.

Penryn Park, Port Hope

LEAKSDALE
At Leaksdale, a plaque on the manse of the local Presbyterian church marks the home of Lucy Maud Montgomery (1874-1942). The author of *Anne of Green Gables* lived in the manse from 1911 to 1926 when her husband served here as minister, and she wrote half her 26 books here. (The manse is private property.)

TYRONE
In the 1840s, when early pioneers in Upper Canada raised wheat for cash and sustenance, each settlement had its own mill to grind the crop into flour. One of the surviving mills still operates at Tyrone. Visitors are welcome to explore the water-powered Tyrone Mill, which once produced as much as 40 to 50 barrels (more than 90 kilograms) of flour daily. The mill's owners, who also operate a sawmill and a feed mill, sell cider from their own press.

The Cone, Port Hope

PORT HOPE
Situated on Lake Ontario at the mouth of the Ganaraska River, Port Hope is noted for its legacy of fine buildings and streets. Originally a fur-trading post, Port Hope was settled by Loyalists in the 1790s. The settlement was known briefly as Toronto, but the name was changed to Port Hope to commemorate a local political figure, Col. Henry Hope. Port Hope became a prosperous industrial and railway center during the mid-19th century, when most of its outstanding buildings were constructed. About 90 local buildings are designated as heritage sites. Today visitors can stroll by blocks of Victorian shops on Walton Street, said to be the best preserved main street in Canada, and admire notable buildings, such as the Town Hall (1851) and Trinity College School (1868). Among the many fine houses that grace Port Hope's quiet residential streets are The Bluestone (1834), The Cone (1847), The Octagon (1856) and Penryn Park (1859), which was used during the filming of *Anne of Green Gables.*

1911 Carter Car, Canadian Automobile Museum, Oshawa

OSHAWA
The economic mainstay of Oshawa (pop. 125,000) is the automobile industry. Production began in 1907 when Col. R. S. McLaughlin (1871-1972) founded his car company, the forerunner of General Motors Canada.
□ Parkwood, McLaughlin's 55-room mansion, contains priceless antiques, tapestries and murals. An art gallery displays paintings by the Group of Seven. The surrounding gardens are adorned with fountains, pools and classical statuary.
□ The Robert McLaughlin Gallery at Oshawa's Civic Centre displays works by contemporary Canadian artists.
□ The Canadian Automotive Museum displays more than 70 historic vehicles from the 1890s to the 1980s.
□ The Oshawa-Sydenham Museum comprises three 19th-century houses, which depict life before the automobile age.

Italian Garden at Parkwood, Oshawa

Lake Simcoe's 'Smiling Beauty,' Muskoka's Autumnal Splendor

Central Ontario

At the point where Lake Simcoe and Lake Couchiching meet is Orillia, immortalized by Stephen Leacock in *Sunshine Sketches of a Little Town*. This humorous classic was one of the many books Leacock wrote in the study of his summer home, now a museum, in Orillia. Explaining his attachment to this area, where he had spent his boyhood, Leacock wrote, "To my way of thinking, nothing will stand comparison with the smiling beauty of the waters, shores and bays of

A Hero Revered by the Chinese

A minister's son born in Gravenhurst in 1890, Norman Bethune interrupted his medical studies in 1914 to join the Canadian army overseas. At the start of the Spanish Civil War in 1936 he established a mobile blood service for the Republican forces. In 1938 Bethune joined the Chinese Communists, then fighting both the Japanese and the Chinese Nationalists. He set up hospitals, organized medical teams and trained army doctors. During a battle-front operation he cut a finger and later died of blood poisoning at Wupaishan, where he was buried. He became a national hero in Communist China. His body was moved to China's Martyrs' Tomb, schools and hospitals were named after him, and his image appeared on Chinese posters and stamps (*right*).

ORILLIA

This year-round resort city (pop. 24,000) was the model for Mariposa in Stephen Leacock's *Sunshine Sketches of a Little Town* (1911). Leacock, economist, historian and well-known humorist, built a lakeshore residence here in 1928. His home, now a museum, remains much as it was when he was alive. It displays several of his handwritten manuscripts.
□ The 12-metre-high Champlain Monument in Couchiching Beach Park is considered one of the finest bronze works in North America.
□ Orillia is an important stop on the Trent-Severn Canal System. The *Island Princess,* a Mississippi-style riverboat, offers daily cruises on nearby Lake Couchiching (July to early October).

BARRIE

This industrial city (pop. 48,000) on Kempenfelt Bay began in 1812 as an outpost on a military road linking Lake Ontario to the upper Great Lakes. It is named for Commodore Robert Barrie, commander of the naval shipyard at Kingston (1818-35).
□ Barrie's Kempenfest, a weekend celebration held in early August, features handicraft exhibitions and a regatta.
□ The Barrie Raceway, a military museum at nearby CFB Borden and a summer season at the Gryphon Theatre are among the city's attractions.
□ Simcoe County Museum and Archives, eight kilometres north of Barrie, describes local development from prehistoric times to the present. A display center re-creates a 19th-century street with a store, a toy shop and an undertaker's parlor. The museum complex also preserves an 1834 log house (furnished in pioneer style) and old-time barns, where blacksmiths and barrelmakers demonstrate their crafts. On the grounds is one of Ontario's few remaining wooden windmills.

Stephen Leacock

GRAVENHURST

Originally a pioneer logging community, Gravenhurst developed a tourist gateway to the scenic Muskoka region during the late 19th century. The town's most famous landmark is the birthplace of native son Dr. Norman Bethune (1890-1939), internationally known for his medical work in Spain and China. The Bethune Memorial House is a museum and a national historic site, which has been restored to the way it was at the time of Bethune's birth. A biographical display on the second floor pays tribute to this exceptional Canadian.
□ The attractively restored Gravenhurst Opera House offers a season of plays and musicals during summer.
□ The historic RS *Segwun,* restored with its 19th-century steam-puffing power, offers lake cruises from early June until early October.

ARROWHEAD PROVINCIAL PARK
Deer and moose frequent this year-round park. Nature trails pass beaver dams, waterfalls and plants such as the cardinal flower, normally found farther south. Park naturalists hold interpretive programs throughout the summer. The park has more than 385 campsites.

Lake Simcoe and its sister lake, Couchiching." The lakeland remains as attractive now as it was when Leacock described it, more than 50 years ago.

Beyond Orillia, the rolling farmland of southern Ontario gives way to the pine and granite landscape of Muskoka. Lumber, cheap land and rumors of gold attracted settlers to this region. But the old bone-rattling Muskoka Road taxed even the hardiest travelers. At its northern end was the tiny lumbering community of McCabe's Bay

(now Gravenhurst) on Lake Muskoka. From here, steamers carried freight and passengers to remote settlements. In summer the last of these ships, the *Segwun*, departs from Gravenhurst on nostalgic lake cruises.

Today's travelers take Highway 11 to reach Gravenhurst, Bracebridge, and Huntsville, gateways to Muskoka's lakes and woods. One of Ontario's popular year-round playgrounds, the region is famed for the beauty of its autumn, when foliage becomes a symphony of gold, red and yellow.

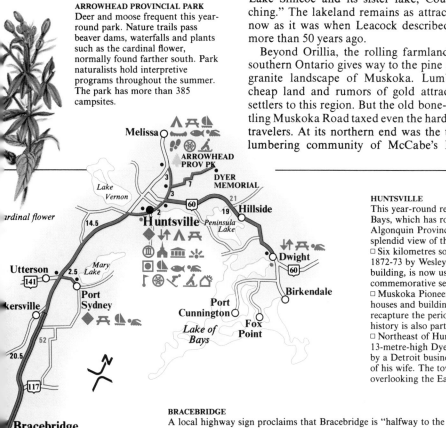

cardinal flower

HUNTSVILLE
This year-round resort town is a gateway to the scenic Lake of Bays, which has roughly 160 kilometres of shoreline, and also to Algonquin Provincial Park. Lion's Lookout Park provides a splendid view of the town and the surrounding area.
□ Six kilometres south of Huntsville is Madill Church, built in 1872-73 by Wesleyan Methodists. The church, a square-timbered building, is now used only for annual United Church commemorative services.
□ Muskoka Pioneer Village, set in scenic woods, includes old-time houses and buildings, which have been restored and furnished to recapture the period from 1860 to 1910. A museum of Muskoka history is also part of this pioneer showplace.
□ Northeast of Huntsville is the 13-metre-high Dyer Memorial, built by a Detroit businessman in memory of his wife. The tower is set in a park overlooking the East River.

BRACEBRIDGE
A local highway sign proclaims that Bracebridge is "halfway to the North Pole" (from the equator). But "arctic" is hardly the word to apply to this year-round resort town. In summer it offers easy access to boating and swimming; in winter, to cross-country skiing, ice fishing and snowshoeing.
□ Bracebridge hosts the month-long Muskoka Cavalcade of Colour (mid-September to mid-October) and a winter carnival of sports and other events (with Gravenhurst and Huntsville) in February.

Madill Church, Huntsville

How Leaves Reveal Hidden Hues

Beneath the top layer of a leaf (the cuticle and the epidermis) are chloroplasts, containing the chlorophyll that uses sunlight to produce food. Under the chloroplasts is a layer of spongy cells, in which carbon dioxide, water and nutrients are mixed. (Carbon dioxide enters the leaf through openings, known as stomata, and water and nutrients, through the viens.) When sunlight strikes the chloroplasts, the chlorophyll sets off a reaction (photosynthesis), in which nutrients and carbon dioxide combine to produce sugar that is fed to the tree. In the cooler autumn weather, chlorophyll production slows, and hidden yellow and orange pigments are exposed. Sugar trapped in the leaves works with the sunlight to produce new red and purple pigments. These, in turn, combine with each other, and with tannin (waste products that turn leaves brown) to give the fall hues.

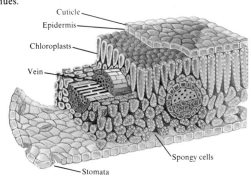

Changing autumn leaves in Muskoka

An Alluring Park—
Inspiration for a Great Painter

Central Ontario

Almost any visitor to Algonquin Provincial Park can see why painter Tom Thomson was inspired by this magnificent wilderness. One need only watch the dance of sunlight on a lake, or the play of shadows among pines, to appreciate what Thomson captured in one of his famous paintings, *The West Wind.*

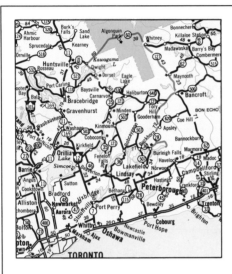

Timber wolves

Tom Thomson's The West Wind

ALGONQUIN PROVINCIAL PARK

This provincial park covers some 7,600 square kilometres. A 56-kilometre stretch of Highway 60, which cuts through the southern corner of Algonquin Park, offers casual visitors easy access to many of the park's attractions.

□ A museum at Kilometre 20 offers audiovisual presentations to introduce visitors to the park's wildlife and geography.

□ A logging exhibit at the park's East Gate features a reconstructed loggers' cabin, a "saddleback" locomotive, and an alligator boat, which could also be used on land.

□ The park contains more than a thousand lakes and 1,500 kilometres of canoe routes. There are a number of short nature trails (along Highway 60) and two overnight backpacking trails. Well-stocked lakes ensure excellent fishing for brook and lake trout, smallmouth bass and walleye.

□ A 12-metre totem pole at Canoe Lake commemorates artist Tom Thomson, who drowned here in 1917.

Algonquin Provincial Park

Locomotive, Pioneer Logging Exhibit,
Algonquin Provincial Park

DORSET

This tiny community on the eastern arm of the Lake of Bays is situated where the Haliburton Highlands (to the southeast) meet Muskoka. A 31-metre tower provides a splendid view of the surrounding region and the Lake of Bays.

□ The Leslie M. Frost Natural Resources Centre is set in a 240-square-kilometre region of lake and forest. The center is a major educational facility for students, adult groups and professionals who are involved in natural sciences. Casual visitors are also welcome. The center has well-marked trails and offers guided tours. Other recreational activities include canoeing, cross-country skiing and snowshoeing.

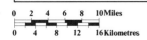

0 2 4 6 8 10 Miles
0 4 8 12 16 Kilometres

A century ago this region was accessible only by canoe. But today visitors arrive by road and air. They can enjoy much of the park from convenient campsites, or they can paddle and camp along its hundreds of canoe routes. Algonquin is the oldest provincial park in Ontario (1893) and one of the biggest in Canada.

Indians roamed the Algonquin region for some 4,000 years without appreciably altering the land; in about 60 years loggers changed it permanently. Early loggers came from Ottawa in the 1840s, attracted by the red, white and jack pines that thrive here. But in felling the pines, the loggers scarred the land and left debris that fed forest fires.

Logging continues within Algonquin Park today. (Roughly 75 percent of the park's area is set aside for this activity.) But careful management restricts its extent. For exam-

ple, logging is forbidden near shorelines and portages, and hauling hours are regulated.

Along Highway 60 there are campsites, picnic grounds and other attractions. Just off the highway are ten interpretive trails—two to five kilometres long—which have been designed for visitors who want a pleasant day's outing in the wild. During summer there are special canoe outings, bird, wildflower and mushroom hikes, and public wolf-howling expeditions (when a wolf pack is located).

The Mystery of Canoe Lake

Canadian artist Tom Thomson spent his last years living alone in Algonquin Park, working as a guide, and sketching and painting. His finest paintings—landscapes which influenced the Group of Seven—were done during this time. Two brilliant canvases from the last year of his life, *The West Wind* (*left*) and *The Jack Pine*, are among the most frequently reproduced.

Thomson was just 39 when he died mysteriously in Canoe Lake in the summer of 1917. His canoe was found in the lake a day or two after he disappeared—it was said he had gone fishing. Six days later his body surfaced. He had a brutal gash on one temple and a fishing line wrapped around his ankle. The coroner's verdict was accidental drowning. One theory was that Thomson had used the line to support a sprained ankle, then had slipped and hit his head before falling overboard. Others were that he killed himself while under pressure to marry a pregnant girl friend—or that he was murdered.

BANCROFT
The Bancroft region, a rock hound's paradise at the edge of the Canadian Shield, yields samples of about 80 percent of the minerals found throughout Canada. Every year Bancroft hosts the four-day Rockhound Gemboree in late July and early August. The biggest of its kind in Canada, the event attracts thousands of collectors from around the world. It features field trips, visits to abandoned mines, and demonstrations of gemstone cutting.
□ Pioneer artifacts are displayed in the Bancroft Historical Museum, a log house built in 1857.
□ The countryside surrounding Bancroft is a haven for bird-watchers and nature photographers and offers excellent hunting and fishing.

Bancroft Historical Museum

SILENT LAKE PROVINCIAL PARK
This 14-square-kilometre park has more than 165 tent and trailer sites, each with a picnic table and a fireplace. The surrounding forest is dominated by sugar maple, hemlock, white pine and white spruce. Wildlife in the forest includes beaver, muskrat, otter, red fox, black bear and deer. Canoes and rowboats are permitted on the lake; powerboats are prohibited.
□ Visitors can explore Silent Lake Provincial Park on foot or, in winter, on cross-country skis. There is a snowmobile trail just west of the park.

Rock hounds near Bancroft

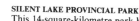

LAKE ST. PETER PROVINCIAL PARK
Visitors to this 26-hectare park can enjoy hiking, canoeing, and fishing for rainbow trout. Facilities include a beach and a picnic area.
□ Just west of the park office, a four-kilometre nature trail leads to a mountain summit that offers a panoramic view of the area.

Rock carvings, Petroglyphs Provincial Park

PETROGLYPHS PROVINCIAL PARK
The park's petroglyphs (rock carvings) are believed to have been done by Algonkian-speaking Indians between 500 and 1,000 years ago. Some 900 figures incised on a 30-by-50-metre sloping limestone wall are identifiable as animals, humans, mythical figures and fertility symbols. A specially designed structure has been constructed to protect the petroglyph site from weather damage. In summer the park offers interpretive programs to explain the significance of the petroglyphs.
□ A 6.5-kilometre hiking trail leads past Minnow Lake to High Falls on Eels Creek, which is situated outside the park.

Where Canals and Locks Link 'Bright Waters and Happy Lands'

Central Ontario

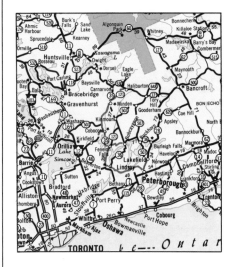

MINDEN

Founded in 1859, this village was the first settlement in the District of Haliburton, and became the county seat in 1874. The oldest remaining building is the square-timber Clergy House (1870), once used by itinerant Anglican missionaries.
□ Each autumn, when the leaves change to brilliant reds, oranges and yellows, the village celebrates a Fall Festival of Color.

Golden-winged warbler

BALSAM LAKE PROVINCIAL PARK

Balsam Lake is the highest point on the Trent-Severn Waterway. The park is an excellent base from which to explore the waterway system and the Haliburton Highlands to the north. It contains more than 485 campsites and offers opportunities for swimming, picnicking and hiking. A nature trail behind the Poplar Plains campground passes through a swamp, a hardwood forest and an open grassland to the top of a lookout hill.

Purdy's Mill, Lindsay

LINDSAY

The first settler in the area, William Purdy, dammed the Scugog River in 1827. In return for a land grant, he built two mills, which still stand. In 1834, a government surveyor named Lindsay was accidentally shot and killed. He was buried in the settlement, and his name was given to the town in 1850.
□ A plaque on the grounds of the Victoria County Historical Society Museum honors Ernest Thompson Seton, naturalist and author, who emigrated from England to a farm near Lindsay in 1866.

"The Highlander," Haliburton

HALIBURTON

This village and the surrounding Haliburton Highlands were named for Judge Thomas Chandler Haliburton, Nova Scotia author and creator of the "Sam Slick" stories. He was chairman of the Canadian Land and Emigration Company, which settled the region in the 1860s.
□ Haliburton has an unusual tourist information center: a Grand Trunk Railway steam locomotive and a wooden caboose (1911) which commemorate the opening of the line here in 1878.
□ The Haliburton Highlands Pioneer Museum displays tools once used in lumbering, farming and trapping.

BOBCAYGEON

Built on three islands and the mainland, the village is the midway point on the Trent-Severn Waterway. A monument records that the first wooden lock and canal on the waterway were constructed here in 1833-3[...]

FENELON FALLS

Maryboro Lodge, built in 1837, houses the Fenelon Falls Museum. Displays focus on pioneer life of the mid-19th century.
□ Sturgeon Lake abounds in muskellunge, largemouth bass and walleye.

Sycamore

Map labels: Head Lake, Drag River, Haliburton, Soyers Lake, 519, 121, 24, 519, Duck Lake, Kashagawigamog Lake, Ingoldsby, 40.5, 35, Minden, Lutterworth, 121, 35, 16.5, Deep Bay, Kilcoo Camp, Gull Lake, Miners Bay, Miners Cr, Black Lake, Moore Falls, Moore Lake, 11, Gull River, 503, Norland, Shadow Lake, Cr, 38.5, 8, Silver Lake, Four Mile Lake, 7, 1, Coboconk, Corben, Corsons, 35, 9, BALSAM LAKE PROV PK, 48, Baddow, Balsam, Kawartha, GRAND ISLAND, Rosedale, Bobcaygeon, ISLA, Lake, 9.5, Cameron Lake, Fenelon Falls, 36, Isaacs Glen, 35A, 16, Kenstone Beach, 6.5, Ancona Point, Birch Point, 121, Lakes, Martin Cr, Sturgeon Lake, 25, 5.5, Cameron, McLaren Cr, 35, Cambray, 13, Scugog, Pigeon Lake, Lindsay, 36, EMILY PROV PK, 7, Reaboro, Hillhead, 18.5, 7, Omemee, 35, Stony Cr, 54.5, River

In the Haliburton Highlands, hundreds of lakes are scattered in a rocky, forested expanse of pine, spruce, maple, oak and balsam. Nestling among the ancient hills are Minden and Haliburton. Proximity to lake and forest has made these villages magnets for boaters, campers and harassed city dwellers.

From the Haliburton Highlands, rivers flow south to a chain of 14 lakes known as the Kawarthas—"bright waters and happy lands" in the Huron language. The lakes drain from one to another, over rapids and falls, to Lake Ontario. The entire chain forms a boundary between Haliburton County and the rolling farmlands near Lindsay and Peterborough.

The Kawartha Lakes are connected by the canals and locks of the 380-kilometre Trent-Severn Waterway, which links Lake Ontario and Georgian Bay. The construction of the waterway began in the 1830s, tracing a canoe route used by Indians and explorers. Bypassing treacherous rapids, the waterway eased the passage of barges carrying lumber from local mills and steamers bringing visitors to the area.

Shipping on the Kawartha Lakes declined as the lumber industry died out. Commercial use of the waterway ceased by the 1930s. The remaining waterway trade was transferred to a new system of roads. These made the lakes more accessible to sportsmen, particularly boating enthusiasts. Today, where barges and steamers once plied, pleasure craft sail each summer.

Two Chroniclers of Wilderness Life

Susanna Moodie (*left*) and Catharine Parr Traill (*right*) were two of Canada's "gentle pioneers" who joined the early 19th-century wave of British immigration to this country. The two sisters and their husbands came to Upper Canada from England in 1832. Catharine adapted cheerfully to life in Douro Township, near Peterborough, and in *The Backwoods of Canada* (1836) and *The Female Emigrant's Guide* (1854) gave practical advice to would-be settlers.

Susanna was less enthusiastic about frontier life. In *Roughing It in the Bush* (1852) she wrote of feeling like "a condemned criminal." She survived a forest fire and being chased by a bear and, in 1853, produced a more optimistic book, *Life in the Clearings.*

LAKEFIELD
In the cemetery of the village church (1853) is the grave of Major Samuel Strickland, a former British army officer and the founder of Lakefield. After establishing a farm in the wilderness here, he chronicled his adventures in *Twenty-seven Years in Canada West.* His sisters, Susanna Moodie and Catharine Parr Traill, also recorded their pioneer lives in books.

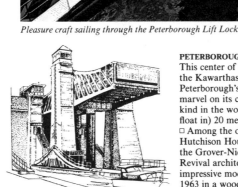

Pleasure craft sailing through the Peterborough Lift Lock

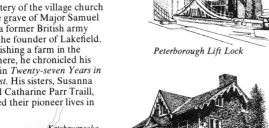

Peterborough Lift Lock

PETERBOROUGH
This center of more than 60,000, often called the "Queen City of the Kawarthas," is a major link on the Trent-Severn Waterway. Peterborough's Hydraulic Lift Lock, which was an engineering marvel on its completion in 1904, is still among the highest of its kind in the world. It can lift vessels (along with the water they float in) 20 metres straight up.
□ Among the oldest buildings in Peterborough are the handsome Hutchison House, built in 1837 for the town's first physician, and the Grover-Nicholls House (1847), an excellent example of Greek Revival architecture, rare in Ontario. In striking contrast is the impressive modern architecture of Trent University, established in 1963 in a wooded setting on both sides of the Otonabee River.
□ The Peterborough Centennial Museum has a military exhibit that includes armor, medals and uniforms of different periods from the Battle of Waterloo to the Korean War, a collection of photographs that covers a century of local history, and a display of sleighs, carriages and dolls dating from 1800.

Hutchison House, Peterborough

Grover-Nicholls House, Peterborough

Trent University, Peterborough

Sawmills by the Stream,
Stately Houses by the Roadside

Central Ontario

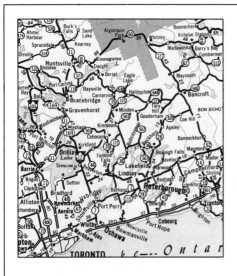

WARSAW CAVES CONSERVATION AREA
Uncounted potholes, passages and underground streams—and a "vanishing" waterfall—have been carved in limestone by the Indian River. On cave walls are fossil remains of prehistoric fish, plants, snails and a giant dragonfly. Above ground are hundreds of potholes, called kettles, formed by boulders caught in river whirlpools. In summer, a four-metre waterfall dries up and the river's reduced flow follows an underground course.

RICE LAKE
This 40-kilometre-long lake takes its name from the wild rice that grows in profusion along its shores. To local Indians, the gourmet delicacy is a principal source of income. Rice Lake is on the route followed by Champlain in 1615 when he journeyed with Huron allies to attack the Iroquois near present-day Syracuse, N.Y.

Victoria Hall courtroom

COBOURG
This port and popular resort glories in its 19th-century buildings and palatial summer homes.
□ Victoria Hall (1860) is one of Ontario's finest municipal buildings and was officially opened by the Prince of Wales (later Edward VII). It contains a replica of a courtroom in the Old Bailey, London.
□ Victoria College (1838) is now part of the University of Toronto. The college building is part of the Ontario Hospital of Cobourg.
□ The birthplace of stage and screen star Marie Dressler (1869-1934), now a restaurant and tavern, has been restored to the 1830s style.
□ Among the attractive features of the town is Victoria Park, an ideal spot for a lakeside picnic.
□ The Art Gallery of Northumberland exhibits paintings, ceramics and other works by Canadian, American and European artists.

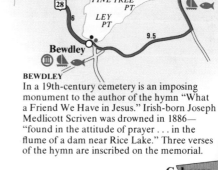

BEWDLEY
In a 19th-century cemetery is an imposing monument to the author of the hymn "What a Friend We Have in Jesus." Irish-born Joseph Medlicott Scriven was drowned in 1886— "found in the attitude of prayer . . . in the flume of a dam near Rice Lake." Three verses of the hymn are inscribed on the memorial.

Victoria Hall, Cobourg

Map labels
WARSAW CAVES CONSERV AREA
5.5
Warsaw
7.5
Douro
31.5
134
14.5
7
HOPE SAWMILL
Lang
LANG PIONEER VILLAGE
4
Keene
Mathers Corners
4
SUGAR I
WHITE ISLAND
SERPENT MOUNDS PROV PK
Rice
Roseneath
Alderville
SHEARER PT
CURTIS PT
IDYLWILDE PT
Otonabee
25
River
22
45
Fenella
55.5
Squirrel Cr
Bensfort Corners
31
COW I
Lake
Harwood
Burnley
South Monaghan
LONG ISLAND
Gores Landing
16
Bailieboro
28
PINE TREE PT
LEY PT
6
9.5
Brook
Bewdley
N
Cobourg
Baltimore
Creighton Heights
Macdonald-Cartier
8
Cobourg
401
12
45
LU PT
COBOURG CONSERV ARE
Brook
Lake Ontario

0　1　2　3　4　5 Miles
0　2　4　6　8 Kilometres

Of all pioneer buildings, few are as romantic, or conspicuously practical, as the mill. Near Keene are two fine old mills on the banks of the Indian River. The Lang gristmill, part of Century Village, was built in 1846 to grind flour for local and export markets. Upriver is the Hope sawmill, which milled logs from farmers' woodlots into dressed lumber for barns and houses.

At Keene, rolling farmlands slope down to the inlets and marshes of Rice Lake.

During the 19th century, steamboats from small settlements on the lake, such as Gore's Landing, carried settlers to destinations in the Kawartha Lakes and Haliburton Highlands. Today marinas in the lakeside towns attract boating enthusiasts and fishermen.

South of Rice Lake is Cobourg, whose town hall, opened in 1860, is an impressive reminder of the town's importance during the 19th century, when it was a major port of Lake Ontario. Between Cobourg and Trenton, travelers can take Highway 2. This is part of the Heritage Highway, the historic route that was once the only road link between Upper and Lower Canada. The building of the Macdonald-Cartier Freeway, a few kilometres to the north, has helped to preserve the character of the area. The traveler passes through a tranquil landscape, where red brick and white frame houses built by early settlers in a solid Georgian style stand proudly by the roadside.

Lang Grist Mill (opposite) *and Lang Pioneer Village blacksmith* (above)

KEENE
The restored buildings at the Lang Pioneer Village, just north of Keene, include a blacksmith shop, sawmill, shingle mill, clapboard church, log house and general store. The Lang Grist Mill (1846), beside the Indian River, was the most up-to-date operation of its day. It was here that the first Red Fife wheat, a hybrid developed in Peterborough, was ground. (At the community of Lang, an interpretive museum describes pioneer life in this area.)
□ The water-powered Hope Sawmill (1836) is still operating, and its exhibits include an extensive wood tool collection.

Bones, Beads and Spears from Elaborate Burial Mounds

At Serpent Mounds Provincial Park are Canada's best preserved and most elaborate burial mounds. Beneath the mounds lie the remains of the Point Peninsula Indians who occupied this region 2,000 years ago. They built nine mounds, the largest of which (seven metres high and two metres wide) snakes for 60 metres on a bluff overlooking Rice Lake. Eight smaller, egg-shaped mounds surround it. All contain mass graves associated with elaborate burial rituals. As late as A.D. 1000 small groups of Indians visited the site to bury their dead in pits nearby. Archaeologists have unearthed shell beads, animal bones, copper spears and loon beaks. Some exhumed skeletons are intact; others, fragmented or partially cremated.

A visitor center displays local artifacts and describes the area's history.

Serpent Mounds Provincial Park

GRAFTON
The neoclassic Barnum House was built in 1817 by Col. Eliakim Barnum, a Loyalist who emigrated from Vermont. Restored in the style of a 19th-century gentleman's residence, the building is now a museum. The mansion's showpiece is the elegant, hand-carved mantel.

Barnum House, Grafton

TRENTON
This attractive city (pop. 15,300) is at the southern end of the 280-kilometre Trent-Severn Waterway, which links Lake Ontario and Georgian Bay. The city is also the western gateway to scenic Quinte's Isle and is an access point to the Bay of Quinte, where sailing, swimming and fishing are popular summer activities.
□ Just east of the city is CFB Trenton, one of largest armed forces air bases in Canada. During the Second World War, it was an important training base for Commonwealth pilots.

Trenton · BAY OF QUINTE · Smithfield · Cankerville · PROCTOR PARK CONSERV AREA · Lovett · Brighton · Little Lake · Gosport · Presqu'ile Point · WELLERS BAY · Purdy Corners · Salem · POPHAM BAY · PRESQU'ILE BAY · Wicklow · Colborne · Lake Ontario · PRESQU'ILE PROV PK · Grafton · Lakeport · CHUB PT

14.5 · 27 · 30 · 12.5 · 9 · 401 · 2 · 8.5 · 4 · 24.5 · 33

Common tern, Presqu'ile Provincial Park

WICKLOW
The oldest Baptist church in Ontario, Wicklow Church (1824), is a simple frame building that served a congregation organized in 1798.

Proctor House, Brighton

BRIGHTON
A local architectural gem is Proctor House, a 19th-century merchant's residence and now a museum.
□ Nearby Presqu'ile Provincial Park, a curved spit of land jutting into Lake Ontario, contains marshes, forests, meadows and beaches. The old lighthouse keeper's house is now a visitors' center with displays about local history and wildlife. More than 310 species of birds have been sighted in the park; 125 breed here. Large colonies of gulls, as well as ducks, cormorants, terns and herons, nest on two small offshore islands.

A Lake on the Mountain and a Loyalist Legacy

Southeastern Ontario

Just once in its smooth sweep, the north shore of Lake Ontario reaches out into the blue waters. This peninsula appears on the map as Prince Edward County, better known as Quinte's Isle.

With 800 kilometres of shoreline, Quinte's Isle is popular with vacationers. Pleasure craft of all kinds ply its bays and reaches. On the western shore, youngsters romp in the Sandbanks Provincial Park, with its hills of gleaming white sand, or challenge the breakers rolling in on the fine

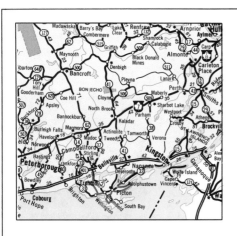

BELLEVILLE

Early Loyalist settlers established two mills on the Moira River here. Belleville, the town that grew up around the mills, became so prosperous that its citizens petitioned Queen Victoria to make their community the capital of Canada.
□ The Hastings County Museum is in Glanmore House, a fine example of Victorian architecture. Lighting devices that range from boat, buggy and bicycle lamps to ancient Roman candles are on display.
□ A monument on the lawn of the Belleville Armory honors Sir Mackenzie Bowell, prime minister of Canada in 1894-96. A printer's apprentice at the Belleville *Intelligencer* as a youth, Bowell later became owner of the newspaper.

Hastings County Museum, Belleville

SANDBANKS BEACH PROVINCIAL PARK

A sandy spit of land, this park was once completely covered by water. It was formed when deposits carried by wind and waves created a sand bar across the mouth of a large bay in Lake Ontario. Natural and planted vegetation have taken hold and made permanent this strip of parkland. There is lake swimming along 10 kilometres of white beach backed by high sand dunes. By following a self-guiding trail, visitors can learn how dunes are formed.

Sandbanks Beach Provincial Park

Black locust

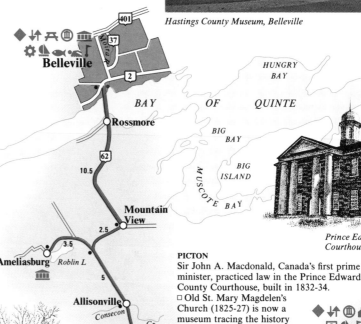

Prince Edward County Courthouse, Picton

PICTON

Sir John A. Macdonald, Canada's first prime minister, practiced law in the Prince Edward County Courthouse, built in 1832-34.
□ Old St. Mary Magdelen's Church (1825-27) is now a museum tracing the history of Prince Edward County.

Belleville

Rossmore

10.5

62

Mountain View

2.5

3.5

Ameliasburg   Roblin L

5

Allisonville

Consecon   Cr

2

8.5

PRINCE EDWARD

COUNTY

14

Bloomfield

66

9.5

33

Wellington   1

West Lake

West Lake

East Lake

30

Woodrous

Cherry Valley

Picton

MACAU MOUNT CONSER AREA

PICTO

49

SANDBANKS BEACH PROV PK   ATHOL BAY

BAY   OF   QUINTE

HUNGRY BAY

BIG BAY

BIG ISLAND

MUSCOTE BAY

0   1   2   3   4   5 Miles

0   2   4   6   8 Kilometres

beaches. On the eastern shore, travelers explore the winding roads that overlook Lake Ontario, and marvel at the Lake on the Mountain, high above the Bay of Quinte.

From Glenora, just below the Lake on the Mountain, a free ferry connects Quinte's Isle to Adolphustown. Here, on the shores of Adolphus Reach, is a memorial to the first settlers in this area—the United Empire Loyalists. The first group of pro-British refugees arrived here in 1784.

With determination and patience, these settlers successfully established themselves here. Reminders of the Loyalist past can be seen today in local museums, Georgian-style houses and old churches kept reverently in repair. Loyalist support for British rule is still reflected in the motto of Ontario: *Ut incepit fidelis sic permanet* (Loyal she began, loyal she remains).

Car ferry to Adolphustown

White House, Amherstview

ADOLPHUSTOWN
A plaque that records the landing of one small group of Loyalists on the shores of Adolphus Reach in 1784 bears these words from Exodus—"Put off thy shoes from off thy feet for the place whereon thou standest is holy ground." In a nearby cemetery many Loyalists lie in graves now unmarked. A stone wall, with many of the original headstones embedded in it, and an obelisk were erected in memory of the settlers.
□ The United Empire Loyalist Museum, in an 1877 house, displays maps of the early settlements, "muster rolls" of Loyalists who served in various royal regiments, and pioneer documents, portraits, tools, utensils and furnishings.
□ On the shores of Hay Bay north of Adolphustown is Upper Canada's earliest Methodist chapel, built in 1792. Near the church a cairn marks the site of the boyhood home of Sir John A. Macdonald.

AMHERSTVIEW
A magnificent example of colonial architecture, the White House was built in 1793 by William Fairfield, Sr., and is still in the Fairfield family five generations later. Few houses of the same period are as well preserved.
□ In nearby Bath is the restored home (1796) of Fairfield's son, William, Jr.

Bonaparte's gull

AMHERST ISLAND
Migratory waterfowl crowd the island's beaches and bays each spring and fall. The gravel beaches of the east end are nesting sites for shorebirds. Bonaparte's gulls are sighted in April and October on the island's southwest tip, accessible only by foot.
□ A plaque at his Amherst Island home honors 19th-century painter Daniel Fowler. A number of the artist's bold watercolors hang in the National Gallery in Ottawa.

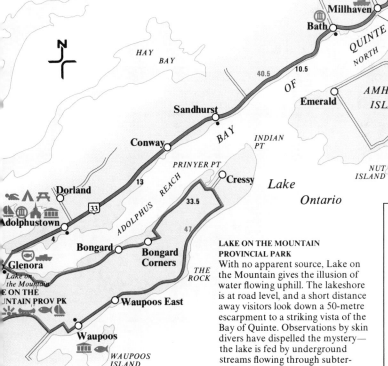

LAKE ON THE MOUNTAIN PROVINCIAL PARK
With no apparent source, Lake on the Mountain gives the illusion of water flowing uphill. The lakeshore is at road level, and a short distance away visitors look down a 50-metre escarpment to a striking vista of the Bay of Quinte. Observations by skin divers have dispelled the mystery— the lake is fed by underground streams flowing through subterranean layers of limestone.

WAUPOOS
The North Marysburgh Museum is in an early settler's house (c. 1818), with kitchen, parlor and bedrooms furnished in rural, 19th-century style. In the restored loft is a display that includes a pedal-operated melodeon (c. 1850), a horse-drawn hay rake (c. 1824), a Quaker doll (1842) and needlecraft, lacework, quilts and handwoven blankets and rugs.

Horse-High, Bull-Strong and Skunk-Tight

Pioneer farmers needed fences that were "horse-high, bull-strong and skunk-tight." They made them from boulders and fieldstones, from tree stumps laid on their sides, and from cedar logs split into rails. One of the most popular fences was the snake rail (*below*), which can still be seen in rural areas of southern Ontario. With its angles and interlocking joints it was strong and easy to build. It zigzagged across the rolling landscape, avoiding obstacles and turning awkward corners. But weeds flourished in its corners and its wasted space. When a snake rail fence was replaced with a straight rail fence, neighbors disagreed over who owned the newly available land.

Once Canada's Capital, a City Steeped in History

Eastern Ontario

View of the Royal Military College, Kingston, from Old Fort Henry

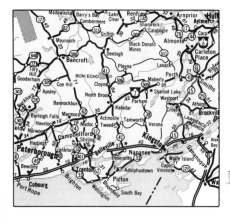

Bellevue House, Kingston

General meeting hall, Kingston City Hall

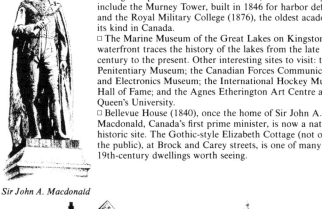

Sir John A. Macdonald

1 Penitentiary Museum
2 Bellevue House
3 International Hockey Museum Hall of Fame
4 Queen's University
5 Murney Tower Museum
6 St. Mary's Cathedral
7 Marine Museum of the Great Lakes
8 St. George's Cathedral
9 City Hall
10 Tourist Information
11 Canadian Forces Communications and Electronics Museum
12 Old Fort Henry
13 Royal Military College Museum

KINGSTON

The city is proud of its impressive concentration of historic buildings. Some recall the years when Kingston was Canada' capital in 1841-43. The city hall, for example, was designed a national legislature, but never served this purpose because capital was moved to Montreal after construction began.

□ Old Fort Henry evokes Kingston's military past. The fort, built during the War of 1812 and reconstructed in 1832-36, displays 19th-century military equipment. (In summer the fort's guard performs a traditional drill.) Other military sites include the Murney Tower, built in 1846 for harbor defense, and the Royal Military College (1876), the oldest academy o its kind in Canada.

□ The Marine Museum of the Great Lakes on Kingston's waterfront traces the history of the lakes from the late 17th century to the present. Other interesting sites to visit: the Penitentiary Museum; the Canadian Forces Communications and Electronics Museum; the International Hockey Museum Hall of Fame; and the Agnes Etherington Art Centre at Queen's University.

□ Bellevue House (1840), once the home of Sir John A. Macdonald, Canada's first prime minister, is now a national historic site. The Gothic-style Elizabeth Cottage (not open to the public), at Brock and Carey streets, is one of many early 19th-century dwellings worth seeing.

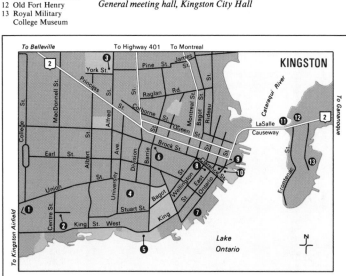

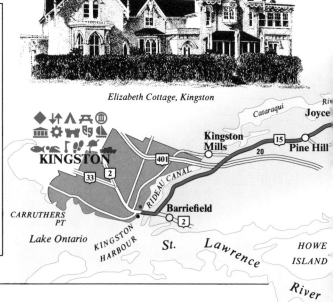

Elizabeth Cottage, Kingston

Kingston has been an Indian village, a French fortress, a British citadel—even, briefly, the capital of Canada (1841-43). The past speaks through the gray limestone walls of the old city, through monuments and museums, and through the battlements of Fort Henry, where 19th-century military routine is daily reenacted.

Governor Frontenac of New France built a wooden stockade here in 1673. The explorer La Salle, named fort commander, replaced the stockade with stone bastions and called it Fort Frontenac. It was a French trading and military post until 1758, when it fell to the British.

In 1784, after the American Revolution, 1,500 Loyalists colonized the site and named it in honor of George III. During the War of 1812, Kingston was the major naval base in Upper Canada. Later it became the seat of government, and home of Sir John A. Macdonald. Today Kingston, with more than 60,000 people, is a center of industry, services and education.

The Rideau Canal, built in 1826-32, for a time added to Kingston's strategic and commercial importance. For 30 kilometres north of Kingston the canal follows the Cataraqui River through a series of lakes. This stretch of the canal has heavily wooded shores and small rocky islands. Roads lead to picnic sites along many of the canal's hand-operated locks.

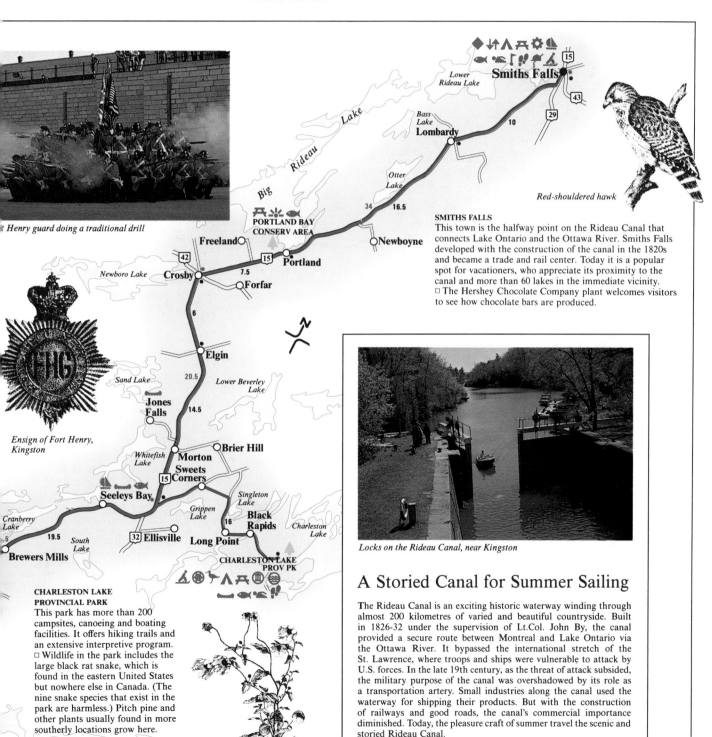

Henry guard doing a traditional drill

Red-shouldered hawk

Ensign of Fort Henry, Kingston

SMITHS FALLS

This town is the halfway point on the Rideau Canal that connects Lake Ontario and the Ottawa River. Smiths Falls developed with the construction of the canal in the 1820s and became a trade and rail center. Today it is a popular spot for vacationers, who appreciate its proximity to the canal and more than 60 lakes in the immediate vicinity.
□ The Hershey Chocolate Company plant welcomes visitors to see how chocolate bars are produced.

Locks on the Rideau Canal, near Kingston

A Storied Canal for Summer Sailing

The Rideau Canal is an exciting historic waterway winding through almost 200 kilometres of varied and beautiful countryside. Built in 1826-32 under the supervision of Lt.Col. John By, the canal provided a secure route between Montreal and Lake Ontario via the Ottawa River. It bypassed the international stretch of the St. Lawrence, where troops and ships were vulnerable to attack by U.S. forces. In the late 19th century, as the threat of attack subsided, the military purpose of the canal was overshadowed by its role as a transportation artery. Small industries along the canal used the waterway for shipping their products. But with the construction of railways and good roads, the canal's commercial importance diminished. Today, the pleasure craft of summer travel the scenic and storied Rideau Canal.

CHARLESTON LAKE PROVINCIAL PARK

This park has more than 200 campsites, canoeing and boating facilities. It offers hiking trails and an extensive interpretive program.
□ Wildlife in the park includes the large black rat snake, which is found in the eastern United States but nowhere else in Canada. (The nine snake species that exist in the park are harmless.) Pitch pine and other plants usually found in more southerly locations grow here.

Black-eyed Susan

Stonemasons' Gems Built
Beside Scenic Waterways

Eastern Ontario

Canada has its own Mississippi River—a tranquil, little-known waterway that is a tributary of the Ottawa River. In the last century it was crowded with flat-bottomed barges and log booms. Today, only a few restored mills recall the river's busy past.

Just after the War of 1812, the British government brought settlers here from Scotland and Ireland. Many, ex-soldiers, were rewarded with tracts of land for service to the Crown. Small shipping ports

ALMONTE
During the First World War Robert Tait McKenzie became famous for rehabilitative methods he developed as a British army medical officer. After the war he bought and restored the Mill of Kintail. McKenzie's fame as a sculptor competed with his renown as a surgeon: he produced hundreds of sculptures, medals, and war memorials. The mill's museum has more than 70 of his works.

*The Sprinter,
Mill of Kintail, Almonte*

Matheson House, Perth

CARLETON PLACE
This community was founded by William Dorphy in 1818. The town hall is one of six local buildings officially designated as heritage property.
□ A plaque in Memorial Park honors Arthur Roy Brown, the World War I airman credited with shooting down German air ace Manfred von Richthofen—the "Red Baron"—in 1918. Brown was born here in 1893.

PERTH
The town, which is named for the Scottish city, has two claims to fame. It is the site of the last fatal duel in Canada. And it was also the place where the Mammoth Cheese was created in 1893.
□ Walking tours of Perth begin at the town hall. Visitors can admire the Perth Hotel (1838), the Matheson House (1840) and the Inge-Va House (1823).

A Fatal Duel in the Rain

Robert Lyon, who "fell in mortal combat"—as is recorded on his gravestone in the Old Burying Ground in Perth—was killed in Canada's last fatal duel on June 13, 1833.

Lyon, 20, made an insulting remark about Elizabeth Hughes, the fiancée of a fellow law student, John Wilson, and Wilson issued a challenge. The duel was fought on the banks of the Tay River. It was raining hard, and both men missed on the first shot, but Lyon was fatally wounded in the second exchange. Wilson, charged with murder, pleaded his own case, contending he had been forced into the duel to preserve his honor. He was acquitted, married Miss Hughes, and later became a judge of the Ontario Supreme Court.

The Mammoth Cheese

At Perth, a model of the Mammoth Cheese celebrates an amazing culinary feat. The world's largest cheese—one of Canada's exhibits at the 1893 Columbian Exposition in Chicago—was made by dairy farmers in a CPR freight shed in Perth. The cheese, which weighed 9,997 kilograms, was shipped to Chicago on two railway flatcars.

Hundreds of people arrived at the station as the cheese left on a special train. Crowds collected at every station between Perth and Windsor as the train passed. When it was unloaded at Chicago and placed with the Canadian display, the cheese crashed through the floor and had to be moved to a reinforced area in another building.

After the fair the cheese was shipped to Liverpool, England. It was bought by a London caterer and cut up by four men working with garden spades.

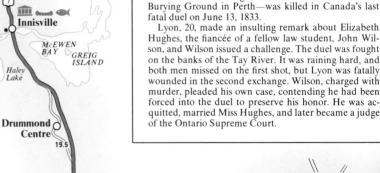

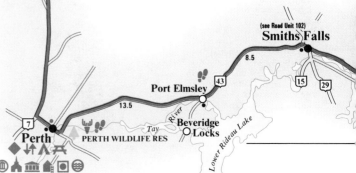

(see Road Unit 102)

Smiths Falls

Port Elmsley

Beveridge Locks

PERTH WILDLIFE RES

Perth

ALMONTE
MILL OF KINTAIL
Appleton
GLEN ISLAND
Carleton Place
Lake Park
Mississippi Lake
McCrearys
Boyds
Innisville
McEWEN BAY
GREIG ISLAND
Haley Lake
Drummond Centre

| 0 | 1 | 2 | 3 | 4 | 5 Miles |
| 0 | 2 | 4 | 6 | 8 Kilometres |

and mill towns sprang up and, for a time, became thriving commercial centers.

This prosperity is reflected in the fine stone buildings for which the area is noted, many built by the skilled stonemasons who worked on the Rideau Canal. Standing where the Rideau River splits around Long Island at Manotick, Watson's Mill is a splendid five-story gristmill made of river limestone. Equally impressive is the Mill of Kintail, built in 1830 of multicolored fieldstones. Other mills and homes, many of them museums, are treasure houses of local history and Canadiana.

One of the best ways to explore the area is by water. Meandering through historic Lanark County, the Mississippi is at its most active at Almonte, where it drops down Upper and Lower Falls—popular cooling-off spots in summer. The Tay River courses over a pink granite bed, its banks riddled with marine fossils. The Rideau Waterway offers almost 200 kilometres of pleasure boating between Ottawa and Kingston.

This region has attractions for the sportsman and the nature lover. At Rideau River Provincial Park there is fishing for walleye, maskinonge, northern pike and perch. Baxter Conservation Area has interpretive nature trails and programs. A three-kilometre trail at the Perth Wildlife Reserve has been laid out for visitors interested in wildlife management techniques.

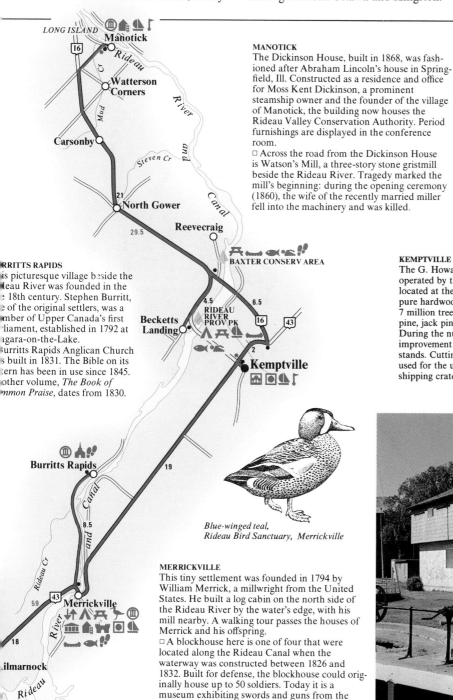

MANOTICK
The Dickinson House, built in 1868, was fashioned after Abraham Lincoln's house in Springfield, Ill. Constructed as a residence and office for Moss Kent Dickinson, a prominent steamship owner and the founder of the village of Manotick, the building now houses the Rideau Valley Conservation Authority. Period furnishings are displayed in the conference room.
□ Across the road from the Dickinson House is Watson's Mill, a three-story stone gristmill beside the Rideau River. Tragedy marked the mill's beginning: during the opening ceremony (1860), the wife of the recently married miller fell into the machinery and was killed.

Watson's Mill, Manotick

KEMPTVILLE
The G. Howard Ferguson Forest Station, a vast tree nursery operated by the Ontario Ministry of Natural Resources, is located at the edge of town. Here nursery stock and mixed and pure hardwoods are grown. Annual production is approximately 7 million trees—the principal species include red pine, white pine, jack pine, Carolina poplar, white cedar and silver maple. During the nursery's off-season—late fall to early spring—improvement work is done on the hardwood and mixed timber stands. Cuttings taken at this time are processed into lumber and used for the upkeep of buildings and equipment and for making shipping crates.

BURRITTS RAPIDS
[Th]is picturesque village beside the [Rid]eau River was founded in the [late] 18th century. Stephen Burritt, [on]e of the original settlers, was a [me]mber of Upper Canada's first [par]liament, established in 1792 at [Ni]agara-on-the-Lake.
[B]urritts Rapids Anglican Church [wa]s built in 1831. The Bible on its [lect]ern has been in use since 1845. [An]other volume, *The Book of [Co]mmon Praise*, dates from 1830.

Blue-winged teal, Rideau Bird Sanctuary, Merrickville

MERRICKVILLE
This tiny settlement was founded in 1794 by William Merrick, a millwright from the United States. He built a log cabin on the north side of the Rideau River by the water's edge, with his mill nearby. A walking tour passes the houses of Merrick and his offspring.
□ A blockhouse here is one of four that were located along the Rideau Canal when the waterway was constructed between 1826 and 1832. Built for defense, the blockhouse could originally house up to 50 soldiers. Today it is a museum exhibiting swords and guns from the 1800s, medals, a treadmill, butter churns and wooden scythes. The old powder magazine can still be seen in the cellar.

Blockhouse on the Rideau Canal near Merrickville

Our 'Westminster of the Wilderness,' a Lively City of Parks and Landmarks

W hen Queen Victoria picked Ottawa as Canada's capital in 1857, the royal decision dashed the hopes of Montreal, Toronto and other contenders for the position. It also provoked a fierce outcry. According to Goldwin Smith, Ottawa was "a subarctic lumber village converted . . . into a political cockpit." Nevertheless, the ground was broken for Parliament Buildings in 1859 and Ottawa's status was confirmed by the British North America Act in 1867.

Ottawa was first settled by Nicholas Sparks in the early 1800s. His homestead, near present-day Sparks Street, remained isolated until Col. John By began work on the Rideau Canal in 1826. By set up his headquarters at the junction of the Ottawa and Rideau rivers and founded a lumbering community, which became known as Bytown. This name was changed in 1855—Ottawa was deemed a more suitable name for a capital—and two years later the city became the "Westminster of the Wilderness."

From the lumber and rail center of bygones days, Ottawa has blossomed into a modern capital. Much has been done by the federal government to improve and develop the natural surroundings, and to preserve the city's famous national landmarks. Today, scenic driveways, parks and other specially developed areas, notably the Rideau Canal, provide an abundance of green space, as well as recreation facilities for local citizens. An impressive array of new museums, galleries and other attractions enliven the dignity of official Ottawa and enhance visitors' enjoyment of the nation's capital.

Arts Court (29)
The municipal art center of Ottawa is located in the former Carleton County Courthouse. Art exhibits, performances of music, theater and dance, as well as lectures and workshops, take place here year-round.

Billings Estate Museum (5)
Braddish Billings' first home, a small log cabin (1813), became a summer kitchen for a larger home built here in 1828.

Bytown Museum (15)
Located at the Ottawa Locks, the Bytown Museum is housed in Ottawa's oldest building (1827). The three-story stone structure was used by Col. John By during the construction of the Rideau Canal. The museum exhibits artifacts from the canal and the early community of Bytown.

Byward Market (27)
This lively market dates from the 1830s. Some of its original buildings, preserved and

Historic Rideau Canal (below), built for military purposes, winds through Ottawa, providing a scenic waterway for modern pleasure craft. In winter, an eight-kilometre-long stretch of the canal (right) in the heart of the city becomes the world's largest rink.

renovated, provide premises for hundreds of restaurants, boutiques and stalls.

Canadian Centre for Caricature (25)
Located in the Byward Market, this museum presents theme displays from its collection of more than 20,000 political cartoons.

Canadian Ski Museum (26)
The museum uses exhibits of skiing equipment to trace the development of the sport, particularly in Canada.

Canadian War Museum (21)
A solid brass cannon cast in 1732 and a Gatling gun used to suppress the Northwest Rebellion in 1885 are part of a collection tracing Canada's military history.

Carleton University (4)
Roughly 19,500 students attend this university (founded in 1942) on the banks of the Rideau River. Elegant modern buildings include the 22-story Arts Tower. In the Henry Marshall Tory Science Building is a 3-by-50-metre mosaic mural by Gerald Trottier.

Central Experimental Farm (2)
This 500-hectare farm in the heart of Ottawa is the headquarters and research branch for Agriculture Canada. Horse-drawn wagon tours pass flower beds, ornamental gardens and the oldest arboretum in Canada.

Changing of the Guard (14)
Every morning at 10 o'clock during summer, guardsmen in scarlet tunics and bearskin busbies enact this traditional military ceremony on the grounds of Parliament Hill.

City Hall (35)
This eight-story building (1958) on Green Island, near Rideau Falls, is graced with a striking freestanding stairway of white marble and aluminum. Swans—a gift from the Queen—float along the Rideau River from City Hall to Carleton University.

Currency Museum (9)
The Bank of Canada's exhibition traces the origins and history of Canadian currency from beads, wampum and whale teeth to such curiosities as Chinese knife money and a three-ton Yap stone from the Pacific.

Earnscliffe (31)
This three-story house (1855), Sir John A. Macdonald's home in 1883-91, is the residence of the British high commissioner.

Garden of the Provinces (6)
Provincial flags fly above enameled bronze plaques depicting the provincial flowers.

Kitchissippi Lookout (1)
A plaque here honors Canadian voyageurs who guided an 1884 British expedition led by

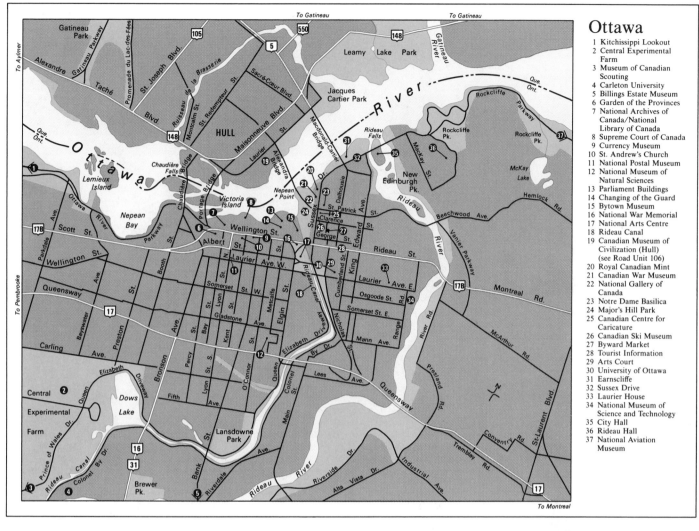

Ottawa

1. Kitchissippi Lookout
2. Central Experimental Farm
3. Museum of Canadian Scouting
4. Carleton University
5. Billings Estate Museum
6. Garden of the Provinces
7. National Archives of Canada/National Library of Canada
8. Supreme Court of Canada
9. Currency Museum
10. St. Andrew's Church
11. National Postal Museum
12. National Museum of Natural Sciences
13. Parliament Buildings
14. Changing of the Guard
15. Bytown Museum
16. National War Memorial
17. National Arts Centre
18. Rideau Canal
19. Canadian Museum of Civilization (Hull) (see Road Unit 106)
20. Royal Canadian Mint
21. Canadian War Museum
22. National Gallery of Canada
23. Notre Dame Basilica
24. Major's Hill Park
25. Canadian Centre for Caricature
26. Canadian Ski Museum
27. Byward Market
28. Tourist Information
29. Arts Court
30. University of Ottawa
31. Earnscliffe
32. Sussex Drive
33. Laurier House
34. National Museum of Science and Technology
35. City Hall
36. Rideau Hall
37. National Aviation Museum

Col. Garnet Wolseley through the Nile rapids to rescue Gen. Charles Gordon who was besieged at Khartoum.

Laurier House (33)
This fine 1878 stone mansion was once the residence of Sir Wilfrid Laurier and William Lyon Mackenzie King. It is filled with its former famous occupants' photographs, documents and furniture, including a prie-dieu (c. 1550) from Mary Queen of Scots' castle and an oak chair said to have been used at the coronation of James I of England. The house also displays the contents of the study of a third prime minister, Lester B. Pearson.

Major's Hill Park (24)
A cannon cast in 1807 is fired at noon on weekdays and 10 a.m. on Sundays in a tradition that dates from 1869. Two stones from the Sappers' Bridge that crossed the Rideau Canal mark the site of Colonel By's house.

Museum of Canadian Scouting (3)
Exhibits telling the story of the Boy Scout movement in Canada include an illustrated log kept by Lord Baden-Powell on his visit to Canada in 1910.

National Archives of Canada (7)
The collection includes some 100,000 books, as well as maps, manuscripts, photographs, pamphlets and other material relating to the history of Canada and the Canadian gov-

ernment. The Constitution Act of 1982 is housed here.

National Arts Centre (17)
This complex on the west bank of the Rideau Canal near Confederation Square contains a 2,300-seat Opera House, an 800-seat theater and a smaller experimental stage, and a hall for receptions and recitals. The center presents a year-round program of music, dance and drama.

National Aviation Museum (37)
The museum at Rockcliffe Airport has more than 100 aircraft, including a replica of the *Silver Dart*, which made the first heavier-than-air flight in the British Empire at Baddeck, Nova Scotia, in 1909. Visitors can follow the periods of aviation history along the Walkway of Time.

National Gallery of Canada (22)
Canada's most extensive art collection is housed in an impressive glass and granite structure, designed by Moshe Safdie and opened to the public in 1988. The museum's paintings, sculptures, prints and other works of art are displayed in skylit galleries. The Canadian galleries contain a comprehensive array of Canadian paintings from the 19th century to the present. The museum also has works by European masters, such as Canaletto, Rubens, Rembrandt, El Greco, Turner,

The former residence of two prime ministers, Laurier House (1878) is now a museum.

Corot, Daumier, Degas, Cézanne and Mondrian. At the heart of the National Gallery is the reconstructed Rideau Chapel, now a repository of sacred art.

National Library of Canada (7)
This storehouse of Canadian books, periodicals, newspapers, sheet music, sound recordings and other materials contains about 3 million items. The Glenn Gould Collection includes the pianist's own grand piano.

National Museum of Natural Sciences (12)
Preserved specimens of mammals and birds from across Canada are positioned in recreations of natural habitats. Displays of

Blossoming tulips (right) turn Ottawa into a riot of color. With some 3 million blossoms, the city has North America's largest tulip display. One of the most stirring sights in Canada is the 30-minute Changing of the Guard on Parliament Hill (below). Men of the Governor-General's Foot Guards and the Canadian Grenadier Guards, with two bands, take part. Coats of arms of the provinces are carved in the limestone arches of Confederation Hall (bottom).

fossils, minerals, plants and animals illustrate the geologic and natural history of the earth. The museum is housed in the castle-like Victoria Memorial Building (1911).

National Museum of Science and Technology (34)

Working exhibits ranging from huge locomotives and vintage automobiles to a Van de Graaff generator encourage visitors to touch, push, pull, twist, climb and observe. An observatory has a 37-centimetre refracting telescope.

National Postal Museum (11)

A re-created turn-of-the-century post office and a railway mail car are two features of

A fanciful lion, its fierce stare frozen in stone, is one of many carved figures on Parliament Hill.

this museum, which contains a vast collection of Canadian and world stamps.

National War Memorial (16)

This monument on Confederation Square honors all Canadian war veterans.

Notre Dame Basilica (23)

Above the Gothic-style choir stalls are Philippe Hébert's statues of prophets, evangelists and patriarchs of the church. The basilica, begun in 1841, has 54-metre twin towers. A memorial honors Msgr. Joseph-Eugène Guigues, founder of the University of Ottawa.

Parliament Buildings (13)

Canada's Parliament Buildings on the bluffs high above the Ottawa River comprise three Gothic-revival buildings: the Centre Block (House of Commons and Senate), the East Block (governor-general's, privy council's and prime minister's offices and cabinet

First World War soldiers silhouetted against an Ottawa sky (left) are part of the National War Memorial in Confederation Square. George VI unveiled the memorial in May 1939. Newly minted coins gleam at the Royal Canadian Mint (above). An airmail pioneer of the 1920s (below right) is one of 110 vintage airplanes at the National Aviation Museum at Rockcliffe Airport. The National Gallery of Canada (below left), designed by Israeli-born architect Moshe Safdie, is one of the many splendid museums that enrich Ottawa.

purposes, but served instead as a commercial waterway in the 19th century. Now the canal is used by pleasure craft during summer. Every winter, an illuminated eight-kilometre stretch of the canal in the heart of Ottawa becomes the world's longest skating rink. The canal is the focus of Ottawa's Winterlude Carnival.

Rideau Hall (36)
This three-story limestone house, built in 1838, is the residence of the governor-general of Canada. The grounds are open to the public every day during July and August, and on weekends and holidays throughout the year. Group tours of Rideau Hall and the private grounds can be arranged.

Royal Canadian Mint (20)
The mint produces millions of coins and blanks for other countries. Visitors are welcome to watch the manufacturing process. A small museum displays Canadian and foreign coins and medals.

St. Andrew's Church (10)
The pews in this stone Presbyterian church (1872) are arranged in a semicircle around the pulpit. The lectern was presented to the church by Queen Juliana of the Netherlands, who joined the congregation while living here during the Second World War.

Supreme Court of Canada (8)
Tours of this impressive stone building include the two Federal Courts, the Supreme Court and the judges' chambers. The building was designed by the renowned Quebec architect Ernest Cormier (1885-1980).

Sussex Drive (32)
This thoroughfare, which stretches from downtown Ottawa to Rideau Hall, links a number of Ottawa's major sites: Notre Dame Basilica, the National Gallery of Canada, the Canadian War Museum and the Royal Canadian Mint, External Affairs Canada and 24 Sussex Drive, the home of the Prime Minister.

University of Ottawa (30)
The oldest bilingual university in Canada (founded as Bytown College in 1848) is also the largest, with a student enrollment of more than 23,600.

chamber) and the West Block (offices and committee rooms). The three buildings were built between 1859 and 1865. The Centre Block was rebuilt after fire destroyed it in 1916. The only part to survive was the cone-shaped library, noted for its vaulted ceiling and intricate woodwork.

At the front of the Centre Block, the Peace Tower with its carillon of 53 bells rises 93 metres high. (The largest bell weighs more than 10 tonnes.) Atop the tower, a white light burns while Parliament is sitting. Below the carillon, the Memorial Chamber houses the four Books of Remembrance listing the names of Canadians who gave their lives in wars. The 14-metre-high sandstone walls are engraved with poems by John McCrae, Rudyard Kipling, Victor Hugo and John Bunyan. The floor is paved with stones from the battlefields of France and Belgium.

The entrance to the Centre Block through the Peace Tower leads to Confederation Hall, whose pillars symbolize Confederation and the provinces. Hand-painted Irish linen covers the ceiling of the Commons. The speaker's chair is a replica of the one in the British House of Commons. In the Commons foyer, a 36-metre-long limestone frieze depicts the history of Canada. Murals of the First World War battlefields and a gilded ceiling decorate the Senate Chamber. There are conducted tours of the Centre Block. Visitors can watch parliamentary proceedings from the Commons gallery.

At the front of the Parliament Buildings, an eternal flame commemorates 100 years of Canadian nationhood.

Rideau Canal (18)
Built between 1826 and 1832, the Rideau Canal was originally designed for military

A Capital's Playground Nestling in Rolling Wooded Hills

Gatineau Park

A playground set in wilderness, Gatineau Park lies within sight of Ottawa's Parliament Buildings. Neither national nor provincial, the park was established in 1938 and is administered by the National Capital Commission.

The park's rolling hills are the stumps of ancient mountains rounded by glaciers. The ice disappeared about 12,000 years ago, leaving the land bleak and devoid of life. Then began the great invasion of plants and animals that continues even today.

WAKEFIELD (LA PÊCHE)
The local Musée historique de la Gatineau is open year-round. The museum depicts 19th-century life in the Gatineau region. The nearby Maclaren gristmill welcomes visitors during summer and early autumn. Built in the 1830s, the three-story stone structure on the La Pêche River was sold a decade later to James and John Maclaren, who used it to supply their Gatineau lumber camps.
□ Lester B. Pearson, Canada's 14th prime minister, is buried in Maclaren Cemetery.

Gatineau Hills

GATINEAU PARK
This park covers roughly 356 square kilometres of rolling, forested wilderness. Bordered on the east by the Gatineau River and on the south by the Ottawa River, Gatineau Park begins just outside Hull and stretches about 50 kilometres into the Canadian Shield. There is a visitor center at Old Chelsea.
□ The southern part of Gatineau Park contains a number of historic and politically significant sites: the Mackenzie King estate, the official summer residence of the prime minister at Harrington Lake and the Meech Lake conference center. The park's recreational areas include Philippe and La Pêche lakes.
□ Gatineau Park offers a full range of recreational activities. In summer, there is boating, camping (at designated sites), fishing, and swimming (at supervised beaches only). A 190-kilometre network of trails crisscrosses the park. The summer hiking paths become cross-country ski trails in winter. There are also two downhill skiing areas.

From Hilltop to Lowland— a Forest Renewed

Centuries of logging, land clearing, fires and floods have left their mark on the three types of forest in Gatineau Park. Half the trees grow in shallow soil along ridgetops and upper slopes. Fires have swept away many older stands, and most trees are less than 60 years old. Here are the hardwoods—gnarled red oak, ironwood and white ash, and the aspens and white birch which take over cleared land. There are mixed-wood stands of hemlock and red maple, and a few softwood groves of white, red and jack pines.

Shade-tolerant hardwoods such as sugar maple and beech thrive on moist middle and lower slopes. Balsam fir and white spruce grow in softwood thickets on abandoned farmland.

Along streams and wet lowlands, mixed woods—black ash and cedar—and softwood stands of black spruce, larch and tamarack are most common.

Larch

Balsam fir

Red oak

AYLMER
This community is a golfer's paradise. There are six local golf courses, including the Kingsway Park and Country Club. The Canadian Golf Museum at the Kingsway club displays vintage golf balls, one-piece wooden clubs, as well as brassies, mashies, spoons and niblicks—forerunners of today's numbered woods and irons. Other exhibits include a leather-faced wooden spoon, which was used by Willie Park, winner of the first British Open in 1860.
□ Among some 170 historic buildings in the Aylmer area are the Symmes Hotel (1832), the British Hotel (1841) and the Town Hall (1842), which served as a courthouse and is now a library.
□ Musée d'Aylmer is housed in the John McLean House (1840). The museum describes Aylmer's history, with emphasis on its pre-1850 steamship days.

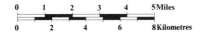

0 1 2 3 4 5 Miles

0 2 4 6 8 Kilometres

Indians settled in the valley of the Ottawa River 4,000 years ago, but it was not until the fur trade era that man's presence was felt in the Gatineau region in a major way. Settlers and loggers arrived early in the 19th century. Because the terrain was suitable only for sheep grazing, most settlers had left by the turn of the century. But the loggers stayed until lumbering ended in the 1920s. With their departure, man invaded the Gatineau region, this time for the sheer enjoyment of the wooded terrain.

Today, Gatineau Park preserves this region for visitors. The scenic Gatineau and Fortune Lake parkways lead travelers to the Champlain Lookout, which offers a spectacular view of the park's rolling hills and forests. Sparkling lakes beckon to canoeists and fishermen. A network of trails attracts summer hikers and winter skiers. Picturesque beaches and roadside sites invite campers and picnickers to stop awhile and enjoy the timeless atmosphere that only an unspoiled wilderness can impart.

Gatineau River

GATINEAU RIVER
This 386-kilometre-long river empties into the Ottawa River at Hull. The origin of the river's name puzzles historians. It is thought to be named for Nicolas Gastineau, Sieur Duplessis, who came to Canada in 1650. He was a fur trader in this region and possibly drowned in the river in 1683.

MEECH LAKE (LAC MEECH)
The lake is named for Asa Meech, an American who settled here in the 1820s.
☐ In 1906, Canadian inventor Thomas "Carbide" Willson (1860-1915) bought property on Meech Lake, where he built an experimental factory. Willson House, purchased by the Federal Government in 1979, is now a conference center. It was the site of the 1987 negotiations leading to the Meech Lake Accord.

The Great Days of the Gatineau Logger

Lumbering was Canada's biggest industry during most of the mid-19th century—and some of the finest stands of white pine needed for the British square-timber trade were in the Gatineau forests.

Trees were felled in winter, when logs could be skidded along the frozen ground. The men who felled and squared the logs also shepherded them on the long river drives, and so were hired "from freeze-up to Quebec."

Loggers worked in pairs, taking alternate swings at a tree. Logs were hauled to a river's edge by oxen and stacked there for the spring drive. When the ice broke, the tumbling logs had to be herded down rivers and streams to the Ottawa River, where they were bound into rafts to be guided to Quebec. It was dangerous, exhausting work. Lumbermen in town after being paid off in July were like "a roistering plague." Many a man's pay—up to $300—was lost in a few nights of drinking, wenching and brawling.

KINGSMERE
This 230-hectare estate was the summer residence of William Lyon Mackenzie King, prime minister in 1921-30 and 1935-48, who bequeathed the property to the Canadian government. The Cloisters (*right*) is one of the picturesque "ruins" assembled on the estate by King from demolished buildings. Some of the stones were saved from the first Canadian Parliament Building (destroyed by fire in 1916) and the House of Commons in London, bomb-damaged during World War II. King's residence, Moorside, is now a museum.

HULL
Founded in 1800, Hull was the first permanent community on the Ottawa River. The first settler was an American, Philemon Wright, who arrived with a small group of his countrymen. Originally an agricultural settlement, Hull became a lumbering center during the 19th century. In 1851, another American, Erza Butler Eddy, set up his match factory here and later became a leading pulp-and-paper producer.
☐ Today, Hull's development is closely linked to neighboring Ottawa. The federal civil service is Hull's principal employer. Since the 1970s, federal government complexes, such as Place du Portage, have dominated Hull's cityscape.
☐ The Canadian Museum of Civilization in Hull is magnificently situated across the river from the Parliament Building in Ottawa. This impressive museum, designed by Alberta-born architect Douglas Cardinal, traces the nation's history from prehistoric times to the present.

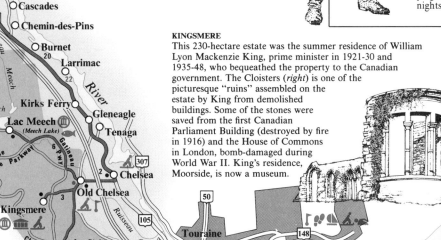

Canadian Museum of Civilization, Hull

Legendary Pieces of Paradise Dropped from a God's Blanket

The Thousand Islands

Some are lushy forested. Others support only a few ragged pines perched precariously over the water. These are the lovely Thousand Islands (perhaps 995, maybe 1,010) that lie in a 56-kilometre stretch between Gananoque and Brockville. They range in size from a protruding boulder to large islands with attractive summer homes and marinas.

By day the islands appear as splashes of green on a river whose blues change color with every different shade of light; when

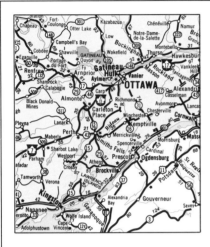

By Boat to Boldt Castle

George Boldt, an immigrant from Germany in the late 1800s, began work in North America as a dishwasher. His rise from poverty to riches was quick. He helped establish the Waldorf-Astoria Hotel in New York City, acquired control of several major businesses—and became a millionaire.

Boldt's dream was to build a castle for his wife. In the 1890s he purchased one of the Thousand Islands, had it reshaped as a heart, and ordered the construction of his castle. But before the structure was completed, Boldt's wife died. Grief-stricken, he ordered the work halted. Boldt never returned to his ornate dream castle on Heart Island. Boats to the island leave from Gananoque, Ivy Lea, Kingston and Rockport.

Boldt Castle, Heart Island

Thousand Islands International Bridge, near Ivy Lea

THOUSAND ISLANDS PARKWAY
Trees along the 38-kilometre parkway sometimes screen the St. Lawrence but lookouts every few kilometres give fine views of the river. Above the road, near Brown's Bay, is a kilometre-long slab of rare light gray sandstone atop the reddish granite common in this area.

The largest stand of pitch pine in mainland Canada grows along this route; the trees are especially thick among the red and white oaks between Rockport and Ivy Lea. Great blue herons and American bitterns feed in roadside marshes.

MALLORYTOWN LANDING
Located on the north shore of the St. Lawrence River, this is the only part of St. Lawrence Islands National Park accessible by car. Swimming, fishing and fine beaches are major attractions.

Pitch pine

Thousand Islands Skydeck, Hill Island

GANANOQUE
Situated in the heart of the Thousand Islands, the popular resort town of Gananoque (pronounced gan-an-ock-way) is a departure point for 1½- to 3-hour boat cruises through the scenic islands.
□ The Gananoque Museum, housed in the old Victoria Hotel (1863), displays 19th-century furnishings and a collection of military artifacts.
□ Gananoque's graceful brick Town Hall was built in 1830 by wealthy merchant John McDonald for his young bride Henrietta Mallory.

HILL ISLAND
Hill Island is between spans of the Thousand Islands International Bridge. A plaque commemorates the opening of the bridge by Prime Minister Mackenzie King and President Franklin D. Roosevelt in 1938.
□ The view from the Thousand Islands Skydeck, 120 metres above the St. Lawrence River, is 65 kilometres on a clear day. Three observation levels are reached by an elevator.

```
0    1    2    3    4    5 Miles
0    2    4    6    8 Kilometres
```

night descends, cottage lights and campfires wink from among the trees and cast flickering reflections across the water.

Indians called the Thousand Islands the Garden of the Great Spirit and believed the region was once a great expanse of open water. According to legend, the Great Spirit created a garden paradise along the shore in an effort to bring peace to warring tribes. Still they fought. So he bundled paradise into a blanket and flew toward his home in the heavens. But the blanket tore and paradise crashed into the water, breaking into hundreds of pieces.

There is also a geological explanation. Some 900 million years ago mountains as majestic as the Rockies rose where the St. Lawrence River now flows. Rivers and glaciers reduced the peaks to low hills that now are islands and shoals.

In the late 19th century the islands were a millionaires' playground where tycoons built lavish waterfront mansions and spent summers in idyllic luxury. Today the islands are among Canada's most popular tourist areas. Scenic boat tours, nature trails, country fairs, water sports and some of the world's best freshwater fishing make the Thousand Islands a near perfect family vacationland.

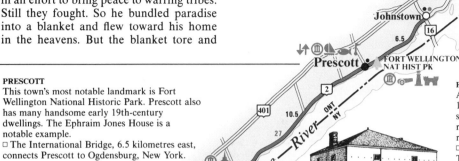

PRESCOTT

This town's most notable landmark is Fort Wellington National Historic Park. Prescott also has many handsome early 19th-century dwellings. The Ephraim Jones House is a notable example.
□ The International Bridge, 6.5 kilometres east, connects Prescott to Ogdensburg, New York.

MAITLAND

The graveyard at the clapboard Blue Church (1845) is the burial place of Barbara Heck (1734-1804), one of the early founders of Methodism in North America. Irish-born Heck and her husband emigrated to New York in 1760. Eight years later, she helped to establish a Wesley chapel, in New York City, considered to be the first in North America. The Hecks were Loyalists, who settled in Canada after the American Revolution. Barbara Heck continued to work for the Methodist cause in this country until her death.
□ The Old Distillery (1828) also served as a gristmill and a shot tower, which was used to make bullets.

Blockhouse, Fort Wellington National Historic Park

FORT WELLINGTON NATIONAL HISTORIC PARK

A three-story blockhouse, dating from the late 1830s, is the main attraction of this historic park, situated in Prescott. Built in 1812, the fort was reconstructed in 1838 during the Canadian rebellions of 1837-38. It was last garrisoned in 1885.
□ The blockhouse has stone walls 1.3 metres thick. The ground floor, which consists of a guardroom, storeroom, armory and powder magazine, is now a museum.
□ From mid-May to early September, traditional military drills are held daily. As part of Prescott's ten-day Loyalist Days festivities, a military pageant is held. Opposing forces in period costume attack and defend the fort in mock battle.
□ On a nearby spit of land, a 20-metre stone tower (1820) commands a view of the St. Lawrence River. Originally a windmill, the tower was a rebel stronghold late in the rebellions of 1837-38.

Blue Church, Maitland

BROCKVILLE

Founded in 1784, Brockville was one of the first Loyalist settlements in Upper Canada. It was named after Maj. Gen. Sir Isaac Brock, the War of 1812 hero.
□ Along the city's clean, tree-lined streets are many fine old homes. Brockville Courthouse, constructed in 1842, is one of Ontario's oldest public buildings. Other well-preserved structures include The Carriage House Hotel (1820), Victoria School (1855) and the Orange Lodge (1825).
□ The Brockville Railway Tunnel, Canada's oldest, was built in 1854-60 to enable trains of the Brockville and Ottawa Railway to reach the riverfront. The tunnel was last used in 1954.
□ Nearby Blockhouse Island was used as a quarantine station during a cholera outbreak in the 1830s.

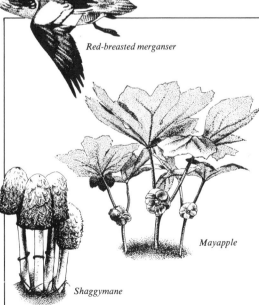

Red-breasted merganser

Mayapple

Shaggymane

A Boater's Paradise in a Park of Islands

A small mainland area, 18 heavily wooded islands and 80 rocky islets between Kingston and Brockville form St. Lawrence Islands National Park. Its scenic beauty and sheltered waters have earned it a reputation as a boater's paradise.

The park supports a rich diversity of flora and fauna, much of it usually found farther south. Among 800 plant species are black oak, mayapple and shaggymane, Canada's only deerberry and the world's most northerly growth of rue anemone. Some 65 species of birds sighted here include cardinals, Carolina wrens, wild turkeys, bald eagles and red-breasted mergansers; 28 species of reptiles and amphibians include eastern ribbon snakes and blue-spotted salamanders. There are some 35 species of fish in this region.

The islands, with such poetic names as Camelot, Mermaid and Endymion, were rounded by glaciers and rivers some 500 million years ago. Almost all of the islands have docks, campsites, wells and kitchen shelters.

Hiking, canoeing and supervised swimming are among the park's main attractions.

Across an 1840 Bridge
to a Village of Yesteryear

Southeastern Ontario

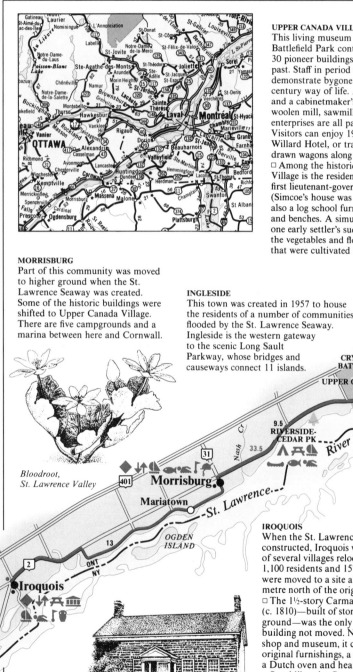

UPPER CANADA VILLAGE

This living museum in Crysler Farm Battlefield Park contains more than 30 pioneer buildings from Ontario's past. Staff in period costume demonstrate bygone skills and re-create a 19th-century way of life. A bakery, a blacksmith's forge and a cabinetmaker's shop, a cheese factory, a woolen mill, sawmills and other pioneer enterprises are all part of the village scene. Visitors can enjoy 19th-century cuisine at the old Willard Hotel, or travel on oxcarts or horse-drawn wagons along quiet back roads.
□ Among the historic houses at Upper Canada Village is the residence of John Graves Simcoe, first lieutenant-governor of Upper Canada. (Simcoe's house was built before 1783.) There is also a log school furnished with rough-hewn desks and benches. A simulated farm tells the story of one early settler's success. Oxen plow the fields; the vegetables and flowers in the garden are those that were cultivated by pioneers.

Sightseeing barge, Upper Canada Village

*Cheese factory,
Upper Canada Village*

MORRISBURG

Part of this community was moved to higher ground when the St. Lawrence Seaway was created. Some of the historic buildings were shifted to Upper Canada Village. There are five campgrounds and a marina between here and Cornwall.

INGLESIDE

This town was created in 1957 to house the residents of a number of communities flooded by the St. Lawrence Seaway. Ingleside is the western gateway to the scenic Long Sault Parkway, whose bridges and causeways connect 11 islands.

*Bloodroot,
St. Lawrence Valley*

CRYSLER FARM BATTLEFIELD PARK

The park's monument commemorates those killed at the Battle of Crysler's Farm on Nov. 11, 1813. An interpretive center describes the battle in which 800 British soldiers, Canadians and Indians routed 4,000 American invaders.

IROQUOIS

When the St. Lawrence Seaway was constructed, Iroquois was the largest of several villages relocated: about 1,100 residents and 157 buildings were moved to a site about one kilometre north of the original.
□ The 1½-story Carman House (c. 1810)—built of stone on high ground—was the only Iroquois building not moved. Now a craft shop and museum, it contains many original furnishings, a stone sink and a Dutch oven and hearth.
□ Straddling the Canada-U.S. border is a huge international dam which maintains the St. Lawrence River at the best level for navigation.

UPPER CANADA MIGRATORY BIRD SANCTUARY

This 1,416-hectare refuge, five kilometres east of Upper Canada Village, is a spring and fall stopover for Canada goose and other birds. It contains an interpretive center, observation tower and six kilometres of nature trails.

Iroquois lock, St. Lawrence Seaway

Carman House, Iroquois

Houses, churches, taverns and shops of the era from 1784 to 1867 have been restored and reconstructed at Upper Canada Village, east of Morrisburg. Some of the buildings were moved here when their original sites were submerged during construction of the St. Lawrence Seaway in the late 1950s. The authentic flavor of village life involved painstaking research by architects, historians and horticulturists.

Visitors enter the village's main street—the King's Highway—over an 1840 bridge.

Clustered along one side of the highway are houses whose interiors mirror pioneer existence in the smallest detail. Fabrics, paints and wallpapers match those in use before Confederation. Every hand-forged nail and door latch, every hand-dipped candle is authentic or was reproduced with 19th-century tools and methods.

Lunaria, hollyhocks, love-in-a-mist and McIntosh apple trees—the first McIntosh Reds were produced north of here at Dundela—bloom at Crysler Hall. This imposing

mansion, which is located in the middle of Upper Canada Village, presents an orientation film and a number of other displays about the re-creation of this pre-1867 community and the flooding of the region. The builder of the mansion was a son of John Crysler, whose farm was the site of a decisive victory in the War of 1812. That site is now submerged, but the battle is commemorated by a monument in Crysler Farm Battlefield Park, which contains Upper Canada Village.

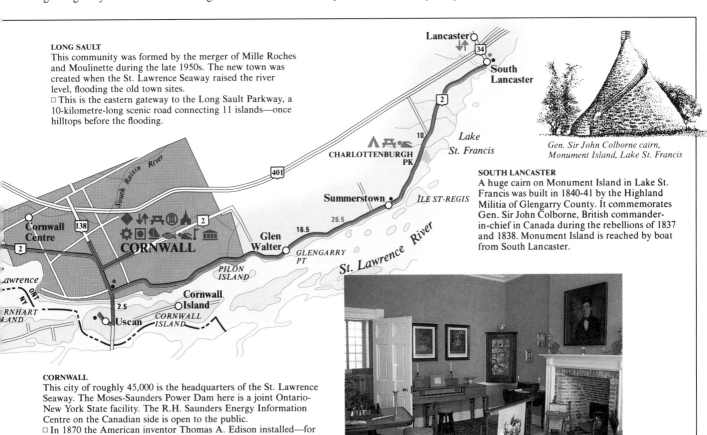

LONG SAULT
This community was formed by the merger of Mille Roches and Moulinette during the late 1950s. The new town was created when the St. Lawrence Seaway raised the river level, flooding the old town sites.
□ This is the eastern gateway to the Long Sault Parkway, a 10-kilometre-long scenic road connecting 11 islands—once hilltops before the flooding.

Gen. Sir John Colborne cairn, Monument Island, Lake St. Francis

SOUTH LANCASTER
A huge cairn on Monument Island in Lake St. Francis was built in 1840-41 by the Highland Militia of Glengarry County. It commemorates Gen. Sir John Colborne, British commander-in-chief in Canada during the rebellions of 1837 and 1838. Monument Island is reached by boat from South Lancaster.

CORNWALL
This city of roughly 45,000 is the headquarters of the St. Lawrence Seaway. The Moses-Saunders Power Dam here is a joint Ontario-New York State facility. The R.H. Saunders Energy Information Centre on the Canadian side is open to the public.
□ In 1870 the American inventor Thomas A. Edison installed—for the first time anywhere—electrical lighting in a Cornwall cotton mill. Some of Edison's equipment is displayed at United Counties Museum, housed in an 1840 stone house.
□ Other local sites include the Inverarden Regency Cottage Museum (1816) and the Museum and Indian Village on Cornwall Island.

Interior view, Inverarden Regency Cottage Museum at Cornwall

The St. Lawrence Seaway—
Gateway to North America's Heartland

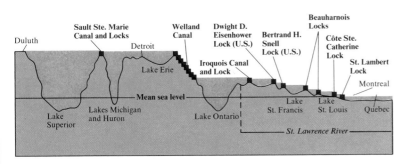

When the Great Lakes–St. Lawrence Seaway was completed in 1959, large, oceangoing ships could travel to the heartland of North America—from the Atlantic Ocean all the way to Lake Superior. Until then, passage had been limited to canal boats, using channels dug before 1903 to bypass shoals and rapids on the St. Lawrence between Montreal and Prescott. In 1954 Canada and the United States agreed upon a joint project to improve the St. Lawrence–Great Lakes System, in all some 3,800 kilometres of canals, lakes and river.

Seven new locks were built, and existing channels dredged to deepen the waterway. Ontario and New York State carried out their own joint project, building three huge dams to harness the power of the International Rapids section near Cornwall.

Today, the seaway raises vessels 183 metres from the Atlantic into Lake Superior through 20 locks. Computers regulate traffic. The ships now accommodated carry loads three times greater than the largest of the old canal boats. Grain and iron ore account for more than half the cargo.

A Wee Bit of Scotland on the Raisin River

Southeastern Ontario

Glengarry County was the first Scottish settlement in Ontario. Western Highlanders arrived in 1784 from New York's Mohawk Valley, where they had settled before the American Revolution. Two years later 500 parishioners of the Rev. Alexander Macdonell of Glengarry, Scotland, joined them. Others followed in the next 50 years, including 400 Highlanders in 1802, one quarter of them named MacMillan.

The preponderance of Scottish names was a postmaster's nightmare. At one time

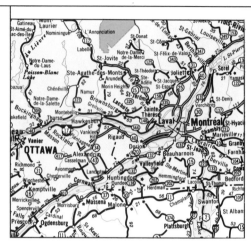

County courthouse, L'Orignal

L'ORIGNAL
This is one of the oldest communities in the Ottawa Valley. The area belonged to a Quebec seigneury when Nathaniel Hazard Treadwell bought the land for settlement in the late 1790s. The name of the town is French-Canadian for moose.
□ Ontario's oldest remaining courthouse, for many years the judicial and administrative center of the old Ottawa district, is in this town. The central portion, built in neoclassic style, was completed in 1825.

DUNVEGAN
In three square-timber buildings here are artifacts of Scottish and Loyalist pioneers who settled Glengarry County nearly 200 years ago. The restored Glengarry Pioneer Inn (c. 1830) has its original bar, wainscoting and broad pine floors. In a coach shed are early 19th-century sleighs, wagons and a log pump drill. Hand tools are displayed in a log barn (c. 1850).

Massed pipe bands, Maxville

Caber toss, Maxville Highland Games

Pioneer Life in Best-Selling Yarns

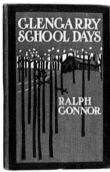

Ralph Connor liked good yarns about people who worked hard and fought well. Others liked them too—and bought five million copies of books he wrote. But writing was only a hobby: Connor was the pseudonym of Charles William Gordon (1860-1937), a prominent Presbyterian clergyman.

Gordon's first ministry, in the Rockies near Banff, Alta., provided the background for *Black Rock* (1898). *The Sky Pilot* (1899), a tale of prairie settlers, and *The Man from Glengarry* (1901) and *Glengarry School Days* (1902)—both set in the backwoods of the author's boyhood—enhanced his popularity. Gordon wrote 25 books in all, but obligations to his church came first. He was pastor of a Winnipeg church from 1895 to 1915, and from 1919 until his death, and was a chaplain in the First World War.

MAXVILLE
The Glengarry Highland Games, one of the biggest gatherings of its kind in North America, have been a major event in Maxville since 1948. The games, held in August, include the North American Pipe Championships, as well as drumming and drum majors' contests.
□ This is the part of southwestern Ontario where Ralph Connor (the Rev. Charles William Gordon) set his novels *The Man from Glengarry* and *Glengarry School Days*. Gordon was born at St. Elmo, just north of Maxville, in 1860, and died at Winnipeg in 1937.

ST. ANDREWS
The oldest remaining stone structure in Ontario erected as a place of worship is old St. Andrew's Church (1801), now a parish hall. It was the first church built by Roman Catholic Scottish Highlanders in Upper Canada. In a graveyard opposite new St. Andrew's Church (1860) is the grave of the explorer Simon Fraser.

St. Andrew's Church, St. Andrews

as many as 500 Macdonalds received mail from the Alexandria post office. The town of Maxville may have been so named because most of its residents had names beginning with "Mac."

These Scottish settlers carved today's prosperous dairy farms out of a forest wilderness on the Raisin River. Some sought further adventure and, as partners and employees of the fur-trading North West Company, helped open up Canada's North and West. They were replaced here by farmers from Quebec and half of today's population is French-speaking.

Glengarry's pioneers achieved prominence in education, politics, industry and business. A proud military history, dating from the Glengarry Light Infantry's role in the War of 1812, has been handed down to the present-day Dundas, Stormont and Glengarry Highlanders. The traditions of Scottish music, dance and athletics live on in the Glengarry Highland Games, held annually at Maxville.

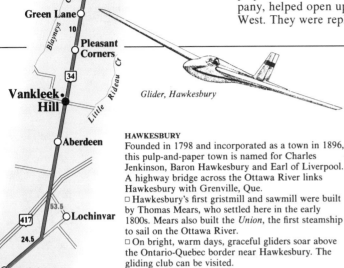

Glider, Hawkesbury

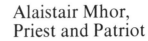

HAWKESBURY
Founded in 1798 and incorporated as a town in 1896, this pulp-and-paper town is named for Charles Jenkinson, Baron Hawkesbury and Earl of Liverpool. A highway bridge across the Ottawa River links Hawkesbury with Grenville, Que.
□ Hawkesbury's first gristmill and sawmill were built by Thomas Mears, who settled here in the early 1800s. Mears also built the *Union*, the first steamship to sail on the Ottawa River.
□ On bright, warm days, graceful gliders soar above the Ontario-Quebec border near Hawkesbury. The gliding club can be visited.

Alaistair Mhor, Priest and Patriot

A leading spokesman for Glengarry's settlers was the Most Rev. Alexander Macdonell, known as Alaistair Mhor (Big Alexander)—to distinguish him from a predecessor at St. Raphaels. Father Macdonell was 42 when he led the disbanded Glengarry Fencibles—a Roman Catholic Highland regiment he had organized—from Scotland in 1804. The Glengarry Light Infantry he formed in the War of 1812 fought in 14 battles.

After the war Macdonell opened his home to students for the priesthood. He became Upper Canada's first Roman Catholic bishop in 1820, and a member of the legislative council in 1831. He died in 1840 in Scotland.

ST. RAPHAELS
The ruins of St. Raphael's Church make an impressive sight. The stone church, built in 1821, was destroyed by fire in 1970.
□ A cairn commemorates an early pastor, Alexander Macdonell, who was the first Roman Catholic bishop of Upper Canada and the founder of the Glengarry Light Infantry.
□ A plaque marks the birthplace of John Sandfield Macdonald, joint prime minister of Canada in 1862-64 and first premier of Ontario in 1867-71.

MARTINTOWN
The Raisin River, its level raised more than two metres by spring meltwaters, becomes a white-water canoe route each April. Some 100 persons compete in races from here to St. Andrews.
□ A favorite of artists is a three-story, fieldstone gristmill, built at the turn of the century. It is occupied by descendants of the original miller.

Ruins of St. Raphael's Church

WILLIAMSTOWN
The Williamstown Fair, the oldest regularly operated country fair in Canada, is held every year during the second week of August. It was started in 1810 by Sir John Johnson, the leader of a group of Loyalists who came here in 1784 from New York. Johnson's red-roofed, white clapboard manor (c. 1790) is one of many noteworthy houses in this area. Another is a white frame house built by the Rev. John Bethune, who founded Ontario's first Presbyterian congregation in 1787. Fraserfield (c. 1872), a 23-room stone structure, is also a fine historic house.
□ The Nor'Westers and Loyalist Museum is in a red brick Georgian building (1862).

Sir John Johnson's manor house, Williamstown

Where Voyageurs Once Sang Their 'Parting Hymn'

Lac Saint-Louis

In the late 1700s and early 1800s Lachine was the embarkation point of the North West Company fur brigades heading west. The starting point was above the treacherous Lachine Rapids, near present-day Promenade du Père-Marquette. In spring voyageurs loaded food, supplies and trade goods into birchbark canoes. (In autumn they would return, their canoes laden with beaver pelts.) As the voyageurs paddled off, they sang rousing songs that gave rhythm to their strokes. Their first stop was

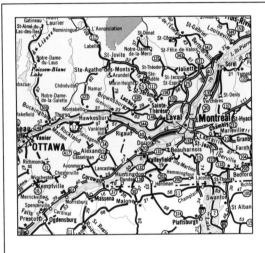

SAINTE-ANNE-DE-BELLEVUE
Situated at the western tip of the Montreal Island, this community was first settled in the late 17th century. During the fur-trading period, Sainte-Anne was the departure point for voyageurs heading west. Surviving from this period is a stone house (1793) that was once the residence of fur trader and explorer Simon Fraser (1776-1862). Fraser's house, on St. Anne Street, is now a restaurant.
□ St. Anne Church (1853-58) displays a painting of Saint Anne, the patron saint of the voyageurs, guiding canoeists ashore. (Marguerite Bourgeois Convent occupies the site of the chapel where the voyageurs once stopped to pray.)
□ St. Anne Locks, which link Lac des Deux Montagnes and Lac Saint-Louis, were built in 1840 for commercial and military purposes. Today the historic locks are used primarily by pleasure craft.
□ The Morgan Arboretum at Macdonald College (part of McGill University) covers roughly 245 hectares. About 80 percent of the area is forested and contains 150 tree species. Open year-round, the property also has 19 kilometres of trails for hiking and cross-country skiing.

18th-century windmill, Pointe-Claire

Vaudreuil-Soulanges Regional Museum

VAUDREUIL
A stone school, built in 1859, houses the Vaudreuil-Soulanges Regional Museum. The museum presents exhibitions assembled from its collection of 19th-century furniture, tools and other items.
□ Saint-Michel Church (1787) has a pulpit, altars, candlesticks, and two statues, all carved between 1792 and 1798 by Philippe Liébert. Behind the main altar, a life-size William Berczy painting (1809) depicts Saint Michel, with a sword in hand and a foot planted firmly on Satan's chest.
□ Just opposite Saint-Michel Church, a plaque commemorates Pierre de Rigaud, marquis de Vaudreuil-Cavagnial, last governor of New France, who surrendered this region to the British in 1760.

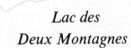

COTEAU-DU-LAC NATIONAL HISTORIC PARK
This park preserves the remnants of the first lock canal in North America, built by the British in 1779-80. A forerunner of the St. Lawrence Seaway, the Coteau-du-Lac canal was an important transit point for military and commercial shipping between Montreal and Kingston until the 1850s. Originally, it was 300 metres long and 2.5 metres wide, and it was used to raise and lower ships about 2.7 metres.
□ Between 1781 and 1814, the British fortified the canal with a bastion and several blockhouses, but only traces of these buildings remain in the park. Visitors can see a collection of British military supplies in an octagonal blockhouse (a reconstruction of an 1812 structure). A reception center has a model of the fort and a display about navigation on the St. Lawrence, as well as artifacts unearthed here by archaeologists.

Octagonal blockhouse, Coteau-du-Lac

POINTE-DES-CASCADES
This village is divided by the Soulanges Canal, built in the 1890s to bypass rapids on the St. Lawrence River between Lac Saint-François and Lac Saint-Louis. The canal became obsolete with the opening of the St. Lawrence Seaway. The village provides a view of the nearby dams, locks and powerhouses along the seaway.
□ Parc des Ancres at Lock No. 3 displays a collection of ship anchors salvaged from the St. Lawrence during the last 200 years.

Map labels: ÎLE BIZARD · Lac des Deux Montagnes · Senneville · Kirkland · Trans-Canada Highway · Beaconsfield · Baie-d'Urfé · BAIE DE VAUDREUIL · Vaudreuil · R Quinchien · Ile-Perrot · Ste-Anne-de-Bellevue · Dorion · Pincourt · Notre-Dame-de-l'Ile-Perrot · Pointe-du-Moul · ÎLE PERROT · PTE-À FOURNEA · St-Dominique · 6.5 · 11.5 · 25.5 · CANAL DE SOULANGES · Pointe-des-Cascades · Village-sur-le-Lac · R Delisle · Coteau-du-Lac · St. Lawrence River · Les Cèdres · ÎLE DE SALABERRY · COTEAU-DU-LAC NAT HIST SITE · 18 · 24.5

0 1 2 3 4 5 Miles

0 2 4 6 8 Kilometres

at Sainte-Anne-de-Bellevue. It was here, in 1804, that Thomas Moore, the Irish poet, may have heard the "parting hymn" of the voyageurs, which inspired his *Canadian Boat Song:*

Faintly as tolls the evening chime,
Our voices deep tune and our oars keep time.
Soon as the woods on shore look dim,
We'll sing at Ste. Anne's our parting hymn.
Row, brothers, row, the stream runs fast,
The Rapids are near, and the daylight's past.

The fur trade was waning when the Lachine Canal was opened in 1825. The canal, built to bypass the hazardous rapids, became a gateway to the Great Lakes. For 130 years it carried more shipping traffic than any other Canadian canal.

During the 19th century running the Lachine Rapids was a major attraction for thrill-seekers. (A traveler of 1854 described the treacherous waters as "terror in its most exhilarating form.") Canada Steamship Lines introduced daily cruises on the *Rapids*

King, the *Rapids Prince* and the *Rapids Queen.* The last passenger vessel to make the run was the *Rapids Prince* in 1940. Less than two decades later the rapids were tamed by the construction of the St. Lawrence Seaway. Only pleasure craft bound for Lac Saint-Louis use the Lachine Canal today. In summer, their billowing sails are mirrored in the lake that once resounded to the songs of the voyageurs.

POINTE-CLAIRE
Stewart Hall (1916) is a half-scale model of a castle on Mull Island, Scotland. Now a cultural center, it was one of the mansions built here at the turn of the century by wealthy Montrealers.
□ On the point for which this city is named stands a windmill dating from 1709. It was used for grinding grain and as a refuge during Indian raids. The community has adopted the weather vanes of the windmill as its civic emblem.

Lachine Canal—A Gateway to the Great Lakes

In the early 1600s, fur brigades on the final stage of their journey from the west faced a formidable obstacle just outside Montreal—the Lachine Rapids. The daring vogageurs who braved the rapids often lost their canoes, cargoes and lives. Most chose to make a 14-kilometre portage around the rapids' treacherous waters.

A 17th-century plan called for the excavation of a rudimentary canal—just wide and deep enough to float fur trade canoes—to overcome the rapids. Lack of money, manpower and government interest thwarted the scheme.

Commercial motives eventually prompted the construction of the Lachine Canal in the early 1820s. Montreal entrepreneurs, eager to expand steamship traffic on the St. Lawrence, financed the project, which began in 1821. Four years later, the 14-kilometre Lachine Canal opened the St. Lawrence, providing a shipping gateway to the Great Lakes. The waterway was enlarged between 1843 and 1848, and in 1884, to accommodate growing traffic and larger vessels.

During the 19th century, an industrial district developed on either bank of the Lachine Canal. But it declined rapidly after the 1959 opening of the St. Lawrence Seaway. Today the banks of the canal are a ribbon of parkland with picnic tables and paths for cycling, jogging or just strolling.

Lachine Canal in the 19th century

POINTE-CLAIRE

Dorval

LACHINE

MONTRÉAL
(see Road Unit 112)

CANAL DE LACHINE

River

St. Lawrence

Lac St-Louis

RAPIDES DE LACHINE

LACHINE
The city occupies land once granted to the French explorer René-Robert Cavelier de La Salle (1643-87). The land was named "la Chine" by the explorer's detractors, who ridiculed his dream of finding a route to China. A 3.7-metre-high stone monument at Lachine City Hall honors La Salle who failed to find China but discovered the Mississippi River instead.
□ Several plaques near the La Salle monument recall the Lachine Raid of 1689, in which the Iroquois attacked the village, killed 24 settlers and took 60 hostages.
□ A stone shed, built by the North West Company in 1803 to store fur pelts, is the centerpiece of The Fur Trade in Lachine National Historic Park on the shores of Lac Saint-Louis. The shed was later used as a warehouse after the Hudson's Bay Company and the North West Company merged in 1820. The museum describes the key roles of Lachine and Montreal in the 18th and 19th centuries, the heyday of the fur trade.
□ The Lachine Canal Interpretation Centre records the canal's history.
□ The Lachine Museum comprises a complex of buildings, which includes the French colonial house built between 1669 and 1685 by Jacques Le Ber and Charles Le Moyne. The restored house is one of the oldest in Canada. The museum's exhibits focus on life in New France and the industrial development of Lachine in the 19th century.

Sailboats on Lac Saint-Louis

ÎLE-PERROT
In the early 18th century, Joseph Trottier Desruisseaux, the seigneur of Île Perrot, built a windmill to grind his tenants' grain. Today Pointe-du-Moulin Historical Park contains the restored stone windmill (1705) and the miller's house (1785). Exhibits at the interpretation center and the miller's house describe the operation of the mill. In summer, performers reenact events from the 18th-century life of the island. The 12-hectare park also has picnic sites and nature trails.

Old Conflicts and Fur Trading on the 'Grand River of the North'

Lower Ottawa River Valley

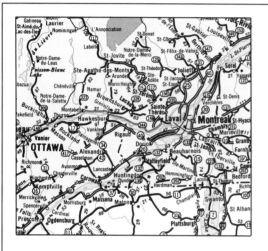

Argenteuil Historical Museum, Carillon

GRENVILLE
Founded in 1809 as a trading post, Grenville was at the western end of the Carillon Canal. Locks at Grenville, Carillon and Sainte-Anne-de-Bellevue (at the western tip of the Island of Montreal) ensured the uninterrupted passage of ships between Montreal and Ottawa. The old Grenville lock, built between 1825 and 1829 by British military engineers, was submerged when the Carillon power station was built in the early 1960s.

CARILLON
A monument at Carillon commemorates the bravery of 25-year-old French soldier Dollard des Ormeaux and his 16 companions at the Battle of the Long Sault in May 1660.
□ Carillon was the eastern entrance to the old Carillon Canal, built between 1819 and 1833. Visitors can still explore the remains of the Carillon lock (1825-33). A new canal was built in the early 1960s as part of the Carillon power station. The power station, the largest on the Ottawa River, can be toured.
□ The old Carillon Barracks houses Argenteuil Historical Museum. The four-story stone structure was built between 1834 and 1837 for British troops guarding the Carillon Canal. The museum has Indian, French and Loyalist artifacts.

PAPINEAUVILLE
A farming and industrial village, Papineauville is named for the *Patriote* leader and chief architect of the Rebellion of 1837, Louis-Joseph Papineau.

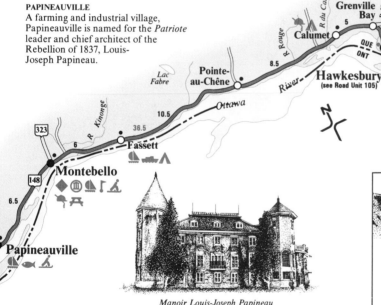

Manoir Louis-Joseph Papineau

MONTEBELLO
This resort community is named for the stone manor built here in 1850 by Louis-Joseph Papineau (1786-1871), lawyer, politician and leader of the 1837 rebellion of Lower Canada. The Manoir Louis-Joseph Papineau, now a museum, and the chapel where Papineau is buried are on the grounds of the Chateau Montebello Hotel. The museum is open from mid-April to early November. The chapel can be visited by appointment.
□ The Chateau Montebello, said to be the "largest log cabin in the world," was inaugurated in July 1930. Built from 10,000 logs in four months, the structure was originally a resort for executives and later an exclusive club. It was opened to the public in the early 1970s. Canada hosted the 1981 world economic summit at the Chateau Montebello.

Along the Voyageurs' Route— the First 'Trans-Canada'

During the late 18th and early 19th centuries, the Ottawa River was the first stretch of a "Trans-Canada Highway" of interconnecting lakes, rivers, streams and rapids traveled by the canoes of Indians, missionaries, merchants and fur traders. Every spring, fur brigades in canoes heavily laden with trade goods and supplies headed westward from their headquarters at Lachine and Montreal to outposts scattered throughout the remote Canadian interior.

The first stopover was Sainte-Anne-de-Bellevue, at the western tip of Montreal Island, where the voyageurs sang a "parting hymn." The next day they skimmed the roiling 20-kilometre stretch of the Long Sault rapids. At the riverside settlements of Carillon and Grenville, they sighted the outline of distant hills marking the edge of the Laurentian wilderness. Today travelers on the highways running parallel with the Ottawa River can still glimpse this spectacular scene.

0 1 2 3 4 5 Miles
0 2 4 6 8 Kilometres

To the early French explorers and fur traders, the Ottawa River was the "Grand River of the North." The first European to ascend the river was Etienne Brûlé, in 1610. Champlain followed in 1613 and again in 1615 on what later became Canada's main fur-trade route—up the Ottawa to the Mattawa River and across to Lake Nipissing. Echoes of the colorful and sometimes violent history of the river still linger at certain places on its north shore.

Lac des Deux Montagnes, where the Ottawa widens at its outlet, was once a stopping place for fur traders heading into the West. The French and Indians clashed fiercely along the river. Monuments at Carillon commemorate one of the bloodier battles—the heroic stand of Adam Dollard des Ormeaux in 1660. Hostilities impeded the settlement of the Ottawa River until the 18th century. One of the few French seigneuries in this area, La Petite Nation, was acquired in the early 1800s. Here, in 1850, Louis-Joseph Papineau, leader of the 1837 rebellion in Lower Canada, built his manor at Montebello, now a museum.

In the early 19th century the fur trade gave way to the lumber industry. Canals and, later, railways were built to bypass the hazardous rapids between Carillon and Grenville. Loyalists, Scots and Americans came to the banks of the Ottawa and established communities that have become farming, industrial and resort towns. In this century, the Ottawa has been turned to modern use by vast power developments.

SAINT-PLACIDE
This resort center on the Lac des Deux Montagnes is the birthplace of Sir Adolphe-Basile Routhier (1839-1920), author of the French lyrics to *O Canada*. A lawyer, poet, novelist and playwright, Routhier served as chief justice of Quebec and president of the Royal Society of Canada.

SAINT-ANDRÉ-EST
This was the first settlement of the seigneury of Argenteuil and birthplace of Sir John J. C. Abbott, the first Canadian-born prime minister (1891-93).
□ A plaque records that Canada's first paper mill was built here in 1803-05 by a group of New England immigrants.

SAINT-EUSTACHE
Situated in rich farming country, Saint-Eustache was founded in 1768 and named for local seigneur Eustache Lambert. The community was a *Patriote* stronghold and the site of the battle that ended the first phase of the 1837 rebellion. The walls and twin towers of St. Eustache Church bear the marks of cannon shot. The church, built between 1813 and 1841, is used for recording sessions by the Montreal Symphony Orchestra.
□ Moulin Légaré, built in 1762-63, is said to be the oldest continuously operating water mill in Canada. It was originally built to serve the local Rivière-du-Chêne seigneury and today its products are still sold locally. Visitors can watch the miller grind grain into flour.

OKA
This is the site of one of the oldest monasteries in North America. The Sulpician Fathers gave the property to French Trappist monks, who settled here in the early 1880s. The monks set up an agricultural school and experimental farm, where they created the famous Oka cheese. Visitors can tour the chapel, the gardens and the dwelling where the Trappists first lived on their arrival here.
□ The Oka Calvary (Stations of the Cross), built in 1740-42, is the oldest in Canada. Today only three of the seven original stone chapels remain. On September 14 each year, local people and pilgrims gather here to celebrate the Feast of the Holy Cross. The walk to the calvary leads to a superb view of the region around the Lac des Deux Montagnes.

Scars of a Brave Rebellion

Pockmarked by cannon shot, the walls of the Saint-Eustache church bear witness to the bloodiest battle of the Rebellion of 1837. General Sir John Colborne, commander of British forces in Lower Canada, marched to Saint-Eustache to crush the French-Canadian rebel movement. Some 250 *Patriotes*, led by Jean-Olivier Chénier, barricaded themselves into the church. The British troops slowly advanced behind heavy cannon and musket fire, broke into the church and set it aflame. Some 100 rebels were killed, among them Chénier, whose monument stands at Sacré-Coeur School. In 1841 the reconstructed church was blessed by the Bishop of Montreal.

Cannon marks, St. Eustache Church

The chapel at the Oka Monastery

Stone chapels near Oka

PARC PAUL-SAUVÉ
This park on Montreal's outskirts was part of the seigneury of Lac des Deux Montagnes, given to the Sulpician Fathers in 1717. The park, which is named for Paul Sauvé, a former premier of Quebec (1959-1960), contains a hardwood forest of ash, oak, hickory and walnut trees. A beach, roughly 3.2 kilometres long, slopes gently to the lake. In summer, this park is a popular place for camping, hiking, picnicking and windsurfing. In winter, it attracts cross-country skiers and snowmobilers.

Our Most Cosmopolitan City—
Varied, Vibrant, Ever-Changing

Old and new exist easily in Montreal. The elegant Château Ramezay Museum (above), built in 1705, once served as the residence of French governors in Montreal. The city's rapidly changing skyline (left) attests to economic and cultural buoyancy.

Montreal combines modern dynamism and old-world charm. With a population of more than 3 million, Montreal exudes the energy of a North American metropolis. The city's position as a major commercial, financial and transportation center continues despite the loss of its historic role as Canada's leading city to Toronto. Moreover, its international reputation, firmly established by Expo 67 and the summer Olympics of 1976, endures, while its importance as the home of a self-sufficient French culture in North America grows. Since the 1960s, extraordinary civic, commercial and cultural endeavor has enriched Montreal with an impressive array of skyscrapers, subways and sports centers, as well as museums, galleries and theaters.

For visitors, however, Montreal's greatest attraction is its cosmopolitan, almost European atmosphere. The meeting of French and English cultures and the addition of other ethnic influences have created a blend unmatched in North America and, possibly, in the world. The city's reputation for good living is proverbial. Its varied and vibrant neighborhoods, such as Old Montreal with its picturesque cobbled streets and historic gray limestone buildings, or the "Latin Quarter" of St. Denis Street with its lively outdoor cafés, provide a refreshing, ever-changing urban panorama.

Bank of Montreal (27)
Canada's oldest bank (1817) moved to St. Jacques Street from its original site on St. Paul Street in 1847. The building has a classic portico of Corinthian columns, an elegant dome and a monumental lobby. The bank's museum displays rare coins, bills, gold and other memorabilia.

Bonsecours Market Building (35)
This silver-domed, cut-stone building housed Canada's parliament in 1849-52, then served as Montreal's city hall until 1878, when it became a market. Restored in 1964, it now contains municipal offices.

Botanical Garden (14)
Founded in 1931 by renowned Quebec botanist Frère Marie-Victorin (1885-1944), the garden is the third largest in the world after London's Kew Gardens and the Berlin gardens. The 73-hectare garden contains some 26,000 plant species and varieties from many parts of the world. It encompasses 10 exhibition greenhouses and 30 outdoor gardens, including a Japanese and a Chinese garden.

Canadian Centre for Architecture (6)
This museum and research institute is the only one of its kind in Canada and one of the few in the world devoted to the study of architecture. Its archives include 20,000 prints and drawings, 135,000 books and 45,000 photographs. The imposing building, opened in 1989, incorporates the Shaughnessy Man-

sion (1874), a fine example of Victorian residential architecture. A sculpture garden by Melvin Charney is opposite the centre on René Lévesque Boulevard.

Centaur Theatre (28)
Montreal's main English-language theater is housed in a handsome Beaux-Arts building (1903), which served as the city's stock exchange until 1965.

Château de Ramezay Museum (33)
This fieldstone house (1705) has been used at different times by French, British and Canadian governments and served as headquarters for an invading American Army in 1775-76. Exhibits depict life in Quebec during the 18th and early 19th centuries, and include furniture, paintings and clothes.

Château Dufresne (13)
The interiors of this restored Beaux-Arts mansion (1915-18) reflect the opulent taste of its builders, the Dufresne brothers. The mansion now houses the Montreal Museum of Decorative Arts, which presents a collection of modern decorative objects.

City Hall (32)
This ornate five-story example of Second Empire architecture was built in 1872-78, and rebuilt and enlarged after a 1922 fire gutted its interior.

Complexe Desjardins (26)
Three office towers and a hotel surround a glass-roofed shopping mall with a spacious promenade area.

Dow Planetarium (19)
This 385-seat planetarium uses a Zeiss projector and 100 auxiliary projectors to create astronomical shows on its dome, which is 20 metres in diameter.

Fort Towers (4)
A pair of stone towers, two of Montreal's oldest structures, stand on the grounds of the Sulpician seminary. Built between 1683 and 1694 (the date is uncertain), the towers were part of a fort used to protect the seminary.

Habitat (8)
Built for Expo 67, Moshe Safdie's experimental housing development on the Cité du Havre pier is a landmark of contemporary architecture.

Lafontaine Park (11)
This 40-hectare park contains two small man-made lakes (for boating in summer and

skating in winter) and an open-air theater for family entertainment.

Mary Queen of the World (18)
This imposing cathedral, built between 1870 and 1894, is a replica of St. Peter's in Rome, about one third the size of the original. The statues above the facade are the patron saints of Montreal.

McCord Museum of Canadian History (21)
The museum exhibits paintings, furniture

Palais de la Civilisation, Notre-Dame Island

and costumes from the 18th century to the present. It also has the Notman photographic collection, which provides a visual record of Canada between 1856 and 1934.

McGill University (20)
Founded in 1821, McGill has a student population of more than 21,500. The campus occupies 30 hectares in the heart of Montreal.

Montreal Museum of Fine Arts (16)
This museum, the oldest art institution in

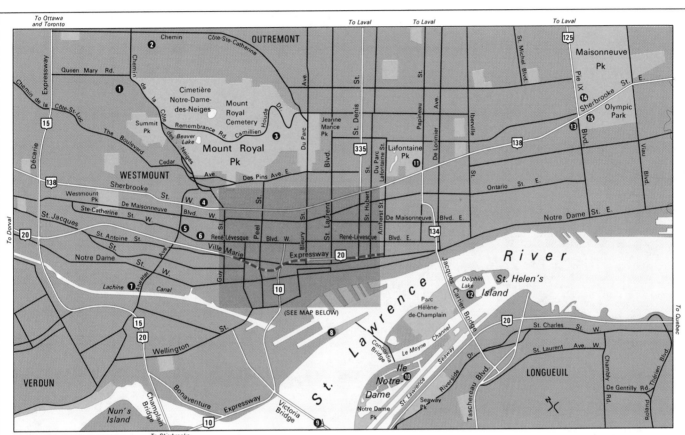

(METROPOLITAN MONTREAL)

Montreal

1 St. Joseph's Oratory
2 Université de Montréal
3 Mount Royal Park
4 Fort Towers
5 Montreal Forum
6 Canadian Centre for Architecture
7 Lachine Canal (see Road Unit 110)
8 Habitat
9 St. Lawrence Seaway
10 Notre-Dame Island
11 Lafontaine Park
12 St. Helen's Island
13 Château Dufresne
14 Botanical Garden
15 Olympic Park

16 Montreal Museum of Fine Arts
17 Tourist Information
18 Mary Queen of the World
19 Dow Planetarium
20 McGill University
21 McCord Museum of Canadian History
22 Place Ville-Marie
23 Place Victoria
24 Place d'Youville
25 Place des Arts
26 Complexe Desjardins
27 Bank of Montreal
28 Centaur Theatre
29 Notre-Dame Basilica
30 Place Royale
31 Old Montreal (Vieux-Montréal)
32 City Hall
33 Château de Ramezay Museum
34 Old Port (Vieux-Port)
35 Bonsecours Market Building
36 Notre-Dame-de-Bon-Secours Chapel
37 Sir George Etienne Cartier House

- - - - - Underground Highway

(DOWNTOWN MONTREAL)

Canada, was founded in 1860. The neoclassic building on the north side of Sherbrooke Street was built in 1912 and renovated between 1973 and 1976. The museum hosts important international exhibitions. The permanent collection includes examples of the work of many major European and Canadian painters and sculptors. The museum also displays furniture, silver and decorative objects, as well as Oriental, pre-Columbian and Amerindian art and artifacts.

Montreal Forum (5)
This 16,500-seat sports and recreation center is home to the Montreal *Canadiens*, which has won the Stanley Cup more times than any other National Hockey League team. Built in 1924 and remodeled in 1968, the Montreal Forum also presents boxing, wrestling and other sports events, ice shows and rock concerts.

In summer, outdoor cafés lend charm to historic Place Jacques-Cartier (above) in the heart of Old Montreal. Domes and spires of Bonsecours Market Building, Notre-Dame-de-Bon-Secours and Montreal City Hall (left) rise above the Old Port, now a center for entertainment and recreation. Montreal houses of a bygone era (below) are graced with flamboyant gingerbread roofs and wrought-iron balconies. Masterworks of the woodcarver's art glorify Notre-Dame Basilica (below left). The Japanese Garden (bottom) is a place of beauty and peace at the Montreal Botanical Garden.

Mount Royal Park (3)
This 200-hectare park at the summit of Mount Royal was designed by 19th-century American landscape architect Frederick Law Olmstead, who created New York's Central Park. Only a short distance from the heart of Montreal, the park has lookouts at the Chalet and along Camille Houde Parkway that provide superb views of the Montreal region. A 30-metre-high illuminated cross commemorates the one put up in 1643 by Montreal's founder Paul de Chomedey, Sieur de Maisonneuve. In summer, visitors can enjoy rides in horse-drawn calèches. Winter recreations include skating on Beaver Lake and cross-country skiing.

Notre-Dame Basilica (29)
This Gothic Revival church, built between 1824 and 1829, was designed by American architect James O'Donnell. The twin 67-metre-high towers were completed in the 1840s, and the richly decorated interior by Victor Bourgeau, in the late 1870s. The church museum exhibits sacred objects, church vestments and 17th-century silverware. The adjacent Sulpician Seminary (1685) is Montreal's oldest building.

Notre-Dame-de-Bon-Secours Chapel (36)
Known as the sailors' chapel, the present Notre-Dame-de-Bon-Secours dates from 1885. It occupies the site of a 1657 chapel built by Marguerite Bourgeoys (1620-1700), Montreal's first teacher and the founder of the Congregation of Notre-Dame nuns, whose life is illustrated in the chapel's museum. A nine-metre-high copper statue of the Virgin Mary with a crown of stars stands atop the chapel's octagonal tower.

Notre-Dame Island (10)
Among the attractions of this man-made island, built for Expo 67, are a floral park, the Gilles-Villeneuve racing track and the Palais de la Civilisation, the former French pavilion, now used for major art exhibits.

Old Montreal (Vieux-Montréal) (31)
This 38-hectare historic district covers the area occupied by Montreal at the beginning of the 19th century. Rue St. Paul, the city's oldest thoroughfare (1672), crosses the core of Old Montreal. Hotels and outdoor cafés flank Place Jacques-Cartier, once a marketplace and now a boulevard. Nelson's Column, Montreal's oldest monument (1809), rises at the north end of the square.

Old Port (Vieux-Port) (34)
Montreal's waterfront is now a year-round recreation and entertainment complex.

Olympic Park (15)
The centerpiece of the 46-hectare park is the 55,000-seat Olympic Stadium, popularly known as the "Big O," the main site of the 1976 Olympic Games. This immense cement structure, designed by French architect Roger Taillibert, is now home for the Montreal Expos baseball team and is used for baseball and special events. A cable car carries visitors to an observation deck at the top of the

Olympic Stadium

190-metre-high Olympic Park Tower, the world's highest inclined tower.

Place des Arts (25)
This performing arts complex comprises four theaters: Salle Wilfrid-Pelletier (3,000 seats), used for concerts, ballet and opera; the Maisonneuve (1,300); the Port-Royal (800) and the 138-seat Café de la Place.

Place d'Youville (24)
The former fire station (1903) in Place d'Youville is now the Montreal History Centre, which describes the growth of the city from the first Indian settlement to recent times. Nearby Youville Stables—three restored 18th-century fieldstone warehouses—house boutiques, offices and a restaurant.

Place Royale (30)
The 1837 Customs building dominates Place Royale, once Montreal's main square. Nearby Pointe-à-Callières is the site of Ville Marie, the first permanent settlement, founded by Sieur de Maisonneuve in 1642.

Place Victoria (23)
This 47-story tower, the tallest building in Montreal, contains the city's stock exchange.

Place Ville-Marie (22)
The main structure of this business, shopping and entertainment complex is the 45-story Royal Bank of Canada tower, the world's largest cruciform building.

St. Helen's Island (12)
This island offers many attractions, including La Ronde (a summer amusement park); the Montreal Aquarium; and the Old Fort (1822), with the David M. Stewart Museum, which displays old maps, scientific instruments and navigational aids.

St. Joseph's Oratory (1)
Built between 1924 and 1955, St. Joseph's Oratory was inspired by Brother André (1848-1937), who put up a chapel here in 1904 and was known as a faith healer. The

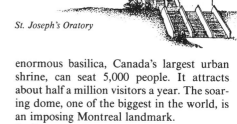
St. Joseph's Oratory

enormous basilica, Canada's largest urban shrine, can seat 5,000 people. It attracts about half a million visitors a year. The soaring dome, one of the biggest in the world, is an imposing Montreal landmark.

St. Lawrence Seaway (9)
In summer, visitors can watch passing ship traffic from an observation deck atop the Seaway Authority building by the St. Lambert Locks, at the south end of Victoria Bridge. Guided tours are available.

Sir George Etienne Cartier House (37)
This site comprises two adjacent residences of the 19th-century politician Sir George Etienne Cartier (1814-73). The west house has been restored to its bygone elegance; the east house serves as an exhibition space.

Université de Montréal (2)
With 50,000 students, the university is the largest in Quebec and one of the largest in the French-speaking world. The mountainside university with its distinctive tower was designed by renowned Quebec architect Ernest Cormier (1885-1980).

Underground Retreats, Spacious Promenades

Beneath Montreal's skyscrapers and busy streets is the world's most extensive underground pedestrian system. About 22 kilometres of passageways connect virtually all the city center's offices, hotels, high-rise apartments, conference halls, exhibition spaces, department stores, boutiques, restaurants and theaters.

The main link in this underground world is the Métro, a 65-kilometre-long subway system (*far left, bottom*), whose trains travel on quiet rubber wheels to 65 stations. Each station has its own special decor, which gives color and identity to what might be drab and impersonal spaces. One of the most striking adornments is the stained-glass mural (*far left, top*), designed by Montreal artist, Frédéric Back, at the Place des Arts station.

The subterranean network also provides protection from Montreal's capricious climate. In winter, Montrealers can retreat here from snowfalls and freezing temperatures. In summer, office workers, shoppers and out-of-towners can escape the heat (and sudden downpours) by strolling through the air-conditioned underground promenades that connect Les Cours Mont-Royal (*left*), Place Montréal Trust, Les Promenades de la Cathédrale and other spacious shopping malls.

Year-Round *Joie de Vivre* in a Vital Vacationland

The Laurentians

Northwest of Montreal is one of the most accessible areas of the Laurentian wilderness in Quebec. The Laurentians, also called the Laurentides in Quebec, are part of the Canadian Shield. The region extends from the Ottawa River to the Saguenay River and embraces rugged hills, deep valleys, dense forests and a myriad of lakes, streams, rivers and falls.

The route from Saint-Jérôme to Parc du Mont-Tremblant passes through what is perhaps the most highly developed resort area

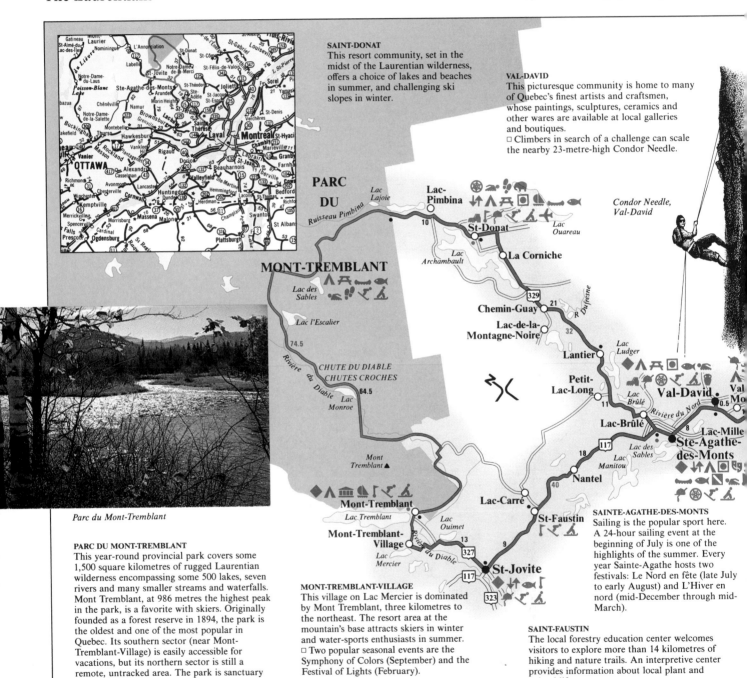

Parc du Mont-Tremblant

SAINT-DONAT
This resort community, set in the midst of the Laurentian wilderness, offers a choice of lakes and beaches in summer, and challenging ski slopes in winter.

VAL-DAVID
This picturesque community is home to many of Quebec's finest artists and craftsmen, whose paintings, sculptures, ceramics and other wares are available at local galleries and boutiques.
□ Climbers in search of a challenge can scale the nearby 23-metre-high Condor Needle.

Condor Needle, Val-David

SAINTE-AGATHE-DES-MONTS
Sailing is the popular sport here. A 24-hour sailing event at the beginning of July is one of the highlights of the summer. Every year Sainte-Agathe hosts two festivals: Le Nord en fête (late July to early August) and L'Hiver en nord (mid-December through mid-March).

SAINT-FAUSTIN
The local forestry education center welcomes visitors to explore more than 14 kilometres of hiking and nature trails. An interpretive center provides information about local plant and animal life.

SAINT-JOVITE
This bustling community on the road to Parc du Mont-Tremblant is the site of the oldest resort hotel in the Laurentians, Gray Rocks, which was established in 1906.

PARC DU MONT-TREMBLANT
This year-round provincial park covers some 1,500 square kilometres of rugged Laurentian wilderness encompassing some 500 lakes, seven rivers and many smaller streams and waterfalls. Mont Tremblant, at 986 metres the highest peak in the park, is a favorite with skiers. Originally founded as a forest reserve in 1894, the park is the oldest and one of the most popular in Quebec. Its southern sector (near Mont-Tremblant-Village) is easily accessible for vacations, but its northern sector is still a remote, untracked area. The park is sanctuary for moose, white-tailed deer, black beaver and fox. Some 200 bird species have been recorded here. The waters contain a dozen species of fish, including speckled trout and pike.

MONT-TREMBLANT-VILLAGE
This village on Lac Mercier is dominated by Mont Tremblant, three kilometres to the northeast. The resort area at the mountain's base attracts skiers in winter and water-sports enthusiasts in summer.
□ Two popular seasonal events are the Symphony of Colors (September) and the Festival of Lights (February).

Speckled or brook trout

0 2 4 6 8 10 Miles
0 4 8 12 16 Kilometres

in Canada. Some 20 lively communities, all within easy reach of Montreal, serve vacationers year-round. The development of many of these communities began with the growing enthusiasm for skiing in the 1920s. From the early 1930s onward, the legendary ski pioneer Herman Smith "Jack Rabbit" Johannsen (1875-1987) helped create this skiers' paradise by establishing many of the ski trails and runs still in use today.

There has been summer activity at Sainte-Agathe and other Laurentian communities since the 1890s. In 1894 Parc Mont-Tremblant, still one of the most popular parks in Quebec, was opened. Its northern sector remains an unspoiled wilderness for adventurous campers, canoeists and fishermen. This region is also a haven for writers, artists and craftsmen. The region's art galleries, craft workshops and theaters are among its most appealing attractions.

Skiing in the Laurentians

PRÉVOST (SHAWBRIDGE)

Between 1932 and 1935, Norwegian-born ski pioneer "Jack Rabbit" Johannsen organized the 96-kilometre-long Maple Leaf Trail from Prévost to Mont Tremblant. This was one of the many trails created in the Laurentian region by Johannsen, who was instrumental in opening up the entire region to all forms of the sport. The legendary Johannsen, who was one of Norway's best skiers when he settled in Canada in 1919, received the Order of Canada in 1972.

□ North America's first rope tow for skiers was built here in 1929. The tow was improvised from a car engine, lines and tackles, and heavy concrete blocks. The price for using the tow was five cents.

SAINT-SAUVEUR-DES-MONTS

This ski center was established in 1930 and is the oldest of the Laurentians. Canada's second rope tow was built here in 1934; the first was at Prévost. The slopes of Mont Avila, Mont Christie, Mont Habitant and Mont Saint-Sauveur draw ski crowds to this area.

Labelle of the Laurentians — A Priestly 'King of the North'

In 1870 there were barely a dozen communities north of Saint-Jérôme and settlers were steadily leaving Quebec to work in the United States. But by 1891 the Most Rev. Antoine Labelle had changed all that. This fiercely determined leader traveled into the Laurentian wilderness, exploring sites for new settlements and creating some 20 new parishes. He brought European settlers to Quebec and persuaded the government to route the Montreal-Quebec railway through Saint-Jérôme. Curé Labelle once told his struggling parishioners: "You who with infinite toil have carved yourselves farms from the wilderness, stay on! Persevere! In another 50 years strangers will flock here, and they will scatter gold by the handful." Today Saint-Jérôme is the gateway to one of Quebec's finest year-round resort areas.

SAINT-JÉRÔME

The impressive triple-spired Cathédrale de Saint-Jérôme, the largest church in the Laurentians, was built in 1897-99 and opened in 1900. A massive portable altar, a silver chalice presented by Pope Leo XIII and other mementos of the Most Rev. Antoine Labelle are housed here. During the 1870s and '80s Curé Labelle founded 20 parishes in the Laurentians. A bronze statue by Canadian sculptor Alfred Laliberté honors Curé Labelle.

SAINTE-ROSE

This tranquil rural community was founded in 1845. St. Rose Church, built in 1856, was designed by a prominent 19th-century architect, Victor Bourgeau. The church contains a carved 18th-century altar.

Village de Séraphin, Sainte-Adèle

SAINTE-ADÈLE

This community, built on Lac Rond and the slopes of Mont Sainte-Adèle, is haven for artists and writers.

□ Sainte-Adèle is the birthplace of Quebec writer Claude-Henri Grignon (1894-1976), whose famous 1933 novel *Un homme et son péché* (translated as *The Woman and the Miser*) recounts the turn-of-the-century way of life in this region. The Village de Séraphin re-creates the hamlet described in the novel. It contains an old-fashioned post office, general store, school, church and doctor's office.

MIRABEL

This city of some 14,000, created in 1970 to accommodate Montreal's principal international airport, covers some 750 square kilometres. It was named for the village that now no longer exists. Although Mirabel Airport is reputedly the world's largest in size, the distance between the terminal entrances and the boarding gates is only 85 metres (about 280 paces). Special vehicles shuttle passengers between the boarding gate and the aircraft.

Terminal building, Mirabel International Airport

A Quiet Corner of Quebec
Where Laurier Spent His Boyhood

The Laurentians

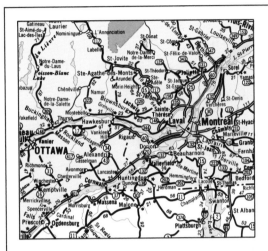

Northeast of Montreal, across the Rivière des Prairies, is a region of quiet farming towns and picturesque Laurentian lakes and woods. Highway 138 follows the north shore of the St. Lawrence River through L'Assomption County, one of the smallest in Quebec, and Berthier County.

The road passes through Repentigny,

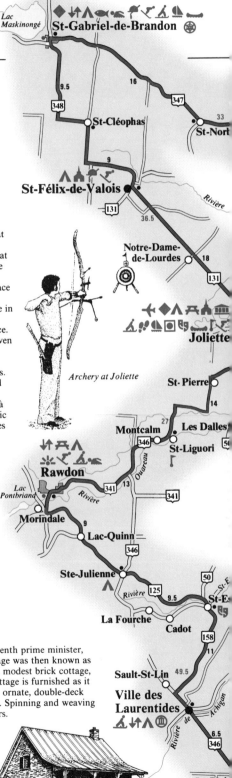

Archery at Joliette

SAINT-GABRIEL-DE-BRANDON
This early settlement, set in magnificent Laurentian scenery, was known as the Mission of Lac Maskinongé until 1837 when its name was changed to Saint-Gabriel-du-Lac-Maskinongé. In 1840 it was renamed Saint-Gabriel-de-Brandon, after an English village.
□ Lac Maskinongé is popular with swimmers, water-skiers and fishermen.

JOLIETTE
This city (pop. 17,000) welcomes world-renowned classical and popular musicians at the summer-long Festival international de Lanaudière. Concerts are held in a 2,000-seat amphitheater. Grassy slopes just outside the amphitheater provide seating for another 8,000 people. Festival concerts also take place in local churches.
□ Joliette also presents the Festival Parallèle in July. This event includes theater, dance, outdoor art exhibitions and live performance.
□ The Musée d'Art de Joliette comprises seven galleries, whose collection ranges from medieval religious art to modern works, including European and Canadian paintings.
□ Maison Antoine-Lacombe (1847), a noted historic site, is open to the public.
□ The wooded area around the Club de tir à l'arc de Joliette, the site of the 1976 Olympic archery competitions, offers eight kilometres of hiking and cycling trails.

RAWDON
A one-room schoolhouse, a settler's cabin, a smithy and an ice cream parlor are among the 19th-century buildings in Earle Moore's Canadiana Village. A covered bridge (1888) spans a river that flows through the village.
□ At nearby Dorwin Falls is a rock formation in the shape of an Indian's head. Legend says it is the head of a sorcerer who was turned to stone.

VILLE DES LAURENTIDES
Sir Wilfrid Laurier, Canada's seventh prime minister, was born here in 1841. (The village was then known as Saint-Lin.) His boyhood home, a modest brick cottage, is a national historic site. The cottage is furnished as it was when Laurier lived here. An ornate, double-deck wood stove stands in the kitchen. Spinning and weaving rooms and a bedroom are upstairs.

Joliette Museum of Art

A Mighty Fighter

The deep waters of the lakes and rivers in this region teem with muskellunge, Canada's second largest freshwater fish (after sturgeon). The powerful fish is a fighter, and landing one is a thrilling experience. The average fish caught is between 2 and 16 kilograms but some 45-kilogram giants, 183 centimetres long, have been recorded.

Muskellunge are caught mainly by trolling, but it takes patience: the angler may fish for days without a strike. But when the fish are hungry, they will bite at anything, and several can be caught in a day.

*Wilfrid Laurier House,
Ville des Laurentides*

0	1	2	3	4	5 Miles
0	2	4	6		8 Kilometres

where the modernity of Notre-Dame-des-Champs Church contrasts with the simplicity of the town's 18th-century parish church, and Lanoraie, whose Hétu and Hervieux houses are fine examples of 19th-century Quebec architecture. At Berthierville, there is the Cuthbert Chapel, the first Protestant church in Quebec. The town is linked by bridge and road to Île Dupas and other small, tranquil islands.

This route passes through tobacco-growing country. Hothouses, curing sheds and shrubbery windbreaks, essential to the crop's cultivation, dot the landscape. (Near Berthierville, tobacco thrives on a strip of reclaimed land, once marshy channels of the St. Lawrence.) The tobacco belt extends to the farmlands near Joliette. Sandy soil, some 125 frost-free days annually, and adequate rainfall during the growing season have made this one of Canada's major tobacco-growing areas.

North and east of Joliette is the wooded and mountainous landscape of the Laurentians. Both Saint-Gabriel-de-Brandon and Rawdon offer year-round recreational activities. Rawdon boasts five waterfalls; the most spectacular is the 30-metre-high, 15-metre-wide Dorwin Falls.

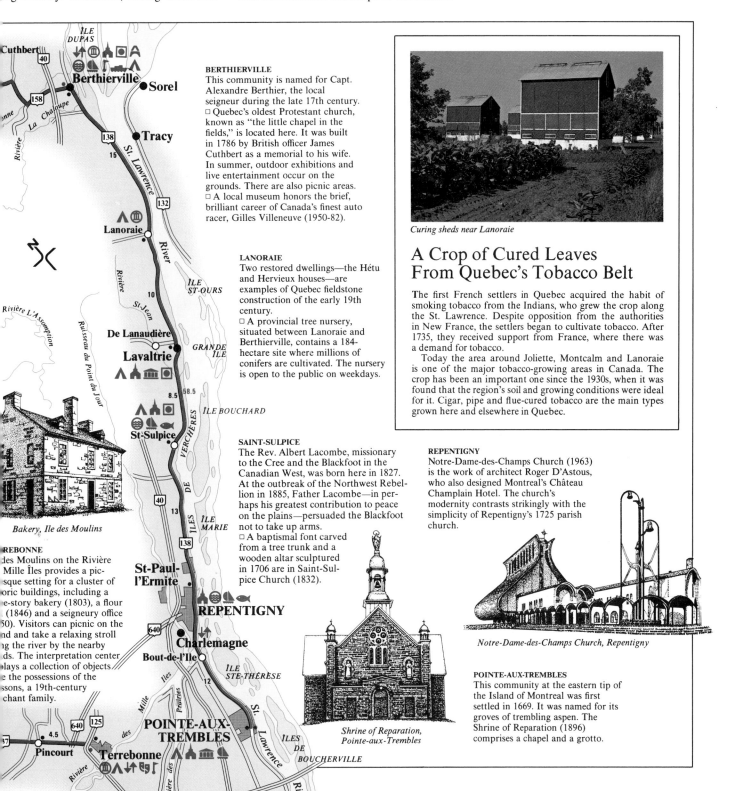

Curing sheds near Lanoraie

BERTHIERVILLE
This community is named for Capt. Alexandre Berthier, the local seigneur during the late 17th century.
□ Quebec's oldest Protestant church, known as "the little chapel in the fields," is located here. It was built in 1786 by British officer James Cuthbert as a memorial to his wife. In summer, outdoor exhibitions and live entertainment occur on the grounds. There are also picnic areas.
□ A local museum honors the brief, brilliant career of Canada's finest auto racer, Gilles Villeneuve (1950-82).

LANORAIE
Two restored dwellings—the Hétu and Hervieux houses—are examples of Quebec fieldstone construction of the early 19th century.
□ A provincial tree nursery, situated between Lanoraie and Berthierville, contains a 184-hectare site where millions of conifers are cultivated. The nursery is open to the public on weekdays.

A Crop of Cured Leaves From Quebec's Tobacco Belt

The first French settlers in Quebec acquired the habit of smoking tobacco from the Indians, who grew the crop along the St. Lawrence. Despite opposition from the authorities in New France, the settlers began to cultivate tobacco. After 1735, they received support from France, where there was a demand for tobacco.

Today the area around Joliette, Montcalm and Lanoraie is one of the major tobacco-growing areas in Canada. The crop has been an important one since the 1930s, when it was found that the region's soil and growing conditions were ideal for it. Cigar, pipe and flue-cured tobacco are the main types grown here and elsewhere in Quebec.

Bakery, Ile des Moulins

...REBONNE
...des Moulins on the Rivière ...Mille Îles provides a pic-...sque setting for a cluster of ...oric buildings, including a ...e-story bakery (1803), a flour ...(1846) and a seigneury office ...0). Visitors can picnic on the ...nd and take a relaxing stroll ...g the river by the nearby ...ds. The interpretation center ...lays a collection of objects ...e the possessions of the ...ssons, a 19th-century ...chant family.

SAINT-SULPICE
The Rev. Albert Lacombe, missionary to the Cree and the Blackfoot in the Canadian West, was born here in 1827. At the outbreak of the Northwest Rebellion in 1885, Father Lacombe—in perhaps his greatest contribution to peace on the plains—persuaded the Blackfoot not to take up arms.
□ A baptismal font carved from a tree trunk and a wooden altar sculptured in 1706 are in Saint-Sulpice Church (1832).

REPENTIGNY
Notre-Dame-des-Champs Church (1963) is the work of architect Roger D'Astous, who also designed Montreal's Château Champlain Hotel. The church's modernity contrasts strikingly with the simplicity of Repentigny's 1725 parish church.

Notre-Dame-des-Champs Church, Repentigny

Shrine of Reparation, Pointe-aux-Trembles

POINTE-AUX-TREMBLES
This community at the eastern tip of the Island of Montreal was first settled in 1669. It was named for its groves of trembling aspen. The Shrine of Reparation (1896) comprises a chapel and a grotto.

Farms and Orchards
in a Region Graced with Serenity

Southwestern Quebec

After the bustle of nearby Montreal, the peaceful orchards and fertile valleys of southwestern Quebec offer a pleasant change of pace.

Across the St. Lawrence River from Montreal, Indian village of Kahnawake reflects the region's history. French Jesuits established a mission here in the late 17th century for Indian converts to Christianity. In the days of New France the mission Indians carried on a lively contraband trade in furs with the Dutch settlers in what is now

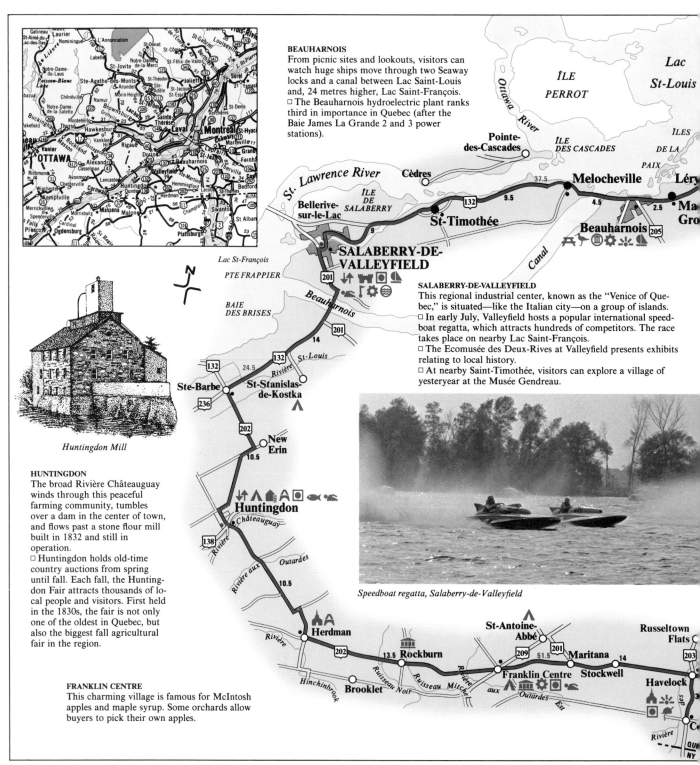

BEAUHARNOIS
From picnic sites and lookouts, visitors can watch huge ships move through two Seaway locks and a canal between Lac Saint-Louis and, 24 metres higher, Lac Saint-François.
□ The Beauharnois hydroelectric plant ranks third in importance in Quebec (after the Baie James La Grande 2 and 3 power stations).

SALABERRY-DE-VALLEYFIELD
This regional industrial center, known as the "Venice of Quebec," is situated—like the Italian city—on a group of islands.
□ In early July, Valleyfield hosts a popular international speedboat regatta, which attracts hundreds of competitors. The race takes place on nearby Lac Saint-François.
□ The Ecomusée des Deux-Rives at Valleyfield presents exhibits relating to local history.
□ At nearby Saint-Timothée, visitors can explore a village of yesteryear at the Musée Gendreau.

Huntingdon Mill

HUNTINGDON
The broad Rivière Châteauguay winds through this peaceful farming community, tumbles over a dam in the center of town, and flows past a stone flour mill built in 1832 and still in operation.
□ Huntingdon holds old-time country auctions from spring until fall. Each fall, the Huntingdon Fair attracts thousands of local people and visitors. First held in the 1830s, the fair is not only one of the oldest in Quebec, but also the biggest fall agricultural fair in the region.

FRANKLIN CENTRE
This charming village is famous for McIntosh apples and maple syrup. Some orchards allow buyers to pick their own apples.

Speedboat regatta, Salaberry-de-Valleyfield

KAHNAWAKE

A Mohawk maiden, Kateri Tekak-witha, expected to become the first North American Indian saint, is revered in this village where she died in 1680. Her relics lie in a white marble tomb in the Mission Church of St. Francis Xavier (1717). □ In the sacristy chapel of the mission church is an elegant tabernacle believed built in France about 1700. In the adjacent field stone presbytery (1717-18) are an old Iroquois grammar book (1813-53) and dictionaries.

New York State. Today the men of Kahna-wake, representing seven Indian tribes, are famous for their work as high-steel riggers on skyscrapers.

The clays and silts of Rivière Châteauguay support the most intensive dairy farming in Canada. Forerunners of the black Canadian breed were imported by Champlain before 1610 and flourished in southwestern Quebec. Today herds of black-and-white holsteins are a familiar sight in roadside fields.

Along the winding roads are other samples of an agricultural way of life almost three centuries old. The Grey Nuns of Châteauguay were the first to cultivate apple trees here in the late 1700s; dozens of orchards now prosper. In spring, wisps of smoke curl from sugar shacks deep within area maple groves. Silhouettes of huge old elm trees—dead but still standing—punctuate fields that have been tilled, seeded and harvested since the 17th century.

Statue of Kateri Tekakwitha,
Tekakwitha School, Kahnawake

LA PRAIRIE

La Prairie was one terminus (the other was Saint-Jean) of Canada's first railway. A plaque records that this 25-kilometre line was built in 1836. □ The Church of the Nativity, in Italian baroque style, dates from 1839. The pulpit was carved by Victor Bourgeau. □ A cairn commemorates a 1691 battle in which French settlers repelled an invading force of New Englanders and averted an attack on Montreal.

Saint-Joachim Church, Châteauguay

CHÂTEAUGUAY

Local points of interest include: St. Joachim Church, which is more than 200 years old; Lang House, originally built for the Hudson's Bay Company; and a windmill on Île Saint-Bernard dating from 1687. □ A national historic park, southwest of Châteauguay at Ormstown, commemorates the battle of Oct. 26, 1813, where Lt.Col. Charles-Michel de Salaberry and 300 French-speaking Canadian troops defeated an American force of 3,000. The victory saved Montreal.

Sleepers, Cabooses, and a Schoolhouse on Wheels

A locomotive that was built in 1887 and—73 years later—was the last steam engine to haul a CPR train is exhibited in the Canadian Railway Museum at Saint-Constant.

A sleek, powerful 1937 locomotive of the type that set a world record of 126 miles an hour (202 kilometres an hour) for steam locomotives is also here.

The museum has many Montreal streetcars, including the city's first electric tram (1892) and the Golden Chariot open cars used on scenic tours. There are cabooses, sleepers, tank and freight cars and a carriage once used in northern Ontario as a mobile schoolhouse. On the museum site are a turntable, a water tank, a roundhouse and a rural station of the 1880s.

The *John Molson* (*right*), similar to the locomotive used on Canada's first railway in 1836, operates on scheduled days.

HEMMINGFORD

At Hemmingford, the 112-hectare Parc Safari Africain contains one of the largest collections of wildlife in Canada. Drivers can follow a six-kilometre road through open country, where bison, camels, giraffes, and zebras roam freely. Visitors can also observe exotic creatures from an elevated walkway. On a stroll through The Enchanted Forest, children and parents can pet deer and other tame animals. □ The park also has rare square-lipped rhinoceros, known as "white rhinos." The three-tonne beasts are the largest of their species.

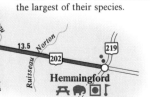

White rhino,
Parc Safari Africain, Hemmingford

Parc Safari Africain, Hemmingford

Echoes of Wars Past
on the Banks of a Welcoming River

Richelieu River Valley

The 130-kilometre-long Richelieu River has its source in Lake Champlain on the Quebec-Vermont border. It flows almost due north and merges with the St. Lawrence at Sorel. During the 19th century, canals at Chambly and Saint-Ours opened the river to commercial vessels carrying goods between Montreal and New York State. Although this traffic has virtually ceased, the locks still ease the passage of pleasure craft on the scenic Richelieu River. Visitors can also take boat cruises from Saint-Charles-sur-Riche-

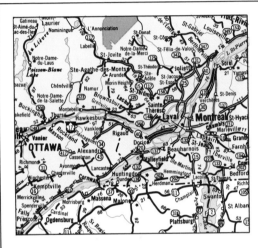

Eight Peaks of the Plain

The Monteregian Hills rise abruptly from the flat lowlands of southwestern Quebec. There are eight peaks in all: Johnson, Brome, Shefford, Yamaska, Rougemont, Saint-Bruno, Saint-Hilaire and Montreal's Mount Royal. The name derives from the Latin *Mons Regius*—royal mountains.

Geologists believe the hills were formed when molten rock rose from below the earth's crust some 120 million years ago. The molten rock thrust into layers of soft, porous sedimentary rock near the earth's surface (Figure 1), then cooled and solidified into igneous rock. Millions of years of erosion wore down the sedimentary rock, exposing the hard igneous rock (Figure 2). Ancient sea beaches and marine shells indicate that the hills were once partially submerged by the Champlain Sea—a body of water that covered the St. Lawrence lowlands when glaciers were receding. Fossils can be found in the sand on the foothills of Mont Saint-Hilaire.

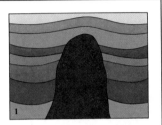

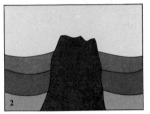

Fort Chambly

FORT CHAMBLY NATIONAL HISTORIC PARK
This great, square fort was built by the French (1665, 1709-11) and abandoned to the British in 1760. American revolutionary troops held the fort in 1775-76. Recaptured in 1777 by the British, Fort Chambly was garrisoned until the mid-19th century, and served as a prison during the War of 1812 and the uprising of 1837. It has been extensively restored.
□ Near the fort are the oldest locks of the Chambly Canal (c. 1843). River traffic still uses the canal to bypass rapids here.
□ In Chambly are a statue and the grave of Charles-Michel de Salaberry, who commanded the Canadian forces that defeated the Americans at Lacolle and Châteauguay in 1813.

SAINT-JEAN-SUR-RICHELIEU
A cairn marks the site of Fort Saint-Jean besieged in 1775 by American forces for 45 days. The Americans occupied the fort before burning it down the following year.
□ A tablet at the CN station commemorates the building of Canada's first railway between here and La Prairie in 1836.

FORT LENNOX NATIONAL HISTORIC PARK
The fort is located on Île-aux-Noix, which can be reached by ferry.
□ The French fortified the island in 1759. The British took possession the next year and held Île-aux-Noix until it was captured in 1775 by an American army. The Americans abandoned the island in 1776 after their failure to capture Quebec.
□ The British built a fort here in 1783. Following the War of 1812, the British reinforced this stronghold as part of a defense against a possible future American invasion. They renamed it Fort Lennox. A barracks, commissary, guardhouse, officers' quarters, and canteen have been restored.

*Fort Lennox,
Ile-aux-Noix*

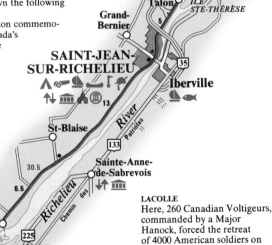

LACOLLE
Here, 260 Canadian Voltigeurs, commanded by a Major Hanock, forced the retreat of 4000 American soldiers on May 13, 1814.

0 1 2 3 4 5 Miles
0 2 4 6 8 Kilometres

lieu and other small riverside communities.

In 1609 the French explorer Samuel de Champlain ascended the Richelieu to make the first fateful French attack on the Iroquois. The river was known as the "River of the Iroquois" until it was renamed, in 1642, in honor of French Cardinal Richelieu.

During the early days of settlement, the Richelieu served as the route by which French and English colonists repeatedly attacked each other. In 1760 an English army advanced up the river to Montreal. Invading American forces followed this route in 1775 without success and, during the War of 1812, they were repelled at present-day Lacolle. The clash of arms was last heard here during the rebellion of 1837.

Rising some 400 metres above the Richelieu is Mont Saint-Hilaire, one of the eight Monteregian Hills lying between Montreal and the Appalachian uplands to the south.

Visitors can drive as far as Lac Hertel at the side of the mountain. A footpath leads from there to a summit lookout that gives a panoramic view of the scenic and historic Richelieu River valley extending as far south as Lake Champlain.

Patriote monument, Saint-Denis

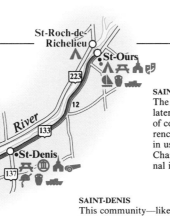

SAINT-CHARLES-SUR-RICHELIEU
On Oct. 23, 1837, rebels gathered in Saint-Charles, planted a tree of liberty, proclaimed a republic (the Confederation of the Six Counties) and called for an uprising. A stone monument commemorates the *Patriote* meeting and the uprising that began on November 21. Hundreds of rebels occupied Saint-Charles. After a bloody combat with government troops, they were defeated and 30 were taken prisoner.
□ Boat trips on the Richelieu River are available here.

SAINT-OURS
The Saint-Ours Canal, built in 1849 and later enlarged, was designed to ease the flow of commercial traffic between the St. Lawrence River and Lake Champlain. It is still in use. (The other canal in this system is at Chambly.) The Parc des Écluses by the canal is ideal for picnics.

SAINT-DENIS
This community—like neighboring Saint-Charles-sur-Richelieu—was the scene of many tumultuous events during the 1837 rebellion. A larger-than-life statue of a *Patriote* commemorates 12 rebels killed on Nov. 23, 1837 at Saint-Denis. The Maison nationale des Patriotes, housed in the Maison Jean-Baptiste Mâsse, traces the course of the uprising. A cairn marks the site of Maison Saint-Germain, where some 300 rebels held out against a force of 500 British soldiers.

MONT SAINT-HILAIRE NATURE CONSERVATION CENTRE
This is the highest of the Monteregian Hills of southwestern Quebec. Scenic Lac Hertel, just at the side of the mountain, can be reached on foot. The conservation area contains a network of trails, which can be used for hiking, bird-watching, cross-country skiing and snowshoeing.

Seigneurial land pattern: an aerial view, near Saint-Denis

A Land of Loyal Seigneurs and Industrious Habitants

Some Quebec farmers still pay rent under contracts laid down in the 17th century. The fertile land along the St. Lawrence and Richelieu rivers was distributed to seigneurs, "persons of rank," by Louis XIV. Seigneurs who pledged loyalty to the King were granted waterfront lots which they parceled out to tenant farmers, who had to clear the land. (Seigneurs divided their land into thin strips so that each tenant had river frontage.) The seigneur was obliged to live in a manor house on his land and to run a flour mill for his tenants, who paid about $35 a year for a 40-hectare farm. Industrious habitants grew wheat, oats, peas and beans, and raised cattle, sheep, pigs and chickens—and prospered; impoverished seigneurs often went hungry to keep up an appearance of gentility.

Cerulian warbler

MONT-SAINT-HILAIRE
The 1837 church in the town of Mont-Saint-Hilaire has a Gothic interior and a fieldstone exterior. On the interior walls are 11 frescoes, murals, Stations of the Cross, and bas-reliefs by Osias Leduc. The presbytery dates from 1798. Several water mills from about 1800 have been converted into houses at the foot of the mountain. Two imposing stone manor houses along the Rivière des Hurons date from about 1850.

Lac Hertel, Mont Saint-Hilaire

Apples, Cheeses and Mushrooms From the 'Garden of Quebec'

Eastern Townships

Lac-Brome

GRANBY

This industrial center of the Eastern Townships (pop. 38,000) has some fine period houses, such as Brownies' Castle, built by Palmer Cox (1840-1924), the creator of the *Brownies* books for children. The Vittie House accommodates the Shefford County Museum. Granby's many fountains are a source of civic pride. A 3,200-year-old Greek fountain and a replica of Rome's Trevi Fountain adorn LeClerc Boulevard. A first-century Roman fountain is the centerpiece of Pelletier Park.
□ Granby Zoo, one of Canada's largest, features more than 1,300 animals, representing 300 different species.

ROUGEMONT

This community is well known for its apples and cider. Apple orchards occupy about 40 percent of the nearby farmland. An interpretive center at Rougemont describes apple-growing techniques. Roadside stands sell apples and related products, and some farmers welcome visitors who wish to pick their own apples.

Rural Charm and Superb Skiing

The Eastern Townships (or *Les Cantons de l'Est*) extend east from the Richelieu River to the Chaudière River, and south from the St. Lawrence lowlands to Quebec's border with the United States. The area is famed for its rural charm. Its scenic lakes, rivers and mountains make it a year-round resort area, and its ski hills, such as Mont Orford, rival those of the Laurentians.

BROMONT

This town was founded in 1964 by the nine Desourdy brothers—all members of a local family prominent in the construction business. An industrial park, including an airfield, attracted new business to the area and the venture prospered. With 10 mountain peaks and two lakes nearby, the town is also a popular year-round resort.

American woodcock

COWANSVILLE

The handsome houses on Main and South streets are among the finest examples of Victorian domestic architecture in Quebec. Cowansville was founded by Loyalist settler Jacob Ruiter, who built a gristmill and a sawmill on the Yamaska River. Once known as Nelsonville, Cowansville absorbed neighboring Sweetsburg (originally Churchville), which was also an early Loyalist community.

STANBRIDGE EAST

The three-story brick Cornell Mill, built in 1832, is one of three structures at Missisquoi Museum. The second floor of the mill has been redone as the interior of a Victorian house.
□ Nearby Hodge's Store is a two-story brick house (1843), which was converted to an old-time country store with late-19th- and early-20th-century merchandise. Most of the merchandise was found intact during renovations. Bill's Barn has old agricultural equipment.

Quebec's Eastern Townships were first settled by United Empire Loyalists who fled here in the 1790s after the American War of Independence. (The region was given its name to distinguish it from the townships to the west of Montreal in what is now Ontario.) During the early 19th century the Loyalists were followed by successive waves of immigrants: Americans, Irish, Scots and English. After 1840, French Canadians came to the townships, where they predominate today.

Known as the "Garden of Quebec," the townships have many of the province's best dairy and livestock farms. The abundance of local produce is the foundation of food industries at Granby and Rougemont. The Benedictine Abbey at Saint-Benoît-du-Lac makes two distinctive cheeses, *Ermite* and *St. Benoît*. Canada's largest producer of mushrooms is at Waterloo. Ducks are raised commercially at Lac Brome.

In summer and early autumn roadside stands offer farm produce, maple-sugar products, homemade preserves—and apples. The largest apple orchards in Quebec are found in this region. The first orchards were planted near Rougemont in the 1860s by the Sulpician Fathers. Early apple varieties, such as the Fameuse or Snow apple, have been replaced by the Melba, Lobo, McIntosh and Cortland. From the plentiful apple crop, hard cider is made. Some local cideries can be toured and their delicious product sampled.

WATERLOO

The first settlers here arrived in the late 18th century, and the settlement was named Waterloo in 1815, the year of the famous battle. Waterloo was incorporated as a village in 1867 and as a town in 1890. One of Waterloo's pleasing features is its heritage of Victorian buildings. The town is home to Slack Bros., Canada's largest mushroom producer.
□ Waterloo is the site of the Musée québécois de la chasse. This hunting museum, said to be the only one of its kind in North America, has collections of stuffed animals and antique guns.

Brown trout

LAC-BROME (KNOWLTON)

The town of Lac-Brome includes Knowlton and other small communities. The area is a year-round recreational playground. The village of Knowlton retains the spirit of its Loyalist and Victorian past. Many handsome Victorian houses grace its streets.
□ Brome County Historical Museum comprises five period buildings. A white brick building, once the Knowlton Academy (1854), contains pioneer artifacts and archives. The Martin annex displays a First World War German Fokker aircraft. Other buildings include Tibbits Hill Schoolhouse (1884) and the old 19th-century fire hall.

Orford Arts Centre

Benedictine Abbey, Saint-Benoît-du-Lac

PARC DU MONT-ORFORD

In winter, this 58-square-kilometre provincial park swarms with skiers. Mont Orford, at a height of 852 metres, offers several challenging slopes. In summer the park reverts to campers, boaters and golfers.
□ The park is the setting for the Orford Arts Centre, which presents a summer-long festival of classical and popular music concerts and art exhibitions. It also offers advanced music training to roughly 500 students from around the world. The complex comprises residences for teachers and students, a central building (where visitors can dine) and a large multi-use facility. The Man and Music Pavilion, built for Montreal's Expo 67 and moved here in 1972, has classrooms, and assembly and exhibition halls. The Gilles Lefebvre Concert Hall seats 500. The grounds are used to exhibit sculpture.

SAINT-BENOÎT-DU-LAC

The Benedictine Abbey overlooking Lake Memphrémagog here is a striking combination of octagonal and square towers, triangular gables and long, thin, pointed windows. Inside are intricately tiled floors and graceful arches in mosaics of brick. The abbey's design was influenced by French-born Dom Paul Bellot, who immigrated to Canada in 1937, and became one of Quebec's foremost ecclesiastical architects. His most famous work is the dome of St. Joseph's Oratory in Montreal. His grave is in the abbey grounds.
□ Visitors can buy cheese made by the monks. Their distinctive *Ermite* is a blue cheese. *St. Benoît* has a nutty, somewhat sweet flavor, and looks like Swiss cheese.

Benedictine Abbey, Saint-Benoît-du-Lac

Where Backwoods Roads Lead to Country Fairs and Covered Bridges

Eastern Townships

This lively and picturesque corner of the Eastern Townships offers year-round recreations. In summer visitors enjoy fishing and boating on the sparkling waters of Lac Memphrémagog and its smaller neighbor, Lac Massawippi. Hikers are drawn to the high wooded hills surrounding the lakes. In winter skiers flock to Parc du Mont-Orford, one of Quebec's major winter sports centers, near the town of Magog.

Entertainment as well as recreation thrives here. Theatrical and musical attrac-

The Piggery, North Hatley

NORTH HATLEY
This all-seasons resort town north of Lake Massawippi is home to numerous painters, sculptors, potters and writers. The Piggery offers a summer program of drama and musicals. Evening concerts are combined with exhibitions of local art and handicrafts.
□ Two of North Hatley's oldest houses, Hovey Manor and the Hatley Inn, have been converted into hotels. Both were built about 1900.
□ Hatley, south of here, has clapboard houses and two wooden churches, all dating from 1850.

MAGOG
Established in 1799 by United Empire Loyalists, Magog is a popular year-round sports center. Northwest of the town is a major ski center at Parc du Mont-Orford.
□ To the south of the town is Lac Memphrémagog—an Indian word meaning great stretch of water. (The name of the town is an abbreviation of this word.) One fifth of this 52-kilometre-long lake lies in Vermont. Boat tours of the lake are available from Magog. The cruises offer views of local scenic landmarks such as Mont Orford, Owl's Head and Three Sisters Islands.
□ At Magog Lac Memphrémagog empties into the Magog River which, in turn, flows into the Saint-François River at Sherbrooke. During the 19th century, commercial shipping traffic traveling from the United States crossed the lake to reach the Saint-François.

AYER'S CLIFF
This resort community at the southern end of Lake Massawippi possesses one of the last Victorian bandstands in Quebec, sometimes used for concerts. A public boat ramp provides easy access to the lake. Windsurfing is a popular local recreation. The lake also offers excellent fishing for brown trout and yellow perch.

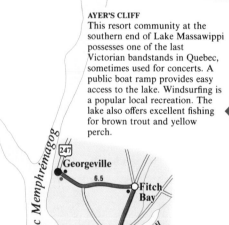

ROCK ISLAND
The Haskell Opera House in the twin towns of Rock Island, Que., and Derby Line, Vt., straddles the international border. Theatergoers sit in the United States to watch performances on a stage in Canada. Downstairs in the Haskell Library the adult section is in the U.S., and the children's section is in Canada. The Opera House, built in 1901-04, is a replica of the old Boston Opera House.

BEEBE PLAIN
The prosperity of this village is based on four granite quarries. Some stonecutters' workshops are open to the public. Visitors are welcome at the Stonecutters' Festival in May. The village's Canusa Street (*Ca*nada and *USA*) is named for the international border just south of the village.

Haskell Opera House, Rock Island

Bishop's University, Lennoxville

tions are presented at local summer theaters, such as the Piggery in North Hatley and the Théâtre du Vieux-Clocher in Magog. The 650-seat Centennial Theatre of Bishop's University, Lennoxville, offers Canadian plays year-round.

In this area are towns and villages that tempt the traveler to linger and enjoy the rural charm and peace of a bygone age. Mementos of the past are displayed in museums at Rock Island, Beebe Plain and Coaticook. Lively country fairs and festivals are still held every autumn in towns like Ayer's Cliff and Magog.

Outside the towns the visitor can explore quiet backroads winding through woodlots, meadows and furrowed fields. Covered bridges still span the rivers near Compton, Fitch Bay and Lennoxville. At the turn of the century Quebec had more than a thousand covered bridges, but today only 100 remain. The 18 survivors in this unspoiled region are eloquent reminders of horse-and-buggy days.

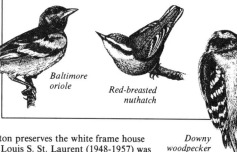

LENNOXVILLE
During the French Regime, this town where Massawippi, Coaticook and other rivers meet was known as Les Petites Fourches (The Little Forks). By contrast, nearby Sherbrooke was known as Les Grandes Fourches at this time. Lennoxville was settled in the 1790s by Loyalists from Vermont and was named for Charles Lennox, Duke of Richmond, governor in chief of Canada, 1818-19.
□ The town is the seat of Bishop's University, established in 1843 and granted university status in 1853. This institution is modeled on the colleges of Oxford University. St. Mark's Chapel, built in 1853 and enlarged in 1875, is one of the university's noteworthy buildings.
□ The Lennoxville-Ascot Historical Society Museum exhibits pioneer artifacts. The local agricultural research station, established in 1914, offers audiovisual presentations and group tours.

Birds of the Townships

Red-breasted nuthatches and downy woodpeckers are year-round residents in the wooded Eastern Townships. The downy woodpecker, a black and white bird, is the smallest of its species found in Canada. It nests in a hole drilled high in a tree. A strong skull enables the woodpecker to withstand the pounding of its bill as it bores into trees.

Abandoned woodpecker holes are favorite nesting places of the tree-climbing red-breasted nuthatch. It lines the nesting cavity with shredded bark, grasses and roots. The nuthatch feeds on nuts and, using its long toes and claws to climb, it forages up and down tree trunks for insects.

In early May the first Baltimore orioles appear in the Eastern Townships. The male has fiery orange markings. The female is a duller, dusky orange. Other birds found in this area include yellow-throated vireos, warbling vireos, chestnut-sided warblers, scarlet tanagers and pine siskins.

Baltimore oriole

Red-breasted nuthatch

Downy woodpecker

COMPTON
A national historic site at Compton preserves the white frame house where Canadian Prime Minister Louis S. St. Laurent (1948-1957) was born in 1881. The site also contains his father's general store and warehouse. The store was often the setting for local political discussions involving St. Laurent. Visitors can listen by earphone to re-creations of these discussions. The warehouse also presents a sight-and-sound show about St. Laurent's career. St. Laurent, who died in 1973, is buried at the parish cemetery of St. Thomas Aquinas, Compton.

COATICOOK
The name of the town derives from the Abenakis Indian word *koatikeku,* which means "river of the land of pines." The Coaticook region was settled by Loyalists after 1818.
□ A suspended footbridge, said to be the longest in Canada, crosses a 70-metre-deep gorge on the Coaticook River. The bridge leads to a 20-metre-high observation tower, which offers a panoramic view of the Coaticook region.
□ Beaulne Museum, housed in the splendid turn-of-the-century Norton Mansion, shows period fashions and textiles.

BALDWIN MILLS
Visitors to the Baldwin Hills' fish hatchery (one of the largest in Quebec) can inspect an indoor aquarium and outdoor pools. The hatchery breeds eight species of fish, including gray trout.
□ Rozynska Pottery displays its distinctive wares at nearby Ways Mills.

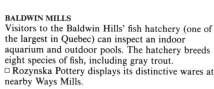

Rozynska Pottery, Ways Mills

Coaticook River gorge

Asbestos, Hockey Sticks and Scenic Hardwood Forests

Eastern Townships

The region between Sherbrooke and Victoriaville exudes rural tranquillity. Here are rolling, forested hills; poultry and dairy farms and lush meadows; weathered wooden barns, old mills and covered bridges. But here, too, are the bustling pulp-and-paper towns of Bromptonville and Windsor, the mining center of Asbestos, and Victoriaville, which has the world's leading manufacturer of hockey sticks.

The largest center in this region is Sherbrooke, unofficial "capital" of the Eastern

Restored gristmill, Denison Mills

RICHMOND
A cairn at Richmond commemorates the Craig Road, the first road to link the Eastern Townships with Quebec City. Its construction began in 1809 under the direction of Sir James Craig, the governor of Lower Canada (1807-11). It replaced a rough and often impassable trail. Today parts of the Craig Road are paved, but much of the original road has been abandoned.

MELBOURNE
The local county historical society preserves a mid-19th-century farmhouse at Melbourne. The exhibits re-create Victorian life in this region.

Sanctuary of the Sacred Heart, Beauvoir

BEAUVOIR
The sanctuary of the Sacred Heart is situated on the top of a hill overlooking the Rivière Saint-François at Beauvoir. The fieldstone shrine has attracted the faithful since it was built in 1920. Outdoor services are still held every Sunday (weather permitting) from early May to late October. The site offers a fine view of the surrounding region.

1 Université de Sherbrooke
2 Parc Blanchard
3 Parc Jacques-Cartier
4 Domaine Howard
5 Mont Bellevue
6 Old North Ward
7 St. Peter's Church
8 Old Court House
9 Léon Marcotte Exhibition Centre
10 Seminary Museum of Natural History
11 St. Michael's Cathedral
12 Tourist Information
13 Aylmer Bridge
14 Parc Victoria

King Street, Sherbrooke

SHERBROOKE
This administrative, industrial and educational center, situated at the junction of the Magog and Saint-François rivers, has a wide range of recreational and cultural things to do.
□ Sherbrooke's downtown area is a lively place with cafés and restaurants. Its notable sites include St. Peter's Anglican Church (1844), St. Michael's Cathedral, the Old Court House, the Leon Marcotte Exhibition Centre (for traveling exhibitions) and the Seminary Museum of Natural History. The Université de Sherbrooke (1954) on the city's western outskirts presents art shows at its cultural center.
□ The Old North Ward is a district of handsome 19th-century houses. Domaine Howard, formerly the estate of Charles Howard, has been converted into a museum of local history.
□ Sherbrooke has some fine green spaces: Lac des Nations offers swimming and waterskiing in summer, and Mont Bellevue, skiing in winter.

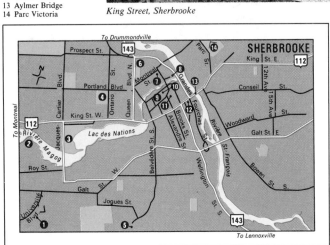

0 1 2 3 4 5 Miles
0 2 4 6 8 Kilometres

Townships. It is attractively situated on hills at the point where Rivière Magog plunges into the Saint-François. (There is a magnificent view of the city from Mont Bellevue on the southern outskirts.)

Sherbrooke's founder was Gilbert Hyatt, a Loyalist from Vermont, who built a gristmill by Rivière Magog in 1794. The community that grew up around it was named for Sir John Sherbrooke, governor-general of Canada in 1816-18. Local industrial development began in the 1840s. Today Sherbrooke has

become Quebec's sixth largest city (pop. 74,500) and a major manufacturing center.

Northeast of Sherbrooke is Warwick, famed for its picturesque gardens and covered bridge. This small community is the gateway to the Bois-Francs, a region noted for its hardwood forests. It is here that the farmland of the St. Lawrence River valley gives way to the rugged, scenic landscape of southwestern Quebec.

Arthabaska, in the heart of Bois-Francs country, claims two famous sons: the painter

Marc-Aurèle de Foy Suzor-Côté (1869-1937) and Sir Wilfrid Laurier. (The house where Laurier lived from 1876 to 1897 is a museum.) Asbestos, south of Warwick, takes its name from the fibrous mineral extracted locally from a vast terraced open-pit mine, one of the largest in the world. Its size dwarfs the men and machines that continually enlarge it.

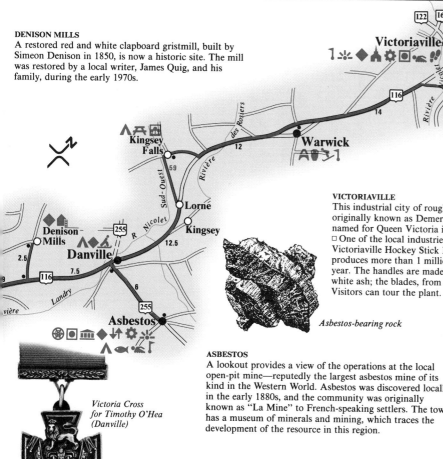

DENISON MILLS
A restored red and white clapboard gristmill, built by Simeon Denison in 1850, is now a historic site. The mill was restored by a local writer, James Quig, and his family, during the early 1970s.

White ash

Asbestos-bearing rock

VICTORIAVILLE
This industrial city of roughly 22,000, originally known as Demersville, was named for Queen Victoria in 1861.
□ One of the local industries, the Victoriaville Hockey Stick Ltd., produces more than 1 million sticks a year. The handles are made from local white ash; the blades, from hard maple. Visitors can tour the plant.

ARTHABASKA
First settled in the 1830s, Arthabaska (pop. 7,244) is dominated by Mont Saint-Michel, originally known as Monte Cristo, which provides a superb view of the surrounding region.
□ Arthabaska is also the site of Wilfrid Laurier's summer home (now a museum). The renowned painter Marc-Aurèle de Foy Suzor-Côté was born in Arthabaska in 1869. From 1891 to 1912, he traveled widely and worked in Europe and the United States, but after 1912, spent his summers here. His house, still a private residence, is marked with a plaque.

ASBESTOS
A lookout provides a view of the operations at the local open-pit mine—reputedly the largest asbestos mine of its kind in the Western World. Asbestos was discovered locally in the early 1880s, and the community was originally known as "La Mine" to French-speaking settlers. The town has a museum of minerals and mining, which traces the development of the resource in this region.

Victoria Cross for Timothy O'Hea (Danville)

DANVILLE
Situated in rich farming country, Danville was settled by Loyalists in the early 19th century. A number of residences from the Loyalist period still survive on Grove and Du Carmel streets.
□ A plaque at Danville honors a 20-year-old British soldier, Timothy O'Hea, the very first recipient of the famous Victoria Cross "for conspicuous bravery in the presence of the enemy." O'Hea won his award far from the field of battle. In June 1866 the young soldier single-handedly extinguished a fire that threatened to ignite an ammunition train in the Danville railway yard. (The award, subsequently won by 93 Canadians, was replaced by a Canadian government award in 1972.)

An Elegant Setting for a Political Leader

Wilfrid Laurier, prime minister of Canada in 1896-1911, lived in Arthabaska for some 20 years. The elegant brick house he built here in 1876 is now a museum. The house—perhaps a bit beyond Laurier's means at the time—is furnished as in his day. Historical documents and many personal possessions of Laurier and his wife, Zoë, are displayed.

Laurier practiced law and ran a weekly newspaper in Arthabaska—the chief town of Quebec's Bois-Francs region. The voters of Drummond-Arthabaska, attracted by Laurier's moderate political views, elected him their Member of Parliament in 1874. For the next 13 years, Laurier's eloquence and ability won the respect of the Liberal Party. In 1887 the Liberals made him national leader.

Living room, Laurier House, Arthabaska

Lively Folk Songs and Sugar Shacks Along the Chaudière

Eastern Townships

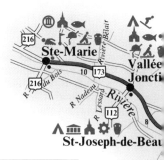

Pottery making, Saint-Joseph-de-Beauce

Gentle Lullabies, Drinking Songs, and the Famous *Alouette*

Writer and folklore expert Marius Barbeau—born at Sainte-Marie in 1883—collected, recorded and transcribed thousands of French-Canadian folk songs.

Barbeau traveled Quebec, the Maritimes and New England in his search for traditional songs. Many of the songs had been passed down for generations, but had never been put in written form. The singers were fishermen, lumbermen, and women who sang as they worked at spinning and weaving. Some had memorized more than 100 songs. There were songs of the fur traders, voyageurs and coureurs de bois; work songs of the habitant farmers who cleared land along the St. Lawrence; lullabies and drinking songs. Old French songs—brought to Quebec by early settlers—sometimes dated back to the 16th century.

One of the best known Canadian songs in Barbeau's collection is *Alouette*, in which an unfortunate lark is told: "I will pluck your head, your beak, your nose, your eyes . . ."

Barbeau studied at Université Laval then at Oxford and the Sorbonne. He worked as an anthropologist at the National Museum of Canada from 1911 to 1958, and produced a number of books on French-Canadian and Indian folklore and arts and crafts, collections of legends and folk tales, and two novels. Barbeau died in 1969 in Ottawa.

SAINTE-MARIE
The shrine of Sainte-Anne-de-Beauce (1892) is next to the Maison Taschereau (1809), the birthplace of the first Canadian-born cardinal, Elzéar-Alexandre Taschereau (1821-98). Other important structures include Maison Lacroix, the region's only stone house, and St. Marie Church (1856).

SAINT-JOSEPH-DE-BEAUCE
This community was named for Joseph de la Gorgendière, who was granted the seigneury in 1736. A complex of five historic buildings includes St. Joseph de Beauce Church, built of local fieldstone in 1867, and an 1889 convent, which houses the Musée Marius-Barbeau.

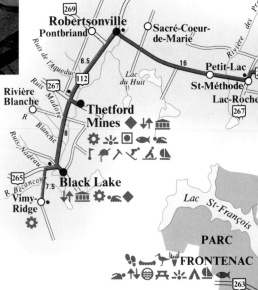

THETFORD MINES
A monument at Thetford Mines city hall honors Joseph Fecteau who discovered asbestos here in 1876. Today Thetford Mines—the largest producer of the mineral in the Western World—has both open-pit and underground mines. (The open-pit mines can be viewed from observation posts.) The Musée minéralogique et minier displays samples of asbestos and other minerals from around the world, as well as mining equipment. Thetford Mines celebrates the mineral that made its fortune during the Asbestos Festival in late June and early July.

Beauce Country

0   2   4   6   8   10 Miles

0   4   8   12   16 Kilometres

During the American invasion in the winter of 1775-76, Gen. Benedict Arnold led 1,100 American troops along the Rivière Chaudière from northern Maine to Quebec City. Nearly half the invaders died in forests and swamps. Starving survivors ate soap, grease and boiled moccasins. They reached Quebec City, but were repulsed on Dec. 31, 1775, by troops of Governor Guy Carleton.

The forests have been cleared and the swamps drained in what now is known as the Beauce Country. The Chaudière, which flows through gently rolling terrain, is bordered by long, narrow farms. (During the French regime seigneurs divided their land into thin strips so that each tenant farmer had river frontage.) Quebec's longest covered bridge (155 metres) spans the river at Notre-Dame-des-Pins. The Chaudière's source is Lac Mégantic, noted for its ouananiche (landlocked salmon).

Maple trees here yield most of the maple syrup produced in Canada. Wooden shacks (*cabanes à sucre*) in the hills are used for "sugaring off" parties. Families and friends gather to dance, sing and sample maple syrup in celebration of spring.

NOTRE-DAME-DES-PINS
Local artisans sell fine linen and woolen goods, pottery, wood sculptures, and handmade dolls and toys at Les Créativités Beauceronnes in Notre-Dame-des-Pins.
□ The community is justly proud of its 155-metre-long covered bridge, built in 1929. It is the longest of its kind in Quebec.

SAINT-GEORGES-OUEST
A replica of Louis Jobin's five-metre-high statue of saint George slaying a dragon stands in front of the community's church. The original, sculpted in 1912, was moved into the church to protect it from weather damage.
□ Parc des Sept-Chutes, about three kilometres north of town, is named for the seven waterfalls that tumble 38 metres into a gorge on the Rivière Pozer.

Sugaring-off party, Saint-Benoît-Labre

Tire sur la neige—
Hot Maple Syrup on Snow

Maple trees were the only source of sugar for the early settlers in New France. Before their arrival, the Indians had been familiar with the process of making maple syrup and sugar. Each spring, when the sap began to run freely, the Indians tapped the maple tree by cutting a diagonal incision in the trunk. In the lower end of the incision, they placed a concave piece of bark which piped the sap into a hollowed log.

The pioneers borrowed and improved upon the Indian techniques of tapping the maples and refining its sap. (The earliest record of Canadian maple-sugar production is dated 1706.) After the sap was gathered, it was boiled in a large kettle over an open fire. The maple sugar was formed into cakes for later use.

Today the sap is processed in sugar shacks, where evaporator pans over furnaces convert it rapidly into syrup and sugar. Modern production methods yield some 4.5 million litres of maple syrup annually in Canada. Ninety percent comes from rural regions of Quebec, such as the Beauce Country.

Although maple syrup is now produced commercially in large quantities, many families save small amounts for "sugaring off" parties each spring. The hot syrup is poured on clean snow and the sweet taffy (called *tire*) is eagerly eaten.

Maple syrup is often associated with Canadian cuisine, especially that of Quebec. Two famous recipes are maple sugar pie, a custardlike dish with maple syrup thickened with cornstarch, and *grands-pères au sirop d'érable* (maple syrup dumplings).

PARC FRONTENAC
This park is divided into two main sectors. The Saint-Daniel sector, on the north shore of Lac Saint-François, is designed for water sports; the southern sector, on the opposite shore, for anglers and wildlife enthusiasts. The southern sector offers rental chalets.

Gray partridge

LAC-MÉGANTIC
Situated in one of Quebec's most mountainous regions, Lac-Mégantic was settled by Scots in the late 1880s. Today it is a recreational center for summer hikers and winter skiers. Boat trips on the lake are available.
□ Nearby Mount Megantic Observatory and St. Joseph's Shrine are two points of interest. Visitors can ask at the observatory's reception center about summer stargazing outings.

Rivière-des-Plantes
16
50
Rivière-Gilbert
Beauceville-Est
Beauceville
Chaudière
108
Notre-Dame-des-Pins
204
16
173
Lacroix
St-Georges
Pozer
12
St-Georges-Ouest
271
St-Benoît-Labre
Lac-Poulin
Victor
St-Ephrem-Station
12.5
31
8
St-Ephrem-de-Tring
6.5
.5
5
Guadeloupe
269
St-Evariste-de-Forsyth
20
Courcelles
108
Lambton
263
St-Romain
R
des-Indiens
10.5
Félton
Stornoway
161
13
25.5
Lac Whitton
Nantes
263
Lac de l'Original
12.5
Lac Mégantic
204
Lac-Mégantic

Work in Silver and Wood by Quebec's Early Artisans

South Shore, St. Lawrence River

The south shore of the St. Lawrence River is redolent with history. This was the land Jacques Cartier saw in 1535. Chagrined that the broad blue river was not a route to the Orient, Cartier sailed away. But other Frenchmen followed—explorers, fur traders and missionaries. These adventurous men pushed westward from New France until, by the early 1700s, they had explored the vast interior of North America.

A monument in a Boucherville park honors one of these explorers—the Rev. Jac-

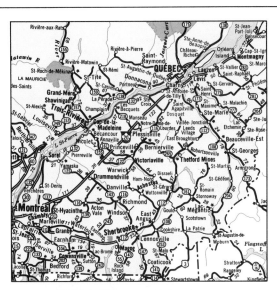

Sorel

Short-billed marsh wren

LAC SAINT-PIERRE

A seafood fricassee, *gibelotte de poissons,* is the regional specialty in restaurants on a cluster of islands opposite Sorel, and just north of the town. The islands, favorite haunts of duck hunters and fishermen, are at the entrance to Lac Saint-Pierre, a shallow, 11-by-22-kilometre bulge in the St. Lawrence River.
□ Common gallinules, long-billed and short-billed marsh wrens are found by the shores of Lac Saint-Pierre. Large colonies of seabirds, ducks, bustards and snipes also breed in the reedy, lakeside marshes. This is the only place in the St. Lawrence Valley inhabited by red-spotted turtles, which normally avoid subzero winters. They are believed to be survivors from a warmer, wetter period that followed the last ice age.

SOREL

Situated on the south shore of the St. Lawrence River at the mouth of the Richelieu River, Sorel is a year-round port, an industrial and ship building center, and the commercial hub of the agricultural Richelieu Valley. The provincial marina is one of the most important in Quebec.
□ Established in 1642, Sorel is Canada's fourth oldest city. One of its most notable buildings is La Maison des Gouverneurs, built by Governor in chief Sir Frederick Haldimand (1718-91) in 1781. This house, once the residence of the governors-general of Canada, is now a conference hall and exhibition center.
□ From nearby Sainte-Anne-de-Sorel, visitors can take boat rides around the offshore islands. Moonlight cruises are also available.
□ Île au Pée was the home of Germaine Guèvremont (1893-1968), the popular Quebec writer, who described the Sainte-Anne-de-Sorel area in her novel *Le Survenant* (translated as *The Outsider*).

Common gallinule

Madeleine de Verchères statue Verchères

BOUCHERVILLE

Sainte-Famille Church, built in 1801, contains an important collection of religious art and has been designated an historic monument. Among many wood sculptures is a tabernacle carved about 1745 by Gilles Bolvin. Side altars (1807-08) are by Louis Amble Quevillon, and baptismal fonts (c. 1880) by Nicolas Manny.
□ Other historic sites include La Chaumière (1741), the oldest house in Boucherville, and the Lafontaine House (1780), birthplace of Louis-Hippolyte Lafontaine, joint premier (with Robert Baldwin) of the Province of Canada in 1842-48.

VARENNES

A huge wooden calvary overlooks the St. Lawrence River here. The figure of Christ is on a cross 24 metres high, those of the two thieves on crosses about 23 metres high. The calvary was sculpted in 1776 by Michel Brisset.
□ A shrine honors Mother Marguerite d'Youville, foundress of the Order of the Gray Nuns, who was born here.

VERCHÈRES

Three times life-size, this bronze statue of Madeleine de Verchères commemorates the 14-year-old's defense in 1692 of her father's seigneurial fort. Sculpted in 1913 by Philippe Hébert, the statue is at the site of the girl's heroic encounter with the Iroquois.
□ A plaque marks the site of a house in which Ludger Duvernay, founder of the Saint-Jean-Baptiste Society (1834), was born in 1799. Verchères was also the birthplace of Calixa Lavallée (1841-1919), who composed the music of *O Canada*.

ques Marquette. The Jesuit was interpreter to Louis Jolliet on his 1673 voyage of discovery down the Mississippi River. In the parish archives at Boucherville is a baptismal certificate of an Indian child, dated May 20, 1668, and signed by Marquette.

Sainte-Famille Church, at Boucherville, contains the work of one of Quebec's greatest wood-carvers, Louis Amble Quevillon (1749-1823). By drawing on the Canadian scene for motifs and designs, Quevillon and his contemporary, François Baillargé

(1739-1819), created a distinctive and original style of church decoration. At Lotbinière, examples of Baillargé's sculpture can be seen in Saint-Louis Church—one of the most richly decorated in Quebec.

Church silver was another craft that was brought to a high state of artistic development in Quebec during the late 1700s and the early 1800s. The fine work of François Ranvoyzé (1739-1819), the foremost silversmith of his time, is found in Saint-Edouard Church at Gentilly.

Saint-Louis de Lotbinière Church

SAINT-PIERRE-LES-BECQUETS
This resort community offers a panoramic view of the St. Lawrence River as far upstream as Trois-Rivières. It is famous for its tomato crop. In summer visitors can buy local produce from the area's market gardens.

BÉCANCOUR
This industrial community of 10,500, almost opposite Trois-Rivières on the south shore of the St. Lawrence, includes villages such as Saint-Grégoire, Sainte-Angèle and Gentilly. The Gentilly nuclear power station exemplifies modern development; the area's churches and historic buildings evoke the past. At Bécancour, Saint-Grégoire Church, built in 1892, has a 55-metre-high steeple. At Gentilly, Saint-Edouard Church, built of fieldstone in 1848, contains work by Quebec silversmiths François Ranvoyzé and Laurent Amyot.

LOTBINIÈRE
This village has some fine old dwellings: Maison Bélanger (1740-84), Maison Page (1785), and Maison Chavigny de la Chevrotière (1817). Saint-Louis de Lotbinière Church dates from 1818. The two-story stone Moulin du Portage, just east of the village, is a delightful place for a picnic.

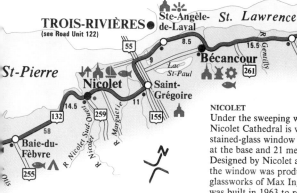

NICOLET
Under the sweeping white front arch of Nicolet Cathedral is what may be the largest stained-glass window in the world, 52 metres at the base and 21 metres high at the center. Designed by Nicolet artist Jean Charland, the window was produced in the Paris glassworks of Max Ingrand. The cathedral was built in 1963 to replace one that had to be demolished after a landslide in 1955.
□ Quebec artist Rodolphe Duguay (1891-1973) lived and died at Nicolet. Duguay's house and studio are open to the public.

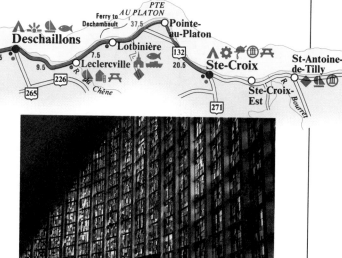

Stained-glass window, Nicolet Cathedral

ODANAK
The Abenaki Indians on the Odanak reserve maintain a museum, which contains a model of the 17th-century Abenaki fort, a traditional skin tent and the biblical scriptures translated into the Abenaki language. An 1828 stone church on the reserve is decorated with native sculpture.

Stone chapel, Odanak Indian Reserve

A Heroine of New France

Madeleine de Verchères, who led the defense of her father's seigneury against an Iroquois war party in 1692 when she was 14, wrote the best-known account of her feat 30 years later. She claimed she ran in from the fields ahead of 45 Indians, repaired the fort and, with two soldiers, an old man and two younger brothers, held out for seven days (*right*) until help arrived from Montreal. In 1699 she had written a more plausible account: she struggled free of one Iroquois who grabbed her neckerchief, and with one soldier she fought off attackers for two days. Whichever story is to be believed, Madeleine remains a heroine. In 1722 when her husband, Pierre-Thomas de La Pérade, was attacked by two Indians, she disabled one and saved her husband's life.

Canada's First Iron Foundry and Second Oldest City

Saint-Maurice River Valley

LA MAURICIE NAT PK

Common loon

Lac Wapizagonke, La Mauricie National Park

LA MAURICIE NATIONAL PARK

This heavily wooded, 549 square-kilometre park in the Saint-Maurice River valley has campsites, beaches, wilderness and wildlife areas, and 154 lakes. Lac Wapizagonke, a favorite of canoeists and sailing enthusiasts, is the park's chief lake. It is boxed into a narrow valley by cliffs formed millions of years ago by a massive movement of the earth's crust. Here and there are tiny coves with waterfalls and sandy beaches.

□ A paved 60-kilometre road divides the park into two sectors. The southern (and smaller) sector has been developed for campers; the northern sector is still a Laurentian wilderness. Saint-Jean-des-Piles, the main entry point for the park's visitors, has an interpretive center.

□ Moose, bear, deer, lynx, beaver, wolves, and many small mammals inhabit the park's rolling hills.

SHAWINIGAN

This city (pop. 21,400) began to develop in 1899 when a dam was built here to harness the power of the 45-metre-high Shawinigan Falls on the Saint-Maurice River. Within five years, Shawinigan was supplying electricity to Montreal. Cheap local power also attracted aluminum, chemical and other industries.

□ A promenade along the Saint-Maurice River provides a spectacular view of thundering Shawinigan Falls. The local Hydro-Québec plant can be visited.

□ The Shawinigan Cultural Center has painting and sculptures by outstanding Quebec artists. The walls of the Church of Notre-Dame-de-la-Présentation at Shawinigan-Sud are covered with paintings by Osias Leduc (1864-1955).

Anchors, Plowshares and Pots From Master Ironworkers

A towering stone chimney (*right*), once part of Canada's first iron foundry, dominates Les Forges du Saint-Maurice National Historic Park. The foundations of the *Grande Maison*—home of the ironmasters—are also in the 50-hectare park.

The foundry, established in 1730, marked the start of industrialization in the region. Local iron ore and wood were used to produce stoves, pots, tools, plowshares and anchors.

François Poulin de Francheville, seigneur of Saint-Maurice, built the ironworks after he was granted iron-mining rights by Louis XV. By 1741, with the help of master ironworkers from France, the foundry had become the most important industry in New France. At peak production, its blast furnaces were fired around the clock by stokers working in six-hour shifts. In 1833 the plant produced 1,500 cast-iron stoves in only four months. Competition from modern foundries and a dwindling supply of local raw materials eventually forced the Saint-Maurice works to close. The foundry was abandoned in 1883.

In Quebec, major cities have developed where important tributaries flow into the St. Lawrence River, the backbone of Canada's transportation system for more than three centuries. Canada's second oldest city, Trois-Rivières was established in 1634 at the confluence of the Saint-Maurice and the St. Lawrence. There was a fur market at Trois-Rivières as early as 1610, and the settlement was a major fur-trading center until 1665, by which time Montreal had become the primary marketplace.

Les Forges du Saint-Maurice, the first iron foundry in Canada, was established north of Trois-Rivières in 1730. It became the most important industry in New France, but competition from more modern foundries forced it out of business in 1883.

In 1852 a slide was built at the falls upstream at Shawinigan so that logs from the immense forests of the Saint-Maurice Valley could be floated to the mouth of the river. By 1854 some 80 sawmills were operating at Trois-Rivières. Today about 25 per-cent of the city's work force is in the pulp and paper industry.

North of the industrial centers of Trois-Rivières, Shawinigan and Grand-Mère is the wild grandeur of the Laurentian hills. This wilderness is preserved in La Mauricie National Park. Here, in a pristine forest that is ablaze with color in the fall, are 35 kinds of deciduous trees and 11 evergreen species. In spring and summer the park is bright with asters, goldenrod, fireweed, violets and numerous other wildflowers.

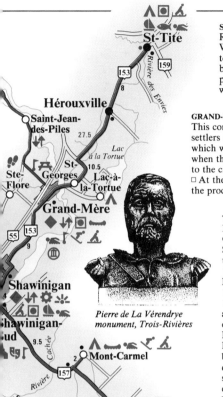

Pierre de La Vérendrye monument, Trois-Rivières

SAINT-TITE
Rodeos are part of the excitement at the 10-day Western Festival held here in September. The town's leather industry, which produces western boots, has inspired this event. About 80,000 people—some dressed in stetson hats and colorful western shirts—attend the festivities.

GRAND-MÈRE
This community (pop. 14,850) was named by its early settlers for a rock outcrop ressembling an old woman, which was situated at the base of the local falls. In 1916, when the local dam was constructed, the rock was moved to the city's municipal park.
□ At the Consolidated-Bathurst plant, visitors can watch the process by which logs are made into paper.

TROIS-RIVIÈRES
Founded in 1634, Trois-Rivières (pop. 100,000) is Canada's second oldest city (after Quebec City). Some of the notable French regime buildings that survived a devastating 1908 fire include the 1697 Ursuline monastery (now a museum), the Manoir Boucher-de-Niverville (1730), and the 18th-century Manoir de Tonnancour (rebuilt in 1974). St. James' Anglican Church is housed in a Récollet convent, which was built in 1697. The old prison (1816), the Maison Hertel-de-la-Fresnière (1821) and the Cathédrale de Trois-Rivières (1854-58) are outstanding 19th-century buildings. Monuments honor native son Pierre de La Vérendrye and other explorers. A granite shaft (Le Flambeau) was put up in 1934 to commemorate the city's 300th anniversary.
□ The Musée Pierre-Boucher evokes Trois-Rivières' colorful history. On the city's outskirts are Les Forges du Saint-Maurice and the Université du Québec's archaeological museum.

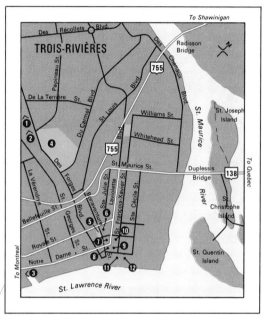

1 Les Forges du Saint-Maurice	4 Exhibition Grounds	9 De Tonnancour House
2 Université du Québec à Trois-Rivières	5 Champlain Park	10 Place d'Armes
3 Moulin seigneurial de Tonnancour	6 Cathedral of the Immaculate Conception	11 St. James' Anglican Church
	7 Tourist information	12 Ursuline Convent
	8 Le Flambeau	

De Tonnancour House, Trois-Rivières

POINTE-DU-LAC
On the shore of Lac Saint-Pierre (actually a widening of the St. Lawrence River), this community is a popular spot for windsurfers.
□ Two local attractions include the church and the old mill (Moulin seigneurial de Tonnancour), which was built between 1765 and 1788. Tours are available, and exhibitions and concerts are held here.

Trois-Rivières, as seen by painter Pierre Labreque

An Old Royal Road and a Place of Pilgrimage

North Shore, St. Lawrence River

Echoes of Quebec's history pervade this scenic stretch of road along the north shore of the St. Lawrence. Highway 138 follows Canada's first carriageway, *le chemin du Roy* (the King's road).

Completed in 1737, the old royal road provided an important link between Montreal and Quebec City. Along this route there were some 30 relay stations—usually country dwellings or inns—where weary travelers stopped to rest and change horses. Many of these early houses, now attractively restored,

LA PÉRADE
In January and February the frozen Rivière Sainte-Anne blossoms with the cabins of thousands of anglers fishing for tommycod through holes in the ice. A local carnival celebrates this annual winter event. Festivities feature ice sculptures, parades, singing and dancing. Prizes are awarded for the longest fish caught. The daily catch can vary from 200 to 1,200 fish.
□ In La Pérade are the ruins of a 1676 seigneurial house and the well-preserved Gouin (1669), Tremblay (1669), Dorion (1719) and Baribeau (1717) houses.

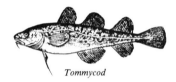

Tommycod

Cabins on the frozen Rivière Sainte-Anne, La Pérade

BATISCAN
Near here in 1609 Champlain first met with the Huron Indians, who thereafter were allies of the French.
□ A handsome 17th-century fieldstone house—the rectory and manor house of Jesuit priests who were Batiscan's first seigneurs—is preserved in a small provincial park.

CAP-DE-LA-MADELEINE
This industrial community (pop. 32,800)—popularly known as "le Cap"—is situated at the mouth of the St. Maurice River across from Trois-Rivières. The Shrine of Our Lady of the Rosary is the best-known site. A stone chapel, built in 1714, contains a statue of the Blessed Virgin considered miraculous. (In 1888 Father Frédéric Jansoone and two others claimed they saw her eyes open momentarily.) Today the site is Canada's national shrine to the Virgin Mary and ranks third in importance among places of pilgrimage in Quebec. Beside the chapel is the magnificent, octagonal Basilica of Our Lady of the Rosary, which was constructed in the 1960s.

Basilica of Our Lady of the Rosary, Cap-de-la-Madeleine

CHAMPLAIN
A sanctuary lamp carved in maple and painted white with gilt trim serves as a baptismal font in the Church of Notre-Dame-de-la-Visitation. It was used in an earlier church (1710). In the present church, built in 1879, Mass is said on a consecrated stone given to the parish in 1681 by Jean-Baptiste de la Croix de Chevrières de Saint-Vallier, second Roman Catholic bishop of Quebec.

TROIS-RIVIÈRES
(see Road Unit 122)

0 1 2 3 4 5 Miles
0 2 4 6 8 Kilometres

still survive by the roadside at Batiscan, Deschambault, Neuville, Portneuf and other small communities.

Stout masonry and harmonious lines proclaim the fine architectural quality of these buildings. Their other distinctive—and appealing—features include imposing chimneys, multipaned dormer windows, and steep roofs with bell-cast curves.

The ancient, richly decorated churches of this region display some of the finest work by Quebec's greatest 18th- and 19th-century artists and craftsmen. For example, the church at Deschambault was designed by Thomas Baillargé (1791-1859). Paintings by Antoine Plamondon (1804-95) and sculpture by Louis Jobin (1845-1928) adorn the church at Neuville.

The region's most famous religious structure is a small stone chapel at Cap-de-la-Madeleine. Built in 1714, the chapel has been a place of pilgrimage since the late 19th century. Today it is a national shrine to the Virgin Mary and attracts thousands of visitors every year.

Manoir Langlois, Portneuf

PORTNEUF
This industrial town at the mouth of Rivière Portneuf is on the site of a Huron village, which was named Achelay by the French explorer Jacques Cartier. The first settlers, who arrived in the 17th century, called their community Port; later, a local seignior, Sieur de Neuf, added his name to it.
□ Like many other towns along the route between Cap-de-la-Madeleine and Neuville, Portneuf has its architectural gems. One of the most outstanding is the one-story frame Manoir Langlois, built in the early 19th century and regarded as a fine example of domestic architecture from this period.

NEUVILLE
A half-domed sanctuary that dates from 1697 is part of Saint-François-de-Sales Church. The church's treasures include a wooden baldachin (altar canopy) dating from 1775, three late-18th-century altars sculpted by François Baillargé and 21 Antoine Plamondon paintings.
□ Neuville's fine old buildings include a convent (1716), a procession chapel (1735), and the Soulard (1760-80), Denis (c. 1780) and Anger (1797) houses.

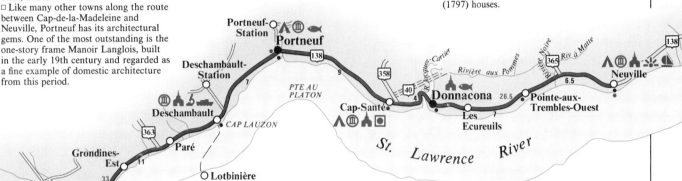

DESCHAMBAULT
Saint-Joseph-de-Deschambault Church (1837) and the rectory (1815), now a cultural center, are historic monuments. Another, the Chevrotière Mill (1830), houses a crafts school where artisans work in wood and stone.
□ Descendants of horses and cattle brought to New France by Intendant Jean Talon in 1665-71 are raised at a provincial government experimental farm.
□ The ruins of a small fort built by Champlain are on an island in the St. Lawrence River.
□ A third of Deschambault's houses are at least one century old.

CAP-SANTÉ
The site of historic Fort Jacques-Cartier, the last place in New France to capitulate to the English, is marked by a stone at the head of a private road five kilmetres east of the village. The fort held out until Sept. 13, 1760, five days after Montreal surrendered.
□ Cap-Santé's church was built in 1755. A house on the Morisset farm, at the village's outskirts, dates from the early 18th century.

Sturdy Stone Walls, Steep-Slanted Roofs

Jesuit rectory, Batiscan

Manor house, Neuville

Manoir Gorgendière, Deschambault

Stone houses of 17th-century New France were square and sturdy, with single chimneys and steep-slanted roofs. Walls sloped inward to support the roof better. Dormers were added when growing families needed top stories for bedrooms.

Typical of this style of architecture is the Manoir Gorgendière, built in the 1660s in Deschambault. A modification of this style is the Jesuit rectory at Batiscan—rectangular with triple chimneys and eaves flared to protect the walls from the elements. By the 18th century, the projection of the eaves became larger—and was supported by posts. This created a veranda, as in the manor house on Neuville's main street.

Examples of styles favored by 19th-century builders are the steep roof, multipaned dormer windows and two chimneys of Manoir Langlois at Portneuf.

Where New France Was Born, an Ancient City Thrives

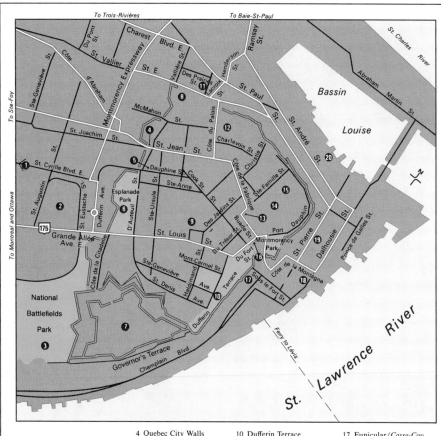

Quebec

1 Grand Théâtre de Québec
2 Hôtel du Parlement (National Assembly)
3 National Battlefields Park
4 Quebec City Walls and Gates
5 Jesuit Chapel
6 Tourist Information
7 The Citadel
8 Artillery Park
9 Ursuline Convent
10 Dufferin Terrace
11 Talon's Vaults
12 Hôtel-Dieu Hospital
13 Basilica of Notre-Dame
14 Quebec Seminary
15 Seminary Museum
16 Fort Museum
17 Funicular/Casse-Cou Stairs
18 Place Royale
19 Museum of Civilization
20 Port of Quebec in the 19th Century

The Château Frontenac, perched on the heights of Cape Diamond, rises majestically above Place Royale, the heart of Quebec City's historic Lower Town.

F ew cities in North America can rival Quebec City in historic riches. The old core of the city—Lower Town by the St. Lawrence and Upper Town atop lofty Cape Diamond—became a United Nations World Heritage Site in 1985. The accolade recognized Quebec's unique status as North America's only walled city north of Mexico and its role as the wellspring of French culture on this continent.

Roughly four centuries of cultural, military and religious activity and achievement imbue Quebec City with an old-world atmosphere. The stout walls and ornate gates that enclose Upper Town evoke the city's stormy past. The steep-roofed stone houses and the narrow, cobbled streets of Lower Town, once the site of Champlain's original 1608 settlement, recapture the spirit of New France during the 17th and 18th centuries.

Artillery Park (8)
This national historic park was used for military purposes from the early 1700s until the 1960s. Three of its landmarks—the Dauphine Redoubt (1712), the Officers' Quarters (1820) and a 1903 foundry (now an interpretation center)—are open to the public.

Basilica of Notre-Dame (13)
The church of Canada's oldest parish (1659) was begun in 1647. The facade was designed by Thomas Baillargé (1791-1859).

The Citadel (7)
This star-shaped fortress, built by the British between 1820 and 1852, comprises 25 buildings, including a 1693 redoubt, a museum, an officers' mess, and the official Quebec residence of the governor-general of Canada.

Dufferin Terrace (10)
This boardwalk, which offers a superb view of the St. Lawrence, runs along the top of the

cliff beside the Château Frontenac Hotel (1893-95 and 1925) and connects with the Governor's Promenade and National Battlefields Park. From the terrace, visitors can take *L'Escalier casse-cou* (breakneck stairs) or the cliffside funicular (17) to the Place Royale and Petit-Champlain quarters in Lower Town, Quebec's oldest district.

The Fort Museum (16)
A sound-and-light show re-creates the six sieges of Quebec, including the Battle of the Plains of Abraham (1759) and the American invasion of 1775.

Grand Théâtre de Québec (1)
This arts complex is the home of the Quebec Symphony Orchestra, Théâtre du Trident and Club musical de Québec.

Hôtel-Dieu Hospital (12)
Founded in 1637, the Hôtel-Dieu is Canada's first hospital. Its museum displays antique furniture, silverware and paintings.

Hôtel du Parlement (2)
Quebec's National Assembly meets in this elegant Renaissance-style building, which was built in 1886. Fifteen bronze statues of Quebec historical figures by Quebec sculptor Louis-Philippe Hébert (1850-1917) adorn the niches on the facade. In the National Assembly Chamber, a painting by Charles Huot (1855-1930) depicts the first parliament of Lower Canada in 1792.

Jesuit Chapel (5)
A reliquary contains some bones of three Canadian martyr saints: Jean de Brébeuf, Charles Garnier and Gabriel Lalemant.

Museum of Civilization (19)
This museum, opened in 1988, is located at the old port of Quebec. Its exhibits highlight five themes: the human body, matter, society, language and thought.

National Battlefields Park (3)
Granite markers in this 100-hectare national historic park describe the course of the Bat-

tle of the Plains of Abraham (Sept. 13, 1759), where British forces under Gen. James Wolfe defeated the French led by the Marquis de Montcalm. A monument to St. Joan of Arc honors those who fought at the Plains of Abraham and at nearby Sainte-Foy the following spring. *O Canada* was reputedly first performed in public on June 24, 1880, in a garden beside the monument.

Place Royale (18)

Once the site of Samuel de Champlain's original 1608 settlement, Place Royale in Lower Town contains about 80 carefully restored 17th- and 18th-century structures. Hazeur House (1684) is the oldest building in Place

The star-shaped Citadel (above), beside the Plains of Abraham, recalls Quebec City's stormy past, while the steep-roofed houses of Lower Town (right) evoke the spirit of 17th- and 18th-century New France.

Royale, and Notre-Dame-des-Victoires Church (1688) is one of the oldest churches in Quebec. Chevalier House (1752), with two adjoining houses, Frérot (1675) and Chenaye de la Garonne (1695), presents cultural and historical exhibits. Information centers in the Bruneau, Fornel and Soudmandre houses describe different aspects of the history of Place Royale. The Royal Battery, built in 1691 and used to defend Quebec in 1759, has been restored as a park.

Port of Quebec in the 19th Century (20)

This national historic park describes Quebec's major role in the timber trade and shipbuilding during the 19th century.

Quebec City Walls and Gates (4)

Lord Dufferin, governor-general of Canada in the 1870s, saved the walls and gates of Quebec from demolition. Today, visitors can stroll along almost five kilometres of the fortifications that enclose Quebec's Upper Town and make it the only walled city north of Mexico. Three of the old city gates —Saint-Louis, Kent and Saint-Jean—were elaborately rebuilt in the late 19th century. Prescott Gate, just below Place d'Armes, was reconstructed in the 1980s.

The Quebec Seminary (above) was founded in 1663 by François de Laval, the first bishop of Quebec.

Seminary Museum (15)

This museum has paintings by Plamondon and Suzor-Côté; silverware by Ranvoyzé and Amiot; and a display of playing card money (legal tender in New France in 1658-1717 and 1729-59). There are guided tours of the nearby Quebec Seminary (14), whose founder, Bishop Laval, is buried here.

Talon's Vaults (11)

In 1688, Intendant Jean Talon built Canada's first commercial brewery, hoping to encourage early colonists to drink beer rather than brandy. Its vaults now contain an interpretation center, with displays about the history of Quebec City.

Ursuline Convent (9)

Founded in 1624, this convent is the oldest in Canada. Its museum has paintings and embroidery, the work of Ursuline nuns who lived here during the 17th, 18th and 19th centuries. Marquis de Montcalm's tomb is within the convent's walls.

Parades, Giant Snowmen and an Icy Canoe Race

Launched by winter-weary Quebecers, the Quebec Winter Carnival doubles the city's population for 10 days in either January or February as the city erupts with street dances, beauty contests, hockey tournaments, winter sports and parades (*above*). Streets are ablaze with lights and decorations during the pre-Lent festival, and fanciful ice sculptures (*left*) are carved in parks and squares. One highlight is a canoe race across the ice-choked St. Lawrence River. The celebrations are presided over by Bonhomme Carnaval, a jovial giant snowman.

A Famous Flagship
Beyond the City Walls

Around Quebec City

In suburbs and towns surrounding Quebec City are a modern aquarium, zoo and university campus—and buildings as historic as those in the walled capital.

Sillery, an elegant residential suburb, has one of Canada's most important historic sites. In front of the Old Jesuit House (c. 1700) are the foundations of an older Jesuit House (1637) and Saint-Michel Church (1644), the first stone church built in New France. Bois de Coulonge park, once the estate of Quebec's lieutenant governors,

Artisan at work, Wendake

UNIVERSITÉ LAVAL
The oldest French-language university in North America (1852) is located at Sainte-Foy. About 26,000 full-time and 10,000 part-time students attend Laval, which is noted for its summer school language programs. Group tours of the campus can be arranged. (Reservations are required.)
□ A museum in the Casault Pavilion houses the university collections. The Koninck Pavilion displays Greek and Inuit artifacts. Pouliot Pavilion has a mural by Jodi Bonnet.

WENDAKE
Visitors to this Indian reserve, founded in 1697, can see Huron artisans make snowshoes much as their ancestors did three centuries ago. A reconstructed Indian village is open to the public from the beginning of May to mid-October.
□ The whitewashed stone chapel of Notre-Dame-de-Lorette was built in 1730 by François Vincent, a Huron who apprenticed to sculptor François-Noël Levasseur. In the chapel are a silver sanctuary lamp (1730) by François Ranvoyzé and a wooden statue of the Madonna sculpted by Levasseur. The Stations of the Cross are by Médard Bourgault.

AQUARIUM DU QUÉBEC
This aquarium at Sainte-Foy which exhibits more than 300 species of fish, has a splendid setting on a cliff overlooking the St. Lawrence River. Sturgeon, northern pike, cod, eel and salmon and tropical fish, such as angelfish and piranha, are displayed in 32 freshwater and 12 saltwater tanks. Snakes, crocodiles, turtles and lizards are exhibited in four terraria. Marine mammals, such as harbor and gray seals, are kept in four outdoor pools.

PONT DE QUÉBEC
This bridge, spanning the St. Lawrence near Quebec City, was one of Canada's most daring—and tragic—engineering feats. Construction began in 1899. A section collapsed in 1907, killing 71 steelworkers. Another 13 died in 1916 when a central section plunged into the river as it was being hoisted into position. When completed, the bridge was the world's longest cantilever span (548 metres). It is still the longest bridge of this kind in North America. Officially inaugurated in 1918 by the Prince of Wales (the future King Edward VIII), the bridge has a railroad track, a highway and a footpath.
□ Nearby is the modern Pont Pierre-Laporte, Canada's longest suspension bridge (668 metres).

Pont de Québec

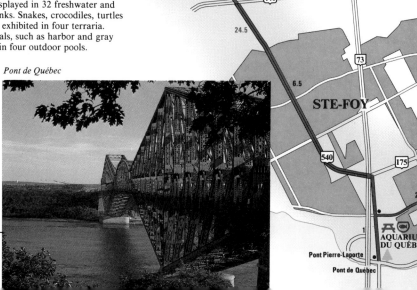

| 0 | 0.5 | 1 | 1.5 | 2 | 2.5 Miles |
| 0 | 1 | 2 | 3 | 4 Kilometres |

delights the eye with flower gardens, trees, lawns and a splendid view of the St. Lawrence River.

The Sainte-Foy campus of Université Laval has distinctive modern architecture: a striking, flat-roofed church has towers and arched windows that give it the appearance of a Gothic cathedral. The Sainte-Foy aquarium overlooks the Pont de Québec, which spans the St. Lawrence.

Rivière du Berger flows through the lush gardens and wooded grounds of the Orsain-ville zoo, where zebras, wapiti and caribou graze.

Charlesbourg, settled in 1659, has a central square with streets radiating from it like spokes.

Jacques Cartier, the first European here, wintered beside the Rivière Saint-Charles in 1535-36. A national historic park at the site has a replica of his flagship, *La Grande Hermine*.

ORSAINVILLE
The local zoo was opened in 1931. Today it exhibits some 45 mammal species, such as polar bears and llamas, and some 120 bird species including condor, peacock and pheasant. The Rivière du Berger, which has been dammed to create pools for sea lions and beavers, flows through the lush grounds where replicas of old Quebec mills and farmhouses stand. Also displayed is a 1865 totem pole carved by British Columbian Indians.

La Grande Hermine,
Cartier-Brébeuf National Historic Park

CARTIER-BRÉBEUF NATIONAL HISTORIC PARK
A 24-metre replica of *La Grande Hermine*, Jacques Cartier's flagship, is the focal point of this 6.5-hectare park. The furnished vessel was built in 1966 using 16th-century tools and methods. Nearby is an interpretive center.
□ Also in the park is an eight-metre granite cross erected in 1935 where Cartier raised a wooden cross four centuries earlier. The park is believed to be the site of a house built in 1626 by Saint Jean de Brébeuf, who is commemorated here with a granite monument. Brébeuf, a Jesuit missionary who was tortured and killed by the Iroquois in 1649, was proclaimed a patron saint of Canada in 1940.

CHARLESBOURG
Intendant Jean Talon's design for this community is still evident after three centuries. Streets radiate from the Trait-Carré (central square), which is dominated by the Saint-Charles-Borromée Church (1825). Talon's design put the church at the center with wedge-shaped farms extending outward from the square. Three historical houses near the Trait-Carré can be visited.
□ The two-story stone L'Heureux House dates from 1684.

L'Heureux House, Charlesbourg

View of the St. Lawrence from Bois de Coulonge

BOIS DE COULONGE
Visitors strolling among flower gardens and stately pines, maples and elms in this park have a fine view of the St. Lawrence River and Ile d'Orléans. Plays, concerts and poetry readings are presented in an outdoor theater.

SILLERY
A two-story stone house built by Jesuits about 1700 is a museum with audiovisual presentations that tell the history of the order in North America. Exhibits include Indian relics, a 1635 weather vane from the Jesuit College, 17th-century axes, historical photographs, books and documents. Nearby are the foundations of a mission, built in 1637, where the first Jesuit in North America, the Rev. Enemond Massé, and six of the Canadian martyr saints once lived.

JARDIN ZOOLOGIQUE DE QUÉBEC

2.5

Orsainville

73

13

358

2

369

CHARLESBOURG

40   5

138

440

CARTIER-BRÉBEUF NAT HIST PK

Rivière   St. Charles

ESTUAIRE DE LA RIVIÈRE ST-CHARLES

QUÉBEC

BASSIN LOUISE

NATIONAL BATTLEFIELDS PARK

BOIS DE COULONGE

175

UNIVERSITÉ LAVAL

Sillery

3

MAISON DES JÉSUITES

1

2

St. Lawrence River

An Idyllic, Fertile Island Where Time Stands Still

Ile d'Orléans

Île d'Orléans is so vital a reminder of Quebec rural life in the 1700s that the entire island has been designated a historic region. Its centuries of isolation in the St. Lawrence River ended in 1935 when a bridge linked it with the north shore. But islanders still cling to the old ways, proud of the churches, houses and farms that have been here for two to three hundred years—symbols of Quebec's historic beginnings.

Jacques Cartier first called the island Bacchus, for the Roman god of wine, be-

SAINTE-PÉTRONILLE
Although this community was established only in 1870, the site had already served as General Wolfe's headquarters in 1759. His force numbered 40,000 and a fleet of 100 ships. From here the British general bombarded Quebec and the Beaupré coast. In the late 19th century, Sainte-Pétronille became a popular resort.
□ Rue Horatio-Walker is named for the famous 19th-century painter. This picturesque street offers a view of Quebec City, Beauport Bay, Montmorency Falls and other sites on the north shore of the St. Lawrence River.

SAINT-PIERRE
The parish church, built in 1716-18, has been restored. The striking altar and sanctuary carvings were created by Charles Vézina in the 1730s. Although the church is no longer used for services, it is open to the public.
□ Saint-Pierre was the home of Quebec's famed singer, composer and writer Félix Leclerc (1914-88).

SAINT-LAURENT
Founded in the late 17th century, Saint-Laurent was an important shipbuilding community in the early 19th century, when as many as 30 "chalouperies" (family shipyards) were located here. As if to remind visitors of its past, the community has a marina—the only one on the island.
□ Saint-Laurent's church (1732) has a pulpit carved by renowned sculptor Jean Gosselin. A nearby plaque marks the site where General Wolfe landed in 1759.
□ Moulin Gosselin (1635), a four-story stone flour mill, has been converted into a restaurant.

Evening, Ile d'Orléans, *by Horatio Walker*

A Painter of Island Scenes

Artist Horatio Walker lived and worked on Ile d'Orléans for more than 50 years. By 1907 he had become the most famous Canadian-born painter, winning international acclaim for his portrayals of the island's farming life.

Walker was born at Listowel, Ont., in 1858, and moved to Toronto at age 15 to work as a staff artist at the Notman and Fraser photographic studios. A few years later he went to New York to study and paint, made several visits to European art galleries, and in 1883 settled on Ile d'Orléans. In 1915 he became president of the Canadian Art Club, and in 1925 president of the Royal Canadian Academy. Walker died at Sainte-Pétronille in 1938.

Artisans at work, Saint-Laurent

cause of its wild grapes, then renamed it in honor of the Duke of Orléans, son of Francis I. Settlement started in 1648 and the first chapel was built five years later. By 1712 there were five prosperous parishes. There are now six, each with a beautiful stone church.

At Sainte-Famille, one of the island's finest churches, built in 1742-48, has superb wood carvings and three bell towers. Some of the island's old barns and sturdy fieldstone houses with their steep, Norman-style roofs are now restaurants, art galleries and theaters.

Potatoes and other vegetables are grown on long, narrow farms, each extending to the river. Orchards yield apples and plums. The island is noted for its strawberries.

Near Saint-Pierre is a splendid view of Montmorency Falls on the north shore of the St. Lawrence. North of Saint-François, visitors can look across the river to Cap-Tourmente and the Laurentians.

Restaurant L'Atre, Sainte-Famille

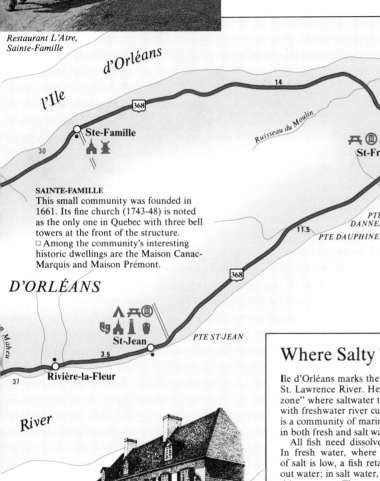

Parish church, Saint-François

SAINTE-FAMILLE
This small community was founded in 1661. Its fine church (1743-48) is noted as the only one in Quebec with three bell towers at the front of the structure.
□ Among the community's interesting historic dwellings are the Maison Canac-Marquis and Maison Prémont.

SAINT-FRANÇOIS
The parish church (1734) has a gilded pulpit carved by Louis-Xavier Leprohon in 1845. The vault and cornice (1832-40) are by André Paquet, the churchwarden's seat (1840) by Thomas Berlinguet, the baptismal fonts (1854) by Olivier Sanson.
□ Late 17th-century buildings include the Imbeau, Roberge and Ginchereau houses, and the École de Fabrique.
□ An observation tower overlooks Argentenay Point and the north shore of the St. Lawrence River.

Mauvide-Genest Manor, Saint-Jean

SAINT-JEAN
Manoir Mauvide-Genest (1734) bears the scars of English cannonballs fired during the 1759 siege of Quebec. The house was built by Jean Mauvide, the first doctor on the Île d'Orléans, who lived here until his death in 1782. The manor now has a restaurant on the ground floor and a museum on the first floor. Behind the manor is Théâtre Paul-Hébert, which is open in the summer months.
□ The presbytery (1879), the Dubuc house (1750) and the parish church (1732-34), which has paintings by Antoine Plamondon (1804-95), are notable buildings worth a visit.

Where Salty Tides Meet Freshwater Currents

Ile d'Orléans marks the tidal divide of the St. Lawrence River. Here is the "brackish zone" where saltwater tides meet and mix with freshwater river currents. In the zone is a community of marine life that can live in both fresh and salt water.

All fish need dissolved salts to survive. In fresh water, where the concentration of salt is low, a fish retains salt and keeps out water; in salt water, a fish must reverse this process. The passage through the brackish zone is impossible for most fish. A fish swimming from fresh to salt water could take in too much salt and shrivel. In salt water, the fish could take in too much water and become bloated. In the brackish zone, certain fish overcome these problems by eliminating excess salt when they are in the ocean, and by retaining salt in the river. This ability to adapt is common to the sea-run brook trout, stickleback, lamprey and American eel.

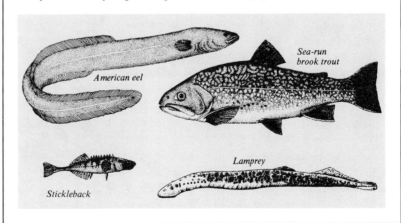

American eel

Sea-run brook trout

Stickleback

Lamprey

A Faith-Healing Shrine on the Broad Beaupré Coast

North Shore, St. Lawrence River

The Beaupré Coast—a broad plain on the north shore of the St. Lawrence River between Quebec City and Cap-Tourmente—is most famous for a faith-healing shrine in Sainte-Anne-de-Beaupré. In 1658 Etienne Lessard, one of the town's early settlers, built a chapel dedicated to Saint Anne. Through the years, the chapel's reputation as the source of miraculous cures grew. As early as 1665, Marie de l'Incarnation, the founder of Quebec's Ursuline Convent, wrote: "Seven leagues from here is . . . a

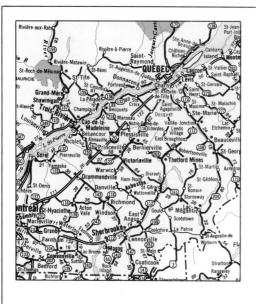

Where Oven-Fresh Bread is Still Baked Outdoors

Bread is still baked in two old outdoor ovens—*les fours Turgeon*—alongside the highway in Château-Richer. Outdoor ovens, once common in Quebec villages, were often shared by several families to bake bread, beans and tourtières. The ovens—traditionally made of hard-packed earth or clay, or of stones or bricks—burned wood. Wooden roofs keep off rain and snow.

Old masonry root cellars, embedded in steep slopes along the north side of the road through Château-Richer and L'Ange-Gardien, can also be seen. Some of the cellars are still used for winter storage of vegetables.

Outdoor oven, Château-Richer

MONTMORENCY FALLS
The 83-metre-high falls are about 30 metres higher than Niagara Falls. Roughly 35,000 litres of water per second flow over the falls, but this amount can swell to 125,000 litres during the spring runoff. A huge cone of ice, known as the "sugar loaf," forms at the base of the falls in winter. There are lookouts and picnic grounds at both the summit and the base of the falls.

□ Manoir Montmorency, built in 1781 by Sir Frederick Haldimand, then Governor-General of Canada, offers a superb view of the falls. The manor is now a hotel, but its gardens and the nearby Sainte-Marie Chapel (1904) are open to the public.

Manoir Montmorency

Montmorency Falls

BEAUPORT
This community of more than 60,000, which now is part of greater Quebec City, was the first settlement on the Beaupré Coast (1634). An outstanding local historic house is the Norman-style Maison-Bellanger-Girardin. The present structure, built between 1722 and 1735 on the site of an earlier (1673) timber dwelling, serves as a local art gallery.

L'ANGE-GARDIEN
Chapels commemorate the La Berge and Brisson families who came here in the 1660s. Part of the La Berge House, a private residence, is thought to date from the 1670s. A monument is at the site of the Trudelle House in which the town's first Mass was celebrated in 1664.

0 .5 1 1.5 2 2.5 Miles
0 1 2 3 4 Kilometres

church of Saint Anne [where] paralytics walk, the blind recover their sight, and the sick, whatever be their malady, recover their health." Today the shrine attracts more than 1.5 million pilgrims each year.

The Beaupré Coast was first settled in the first half of the 17th century. Some of the region's earliest structures still survive at Château-Richer, L'Ange-Gardien and other local villages. Along Highway 360, visitors can glimpse many vestiges of the past—wayside chapels, root cellars and outdoor ovens.

Cross-country skiing, Parc du Mont-Sainte-Anne

But there is more to the Beaupré region than the reminders of its fascinating past. Its popular attractions include Montmorency Falls, which is 30 metres higher than Niagara Falls, and Cap-Tourmente, a wildlife sanctuary where thousands of migrating geese gather in spring and autumn. There is also Parc du Mont-Sainte-Anne, where sports enthusiasts can enjoy year-round recreational opportunities.

SAINTE-ANNE-DE-BEAUPRÉ
The town's famous shrine has attracted pilgrims since the mid-17th century. Many arrive during the week before the saint's feast day on July 28.
□ The immense Basilica of Sainte-Anne-de-Beaupré, built in the mid-1920s, combines Romanesque and Gothic architectural elements. Its interior is graced with beautiful stained glass windows and a statue of the saint, which stands on a marble pedestal atop an onyx shaft.
□ The Memorial Chapel (1878) contains a 1702 altar carved by Charles Vézina, an 1807 pulpit by Thomas Baillargé and other treasures.
□ The Scala Santa chapel (1871) has a replica of the 28 steps that Christ ascended when he appeared before Pontius Pilate.
□ The hillside Chemin de la Croix (the Way of the Cross) is lined with life-size, cast-iron statues. In summer, torchlight processions are held here.
□ The Historial displays waxwork tableaux depicting the life of Saint Anne.

CHÂTEAU-RICHER
Some of the dwellings here—the Côté, Caughon, Simard and Gravel houses—are nearly as old as this town, which was founded in 1640.
Moulin du Petit Pré (1695) houses an interpretive center that contains displays about the history of the Beaupré Coast.

Raccoons

PARC DU MONT-STE-ANNE

◆∧⩽☀⌠‼◉⌇⚊

▲ Mont Ste-Anne

PARC DU MONT-SAINTE-ANNE
This year-round park is a prime ski area. There are 40 downhill runs, which are registered on the World Cup circuit, and 181 kilometres of cross-country ski trails. The park is more than a winter sports paradise. In summer visitors can explore its hiking trails and cycling paths. An 800-metre cable car ride climbs to the summit, where there is a magnificent view of the surrounding region.

SAINT-JOACHIM
A house called La Petite Ferme, once Bishop François de Laval's seigneurial manor, is on the site of a farm operated by Samuel de Champlain in 1626.
□ The Saint-Joachim parish church (1779) has wood sculptures by François and Thomas Baillargé.

Basilica of Sainte-Anne-de-Beaupré

CHUTES STE-ANNE ☀⌐

Ste-Anne-de-Beaupré-Ouest

Beaupré

St-Joachim

Cap-Tourmente

CAP TOURMENTE NAT WILDLIFE AREA

Ste-Anne-de-Beaupré
◆∧⌂⚑🏛☀⛾🀰

St. Lawrence **River**

Sault-à-la-Puce

Château-Richer
⛯🀰⛾⚓⚊

ÎLE D'ORLÉANS

Snow geese, Cap-Tourmente National Wildlife Area

La Petite Ferme, Saint-Joachim

CAP TOURMENTE NATIONAL WILDLIFE AREA
A trail leads to a cliff where visitors can observe some 100,000 snow geese dappling the St. Lawrence River for six weeks in spring and fall. Geese stop at Cap-Tourmente on their migration between breeding grounds on Baffin Island and wintering grounds in Virginia and North Carolina. At low tide they feed on bulrushes that grow in the mud flats. Some 250 other bird species, including Canada geese, are also found in the sanctuary. An interpretive center gives the life history and habits of snow geese and local songbirds. Naturalists conduct walks through the wildlife area. A trail leads to the summit of Cap-Tourmente.

Where the Wild Laurentians Overlook a Quaint Town and Its Broad Bay

North Shore, St. Lawrence River

Charlevoix County—on the north shore of the St. Lawrence between Baie-Saint-Paul and Baie-Sainte-Catherine—is a region of stunning beauty. Its rugged hills and coast, fertile river valleys, and picturesque fishing and farming communities have long inspired artists—and have been an irresistible lure to tourists.

Baie-Saint-Paul's narrow streets and fieldstone houses were captured on canvas by Clarence Gagnon, Marc-Aurèle Fortin and

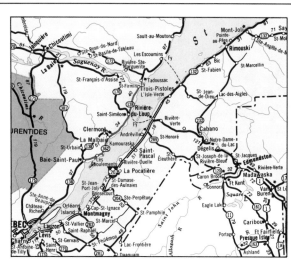

Clarence Gagnon's Evening on the North Shore, *painted in 1916 at Baie-Saint-Paul*

La Maison Croche,
Saint-Bernard-sur-Mer, Île aux Coudres

ÎLE AUX COUDRES

Time seems to have stopped on Île aux Coudres. The metre-thick stone walls of its farmhouses, the lazy look of its windmills, the pace and the peace of this little island keep it a living miniature of 18th-century New France. Eleven kilometres by three, Île aux Coudres is linked by ferry with Saint-Joseph-de-la-Rive on the north shore.
□ Jacques Cartier named the island for its hazel trees. (Île aux Coudres means "hazel island.") The French explorer landed here on September 7, 1534 and celebrated mass—the first on Canadian soil—on the same day.
□ A monument at Saint-Bernard-sur-Mer commemorates Cartier's arrival. The community's church has a painting that depicts the same event. La Maison Croche (the crooked house) is a local curiosity.
□ At Saint-Louis, the Musée de l'Isle-aux-Coudres describes local history and customs. Les Moulins de l'Île preserves a watermill (1824), a windmill (1836), as well as a blacksmith shop and the miller's house. Guides escort visitors around the site. Another museum—Musée Les Voitures d'Eau—tells the story of inshore navigation on the St. Lawrence.
□ The road that crosses the Île aux Coudres between Saint-Bernard and La Baleine is called the chemin de la Tourbière (the peat bog road). The peat bogs on either side of the road are "harvested"—often to a depth of six metres—with vacuum equipment.

BAIE-SAINT-PAUL

A superb setting, between two promontories at the mouth of the Rivière du Gouffre and opposite Île aux Coudres, has made Baie-Saint-Paul a favorite subject for Clarence Gagnon (1881-1942), Marc-Aurèle Fortin (1888-1970), and other painters. (After Montreal and Quebec City, the Baie-Saint-Paul area is the most frequently depicted site in Quebec among the paintings in the National Gallery of Canada.)
□ Every year artists flock here to paint and photograph its picturesque streets and houses, as well as the surrounding farmland and high hills. (Rising about 1,200 metres, the peaks just inland from Baie-Saint-Paul are the highest in the Laurentians.) The town's numerous galleries give visitors plenty of opportunity to discover the work of well-known and budding local artists.
□ Gliding (particularly at summer's end) and sailboarding (at high tide) are popular local recreations. The surrounding area abounds in cycling paths, hiking paths, picnic sites and lookouts.

Arctic char (Quebec red trout)

Windmill, Île aux Coudres

other famous painters. Wild, broken Laurentian hills that overlook the town and its broad bay are softened by green farmland in the valley of the Rivière du Gouffre.

Guarding the entrance to Baie-Saint-Paul is a haven of tranquillity and tradition—Île aux Coudres. In 1535 Jacques Cartier celebrated Canada's first Mass on this island. New France seems to live on in its stone windmills, wayside chapels and apple and plum orchards.

La Malbaie, North America's oldest resort, has long attracted visitors. (The first were Scottish soldiers who came to fish in the area during the late 1760s.) The town is dominated by the Manoir Richelieu. This long-established grand hotel overlooks the St. Lawrence, its opposite shore merely a narrow blue line on the horizon.

The coast is more rugged at Saint-Siméon, where craggy granite cliffs line the river. Here Highway 138 turns inland, climbs the Laurentians and skirts sparkling lakes amid forests of cedar and white spruce.

Devastating Tremors That Toppled a Mountain

In 1663 a series of devastating earthquakes shook New France. An Ursuline nun in Quebec wrote of "a horrible confusion of overturning furniture, falling stones, parting floors, and splitting walls." Frightened Indians believed that "the streams were full of firewater and the forests were drunk."

The first quake, one of the worst ever in North America, was centered near the mouth of the Saguenay River. Thirty-two more followed during the next seven months, transforming the countryside. Waterfalls vanished, forests were destroyed, crevices opened and swallowed up whole houses. The face of a mountain toppled into the St. Lawrence River near the present-day town of Les Eboulements (French for landslides).

Many colonists believed the tremors were the result of God's displeasure, and priests were kept busy day and night with confessions. Dishonest fur traders cleaned up their business dealings, and the liquor trade was abolished. When the earthquakes finally ended, not one person had been killed or injured—and many penitents no doubt returned to their sinful ways.

BAIE-SAINTE-CATHERINE

The Pointe-Noire rest area on Highway 138 offers a superb view of the Saguenay fjord and the vast St. Lawrence River. From an observation tower here, visitors can also see beluga and other species of whales that live in the offshore waters. There is an interpretive center and a nature trail.

Brown-headed cowbird

SAINT-SIMÉON

At Les Palissades, a provincial nature appreciation center northwest of here, are glacial lakes, waterfalls and 244-metre-high jagged cliffs with magnificent views of the valley of Rivière Noire.

PORT-AU-PERSIL

A brook cascades into this small harbor, dominated at low tide by a rocky islet. The waterfall is a favorite playground of children. Thousands annually visit this charming hamlet.

Port-au-Persil

LA MALBAIE

Champlain came here in 1608, anchored at high tide, found his ship hard aground by morning, and called the place *malle baye* (bad bay). Many visitors know the village as Murray Bay.
□ A local museum honors Laure Conan, Canada's first woman novelist of renown. The author of *L'Oublié*, whose real name was Félicité Angers, was born here in 1845.

POINTE-AU-PIC

Perched on a 213-metre cliff is the imposing Manoir Richelieu (c. 1910), one of Quebec's oldest resort hotels. Scores of splendid old summer homes are in this village.
□ The grave of William Hume Blake, a lawyer who wrote *Brown Waters, In a Fishing Village,* and *A Fisherman's Creed,* is in the yard of the Murray Bay Protestant Church.

Saguenay River

Tadoussac

138

PTE NOIRE
PTE AUX VACHES

Baie-Ste-Catherine
BAIE STE-CATHERINE
PTE AUX ALOUETTES

Rivière aux Canards

Pointe-au-Bouleau

138

PTE AU BOULEAU

Lac du Basque
25.5

34.5

CAP DU BASQUE

CAP DU NID AUX CORBEAUX

St. Lawrence River

BAIE DES ROCHERS

Baie-des-Rochers
Lac de la Baie des Rochers

LES PALISSADES

Rivière du Port aux Quilles

Port-aux-Quilles

CAP DE LA TÊTE AU CHIEN

13

Rivière Noire

170

9

PORT AUX QUILLES

Rivière-Noire

St-Siméon

St-Chrétien
5

Ferry to Rivière-du-Loup

Port-au-Persil
PORT AU PERSIL

12 138

Anse-au-Saumon

Port-au-Saumon

PTE DES ROCHERS

Bas-de-l'Anse
35

Mont-Murray 13

St-Fidèle-de-Mont-Murray

PORT AU SAUMON

GROS CAP À L'AIGLE

La Malbaie
5

4.5
LA MALBAIE

Cap-à-l'Aigle

Pointe-au-Pic
8.5

362

St. Lawrence River

Irénée
9

CAP DE LA CORNEILLE

Cap-aux-Oies
CAP AUX OIES

Wood-Carvers and Famous Sons of an Island-Dotted Shoreline

South Shore, St. Lawrence River

The road between Lévis and Rimouski climbs and dips along the rugged south shore of the island-dotted St. Lawrence River. On the north shore is the blue outline of the Laurentian hills.

Many islands, including Ile aux Grues, Ile du Bic and Les Pèlerins, are frequented by thousands of seabirds and shorebirds. Grosse Ile was a 19th-century immigrant quarantine station. On Ile aux Basques are furnaces used by 16th-century Basque fishermen to extract whale oil.

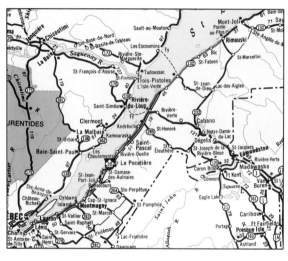

L'ISLET-SUR-MER
Almost three centuries of seafarers born and raised here have earned this village the name *la patrie des marins,* the sailors' homeland. The marine museum honors Capt. Joseph-Elzéar Bernier (1852-1934), a native son whose seven voyages between 1904 and 1925 established Canada's sovereignty over the Arctic islands. An octant (a navigational instrument) from his ship *Arctic* is in the museum. A monument to Bernier in a park next to the museum is an aluminum globe on which his Arctic voyages are indicated.

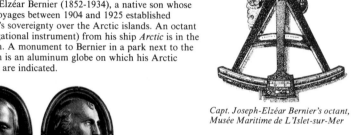

Capt. Joseph-Elzéar Bernier's octant, Musée Maritime de L'Islet-sur-Mer

Wood carvings of St. Paul and St. Peter, Saint-Romuald-d'Etchemin Church

SAINT-ROMUALD-D'ETCHEMIN
The church (1855) contains *Le Père Jean de Brébeuf évangélisant deux jeunes Indiens* and other works by local sculptor Lauréat Vallières, who died here in 1973. Wood carvings of St. Peter and St. Paul by Ferdinand Villeneuve and Louis Saint-Hilaire decorate the ornate wooden pulpit.

BERTHIER-SUR-MER
A lookout affords a view of the St. Lawrence River, Grosse Ile and Ile de Bellechasse. A monument on Grosse Ile marks where an immigrant quarantine station was established during an 1832 cholera epidemic. Some 5,000 Irish immigrants died there during an outbreak of typhus in 1847-48.
□ The town's beach is one of the finest on the south shore of the St. Lawrence River.

LÉVIS
A walkway and a ferry service (in operation since 1816) link Lévis and Quebec City. The terrace along the St. Lawrence at Lévis provides a superb view of the river and the provincial capital on the opposite shore.
□ Maison Alphonse-Desjardins (1882-84), the home of the founder of the *caisse populaire* (credit union) movement in Quebec, is open to the public. An interpretive center explains Desjardins' life and work.
□ At nearby Lauzon, a national historic site preserves Fort No. 1, one of three local fortifications built between 1865 and 1872.

MONTMAGNY
The restored two-story wooden Manoir Couillard-Dupuis, built in 1789, contains a tourist information center and a handicrafts shop. A feature of the house is a large stone bread oven.
□ Visitors can also inspect the house of Sir Etienne-Paschal Taché (1795-1865), prime minister of the Province of Canada (1856-57 and 1864-65) and a Father of Confederation. He was born in Montmagny and practiced medicine here. The town memorialized Taché with a granite statue by the famous wood-carver Jean-Julien Bourgault of Saint-Jean-Port-Joli.
□ The offshore Île aux Grues and Île aux Oies are a sanctuary for as many as 200,000 snow geese in spring. (Mallard, snipe and blue-winged teal can also be seen on the islands.) Montmagny honors its migratory visitors with a Snow Goose Festival in October.

Manoir Couillard-Dupuis, Montmagny

A wood-carver in his studio, Saint-Jean-Port-Joli

(Map labels:)
QUÉBEC · St-Romuald-D'Étchemin · Lévis · Lauzon · ÎLE D'ORLÉANS · St-David-de-l'Auberivière · Beaumont · St-Michel-de-Bellechasse · St-Vallier · Berthier-sur-Mer · St-François-Montmagny · Montmagny · ÎLE AUX GRUES · Cap-St-Ignace · St-Jean-Port-Joli · L'Islet-sur-Mer · L'Islet · Trois-Saumons · Village-des-Aulnaies · St-Jean-Port-Joli · St-Roch-des-Aulnaies · La Poca · St-Gab · Kamoura · Rivi Ou

Sandy beaches line many of the area's bays and coves. At Rivière-du-Loup visitors can picnic beside a 38-metre waterfall.

This region is famous for its wood-carvers, many of whom live in Saint-Jean-Port-Joli. They follow a tradition that goes back three centuries in Quebec. Local churches, museums and other public buildings are decorated with their meticulous carvings.

Throughout this region, outstanding local figures are honored. At L'Islet-sur-Mer, for example, the achievement of Arctic explorer Capt. Joseph-Elzéar Bernier is commemorated at a museum in L'Islet-sur-Mer. At Lévis, the restored residence of Alphonse Desjardins, journalist and founder of Quebec's *caisse populaire* movement, is an interpretive center to his life and work. And at Montmagny, the residence of the 19th-century politician Sir Etienne-Paschal Taché is also open to the public.

Weir traps for eels, Kamouraska

KAMOURASKA

In the St. Lawrence River here eels are caught in weir traps—rows of stakes that divert the fish into enclosures where they are netted.
□ Large colonies of black-crowned night herons occupy the six islands opposite Kamouraska. At low tide, visitors can walk from the village to the islands.
□ Two points of interest are the local museum, housed in an old convent, and an earthwork dike (*L'Aboiteau*), which protects local farmland from river flooding.

ÎLE DU BIC

As many as 8,000 eider ducks nest on islands in the St. Lawrence River here; sea otters and harbor and harp seals sun on reefs and rocky shores.
□ Ile du Massacre, where 200 Micmacs were trapped and slaughtered by Iroquois in 1533, is accessible at low tide. Visitors can see the cave in which the Micmacs hid.

SAINT-JEAN-PORT-JOLI

This town is the wood-carving capital of Quebec. Some 50 studios (many are open to the public) display life-size religious and historical figures, sculptured murals, Quebec landscapes, miniature birds and animals, abstract forms, and some of the finest miniature sailboats in the world. Many sculptures have rustic themes: a trapper on snowshoes, a logger swinging an ax, the ever-popular habitant. Other artists and craftsmen produce copper-enamel art, jewelry and leather goods.

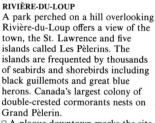

Double-crested cormorants

RIMOUSKI

This city (pop. 33,000), the administrative and cultural center for eastern Quebec, is built on three levels, rising from the banks of the St. Lawrence to a terrace that overlooks the area.
□ The multipurpose marina at Rimouski-Est is the scene of major events, including a jazz festival and an international film festival, both held in September.
□ Art, historical and scientific exhibitions are presented in the bright, open galleries of the Rimouski Regional Museum, housed in an old, converted church. Among the artists past and present whose works appear here are Antoine Plamondon, Charles Huot, Rodolphe Duguay, and Frédéric Taylor.

TROIS-PISTOLES

On Île aux Basques in the St. Lawrence River are the restored remains of three stone furnaces that early Basque whalers used to convert blubber to oil. A monument on the island and a plaque at Trois-Pistoles commemorate the Basques who hunted baleen whales at the mouth of the Saguenay River in the 1500s.
□ Île aux Basques and the two Razade islands are a sanctuary where double-crested cormorants may be photographed.

A Tradition Revived

Most of the wood carving in Saint-Jean-Port-Joli's church (1779) dates from the late 18th and early 19th centuries. But the magnificent pulpit, installed in 1937, is the work of the Bourgault brothers. The tradition they follow goes back to the 1670s when Bishop Laval encouraged the teaching of arts and crafts. For two centuries artists in wood were in demand for decorating public buildings. Wood carving declined with the mass production of furniture and building materials but farmers and seamen kept it alive as a pastime.

One seaman, Médard Bourgault, opened a studio in 1936, with his brothers André and Jean-Julien. Today their work can be seen at the Musée des Anciens Canadiens, Saint-Jean-Port-Joli. Médard's *Stations of the Cross* is at the L'Islet-sur-Mer Church, and Jean-Julien's *Town Council* is at l'Auberge du Faubourg, Saint-Jean-Port-Joli.

RIVIÈRE-DU-LOUP

A park perched on a hill overlooking Rivière-du-Loup offers a view of the town, the St. Lawrence and five islands called Les Pèlerins. The islands are frequented by thousands of seabirds and shorebirds including black guillemots and great blue herons. Canada's largest colony of double-crested cormorants nests on Grand Pèlerin.
□ A plaque downtown marks the site of the house in which the Most Rev. Alexandre-Antonin Taché was born in 1823. He was sent to the Red River as a missionary in 1845 and became bishop of St. Boniface, Man., in 1853. Deeply sympathetic to the Métis, Taché was influential in restoring order after the Red River Rebellion in 1870.

St. Lawrence River near Rivière-du-Loup

A Sportsman's Paradise in Cartier's 'Saguenay Kingdom'

Lac Saint-Jean

Rich, fertile plains and ancient hills border 1,002-square-kilometre Lac Saint-Jean. It is a part of the immense territory on which Jacques Cartier conferred the name "Saguenay Kingdom," but it is perhaps the most impressive part, the richest in contrasts.

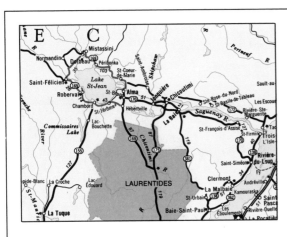

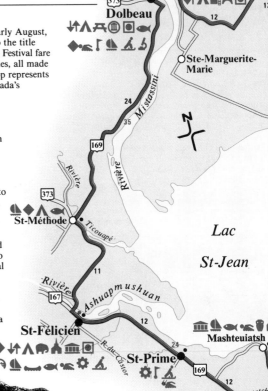

MISTASSINI
A blueberry festival, held in early August, celebrates Mistassini's claim to the title of the world's blueberry capital. Festival fare includes tempting pies and wines, all made from blueberries. The local crop represents a significant proportion of Canada's blueberry production.

DOLBEAU
A monument honors the Rev. Jean Dolbeau, who came here as a missionary to the Montagnais Indians in 1615—more than 300 years before the founding of the town. Dolbeau owes its existence to the local Domtar newsprint plant, which opened in 1927.
□ Centre Astro (affiliated with the Observatoire de Paris) comprises an auditorium, an observatory and a natural science pavilion. Open to the public, it presents astronomical shows (on clear nights) and scientific exhibitions.
□ For ten rip-roaring days in July, Dolbeau hosts a western festival, with a rodeo, riding contests and a barbecue.

Zoological Garden, Saint-Félicien

Yaks, Zoological Garden of Saint-Félicien

Rose-breasted grosbeak

SAINT-FÉLICIEN
This pulp-and-paper center (pop. 9,300) lies on the Rivière Ashuapmushuan, a major spawning ground for landlocked salmon.
□ At the 400-hectare Saint-Félicien zoo, visitors can ride on a small train with screened cars through natural settings where moose and other creatures roam freely. The zoo has about 200 different species of North American and exotic birds, reptiles and animals. Other attractions on the grounds of the zoo include a visitors' center, nature trails and reconstructions of a logging camp, a fur-trading post and an Indian village.
□ Saint-Félicien is the gateway to the mines and forests of the Chibougamau region to the northwest. Highway 167 crosses this vast area, which contains the 11,000-square-kilometre Ashuapmushuan wildlife reserve.

MASHTEUIATSH (POINTE-BLEUE)
At a local museum, the Montagnais Indians bring their ancient culture to life through displays of costumes, artifacts and archaeological finds, as well as art exhibitions, films and slide presentations.

ROBERVAL
The only city (pop. 11,000) on Lac Saint-Jean, Roberval is a regional commercial and tourism center. The local maritime museum focuses on the history of the lake. Half-day lake cruises are available on *Le Cépal,* a sailing catamaran.
□ In July, swimmers from more than a dozen countries gather at Roberval to compete in the 64-kilometre International Crossing of Lac Saint-Jean. The swim (between Roberval and Péribonka, and back again) was first held in 1955 and has become a long-distance classic. It concludes Roberval's eight-day summer festival, the Huitaine de gaieté.

0 1 2 3 4 5 Miles

0 2 4 6 8 Kilometres

The almost circular lake is an ancient glacial trough that was once an arm of the sea. The Péribonca, largest of the rivers that cascade down from the Laurentians to feed Lac Saint-Jean, is 494 kilometres long. The Métabetchouane is 142; the Ashuapmushuan, 178; and the Mistassini, 286. All this tumbling water, temporarily stilled by the lake, soon rushes through two channels worn in the bedrock of the Canadian Shield. Then the two become one: the seething, torrential Saguenay.

A tour around the lake crosses all these rivers. At the western end of the lake the road leads to Saint-Félicien, gateway to the vast Ashuapmushuan and Mistassini reserves, then bends northeast toward the logging town of Mistassini.

The north shore, on the edge of the Laurentian hills, is strewn with granite outcrops and glacial debris as high as three-story buildings. The south shore is gently rolling and fertile. Here, good pastures and clear waters support prosperous dairy farms. In unspoiled towns such as Hébertville (where settlement of the region began in 1849), charming 19th-century houses hug the narrow streets.

For the sportsman, Lac Saint-Jean is a region of fine fishing and hunting, of hiking, climbing and horseback riding. The lake provides some of the province's best fishing for landlocked salmon. Here and there are sparkling waterfalls and lakeside recreation areas. And everywhere is the wild beauty of the countryside.

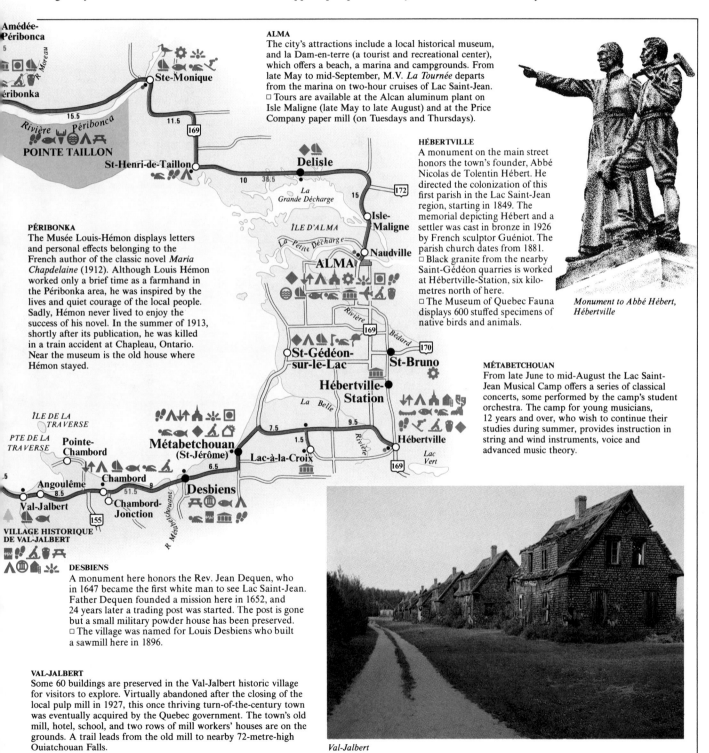

ALMA
The city's attractions include a local historical museum, and la Dam-en-terre (a tourist and recreational center), which offers a beach, a marina and campgrounds. From late May to mid-September, M.V. *La Tournée* departs from the marina on two-hour cruises of Lac Saint-Jean.
□ Tours are available at the Alcan aluminum plant on Isle Maligne (late May to late August) and at the Price Company paper mill (on Tuesdays and Thursdays).

HÉBERTVILLE
A monument on the main street honors the town's founder, Abbé Nicolas de Tolentin Hébert. He directed the colonization of this first parish in the Lac Saint-Jean region, starting in 1849. The memorial depicting Hébert and a settler was cast in bronze in 1926 by French sculptor Guéniot. The parish church dates from 1881.
□ Black granite from the nearby Saint-Gédéon quarries is worked at Hébertville-Station, six kilometres north of here.
□ The Museum of Quebec Fauna displays 600 stuffed specimens of native birds and animals.

Monument to Abbé Hébert, Hébertville

PÉRIBONKA
The Musée Louis-Hémon displays letters and personal effects belonging to the French author of the classic novel *Maria Chapdelaine* (1912). Although Louis Hémon worked only a brief time as a farmhand in the Péribonka area, he was inspired by the lives and quiet courage of the local people. Sadly, Hémon never lived to enjoy the success of his novel. In the summer of 1913, shortly after its publication, he was killed in a train accident at Chapleau, Ontario. Near the museum is the old house where Hémon stayed.

MÉTABETCHOUAN
From late June to mid-August the Lac Saint-Jean Musical Camp offers a series of classical concerts, some performed by the camp's student orchestra. The camp for young musicians, 12 years and over, who wish to continue their studies during summer, provides instruction in string and wind instruments, voice and advanced music theory.

VILLAGE HISTORIQUE DE VAL-JALBERT

DESBIENS
A monument here honors the Rev. Jean Dequen, who in 1647 became the first white man to see Lac Saint-Jean. Father Dequen founded a mission here in 1652, and 24 years later a trading post was started. The post is gone but a small military powder house has been preserved.
□ The village was named for Louis Desbiens who built a sawmill here in 1896.

VAL-JALBERT
Some 60 buildings are preserved in the Val-Jalbert historic village for visitors to explore. Virtually abandoned after the closing of the local pulp mill in 1927, this once thriving turn-of-the-century town was eventually acquired by the Quebec government. The town's old mill, hotel, school, and two rows of mill workers' houses are on the grounds. A trail leads from the old mill to nearby 72-metre-high Ouiatchouan Falls.

Val-Jalbert

A Mighty 'Fjord'
Where the Sea Surges Inland

Saguenay River

For centuries the Saguenay River was the only gateway to the furs and forests of the region around Lac Saint-Jean. Today Highway 170, leading to the bustling centers of Chicoutimi and Jonquière, parallels the Saguenay River. From the road the spectacular grandeur of its steep south bank can be glimpsed.

The Saguenay once leaped and plunged for 56 kilometres of rapids and falls from Lac Saint-Jean to Chicoutimi, dropping more than 90 metres along the way. Now

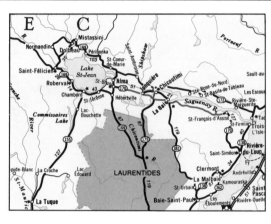

Notre-Dame-de-Fatima Church,
Jonquière

JONQUIÈRE
This industrial center (pop. 60,354) was formed with the amalgamation of Arvida, Jonquière and Kenogami municipalities and the village of Jonquière in 1975. Its key industries are aluminum, and pulp and paper (plant tours are available).
□ The Aluminum Bridge, which spans the Saguenay, was the first of its kind in the world when it was erected in 1950.
□ Nearby Shipshaw Dam was built during the Second World War to increase the power supply for aluminum smelting. Tours are available.
□ Notre-Dame-de-Fatima Church is shaped like a tepee split vertically, the two halves slightly offset but joined with modern stained-glass windows created by Chicoutimi artist Jean-Guy Barbeau.

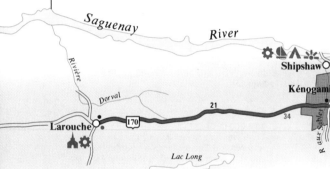

LAROUCHE
This farming and industrial village was founded in 1921 after a sawmill was established here. Saint-Gérard-Majella Church, built in 1960, is distinctively modern in architecture but traditional in form. The roof, sweeping up in two curved planes to its highest point above the altar, is supported by white concrete walls. They describe four quarter-arcs to form the conventional cross-shaped ground plan.

CHICOUTIMI
This city of more than 60,000 is situated at the junction of the Chicoutimi and Saguenay rivers, where deep-water navigation ends.
□ Now the hub of the Saguenay-Lac Saint-Jean region, Chicoutimi started as a trading post in the 17th century. It began to develop in 1842, when Peter McLeod, Jr., built a local sawmill here. McLeod's gold watch and other possessions are displayed at the Saguenay-Lac Saint-Jean Museum.
□ The Old Pulp Company (*La Pulperie*), which operated from 1896 until 1930, is the oldest industrial site of its kind in Quebec. The site has an interpretive center and guided tours.
□ Each year Chicoutimi celebrates the mid-19th-century settlement of the region. During the eight-day *Carnaval-Souvenir* in February, local people put on period costumes and take part in sports contests, dances, plays and parades.

Peter McLeod's gold watch,
Saguenay Museum,
Chicoutimi

Carnaval-Souvenir, Chicoutimi

modern hydroelectric dams have tamed the mighty torrent.

Between Chicoutimi—an inland seaport and a chief city of the region—and the St. Lawrence River the Saguenay is a "fjord," an ice age relic by which the sea penetrates deep into the continent. In the fjord, cold seawater from the St. Lawrence pushes under warmer freshwater from Lac Saint-Jean and the Saguenay becomes a two-level river: on top it is warm and slightly saline; the lower level is icy and almost as salty as the sea itself. The river's depth, which averages 240 metres, makes the waters appear deep amber or black. Much of the fjord is flanked by barren, ash-colored rocks. Here and there are patches of vegetation: a clump of birches, a lone spruce, a slender poplar.

Near L'Anse-Saint-Jean a trail leads to the top of the Cap Trinité, some 500 metres above the water. It offers an impressive view of the Saguenay. Beyond the river's austere cliffs, the forested Laurentians—ancient hills that cradle some 1,500 lakes and 700 rivers—seem to undulate to the ends of the earth.

Monument to pioneers, La Baie

LA BAIE
This industrial center—a merger of Bagotville, Port-Alfred and Grande Baie—has a deep-water port at the head of Baie des Ha! Ha! on the Saguenay. (The bay's name derives from the French *ha,ha!*, which once meant dead end.) Oceangoing freighters arrive with bauxite for La Baie's aluminum smelter and depart with local newsprint.
□ A stone statue of a settler commemorates La Baie's 19th-century pioneers.

L'ANSE-SAINT-JEAN
This picturesque agricultural village is on a bay where Rivière Saint-Jean flows into the Saguenay. Before the first colonists arrived here in 1838, L'Anse-Saint-Jean was the site of an Indian mission.
□ In the village, a 37-metre covered bridge spans Rivière Saint-Jean. There are picnic areas and lookouts beside waterfalls on the river.

L'Anse-Saint-Jean

[Map showing the Saguenay River region with labels: Ste-Rose-du-Nord, CAP DE L'EST, Saguenay River, CAP TRINITÉ, BAIE ÉTERNITÉ, CAP ÉTERNITÉ, L'Anse-Saint-Jean, POINTE AU BOEUF, Lac à la Croix, Lac Otis, Rivière Éternité, PARC DU SAGUENAY, Anse St-Jean, R Petit Saguenay, Petit-Saguenay, Rivière-Eternité, St-Félix-d'Otis, Lac à la Truite, Rivière St-Jean, L'Anse-St-Jean, R du Cabanage, 25, 19, 16.5, 49.5, 5.5, 170, 14]

PARC DU SAGUENAY
This 288-square-kilometre provincial park occupies strips of land on either side of the Saguenay River. Rivière Éternité has a visitors' center and is one of the main access points for hikers and campers wishing to explore the park's interior.
□ From L'Anse-Saint-Jean, a hiking trail leads along the river to Cap Éternité (549 metres high) and Cap Trinité (518 metres), which overlook the Saguenay fjord. Cap Trinité is the site of a huge statue of Our Lady of the Saguenay, erected in 1881.

The Barber-Painter of Chicoutimi

In 1957 Arthur Villeneuve (1910-90), a Chicoutimi barber for 31 years, decided to become a painter. He started on his house and didn't stop until he had run out of walls—inside and out—and ceilings. His wife forbade him to paint the stove and refrigerator. Some years later she said, "I even bought two gallons of white paint to cover up what he had done to the walls." His neighbors called him a fool. But Villeneuve was not discouraged. He painted for two years, and then opened his house to the public. Scenes of Chicoutimi spread from room to room; the Saguenay River flowed beside the staircase. Visitors left with growing respect for the artist's talent.

When Villeneuve ran out of walls, he switched to canvas. His paintings, lauded as "authentic primitives," began to sell. In 1972, a one-man show at the Montreal Museum of Fine Arts confirmed the art world's acceptance of the barber-painter. Villeneuve's house, now a museum, is still open to visitors.

Le train de la parenté, by Arthur Villeneuve

Le Conte's sparrow

PETIT-SAGUENAY
In 1848 William Price purchased a sawmill and established a warehouse and an administrative center here for his logging operations in the area.
□ This tiny village nestles in the steep-sided valley of Rivière Petit Saguenay. Salmon use a fish ladder to bypass two nearby waterfalls on the Petit Saguenay.
□ From June to the end of August speckled trout can be caught in a government fishing reserve here.

An Awakening Frontier—
Rich in Minerals and Power

North Shore, St. Lawrence River

Until the 1930s settlement of this stretch of the St. Lawrence, called the "North Shore," was limited to a string of small fishing villages joined by primitive roads and connected with the outside world by coastal vessels. But exploitation of the region's vast natural resources—wood and water in a 200-kilometre-wide coastal strip and iron ore in the northern hinterland—led to spectacular developments.

Pulp mills came first, in the 1930s. Two decades later iron ore was discovered near

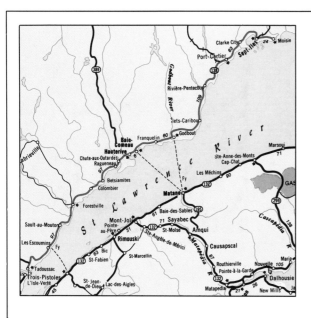

Whale-Watching on the St. Lawrence

Whales by the score can often be seen where the Saguenay joins the St. Lawrence. The shallow waters at the confluence of the two rivers are a rich feeding ground. The Saguenay is the home of the beluga whale, a variety of white arctic porpoise, once known as the St. Lawrence whale. The beluga is attracted by abundant shrimp and capelin, and its young are believed to be born in the Baie Sainte-Marguerite area. Whalers once hunted and killed the beluga for its oil. Now, if hunted at all, belugas are taken alive for shipment to zoos.

Other species of whale reported near the mouth of the Saguenay include finbacks, humpbacks and blues.

Trips can be arranged at Tadoussac. Saguenay cruise ships provide opportunities to catch sight of the beluga.

Cruise ships near the Saguenay River

Sand dunes, Tadoussac

TADOUSSAC
Situated at the junction of the Saguenay and St. Lawrence, Tadoussac is a center for tourism and forestry. The bay sheltered the ships of French explorers Jacques Cartier in 1534 and Samuel de Champlain in 1603. In 1600 Pierre Chauvin was granted a fur-trading monopoly in this region and chose this location as his headquarters. A reconstruction of Chauvin's house—Canada's first trading post—is open to the public.
□ A wooden chapel, built in 1747, is the oldest in North America. In its tower hangs the bell from a 1641 church that stood on the same site.

CHUTE-AUX-OUTARDES
The community developed when a dam was built nearby on the Rivière aux Outardes in 1925. This dam was replaced by larger ones upriver in the 1960s, but its remains can still be seen.
□ Just off Highway 138, east of Chute-aux-Outardes, a 12-kilometre road leads to the Manicouagan Peninsula, which has some of the finest beaches in North America.
□ Parc régional de Pointe-aux-Outardes contains salt marshes, sand dunes and pine forests. Visitors can follow nature trails to explore the park's different habitats.

Wooden chapel, Tadoussac

GRANDES-BERGERONNES
A superb local lookout provides visitors with opportunities to observe great blue whales, which play close to the nearby shores of the St. Lawrence River. There is also an interpretive center, which supplies binoculars and telescopes. Whale-watching excursions by boat are also available. This tiny community (and its neighbor, Petites-Bergeronnes) celebrates the presence of the whales with a four-day festival in August.

Schefferville (Que.) and Wabush (Labrador). Railway links between the mines and the natural harbors of the North Shore such as Port-Cartier and Sept-Îles brought radical economic change. Sept-Îles, for instance, was a fishing village of 1,500 people in 1950. Today, it is a shipping and administrative center of more than 25,000.

In the 1960s came hydroelectric developments. Dams and generating plants harnessed rivers such as the Betsiamites, Outardes, Manicouagan and Toulnustouc. A dam at Labrieville on the Betsiamites (84 kilometres northwest of Forestville) creates a reservoir 770 square kilometres large. The 214-metre-high Manic 5 Dam on the Manicouagan, 210 kilometres north of Baie-Comeau, is one of the world's largest. High-energy-consuming aluminum refineries and other industries are located near this source of electric power. Despite these developments, much of this region remains a wilderness offering thrilling experiences for canoeists and fishermen.

Robert R. McCormick statue, Baie-Comeau

AIE-COMEAU

‍ie industrial development of the once-isolated North Shore d its beginning here in 1936 when Chicago publisher Col. ‍obert R. McCormick built a pulp-and-paper mill to feed ‍s newspapers in the United States. McCormick is honored ‍ a statue at Baie-Comeau. Development boomed in the ‍50s and 1960s: an aluminum refinery and grain elevators ‍ere built here, and the Rivière Manicouagan and the Rivière ‍x Outardes were harnessed to produce electricty.

‍The town is named for the renowned Quebec naturalist of ‍uebec's North Shore, Napoléon-Alexandre Comeau (1845-‍23), who was born at Colombier.

‍Baie-Comeau is the birthplace of Prime Minister Brian ‍ulroney.

POINTE-AUX-ANGLAIS
When Saint-Paul-de-Pointe-aux-Anglais Church was erected in 1962, some 120 parishioners each carried 40 stones five kilometres from a Gulf of St. Lawrence beach to the construction site. Bas-relief Stations of the Cross by Médard Bourgault are of basswood on walnut backgrounds. Above the altar is an oak crucifix, also sculpted by Bourgault.

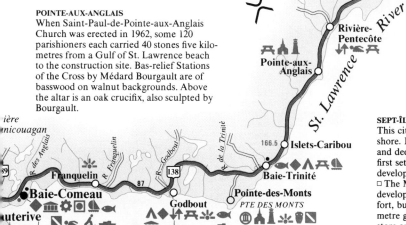

PORT-CARTIER
Situated where two rivers flow into the St. Lawrence, Port-Cartier grew rapidly during the mining boom of the 1960s. In the heart of the town are Patterson and McCormick Islands, which have recreational facilities.
□ Just north of Port-Cartier, the vast expanse of the Sept-Îles-Port-Cartier wildlife reserve offers fishing, hunting, camping and hiking. There are also boat-launching sites, lookouts and picnic grounds.

SEPT-ÎLES
This city of about 25,000 is the regional center for Quebec's north shore. Its almost circular bay is some 35 kilometres in diameter and deep enough for oceangoing vessels. Although Sept-Îles was first settled in the 17th century, its expansion began only with the development of the Quebec and Labrador iron mines in the 1950s.
□ The Musée de la Côte-Nord describes the history of local development. The Vieux-Poste is a reconstruction of a local log fort, built in 1661 and burned down in 1692. The site has a 27-metre guard tower, two dwellings, a chapel, a powder magazine, store and stable.

Islands Shaped by Wind and Waves

The Mingan Islands National Park Reserve, about 220 kilometres east of Sept-Îles, is ideal for travelers seeking a remote and remarkable destination. The islands are located 3.5 kilometres off the North Shore of the St. Lawrence River in Jacques Cartier Strait, north of Anticosti Island. They form a chain of 15 islands and more than 40 islets, which stretch for a distance of more than 150 kilometres. Spectacular rock formations—the product of erosion by wind and waves—are outstanding features of the islands. Particularly fascinating are the picturesque "flowerpots" (top-heavy rock pillars) on the shorelines. The islands are largely covered with coniferous forest. But they also support a wide variety of plants usually found farther north. The islands are sanctuary for migratory birds, and the offshore waters attract whales.

The Mingan Islands are accessible by Highway 138, which goes as far as Havre-Saint-Pierre, where a visitors' center is located. From June to mid-October, boat trips through the islands depart from Havre-Saint-Pierre. The offshore waters are ideal for boating, fishing and scuba diving.

Arctic Flowers on the Mountain, Rare Caribou in the Park

Gaspé Peninsula

The Gaspé Peninsula is a world of farms, fishing villages, and rugged mountains. The Gaspé's isolation ended when the Perron Boulevard (now Highway 132) was built around the perimeter of the peninsula in 1929. Although much of the region is easily accessible today, it retains its traditional charm and beauty.

The Jardins de Métis has formal gardens that were once part of the estate of George Stephen (1829-1921), first president of the Canadian Pacific Railway. In summer Ste-

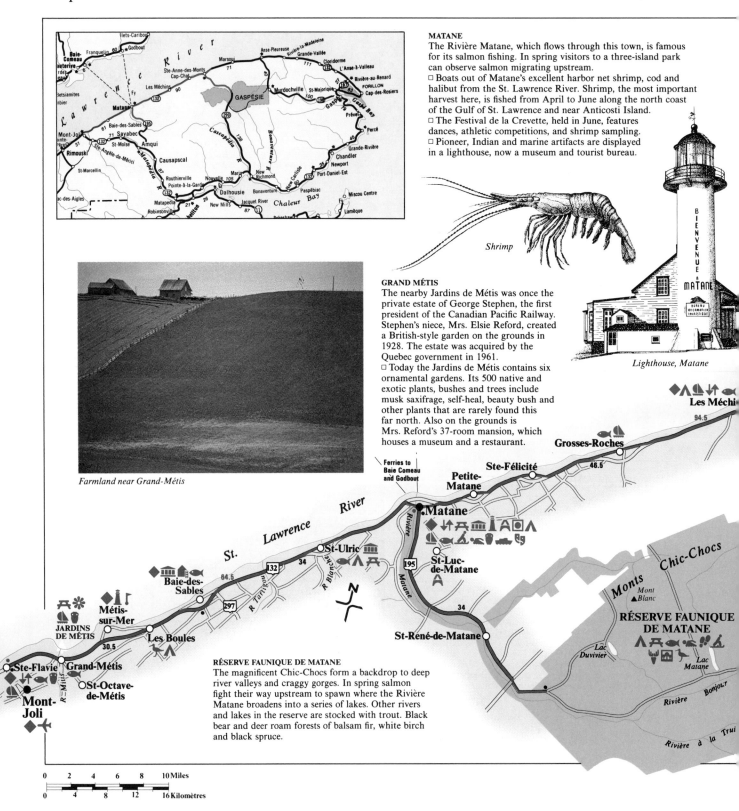

MATANE
The Rivière Matane, which flows through this town, is famous for its salmon fishing. In spring visitors to a three-island park can observe salmon migrating upstream.
□ Boats out of Matane's excellent harbor net shrimp, cod and halibut from the St. Lawrence River. Shrimp, the most important harvest here, is fished from April to June along the north coast of the Gulf of St. Lawrence and near Anticosti Island.
□ The Festival de la Crevette, held in June, features dances, athletic competitions, and shrimp sampling.
□ Pioneer, Indian and marine artifacts are displayed in a lighthouse, now a museum and tourist bureau.

Shrimp

Lighthouse, Matane

Farmland near Grand-Métis

GRAND MÉTIS
The nearby Jardins de Métis was once the private estate of George Stephen, the first president of the Canadian Pacific Railway. Stephen's niece, Mrs. Elsie Reford, created a British-style garden on the grounds in 1928. The estate was acquired by the Quebec government in 1961.
□ Today the Jardins de Métis contains six ornamental gardens. Its 500 native and exotic plants, bushes and trees include musk saxifrage, self-heal, beauty bush and other plants that are rarely found this far north. Also on the grounds is Mrs. Reford's 37-room mansion, which houses a museum and a restaurant.

RÉSERVE FAUNIQUE DE MATANE
The magnificent Chic-Chocs form a backdrop to deep river valleys and craggy gorges. In spring salmon fight their way upstream to spawn where the Rivière Matane broadens into a series of lakes. Other rivers and lakes in the reserve are stocked with trout. Black bear and deer roam forests of balsam fir, white birch and black spruce.

phen enjoyed angling in the region's salmon-fishing rivers. Stephen's niece, Mrs. Elsie Reford, who inherited the estate, established the gardens in 1928. Nearby Métis-sur-Mer, the region's oldest resort, has fine beaches and many beautiful old homes.

Inland are wild rolling highlands and the Chic-Chocs, eastern Canada's highest mountains. From the summit of Mont Jacques-Cartier (1,268 metres), the loftiest peak in the range, visitors can see the St. Lawrence River 25 kilometres away.

About 20 Chic-Choc peaks exceed 1,070 metres; some of these are snowcapped as late as July. The summit of Mont Albert, a lake-dotted plateau, has mosses, lichens and stunted shrubs that are usually found in the Arctic.

Réserve faunique de Matane in the Chic-Chocs has rivers teeming with salmon, and lakes and streams stocked with trout. One of Quebec's largest herds of moose ranges the park's black spruce forests.

Much of Parc de la Gaspésie is wilderness—home to moose, Virginia deer and rare woodland caribou.

Highway 132 near Sainte-Anne-des-Monts

SAINTE-ANNE-DES-MONTS
This farming, cod-fishing and lumbering community is on the rocky shore of a bay named by Champlain for Pierre de Monts, the first governor of Acadia (1604).
□ A stately granite church here is dedicated to Saint Anne, patron saint of sailors.

CAP-CHAT
According to local belief, this town is named for a nearby rocky headland that resembles a crouching cat. Cap-Chat is considered to be the dividing line between the St. Lawrence River and the Gulf of St. Lawrence.
□ Mont Logan, 24 kilometres south, has downhill and cross-country skiing. The 1,148-metre peak is part of the Chic-Choc range. The Rivière Cap-Chat is noted for its salmon.

SAINT-JOACHIM-DE-TOURELLE
Two craggy granite pillars stand about five kilometres apart on a beach near here.
□ This agricultural and fishing community, founded in 1916, was partially destroyed by a landslide in 1963.
□ East of town Highway 132 winds between the St. Lawrence River and sheer cliffs.

Rock formation, Saint-Joachim-de-Tourelle

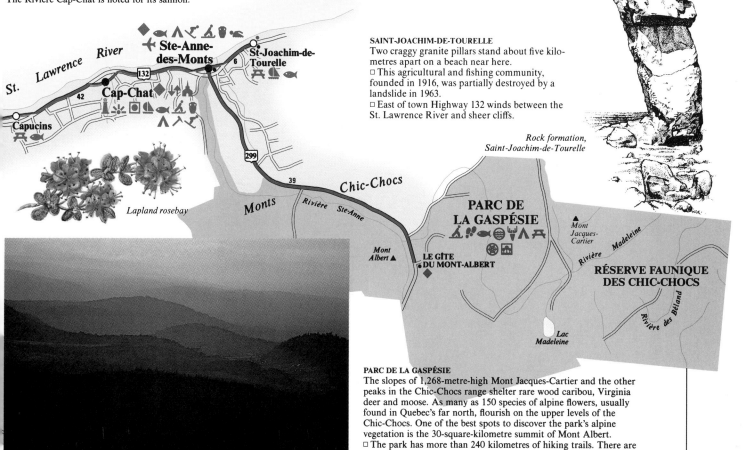

Lapland rosebay

Parc de la Gaspésie

PARC DE LA GASPÉSIE
The slopes of 1,268-metre-high Mont Jacques-Cartier and the other peaks in the Chic-Chocs range shelter rare wood caribou, Virginia deer and moose. As many as 150 species of alpine flowers, usually found in Quebec's far north, flourish on the upper levels of the Chic-Chocs. One of the best spots to discover the park's alpine vegetation is the 30-square-kilometre summit of Mont Albert.
□ The park has more than 240 kilometres of hiking trails. There are three trails leading to the top of Mont Albert. Guides take visitors to the summit of Mont Jacques-Cartier. Fishermen angle for ouananiche (land-locked salmon) and trout in the park's rivers.

Wild Beauty and Sheltering Bays 'Where the Land Ends'

North Shore, Gaspé Peninsula

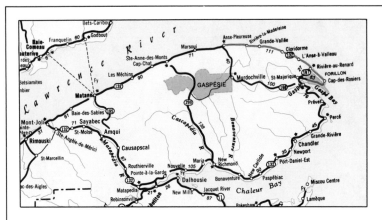

Vigneaux at Cloridorme

CLORIDORME

Large, sonar-equipped trawlers have replaced small wooden fishing boats in recent years, but *vigneaux*—wooden tables with metal trellises used for drying cod—still line the shores of Cloridorme. A portion of the catch, cleaned and salted, is spread out on these racks to dry in the sun.

GRANDE-VALLÉE

A lookout just west of Grande-Vallée provides a fine view of the shores of the St. Lawrence River and the village. Grande-Vallée's "Galipeau" covered bridge evokes bygone days.

RIVIÈRE-AU-RENARD

This community is the fish-processing center of the north shore of the Gaspé Peninsula. Some residents claim to be descendants of Irish sailors shipwrecked off Cap-des-Rosiers in 1856. The local church, Saint-Martin-de-la-Rivière-au-Renard, is in the modern style of the French architect, Benedictine monk Dom Paul Bellot, who designed the abbey at Saint-Benoît-du-Lac.

ANSE-PLEUREUSE

The name of this fishing village at the head of a small bay means "crying cove." According to different local legends, the sound of the wind blowing through the trees can be the moaning of lost children, the sobbing of a murder victim or the cries of shipwrecked ghosts. Nearby Rivière-la-Madeleine also has its wind spirit—the *braillard de Madeleine* (meaning the "sobber of Madeleine").

Rusty blackbird

Pilot whale

FORILLON NATIONAL PARK

Established in 1971, this 240-square-kilometre park embraces a diverse environment. The shoreline has rugged limestone cliffs, long pebble beaches, and small sandy coves. Arctic vegetation grows on the cliffs, and boreal forest predominates within the park. Sand dunes and the saltwater marsh near Penouille support distinctive plant life.

□ More than 200 bird species visit Forillon each year. Herring gulls, black guillemots and double-crested cormorants nest on the cliffs. Pilot whales are the most common of the 12 whale species in Forillon's offshore waters. (Whale-watching excursions are available locally.)

Limestone cliffs, Forillon National Park

The northeast coast of the Gaspé Peninsula is a rich landscape of limestone cliffs, shingly beaches, streams, coves and thickly forested highlands. Small villages dot the coastline in sheltered bays. Fishing boats cluster around wharves much as they have since the 1700s. Cod is still split, salted and dried on wooden racks along the beach.

The wild beauty of the Gaspé (from an Indian word, *Gaspeg*—"where the land ends") reaches its climax at Forillon National Park. Here, visitors stand at one end of the Appalachian Mountains, a chain that extends deep into the southeastern United States. The park appears as a massive, tilted block emerging from the sea. Wind and surf have sculpted 200-metre-high escarpments on sections of the eastern shore. The coast facing the Baie de Gaspé is indented with beaches and small coves hidden between the rocky headlands. On the cliffs grow species of vigorous alpine flora—species whose presence here is not yet understood by botanists. Sheltered from the harsh weather of the gulf are long stretches of sandy beach. Within a hundred metres of shore is a heavy cover of evergreen forest crisscrossed by nature trails.

Thousands of birds visit the peninsula—some migrating from the Arctic to winter in the park, others flying on. Seals in great numbers return each summer to the waters off Forillon, as do pilot whales. Such yearly migrations, like the rugged scenery, give the region a timeless quality.

Forillon: A Stepping-Stone Between Land and Sea

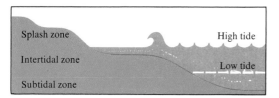

Life between the deep waters of the Gulf of St. Lawrence and the highlands of Forillon National Park is inextricably linked to the rise and fall of the tide. Along the rugged, rocky shore are three life zones: the splash zone, high on the rocks; the intertidal zone, flooded at high tide and exposed at ebb tide; and the subtidal zone, uncovered by only the lowest tides.

Forillon has countless tide pools, each a marine world in microcosm. On and near the rocks are countless communities of sea plants and animals, each specifically adapted to the rigors and demands of its environment. Together the zones illustrate the progress of life from sea to land.

SPLASH ZONE
Only the highest spring tides reach the splash zone. Life here relies on spray for its seawater needs. The rough periwinkle eats minute blue-green algae, scraping them from the rocks with an abrasive tongue. Its rows of microscopic thorns can wear down even rocky surfaces.

Rough periwinkle

INTERTIDAL ZONE
The intertidal zone is covered with water about half the time and animals and plants retain enough to sustain them when the tide is out. Creatures here must be able to anchor themselves against the push and pull of the waves. Each barnacle secretes a strong adhesive and attaches itself to the spot it will occupy the rest of its life.

Barnacle

SUBTIDAL ZONE
Covered by water most of the time, plants and animals of the subtidal zone are poorly adapted to dry land. The starfish eats mussels, oysters and other bivalve mollusks, curving itself around each victim and pulling the shells apart with its hundreds of "suction-tube" feet.

Starfish

L'ANSE-AU-GRIFFON
This fishing community may have been named for the *Griffon,* a vessel that once plied local waters in the 18th century. Or the origin of the name may be *gris fonds,* meaning the "gray depths" of the sea.
□ A nearby historic manor, built in 1840 by John LeBoutillier, an important local 19th-century cod merchant, is open to the public.

CAP-DES-ROSIERS
The French explorer Samuel de Champlain named the cape for the wild roses that thrive on its cliffs.
□ The Cap-des-Rosiers lighthouse (1858) stands on a 37-metre-high site (the highest site for a Canadian lighthouse). It is one of a series of lighthouses built to guide ships safely along the treacherous shores of the St. Lawrence River. Before the use of radio telegraphy, incoming vessels signaled their passing to the station by means of flags. The notice of arrival was then telegraphed to Quebec. Until recently a nine-pounder cannon was fired every hour in fog and snow.

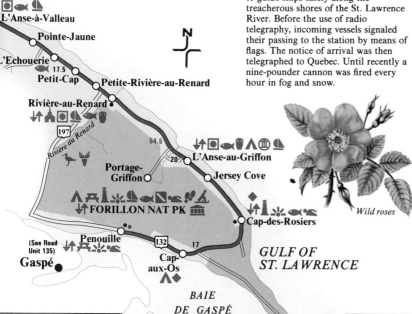

Wild roses

Cap-des-Rosiers

A Great, Shiplike Rock, Sweeping Views of the Gulf

South Shore, Gaspé Peninsula

At the tip of the Gaspé Peninsula, the irregular coastline blends into limestone and shale formations which have been pushed, folded and squeezed by tremendous geological forces. Nowhere is the effect more striking than at Percé Rock, a great shiplike block of limestone rising 86 metres from the sea. Off the mainland near Percé, the French explorer Jacques Cartier anchored his three ships in 1534 to claim the region for France.

At Percé, there is another spectacular off-

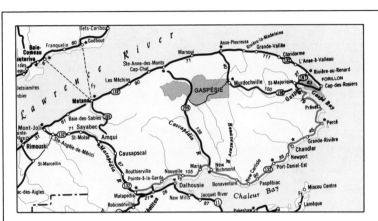

A Haven on the High Cliffs

Île Bonaventure, 3.5 kilometres from the beaches of Percé, is a famous bird sanctuary. Tens of thousands of gannets make their home on the 100-metre-high cliffs from April to October. They constitute the largest colony of these seabirds in the world. Amid the flocks of white gannets are other birds: murres, kittiwakes, arctic puffins, cormorants, gulls and razor-billed auks. The island's bird population finds sustenance in the shallow, cold and nutrient-rich waters which surround it.

During the summer, there is a daily ferry service between Percé and Île Bonaventure. The island's attractions include an interpretive center, a museum, nature trails and picnic sites.

Gannet colony, Ile Bonaventure

POINTE-À-LA-CROIX

A national historic park at Pointe-à-la-Croix marks the site of the Battle of the Restigouche—the last English-French naval encounter of the Seven Years' War—that occurred in July 1760. An interpretation center overlooks the site and exhibits battle relics, including parts of a French supply ship, *Le Machault*, which was raised during an underwater excavation of the site. A short documentary film describes the battle and the life on board 18th-century vessels.

Silver buckle, Capuchin monastery of Sainte-Anne-de-Restigouche

CARLETON

A road leads from the village to the top of Mont Saint-Joseph and the Notre-Dame Oratory. The 555-metre summit gives visitors an exceptional view of the Gaspé coast and the north shore of New Brunswick.

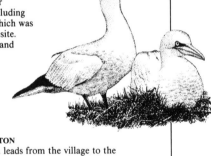

MATAPÉDIA

Highway 132 north of this town passes through farmlands and forests of fir, elm and maple in the Matapédia Valley. Rivière Matapédia offers canoeing and fishing for Atlantic salmon. The region is also noted for the covered "settlers' bridges" that cross the Matapédia.

PARC DE MIGUASHA

The cliffs in this park are a repository of fossils more than 400 million years old. The fossils include 24 species of prehistoric fish. Although the site has attracted scientists since the 1880s, it was established as a provincial park only in 1976. An interpretive center and the cliffs are open to the public.

BONAVENTURE

This Acadian community honors its early settlers at the Musée acadien du Québec. The museum's collection includes cradles, looms, spinning wheels and other antiques.

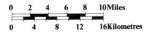

shore site: the gannet colony of Île Bonaventure. Along the island's shorelines, tens of thousands of birds thickly populate rocky ledges. Hiking trails on the island lead to lookouts where the birds' activities can be observed at close range.

Toward the Baie des Chaleurs, the highway winds past the sheltered bays of the Gaspé's south shore. In season, scores of salmon fishermen line the banks of the Dartmouth, York and Saint John rivers. The scenic Matapédia and Cascapédia rivers, known for their salmon fishing, drain into the Baie des Chaleurs. The Chic-Chocs, the mountains with the highest peaks in eastern Canada, rise behind the fishing villages and resort centers strung along the coast. Hiking trails wind through the forested slopes leading to sweeping views of the Gulf of St. Lawrence and Baie des Chaleurs.

Gaspé fishermen

GASPÉ

A nine-metre-high granite cross commemorates the 400th anniversary of Jacques Cartier's landing at this site in 1534. Cartier took possession of the Gaspé in the name of the King of France and raised a wooden cross at Point de Penouille.
□ The Cathédrale de Gaspé (1960)—the only wooden cathedral in North America—contains a stained glass window and a fresco, a gift from France in 1934 to honor Cartier's landing.
□ The Musée de la Gaspésie features displays that trace the history of the Gaspé Peninsula from the time of the Vikings to the present day. The museum also presents art shows and historic exhibitions. There is an impressive monument to Cartier on the museum grounds.
□ Quebec's oldest provincial fish hatchery (built in 1876 and relocated here in 1938) produced as many as a million salmon and trout fry a year. The hatchery is open to the public.

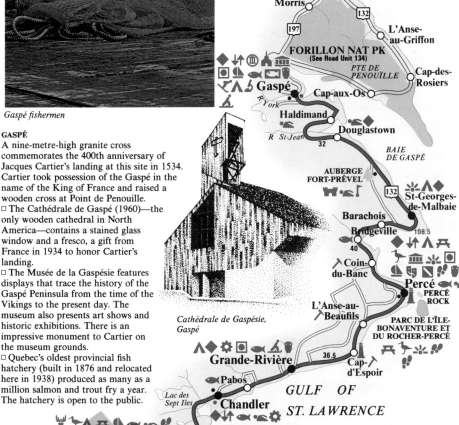

Cathédrale de Gaspésie, Gaspé

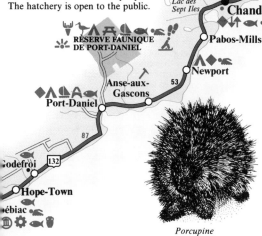

Porcupine

RÉSERVE FAUNIQUE DE PORT-DANIEL

From its headwaters in the Gaspé interior, the Rivière Port-Daniel flows through a deep, forested valley, part of which has been preserved in this park. Most of the lakes in the park have excellent brook trout fishing, and angling for Atlantic salmon is popular on the Rivière Port-Daniel.

Salmon Pie, Gaspé Style

This version of shepherd's pie is a regional dish of the Gaspé, whose rivers are among the finest Atlantic salmon waters in the world.

INGREDIENTS:

2 cups flaked cooked fresh salmon
(or 2 cups canned salmon)
2½ to 3 cups mashed potatoes
½ cup finely chopped onion
3 tablespoons butter
¼ teaspoon savory
pastry dough for one pie crust
salt and pepper

Combine the potatoes, onion, butter, and seasoning. Place half the potato mixture in the bottom of a greased, nine-inch pie plate or individual casseroles. Add salmon, and top with remaining potato. Cover with prepared pastry.

Bake in a 400°F oven for 25 to 30 minutes, or until golden brown. Makes six servings.

PERCÉ

Once the largest fishing port in the Gaspé, Percé is now a tourist and resort town. Behind the village are scenic hills and mountains. A statue of Saint Anne, a landmark for fishermen at sea, is atop 360-metre-high Mont Sainte-Anne.
□ Percé Rock was named by Champlain for the soaring natural arch that distinguishes this enormous block of limestone in the Gulf of St. Lawrence.

Percé Rock

A Mountain Wilderness and Sandy, Pine-Clad Shores

Northern New Brunswick

By late spring the Atlantic salmon are running in the Restigouche Valley. Anglers and their guides, in long, green canoes, head upriver toward the sheltered pools and backwaters where the fish will rest on their way to the spawning grounds. The salmon run continues into early July, and the season ends with a gala festival in Campbellton.

Downriver, the Restigouche flows past Dalhousie into Chaleur Bay. Here, in summer, tourists sunbathe on the bay's sandy,

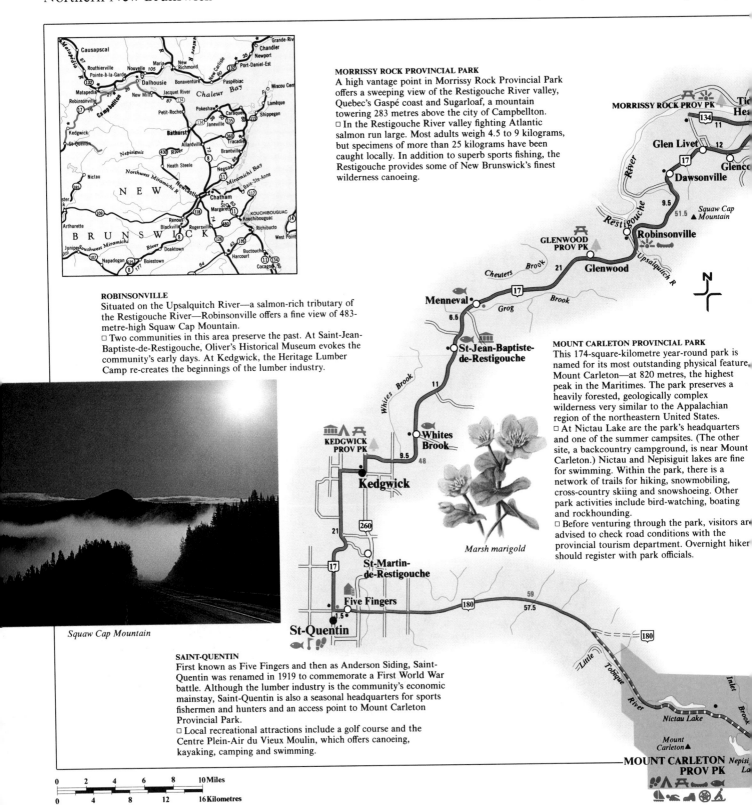

MORRISSY ROCK PROVINCIAL PARK
A high vantage point in Morrissy Rock Provincial Park offers a sweeping view of the Restigouche River valley, Quebec's Gaspé coast and Sugarloaf, a mountain towering 283 metres above the city of Campbellton.
□ In the Restigouche River valley fighting Atlantic salmon run large. Most adults weigh 4.5 to 9 kilograms, but specimens of more than 25 kilograms have been caught locally. In addition to superb sports fishing, the Restigouche provides some of New Brunswick's finest wilderness canoeing.

ROBINSONVILLE
Situated on the Upsalquitch River—a salmon-rich tributary of the Restigouche River—Robinsonville offers a fine view of 483-metre-high Squaw Cap Mountain.
□ Two communities in this area preserve the past. At Saint-Jean-Baptiste-de-Restigouche, Oliver's Historical Museum evokes the community's early days. At Kedgwick, the Heritage Lumber Camp re-creates the beginnings of the lumber industry.

MOUNT CARLETON PROVINCIAL PARK
This 174-square-kilometre year-round park is named for its most outstanding physical feature, Mount Carleton—at 820 metres, the highest peak in the Maritimes. The park preserves a heavily forested, geologically complex wilderness very similar to the Appalachian region of the northeastern United States.
□ At Nictau Lake are the park's headquarters and one of the summer campsites. (The other site, a backcountry campground, is near Mount Carleton.) Nictau and Nepisiguit lakes are fine for swimming. Within the park, there is a network of trails for hiking, snowmobiling, cross-country skiing and snowshoeing. Other park activities include bird-watching, boating and rockhounding.
□ Before venturing through the park, visitors are advised to check road conditions with the provincial tourism department. Overnight hikers should register with park officials.

Marsh marigold

Squaw Cap Mountain

SAINT-QUENTIN
First known as Five Fingers and then as Anderson Siding, Saint-Quentin was renamed in 1919 to commemorate a First World War battle. Although the lumber industry is the community's economic mainstay, Saint-Quentin is also a seasonal headquarters for sports fishermen and hunters and an access point to Mount Carleton Provincial Park.
□ Local recreational attractions include a golf course and the Centre Plein-Air du Vieux Moulin, which offers canoeing, kayaking, camping and swimming.

| 0 | 2 | 4 | 6 | 8 | 10 Miles |
| 0 | 4 | 8 | 12 | 16 Kilometres |

pine-clad shores; swim in its salt water; fish offshore for cod and mackerel; sail before a brisk ocean breeze; or dig for clams on sandbars at the mouth of the Eel River.

In autumn, inland from Campbellton, brilliant foliage transforms the vast forest into a dazzling tapestry splashed with gold and scarlet. Mount Carleton, the Maritime provinces' highest mountain, looms over the land. In this rugged wilderness, outdoor enthusiasts find pleasure in camping, canoeing, hiking, mountain climbing, photography,

bird-watching, rockhounding and fishing. Big-game hunters make their headquarters in villages such as Saint-Quentin, Kedgwick and Robinsonville.

In winter the snow-covered slopes of Sugarloaf, on the outskirts of Campbellton, are speckled with hundreds of brightly clad downhill skiers. At the base of the mountain there are skating ponds and a toboggan run. Cross-country skiers and snowshoers are invigorated by the scent of the pines and the clear, crisp air.

From salmon fishing to big-game hunting, from saltwater swimming to mountain climbing, northern New Brunswick offers an almost unlimited variety of outdoor activities. It is an uncrowded vacationland, and a place for all seasons.

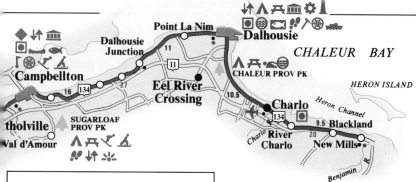

CHALEUR BAY

HERON ISLAND

Heron Channel

DALHOUSIE

This year-round port at the mouth of the Restigouche River offers easy access to saltwater swimming, rockhounding and other recreational activities on Chaleur Bay. Dalhousie is one of New Brunswick's major wood-processing centers.
□ Displays in the Restigouche Regional Museum deal with pioneer days in the Dalhousie area and with the growth of fishing, farming and local early industry. One of the town's major industries—the New Brunswick International Paper Company—offers plant tours.

Sugarloaf Provincial Park

The Phantom Ship of Chaleur Bay

On stormy nights a mysterious, burning, square-rigged warship is said to haunt Chaleur Bay between Campbellton and Bathurst. Is it a ghostly reincarnation or is it a mirage? Witnesses have reported seeing a large, fully rigged, four-masted ship, with masts and sails ablaze. Some claim to have seen men scurrying about the flaming rigging. Those who have tried to approach the ship say it stays out of clear viewing distance. Eventually, it disappears.

Some say the phenomenon is merely the reflection of heat waves. Others insist it is a phantom—the ghost of a French ship that burned and sank in 1760 during the Battle of the Restigouche.

CAMPBELLTON

This community of more than 9,000 is the administrative and commercial center of New Brunswick's north shore. But it is best known as the gateway to the Restigouche region—famed for Atlantic salmon. Sports fishermen come here from all over the world to catch this prize. In summer Campbellton celebrates with an annual salmon festival. It also pays tribute to its prized resource with an 8.5-metre-high model of a leaping salmon—the centerpiece of a waterfront park fountain.
□ The Restigouche Gallery, one of Canada's national exhibition centers, displays local art, as well as work by regional, national and international artists.
□ At Atholville, Sugarloaf Provincial Park—named for the 283-metre-high peak overlooking this area—has year-round outdoor activities. The Sugarloaf summit can be reached by chair lift, which offers striking views of the region. The park also has two winter slides that provide thrilling rides to Sugarloaf's base.

Mount Carleton: A Mixed Forest of Hardwoods and Evergreens

Black spruce   *Red pine*   *Eastern white pine*   *Balsam fir*   *Red spruce*

Beech   *Yellow birch*   *White birch*

More than half of Mount Carleton Provincial Park is, at high, dry elevations, burned-over forest that has regenerated into nearly pure stands of fire-resistant hardwoods. Yellow and white birches grow near lakes and streams. Beeches, with smooth, gray bark and dark green leaves, produce edible, three-cornered nuts. In autumn the vivid foliage of sugar maples brightens the landscape.

Softwoods thrive in the moist, low-lying areas. Stands of black spruce seldom exceed 15 metres. Red pines may reach 38 metres but usually grow to about 20. Moose eat the leaves of the trembling aspen and beavers feed on its pale, greenish white bark. Ground vegetation in the burned-over forest includes Dutchman's-breeches, bloodroot, wild ginger, trilliums and orchids.

The park area untouched by fire is mainly coniferous forest. The balsam fir,

a common Christmas tree, has upright seed-bearing cones. The red spruce has narrow, pendulous, egg-shaped cones that open in autumn and usually remain attached to the tree through winter. The eastern white pine grows to 30 metres and may live 450 years. Its seed cones mature in autumn and drop off in winter; the cones are food for squirrels, chipmunks and birds. Bunchberries, dainty evergreen twinflowers, club mosses and ferns grow on the floor of the park's coniferous forest.

In spring, the brilliant yellow flowers of the marsh marigold or cowslip brighten swamps, marshes and wet meadows. Fragrant water lilies, which float on ponds and slow-moving streams, bloom from June to September. Fish and mammals eat their leaves and protein-rich seeds. Alders, red-osier dogwoods and willows border marshy areas.

Picturesque Seascapes and Fishing Villages

The Acadian Peninsula

All along the Chaleur Bay coast is evidence of Acadian *joie de vivre*, self-reliance and determination to preserve a unique heritage.

The richness of this people's history is captured at the Acadian Historical Village (Village Historique Acadien), near Caraquet. Sod dikes have reclaimed marshes near the river for wheat, oats and hay. Reconstructed houses and public buildings mirror the tiniest details of early Acadian architecture. Small log farmhouses, their

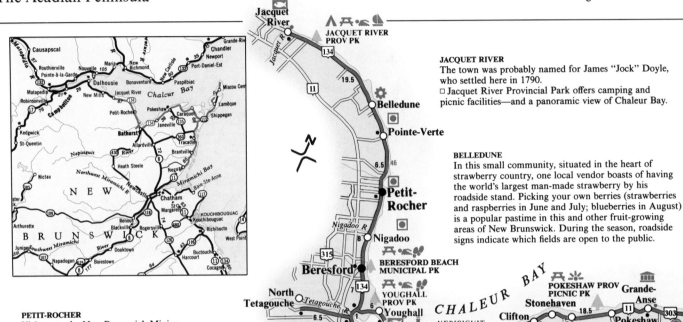

JACQUET RIVER
The town was probably named for James "Jock" Doyle, who settled here in 1790.
□ Jacquet River Provincial Park offers camping and picnic facilities—and a panoramic view of Chaleur Bay.

BELLEDUNE
In this small community, situated in the heart of strawberry country, one local vendor boasts of having the world's largest man-made strawberry by his roadside stand. Picking your own berries (strawberries and raspberries in June and July; blueberries in August) is a popular pastime in this and other fruit-growing areas of New Brunswick. During the season, roadside signs indicate which fields are open to the public.

PETIT-ROCHER
Visitors to the New Brunswick Mining and Mineral Interpretation Centre can take a simulated ride down a mine shaft and explore caverns and mine passageways drilled through mineral deposits. The center also presents exhibits, graphic displays and films about New Brunswick's mining industry.

BATHURST
This industrial city (pop. 14,680) is at the mouth of the Nepisiguit (Micmac for "tumultuous river") River. Long prominent for pulp-and-paper manufacturing, Bathurst has developed as a mining center since the 1950s. Roughly 40 percent of Canada's silver, zinc, lead and copper reserves are found in the area. The mines and mills are about 37 kilometres southwest of the city.
□ Bathurst's origins go back to the mid-17th century. Nicolas Denys, the French "governor of the coasts and islands of the St. Lawrence," established a settlement here in 1652. (Denys' grave and memorial are in downtown Bathurst.) After his death the site was abandoned until Acadians and English settlers came to this area in the late 18th century. Originally called Nepisiguit and then St. Peters, the community was renamed for British colonial secretary Lord Bathurst in 1826. In the 1800s the town was important for its lumber industry and shipbuilding.
□ Bathurst welcomes boaters to the marinas along its harborfront. (Boat tours are available.) In July the city celebrates Hospitality Days.
□ The Herman J. Good, V.C., Memorial Museum (at the Royal Canadian Legion) displays military artifacts.
□ Local beaches—at Youghall Provincial Park, for example—offer saltwater swimming. West of the city are the scenic Tetagouche, Pabineau and Grand falls.

Pokeshaw Island

POKESHAW ISLAND
This stark, flat-topped island just offshore from the village of Pokeshaw is a gathering place for hundreds of seabirds. The island is a favorite of artists and photographers.

0 2 4 6 8 10 Miles

0 4 8 12 16 Kilometres

vegetable gardens planted in neat rows, nestle in clearings cut in stands of white birch. Costumed staff demonstrate pioneer skills: men square timbers, make shingles, dry and barrel salted cod; women spin wool, hook rugs, churn butter and bake bread. A winding country road connects the houses and the buildings in the village. Visitors can tour these on foot or in a *carriole* drawn by horses or oxen.

Acadian gaiety and enthusiasm enliven annual festivals in Pointe-Verte, Nigadoo, Petit-Rocher and Lamèque. In Shippagan and Caraquet, the famous blessings of the fishing fleets highlight summertime Acadian festivals. Also in Caraquet are a bustling fishermen's market, an Acadian museum and a historic chapel more than two centuries old. Elsewhere along the coast are farms, fishing villages, picturesque seascapes, and occasional reminders of the past—an abandoned farmhouse, old and gray, its windows shuttered; or the beached, battered hulk of a fishing boat.

CARAQUET

Founded in the 1750s, Caraquet is a major center of Acadian culture and religious devotion. Exhibits at the Acadian Museum depict pioneer days, and the 200-year-old Sainte Anne du Bocage shrine is the site of an annual pilgrimage that attracts thousands of visitors.

□ Most of the town's 5,000 residents live near the 13-kilometre-long main street—the longest in the Maritimes—which follows the rocky shore of Caraquet Bay. Caraquet's economy revolves around boat-building and commercial fishing: its fleet is one of the largest in New Brunswick and the province's only fisheries school is here.

□ Caraquet's popular annual Acadian festival in mid-August opens with the blessing of the local fishing fleet (a reminder of Christ's blessing of the fishermen of Galilee).

□ Charter boats take tourists deep-sea fishing for giant bluefin tuna. Shellfish and groundfish are sold at the fish market.

Where Acadia's Homespun Heritage Lives On

Acadian haystacks

La Maison Godin, Acadian Historical Village

A pioneer Acadian community has been re-created on a 10.5-square-kilometre site between Grande-Anse and Caraquet. In addition to 10 dwellings, Acadian Historical Village has a smithy, a warehouse, a general store, a one-room schoolhouse, a chapel, and a public tavern. Along the banks of the Rivière du Nord are diked farmlands.

The men, women and children of the village wear colorful homespuns and live as their Acadian forebears lived. Some tend fields and cattle; others churn butter, make clothing, build furniture, split shingles, and perform a myriad of other chores.

Expelled from the Maritimes by the British in 1755, thousands of Acadian refugees spent years of exile in Massachusetts, Virginia, Louisiana and France. Most of them returned to the Maritimes, and between 1780 and 1880 they built primitive settlements along the coast of northeastern New Brunswick.

Some of the reconstructed buildings in the Acadian Historical Village come from as far away as Fredericton and Edmundston. The oldest building is the Martin farmhouse (1783). A log cabin with an earthen floor, it stood for nearly two centuries at French Village, near Fredericton.

[map: showing ÎLE MISCOU ISLAND, Miscou Centre, Petite-Rivière-de-l'Île, Petit-Shippagan, araquet, Bas-Caraquet, POKESUDIE ISLAND, Petite-Lamèque, ÎLE LAMÈQUE, Pigeon Hill, Lamèque, Haut-Pokemouche, SHIPPAGAN PROV PK, Saint-Raphaël-sur-Mer, Shippagan, Sainte-Marie-sur-Mer, Inkerman Le Goulet, GULF OF ST. LAWRENCE, sonnette]

MISCOU ISLAND

The "Land's End" of New Brunswick—only 18 kilometres long and 13 kilometres wide—is linked by toll-free ferry to Ile Lamèque and the mainland. The island has changed little since the first settlers arrived from France and the Channel Islands in the 18th century. Spruce trees—dwarfed by wind and sea spray—overlook picturesque white sand beaches. Deep-sea fishing charters are available summer and fall.

ÎLE LAMÈQUE

Vast bogs here are among Canada's major sources of peat moss. Most of the local product is shipped to the United States as soil conditioner, stable and poultry litter, insulation and packing material.

□ July is the month for local festivals. The seaside village of Lamèque holds its Peat Moss Festival. Sainte-Cécile Church (near the ferry dock) is the setting for an international baroque music festival.

Queen crab

SHIPPAGAN

During the Fisheries Festival in July, visitors can sample tasty seafood platters, watch the blessing of the local fleet, and enjoy festive events, such as street dancing.

□ The aquarium at the Marine Centre displays marine species and explains the development of deep-sea fishing, which dates from the 16th century in this area.

Fishermen's wharf, Shippagan

Lumberjacks, Legends and a Wild Waterfall

Upper Saint John River Valley

Black-crowned night heron

SAINT-JACQUES

Here at the gateway to the Madawaska region is Les Jardins de la République—a provincial park whose facilities include an amphitheater, an adventure playground, a swimming pool, tennis courts, camping sites and nature trails. Vintage cars (from the period 1905 to 1930), early telephones, and other marvels of bygone days are displayed at the Automobile Museum, which is also in the park.

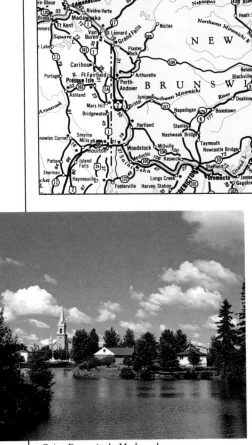

Saint-François-de-Madawaska

SAINT-FRANÇOIS-DE-MADAWASKA

Visitors to Saint-François-de-Madawaska may tour a handicraft center and a blacksmith museum. North of the town, Lac-Baker Provincial Park offers boating, swimming, sailing and waterskiing. Trout fishing in this area is excellent.
□ At Clair an international bridge leads to Fort Kent, Maine. The Daigle/St-Jean House, built in 1848, is open to visitors.

Tau cross by Claude Roussel

EDMUNDSTON

Straddling the junction of the Madawaska and Saint John rivers, this community of 11,500 is a thriving pulp-producing center. (Visitors can tour the Fraser Co. plant and forest nursery.)
□ The city was named in 1848 for Sir Edmund Head, who was lieutenant governor of New Brunswick at that time. The colorful history of the Madawaska region is described at the local regional museum.
□ At Notre Dame des Sept Douleurs Church are intricate wood carvings of the Stations of the Cross by New Brunswick sculptor Claude Roussel. A pre-Christian tau cross, which resembles the Greek capital T, is noteworthy.

Six Red Stars and an Eagle— Symbols of 'la République'

In 1837 the timber-rich Madawaska region was involved in a boundary dispute between New Brunswick and Maine. Lumbermen on both sides of the Saint John River fought in what became known as the Aroostook or "Pork and Beans War." The conflict was resolved in 1842 under the Webster-Ashburton Treaty, but five years of tug-of-war tactics between the American and Canadian governments had created a concept of an independent Madawaska—a *republic* of Madawaska.

The title is thought to have originated with a response given by a colonist to a French official. Thinking the official too inquisitive, the colonist remarked: "I am a citizen of the Republic of Madawaska." The name stuck.

In 1949, recognizing the publicity value of this historical quirk—a republic in the heart of a constitutional monarchy—two New Brunswickers prepared a coat of arms for Madawaska. Edmundston became the republic's capital (mayors of Edmundston automatically hold the title of president of the republic) and an official flag was designed. The flag features a bald eagle, symbol of Madawaska's independent spirit. Six red stars represent the republic's cultural groups: Indian, Acadian, Canadian, English, American and Irish.

Important visitors to the republic are often presented with honorary citizenships, and may even be addressed in the republic's own dialect—known as "Brayon."

0 1 2 3 4 5 Miles

0 2 4 6 8 Kilometres

The Saint John River winds through forest and field and primeval gorge on its journey across Madawaska County. It dominates the rich, gently rolling landscape of this region and at Grand Falls plunges 25 metres over the province's highest escarpment. The river forms almost 110 kilometres of the Canada–United States border, and is skirted for most of its length in New Brunswick by the Trans-Canada Highway.

Malecite Indians were here when explorers de Monts and Champlain named the river on June 24, 1604—the feast day of St. John. The region was later inhabited by settlers from Quebec.

In the 1800s Madawaska was a land of riotous lumber camps. But today the rip-roaring life of the lumberjacks is little more than folklore among a people whose love of dancing and music, work and independence is instantly recognizable.

An effortless bilingualism unites residents of Madawaska—conversations often switch back and forth between French and English. And community celebrations are enjoyed by everyone. One of the most popular is held in Edmundston: "La Foire Brayonne," nine days of colorful festivities ending on the first Monday in August.

SAINT-BASILE

Founded in 1792, this small community is one of the oldest in the Madawaska region. A log replica of the area's first chapel, which was built in 1780, contains a museum that displays pioneer artifacts. □ Saint-Basile hosts the Madawaska County Fair in late August.

John Glasier was a pioneer lumberman in the Madawaska region. Born in 1809, he was the first to drive logs over Grand Falls, and the first to explore the Squatec Lakes in Quebec. A rugged bear of a fellow, he towered over other men and added to his height by wearing a tall black hat—even in bed, according to legend.

Early in life Glasier employed some 600 men to run New Brunswick's largest lumbering operation. As his reputation grew, he acquired the nickname "Main John"—a title that identified him as the man in charge. The expression was later used throughout North America to designate the manager of any large lumber camp.

Glasier became a member of the New Brunswick legislature in 1861. Seven years later he was named to the Canadian Senate. He died in 1894 and was immortalized in a poem by H. A. Cody:

'Main John' Glasier, the First Man to Drive Logs Over Grand Falls

Don't you see the "Main John" striding in the lead?
Clear-eyed, strong and fearless, kith of Bluenose breed;
First to bring a timber drive through the wild Grand Falls;
First to sight the Squattook Lakes where the lone moose calls.
Haunter of the silent ways,
Spirit of the glen,
Dauntless as in olden days
Glasier leads his men.

GRAND FALLS/GRAND SAULT

The town takes its name from Grand Falls on the Saint John River, which plunges roughly 21 metres into a local 1.5-metre-long gorge. The Malecite Indians called the falls *Chik-un-il-pe*—"the destroying giant"—because of its awesome appearance. Since the 1870s, when the railway first reached this region, the falls—one of the largest east of Niagara Falls—has remained a tourist attraction. Interpretative displays describe the action of the falls. Stairs lead to the wells-in-the-rocks—a series of 9-metre-deep potholes in the gorge. The energy of the falls is channeled through a power plant, which supplies electricity for the provincial distribution system.
□ Grand Falls' 38-metre-wide main street, originally a military parade ground, is believed to be the widest in Canada.
□ In early summer the town hosts a festival to celebrate the potato, the major crop of this region.

SAINT-LÉONARD

Linked to the United States by an international bridge over the Saint John River, this busy rural community—founded in 1789—is a center for the surrounding lumbering and agricultural region. (Potatoes are the main crop.)
□ Saint-Léonard is the center for the famous Madawaska Weavers, whose colorful hand-loomed creations include skirts, scarves and ties. Visitors are welcome to tour the Weavers' store and workshops (on the main street).

Weavers at Saint-Léonard

ST-BASILE
COMMUNITY PK
St-Basile

NB
MAINE
8

Rivière Verte
Rivière-Verte
2
9.5

Saint
John
River

Rivière Quisibis
36.5

Ste-Anne-de-Madawaska

Siegas
11

Grande R.
ST-LÉONARD
PROV PK
St-Léonard
17
Van Buren

Bellefleur
18

1
8

10
2
255

MAINE
NB

Grand Falls/Grand Sault
2

Grand Falls

A Tradition of Hospitality in Bountiful Potato Country

Upper Saint John River Valley

DRUMMOND

Since the 1860s, Drummond and its surroundings have prospered from potato farming. The first bushel of potatoes grown here was planted by Barney McLaughlin, an Irishman. Today most Drummond farmers are of French descent. Schools here open in early August so that students can leave for three weeks in September to help with the harvest. The crop is stored in potato cellars or houses—storage sheds partly buried in the ground to protect against frost.

Potato cellar, Drummond

Greens for Gourmets

Fiddlehead greens—the unopened fronds of ostrich ferns—are harvested in the woods and on the riverbanks of New Brunswick in early May. The fast-growing shoots—about 10 to 20 centimetres in length—are packed and frozen by food-processing firms at Florenceville and elsewhere. When boiled, the fiddlehead greens are a succulent delicacy. For centuries, New Brunswick's Malecite Indians have prized fiddleheads as food and medicine. Now the plant is big business and something of a provincial symbol: Fredericton stages an annual fiddlehead festival; a radio station boasts of serving "fiddlehead country," and the University of New Brunswick publishes a literary magazine called *The Fiddlehead.*

BEECHWOOD

Visitors to Beechwood's hydro-electric plant can watch a fish elevator lifting Atlantic salmon over an 18-metre dam on the Saint John River. The plant's grounds feature a floral clock.
□ North of Beechwood, a hillside setting of beech and maple adds to the picnicking and camping pleasures of Muniac Provincial Park.

FLORENCEVILLE

Once known as Buttermilk Creek, Florenceville was renamed for the English nurse and philanthropist Florence Nightingale (1820-1910), who was the heroine of the Crimean War. Today the town is the site of Canada's largest food plant (operated by McCain Foods Ltd.), which prepares potatoes—and the local specialty, fiddleheads, for nationwide consumption.

UPPER WOODSTOCK

Historic documents, costumes, photographs, paintings, an old law book and a blotting sand bottle are preserved in the Old Carleton County Courthouse (1833), whose courtroom, jury and lawyers' rooms have been restored. This elegant, two-story, clapboard museum was the seat of New Brunswick's first county council. It has also been a stagecoach stop, and the scene of agricultural fairs, political rallies and governors' levees. One exhibit recalls Edwin Tappan Adney, a local author, artist, naturalist, authority on heraldic design and expert on North American Indian crafts. Another exhibit includes 1,000 lead soldiers, replicas of British regiments of the 18th and 19th centuries.

Old Carleton County Courthouse, Upper Woodstock

Toy soldiers, Old Carleton County Courthouse

The Saint John River: *Oo-lahs-took* the Indians called it—the goodly river. And goodly it remains to those who till its valley soil. This is potato country—a peaceful, prosperous land where potato festivals (at Grand Falls and Hartland) pay homage to the bounty of the soil, and where bushels of the vegetables roll off production lines as french fries, hash browns and instant mashed. The fields that produced them stretch to the horizon.

Agriculture is a common bond uniting diverse communities in this region. Between Perth-Andover and Woodstock gospel tents dot the countryside, and Bible texts on billboards and barn gables exhort repentence. Stately homes set among elms and maples are the hallmark of Woodstock, "the hospitality town." Its settlers decreed that "no visitor, known or unknown, should pass through this community without sharing its hospitality."

Woodstock's hospitality is particularly warm during Old Home Week, an annual July celebration that includes horse-pulling contests and harness racing. In Woodstock, visitors can see the house outside which, in 1860, Charles Connell, the eccentric provincial postmaster general, lit a bonfire and burned half a million stamps on which he had printed his own portrait.

In spring, travelers on this route can pluck and savor fiddleheads. In any season they can explore one of New Brunswick's most famous landmarks—the world's longest covered bridge at Hartland.

NEW DENMARK

Many of the 1,000 persons in this town wear Danish dress and enjoy traditional dances each June 19—Founders' Day in Canada's largest Danish community. The festivities commemorate 29 immigrants who settled at the junction of the Saint John and Salmon rivers in 1872.
□ The New Denmark Memorial Museum, on the site of the original clearing, displays early tax records, and settlers' clothing, including an old wedding dress and boots from an immigrant's army service in Denmark.

Folk dancing, New Denmark

PLASTER ROCK

At Plaster Rock, gateway to the highlands of northern New Brunswick, the Tobique River loops green and swift through red gypsum hills for which this lumbering and agricultural town is named. The Tobique, main tributary of the Saint John, provides a 137-kilometre canoe route through wilderness inhabited by black bears, moose, white-tailed deer, marten, ruffed grouse and black ducks. The route includes fast water, rapids, tight turns and the calm waters of the Tobique Reservoir. Upriver from Plaster Rock, guides and outfitters cater to hunters and fishermen.

PERTH-ANDOVER

Originally used as logging centers and portages, Perth *and* Andover were settled in the early 1850s by British soldiers, who received land in lieu of pay for military service. Perth-Andover became a single community in 1966.

Tobique River, Plaster Rock

HARTLAND

Where the world's longest covered bridge (391 metres) spans the Saint John River at Hartland, you may cross your fingers, hold your breath and make a wish: according to local lore, dreams come true for those who cross the seven-span giant without exhaling. Built in 1896, it was a toll bridge until 1904.

WOODSTOCK

A two-story wooden dwelling built in the 1820s by Charles Connell is one of several stately old homes here. Connell, postmaster general of New Brunswick in 1858-61, is famous for substituting his own likeness for one of Queen Victoria on an 1860 issue of stamps. In the ensuing protest Connell burned the stamps and resigned.
□ Harness racing, golf, swimming and a weekly farmers' market are among the attractions in Connell Park.

Sheltering Spans of Yesteryear

Wishing or kissing bridges are romantic relics of a bygone age. Wishin' may indeed have become kissin' under those wooden rafters of yesteryear, but it was common sense not dreams and romance that inspired the building of Canada's covered bridges.

An uncovered wooden bridge lasted only 15 years before rot weakened its underpinnings and broad deck planks. Horses, frightened by rushing waters glimpsed through the timber floor, shied and bolted. With a roof and siding—cheap and easy to install—a bridge was good for 80 years. And animals, reassured by the stablelike structure, trotted docilely through.

Covered bridges were "high enough and wide enough to take a load of hay." Snow was spread on the carriageway in winter to ease sled traffic. The bridges served as notice boards for circuses and patent medicines.

Of the thousands of covered bridges built at the turn of the century, there are few still standing, and most of these are in Quebec and New Brunswick. At Hartland, N.B., the world's longest covered bridge (*above*) is a 391-metre giant whose seven spans leap the Saint John River. The original cedar log abutments and rock-filled piers of 1899 were replaced by concrete in 1920.

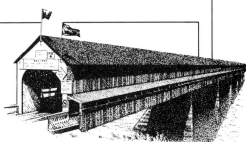

World's longest covered bridge, Hartland

A City of Stately Elms
Where Past and Present Merge

Lower Saint John River Valley

*Legislative Building,
Fredericton*

*Christ Church Cathedral,
Fredericton*

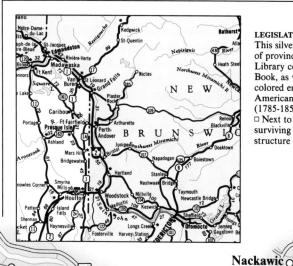

LEGISLATIVE BUILDING
This silver-domed Victorian edifice has been the seat of provincial government since 1882. The Legislative Library contains a 1783 edition of the Domesday Book, as well as a complete set of the 435 hand-colored engravings of the *Birds of America* by American painter and naturalist John James Audubon (1785-1851).
□ Next to the legislature is Fredericton's oldest surviving building. The first floor of the modest stone structure was built in 1816.

CHRIST CHURCH CATHEDRAL
One of the finest examples of decorated Gothic architecture in North America, Christ Church Cathedral was built between 1845 and 1853. The moving force behind its construction was Bishop John Medley, who persuaded British authorities to confer city status—a prerequisite for cathedral building—on Fredericton.
□ The cathedral contains the letters patent—issued by Queen Victoria—elevating Fredericton to a city. Other items include a pulpit hanging made from part of Queen Victoria's coronation robe.

KINGS LANDING HISTORICAL SETTLEMENT
This 121-hectare reconstructed 19th-century New Brunswick settlement—just off the Trans-Canada Highway, 39.5 kilometres west of Fredericton—opened in 1974. Many of the historic buildings were moved to the site from areas that were flooded when the Mactaquac dam (near Mactaquac Provincial Park) was completed. The settlement is open daily from June until October and on Sundays from mid-January until mid-March.
□ A memorial cairn at Meductic, 40 kilometres west of Kings Landing, marks the site of one of the earliest chapels in New Brunswick. It was built by French settlers in 1717.

Warm Hearths and Creaking Oxcarts

The sights and sounds of 19th-century New Brunswick are everywhere at Kings Landing Historical Settlement. Among the site's more than 70 buildings are 10 meticulously restored dwellings. The elegantly furnished Ingraham House typifies the surroundings of a wealthy family of the 1840s. Joslin Farm shows the life of a farm family in the 1860s. The plush parlor and formal dining room of the Hagerman House mirror life of the well-to-do of the 1860s.

Kings Landing also has a church, a school and a small theater, as well as old-time workplaces—a sawmill (*right*), a gristmill, a forge, a carpenter shop and a general store. At the Kings Head Inn visitors can down mugs of draft beer in the cozy taproom, or enjoy old-fashioned cooking in the dining room.

The settlement's costumed staff re-create the rhythms of New Brunswick's rural life between 1820 and 1890. In the old houses, women spin and weave, churn butter and make soap, while fires crackle on open hearths. In the fields, men plant or harvest according to the season. And, along the settlement's winding lanes, creaking oxcarts and horse-drawn buggies carry visitors through the tranquil landscape of yesteryear.

MACTAQUAC
Overlooking the head pond of Mactaquac Dam, New Brunswick's "Super Park"—Mactaquac Provincial Park—is open year-round. Within its 567 hectares are campsites, kitchen shelters and laundry facilities. It contains two beaches, marinas, nature trails, and a championship 18-hole golf course.
□ Other nearby attractions include the Mactaquac generating station and the fish hatchery. Both can be toured.

WOOLASTOOK WILDLIFE PARK
The park highlights animals common to Atlantic Canada. Nature trails lead to enclosures where visitors can view caribou moose, lynx and other species in open or wooded compounds.

Meductic · 122 · Temple · 105 · 2 · 21 Trans-Canada Hwy · 40 · Pokiok Stream · Nackawic · Hawkshaw · 9.5 · Pokiok · Dumfries · Davidson Lake · Saint · 9.5 · 2 · Prince William · 636 · KINGS LANDING HIST SETTLEMENT · 11.5 · John · River · Longs Creek · 3 · Keswick Ridge · 616 · 615 · 2 · 105 · MACTAQUAC PROV PK · 4 · Mactaquac · 9.5 · 2 · 39.5 · Kingsclear · 3 · WOOLASTOOK WILDLIFE · N

Past and present merge in Fredericton (pop. 44,350), New Brunswick's tranquil capital. The historic buildings, gracious homes and stately elms recall the aristocratic Loyalist founders and the wealthy 19th-century merchants and lumber barons. At the same time, the city's modern buildings—notably the Beaverbrook Art Gallery—and sophisticated tourist attractions tell of a place attuned to today.

Fredericton was still wilderness when Loyalist refugees established their "haven for the King's Friends" here in 1783. Within two years, the site—known to earlier Acadian settlers as Sainte-Anne's Point—was designated provincial capital and renamed for George III's son Frederick.

Major Fredericton landmarks, such as the Military Compound and Christ Church Cathedral, are reminders of its importance as an early 19th-century military stronghold and religious center. But the city was also a place of culture and education. The University of New Brunswick—founded in 1828 as King's College—is the oldest provincial university in Canada. Within its precincts are the nation's first astronomical observatory (1851) and engineering school (1854). Campus memorials honor New Brunswick poets Bliss Carman (1861-1929) and Sir Charles G. D. Roberts (1860-1943).

Fredericton abounds with tree-lined streets and open spaces, such as Odell Park and The Green, which enhance its reputation as the "last surviving hometown in North America."

FREDERICTON

Virtually all Fredericton's major attractions—the Legislative Building, Christ Church Cathedral, the Beaverbrook Art Gallery and the Playhouse—are concentrated in the downtown area.

□ The city's 19th-century Military Compound includes the Soldiers Barracks, the Guard House, and the Officers' Quarters. The renovated three-story barracks, completed in 1827, are now offices, although one room has been restored to the 1860s style. The Guard House, built in 1828, contains an orderly room, a guardroom, and a cellblock, all of which have been restored. The Officers' Quarters has two wings—built in 1839-40 and 1851 respectively. The older part houses the York-Sunbury Historical Society Museum.

□ Other important landmarks include the old City Hall (1876); Wilmot United Church, which dates from 1852 and is a fine example of "carpenter's Gothic" decoration; York County Courthouse (1882); the Old York County Gaol (1840-42); and Old Government House (1828).

OLD GOVERNMENT HOUSE

This imposing Georgian structure, opposite Wilmot Park, was the residence of New Brunswick's governors and lieutenant governors from 1828 to 1893. Now the local RCMP headquarters, Old Government House is closed to the public.

Old Government House, Fredericton

OFFICERS' QUARTERS

This remnant of Fredericton's military history contains the York-Sunbury Historical Society Museum. It focuses on central New Brunswick history from the early Indian period to the immediate past.

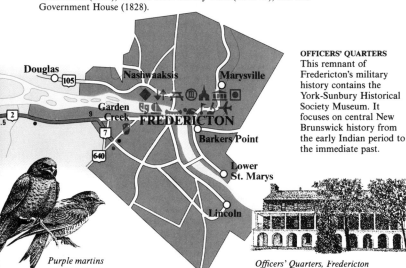

Purple martins

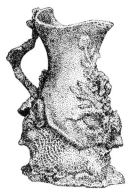

Officers' Quarters, Fredericton

Orderly room, Fredericton Military Compound

Beaverbrook's Gift— a Gallery of Great Pictures

Lord Beaverbrook said that the best picture in Fredericton's Beaverbrook Art Gallery was the view of the Saint John River from the great window in the main gallery. But the painting that attracts most visitors is Salvador Dali's large *Santiago el Grande*. The gallery, one of Beaverbrook's gifts to the city, houses a collection of British art. There are paintings by Reynolds, Gainsborough, Constable, Romney, Turner and Hogarth. Several of Sir Winston Churchill's canvases are here. The Canadian collection includes works by Cornelius Krieghoff, Paul Kane, James Wilson Morrice, Tom Thomson, Arthur Lismer, and Emily Carr. The Lucile Pillow Room contains 130 porcelain pieces representing the best of English artistry between 1743 and 1840. *Right:* a Chelsea Goat and Bee jug (1743).

Fredericton

1 Old Government House
2 Odell Park
3 City Hall
4 Tourist Information
5 Soldiers Barracks
6 The Guard House
7 National Exhibition Centre
8 Officers' Quarters
9 The Playhouse
10 Beaverbrook Art Gallery
11 Legislative Assembly Building
12 The Green
13 Christ Church Cathedral
14 University of New Brunswick
15 St. Thomas University
16 Tourist Information
17 Fort Nashwaak (cairn)
18 Loyalist Cemetery

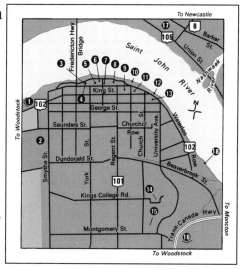

Line-Busting Salmon in a Land of Song

Nashwaak-Miramichi Trail

All morning the angler has been casting over his favorite stretch of water on the Southwest Miramichi.

Suddenly there is a flash of silver and a tug that bows the angler's rod. The reel screams as a salmon takes out line, dashes almost to the opposite shore, then downstream. The fish leaps far out of the water, hangs poised for a breathless second, then falls with a splash. Again the salmon leaps and strikes the water on its side with a sound like breaking glass. With luck, patience will

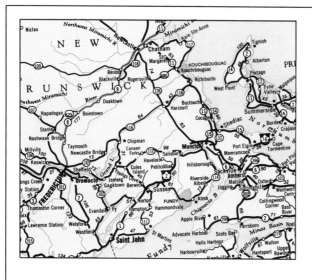

BOIESTOWN

This village, a lumbering and outfitting center, is at the geographical midpoint of New Brunswick. For travelers heading northeast from Fredericton on Route 8, Boiestown provides the first glimpse of the world-renowned salmon river, the 217-kilometre-long Southwest Miramichi. Sports fishermen first appear locally in April and May—during the spring runoff of Atlantic salmon—and others continue to arrive until September. Between Boiestown and Blackville, fishing and hunting camps abound to accommodate the influx.
□ The Woodmen's Museum—just east of Boiestown—presents historic photographs, tools and buildings, which illustrate pioneer life in New Brunswick.
□ At the village of McNamee, roughly 11 kilometres northeast of Boiestown, a 200-metre suspension footbridge—the only one in New Brunswick—spans the Miramichi River.

Salmon angling on the Southwest Miramichi

STANLEY

The mid-August Stanley Fair, first held in 1851, is the longest continuous event of its kind in New Brunswick. Residents—and visitors, too—celebrate the harvest with square dances to the sound of old-time fiddle playing. Local farmers—the descendants of British settlers for the most part—display their produce and livestock.

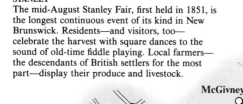

Southwest Miramichi River

DOAKTOWN

The Miramichi Salmon Museum at Doaktown honors the region's valuable game fish with exhibits emphasizing conservation and sportsmanship. The museum, which includes an aquarium displaying the full range of salmon species, presents a year-round schedule of special programs and events.
□ The local heritage park preserves Robert Doak's restored home, which the Scottish settler built in the early 19th century. It survived the great Miramichi forest fire of 1825, which devastated this area.

MARYSVILLE

This Fredericton suburb near the mouth of the Nashwaak River was founded by Alexander "Boss" Gibson, who arrived here in the summer of 1862 and brought the first log drive down the river. He built sawmills and an extensive lumbering empire, and even constructed a railway to consolidate his holdings. In addition to lumber mills, Gibson built a large red brick cotton mill—along with row housing for his workers. He named the town which grew up around the mill, Marysville, in honor of his wife.

0   2   4   6   8   10 Miles
0   4   8   12   16 Kilometres

soon pay off handsomely for yet another sportsman, lured to the Southwest Miramichi River by tales of line-busting Atlantic salmon.

Northbound highway travelers on the Nashwaak-Miramichi Trail first glimpse the Southwest Miramichi at Boiestown, the geographical center of New Brunswick. The trail follows the Nashwaak River north from Fredericton, then heads along the Southwest Miramichi—through the spectacular scenery of central New Brunswick—to the sea, and the thriving ports of Newcastle and Chatham.

Basque and French fishermen came to Miramichi Bay in the early 1500s, though the first recorded voyage was that of Jacques Cartier in 1534. In 1686, Baptiste Franquelin, a French engineer-cartographer, mapped the river and its numerous tributaries, and recorded their Indian names.

Then came the valley's hardy pioneers—lumbermen and shipbuilders—and with them, their songs. Singing remained a major part of Miramichi life in horse-and-buggy days, when songs were carefully chosen to last the length of a journey. Today the people of the region celebrate their love of music at Newcastle's Miramichi Folk Song Festival in late July and early August.

McDonald farmhouse, Bartibog Bridge

BARTIBOG BRIDGE
Overlooking Miramichi Bay is an eight-room sandstone house, built about 1815 by Scottish settler Alexander McDonald. The house is the centerpiece of a provincial heritage park, which re-creates a working farm of the early 19th century.

BLACKVILLE
The region between Boiestown and Blackville is the legendary haunt of the Dungarvon Whooper, the ghost of a lumber camp cook who was robbed and murdered on the bank of the Dungarvon River in the 1860s. After the young man was buried in a shallow grave, people in the area began to hear loud, bloodcurdling screams. Unwary travelers are warned to "beware of the smell of frying bacon"—with which the Whooper tries to lure his murderer.

Lord Beaverbrook monument, Newcastle

MIDDLE ISLAND PROVINCIAL PARK
The island has a shape similar to a nearby lake. The Indians believed that the island was lifted from the mainland and dropped in the middle of the river. A Celtic cross on the island honors the Irish immigrants to this region. The park, which has a beach and picnic sites, is reached by a causeway.

DOUGLASTOWN
Rankin House, which was built in the late 1880s by a shipbuilder, displays ship models, historic artifacts and works by local artists.

CHATHAM
The town's development in the early 19th century was linked to the fortunes of the Cunard shipping dynasty. Joseph Cunard (1799-1865)—whose brother Samuel (1787-1865) founded the famous steamship line—presided over the family's local business interests from 1820 until bankruptcy forced his departure in 1848.
□ Another famous Chatham figure was R. B. Bennett (1870-1947), the only New Brunswick-born Canadian prime minister.
□ The Miramichi Natural History Museum displays Cunard documents and records. Other important Chatham landmarks include the restored Loggie House (now a cultural center) and St. Michael's Historical Museum, which contains local genealogical records.

NEWCASTLE
One of the town's showplaces was the boyhood home of Lord Beaverbrook (1879-1964). During his life, Beaverbrook played many roles—financier, Fleet Street newspaper tycoon and a member of Winston Churchill's wartime cabinet. Beaverbrook—who was born William Maxwell Aitken, son of a Newcastle Presbyterian minister—grew up at the Old Manse, near St. James Church. His former home, open to the public, houses a museum and a library. A monument containing Beaverbrook's ashes and an Italian gazebo (a Beaverbrook gift) are in the town square.
□ Many of Newcastle's spacious frame houses were built by local 19th-century lumber barons after the great Miramichi fire of 1825. The fire leveled all but 12 of the town's 260 buildings, as well as 5,500 square miles of forest in this region—one of the worst disasters of its kind on record.

Fire fighting "air tanker," Upper Blackville

UPPER BLACKVILLE
The Forest Protection Branch of New Brunswick's Natural Resources Department maintains an airstrip and headquarters here for light aircraft that look for fires in the province's dense forests. A fleet of "air tankers" is used to bomb fire outbreaks with chemical retardants.

Come All Ye Down to the Miramichi . . .

Acadian step dances and the traditional songs of New Brunswick's colorful lumbermen are highlights of the Miramichi Folk Song Festival at Newcastle in midsummer. Long narrative chants about great feats and lost loves are sung to the foot-tapping music of fiddle, banjo, accordion and mouth organ.

The Jones Boys, a one-verse ditty, was a favorite of Lord Beaverbrook. The bells he gave to the University of New Brunswick at Fredericton ring out that chorus on the hour. Another popular ballad is *Peter Emberley,* a tale of a young man fatally injured in the Miramichi woods.

Other festival favorites include ballads that begin with "Come all ye jolly lumbermen . . ." and "good night" songs—those once sung at public executions.

My name 'tis Pe-ter Em-ber-ley.

I landed in New Brunswick in a lumbering counterie,
I hired to work in the lumber woods on the Sou-West Miramichi.
I hired to work in the lumber woods where they cut the tall spruce down,
While loading teams with yarded logs I received a deadly wound.

The World's Lobster Capital...
and Its Largest Hayfield

Southeastern New Brunswick

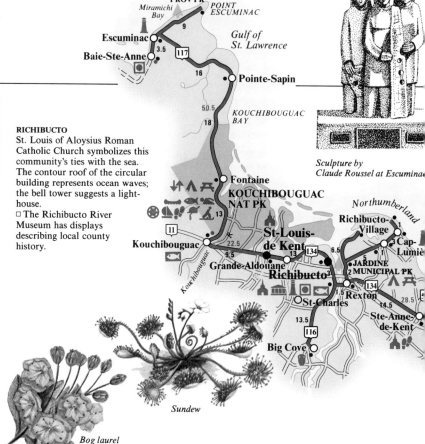

Sculpture by Claude Roussel at Escuminac

ESCUMINAC

A sculpture by New Brunswick artist Claude Roussel commemorates the tragic loss of 35 fishermen in a savage storm on Miramichi Bay in 1959. The sculpture, paid for b[y] New Brunswick's Fishermen's Memorial Fund, symbolizes sea's impact on the lives of those dependent on it.

RICHIBUCTO

St. Louis of Aloysius Roman Catholic Church symbolizes this community's ties with the sea. The contour roof of the circular building represents ocean waves; the bell tower suggests a lighthouse.

□ The Richibucto River Museum has displays describing local county history.

KOUCHIBOUGUAC NATIONAL PARK

Boardwalks in this park on Kouchibouguac Bay lead to a 25-kilometre sweep of offshore sandbars, tidewater lagoons and grassy salt marshes. Marram grass and false heather anchor shoreline dunes. Peat bogs, underlying the marshes and dunes, encourage the growth of bog laurel, lambkill, white-fringed orchids, and insect-eating sundews and pitcher plants. Inland is mixed forest of black spruce, white pine, jack pine, yellow birch and trembling aspen. Some 216 species of birds and 25 species of mammals have been sighted in the 238-square-kilometre park. There is good swimming in the warm water of Northumberland Strait. Other park activities include camping, canoeing, hiking, fishing and cross-country skiing.

Sundew

Bog laurel

REXTON

Bonar Law Historic Park—a nine-hectare area along the Richibucto River—encloses the restored boyhood home of Andrew Bonar Law, who was prime minister of Britain in 1922-23. The park also conserves period farm buildings. From an orientation center, costumed guides escort visitors around the park.

MONCTON

New Brunswick's second largest city (pop. 56,000) was originally settled by Germans, who were followed by Loyalists, Scots and Irish. In 1855 it was named for Lt.Col. Robert Monckton, who had taken nearby Fort Beauséjour a century earlier. (By accident, the letter "k" was deleted when the name was officially designated.)

□ Today more than a third of the city's residents are French-speaking. The Université de Moncton is the only French-language university east of Quebec City.

□ Places of historical interest include the city's oldest building—the Free Meeting House. This one-story structure, built in 1821, was a place of worship for the early German settlers.

□ Moncton Museum has displays about the area from Micmac Indian days to the present. The Acadian Museum (on the university campus) contains paintings, old looms and spinning wheels, a smithy and a 1614 pipe organ. The Lutz Mountain Heritage Museum, located in an old church, preserves genealogies of the city's 1766 founders.

□ Natural features include the tidal bore, which surges up the Petitcodiac River twice daily; Magnetic Hill, where vehicles seem to coast uphill; and Centennial Park, which contains 21 hectares of lake and woodland.

Specialities from Acadian Kitchens

For centuries Acadians have reaped the sea's harvest and tilled the fertile soil of the Maritimes. Fish and vegetables are important ingredients in traditional Acadian cooking. Mackerel, herring or cod is boiled in salted water and served with potatoes; hearty chowder is made with clams, oysters or lobsters, and potatoes and onions. Turnips, cabbages or red beans are often combined with bacon.

Several Moncton area restaurants prepare Acadian specialities like *pot-en-pot*, a chicken stew cooked with homemade noodles, and *poutines râpées*, large balls of grated and mashed potato embedded with diced salt pork and simmered in water. *Poutines râpées* are served with salt and pepper for a main course, or with molasses for a tasty dessert.

0 2 4 6 8 10 Miles

0 4 8 12 16 Kilometres

Lobster traps, homespun sweaters, sea gulls, vesper bells and front-porch rocking chairs—these are the sights and sounds of the Northumberland Shore, in southeastern New Brunswick.

In Kouchibouguac National Park, set in gently rolling mixed forests of spruce, birch, aspen and pine, side roads lead seaward to sand dunes, quiet lagoons and sandy beaches. South of the park are Richibucto, famed for scallops; Rexton, birthplace of Andrew Bonar Law (1858-1923)—the only British prime minister born outside the British Isles; and Bouctouche, birthplace of distinguished Acadian novelist Antonine Maillet. Near Shediac, "lobster capital of the world," fine beaches offer warm saltwater swimming.

A bustling terminus of one New Brunswick–Prince Edward Island ferry is at Cape Tormentine. Inland, across the isthmus of Chignecto, the ruins of Fort Beauséjour overlook the vast, barn-dotted Tantramar marshes—known as the world's biggest hay-field. For 13 grim days in 1755, the marshes were the scene of bitter fighting as 270 British regulars and 2,000 New England volunteers attacked and captured Beauséjour.

Sackville is a quiet, tree-shaded university town; Dorchester boasts some of the province's finest Classical Revival architecture; and Moncton, the transportation hub of the Maritimes, combines English reserve with Acadian *joie de vivre*.

"La Sagouine" as portrayed by New Brunswick actress, Viola Léger

BOUCTOUCHE
The wild and beautiful beaches, warm sands and temperate waters of Bouctouche harbor make this Acadian fishing village a favorite tourist spot. There is excellent local lobster fishing, and the area is known as "the oyster bed of New Brunswick."
□ Kent Museum, which occupies an old convent and educational center, exhibits artifacts on local and county history.
□ Bouctouche is the birthplace of Acadian novelist Antonine Maillet. Her most popular work is *La Sagouine* (1971), the portrait of an aging but indomitable woman who recounts her life in rich Acadian dialect.

SHEDIAC
The "lobster capital of the world" stages a five-day festival in mid-July with parades, folk songs and dancing, sports events and lobster dinners. One of New Brunswick's principal yachting and resort areas, Shediac has several fine beaches on the Northumberland Strait, whose waters are among the warmest north of Virginia. Parlee Beach Provincial Park offers spacious camping facilities and excellent saltwater swimming.

Ruins at Fort Beauséjour National Historic Park

AULAC
Fort Beauséjour, one of the few military posts in Canada to see heavy fighting, was built by the French in 1751-55 to counter the British at Fort Lawrence, near present-day Amherst, N.S. In June 1755 Beauséjour was taken by the British, who renamed it Fort Cumberland and extended its defenses. The old name was reinstated in 1926 when the site was designated a national historic park.

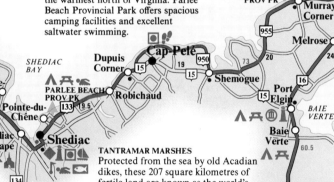

TANTRAMAR MARSHES
Protected from the sea by old Acadian dikes, these 207 square kilometres of fertile land are known as the world's biggest hayfield. Tantramar may be from the French *tintamarre* (loud noise), referring to the sound of the tides or the cacophony of marsh birds.

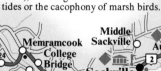

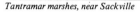

Tantramar marshes, near Sackville

Keillor House, Dorchester

DORCHESTER
Locally quarried stone was used to build Keillor House in 1813. The mansion, which has been restored and is now a museum, has 10 rooms of fine late-18th- and early-19th-century furniture. Outstanding architectural features include nine fireplaces and a three-story spiral staircase.
□ The 1811 Bell Inn—the oldest stone building in New Brunswick—contains a restaurant and a crafts shop.

SACKVILLE
Near the center of town is the parklike campus of Mount Allison University, whose Owens Art Gallery has one of Canada's finest collections of graphics. The gallery has three silk-screened prints by realist painter Alex Colville, who studied at Mount Allison. There are also works by the Group of Seven; pre-1880 English watercolors, etchings and paintings; and 10 prints and a self-portrait in oils by Newfoundland artist Christopher Pratt. Graduates of the university include Grace Ann Lockhart, the first woman in the British Empire to be granted a bachelor's degree (1875).
□ A small harness shop on Main Street is the only one in North America still producing handmade horse collars.

A Friendly Border
Where Old Angers Are Forgotten

Southwestern New Brunswick

The industry and conservatism of Loyalist forebears are imprinted along the route, which is broken by gentle bays and belted by spruce and fir and rolling farmland. Scorned and threatened by the victors of the American Revolution, the Loyalist residents of Castine, Maine, fled from the United States and settled these rugged shores. The Crown rewarded their loyalty with liberal land grants and they prospered.

In St. Andrews, stately homes and quaint inns exude colonial charm, and reflection

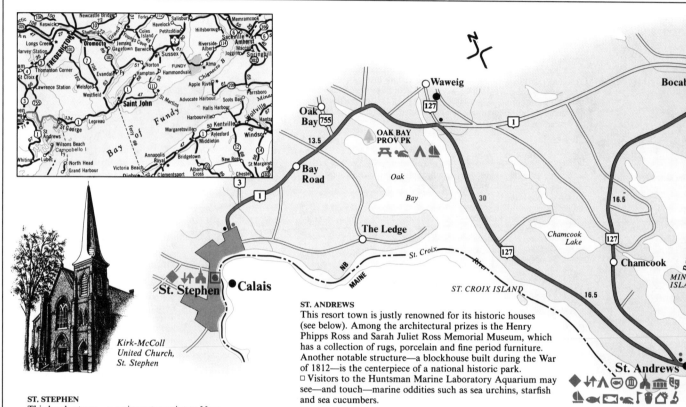

Kirk-McColl United Church, St. Stephen

ST. ANDREWS
This resort town is justly renowned for its historic houses (see below). Among the architectural prizes is the Henry Phipps Ross and Sarah Juliet Ross Memorial Museum, which has a collection of rugs, porcelain and fine period furniture. Another notable structure—a blockhouse built during the War of 1812—is the centerpiece of a national historic park.
□ Visitors to the Huntsman Marine Laboratory Aquarium may see—and touch—marine oddities such as sea urchins, starfish and sea cucumbers.

ST. STEPHEN
This border town—a major entry point to New Brunswick for American tourists—has always maintained amicable relations with Calais, Maine, across the St. Croix River. Both towns celebrate each other's national holidays, share the same water supply, and answer each other's fire alarms.
□ Kirk-McColl United Church is named for Methodist minister Duncan McColl, who helped to keep the peace locally during the War of 1812.
□ St. Stephen was originally a shipbuilding center. (Builders once hauled masts down King Street—formerly known as King's Mast Road.) Today the town's major industry is the Ganong candy factory. Here in 1906 Arthur Ganong invented chocolate bars—blocks of chocolate wrapped in paper—as snacks for a fishing trip. In summer St. Stephen hosts a Chocolate Fest, which includes—at this time only—tours of the candy factory.

Ganong's chocolate box (1920)

Canada's First 'Prefabs'

When the Loyalist founders of St. Andrews fled Castine, Maine, after the American Revolution, some brought their houses, section by section, on barges. A green-roofed, white clapboard dwelling built in Castine in 1770 and reassembled here in 1783 is at 75 Montague Street. Of the 13 other 18th-century buildings in the town, the best preserved one is at Adolphus and Queen streets. It was built about 1790 for John Dunn, county sheriff. A rarer, saltbox design—two-storied front, one-storied rear—is the frame dwelling on Queen Street, near Edward Street, built in 1785 by ship's carpenter Joseph Crookshank. The Pagan-O'Neill House at Queen and Frederick streets was one of the first in the settlement. Chestnut Hall at King and Montague streets was built about 1810 for Col. Christopher Hatch, commander of the garrison.

But the town's architectural gem is Greenock Presbyterian Church, built in 1824 by a shipbuilder, Capt. Christopher Scott. On its white tower is carved a green oak tree (emblem of Scott's Greenock, Scotland, birthplace).

Joseph Crookshank House (1785)

Pagan-O'Neill House (1784)

John Dunn House (1790)

0	1	2	3	4	5 Miles
0		2	4	6	8 Kilometres

of the town's English-American heritage are in historic buildings on almost every street.

For many years tensions ran high between the Loyalists and their American neighbors. The wooden blockhouse opposite Centennial Park was built early in the War of 1812. (Capt. Christopher Scott, a wealthy shipbuilder, paid for construction of the blockhouse when military funds were withheld.)

The Americans never attacked St. Andrews. By the mid-19th century old angers were spent and American vacationers flocked to this Loyalist bastion. The Shiretown Inn (1881), one of Canada's oldest summer hotels, and the gabled Algonquin Hotel (1888, rebuilt 1915) are reminders of St. Andrews's era as the summer playground of wealthy Bostonians and New Yorkers.

Today on Campobello Island an international park dedicated to the memory of U.S. President Franklin Delano Roosevelt symbolizes friendship between Canada and the United States.

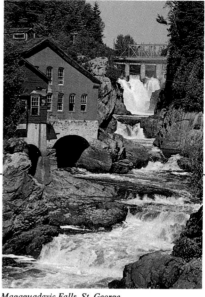

Magaguadavic Falls, St. George

ST. GEORGE
Granite outcrops—and granite markers in the Loyalist cemetery—are reminders of thriving local quarries. Once called "the red granite town," St. George is now a fishing community.
□ Near picturesque Magaguadavic Falls, Atlantic salmon bound for upstream spawning grounds use a concrete fish ladder that bypasses the falls.

Spindle shell

Common periwinkle

Waved whelk

PASSAMAQUODDY BAY
Sheltered Passamaquoddy Bay has a rich variety of marine life. Periwinkles, barnacles, limpets, sand dollars and poisonous moon snails can be found on its shores at low tide. In warm weather, rocky areas yield waved whelks. (Warnings are posted any time these normally edible mollusks contain toxins.) Spindle shells, whose shells once served as whale-oil lamps, are occasionally found here. Clams can be dug from muddy sand. Sea anemones and starfish cling to rocks at or below the low-tide line. The starfish extends its stomach through its mouth to devour barnacles and shellfish. Toad crabs hide in weeds. Shore crabs will threaten intruders but rarely attack. Whales, porpoises, seals, eels and lobsters are found in the bay.

Lobster pounds, Deer Island

DEER ISLAND
Fishing—particularly for lobster—has been the mainstay of Deer Island since the late 18th century. Northern Harbour (on the island's west shore) is the site of the world's three largest lobster pounds. The pounds are inlets, converted by fences and nets into corrals, whose salt water is changed daily by the surging tides. Lobsters, trapped during strictly enforced seasons, are kept alive in the pounds until they can be shipped to market.
□ Old Sow, the world's second largest whirlpool (after Norway's Maelstrom), can be seen best from the high ground at Deer Island Point.

CAMPOBELLO ISLAND
President Franklin D. Roosevelt's 34-room "summer cottage"—a red-shingled, green-roofed Dutch colonial mansion—is the centerpiece of Roosevelt-Campobello International Park. FDR spent most of the summers of his youth on the island until 1921, when he was stricken with polio. Roosevelt came to Campobello on three occasions during his presidency (1933-1945).
□ A toll ferry links Campobello and Deer islands.

FDR statuette, Roosevelt-Campobello International Park

A Storybook Island
Off a Coast of Sheltered Coves

Southwestern New Brunswick

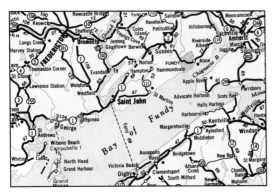

LAKE UTOPIA

For almost a century sightings of a sea monster said to have crawled inland have been reported from Lake Utopia. Despite the rumors, boating, fishing and waterskiing enthusiasts flock to this scenic lake, 11 kilometres northeast of St. George. By the lake, there are camping and picnic sites, and a sandy beach.

□ Northeast of the lake is Utopia Game Refuge, a provincial wildlife sanctuary that is open to the general public except during the hunting seasons.

BLACKS HARBOUR

This community, the terminal for the ferry to Grand Manan Island, is a major fish canning center. Ten local canneries process most of Canada's sardine supply. The annual North American Sardine Packing Championships are held here in early September.

□ Sardines are caught near shore either in giant weirs—circular fenced traps—or by seines in open water. The seine—60 metres deep and roughly 500 metres long—is dropped over the sardines, while the bottom is drawn tight to trap them. The catch is emptied by suction hoses.

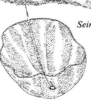

Seining for sardines, Bay of Fundy

GRAND MANAN ISLAND

Geological curiosities and the unhurried pace of life are among the attractions of picturesque Grand Manan, the biggest (142 square kilometres) of the Fundy isles. Local inhabitants harvest dulse (an edible seaweed), and trap lobsters.

□ There are no neon signs or public drinking places here. But there are tranquil forests of spruce, balsam, birch and poplar; awesome cliffs; craggy trails, bright with wildflowers; and off the sheltered east shore a forest of underwater tree stumps.

□ Grand Manan is a fine place for whale-watching, beachcombing or basking on a lonely stretch of seaside sand.

Swallowtail Lighthouse, Pettes Cove, Grand Manan Island

DARK HARBOUR

Soft or leathery, pink or purple, dulse is a seaweed delicacy—and dulse from Dark Harbour is rated the best in the world. This tangy, salty seaweed, rich in iron and iodine, is eaten raw, toasted over a flame, or powdered for use in chowders, casseroles and gravies. It is picked from the rocks at low tide and dried in the sun for five hours. An experienced picker gathers more than 60 kilograms of dulse between tides. Most of Dark Harbour's harvest is shipped throughout Canada and the United States.

Dulse

St. George and Blacks Harbour snuggle in a rugged coastline worn by mighty Bay of Fundy tides. Fishing villages cling to sheltered coves along Fundy's north shore. Lakes and streams teem with fish, and woodlands shelter black bears, moose and white-tailed deer. The swift current and white water of the Lepreau River challenge experienced canoeists.

At St. George, settled nearly 200 years ago, Atlantic salmon dart up a concrete fish ladder on their way to spawning grounds in the northern reaches of the picturesque Magaguadavic River.

From Blacks Harbour, the center of Canada's sardine industry, visitors can take a two-hour ferry journey across the Bay of Fundy to remote Grand Manan Island. (The ferry makes the crossing several times daily.) Long favored by geologists, naturalists, artists and writers, Grand Manan Island has a storybook setting of sheer cliffs, pirate coves, white lighthouses, and getaway cottages.

Tourists can accompany fishermen to herring, pollock, haddock or bluefin tuna grounds; visit a smokehouse where salted herrings hang above smoldering, sawdust-smothered logs; or dig for Captain Kidd's treasure where Money Cove Brook plunges down a 244-metre ravine near Dark Harbour. Offshore there are numerous shipwrecks to interest experienced divers.

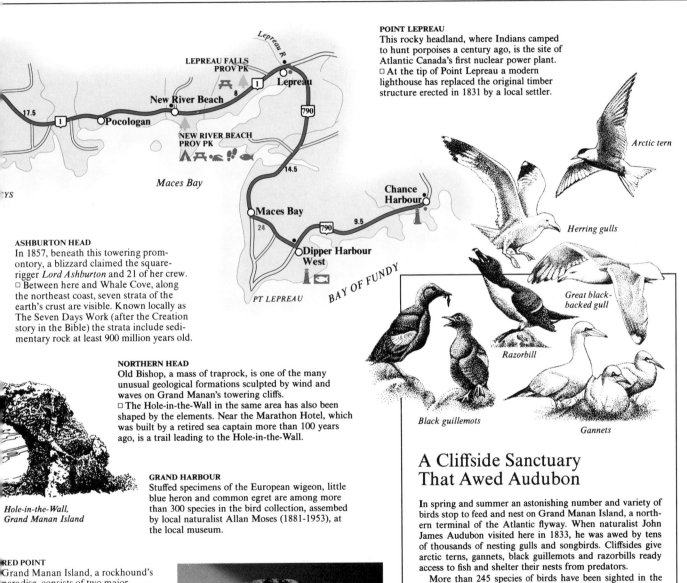

POINT LEPREAU
This rocky headland, where Indians camped to hunt porpoises a century ago, is the site of Atlantic Canada's first nuclear power plant.
□ At the tip of Point Lepreau a modern lighthouse has replaced the original timber structure erected in 1831 by a local settler.

Arctic tern

Herring gulls

Great black-backed gull

Razorbill

Gannets

Black guillemots

ASHBURTON HEAD
In 1857, beneath this towering promontory, a blizzard claimed the square-rigger *Lord Ashburton* and 21 of her crew.
□ Between here and Whale Cove, along the northeast coast, seven strata of the earth's crust are visible. Known locally as The Seven Days Work (after the Creation story in the Bible) the strata include sedimentary rock at least 900 million years old.

NORTHERN HEAD
Old Bishop, a mass of traprock, is one of the many unusual geological formations sculpted by wind and waves on Grand Manan's towering cliffs.
□ The Hole-in-the-Wall in the same area has also been shaped by the elements. Near the Marathon Hotel, which was built by a retired sea captain more than 100 years ago, is a trail leading to the Hole-in-the-Wall.

Hole-in-the-Wall, Grand Manan Island

GRAND HARBOUR
Stuffed specimens of the European wigeon, little blue heron and common egret are among more than 300 species in the bird collection, assembled by local naturalist Allan Moses (1881-1953), at the local museum.

RED POINT
Grand Manan Island, a rockhound's paradise, consists of two major geologic structures formed 700 million years apart. The rugged, uninhabited west is of volcanic origin; the flatter, eastern island is of older, sedimentary rock. At Red Point, on the southeast shore, a line can be seen where gray, volcanic rock overlapped red, sedimentary slabs millions of years ago. Between Dark Harbour and North Head, the collector can find such semiprecious minerals as amethyst, agate, jasper, hornstone and apophyllite.

Specular hematite, Grand Manan Island

A Cliffside Sanctuary That Awed Audubon

In spring and summer an astonishing number and variety of birds stop to feed and nest on Grand Manan Island, a northern terminal of the Atlantic flyway. When naturalist John James Audubon visited here in 1833, he was awed by tens of thousands of nesting gulls and songbirds. Cliffsides give arctic terns, gannets, black guillemots and razorbills ready access to fish and shelter their nests from predators.

More than 245 species of birds have been sighted in the 81-hectare Grand Manan Bird Sanctuary, which is located in Anchorage Provincial Park, between Grand Harbour and Seal Cove. During a typical nesting season, ornithologists have counted more than 2,000 black ducks, 1,200 brant, 200 goldeneyes and 100 buffleheads. Other species here include geese, teal, eiders, ring-necked ducks, mergansers, scaup and pintail. The sanctuary, a refuge in the hunting season and a wintering place, consists of wet heath, spruce and fir woods, and two ponds separated from the sea by a grassy sandbar.

A New Life for an Old Seaport
Where Loyalist Memories Linger

Loyalist House

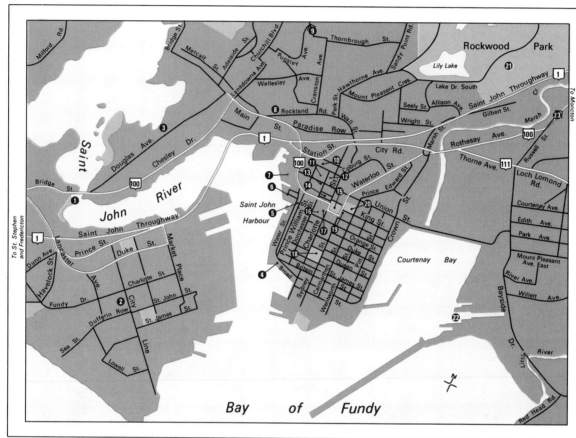

Saint John

1 Reversing Falls
2 Carleton Martello Tower
3 New Brunswick Museum
4 Three Sisters Lamps
5 Barbour's General Store
6 Loyalist Landing Place
7 Market Square
8 Fort Howe
9 University of New Brunswick
10 Saint John's Stone Church
11 Aitken Bicentennial Exhibition Centre
12 Canada Games Aquatic Centre
13 Loyalist House
14 Old City Market
15 King Square
16 Tourist Information
17 Trinity Church
18 Samuel de Champlain Monument
19 County Courthouse
20 Loyalist Burial Ground
21 Rockwood Park
22 Saint John Shipbuilding and Dry Dock
23 Atlantic National Exhibition

Saint John offers an exciting mixture of past and present. Market Square is a notable example. This modern waterfront redevelopment in the heart of the city overlooks Market Slip, where the first United Empire Loyalists landed in 1783. From Market Square, visitors can stroll through the streets of this bustling port and explore its Loyalist dwellings, 19th-century buildings and other handsome reminders of its history.

Although the French explorer Samuel de Champlain discovered Saint John Harbour in 1604, the city took shape only in the 1780s, after the arrival of English-speaking Loyalist refugees from the United States. During the first half of the 19th century, Saint John prospered from the growth of the timber trade and shipbuilding. But, as these industries declined during the 1860s, Saint John's fortunes also faded. The city nevertheless remained an important year-round seaport. Stimulus from urban redevelopment and new investment in business and shipping revitalized Saint John in the 1970s and 1980s.

Aitken Bicentennial Exhibition Centre (11)
This is housed in the old Saint John city library, which was renovated in the early 1980s. Its five galleries feature permanent and traveling displays of art, crafts, photography and science.

Atlantic National Exhibition (23)
The largest fair in Eastern Canada is held here in late August.

Barbour's General Store (5)
Located across from Market Square, Bar-

Carleton Martello Tower

bour's General Store recaptures the atmosphere of an emporium of the 1860s. Also at this site are an old-time barbershop and a small 1850 schoolhouse—just 5 by 6 metres in size—which contains its original double benches.

Canada Games Aquatic Centre (12)
Opened for the Canada Summer Games in 1985, this world-class facility can be visited and its facilities, enjoyed—for a modest fee.

Carleton Martello Tower (2)
The two lower levels of this stone fortification date from 1812; the two upper levels, from 1941. The tower, now a national historic site, provides sweeping vistas of Saint John and its harbor. An audiovisual presentation explains the tower's history.

County Courthouse (19)
A self-supporting, three-story spiral staircase is a notable feature of this courthouse, which was built in the 1820s.

Fort Howe (8)
The reconstructed Fort Howe blockhouse offers a splendid vista of Saint John. Built by the British in 1777-78, Fort Howe was part

of the local defenses for more than 40 years.

King Square (15)
A memorial cross in King Square commemorates the establishment of New Brunswick as a separate British colony on Aug. 16, 1784. Prior to this date, New Brunswick had been a part of Nova Scotia.

Loyalist Burial Ground (20)
The oldest stone tablet marks the grave of Coonradt Hendricks, who died July 13, 1784.

Loyalist House (13)
This 1816 Georgian mansion is among the oldest buildings in Saint John. Once the home of a prosperous 19th-century merchant, Loyalist House has been restored with period furnishings, such as Grecian swooning sofas and Duncan Phyfe tables. The house, which was in the possession of the same family for about 150 years, escaped the 1877 fire that destroyed much of Saint John.

Loyalist Landing Place (6)
A memorial marks the site where thousands of Loyalists came ashore in May 1783.

Market Square (7)
Boutiques, sidewalk cafes, hotels and a trade and convention center are among attractions of the extensive waterfront restoration that has helped revive downtown Saint John. A skywalk links Market Square to the Brunswick Square shopping mall and the Old City Market (14).

New Brunswick Museum (3)
The museum—one of Canada's oldest—was founded in 1842 by Abraham Gesner (1797-1864), who invented kerosene, and now it houses art from international and Canadian sources. Other interesting exhibits include nautical artifacts (ship models, whaling dioramas and whalebone carvings), a collection of mounted birds and animals, the J.C. Webster Canadiana collection, and equipment and supplies retrieved from the clipper ship *Marco Polo,* which sank off Cavendish, P.E.I., in 1883.

Old City Market (14)
Built in 1876 with an interior like an inverted ship's hull, this is one of the oldest markets in Canada. The block-long structure is also one of the few public buildings in Saint John to survive the 1877 fire that destroyed more than half the city. Today, the Old City Market sells fresh fish and produce, as well as antiques and handicrafts.

Reversing Falls (1)
Four-metre-high tides from Fundy Bay surge through a 137-metre-deep gorge into the Saint John River at this point. Twice each day the tide forces the river to flow up-

The old Loyalist Burial Ground (below) evokes memories of the United Empire Loyalists who first settled in Saint John during the early 1780s.

stream in a fury of foam, rapids and whirlpools. Visitors can view the phenomenon from two lookouts.

Rockwood Park (21)
This 870-hectare expanse of parkland and lakes offers year-round recreation. Its attractions include nature trails, a children's farm, and Cherry Brook Zoo, where camels, zebras and other animals can be seen.

Saint John Shipbuilding and Dry Dock (22)
Saint John boasts one of the world's largest dry docks for ship construction and repair. The main dry dock is 350 metres long and 38 metres wide.

Saint John's Stone Church (10)
The city's first stone structure was built in 1825. The stone was brought from England as ship's ballast.

Samuel de Champlain Monument (18)
The monument pays tribute to French explorer Samuel de Champlain who discovered the Saint John River on June 24, 1604. Champlain named the river for the saint whose feast day it was.

Three Sisters Lamps (4)
Since 1848 the Three Sisters Lamps have been a navigation guide for vessels entering

Reliving Loyalist Days in Old Saint John

Early in May 1783, ships bearing the first Loyalist refugees from the newly formed United States anchored in the Bay of Fundy off the mouth of the Saint John River. These refugees—supporters of the British cause during the War of Independence—were seeking sanctuary from the persecution they feared in the young republic.

Today Saint John holds its popular annual Loyalist Days to commemorate their arrival. The week-long event, which is held in mid-July, opens with a reenactment of the landing at Market Slip. After the ceremonial raising of the Union Jack, the heart of Saint John is transformed with parades and other festivities. Among the throngs are local people wearing the 18th-century garb of their Loyalist forebears.

Loyalist Days celebrations include street casinos, horse racing, an antique fair, a family day extravaganza at Rockwood Park and a Miss Saint John Pageant.

A Loyalist Days parade

Market Square (left), where the Loyalists first landed, is a symbol of Saint John's urban renewal, which has brought color and excitement to the heart of the city.

Saint John's harbor. A Celtic cross at this site commemorates 2,000 Irish emigrants who died of cholera at sea and at nearby Partridge Island in 1847. Some 600 of the victims are buried on Partridge Island, now a national historic site containing a museum.

Trinity Church (17)
Built in 1791, Trinity Church was destroyed in the great 1877 fire and rebuilt three years later. The royal coat of arms over the west door was brought to Saint John by Loyalists who took it from the Boston council chamber of the former colony of Massachusetts.

University of New Brunswick (9)
The university's Saint John campus was established in 1964.

In Serene Beauty, a Great River Flows Down to the Sea

Lower Saint John River Valley

Tranquil and ever more picturesque a it approaches the sea, the Saint Joh River flows east past Fredericton and the on to Oromocto. Here it widens befor flowing southward on a winding course t the city of Saint John and the Bay of Fund Travelers can cross the lower reaches o a bridge at Maugerville, or via several fre government-operated ferries.

Downriver from Oromocto is Gagetow a charming, elm-shaded town surrounde by woodlands of white cedar, pine, mapl

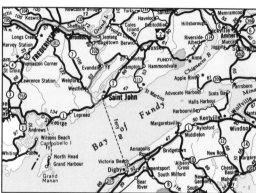

SHEFFIELD
Puritans from Massachusetts built New Brunswick's first Protestant church in nearby Maugerville in 1775. Thirteen years later, after a land dispute, they moved the wooden structure to Sheffield, pushing it eight kilometres along the Saint John River ice. Rebuilt in 1840 with the original lumber, the church is still in use. A cairn commemorating the church's founders was erected in 1926.

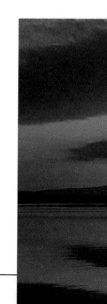

Blue flag

OROMOCTO
Military activity figures prominently in the history of this town of more than 9,500. Fort Hughes, a reconstructed 1777 blockhouse, was designed to protect local pioneers from rebel Americans and hostile Indians. In the 1950s CFB Gagetown, which has the largest military training area in the British Commonwealth, was set up just north of Oromocto. The town's successful expansion to accommodate the base earned it the title "Canada's Model Town."
□ Uniforms, weapons and military memorabilia from the 18th century to the present are displayed in the CFB Gagetown Museum.
□ Oromocto Pioneer Days, usually held in early summer, is a popular local festival.

Fort Hughes blockhouse

MAUGERVILLE
The town of Maugerville (pronounc "Majorville") was named after Josh Mauger, a Halifax merchant who helped New England settlers acquir land here during the early 1760s.
□ The surrounding area is known as New Brunswick's "garden patch." S rich is the silt brought from the upp Saint John River by spring floods th local farmers sometimes harvest two crops in a single growing season.
□ A modern, single-span bridge over the Saint John River links Maugervi with Burton and Oromocto.

Fine Homemade Tartans From Traditional Hand Looms

Handweaving on a four-harness floor loom

The Loomcrofters of Gagetown, designers and weavers of fine tartans, demonstrate handweaving and sell their products in a one-time trading post (built in 1761), which is one of the oldest buildings in the Saint John River valley. The hand-split cedar shingles of the two-story structure are held together with wooden pegs rather than nails. The cellar of the building—known as The Blockhouse—was used to store firearms and ammunition.

The Loomcrofters began as a government-sponsored youth training program in 1939. Today the enterprise includes about 35 weavers working at home on their own looms to produce a wide range of goods, including hand-woven garments, blankets and shawls, and drapery and upholstery fabrics.

The Loomcrofters have woven tartans for British royalty, American presidents, the newspaper baron Lord Beaverbrook (one of New Brunswick's most famous native sons), movie stars and other celebrities from around the world. The tartans created for the Royal Canadian Air Force and the province of New Brunswick are among their best-known designs.

| 0 | 2 | 4 | 6 | 8 | 10 Miles |
| 0 | 4 | | 8 | 12 | 16 Kilometres |

spruce, poplar, and great oaks that sprouted before the first United Empire Loyalists arrived in the 1780s. Lilies of the valley and orchids grow in the woods, but the most abundant flower is the blue flag, a wild iris.

The river is quiet here, so filled with long, low islands that it is often difficult to distinguish the main channel. The islands, swept by floodwater, ice and driftwood in the annual breakup, are used for pasture and hay but seldom for homesteads. Silt dumped by the river each spring makes farmland in the lower Saint John River valley among the most fertile in Canada. Wildlife is abundant. There are deer, muskrat and almost every species of duck and wading bird native to eastern Canada.

South of Evandale is Long Reach. This lake, flanked by impressive hills covered in hardwood and laced with trout streams, is a 32-kilometre stretch of the river. Here, in autumn, the river's placid surface mirrors the brilliant gold-and-scarlet foliage of the Kingston Peninsula on the eastern shore.

Yellow warbler

WHITES COVE
Fruit-and-vegetable stands line the highway here. A one-room schoolhouse has been converted into a shop selling handwoven articles, pottery, blown glass and other New Brunswick crafts.
□ Lakeside Provincial Park has sandy beaches, camping and picnicking sites, and fishing for alewife (a fish resembling the herring) and Atlantic salmon.

LOWER JEMSEG
A cairn marks the site of Fort Jemseg (1659). Built by the British and used for trade with the Indians, it was taken over by the French in 1670. Captured by the Dutch in 1674, the fort was soon retaken by the French, who rebuilt it in 1690, then abandoned it two years later.

GAGETOWN
Tilley House is the birthplace of Sir Samuel Leonard Tilley (1818-96), who was one of the Fathers of Confederation. It was built in 1786 by Gagetown's first physician, Dr. Frederick Stickles. Now restored and a national historic site, it serves as the Queens County Museum. A parlor and bedroom are decorated in Victorian style, and older parts of the house, in Loyalist style.
□ The Loomcrofters, the acclaimed weavers and designers of tartans, have a studio and shop in The Blockhouse—one of the oldest buildings in this region.

OAK POINT
On a low-lying strip of land jutting into the Saint John River is Oak Point Provincial Park, with tree-shaded campsites, a beach and an old lighthouse.
□ Offshore lies Caton's Island, named for Isaac and James Caton—Englishmen who were granted the island in 1760. Traders from France began a short-lived settlement here in 1610. They were New Brunswick's first European settlers.

SAINT JOHN RIVER
Until the 1940s the Saint John River was New Brunswick's principal transport route. Riverboats with names like *May Queen* and *Majestic* chugged and throbbed up this broad and scenic inland waterway. Nowadays, except for farmer's boats and scows, and some ferries, the river carries little but pleasure craft. Canoeing and sailing are popular activities near Gagetown, where the lower Saint John is dotted with long, low-lying islands. Queenstown and Oak Point Provincial Park are ideal spots to enjoy the river's serene beauty.

Queens County Museum, Gagetown

Lower Saint John River

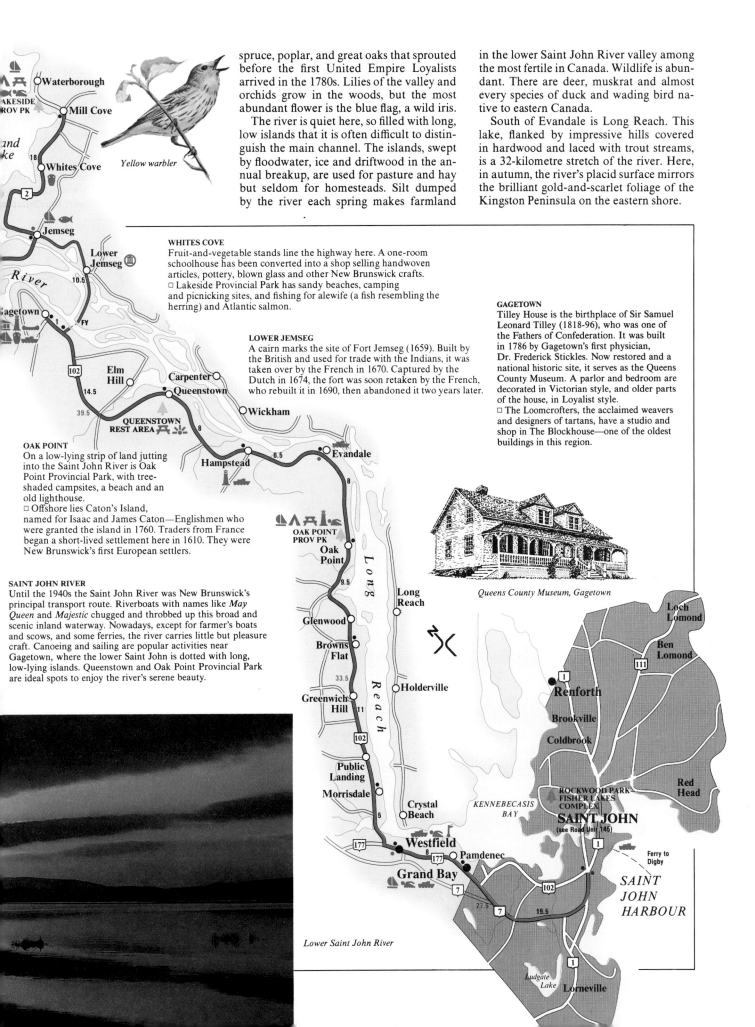

Where Surging Tides Sculpt Towering 'Flowerpots'

Southeastern New Brunswick

Southeastern New Brunswick has dramatic rock formations, rugged cliffs battered by the highest tides in the world, serene dairy farms and woodlands, and sparkling trout streams spanned by quaint covered bridges.

In Fundy National Park coves and inlets cut into steep sandstone cliffs along a spectacular 13-kilometre shoreline. Inland the park is an undulating plateau of forested hills, tumbling brooks, placid lakes and flowered meadows. Armed with cameras

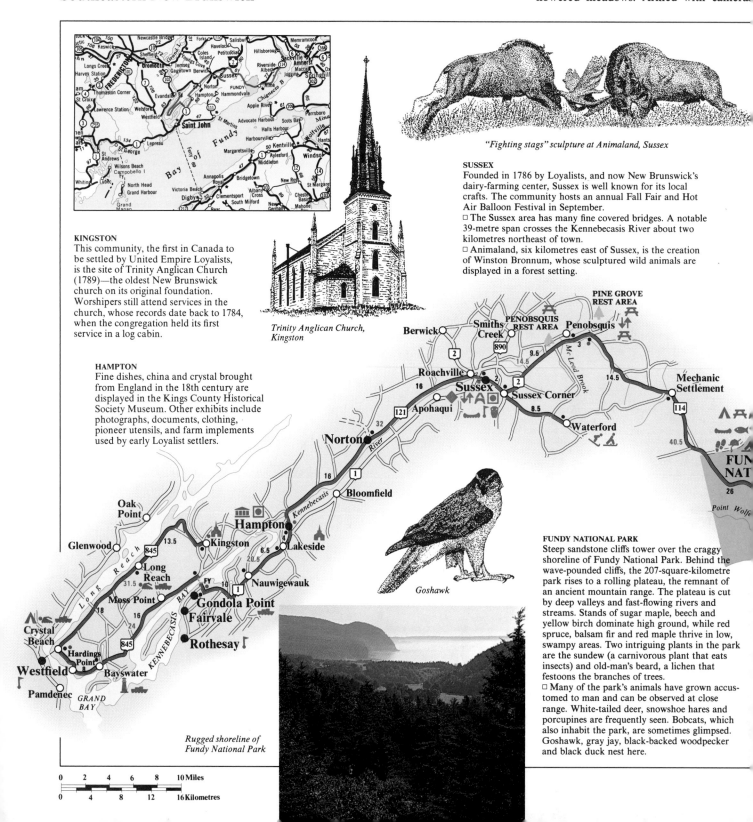

"Fighting stags" sculpture at Animaland, Sussex

KINGSTON
This community, the first in Canada to be settled by United Empire Loyalists, is the site of Trinity Anglican Church (1789)—the oldest New Brunswick church on its original foundation. Worshipers still attend services in the church, whose records date back to 1784, when the congregation held its first service in a log cabin.

SUSSEX
Founded in 1786 by Loyalists, and now New Brunswick's dairy-farming center, Sussex is well known for its local crafts. The community hosts an annual Fall Fair and Hot Air Balloon Festival in September.
□ The Sussex area has many fine covered bridges. A notable 39-metre span crosses the Kennebecasis River about two kilometres northeast of town.
□ Animaland, six kilometres east of Sussex, is the creation of Winston Bronnum, whose sculptured wild animals are displayed in a forest setting.

Trinity Anglican Church, Kingston

HAMPTON
Fine dishes, china and crystal brought from England in the 18th century are displayed in the Kings County Historical Society Museum. Other exhibits include photographs, documents, clothing, pioneer utensils, and farm implements used by early Loyalist settlers.

Goshawk

FUNDY NATIONAL PARK
Steep sandstone cliffs tower over the craggy shoreline of Fundy National Park. Behind the wave-pounded cliffs, the 207-square-kilometre park rises to a rolling plateau, the remnant of an ancient mountain range. The plateau is cut by deep valleys and fast-flowing rivers and streams. Stands of sugar maple, beech and yellow birch dominate high ground, while red spruce, balsam fir and red maple thrive in low, swampy areas. Two intriguing plants in the park are the sundew (a carnivorous plant that eats insects) and old-man's beard, a lichen that festoons the branches of trees.
□ Many of the park's animals have grown accustomed to man and can be observed at close range. White-tailed deer, snowshoe hares and porcupines are frequently seen. Bobcats, which also inhabit the park, are sometimes glimpsed. Goshawk, gray jay, black-backed woodpecker and black duck nest here.

Rugged shoreline of Fundy National Park

| 0 | 2 | 4 | 6 | 8 | 10 Miles |
| 0 | 4 | 8 | 12 | | 16 Kilometres |

and binoculars, bird-watchers can spot some of the more than 215 bird species recorded in the park. Beachcombers can explore tidal pools and other shore features.

East of the park, on the beach at Alma, are rare rock specimens. Countless driftwood souvenirs can be found in a sheltered bay near Cape Enrage. At Hopewell Cape are tide-sculpted rocks and a museum in an old jail. Riverside-Albert has a picnic site and lookout where the view of Crooked Creek is unexcelled.

From Penobsquis, northwest of the park on the Kennebecasis River, a pleasant day trip leads past dairy farms and through small villages such as Sussex, Norton and Hampton, where skilled weavers produce the Kings County tweed. In Sussex exquisite handmade silver jewelry and delicious locally made ice cream can be purchased. At Gondola Point a car ferry crosses the Kennebecasis River to the picturesque Kingston Peninsula.

A circle tour around the peninsula leads through Loyalist settlements dating back to 1783. Here are some of the oldest churches—and some of the finest autumn scenery—in the Maritimes. Here, too, is unforgettable calm and tranquillity.

HILLSBOROUGH
Visitors are welcome at the restored Steeves House, which was once the home of William Henry Steeves (1814-73), one of the Fathers of Confederation. The local Steeves family traces its origins back to Heinrich Steeves (or Stief) who settled here in the 1760s. Steeves had seven sons—and now their more that 150,000 descendants live all over the world. (Many family members are buried in the local cemetery.)
□ Hillsborough hosts its annual Homecoming Days and Exhibition in July.
□ The Salem and Hillsborough Railroad offers train journeys beside the picturesque Petitcodiac River.

Steeves gravestone, Hillsborough

Former county courthouse, Hopewell Cape

HOPEWELL CAPE
The Albert County Museum is housed here in the old county jail (1846), which has cut stone walls that are about 67 centimetres thick. The museum features models and photographs of ships, as well as plans and tools used for shipbuilding. Displays include pioneer candlesticks, whale-oil lamps and chandeliers. The nearby courthouse (1904) and an agricultural building can also be visited.
□ A monument in Hopewell Cape Park honors R. B. Bennett (1870-1947), the only New Brunswicker to become prime minister of Canada. Bennett, who held office during the early 1930s, was born at his grandfather's house near here and grew up in Hopewell Cape.

Flowerpot Rocks, Hopewell Cape, The Rocks Provincial Park

ALMA
Located just outside Fundy National Park, Alma offers arts and crafts programs at the local community center.
□ At low tide, rock hounds can explore the shoreline near the mouth of the Salmon River for rare and colorful stones.

CAPE ENRAGE
A lighthouse warns ships away from this rocky promontory in Chignecto Bay.
□ A sheltered bay, on the west side of Cape Enrage, is noted for its abundance of attractively shaped pieces of driftwood.

THE ROCKS PROVINCIAL PARK
The striking natural features in this park are the top-heavy formations of soft rock, resembling huge flowerpots, which are located at the mouth of the Petitcodiac River. The reddish pillars are capped by balsam fir and dwarf black spruce, which have been shaped by centuries of frost and wind, and by the 14-metre-high tides that surge up the Bay of Fundy. During high tide the tips of the towering "flowerpots"—some as high as 15 metres—become small islands. At low tide visitors can take a stairway to the beach to explore the rock formations and other characteristics of the park's shoreline.

Bobcat

Where Life Moves to the Rhythms of the Sea and the Seasons

Northwestern Prince Edward Island

Spring is a lively season in northwestern P.E.I.—especially in and around Bloomfield and other farming communities in Prince County, where half of the province's potato crop is grown. While potato farmers work through the short planting season—plowing, seeding and fertilizing the red soil—fishermen at Tignish Shore and Northport sort gear, prepare bait, and load their boats with lobster traps and brightly painted buoys. In early May on the first day of the north shore's spring lob-

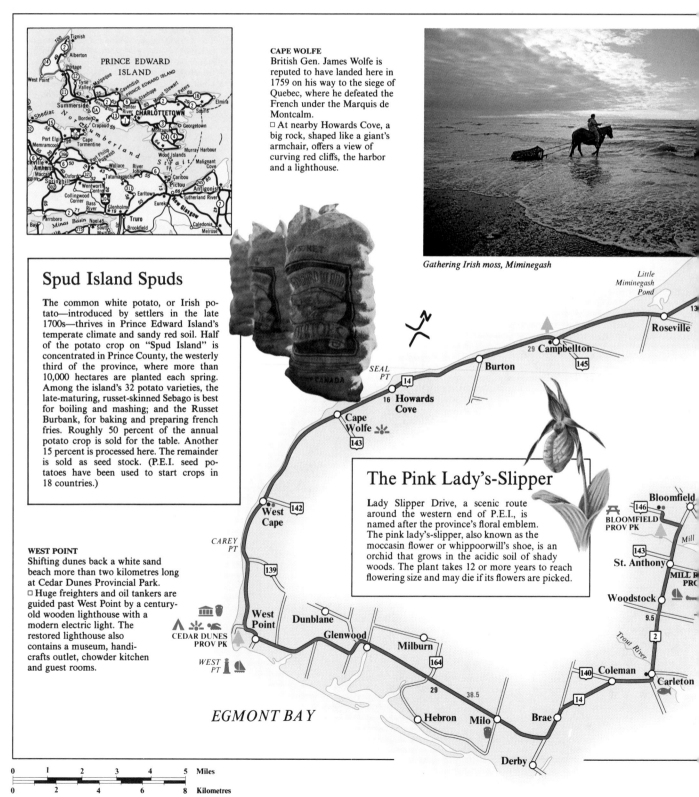

CAPE WOLFE
British Gen. James Wolfe is reputed to have landed here in 1759 on his way to the siege of Quebec, where he defeated the French under the Marquis de Montcalm.
□ At nearby Howards Cove, a big rock, shaped like a giant's armchair, offers a view of curving red cliffs, the harbor and a lighthouse.

Gathering Irish moss, Miminegash

Spud Island Spuds

The common white potato, or Irish potato—introduced by settlers in the late 1700s—thrives in Prince Edward Island's temperate climate and sandy red soil. Half of the potato crop on "Spud Island" is concentrated in Prince County, the westerly third of the province, where more than 10,000 hectares are planted each spring. Among the island's 32 potato varieties, the late-maturing, russet-skinned Sebago is best for boiling and mashing; and the Russet Burbank, for baking and preparing french fries. Roughly 50 percent of the annual potato crop is sold for the table. Another 15 percent is processed here. The remainder is sold as seed stock. (P.E.I. seed potatoes have been used to start crops in 18 countries.)

WEST POINT
Shifting dunes back a white sand beach more than two kilometres long at Cedar Dunes Provincial Park.
□ Huge freighters and oil tankers are guided past West Point by a century-old wooden lighthouse with a modern electric light. The restored lighthouse also contains a museum, handicrafts outlet, chowder kitchen and guest rooms.

The Pink Lady's-Slipper

Lady Slipper Drive, a scenic route around the western end of P.E.I., is named after the province's floral emblem. The pink lady's-slipper, also known as the moccasin flower or whippoorwill's shoe, is an orchid that grows in the acidic soil of shady woods. The plant takes 12 or more years to reach flowering size and may die if its flowers are picked.

EGMONT BAY

| 0 | 1 | 2 | 3 | 4 | 5 | Miles |
| 0 | 2 | | 4 | 6 | 8 | Kilometres |

ster season, the trim boats chug out to the fishing grounds at 5 a.m.

Summer arrives. Colts frolic on new pasture grass. And thousands of tourists, drawn here by the sun and the tang of salt air, enjoy fishing, golfing and clam digging and swimming off magnificent beaches. There are museums and handicraft shops to visit. On bustling wharves, fishermen unload lobsters from rounded traps. The midsummer Potato Blossom Festival in O'Leary (near Bloomfield) and the Prince County Exhibi-tion in Alberton have midways, displays of livestock and farm produce, home-cooking competitions and fiddling and square dancing contests.

As summer ends, fishermen begin to gather the Irish moss that has been uprooted by the ocean's fury. With the arrival of autumn, another crop is ready. Under darkening skies the region's farmers race against time to harvest late-maturing potato crops before the first killing frost. (Even after dark the headlights of tractors trace eerie patterns in the potato fields.) At Howards Cove and other ports along the Northumberland Strait coast, lobster traps are neatly stacked on wharves as the fall season ends in mid-October. Autumn's chill brings a consolation prize of vivid color in fields and woodlots. With summer visitors gone and winter not yet upon the land, this is the favorite season of Islanders.

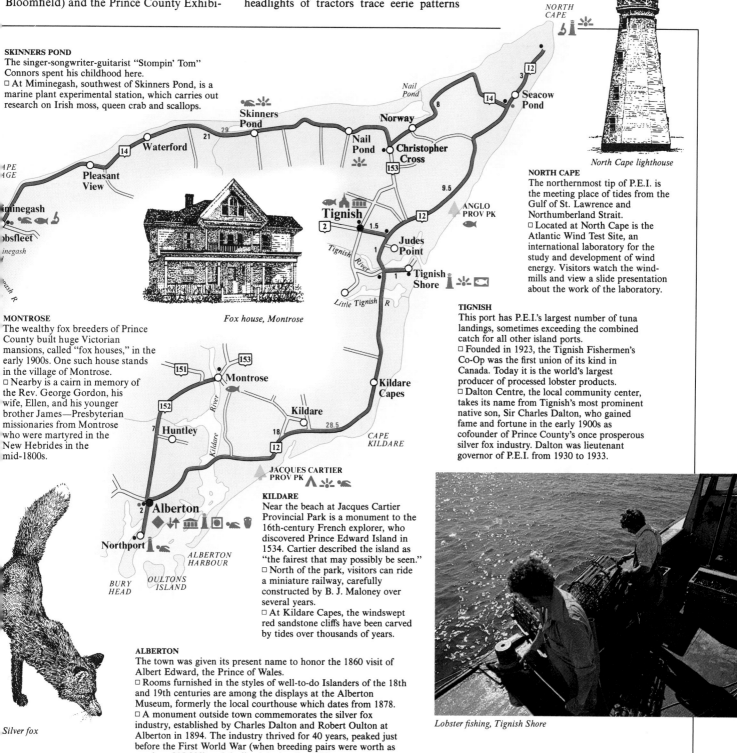

SKINNERS POND
The singer-songwriter-guitarist "Stompin' Tom" Connors spent his childhood here.
□ At Miminegash, southwest of Skinners Pond, is a marine plant experimental station, which carries out research on Irish moss, queen crab and scallops.

Fox house, Montrose

MONTROSE
The wealthy fox breeders of Prince County built huge Victorian mansions, called "fox houses," in the early 1900s. One such house stands in the village of Montrose.
□ Nearby is a cairn in memory of the Rev. George Gordon, his wife, Ellen, and his younger brother James—Presbyterian missionaries from Montrose who were martyred in the New Hebrides in the mid-1800s.

North Cape lighthouse

NORTH CAPE
The northernmost tip of P.E.I. is the meeting place of tides from the Gulf of St. Lawrence and Northumberland Strait.
□ Located at North Cape is the Atlantic Wind Test Site, an international laboratory for the study and development of wind energy. Visitors watch the windmills and view a slide presentation about the work of the laboratory.

TIGNISH
This port has P.E.I.'s largest number of tuna landings, sometimes exceeding the combined catch for all other island ports.
□ Founded in 1923, the Tignish Fishermen's Co-Op was the first union of its kind in Canada. Today it is the world's largest producer of processed lobster products.
□ Dalton Centre, the local community center, takes its name from Tignish's most prominent native son, Sir Charles Dalton, who gained fame and fortune in the early 1900s as cofounder of Prince County's once prosperous silver fox industry. Dalton was lieutenant governor of P.E.I. from 1930 to 1933.

KILDARE
Near the beach at Jacques Cartier Provincial Park is a monument to the 16th-century French explorer, who discovered Prince Edward Island in 1534. Cartier described the island as "the fairest that may possibly be seen."
□ North of the park, visitors can ride a miniature railway, carefully constructed by B. J. Maloney over several years.
□ At Kildare Capes, the windswept red sandstone cliffs have been carved by tides over thousands of years.

ALBERTON
The town was given its present name to honor the 1860 visit of Albert Edward, the Prince of Wales.
□ Rooms furnished in the styles of well-to-do Islanders of the 18th and 19th centuries are among the displays at the Alberton Museum, formerly the local courthouse which dates from 1878.
□ A monument outside town commemorates the silver fox industry, established by Charles Dalton and Robert Oulton at Alberton in 1894. The industry thrived for 40 years, peaked just before the First World War (when breeding pairs were worth as much as $15,000) and declined during the 1930s.

Silver fox

Lobster fishing, Tignish Shore

Memories of the Acadians Near a Bay Famed for Oysters

Western Prince Edward Island

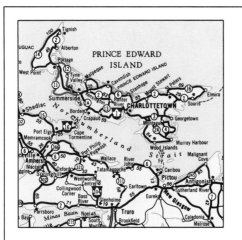

Tonging oysters, Malpeque Bay

Farming Oysters in Malpeque Bay

Prince Edward Island pioneers knew the clean, sharp taste of Malpeque oysters long before they were savored by gourmets around the world. An epidemic in 1917 all but wiped out the tasty mollusks in Malpeque Bay. By the 1930s they had developed a resistance to the disease that was killing them. Nowadays 10 million Malpeque oysters are harvested annually. Modern farming techniques involve the collection of larval oysters, and their subsequent cultivation in tidal bays and estuaries. In spring, when mature oysters begin to spawn, fishermen set down artificial collectors in the water to which the tiny larval oysters attach themselves. Collectors are usually disks of cardboard or plywood coated with concrete and strung on wires between stakes that are planted in the ocean floor. In autumn the young oysters are pried from the collectors and planted out in growing beds, where they feed on minute food particles brought in by the tides. After about 18 months the beds are raked or dredged and the oysters taken to fattening grounds, also in the estuary. The oysters are allowed to grow for about five years, each year adding a new layer to their shell. Then they are gathered and, before marketing, left for a few days in sterile seawater to cleanse them.

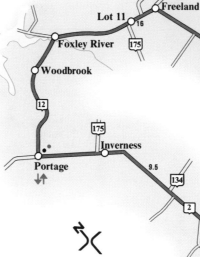
Malpeque oyster

TYNE VALLEY
A midsummer festival in Tyne Valley features not only oysters but also clams and quahogs—as well as fiddling and step-dancing contests.
□ An arts and crafts outlet at Lennox Island Micmac Nation Reserve offers handicrafts by local and other Canadian Indian artists.

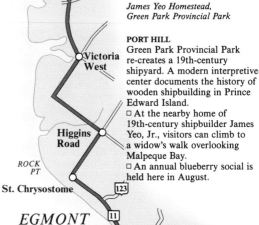

James Yeo Homestead, Green Park Provincial Park

PORT HILL
Green Park Provincial Park re-creates a 19th-century shipyard. A modern interpretive center documents the history of wooden shipbuilding in Prince Edward Island.
□ At the nearby home of 19th-century shipbuilder James Yeo, Jr., visitors can climb to a widow's walk overlooking Malpeque Bay.
□ An annual blueberry social is held here in August.

EGMONT BAY

ABRAM-VILLAGE
Acadian handicrafts, prize livestock and farm produce are displayed at the annual Egmont Bay and Mont-Carmel Exhibition, held in conjunction with the Acadian Festival, on Labor Day weekend.
□ Visitors can buy fresh lobster at the Acadian Fishermen's Cooperative, 10 kilometres south in Cape Egmont.
□ Also at Cape Egmont are three buildings made from roughly 25,000 bottles of different shapes and sizes.

| 0 | 1 | 2 | 3 | 4 | 5 Miles |
| 0 | 2 | 4 | 6 | 8 Kilometres |

West of Summerside, the low-lying central portion of Prince County is thinly populated yet rich in history. Much of this region was molded by the hands of hardy Acadians (French settlers from Nova Scotia), experts at reaping harvests from land and sea.

Twin-spired churches tower by the roadside in seaside villages, such as Egmont Bay and Mont-Carmel. French is still spoken here as it was by the Acadian pioneers of two centuries ago, when the island was called Ile St-Jean. This people's culture, their music, dance, food and crafts can be seen and appreciated at the Acadian Pioneer Village in Mont-Carmel, at the Acadian Museum in Miscouche and at the Acadian Festival in Abram-Village in late August.

The early Acadians survived famine and plague. After the island came under British control in 1763, Acadians often fled to the woods to escape expulsion by the British. Most of the island's present population of 15,000 Acadians are their descendants.

The troubled past of the Acadians contrasts sharply with the history of the shipbuilders who prospered here in the 19th century, when almost every cove and inlet around the island was a scene of bustling shipbuilding activity. Island-built ships sailed to all corners of the world, and for some Islanders lumbering and shipbuilding were sources of great wealth. In Green Park Provincial Park is the restored home (c. 1864) of James Yeo, Jr., one of the island's leading shipbuilders.

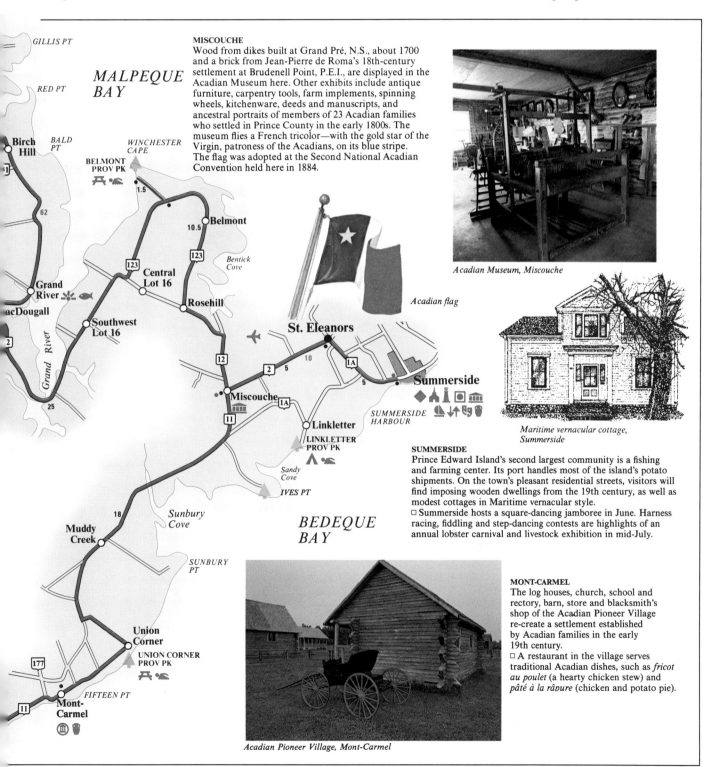

MISCOUCHE
Wood from dikes built at Grand Pré, N.S., about 1700 and a brick from Jean-Pierre de Roma's 18th-century settlement at Brudenell Point, P.E.I., are displayed in the Acadian Museum here. Other exhibits include antique furniture, carpentry tools, farm implements, spinning wheels, kitchenware, deeds and manuscripts, and ancestral portraits of members of 23 Acadian families who settled in Prince County in the early 1800s. The museum flies a French tricolor—with the gold star of the Virgin, patroness of the Acadians, on its blue stripe. The flag was adopted at the Second National Acadian Convention held here in 1884.

Acadian Museum, Miscouche

Acadian flag

Maritime vernacular cottage, Summerside

SUMMERSIDE
Prince Edward Island's second largest community is a fishing and farming center. Its port handles most of the island's potato shipments. On the town's pleasant residential streets, visitors will find imposing wooden dwellings from the 19th century, as well as modest cottages in Maritime vernacular style.
□ Summerside hosts a square-dancing jamboree in June. Harness racing, fiddling and step-dancing contests are highlights of an annual lobster carnival and livestock exhibition in mid-July.

MONT-CARMEL
The log houses, church, school and rectory, barn, store and blacksmith's shop of the Acadian Pioneer Village re-create a settlement established by Acadian families in the early 19th century.
□ A restaurant in the village serves traditional Acadian dishes, such as *fricot au poulet* (a hearty chicken stew) and *pâté à la râpure* (chicken and potato pie).

Acadian Pioneer Village, Mont-Carmel

Warm Beaches, Shifting Dunes, Rugged Cliffs–and a Tireless Wind

North-Central Prince Edward Island

The great dune lands of Prince Edward Island's north shore are like a strip cut from the mighty Sahara and set down between a storybook sea and a neat country garden. The best place to experience both the naturalist's awe at the creation of the dunes and the sunny comfort of some of the finest beaches in North America is in Prince Edward Island National Park. This 40-kilometre stretch of sand, bluffs, salt marshes and freshwater ponds is one of the smallest of the national parks. Yet, each

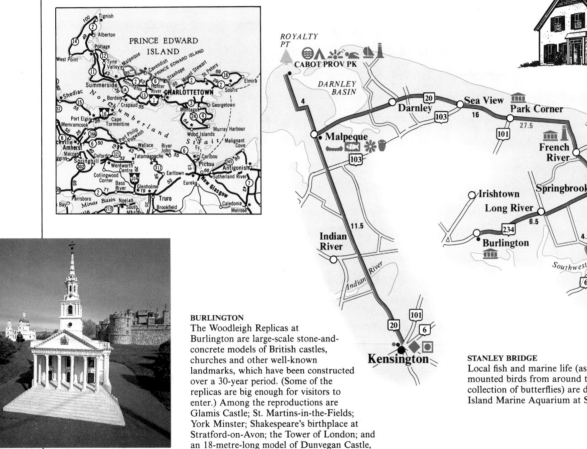

Green Gables, Cavendish

St. Martins-in-the-Fields, Woodleigh Replicas, Burlington

BURLINGTON

The Woodleigh Replicas at Burlington are large-scale stone-and-concrete models of British castles, churches and other well-known landmarks, which have been constructed over a 30-year period. (Some of the replicas are big enough for visitors to enter.) Among the reproductions are Glamis Castle; St. Martins-in-the-Fields; York Minster; Shakespeare's birthplace at Stratford-on-Avon; the Tower of London; and an 18-metre-long model of Dunvegan Castle, with antique furnishings, Scottish artwork and a dungeon. Copies of the British crown jewels are displayed in the White Tower, which is part of the Tower of London replica.

STANLEY BRIDGE

Local fish and marine life (as well as more than 700 mounted birds from around the world and a large collection of butterflies) are displayed at Prince Edward Island Marine Aquarium at Stanley Bridge.

NEW LONDON

A green-trimmed white cottage at New London is the birthplace of Lucy Maud Montgomery, author of *Anne of Green Gables,* which has remained a popular classic since its publication in 1908. Miss Montgomery followed her perennial favorite with seven successful sequels and other novels. Today *Anne* is among the most widely translated novels in the world.

☐ At Park Corner, 10 kilometres north of New London, is the Anne of Green Gables Museum at Silver Bush. Miss Montgomery lived here with her aunt and uncle after her parents died. And it was here that she married Rev. Ewan MacDonald.

Sand-Loving Marram Grass

The botanical name for marram grass, *Ammophila arenaria,* means "sand loving." On north-shore Prince Edward Island the sand desperately needs loving—just to stay put. Marram grass obliges. It is the first growth in nature's system for turning sand into something that can support life. Marram roots reach as much as three metres down in search of water, then spread into a deep, stringy network that helps hold great sand dunes together. The grass survives because it can grow quickly to the surface after being blanketed with sand and because it is impervious to salt spray. But it is not hardy enough to withstand heavy human traffic. Once the grass has gone, the wind often carves small depressions into giant holes called "blowouts." Too many blowouts turn stable dunes into constantly shifting hills unable to support vegetation.

| 0 | 1 | 2 | 3 | 4 | 5 Miles |
| 0 | 2 | 4 | | 6 | 8 Kilometres |

year, more than a million persons come here. Hundreds of thousands make the pilgrimage to Green Gables, the house that helped inspire Lucy Maud Montgomery's classic *Anne of Green Gables*. Other hundreds of thousands find a deeper meaning in the park: a sense of the incredible complexity in the natural forces that make the dune country what it is.

A few metres from the shoreline, white spruce fight to grip the sand. Winds prune them, salt spray stunts them. Strange,

twisted, older than they look (some trees 75 years old are less than a metre high), they are the tough handiwork of the violent elements. Yet farther inland, where the high dunes offer shelter from winds and salt spray, the white spruce grow straight and tall, heralding the start of the coastal forest, with its carpet of rich, emerald-green ferns and mosses.

Along the park's seaward edge great waves roll relentlessly to the land. White breakers curl, collapse, and foam up on the beaches, each in turn tracing a delicate new line of sand at high water. The wind teases and sweeps and scours the dunes and the spits, digging some depressions deeper, filling in others, tirelessly reshaping the sandy shore.

CAVENDISH
Green Gables, the old farmhouse immortalized in *Anne of Green Gables* and other novels by Lucy Maud Montgomery, is a museum in the Cavendish section of Prince Edward Island National Park. Green Gables was the home of Lucy Maud's friends David and Margaret MacNeill. In the novels this house became Anne's home. Places such as Anne's Babbling Brook, the Lake of Shining Waters, the Haunted Woods and the Lovers' Lane are on or near the park's 18-hole golf course. Close by, in Cavendish cemetery, is Miss Montgomery's grave. The world-famous author died in 1942.

Sandstone cliffs, Prince Edward Island National Park

P.E.I. NATIONAL PARK
Fringed by the Gulf of St. Lawrence, this park has some of North America's finest white sand beaches. Near Cavendish is sand tinted pink by the erosion of bleached red clay. Between North Rustico Harbour and Orby Head are more than nine kilometres of red sandstone cliffs up to 30 metres high. At Brackley Beach, wooden walkways pass sand dunes up to 18 metres high. Red foxes prowl the dunes, and mink, muskrat and raccoons are common. Among 210 species of birds are the northern phalarope, Swainson's thrush, marsh hawk and slate-colored junco.
□ The elegant and historic Dalvay-by-the-Sea summer hotel, built in 1895, was once the estate of the Cincinnati oil tycoon Alexander Macdonald.

RUSTICO ISLAND
The island in P.E.I. National Park is summer home to hundreds of great blue herons—some with wingspreads of almost two metres. They nest high in spruce trees and forage for fish in marshes and ponds during summer.

Great blue heron

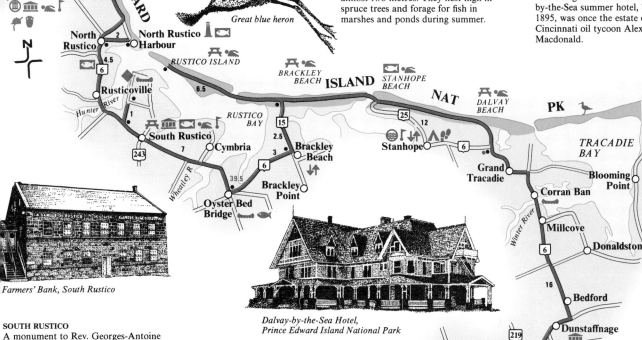

Farmers' Bank, South Rustico

Dalvay-by-the-Sea Hotel, Prince Edward Island National Park

SOUTH RUSTICO
A monument to Rev. Georges-Antoine Belcourt stands between St. Augustine's Church, where he was parish priest from 1859 to 1869, and the Farmers' Bank that he founded in 1864. Belcourt's bank—the smallest ever chartered in Canada—operated as a credit union, roughly 40 years before the credit-union principle was introduced elsewhere in Canada. The two-story brown sandstone bank building (1861-64), which is now the local parish hall, contains a small museum. Exhibits include the bank's own $5 notes.

DUNSTAFFNAGE
Vintage automobiles from the 1910s to the late 1930s, including a 1931 Ford cabriolet—the last in the Model A series—are displayed at the local car museum in Dunstaffnage.

YORK
In Jewell's Gardens and Pioneer Village at York are a reconstructed 19th-century general store, smithy, one-room schoolhouse and chapel. Set among the flowers is an antique glass museum.

The Peaceful Island Capital Where Canada Was Born

South-Central Prince Edward Island

Charlottetown, the cradle of Confederation—with its Victorian homes, stately churches and tree-shaded squares—is the peaceful urban counterpart of Prince Edward Island's idyllic farmlands and seaside villages.

The city's most impressive modern building is the Confederation Centre for the Arts, which was officially opened by Elizabeth II in 1964. Within the complex's great slabbed stone walls, a museum displays contemporary Canadian fine arts, and an art gallery

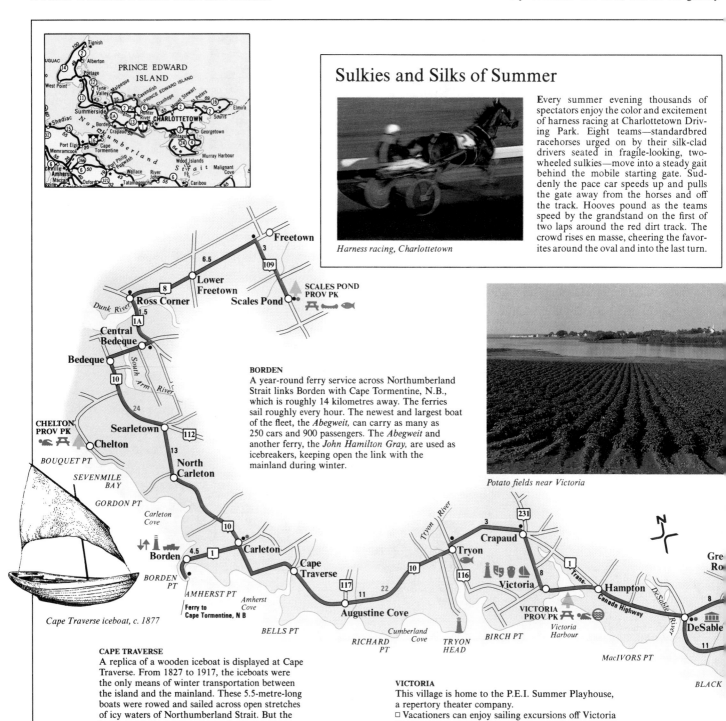

Sulkies and Silks of Summer

Harness racing, Charlottetown

Every summer evening thousands of spectators enjoy the color and excitement of harness racing at Charlottetown Driving Park. Eight teams—standardbred racehorses urged on by their silk-clad drivers seated in fragile-looking, two-wheeled sulkies—move into a steady gait behind the mobile starting gate. Suddenly the pace car speeds up and pulls the gate away from the horses and off the track. Hooves pound as the teams speed by the grandstand on the first of two laps around the red dirt track. The crowd rises en masse, cheering the favorites around the oval and into the last turn.

Potato fields near Victoria

BORDEN
A year-round ferry service across Northumberland Strait links Borden with Cape Tormentine, N.B., which is roughly 14 kilometres away. The ferries sail roughly every hour. The newest and largest boat of the fleet, the *Abegweit*, can carry as many as 250 cars and 900 passengers. The *Abegweit* and another ferry, the *John Hamilton Gray*, are used as icebreakers, keeping open the link with the mainland during winter.

Cape Traverse iceboat, c. 1877

CAPE TRAVERSE
A replica of a wooden iceboat is displayed at Cape Traverse. From 1827 to 1917, the iceboats were the only means of winter transportation between the island and the mainland. These 5.5-metre-long boats were rowed and sailed across open stretches of icy waters of Northumberland Strait. But the boats could also be towed over the ice packs on iron runners attached to both sides of the keel.

VICTORIA
This village is home to the P.E.I. Summer Playhouse, a repertory theater company.
□ Vacationers can enjoy sailing excursions off Victoria Harbour aboard a traditionally rigged schooner.

0 1 2 3 4 5 Miles
0 2 4 6 8 Kilometres

houses more than 1,500 works, such as oil paintings by Canadian masters Robert Harris and Jean-Paul Lemieux. The complex's 1,100-seat theater highlights its year-round program with a gala summer festival of original Canadian musicals. The summer repertoire includes the perennial favorite *Anne of Green Gables,* which is based on the famous novel by Islander Lucy Maud Montgomery.

Across the street is a reminder of the past: the old legislative buildings with the chamber where the Fathers of Confederation first met, in 1864. The chairs they used stand neatly around the table at which they deliberated. A plaque tells that

In the hearts and minds of the delegates who assembled in this room on September 1st 1864 was born the Dominion of Canada. Providence being their Guide, they builded better than they knew.

In August, Old Home Week in Charlottetown features one of Canada's best rural fairs, at the Provincial Exhibition Grounds, along with harness racing at Charlottetown Driving Park. West of the city there is fishing, hiking, sailing in Northumberland Strait, and summer theater at Victoria. And at Rocky Point, in Fort Amherst National Historic Park, is the site of Port la Joie—the island's first European settlement, founded in 1720 by 300 French colonists. The British took it in 1758 and six years later, across the harbor, founded Charlottetown.

Province House, Charlottetown

CHARLOTTETOWN

Canada's smallest provincial capital and the only city in Prince Edward Island. Charlottetown calls itself the birthplace of Canada, for here in September 1864 the Fathers of Confederation met for the first time.

□ Confederation Centre, built in 1964, is a national memorial to the Fathers of Confederation. This complex, covering two downtown blocks, contains a memorial hall, theater, art gallery, museum and a provincial library.

□ Opposite the center is Province House, a three-story, Georgian-style stone structure built in 1843-47. In a high-ceilinged room, now known as the Confederation Chamber, delegates of Britain's North American colonies signed the articles that led to the uniting of present-day Nova Scotia, New Brunswick, Ontario and Quebec into one nation in 1867. Province House also houses the P.E.I. Legislative Assembly.

□ Government House, an imposing white colonial building, home of P.E.I.'s lieutenant governor, was erected in 1834. Beaconsfield, headquarters of the P.E.I. Heritage Foundation, is a Victorian mansion built in 1877. Both buildings overlook Charlottetown harbor and Victoria Park, where a plaque marks the site of Fort Edward, a six-gun battery (c. 1800). The fort was one of a series of strongholds guarding the entrance to the harbor in the early 19th century.

□ St. Dunstan's Basilica, one of Canada's largest churches, is known for its twin Gothic spires, an impressive altar and fine Italian carvings. Murals in St. Peter's Anglican Cathedral are by Robert Harris, the famous Canadian portrait painter.

BONSHAW

The Car Life Museum at Bonshaw displays turn-of-the-century automobiles and tractors, and farm machinery from the 19th and early 20th centuries. Among the car museum's prize exhibits is an 1898 Mason Steamer, a two-cylinder, five-horsepower vehicle that runs on naphtha.

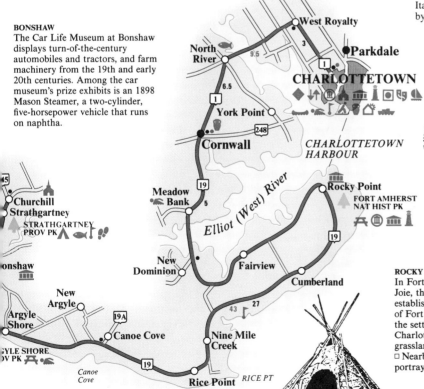

Government House, Charlottetown

Beaconsfield, Charlottetown

ROCKY POINT

In Fort Amherst National Historic Park is the site of Port la Joie, the first European settlement in Prince Edward Island, established by the French in 1720. Only earthworks remain of Fort Amherst, built by the British soon after they captured the settlement in 1758. Overlooking Hillsborough Bay and Charlottetown Harbour, the park's woods and rolling grasslands contain picnic facilities and a museum.

□ Nearby a reconstructed 16th-century Micmac village portrays Indian life before the coming of Europeans.

Birchbark wigwam at Rocky Point

A Trim and Tranquil Corner in the 'Garden of the Gulf'

Southeastern Prince Edward Island

Life is green and calm and unhurried in this southeastern corner of Canada's "Garden of the Gulf." In the summer sun the land is undulating, trim, as picturesque and ordered as a patchwork quilt. It is close to what much of Canada was like at the turn of the century: placid, homespun and friendly.

Visitors experience this sense of the past at the restored 19th-century country crossroads hamlet at Orwell Corner, and in neat, farming communities such as Belfast (prob-

ORWELL CORNER HISTORIC SITE
Musical evenings highlight the summer program at Orwell Corner, where crops and livestock are raised and tended much as they were a century ago. This small rural crossroads, restored to the late 1800s, contains a combined store, post office and farmhouse, with a dressmaker's shop upstairs. There are also barns, a school and a church. The shingled buildings, all on their original sites, date from 1864 to 1896.

MONTAGUE
Among relics of early Prince Edward Island at the Garden of the Gulf Museum are farm implements, a 1698 Bible, clock with wooden works and letters written by Lucy Maud Montgomery, author of *Ann of Green Gables*.
□ A cairn at nearby Brudenell Point commemorates Jean-Pierre de Roma. Depressions in the ground—they were once cellars—are all that remain of his dream of a French settlement in Prince Edward Island 250 years ago. De Roma built wharves, bridges, storehouses and dwellings on the point. But some of his people defected, then crops were destroyed by field mice. In 1745, when the settlement was burned by New England, de Roma and his family hid in the forest and eventually escaped to Quebec.

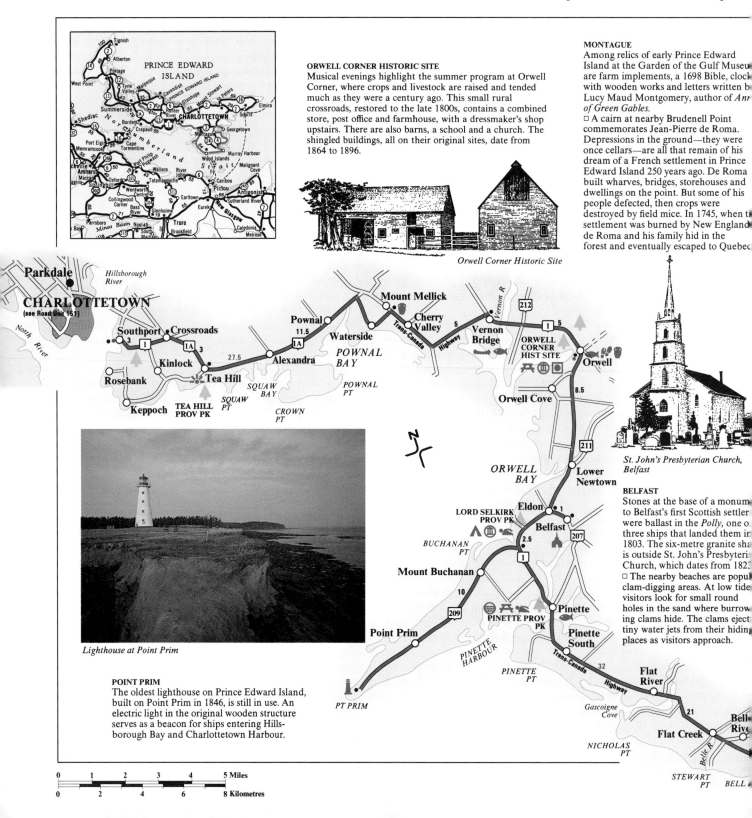

Orwell Corner Historic Site

St. John's Presbyterian Church, Belfast

BELFAST
Stones at the base of a monument to Belfast's first Scottish settler were ballast in the *Polly*, one of three ships that landed them in 1803. The six-metre granite shaft is outside St. John's Presbyterian Church, which dates from 1823.
□ The nearby beaches are popular clam-digging areas. At low tide visitors look for small round holes in the sand where burrowing clams hide. The clams eject tiny water jets from their hiding places as visitors approach.

Lighthouse at Point Prim

POINT PRIM
The oldest lighthouse on Prince Edward Island, built on Point Prim in 1846, is still in use. An electric light in the original wooden structure serves as a beacon for ships entering Hillsborough Bay and Charlottetown Harbour.

0	1	2	3	4	5 Miles

0	2	4	6	8 Kilometres

ably a corruption of *la belle face* to denote the lovely view). On a knoll in Belfast is a memorial to the Selkirk Settlers—800 impoverished crofters brought out from the Isle of Skye by Lord Selkirk in 1803, in one of numerous infusions of Scottish blood. Nearby is a 150-year-old church the settlers built. Its archives contain Selkirk's deed of land for the church and the nearby cemetery.

Some visitors come to the island "from away" and never want to leave. Many families spend summer or fall vacations as pay-ing guests in farm homes. There are farms everywhere, with ample wooden houses, big barns, sturdy fences, fat cattle. Fields surge with golden grain, and, near little places such as Cherry Valley, with great green leaves of tobacco.

Teeming Life Along the Seashore

A myriad of small marine creatures lives close to the water's edge along Prince Edward Island's long stretches of sandy beach.

The starfish, usually found in tidal pools, feeds upon clams, mussels and oysters. It attaches its five powerful arms to the shell of its prey by means of hundreds of suction-tube feet on the underside of each arm. Forcing the shell open by pulling from opposite sides, it lowers its stomach to envelop the prey.

Low tide is best for digging clams. Watch for small round holes in the sand, from which burrowing clams—up to 30 centimetres below the surface—eject streams of water when one walks near.

Hermit crabs, often seen scurrying along tidal pools, are beach scavengers that inhabit the empty shells of marine snails. The crab's rear appendages grasp the inside of the shell; when danger threatens, its two front claws block the shell opening.

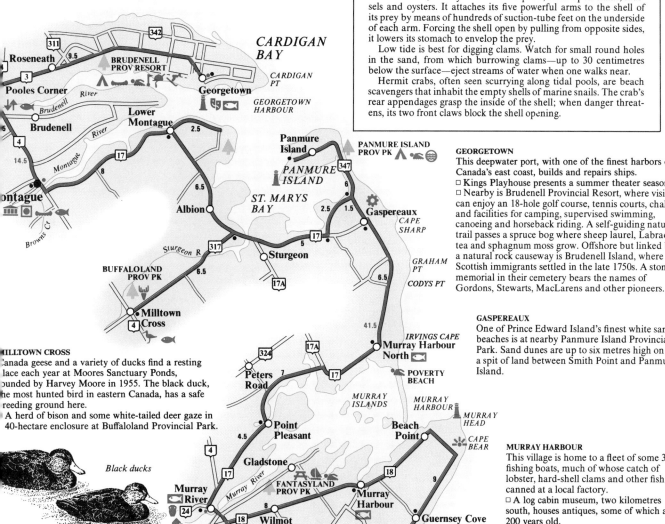

GEORGETOWN
This deepwater port, with one of the finest harbors on Canada's east coast, builds and repairs ships.
□ Kings Playhouse presents a summer theater season.
□ Nearby is Brudenell Provincial Resort, where visitors can enjoy an 18-hole golf course, tennis courts, chalets, and facilities for camping, supervised swimming, canoeing and horseback riding. A self-guiding nature trail passes a spruce bog where sheep laurel, Labrador tea and sphagnum moss grow. Offshore but linked by a natural rock causeway is Brudenell Island, where Scottish immigrants settled in the late 1750s. A stone memorial in their cemetery bears the names of Gordons, Stewarts, MacLarens and other pioneers.

GASPEREAUX
One of Prince Edward Island's finest white sand beaches is at nearby Panmure Island Provincial Park. Sand dunes are up to six metres high on a spit of land between Smith Point and Panmure Island.

MILLTOWN CROSS
Canada geese and a variety of ducks find a resting place each year at Moores Sanctuary Ponds, founded by Harvey Moore in 1955. The black duck, the most hunted bird in eastern Canada, has a safe breeding ground here.
□ A herd of bison and some white-tailed deer gaze in a 40-hectare enclosure at Buffaloland Provincial Park.

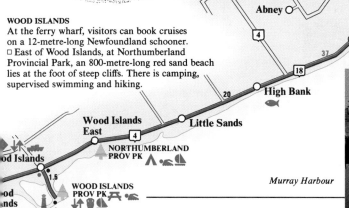

Black ducks

MURRAY HARBOUR
This village is home to a fleet of some 35 fishing boats, much of whose catch of lobster, hard-shell clams and other fish is canned at a local factory.
□ A log cabin museum, two kilometres south, houses antiques, some of which are 200 years old.
□ Near Gladstone, sculptures of storybook characters are displayed in the grounds of Fantasyland Provincial Park.

WOOD ISLANDS
At the ferry wharf, visitors can book cruises on a 12-metre-long Newfoundland schooner.
□ East of Wood Islands, at Northumberland Provincial Park, an 800-metre-long red sand beach lies at the foot of steep cliffs. There is camping, supervised swimming and hiking.

Murray Harbour

An Old Lighthouse, a Modern Ark and a Sea Full of Bluefins

Northeastern Prince Edward Island

At Savage Harbour, Morell, Naufrage, North Lake and other north-shore ports in Prince Edward Island, brightly painted fishing vessels seldom slumber against sunlit wharves. After the lobster season ends in late June, most boats head out to deep-sea fishing grounds in the Gulf of St. Lawrence. Many local skippers welcome tourists aboard for a day spent "jigging" multihooked lines in waters that are alive with mackerel, haddock, cod and herring.

In late summer and early fall, sport fish-

Raking Profits from the Sea

After a storm farmers and fishermen along the north shore of Prince Edward Island gather on the beaches to harvest fresh Irish moss (the common name of red algae). After the ocean's fury uproots the dark, purplish seaweed, harvesters rake Irish moss from the surf or pick it from the beaches. Horse-drawn carts or tractor-drawn trailers are used to transport Irish moss to drying plants. Carrageenan, an emulsifier extracted from Irish moss, is used in the preparation of toothpaste, ice cream, wine and cough syrup. Almost half the world's supply of this valuable crop comes from P.E.I.

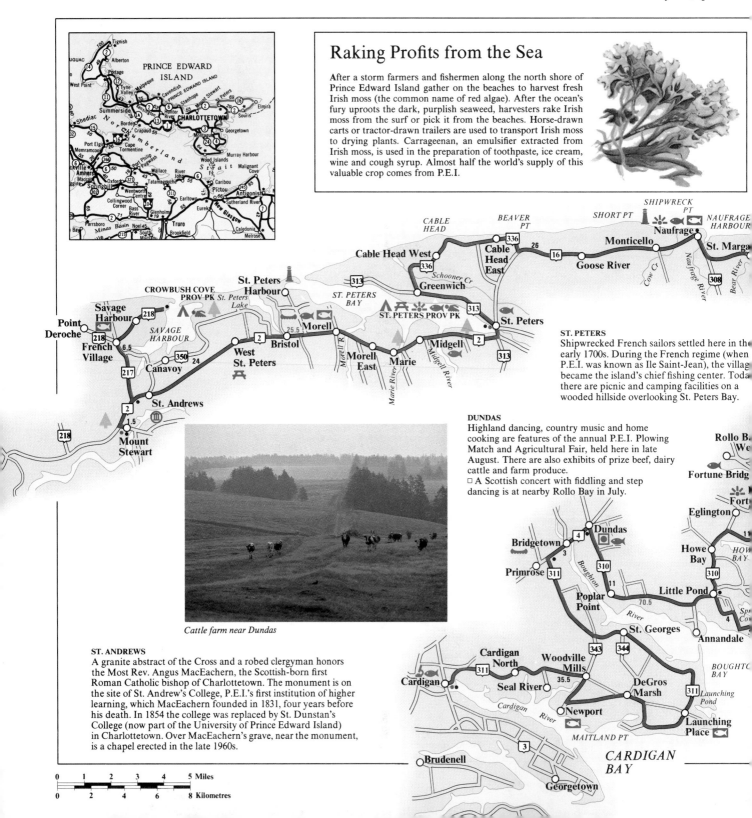

Cattle farm near Dundas

ST. PETERS
Shipwrecked French sailors settled here in the early 1700s. During the French regime (when P.E.I. was known as Ile Saint-Jean), the village became the island's chief fishing center. Today there are picnic and camping facilities on a wooded hillside overlooking St. Peters Bay.

DUNDAS
Highland dancing, country music and home cooking are features of the annual P.E.I. Plowing Match and Agricultural Fair, held here in late August. There are also exhibits of prize beef, dairy cattle and farm produce.
□ A Scottish concert with fiddling and step dancing is at nearby Rollo Bay in July.

ST. ANDREWS
A granite abstract of the Cross and a robed clergyman honors the Most Rev. Angus MacEachern, the Scottish-born first Roman Catholic bishop of Charlottetown. The monument is on the site of St. Andrew's College, P.E.I.'s first institution of higher learning, which MacEachern founded in 1831, four years before his death. In 1854 the college was replaced by St. Dunstan's College (now part of the University of Prince Edward Island) in Charlottetown. Over MacEachern's grave, near the monument, is a chapel erected in the late 1960s.

0 1 2 3 4 5 Miles
0 2 4 6 8 Kilometres

ermen are lured here by the chance of hooking a giant bluefin tuna. (Some of the world's largest bluefins have been caught in these waters, and more than a thousand have been boated in a single season.) When a tuna is hooked, the ensuing battle can last mere seconds or stretch into a marathon of endurance. A successful day ends with the traditional weigh-in ceremony, and the photographs of the victor and the prize. (The victor, incidentally, must surrender the prize to the boat's captain.)

Tuna fishing, North Lake

This corner of the island offers two special summer events. In July, the annual outdoor Scottish fiddling and step-dancing festival is held near Rollo Bay. In the following month, the P.E.I. Plowing Match and Agricultural Fair occurs at Dundas in late August.

At East Point, visitors may tour a lighthouse built in 1867. At Basin Head, there are guided walks over magnificent sand dunes. Here, too, is one of the province's finest museums—a tribute to the proud spirit of the island's commercial inshore fishermen.

NORTH LAKE
Sport fishermen from around the world come here each year (from August to early October) to pit their strength against fighting bluefin tuna. A 680-kilogram giant—one of the world's largest—was caught off North Lake in 1979. Boats usually leave at 9 a.m. for all-day fishing excursions.
□ Three kilometres south is Elmira Station. Restored as a railway museum, this one-story frame structure (c. 1911) has two waiting rooms, a baggage depot and an agent's office.

EAST POINT
Centuries ago Micmac Indians named this area *kespemenagek*—"the end of the island." Today the East Point lighthouse, a wooden colonial structure that may be visited, marks this easternmost tip of Prince Edward Island. Built in 1867, the white tower is one of the island's three remaining manned lighthouses. Of more than 60 around the island, only those at East Point, Souris and Wood Islands are still manned.

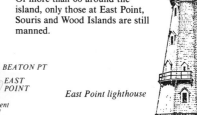

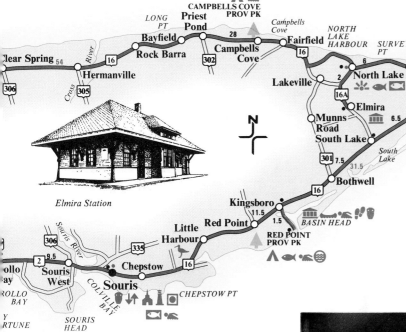

Elmira Station

East Point lighthouse

BASIN HEAD
High on a bluff overlooking the Atlantic Ocean, the Basin Head Fisheries Museum recounts the history of inshore commercial fishing in Prince Edward Island. The museum displays photographs and marine equipment, including ropes, hooks, nets, drying racks and a dory. On the beach below are reconstructed fish shacks; and on the wharf stands an old lobster cannery.
□ The museum's interpretive program offers information about the dune system in this part of the island.
□ In early August, visitors enjoy a seafood festival here.

SOURIS
One of Prince Edward Island's main ports, Souris is noted for its deep-sea fishing and lobster industry, and for its fine beach on Northumberland Strait.
□ A car ferry links Souris with Cap-aux-Meules in the Magdalen Islands.
□ Overlooking Souris harbor is St. Mary's Roman Catholic Church.
□ Souris—French for mice—may have been given this name after plagues of field mice overran the settlement in the 18th century.

Basin Head Fisheries Museum

Windjammer Lore, Scallops and the Picturesque 'French Shore'

Southwestern Nova Scotia

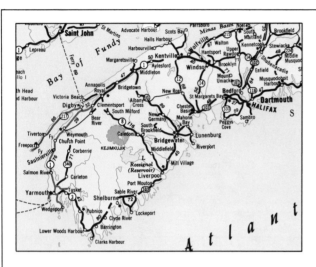

Sunset, Sandy Cove

BRIER ISLAND

Among this island's many attractions are three lighthouses, each with a picnic site. On the island's south side, rock "pillars" extend from the shore hundreds of metres into the sea. (The site—the Giant's Causeway—is remote, but visitors can ask local people for directions.) Bird-watching, rockhounding, whale-watching and deep-sea fishing are popular local activities.

□ At the southern tip of Brier Island a memorial plaque honors mariner and adventurer Capt. Joshua Slocum (1844-1909), the first man to sail around the world alone. Westport was Slocum's home until he went to sea at age 16. Slocum is remembered—by Americans chiefly—for his 1895-98 around-the-world voyage in a 12-metre-long sloop, *Spray*, which weighed less than 12 tonnes.

YARMOUTH

This community of roughly 7,600 is Nova Scotia's largest seaport east of Halifax. Yarmouth holds its most celebrated bash—Seafest—in July. One highlight is a rumrunners' race, but events such as three Acadian festivals, the Western Nova Scotia Exhibition and an international air show also draw visitors.

□ Yarmouth County Museum displays ship models and paintings (one of the largest collections of its kind in Canada), which reflect the town's late 19th-century prominence. A chart in the museum pinpoints the whereabouts of 20 shipyards active locally during the "Golden Age of Sail."

□ The Firefighters Museum of Nova Scotia has two Hunneman engines made in 1840 and an 1880 Silsby steamer. The museum's collection is the largest of its kind in the country.

□ The beam from historic Yarmouth Light—just outside town on Cape Forchu—is visible from 48 kilometres out to sea. The French explorer Champlain named the cape *forchu* ("forked").

Amoskeag steamer (1863), Firefighters' Museum, Yarmouth

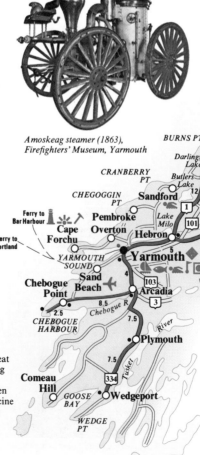

St. Mary's at Church Point

Monument in Town Point Cemetery

CHEBOGUE POINT

A life-size marble monument of a woman reclining on wheat sheaves can be seen at Town Point Cemetery. This touching memorial was placed here by a local doctor, Frederick Webster, in memory of his wife Margaret, who was 45 when she died at Yarmouth in 1864. Webster, who studied medicine at Edinburgh, met Margaret while strolling in the Scottish countryside.

□ *Chebogue* is a Micmac word for "great still water."

WEDGEPORT

Some of the world's best lobster and inshore fishing grounds are along this coast, which is dotted with scores of small islands. Running between the islands is a 1.5-kilometre-wide tide stream—known as the Tusket Tide-Rip or Soldier's Rip—where herring and mackerel feed.

□ Wedgeport celebrates an Acadian festival at the end of June.

A century ago, when 3,000 Nova Scotian windjammers made up one of the world's largest mercantile fleets, the town of Yarmouth was one of the richest ports on the Atlantic coast. Now, Yarmouth thrives on the summer tourists arriving on the daily car ferries from Portland and Bar Harbor, Maine. From the southwest tip of the province, a road leads north along the "French Shore," where picturesque Acadian villages line St. Mary's Bay.

This district of Nova Scotia was settled in 1768 by Acadians who had been expelled by the English some 13 years before. The first to return was Joseph Dugas, his wife and daughter, who made the more than 450 kilometre journey from New England on foot and horseback. Other Acadians straggled back by canoe or schooner, and established small communities, such as Mavillette, Meteghan, Saulnierville, Comeauville, Belliveau Cove and St. Bernard. Most of the nearly 9,000 people who live in these places are of Acadian descent. In mid-July an Acadian festival alternates between Church Point and Meteghan River.

Farther north are the seaside resorts of Smiths Cove and Digby, the latter famed for its scallop fleet and a superb 18-hole championship golf course. Possible side trips from Digby include a day-long excursion out to Westport, on Brier Island. This tiny island at the mouth of the Bay of Fundy was the boyhood home of Capt. Joshua Slocum, the first man to sail around the world alone—between April 1895 and June 1898.

SANDY COVE
This is where a "mysterious" man, known locally as Jérôme, was discovered on the beach in 1854. Jérôme was dressed in clean clothes and had a supply of water and biscuits, but his legs had been amputated above the knees. Unable to speak, he was never able to reveal his origins. Until his death 58 years later, Jérôme was cared for by local people. His grave is at Meteghan.

DIGBY
One of Nova Scotia's most popular summer resorts, Digby offers a wide range of recreational activities—boating, golfing, horseback riding and swimming. Deep-sea fishing for cod, pollack, haddock and halibut is popular here and elsewhere along Digby Neck.
□ Digby is home of one of the world's great scallop fleets. (There are major scallop grounds offshore in Fundy Bay.) The community pays tribute to its prize catch in August when Digby Scallop Days are celebrated. Visitors can also sample "Digby chicks" (smoked herrings), another local delicacy.

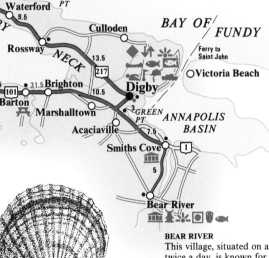

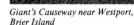

Giant's Causeway near Westport, Brier Island

METEGHAN
La Vieille Maison, an Acadian house built in the 1760s and now a museum, exhibits 18th-century sea chests, butter churns and spinning wheels.
□ St. Mary's Church (1905), north of Meteghan at Church Point, is one of North America's largest wooden churches. Trees from a local parishioner's woodlot were used to make the pillars that support the soaring arches.

GROSSES COQUES
The community is named after the large clams from St. Mary's Bay that kept local settlers alive during their first bitter winter here.
□ Nearby St. Bernard—with a population of about 320—has a magnificent Gothic church, built in 1910-42, that seats a thousand.

Digby scallop

BEAR RIVER
This village, situated on a tidal river that rises about six metres twice a day, is known for its crafts. The candle works is the largest enterprise of its kind in the Maritimes.
□ A picturesque local attraction is *Des Zaaier,* a replica of a three-story Dutch windmill.
□ Only birch was used to build (in 1919) and furnish St. Anne's Birch Chapel, on the grounds of Harbour View House in nearby Smiths Cove.

Unloading Irish moss, Wedgeport

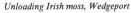

Yarmouth's Golden Age

Shipbuilding in Yarmouth flourished during the Golden Age of Sail in the late 19th century, when thousands of wooden vessels of all shapes and sizes were built in bays and harbors along the Nova Scotia coast. By the late 1870s Canada ranked fourth among shipbuilding and shipowning countries—and Yarmouth led the nation. While the ships and men of the "Bluenose Fleet" won fame around the world, wealth flowed into Yarmouth's two banks and its insurance companies, and to ship chandlers and sailmakers. Ships of the 19th century carried great clouds of sail. Square rigging (hung from transverse yards) caught lots of wind but required big crews working aloft. Fore-and-aft-rigged ships needed fewer men and were more maneuverable near shore. Designs of various ships changed over the years; those pictured (*right*) are typical of the years indicated.

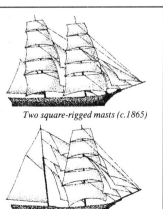

Two square-rigged masts (c.1865)

Mainsail rigged fore and aft (c.1870)

Good Cheer, a Bloodied Fort and a Deep, Woodland Haven

Southwestern Nova Scotia

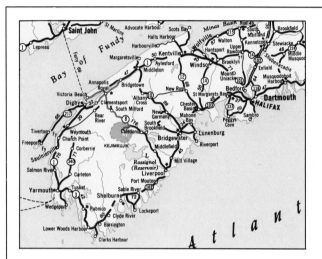

Port Royal Habitation

PORT ROYAL

Here stands a reconstruction of the Habitation that de Monts, Champlain and Poutrincourt established in 1605. The buildings of Port Royal National Historic Park are faithful in every detail to the originals, designed by Champlain. They form a compact square around a courtyard and are fortified by a palisade and a cannon platform. The buildings include the governor's residence, a chapel, a kitchen, a blacksmith shop and a fur-trading room.
□ Here, in 1606, Champlain formed North America's first social club, the Order of Good Cheer. Each member took his turn as Grand Master, responsible for the daily feast of game and wine. Marc Lescarbot, a Paris lawyer, wrote and produced North America's first play here. *Le Théâtre de Neptune* was performed in 1606.

CORNWALLIS

Built during World War II (as HMCS *Cornwallis*, the Commonwealth's biggest naval training base), CFB Cornwallis is now a basic training school. Tours can be arranged.
□ In Clementsport, 2.5 kilometres east, is Old St. Edward's Church, consecrated in 1797 to serve United Empire Loyalist settlers. Coins, household effects, prayer books and a silver communion set from that period are displayed in the church.

VICTORIA BEACH

A pony express that helped speed news from Britain to the United States is commemorated by a national historic plaque here. The express operated in 1849, the year after a telegraph line linked New York with Saint John. Cunard ships brought British dispatches to Halifax. From there the messages were sped 232 kilometres west to Victoria Beach (with fresh horses every 20 kilometres), then by steamer across the Bay of Fundy to Saint John for relay to the United States. At the end of 1849, when Halifax and Saint John were linked by telegraph via Amherst, N.S., the express was suspended.

Kejimkujik National Park

KEJIMKUJIK NATIONAL PARK

This 380-square-kilometre park preserves a wilderness of island-dotted lakes and low-lying hills, which were molded by glaciers thousands of years ago. It contains some of Nova Scotia's finest forests.
□ Information about the year-round park is available at a visitors' reception area. A tower at Kejimkujik Lake offers a panoramic view of the area. Walking and hiking trails lead to the park's forested depths; canoe routes, to its remote lakes. During winter, Kejimkujik is open to snowshoers and cross-country skiers.

Scarlet tanager

Blanding's turtle

A Generous Oasis for Plants and Wildlife

Because Kejimkujik National Park is in a region that has longer, hotter summers than the rest of Nova Scotia, unusual plants and animals exist here: in a lush mixed forest that contains huge hemlocks centuries old, there are greenbrier and witch hazel and such birds as the scarlet tanager, great crested flycatcher and wood thrush. The ribbon snake, Blanding's turtle and the southern flying squirrel—species found nowhere else in the Atlantic provinces—inhabit the park. Kejimkujik has five species of snakes and salamanders, three of turtles and eight of frogs and toads—one of the most varied reptile and amphibian populations in eastern Canada. Several lakes support whitefish, a species common farther west.

Eastern hemlock

Overlooking the broad Annapolis Basin is Port Royal National Historic Park, site of the first successful French colony in the New World. In 1605 Pierre de Monts, and a boatload of French colonists, built a stockaded Habitation in what was then called "Acadie." To brighten their lives, explorer Samuel de Champlain created *l'Ordre de Bon-Temps* (the Order of Good Cheer), which featured banquets of moose pie, roast duck and much wine, followed by songs and music. Today visitors can explore a replica of Port Royal Habitation, with its original well, studded oaken doors, and cobblestoned room where Indians traded beaver pelts.

A few kilometres away, on the south side of the basin, is Fort Anne National Historic Park at Annapolis Royal. The existing earthworks, built by the French in 1690-1708, were later strengthened by the British. The fort has a violent history and was the most fought over place in Canada. In the streets of Annapolis Royal are historic buildings that reveal glimpses of the past.

From Annapolis Royal, the traveler can continue northeast through the verdant Annapolis Valley, a 130-kilometre-long orchard whose fertile land was farmed by French-speaking Acadians as long ago as 1630. But nature lovers take the road which leads south from Annapolis Royal to Kejimkujik National Park. In this woodland haven visitors will find deep solitude and a seemingly endless network of tree-shaded hiking trails and calm canoe routes.

British officers' quarters, Fort Anne

TUPPERVILLE
Visitors can step back into the late 19th century at the local school museum, where classroom exhibits include books, desks, an old school bell, and a potbellied stove.
▫ The grave of Col. James DeLancey—the "Outlaw of the Bronx"—is just east of the museum. DeLancey, who led pro-British partisans during the American Revolution, settled in this area after banishment from the United States in 1783.
▫ Tupperville is named for Nova Scotia-born Sir Charles Tupper (1821-1915), one of the Fathers of Confederation and sixth prime minister of Canada (for ten weeks in 1896).

GRANVILLE FERRY
This tiny community was established by settlers from New England, who began arriving here after 1759. The North Hills Museum occupies a small wood-frame house built in the 1760s with the "saltbox" exterior and "Holy Lord" (H and L) hinges of early 18th-century New England buildings. (The H and L shapes were believed to fend off the powers of witchcraft.) The museum's collection includes Georgian furniture, ceramics, glass and silver.

Interior of British officers' quarters, Fort Anne

ANNAPOLIS ROYAL
This community is one of the oldest in Canada. The French established a fort and a settlement (Port Royal) here in the 1630s. Captured by the British in 1710, and renamed Fort Anne and Annapolis Royal in honor of Queen Anne, this was the seat of British government in Nova Scotia until 1749.
▫ Fort Anne National Historic Park, established in 1917, is the oldest of Canada's national historic sites. Its focal point is the reconstructed British Field Officers' Quarters (1797), which describes the area's history. A French-built powder magazine (1708) and earthwork fortifications from the 1600s also survive.
▫ Among the historic buildings at Annapolis Royal are the Adams-Ritchie House (1712), The Farmer's Hotel (dating from the 1730s), the Robertson-McNamara House (1785) and the O'Dell Inn Museum (1869).
▫ Annapolis Royal Historic Gardens features a number of theme gardens—the Acadian, for example—and a maze.
▫ Annapolist Tidal Power Project—North America's first tidal generating station—on the causeway at Annapolis Royal, contains an interpretive center.

Indian Petroglyphs: Traces of Prehistory

Here and there on the shores of Kejimkujik Lake is fascinating evidence of early human existence. The slate is so soft that, with a harder rock, a knife or piece of bone, men could carve pictures and symbols on it. Some of these petroglyphs, done by Indians, may predate the arrival of the Europeans. There are pictures of animals, of men fishing and hunting, ancient Micmac symbols, and a four-legged bird encircled by stars (probably an Indian god). Later drawings show European traces in Micmac dress and one figure resembles a French cavalier. Some petroglyphs portray sailing ships with flawless rigging (*left*).

A Fertile Valley Famed for Apples, and a Tidy Farm Still Plowed by Oxen

Annapolis Valley

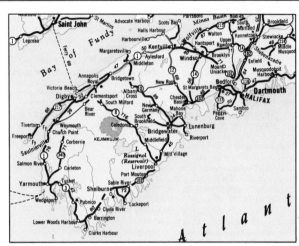

St. Mary's Anglican Church, Auburn

Halls Harbour

HALLS HARBOUR
Overlooking the Minas Channel, where Fundy tides reach world-record heights, this picturesque fishing village is named for the captain of the pirate ship *Mary Jane.* Twice in the early 1800s he successfully raided the settlement. But on the third raid, his crew was defeated by settlers who seized the pirate gold. Legend says the loot was buried ashore, but the location is unknown—and awaits discovery.

AUBURN
Loyalist settlers built St. Mary's Anglican Church in 1790. They made plaster for the walls of the church by powdering the shells of mussels that Acadian refugees ate while in hiding during the winter of 1755-56. (The Acadians had escaped deportation by the English in 1755.) A plaque at St. Mary's commemorates the Rt. Rev. Charles Inglis, first bishop of Nova Scotia (1787), who lived near Auburn for many years.
□ At Morden, 11 kilometres north, a large cross of beach stones honors the estimated 250 Acadians who wintered here in 1755-56. Some of the Acadians died; the survivors escaped by canoe to the north side of Minas Channel in March 1756.
□ Berwick, east of Auburn, is Nova Scotia's largest apple-processing center.

BRIDGETOWN
Fine old houses line the streets of this town, at the head of the Annapolis River. The first settlers—Acadians in the 1650s—were followed by New Englanders in the mid-18th century, and Loyalists after 1776. The James House, built in 1835, is the headquarters of the local historical society, which has displays and art exhibitions there in summer.
□ Valleyview Provincial Park, on the brow of North Mountain, gives a spectacular 80-kilo-metre view of the Annapolis Valley.

Eastern kingbird

LAWRENCETOWN
The Annapolis Valley Exhibition, held here in mid-August, has displays of livestock and farm produce, ox and horse pulls, tugs-of-war and home-cooked meals.
□ Student surveyors are a common sight along highways and railway lines near Lawrencetown: it is the home of the Nova Scotia Land Survey Institute, Canada's only school devoted exclusively to cartography, land surveying and photogrammetry.

GREENWOOD
This community (pop. 9,000) is the site of Canada's largest antisubmarine air base. Established in 1942, the base was originally used for troop training.
□ In the nearby village of Kingston, an annual steer barbecue in early July features sports events, a midway, pony rides and a stage show.

MIDDLETON
Old Holy Trinity Church, built in 1789, is a fine example of colonial church architecture. It still has its original straight-backed pews—each with a numbered door. Guided tours of this Loyalist church—and the adjacent Captain Davis Brass Rubbing Centre—are available on weekdays in summer.
□ The Annapolis Valley Macdonald Museum occupies the oldest consolidated school in Canada. A number of collections, including 150 antique clocks and watches, are displayed.
□ This agricultural community of 1,770 celebrates Heart of the Valley Days in July.

0	1	2	3	4	5 Miles
0	2	4	6	8 Kilometres	

More than three centuries ago, the fertile land of the Annapolis Valley was farmed by Nova Scotia's first permanent settlers, the French-speaking Acadians. Following their expulsion to the Thirteen Colonies in 1755, the area was settled by New Englanders, and then by United Empire Loyalists fleeing persecution at the hands of American revolutionaries. Many of the Loyalists' descendants remain here today, enjoying an easygoing pace of life, in what has become one of the most well-known apple-producing regions in Canada.

Between Bridgetown and Kentville are peaceful farming communities such as Lawrencetown, Middleton, Aylesford, Berwick—and even a village named Paradise. Along the valley road, sea and woodland bird species give way to farm and orchard species such as the ruby-throated hummingbird, the eastern kingbird and the chipping sparrow. In late May and early June, the valley is filled with the fragrance of blossoming trees.

The main highway runs parallel to the Bay of Fundy shore, which is never more than 15 kilometres due north. Side roads branch off to picturesque seaside hamlets such as Hampton, Port George and Margaretsville, where sunny beaches are washed by Fundy's surging tide.

From Kentville, home of the Apple Blossom Festival, a road leads south to Nova Scotia's "living museum" of agriculture: New Ross Farm, fully restored and operating as it did more than a century ago.

Apple Blossom Festival parade, Kentville

KENTVILLE

This is the largest community in the Annapolis Valley. The history of the area, which was settled by New Englanders in the 1760s, is preserved at the Old Kings Courthouse Heritage Museum on Cornwallis Street.
□ When orchards are in full bloom in late May, the annual five-day Apple Blossom Festival is held throughout the Annapolis Valley from Windsor to Digby. Festival highlights include concerts, fireworks, parades, and the coronation of the festival queen. Many of the major events occur at Kentville, which hosted the first festival in 1932.
□ The 183-hectare Kentville Agricultural Research Station can be toured. The history of the local apple industry is recounted at Blair House, a museum at the station.

NEW ROSS FARM

Plows are pulled by oxen and grain is cut by scythe and sickle at this living museum of agriculture. Ross Farm dates from 1816, when Capt. William Ross of the Nova Scotia Fencibles undertook to settle 172 discharged soldiers in the area.
□ In an 1892 red wooden barn are implements illustrating farm technology from 1600 to 1925. In the collection are cant hooks for removing tree stumps, plows and reapers, and threshing and winnowing machines powered by horse or dog treadmills.
□ Barrels and casks are made and repaired in the cooperage at the farm workshop. There are demonstrations of yoke and shingle making and ox shoeing.
□ Rosebank is a two-story frame house built by Captain Ross in 1817 to replace his first log house. It has five fireplaces. Exhibits include a piano (c.1820) that four soldiers carried from Chester, 24 kilometres south.

Crimson Beauties from the Annapolis Valley

Almost all of Nova Scotia's apple orchards are in the Annapolis Valley, where the soil is rich and the climate mild. Settlers who came here from New England in 1760 planted Canada's first commercial orchards. The trees they grew are gone, but many descendants of those settlers still tend Annapolis Valley orchards.

McIntosh, Red and Gold Delicious (*left to right, above*), and Northern Spy are the commonest varieties of apples here; other types include Crimson Beauty, Melba, Bough Sweet and Honeygold. Apples that bruise easily are sold locally; hardier varieties are exported, mainly to Great Britain and the United States. Most types are used for applesauce, juice, jelly and cider.

Rosebank cottage, New Ross Farm

BAY OF FUNDY

Halls Harbour

Vernon Mines — 11
359
221 — Centreville
7
Aldershot
341
Kentville
Cornwallis River

Cambridge — Coldbrook
Waterville — 13
1
7
12
101

South Alton

Gaspereau River

N

Gaspereau Lake

23
40.5
Murphy Lake

New Ross Road

Salmontail River

12

Aldersville
Salmontail Lake
Gold River
Wallaback Lake

Mill Road
Harris Lake
10.5

Lake Ramsay

Lake Ramsay

New Ross

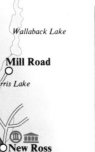

Chipping sparrow

Memories of a Tragic Acadian Heroine and a Comical Yankee Clock Peddler

Central Nova Scotia

Sandstone cliffs overlooking Minas Basin near Blomidon

CAPE BLOMIDON
A 14-kilometre hiking trail between Blomidon Provincial Park and Cape Split runs atop 200-metre sandstone cliffs. Lookouts provide sweeping views of the Annapolis Valley, Minas Basin and the Bay of Fundy. Amethyst and agate can be found along the trail. Blomidon is probably a corruption of Blow-me-down, as the cape was called by early settlers.
□ According to Micmac legend, Cape Blomidon is where the mythical hero Glooscap held court.

STARRS POINT
Prescott House Museum, which is set in a magnificent garden, was built in 1814 by Charles Ramage Prescott, the merchant and pioneer horticulturalist who introduced several apple varieties, including the Gravenstein, into Nova Scotia. The 21-room Georgian mansion has a steep hip roof with four dormers and two massive chimneys. The whitewashed brick walls are nearly a metre thick. Furnishings include four-poster beds, a grandfather clock, Coalport china of the early 1800s, an 18th-century maple desk, Regency dining-room chairs and a portrait of Prescott.
□ At nearby Port Williams, tides rise and fall as much as 12 metres. Ships loading apples and potatoes at low tide are high and dry beside the wharf.

Prescott House, Starrs Point

Fertile Farmland Rescued From the Sea

Old Acadian dikes still remain along the Minas Basin shore near Grand Pré, N.S. (*below*). The dikes held back Bay of Fundy tides and eventually transformed marshes into farmland. More than three metres wide, the dikes were made of stones and logs packed with clay. Built into the base were *aboiteaux*—wooden boxes with clappers hinged to seaward—which prevented sea water from entering at high tide, but allowed marshes to drain at low tide.

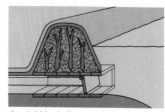

Dikes drained marshes at low tide—

then held back the sea at high tide

WOLFVILLE
This tree-lined university town was founded by New Englanders in the 1760s. Acadia University began as a Baptist academy (1828) and college (1838), and gained university status in 1891. Today more than 3,000 attend classes in its gracious classical buildings. Vaughan Memorial Library on campus preserves the sermons and journals of evangelist Henry Alline, whose preachings helped keep Nova Scotia loyal to the British cause during the American Revolution.
□ The Wolfville Historical Society operates Randall House (c. 1815) as a museum, which contains exhibits about New Englanders and Loyalists who settled here.
□ Works by acclaimed Canadian artist Alex Colville—Wolfville's most famous citizen—are displayed in the Beveridge Arts Centre at Acadia University Art Gallery.

0	1	2	3	4	5 Miles
0	2		4	6	8 Kilometres

The flag of Acadia, a French tricolor with a yellow star in the blue field, flies proudly at Grand Pré National Historic Park, the principal scene of *le grand dérangement*—the expulsion of 1755. That year, as the struggle for North America grew hotter, the Acadians of Nova Scotia refused to swear allegiance to England lest they be forced to fight other Frenchmen. As a result, thousands were shipped south to the English colonies, and abandoned. Ironically, the most moving account of that sad episode, Longfellow's epic *Evangeline*, was written about a girl who lived mainly in the poet's imagination. Yet today, by an ivy-covered chapel, on the very site where the Acadian expulsion was ordered, visitors can toss coins into "Evangeline's well" and gaze at her bronze statue.

Three of Nova Scotia's finest museums are in this area. At Starrs Point is Prescott House, a Georgian mansion built in 1799-1802 by a pioneer horticulturist. At Mount Uniacke is a 19th-century mansion, part of the former estate of one of Nova Scotia's most prominent political families. And at Windsor is the frame house in which Thomas Chandler Haliburton wrote his Sam Slick stories, beginning in 1836 with *The Clockmaker*. It was Sam, the fictional Yankee clock peddler, who first said: "the early bird gets the worm." He coined "jack of all trades and master of none" and countless other "wise saws" on "human nature"—bringing Haliburton international fame as a humorist.

GRAND PRÉ
Old willow trees in Grand Pré National Historic Park are said to have survived from the 1600s and 1700s, when this small community was a major Acadian settlement. A chapel in the park commemorates the church in which the 1755 expulsion notice was read to the Acadians. Outside is a bronze statue of Longfellow's fictional heroine, *Evangeline*. Nearby is "Evangeline's well," a restoration of one that was found when English settlers occupied the lands left by the Acadians.
□ A monument near the park commemorates the 1747 Battle of Grand Pré, in which some 240 Frenchmen and 20 Indians routed an occupying force of 500 New Englanders.
□ Covenanters' Church, built by Loyalists in 1804, has box pews, sounding boards and a pulpit reaching halfway to the ceiling. Square-headed nails join its hand-sawn boards.
□ A marker identifies the boyhood home of Sir Robert Borden (1854-1937), Canadian prime minister during the First World War.

Haliburton's Sam Slick

Evangeline: The Story Behind the Poem

The Evangeline *statue, Grand Pré National Historic Park*

In 1847 American poet Henry Wadsworth Longfellow published *Evangeline: A Tale of Acadie*. With its memorable opening ("This is the forest primeval"), the epic poem about the dispersal of the Acadians became one of his most popular works. Millions now know the story of Evangeline's romance with Gabriel, their separation, and her long, sad search for her lover. The idea to publish the tale came from a Boston minister named Horace L. Conolly. Having heard an account of parted Acadian lovers, Conolly approached novelist Nathaniel Hawthorne to write the story. When Hawthorne declined, Longfellow offered to tell it. The poet began writing *Evangeline* in 1845 at his home in Cambridge, Mass. He relied on published accounts of the Acadian expulsion and never visited Grand Pré.

WINDSOR
"Clifton," the 15-room frame house in which Judge Thomas Chandler Haliburton wrote the Sam Slick stories, is now the Haliburton Memorial Museum. Built in 1834-36, the house contains Haliburton's desk and a Sam Slick shelf clock.
□ Atop a hill overlooking Windsor stands a split-log blockhouse, the oldest in Canada. It was built by the British in 1750 as part of the defenses of Fort Edward.
□ The Hants County Exhibition, first held in 1765 (and run annually since 1815), is North America's oldest agricultural fair. The September exhibition has horse and livestock shows, craft and produce displays, and an ox-pulling competition.
□ Shand House, built in 1890-91, is now a museum. There is a superb view of the surrounding countryside from the ornate tower of this late Victorian dwelling.

SOUTH RAWDON
Nineteenth-century rural Nova Scotia artifacts in the South Rawdon Museum include ice skates (steel blades secured in blocks of wood that were strapped to the skater's boots) and a press for making straw hats. The museum is in a former Sons of Temperance hall, built in 1867.

MOUNT UNIACKE
Original furnishings still grace Uniacke House, an elegant colonial mansion that was once at the center of a huge country estate. Irish-born Richard John Uniacke built the house in 1813-15 while serving as Nova Scotia attorney general. The two-story, eight-bedroom white wooden house later became the summer home of his son, James Boyle Uniacke, a fiery Tory leader who resigned from the Legislative Council in 1837 to join Joseph Howe's reform party. In 1848 Uniacke became Nova Scotia's premier and attorney general—in the British Empire's first responsible government.

Pine grosbeak

HANTSPORT
Ship models and other maritime mementos are displayed at the Hantsport community center in a great three-story house built in 1860 by Ezra Churchill, a shipyard owner who prospered when Hantsport was a major shipbuilding town.
□ A cairn marks the grave of William Hall, the first black and the first Canadian sailor to win the Victoria Cross. The son of a slave brought from Virginia, he served with the Royal Navy in the Crimean War and during the 1857 Indian Mutiny.

Map labels
Avonport Station
Avonport
12
101
32.5
Hantsport
Avon River
Mount Denson
Halfway
11.5
101
DIMOCK PT.
Windsor
Falmouth
14
101
Three-Mile Plains
9
St. Croix
Ellershouse
St. Croix River
215
30
Willow Hill
14.5
Ardoise Hill
1
Meander R.
8.5
Hillsvale
South Rawdon
Cockscomb Lake
Pigott Lake
Lakeland
Lily Lake
Mount Uniacke
6.5
Mount Uniacke
South Uniacke
Oland
1
Lewis Lake
101

White Crescents of Sand
Where Pirates Once Roamed

Southwestern Nova Scotia

On a street corner in the village of Milton, just north of Liverpool, is a privateer cannon placed muzzle down. It was probably placed there to keep carriages to the road and away from a front garden. But the old gun is a reminder of less peaceful times along Nova Scotia's south shore. Settlers from Cape Cod who founded Liverpool in the 1760s spent much of the next 50 years protecting homes, fisheries and shipping from French and Spanish raiders and Yankee privateers. They fought for sur-

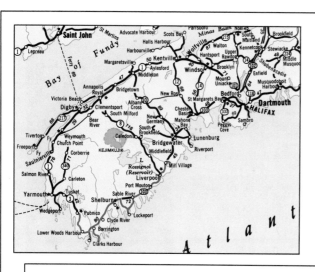

Wool mural at Barrington Woolen Mill

BARRINGTON

This small community boasts the last water-operated woolen mill in eastern Canada. Built in 1884, the Barrington Woollen Mill is now a museum. Exhibits include machines once used for twisting and winding yarn. A wool mural depicts the history of sheep raising in Nova Scotia.
□ Barrington's Old Meeting House, Canada's oldest nonconformist house of worship, was built in 1765 by religious refugees from Massachusetts. Until 1838, the meeting house was also used as a town hall. Narrow steps lead to a wall pulpit (c. 1790). Ceiling beams are braced by "ship's knees"—a common construction device when local carpenters also built ships.

Cape Sable: Graveyard of the Atlantic

At the Archelaus Smith Museum in Centreville on Cape Sable Island, is a self-bailing lifeboat. A relic from the 1890s, it is a reminder of the days when local crews sailed through stormy seas to rescue shipwreck victims—and salvage something from the disaster. When news of a troubled ship reached shore, the wreckers (as local seafarers were called) set out to save lives and—often for their own profit—cargo.

Hundreds of ships have been lost off Cape Sable, where submerged, ship-destroying ledges extend hundreds of metres to sea, and powerful tides sweep around shoals and islands. For centuries the cape

has been known to sailors as one of the graveyards of the Atlantic. (It is not to be confused with another Atlantic graveyard that is just as notorious and has a similar name: Sable Island is a treacherous strip of shifting sand more than 300 kilometres east of Halifax.)

Cape Sable's worst wreck occurred in February 1860, when the steamship *Hungarian*, en route from England to Portland, Maine, foundered on a rocky shoal. All 125 passengers and 80 crewmen drowned. But much of *Hungarian*'s cargo was salvaged, and Cape Sable Islanders considered the rich wreck a gift from providence.

SHAG HARBOUR

Chapel Hill Museum, in what was formerly a church, is located in the center of Shag Harbour. From the belfry, there is a superb view of the sea and the offshore islands: at night you can see the beacons of five lighthouses—at Bon Portage Island, Baccaro Point, Cape Sable, Seal Island and Woods Harbour.

White ibis

CAPE SABLE ISLAND

A 1,200-metre causeway links Cape Sable Island with Barrington Passage. This rocky island—Nova Scotia's most southerly point—is the "birthplace" of the Cape Island boat. Famed for its stability and good handling in shallow water, it was developed at Clark's Harbour in 1907 by Ephraim Atkinson. Inboard motor-powered versions—some 12 metres long—are used mostly by inshore fishermen.
□ In the tiny community of Centreville, the Archelaus Smith Museum exhibits items salvaged from vessels shipwrecked offshore.

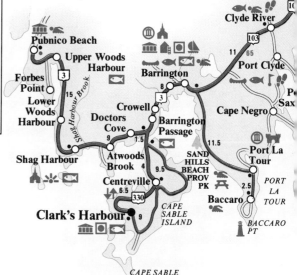

CAPE SABLE

PORT LA TOUR

Nearby are traces of two 17th-century forts. A cairn a few kilometres south of here marks the site of Fort Saint-Louis, built about 1627 by French trader Charles La Tour. Northwest of Port La Tour are traces of Fort Temple (1656), the first English stronghold on the coast of southwestern Nova Scotia.

vival, once in their own streets, often on the high seas, outfitting their own privateers with Royal Navy cannon, and taking wars of retaliation to the New England coast and the Caribbean.

The road south from Liverpool leads past White Point and Hunts Point—resorts fringed by white crescents of sand. Farther on lies Shelburne, a shipbuilding town of 2,300, which was briefly one of the most populous places in British North America, when thousands of Loyalists arrived after the

American Revolution. At Barrington is the Old Meeting House where these settlers gathered more than 200 years ago; here, too, is one of Canada's first water-driven woolen mills. A causeway at Barrington Passage leads to Cape Sable Island, long notorious among sailors as one of the deadliest hazards on the Atlantic coast. At this southernmost tip of Nova Scotia, exotic birds such as the white ibis are sometimes spotted among flocks of Canada geese, black ducks and blue-winged teal.

JORDAN FALLS

An anchor on a cairn of beach stone honors Donald McKay (1810-80), designer and builder of some of the fastest packet ships of the 19th century. Born at Jordan Falls, McKay was an apprentice shipbuilder when he set out at 16 for New York. His reputation was established in 1842, when *Courier*—a packet ship he designed—set speed records. McKay went on to design other famous ships, including *Flying Cloud, Great Republic* and *Sovereign of the Sea*, launching them from the shipyard he built in East Boston, Mass., in 1845.

LIVERPOOL

The Simeon Perkins House was built in 1766 by a Connecticut-born settler who became a prominent local merchant. The house contains 18th-century furnishings and a copy of Perkins' diary, which records more than 40 years of colonial life.
□ Adjacent to the Perkins House is the Queen County Museum, which is housed in a building representing the Perkins' warehouse.

Harbor scene near Hunts Point

LOCKEPORT

On the approach to a sandy crescent beach almost two kilometres long stands Lockeport's first schoolhouse, a five-room structure built about 1845. Restored as the Little School Museum, it reproduces classrooms of a century ago and displays such artifacts as a parlor organ, a potbellied stove and a spinning wheel.

Ross-Thompson House, Shelburne

SHELBURNE

During the mid-1780s, Shelburne's numbers swelled to 16,000 as Loyalists passed through following the American Revolution. (A cairn at the foot of King Street marks their landing place.) Many fine old houses here today survive from that era. The Ross-Thompson House, built in 1784 and now a part of the Nova Scotia Museum, contains a store with period merchandise. The Dory Shop, which operated from 1880 to 1970, preserves a three-story shipbuilding factory. The Rudolph-Williams House, which dates from 1787, is now the Shelburne County Museum.

Lusty Privateersmen of Liverpool

Nova Scotia's dreaded privateer ship, the Liverpool Packet

Nova Scotians practiced privateering with gusto and profit between 1756 and 1815. This legalized piracy ensured the survival of Nova Scotia's West Indian trade, which was threatened by enemy ships during the conflicts of the time—the American Revolution, the War of 1812, and the Napoleonic wars.

Liverpool privateersmen included Capt. Alexander Godfrey of the brig *Rover*, who routed a Spanish squadron and captured its flagship in the Caribbean in 1800; and Capt. Joseph Barss of the schooner *Liverpool Packet*, who captured nearly 100 American ships off the New England coast during the War of 1812.

Smugglers' Haunts, Buried Treasure and the Ghost of a Privateer

Southwestern Nova Scotia

From the rugged shore at Prospect, southwest of Halifax, Nova Scotia's "Lighthouse Route" stretches down a coast where many houses of the old sailing men still have a "widow's walk" looking out to sea. One favorite stop is rockbound Peggy's Cove, the most photographed fishing village in Canada, with about 90 residents and 1,000 sightseers on a typical summer day.

Here the road turns north, winding around the indented shoreline of St. Margarets Bay, where rumrunners loaded boot-

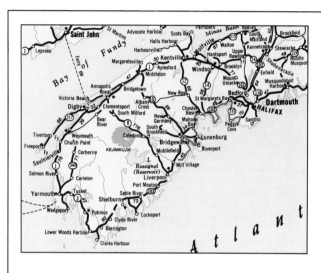

BRIDGEWATER
Among attractions of this thriving community of 6,700 are the DesBrisay Museum, located in a 10-hectare park, and the Dean Wile Carding Mill. The museum, which documents the history of Lunenburg, is named for Judge Mather Byles DesBrisay, who collected some of the objects displayed. Exhibits include an 1841 Micmac birchbark cradle ornamented with dyed woven porcupine quills, and 17th-century German bibles.
□ Built in 1860, the water-powered Wile Carding Mill is now a provincial museum. Its original equipment, which prepared fibers for spinning, has been restored to working order.
□ The South Shore Exhibition and International Ox Pull—a major annual event—is held in July.

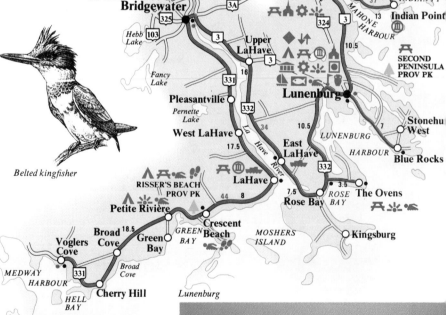

Lunenburg

A 'Living Museum' of Ships and Seafaring

At Lunenburg, veteran fishermen guide visitors through historic ships moored to the quay at the Fisheries Museum of the Atlantic, a branch of the Nova Scotia Museum. *Theresa E. Connor* (launched in 1938), the last of the Lunenburg dory schooners, has been converted below decks to house exhibits of the era of the deep-water

Schooner Theresa E. Connor

fleet and Nova Scotia schooner men. Built by the local Smith and Rhuland shipyard (as were *Bluenose* and her Halifax-based replica, *Bluenose II*), she contains exhibits on the history of the offshore fishery, and *Bluenose*'s wheel and trophies. Also on display is the steel-hulled side trawler *Cape Sable.*

Adjacent museum buildings include an aquarium, a dory shop, and a theater, which presents films on deep-sea fishing.

Belted kingfisher

LAHAVE
French explorer Pierre De Monts landed here in 1604. Fort Point Museum (Fort Sainte-Marie-de-Grâce Historic Site) marks where one of Canada's earliest settlements was established in 1632 by Isaac de Razilly, first governor of New France. It was later captured by the English, and eventually destroyed by Boston privateers in 1705.

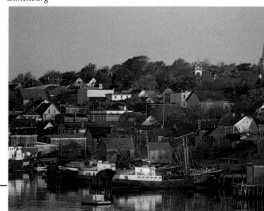

0   1   2   3   4   5 Miles
0   2   4   6   8 Kilometres

leg liquor for the New England coast in the 1920s and early 1930s. Farther on is Mahone Bay, where pirate treasure has been sought on Oak Island since 1795, and where the U.S. privateer *Young Teazer* was blown up in 1813 but still "reappears" in flames on dark, dreadful nights. Some 350 islands and coves make Mahone Bay fascinating to explore.

The most famous port along this coast is Lunenburg, which 50 years ago owned the largest deep-water fishing fleet plying the Grand Banks off Newfoundland. Best of all was the schooner *Bluenose*, whose likeness is on the Canadian dime; she outraced the fastest Yankee ships in the 1920s and 1930s. Now those billowing windjammers have vanished, replaced by modern trawlers. But Lunenburg remains among the most prosperous fishing towns on the Atlantic seaboard.

Nearby is a picturesque haven called Blue Rocks, where fish-drying houses are built on stilts and reached by dory. On the opposite side of Lunenburg Harbour are The Ovens—a series of caves or "blowholes" carved into the cliffs by the pounding sea. The caves can be seen from a concrete viewing platform.

Not far inland, on wooded hills overlooking the LaHave River, lies Bridgewater, the biggest town in Lunenburg County. International horse and ox pulls are an exciting highlight at the South Shore Exhibition held here each August.

CHESTER

The town is situated on a peninsula in Mahone Bay, which has 365 islands. A ferry links Chester with the two largest—Big and Little Tancook islands. No cars are permitted on the ferry.
□ Chester was first settled by New Englanders in 1760. The Sword and Anchor Inn was built in the early 1800s; its annex, Sheet Anchor House, in 1783.

MAHONE BAY

Three churches—Trinity United (1862), St. John's Lutheran (c. 1869) and St. James Anglican (1883)—stand at the head of the town's harbor.
□ Just off Highway 3 north of town is Oak Island, which has lured treasure seekers—often with tragic consequences—for more than half a century. According to legend, Captain Kidd's treasure is buried here, but so far it has eluded discovery. The area is closed to the public.

Peggy's Cove

PEGGY'S COVE

This fishing community (pop. 90)—one of Canada's favorite spots with artists and photographers—is famous for its granite shoreline, its weatherworn wharves and rustic dwellings, and its lighthouse point, which offers a sweeping sea view. (The lighthouse, no longer used for its original purpose, serves as a post office in summer, the only lighthouse in Canada filling this role.)
□ The Fishermen's Monument in William E. deGarthe Memorial Provincial Park depicts 32 local fishermen, their wives and children, a guardian angel with unfurled wings, and Peggy of the Cove (reputedly the lone survivor of a shipwreck off Lighthouse Point after whom the village is named). The monument is the work of local marine artist William deGarthe (1907-83), who planned it as "a lasting monument to Canadian fishermen."

Map labels

GRAVES ISLAND PROV PK
East River
Hubbards
Queensland
Head of St. Margarets Bay
Upper Tantallon
Fox Point Lake
Ingramport
HEAD HARBOUR
Tantallon
Fox Point
Glen Haven
Mill Cove
ST. MARGARETS BAY
Hollahan Lake
French Village
Seabright
MEISNER PT
MAHONE BAY
Deep Cove
Glen Margaret
Aspotogan
Northwest Cove
LITTLE TANCOOK ISLAND
Blandford
SHUT-IN ISLAND
Hacketts Cove
Tancook
Bayswater
BIG TANCOOK ISLAND
Indian Harbour
McGrath Cove
ATLANTIC
Bayside
OCEAN
Peggy's Cove
PEGGY'S PT
West Dover
Shad Bay
East Dover
Whites Lake
Prospect

LUNENBURG

Long one of Canada's great fishing ports, Lunenburg (pop. 3,000) is renowned as the home of the schooner *Bluenose*—the nation's most famous ship. A local monument calls the schooner a symbol of "the transformation of an inland people." The German, French and Swiss farmers who settled here in 1783 tamed the local wilderness before setting out to fish along the coast and—eventually—on Newfoundland's Grand Banks, where their skills rivaled the best of the world's deep-sea fishermen.
□ Among restored vessels at the Fisheries Museum of the Atlantic is *Theresa E. Connor,* the last Canadian schooner to fish the Grand Banks (1962).
□ The annual Nova Scotia Fisheries Exhibition and Fishermen's Reunion in September features fishing industry displays, scallop-shucking competitions, dory races and other events.
□ The Fishermen's Memorial Room in the Community Centre honors men and ships lost at sea.
□ St. John's Anglican Church (1754) is the second oldest Anglican church in Canada. (The oldest is St. Paul's, Halifax.) The steeple of Zion Lutheran Church (1776) has a bell that once rang in the chapel at the Fortress of Louisburg. St. Andrew's Church (1828) serves one of Canada's oldest Presbyterian congregations. Its roots here go back to the 1700s.

Sour Cream and Cabbages

The people of Lunenburg—many of them descended from Germans who settled in Nova Scotia in the 1750s—speak with a musical lilt, keep their houses freshly painted and their gardens neat, and love German cooking.

The fertile soil here nourishes bumper crops of vegetables. Local cabbage, when shredded, salted and fermented, makes tart and tasty sauerkraut. Hodge-podge, a Lunenburg specialty for the past 200 years, is made with fresh, young vegetables. Carrots, onions, green beans, peas and small new potatoes are steamed together, then combined with cream (sweet or sour) and butter and diced salt pork fried to a crisp.

Salt cod, soaked overnight, is boiled with potatoes and garnished with fried onions and crisped salt pork to make hugger-in-buff, a traditional dish of Newfoundland. Lunenburg cooks add a German touch: a cup of sour cream.

An Anchorage in Peace and War...
and the Leader of Atlantic Canada

Throughout its history, Halifax—Nova Scotia's capital and Atlantic Canada's largest city—has thrived as a port and served as a naval and military base. It earned the title "Warden of the North" for its key role in global conflicts, from Wolfe's conquest of Quebec (1759) to the two world wars.

Modern Halifax abounds with reminders of its storied past. At the heart of the city, St. Paul's Anglican Church summons up memories of Governor Edward Cornwallis (1712-76) and the city's first settlers, who arrived in 1749 and built the church in 1750. At the summit of 77-metre-high Citadel Hill, the ramparts of the star-shaped fort recall the city's military past. On the waterfront, the restored Historic Properties—a lively complex of restaurants and shops—brings to life the "golden age of sail" of the mid-1800s.

Visitors to the waterfront can take boat tours of Halifax's large (more than 25 kilometres long) and vital harbor. The bustling, year-round harbor, more than anything else, powerfully evokes the sea and the ships that have shaped Halifax.

Art Gallery of Nova Scotia (22)
The restored and renovated Dominion Building (1863-68) houses the art gallery, whose permanent collection includes paintings by Nova Scotian, British and European artists.

Cathedral Church of All Saints (10)
Built in 1908-10, this Gothic-style cathedral is known for its stained-glass windows and beautiful woodcarvings.

Dalhousie University (3)
Founded in 1818, the university is noted for legal, medical and ocean studies. (The student population numbers about 9,000.) The Dalhousie Arts Centre's collections range from pre-Inca pottery to modern paintings. McCullough Museum at the Life Sciences Building exhibits a collection of mounted birds of Nova Scotia, created by Dalhousie College's first principal Thomas McCullough (1776-1843).

Government House (28)
This stone mansion, the official residence of Nova Scotia's lieutenant governor, was built in 1800-05.

The Old Town Clock (above) *at the base of Citadel Hill is one of the many venerable landmarks that enrich the Halifax cityscape. The high rises of recent times, however, are the dominant features of the city's downtown skyline* (below).

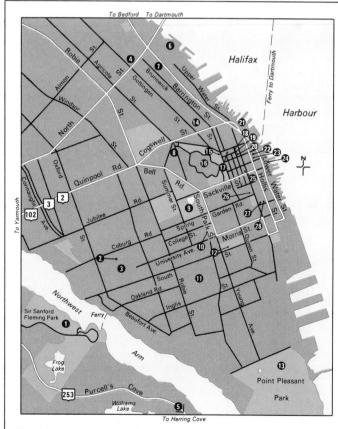

Halifax
1 Sir Sanford Fleming Park
2 University of King's College
3 Dalhousie University
4 Maritime Command Museum
5 York Redoubt
6 H.M.C. Dockyard
7 Old Dutch Church
8 Nova Scotia Museum
9 Public Gardens
10 Cathedral Church of All Saints
11 St. Mary's University
12 Our Lady of Sorrows Chapel
13 Point Pleasant Park
14 St. George's Round Church
15 Old Town Clock
16 Halifax Citadel National Historic Park
17 World Trade and Convention Centre
18 Halifax City Hall/Tourist Information
19 Grand Parade
20 St. Paul's Church
21 Historic Properties/ Tourist Information
22 Art Gallery of Nova Scotia
23 Province House
24 Maritime Museum of the Atlantic
25 Neptune Theatre
26 St. Mary's Basilica
27 St. Matthew's United Church
28 Government House

Grand Parade (19)
The old main square of Halifax—where local troops once drilled and town criers read the news—is the site of the Halifax War Memorial.

Halifax Citadel National Historic Park (16)
Situated on a hill overlooking Halifax, the Citadel is a large star-shaped stone fortress, which was built between 1828 and 1856 on the site of three earlier forts. It was designed to prevent a land attack and remained in use as a military base until after the Second World War. Today, the Halifax Citadel National Historic Park preserves the fortress. Exhibits explain the construction of the Citadel. A sight-and-sound presentation describes the history of Halifax and its defenses.

Halifax City Hall (18)
Just north of the Grand Parade is the Halifax

City Hall, which has a tourist information bureau. The site was originally occupied by Dalhousie College (1820-87).

Historic Properties (21)
These restored waterfront buildings—including the Privateers' Warehouse (1813), once a storehouse for pirated cargoes—house offices, restaurants and boutiques. At Privateers' Wharf, *Bluenose II*—a replica of the renowned schooner (1921-46), depicted on the Canadian dime—is available for harbor cruises during July and August.

H.M.C. Dockyard (6)
Established in 1758, H.M.C. Dockyard—the oldest in North America—was a berth for the brigantines and sloops of the 19th-century "golden age of sail." Today modernized facilities supply destroyers and submarines.

Maritime Command Museum (4)
Located in Admiralty House, CFB Halifax, the museum features artifacts relating to Canadian marine military history.

Maritime Museum of the Atlantic (24)
This branch of the Nova Scotia Museum (8) highlights the region's marine history. It features a restored 19th-century ship chandler's shop, ships' figureheads, ship models and other naval artifacts.

Neptune Theatre (25)
Founded in 1963, the Neptune is one of the most prominent regional theaters in Canada.

Nova Scotia Museum (8)
This is the headquarters for a network of provincal museums throughout Nova Scotia. This museum's exhibits emphasize the province's social and natural history.

Old Dutch Church (7)
Built by German settlers in 1756, the Old Dutch Church—the first Lutheran church in Canada—is only 12 by 6 metres.

Our Lady of Sorrows Chapel (12)
Located in Holy Cross Cemetery, Our Lady of Sorrows is known as "the chapel that was built in a day." Some 1,800 men constructed the chapel in just one day—Aug. 31, 1843.

Old Town Clock (15)
At the foot of Citadel Hill is the Old Town Clock (1803), whose round shape reflects the architectural taste of Queen Victoria's father, Prince Edward, the Duke of Kent (1767-1820), who ordered its construction

while he was in Halifax (1794-1800).

Point Pleasant Park (13)
The 75-hectare park contains the Prince of Wales Martello Tower, built in 1796-97 under the supervision of the Duke of York. The tower—the first structure of its kind in North America—is a national historic site.

Province House (23)
Built between 1811 and 1819, Province House—one of the finest examples of Georgian architecture in Canada—is the oldest, and smallest, provincial legislature in Canada. (Nova Scotia's first responsible government met in the sandstone building on Feb. 2, 1848.) The statue of Nova Scotia journalist and politician Joseph Howe (1804-73) stands outside Province House.

Public Gardens (9)
Opened in 1867, the gardens preserve a formal Victorian landscape in modern Halifax.

St. George's Round Church (14)
This Byzantine-style Anglican church was built between 1800 and 1812. The design—unusual in North America—was supervised by the Duke of York, whose architectural legacy to Halifax also includes the Old Town Clock, the Prince of Wales Martello Tower and York Redoubt.

St. Mary's Basilica (26)
One of Canada's oldest stone churches (1829), St. Mary's Basilica is noted for its 58-metre-high polished granite spire, the tallest in North America.

St. Mary's University (11)
Founded as a church-related institution in 1802, Saint Mary's has about 7,000 students.

St. Matthew's United Church (27)
Opened in 1858, this church is home to Canada's oldest non-Anglican Protestant congregation, whose origins date back to 1749.

St. Paul's Church (20)
Built in 1749, St. Paul's Anglican Church is Halifax's oldest building. It was the cathedral of Nova Scotia's first Anglican bishop Charles Inglis (1734-1816).

Sir Sanford Fleming Park (1)
Popularly known as the Dingle, Fleming Park overlooks the Northwest Arm—the saltwater inlet that serves as Halifax's aquatic playground. The Dingle Tower, built in 1908-12, honors Canada's first legislative assembly, held in Halifax on Oct. 2, 1758.

University of King's College (2)
Established in 1789 at Windsor, N.S., King's College—the oldest university in the British Commonwealth outside Great Britain—was moved to Halifax in 1923.

World Trade and Convention Centre (17)
This complex incorporates the 10,000-seat Metro Centre, which offers concerts, sports and trade shows. The Nova Scotia Sport Heritage Centre—on the promenade level—displays local sports trophies and mementos.

York Redoubt (5)
Located about 13 kilometres south of Halifax, this fortification was set up in 1793 to protect the entrance of Halifax Harbour. Later expanded and reinforced, York Redoubt is now a national historic site, with a collection of muzzle-loading guns.

High Tides and Gemstones in the Land of Glooscap

Central Nova Scotia

This scenic drive follows the north shore of Minas Basin and Cobequid Bay, where tides are among the highest in the world. Glooscap—the legendary hero of the Micmac Indians—is said to have created the tides. According to Micmac lore, Glooscap held court at Cape Blomidon on the other side of Minas Basin. When he slept, his bed was Nova Scotia; his pillow, Prince Edward Island. His anger was thunder and lightning; his peace, the tranquillity of Indian summer. His friends were the Micmac Indians, whose

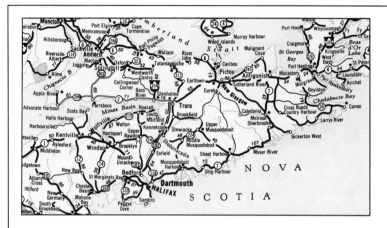

Miners' Monument, Springhill

SPRINGHILL

Coal mining began at Springhill in 1872; a 1,220-metre shaft here was once the deepest in Canada. On Main Street a monument topped by a statue of a coal miner commemorates three tragic mine disasters. An explosion in 1891 killed 125 miners; another in 1956 killed 39; a "bump" in 1958 claimed 76 lives. In the 1958 disaster 12 miners were saved after being entombed for six days; seven more were rescued two days later.
□ Springhill is the hometown of singer Anne Murray. Her achievements are honored in the community-built Anne Murray Centre.

A Roundup for Rockhounds

Amethysts from the Parrsboro region

For rock hounders, the beaches and cliffs near Parrsboro are treasure troves of semi-precious stones such as agates and amethysts. Specimens of such gemstones, as well as other local mineral finds, are displayed at Parrsboro's Geological Mineral and Gem Museum. (The museum also has fossils found in this region.)

Collectors and craftsmen gather at Parrsboro for a three-day Rockhound Roundup in mid-August. The event features an exhibition and sale of Nova Scotia gemstones, handcrafted jewelry and other items, and demonstrations of cutting, polishing and setting rough stones.

Visitors also take field trips to nearby East Bay, where fossils of prehistoric plants, fish, lizards and amphibians are found in cliffs along the shore. The 250-million-year-old footprints of a small dinosaur were discovered here in 1902.

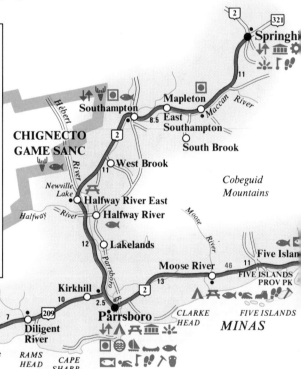

SPENCERS ISLAND

The brigantine *Mary Celeste*, which figures in one of the great mysteries of the sea, was built in this village in 1861. A cairn records that in 1872 she was discovered in the Atlantic—between the Azores and Gibraltar—"with all sails set and everything in order, but not a person was on board or ever found." The ship had been on a voyage from New York to Genoa.
□ At nearby Advocate Harbour is a rock formation known as the Three Sisters—the legendary sisters of Glooscap who were turned to stone by the man-god as a punishment.

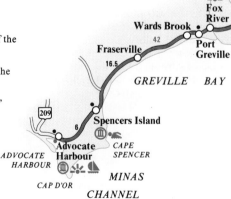

PARRSBORO

When the tide ebbs in Minas Basin, Parrsboro's harbor empties completely. The water level falls as much as 15 metres and recedes more than 1.6 kilometres, leaving fishing boats and lumber freighters in the harbor high and dry.
□ The Parrsboro area is a focal point for rock hounders. The local geological museum displays semiprecious stones found in the Minas Basin area. According to Micmac legend, Glooscap scattered the gems (his grandmother's jewels) along these shores.
□ Moose, deer, and black bears are among the wildlife found at Chignecto Game Sanctuary, north of Parrsboro.

0 2 4 6 8 10 Miles
0 4 8 12 16 Kilometres

lands these were before the arrival of European settlers.

West of Truro, the highway runs along the marshy shores of Cobequid Bay, where traces of old Acadian dikes may still be seen. From Bass River—where a factory operating since 1860 still makes chairs from birch and maple—the highway climbs to the village of Economy, which offers a view of another of Glooscap's creations—the Five Islands (Moose, Diamond, Long, Egg and Pinnacle).

Along the shore near Parrsboro, collectors hunt for semiprecious stones. Seabirds nest in marshy areas behind the beaches. Visitors to Parrsboro may tour a small shipyard where yachts are built, watch weir-fishing, dig for clams or gold along a rocky shore that offers one of Nova Scotia's finest ocean views. To the west lies the village of Spencers Island, where the famous mystery ship *Mary Celeste* was launched in 1861. Farther on is Advocate Harbour, where the French explorer Pierre de Monts found copper in June 1604.

From Parrsboro the road leads inland to Springhill, where coal-mining operations began in 1872. Since then, this courageous town has survived three mine disasters and two major fires. (Guides at the Miners' Museum here are retired miners who have a wealth of stories and a staunch pride in their work.) Here, too, in the highlands called the Cobequid Mountains, the lands of Glooscap remain much as they were— breathtaking in their beauty, and steeped in Indian legend and folklore.

A Town Famed for Courage in the Face of Disaster

The story of a coal-mining town's courage in the face of disaster is told at the Springhill Miners' Museum. Among mining equipment of many kinds—some picks and shovels date from 1885—are rubber air pipes, handsaws, and breathing apparatus dating from the early 1900s. There are a diary and letters of trapped men, and other relics of Springhill's three worst mine accidents. At the museum are a washhouse with miners' clothes, hats and boots, and a lamp cabin with a display of miners' lamps from the 1930s to the present. Retired miners conduct a museum tour that includes a 274-metre descent into a mine shaft.

FIVE ISLANDS PROVINCIAL PARK
Vast stretches of red sand are laid bare here at low tide. A four-kilometre hiking tail winds along the crest of 45-metre cliffs facing Minas Basin. According to Micmac legend, the five offshore islands are great clumps of earth thrown angrily by Glooscap at a mocking foe.

A view of Five Islands, Minas Basin

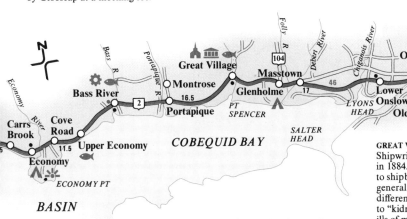

Bobolink

GREAT VILLAGE
Shipwrights built St. James United Church in 1884. It contains a small museum devoted to shipbuilding. The Robert F. Layton general store has a display of relics of a different sort: from hatpins and hardware to "kidney flushers, guaranteed to cure the ills of man."
□ Wentworth Valley, 22 kilometres north, is the oldest ski development in the Atlantic provinces, dating from the 1940s.

TRURO
This manufacturing, railway and shipping center is known as the "hub of Nova Scotia."
□ Truro's tidal bore—a wave of water sometimes 1.5 metres high—surges twice daily up the Salmon River, which passes through the northern outskirts of the city. (A local telephone service gives times for this event.) There are several viewing sites.
□ Among Truro's attractions are the 400-hectare Victoria Park, where wooden walkways lead to two picturesque falls at Lepper Brook; the Colchester Historical Society Museum, which presents local history exhibits; and the Little White School House Museum, which has been restored to the 1930s.

Building an old-fashioned yacht, Parrsboro

Giants and Gristmills, Blueberries and Tidal Bores

Central Nova Scotia

At Amherst, just below the New Brunswick border, highway travelers are greeted by Gaelic signs bidding them *Ciad Mile Failte*—"a hundred thousand welcomes." It is a warm and typical Nova Scotia greeting, and a sentimental farewell.

Leaving the Trans-Canada Highway at Amherst, this is a delightful route across north-central Nova Scotia at its best. It links Joggins (and its fossils), on Chignecto Bay, with the charming Balmoral Mills (and its historic gristmill). It cuts across the narrow

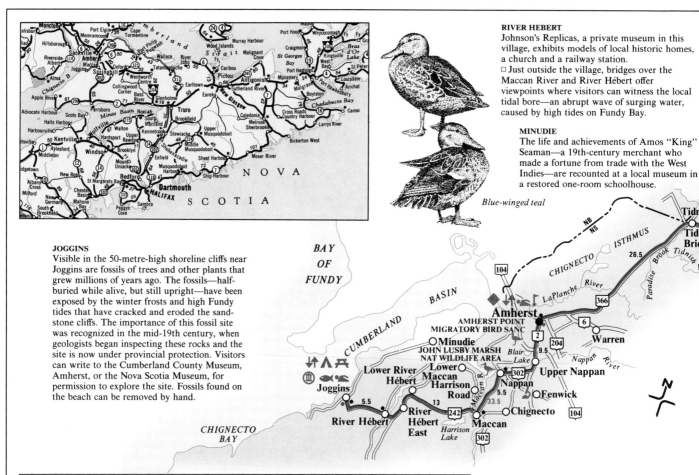

RIVER HEBERT

Johnson's Replicas, a private museum in this village, exhibits models of local historic homes, a church and a railway station.
□ Just outside the village, bridges over the Maccan River and River Hébert offer viewpoints where visitors can witness the local tidal bore—an abrupt wave of surging water, caused by high tides on Fundy Bay.

MINUDIE

The life and achievements of Amos "King" Seaman—a 19th-century merchant who made a fortune from trade with the West Indies—are recounted at a local museum in a restored one-room schoolhouse.

Blue-winged teal

JOGGINS

Visible in the 50-metre-high shoreline cliffs near Joggins are fossils of trees and other plants that grew millions of years ago. The fossils—half-buried while alive, but still upright—have been exposed by the winter frosts and high Fundy tides that have cracked and eroded the sandstone cliffs. The importance of this fossil site was recognized in the mid-19th century, when geologists began inspecting these rocks and the site is now under provincial protection. Visitors can write to the Cumberland County Museum, Amherst, or the Nova Scotia Museum, for permission to explore the site. Fossils found on the beach can be removed by hand.

Blueberry harvest in Cumberland County

Come September, It's Blueberry Time

For three days in early September, "blueberry" is the most often-heard word in Amherst. This is the heart of Cumberland County, which is also the center of Nova Scotia's blueberry country. At the annual Blueberry Harvest Festival, held in early August at Amherst, visitors eat blueberry pancakes, watch (or take part in) a blueberry pie-eating contest, and attend the selection of a Blueberry Queen. The festival program concludes with a blueberry harvest ball.

Blueberries—one of Canada's most valuable native fruits—are a multimillion-dollar export crop. The berries are harvested with hand rakes, air-cleaned (to remove green berries and leaves) and quick-frozen before shipment to food-processing companies, mostly in the United States.

AMHERST

This community (pop. 10,000) is the geographical center of the Maritime Provinces and the gateway to Nova Scotia for anyone entering from New Brunswick. It sits on high ground above the Tantramar marshes, sometimes called the "world's biggest hayfield." The marshland is actually more than 200 square kilometres of fertile farmland, which was first won from the sea by Acadian settlers, who stemmed the high Fundy tides with a system of dikes that remain today.
□ Amherst boasts four Fathers of Confederation: Edmund Barron Chandler (1800-80), Robert Barry Dickey (1811-1903), Jonathan McCully (1809-77) and Sir Charles Tupper (1821-1915). Grove Cottage, built in 1831 and long the Dickey family home, is now a museum with displays on local history and industrial development.

0   2   4   6   8   10 Miles

0   4   8   12   16 Kilometres

Chignecto Isthmus and skirts the Northumberland Strait shore. Along the route are the town of Tidnish and the old French community of Tatamagouche.

Attractions here are both interesting and unique: the Fundy tides in action, a century-old operating gristmill, the giantess of Nova Scotia, the "world's biggest hayfield" near Amherst, the ruins of an ambitious ship railway. At various places there are cairns and plaques recording the stormy history of the area in Acadian times. There are colorful local celebrations, such as the gathering of the clans at Pugwash and a blueberry festival at Amherst. This region also is rich in wildlife, some of which may be observed at the John Lusby Marsh and Amherst Point Migratory Bird Sanctuary.

Ship railway culvert at Tidnish

TIDNISH

In the 1890s work began here on the 27-kilometre Cumberland Ship Railway, which was designed to carry 5,000-tonne schooners overland between the Fundy Bay and Tidnish. The scheme's backers hoped to reduce shipping costs by eliminating the 1,040-kilometre voyage around the southern tip of Nova Scotia. Unfortunately, they underestimated railway construction costs. Some track was laid but, after five years, money ran out and the scheme collapsed. The remains can still be seen: the old roadbed, crumbling masonry, and an abandoned culvert in Tidnish.

PUGWASH

Bagpipes skirl and Highland dancers whirl at the annual July 1 Gathering of the Clans in Pugwash, a community whose street signs are in English and Gaelic.
□ Pugwash has one of Nova Scotia's best harbors—the big freighters and tankers are a major tourist attraction—and nearby golf, boating and fine sand beaches, all enriched by the tang of salt air. Charter boats are available for deep-sea fishing; several streams in the area have trout and salmon. In the fall, lakes and marshes are popular with waterfowl hunters.

WALLACE

Sandstone quarried at Wallace has been used in the construction of major Canadian public buildings, such as Province House in Halifax and the Parliament Buildings in Ottawa.
□ A local monument commemorates world-famous astronomer Simon Newcomb (1835-1909), who spent his boyhood here.

Drysdale Falls, near Balmoral Mills

BALMORAL MILLS

Many old millstones remain in Nova Scotia—as doorsteps and curios—but only a few old-time water-powered mills survive. One such survivor is the Balmoral Gristmill, built in 1874, and now restored to working order on Matheson's Creek. The original 1.5-tonne stones still grind wheat, oats, barley and buckwheat for visitors between mid-May and the end of October.
□ Nearby, on Bayleys Brook, is the seven-metre-high Drysdale Falls.

TATAMAGOUCHE

The startlingly large clothing of Anna Swan, 2.41-metre (7 feet 11 inches) "giantess of Nova Scotia," is displayed in the Fraser Culture Centre. Swan was born in nearby New Annan in 1846—an eight-kilogram baby—and for years was in P. T. Barnum's "Greatest Show on Earth." Later she took a giant husband, 2.35-metre Capt. Martin Van Buren Bates, an American and another of Barnum's oddities. The museum's collection also includes detailed records of an 1867 open vote (no secret ballot) won by Charles Tupper, later Canadian prime minister. Opposite each Cumberland riding voter's name is the name of the candidate who received the vote.

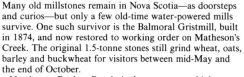

Balmoral Mills

A Pride in Old Ways, in a Land Like Home

Central Nova Scotia

The Scots who settled this part of Nova Scotia in the late 1700s and early 1800s found a land that reminded them of home. Thousands, drawn by the promise of free land, came to Nova Scotia in the wake of political unrest in Scotland. They sank deep roots in the rolling hills and, while visitors here will encounter many an Indian and French place-name, the shores of Northumberland Strait and St. George's Bay are truly a bit of old Scotland.

Loch Broom, New Glasgow, MacPher-

PICTOU

This community (pop. 4,400) proudly claims the title "the birthplace of New Scotland." A statue of a Scotsman, with ax in one hand and a rifle in the other, honors the settlers—farming families bent on a new life in a hostile land—who came here from Scotland on the bark *Hector* in 1773.
□ Two important landmarks are the McCulloch House and the Burning Bush Centre-Museum. The latter, built in 1848 for the local Presbyterian congregation, has displays and documents on local church history.
□ Grohmann Knives, an important local manufacturer, offers plant tours.

Pictou's monument to early Scottish settlers

LOCH BROOM

This tiny community is named for Loch Broom in the Scottish Highlands.
□ One of the first Presbyterian churches in Pictou County was built here in 1787. (The first service was in Gaelic.) The replica seen today was built as a community project in 1973. The church can be visited on weekdays in summer. There is a service on Sunday afternoon.

STELLARTON

Coal and steel and early railroading play important roles in the history of Stellarton and the neighboring towns of New Glasgow and Trenton.
□ Coal was discovered at Stellarton in 1798 and was mined continuously until recent years. The Foord Seam (no longer mined) was up to 14 metres thick, thought to be the world's thickest. Canada's first stationary engine went into operation here in 1827; the first iron rails in North America were cast here a year later.
□ In the Stellarton Miners Museum are helmets and equipment dating from the early days of coal mining, and the locomotive *Albion*, which went into service in 1854 for the General Mining Association. Another historic locomotive, the first to run on steel rails, is the *Samson*, on display at the Pictou County Historical Museum in New Glasgow.

MacPHERSONS MILLS

The wide boards and hand-hewn beams of this old gristmill, its cogwheels and belts, are all clues to busy days long ago when the mill ran day and night—when season and water were right. It was first a sawmill (1861); later its three sets of millstones ground oats, wheat and buckwheat. For years it also served as a post office, barbershop, general store and community center. Nearby is the restored MacPherson homestead, a fine representation of a 19th-century Pictou County farm dwelling.

Historic Pictou Homes

Settlement began at Pictou June 10, 1767, with the arrival of six families from Pennsylvania and Maryland. Six years later, in the bark *Hector,* came some 180 Scots—33 families and 25 unmarried men. This was the first of many waves of immigrants from Old Scotland to "New" Scotland—Nova Scotia. The town was named Coleraine, then New Paisley, Alexandria, Donegal, Southampton and Walmsley, until Pictou (the original Indian name) was chosen in 1790. Pictou's oldest building is a cottage built in 1788 by John Patterson, a *Hector* passenger. Other historic sites include Scottish-style stone dwellings, such as McCulloch House (*above*), which was built by the Reverend Thomas McCulloch (1776-1843), founder of Pictou Academy and first president of Dalhousie College (later University) in Halifax. The 1806 House, now a museum and archive, is open to the public.

MacPhersons Mills

sons Mills, Heatherton, Auld Cove ... all speak of Scottish origins. But there are Scots in Pictou as well, and Antigonish, Tracadie and Merigomish—all towns with Indian names—and at Pomquet and Havre Boucher and other old Acadian settlements. Gaelic is still heard—although less and less—as are the pipes in all their glory at Antigonish's famous Highland games. It is a land of seascapes and fine beaches; of old churches and simple, certain beliefs; of miners museums and modern manufac-

turing; of lobster suppers and a superb coastal drive past Cape George.

In rural districts, and in towns like Pictou, visitors will discover century-old houses, barns, gristmills, iron foundries, and stores that are being carefully restored to their original state. Many of these buildings are associated with major occupations of a hundred years ago—spinning and weaving, coal mining and iron forging, shipbuilding, and, of course, fishing and farming. Two 19th-century locomotives, the *Samson* (at

New Glasgow) and the *Albion* (at Stellarton Miners Museum), once hauled local ores to foundries and mills that produced everything from cast-iron kettles and ship's knees to stoves and fancy tombstones. This pleasant corner of Nova Scotia is pure delight for history buffs and vacationers—whether Scots-descended or not. It offers swimming and beachcombing, hiking and fishing, sight-seeing and a hundred other pursuits—with pride in its rich past and enjoyment of the present.

The Caber, the Kilt, and the Wail of the Pipes

They are called "Canada's Braemar," after the world-famous Highland Games of the Royal Braemar in Scotland. The Antigonish games, oldest in Canada, have been held each July since 1863, an explosion of caber tossing, hammer throwing (and today high jumping, broad jumping, shot putting) in which young and old still feel the pull of Highland origins. Scots (and "the others") revel in this pageant of Highland history and customs, all to the wondrous wail of Scottish bagpipes.

Highland dances, Antigonish

MALIGNANT COVE
This hamlet (pop. 64) takes its name from the British man-o'-war HMS *Malignant,* which was wrecked offshore during the American Revolution.
☐ The road between Malignant Cove and Antigonish Harbour passes through a tranquil countryside, often within sight and sound of the sea. Along the route are the small communities of Georgeville, Livingstone Cove, Ballantynes Cove, Lakevale, Morristown and Crystal Cliffs, many of which have good swimming beaches.
☐ From Cape George, visitors can glimpse Cape Breton and Prince Edward Island on clear days.

Cape George

NORTHUMBERLAND STRAIT

Map labels: Livingstone Cove • CAPE GEORGE • Ballantynes Cove • Cape George • Georgeville • Malignant Cove • ARISAIG PROV PK • Doctors Brook • DUNN PT • McArras Brook • Mount MacDonald • Lismore • Arisaig • Knoydart • Lakevale • Wallace Brook • ST. GEORGES BAY • Lower Barneys River • Bailey Brook • Bailey Brook • South Rights River • Rights River • Malignant Brook • CRIBBENS PT • Morristown • Crystal Cliffs • DUNNS BEACH • Antigonish • ANTIGONISH HAR • Lower South River • Southside Antigonish Harbour • Salt Springs • Pomquet • Bayfield • Bayfield Road • Tracadie • Heatherton • Monastery • Linwood • CAPE JACK • Havre Boucher • Frankville • Summers Lake • Auld Cove • Trans-Canada Highway • STRAIT • Troy • Port Hastings • OF • CANSO

...MORE
...a beach near here is a cairn in memory of Angus MacDonald, Hugh MacDonald and John MacPherson— ...ldiers of Prince Charlie," who were ...ong the Scots defeated by the ...glish at Culloden in 1746. They ...led here around 1790. St. Mary's ...urch, built by Roman Catholic ...ts, dates from 1834.

ANTIGONISH
This is the home of St. Francis Xavier University. During the 1920s, the university sponsored the Antigonish Movement—a program of self-help through adult education—that brought it considerable renown. The program continues today at the university's Coady International Institute, which trains students from around the world. The Angus L. Macdonald Library, located on campus, contains the Hall of Clans, whose walls are decorated with Scottish crests.
☐ Antigonish is also home of Canada's oldest Highland games, which have been held here continuously since 1861.

MONASTERY
St. Augustine's Monastery—the first Augustinian institution in Canada—was founded here in 1938. The site originally belonged to the Trappists, who came here in 1825 and built the monastery that gave the local community its name. None of the Trappist buildings remain today. The Augustinians' modern chapel is open to the public. Its paintings and stained glass depict Saint Augustine and other saints revered by the Augustinian order.

Where a Stately House Recalls the Age of Sail

Central Nova Scotia

In the 19th century, the forests of Nova Scotia supplied lumber for shipyards that launched thousands of barks, brigs and schooners—and the province's worldwide reputation for shipbuilding. One of Canada's largest wooden ships, a magnificent windjammer named the *William D. Lawrence*, was built virtually at the doorstep of her owner's house beside the Shubenacadie River at Maitland. The elm-shaded W.D. Lawrence House is now a museum and national historic site. This 2½-story

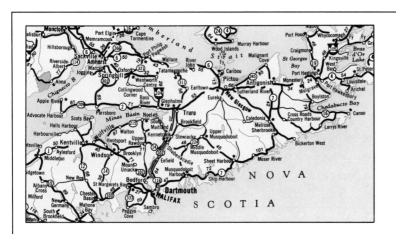

Low tide on Cobequid Bay, near Noel

DARTMOUTH
Among Dartmouth's many attractions are the city's oldest house (c. 1785), the Historic Quaker Whalers' House, which commemorates the Quakers who resided here briefly until 1792; Evergreen House, a restored 1867 Victorian house and former home of Nova Scotian author and folklorist Dr. Helen Creighton; and Dartmouth Heritage Museum, which recounts local history and has a marine section.
□ Dartmouth is also the site of Canada's largest center for marine research, the Bedford Institute of Oceanography. The institute is the third largest in North America and the fifth largest in the world.

Restored Quaker Whalers' House, Dartmouth

EASTERN PASSAGE
One of the greatest escapes of the American Civil War occurred in these waters. In 1864 local pilot "Jock" Flemming steered the Confederate gunboat *Tallahassee* through this treacherous channel to help it evade the northern warships lying in wait at the entrance to Halifax Harbour.
□ The air force museum at nearby CFB Shearwater describes the development of the base from 1918 to the present. An international air show is held at the base in September.

FALL RIVER
From Fall River, the Old Guysborough Road leads to Soldier Lake, which is the only entry point to Waverley Game Sanctuary. Fishing and camping are permitted in this wilderness area.

WELLINGTON
This community is an access point to the waters of Shubenacadie Grand Lake and Shubenacadie River, where landlocked salmon, striped bass and brook trout are prized catches.

WAVERLEY
The name of the town was bestowed by an admirer of Sir Walter Scott's *Waverley* novels. In 1861 a gold rush transformed what was then a hamlet of 20 houses into a town of 2,000 overnight. During the 1860s, mining equipment was brought to Waverley (and nearby Montague Gold Mines) on the Shubenacadie Canal. Built in 1826, the canal linked Darmouth and Fundy Bay, and operated intermittently until 1870. Locks survive at Lake Banook, Portobello, Fletcher's Lake and other local sites. An interpretive center and a canal walk are near Dartmouth Medical Centre.

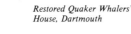

0 1 2 3 4   5Miles
0   2   4   6   8 Kilometres

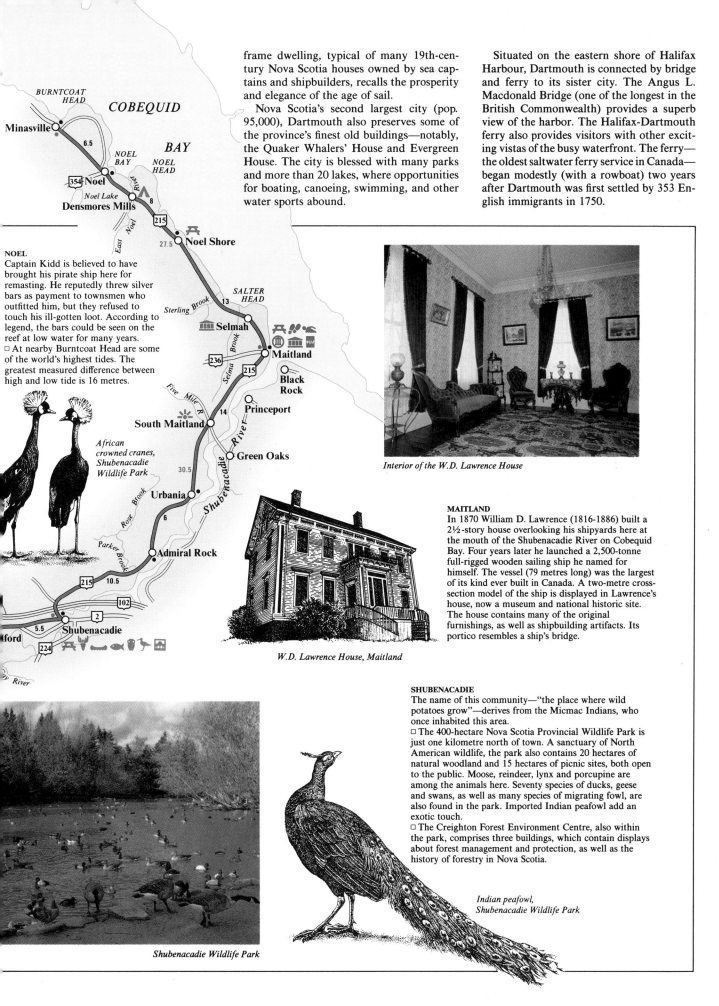

frame dwelling, typical of many 19th-century Nova Scotia houses owned by sea captains and shipbuilders, recalls the prosperity and elegance of the age of sail.

Nova Scotia's second largest city (pop. 95,000), Dartmouth also preserves some of the province's finest old buildings—notably, the Quaker Whalers' House and Evergreen House. The city is blessed with many parks and more than 20 lakes, where opportunities for boating, canoeing, swimming, and other water sports abound.

Situated on the eastern shore of Halifax Harbour, Dartmouth is connected by bridge and ferry to its sister city. The Angus L. Macdonald Bridge (one of the longest in the British Commonwealth) provides a superb view of the harbor. The Halifax-Dartmouth ferry also provides visitors with other exciting vistas of the busy waterfront. The ferry—the oldest saltwater ferry service in Canada—began modestly (with a rowboat) two years after Dartmouth was first settled by 353 English immigrants in 1750.

NOEL

Captain Kidd is believed to have brought his pirate ship here for remasting. He reputedly threw silver bars as payment to townsmen who outfitted him, but they refused to touch his ill-gotten loot. According to legend, the bars could be seen on the reef at low water for many years.
□ At nearby Burntcoat Head are some of the world's highest tides. The greatest measured difference between high and low tide is 16 metres.

African crowned cranes, Shubenacadie Wildlife Park

Interior of the W.D. Lawrence House

W.D. Lawrence House, Maitland

MAITLAND

In 1870 William D. Lawrence (1816-1886) built a 2½-story house overlooking his shipyards here at the mouth of the Shubenacadie River on Cobequid Bay. Four years later he launched a 2,500-tonne full-rigged wooden sailing ship he named for himself. The vessel (79 metres long) was the largest of its kind ever built in Canada. A two-metre cross-section model of the ship is displayed in Lawrence's house, now a museum and national historic site. The house contains many of the original furnishings, as well as shipbuilding artifacts. Its portico resembles a ship's bridge.

SHUBENACADIE

The name of this community—"the place where wild potatoes grow"—derives from the Micmac Indians, who once inhabited this area.
□ The 400-hectare Nova Scotia Provincial Wildlife Park is just one kilometre north of town. A sanctuary of North American wildlife, the park also contains 20 hectares of natural woodland and 15 hectares of picnic sites, both open to the public. Moose, reindeer, lynx and porcupine are among the animals here. Seventy species of ducks, geese and swans, as well as many species of migrating fowl, are also found in the park. Imported Indian peafowl add an exotic touch.
□ The Creighton Forest Environment Centre, also within the park, comprises three buildings, which contain displays about forest management and protection, as well as the history of forestry in Nova Scotia.

Indian peafowl, Shubenacadie Wildlife Park

Shubenacadie Wildlife Park

On a Shore of Strange Place-Names— a 'Wine Harbour' and a 'Sober Island'

Southeastern Nova Scotia

From Lawrencetown to Auld Cove is a drive that combines history, recreation and magnificent scenery. Much of this route winds along Nova Scotia's eastern shore—a region of sheltered coves, friendly fishing villages, and quiet woodlands embroidered by brooks and streams.

History is alive here—notably at Sherbrooke Village. This ongoing restoration recaptures the spirit of Nova Scotian community life from 1860 to 1880. Visitors can stroll the village streets and explore some

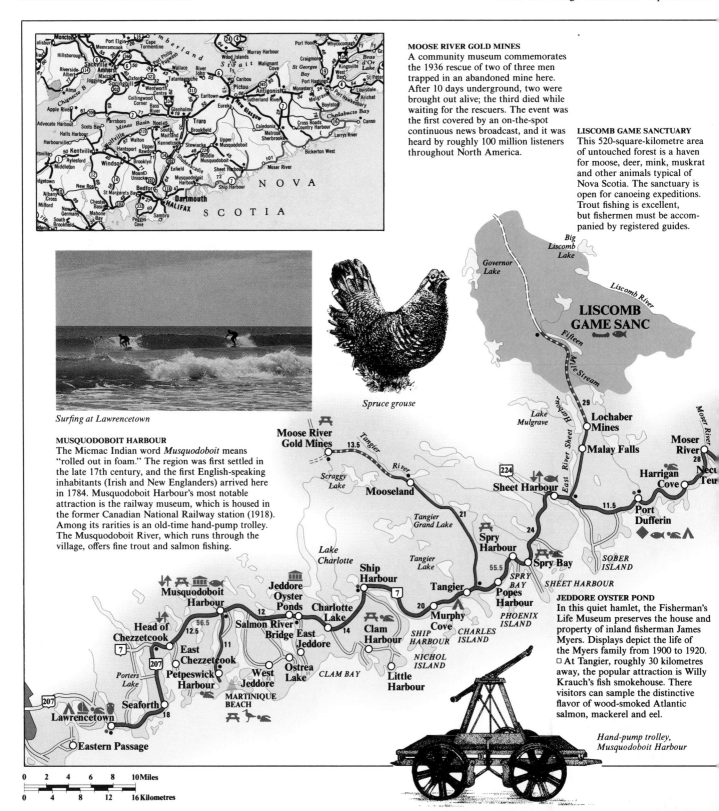

Surfing at Lawrencetown

Spruce grouse

MOOSE RIVER GOLD MINES
A community museum commemorates the 1936 rescue of two of three men trapped in an abandoned mine here. After 10 days underground, two were brought out alive; the third died while waiting for the rescuers. The event was the first covered by an on-the-spot continuous news broadcast, and it was heard by roughly 100 million listeners throughout North America.

LISCOMB GAME SANCTUARY
This 520-square-kilometre area of untouched forest is a haven for moose, deer, mink, muskrat and other animals typical of Nova Scotia. The sanctuary is open for canoeing expeditions. Trout fishing is excellent, but fishermen must be accompanied by registered guides.

MUSQUODOBOIT HARBOUR
The Micmac Indian word *Musquodoboit* means "rolled out in foam." The region was first settled in the late 17th century, and the first English-speaking inhabitants (Irish and New Englanders) arrived here in 1784. Musquodoboit Harbour's most notable attraction is the railway museum, which is housed in the former Canadian National Railway station (1918). Among its rarities is an old-time hand-pump trolley. The Musquodoboit River, which runs through the village, offers fine trout and salmon fishing.

JEDDORE OYSTER POND
In this quiet hamlet, the Fisherman's Life Museum preserves the house and property of inland fisherman James Myers. Displays depict the life of the Myers family from 1900 to 1920.
□ At Tangier, roughly 30 kilometres away, the popular attraction is Willy Krauch's fish smokehouse. There visitors can sample the distinctive flavor of wood-smoked Atlantic salmon, mackerel and eel.

Hand-pump trolley, Musquodoboit Harbour

30 Victorian buildings, where costumed staff bring to life the tasks and crafts of yesteryear.

Equally popular here are a wide range of sports activities—sailing, surfing, swimming and scuba diving. Fishermen seek local salmon and trout streams, or find excitement in snaring tuna and swordfish offshore. Inland hikers follow the trails that wind through hills above the rugged coastline.

Almost everywhere on this shore are place-names to stir the traveler's imagination. Some are from Micmac times: *Jeddore* (a place of sea ducks) and *Necum Teuch* (a beach of fine sand). Others tell a tale: Wine Harbour was named when a wine cargo spilled into the sea; Sober Island, when an early surveying party found there was no local liquor.

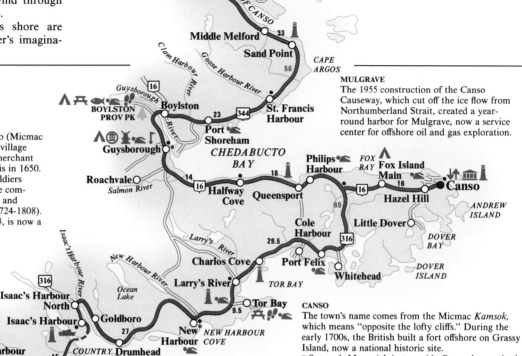

GUYSBOROUGH

Situated at the head of Chedabucto (Micmac for "great long harbor") Bay, this village began when French mariner and merchant Nicholas Denys built Fort St. Louis in 1650. Loyalists and disbanded British soldiers settled here in 1785 and named the community in honor of British general and administrator Sir Guy Carleton (1724-1808). The local courthouse, built in 1843, is now a museum devoted to local history.

MULGRAVE

The 1955 construction of the Canso Causeway, which cut off the ice flow from Northumberland Strait, created a year-round harbor for Mulgrave, now a service center for offshore oil and gas exploration.

CANSO

The town's name comes from the Micmac *Kamsok*, which means "opposite the lofty cliffs." During the early 1700s, the British built a fort offshore on Grassy Island, now a national historic site.

□ Seamen's Memorial, just outside Canso, honors both townspeople lost at sea and the town's enduring bond with the Atlantic.

□ In 1884 Western Union landed its first transatlantic cable at Canso. Some of the company's houses, built then, still overlook the sea.

SHERBROOKE

The town's oldest section—Sherbrooke Village—has been restored to re-create the prosperous port and gold-mining center of more than a century ago. Costumed guides escort visitors through the historic buildings, which include a blacksmith shop, a general store, a post office, a courthouse and jail, some residences, two churches and a school. There are demonstrations of old-time skills—carding, spinning and weaving woolen yarn, hooking rugs and quilt making. Visitors are welcome to lend a hand.

Sawmill, Sherbrooke Village

Blacksmith shop, Sherbrooke Village

The Swordfish— a Tasty Fighter

The highly prized swordfish is common in waters off eastern Nova Scotia. Its flat, rapierlike snout and upper jaw are up to one-third its body length. It feeds by thrashing its sword among a school of fish, then cruising back and forth to eat chunks of flesh. Averaging 320 kilograms, this pugnacious fish has been known to pierce ships' timbers and even whales (probably accidentally) with its sword. Sport fishermen eager to land this tasty fighter can charter boats along the southeastern coast of Nova Scotia.

A Spectacular Highland Trail and a Misty Island's Beauty

Cape Breton Island

Lone Shieling, near Pleasant Bay

Petit point embroiderers, Chéticamp

A Breathtaking Drive by the Sea

The 286-kilometre Cabot Trail is the high road to Cape Breton Island's shores and highlands. The road is named for the Italian explorer and navigator John Cabot (1450-1499), who may have seen the island's northern tip in 1497 while exploring North America for the English crown. The road skirts peaks, waterfalls, swift streams and rugged headlands. Seldom far from the sea, the Cabot Trail is breathtakingly beautiful at almost any season, but some visitors prefer it during autumn, when the highlands are bright with color.

From South Gut St. Anns, the Cabot Trail parallels Cape Breton's Atlantic coast, with its rocky coves wet with spindrift. At Sunrise Valley, along the North Aspy River, the trail turns west to the Gulf of St. Lawrence. Now vista after vista unfolds along the rugged shore. The road goes south through small Acadian communities (Chéticamp, Grand Etang, Belle Côte), winds through the pastoral Margaree Valley, and then returns to Baddeck and South Gut St. Anns.

Cabot Trail, near Chéticamp

CHÉTICAMP

This Acadian fishing village, just at the entrance to Cape Breton Highlands National Park, presents treasured objects from its past—antiques, glassware and looms—at a museum in Les Trois Pigeons, a cultural, genealogical and community information center. In a gallery at the center are hooked rugs and tapestries by world-famous native-born artist Dr. Elizabeth LeFort, as well as other local artists.
□ St. Peter's Church was built in 1883 with stone quarried on nearby Chéticamp Island and hauled on horse-drawn sleigh over the ice in winter.

MARGAREE HARBOUR

The restored schooner *Marion Elizabeth*, now a museum and restaurant, is docked in the harbor. The vessel was built in 1918 by the Lunenberg company which constructed *Bluenose*.
□ Boats can be chartered here to view the seabird colonies at Margaree Island National Wildlife Area.

MARGAREE FORKS

This village is at the junction of the Southwest and Northwest Margaree rivers—and the Cabot and the Ceilidh (pronounced *Kay-lee*) trails. (The latter route begins at Port Hastings and runs along Cape Breton's western shore.) The community hosts a festival in July.

NORTHEAST MARGAREE

The Margaree River is one of the best (and most beautiful) salmon-fishing streams in Canada. The profusion of salmon pools—the Forks, Thornbush, Hut and others—along the river is a mecca for fishermen. The Margaree Salmon Museum describes the river's features and history, and displays rods, spears, jig hooks and *flambeaux* (torches for night fishing).
□ The Museum of Cape Breton Heritage, also at Northeast Margaree, focuses on early spinning and weaving and has a collection of drafts (Scottish weaving patterns).

Red R

Pleasant Ba

WHITE CAPES

39.5

CAP ROUGE

CAVEAU PT

CHÉTICAMP I

Petit Etang

Chéticamp

Belle Marche

Point Cross

10.5

Grand Etang

13.5

48.5

Margaree Harbour

Belle Côte

GREY PT

East Margaree

12

Margaree Centre

Margar Valley

Rossville

Margaree Forks

Northeast Margaree

12.5

Alexander Graham Bell wrote, "I have traveled around the globe. I have seen the Canadian Rockies, the Andes and the Highlands of Scotland. But for simple beauty, Cape Breton outrivals them all."

Bell's accolade is supported by the spectacular Cabot Trail, the highway around the northern part of Cape Breton Island.

The route curves around sea-swept headlands, clings to the edge of cliffs that drop 300 metres to the sea, and threads dark river gorges amid ancient hills. More than one-third of the road's length is in Cape Breton Highlands National Park.

Cape Bretoners are fiercely proud of their island, yet share their ancestors' yearning for the Highlands of Scotland, the homeland of many of the earliest settlers.

A lament for the old country is expressed near Pleasant Bay at the Lone Shieling, a replica of a stone hut used by crofters when tending sheep. On a plaque are these words from the "Canadian Boat Song":

From the lone shieling of the misty island
Mountains divide us, and the waste of seas—
Yet still the blood is strong, the heart is High-
land,
And we in dreams behold the Hebrides!

Traditional ties are renewed at the Nova Scotia Gaelic Mod—an August festival of Scottish music and dance—at St. Anns. The local Gaelic College ensures that the language and lore of the clans survive among those with Scottish forebears.

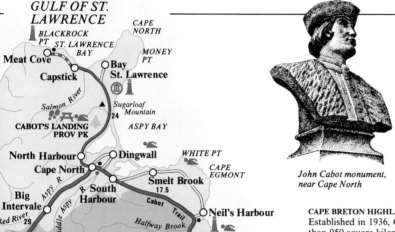

John Cabot monument,
near Cape North

CAPE NORTH
From the summit of Big Intervale, there is a splendid view of farms and forests in Sunrise Valley, through which the Aspy River flows to the sea. The village of Cape North—the most northerly point on the Cabot Trail—has a museum of local history.
□ Nearby Aspy Bay was briefly (1856-57) the western terminal of the first under-the-sea telegraph cable between Nova Scotia and Newfoundland. The first Atlantic cable was landed locally—at Money Point—in 1876.
□ At Cabot's Landing Provincial Picnic Park on Aspy Bay, a monument honors explorer John Cabot. Sugarloaf Mountain, eight kilometres away, is the site of Cabot's presumed landing on June 24, 1497. Each year on this date the event is reenacted on Cabot's Landing beach.

CAPE BRETON HIGHLANDS NATIONAL PARK
Established in 1936, Cape Breton Highlands National Park covers more than 950 square kilometres of scenic upland. Visitors can enter the park at Chéticamp and Ingonish Beach (the park's headquarters). The Cabot Trail, which skirts the park's shorelines and its northern boundary, offers superb vistas at every turn. Among the park's most spectacular sights are the 300-metre-high western headlands rising abruptly from the sea. Scenic spots within the park include Beulach Ban Falls—a lacy ribbon of water slipping over granite some three kilometres southwest of Big Intervale. Near Pleasant Bay there is the Lone Shieling, a replica of a crofter's cottage built in 1942 to commemorate Cape Breton's Scottish settlers.
□ Along the Cabot Trail are numerous beaches, campsites, lookouts and picnic grounds, where visitors can stop and linger. Just off the road, hiking trails lead to the park's interior, a place of wind-stunted spruce, bogs and mires, and patches of dry heath. Wildlife in the park includes beaver, black bear, bobcat, lynx, mink, moose and white-tailed deer. The deer are sometimes glimpsed on the highway. Among the more than 200 bird species are bald and golden eagles, ospreys, and boreal and snowy eagles.

ENGLISHTOWN
Earthworks here date from 1713, when the French fortified the settlement of Sainte-Anne and renamed it Port Dauphin. Sainte-Anne, founded in 1629, was Cape Breton Island's first French colony. A cairn marks the site.
□ In a cemetery here is the grave of the Cape Breton giant, Angus McAskill (2.4 metres tall and more than 180 kilograms). He died at St. Anns in 1863, aged 38.

SOUTH GUT ST. ANNS
In the early 1820s a group of Highland Scots whose ship had been blown off course landed here and decided to stay. South Gut St. Anns' continuing pride in its Scottish heritage is evident at the Nova Scotia Gaelic College of Arts and Culture (the only institute of its kind in North America). In summer it offers courses ranging from bagpipe playing to tartan weaving. The Great Hall of the Clans, at Gaelic College, recounts Scottish history and culture.
□ Visitors can take cruises to view the nearby Bird Islands, which are inhabited by different species of cormorants, guillemots and terns.
□ Visitors to South Gut St. Anns sometimes include New Zealanders trying to trace their roots. They are descendants of 130 local inhabitants who settled in New Zealand in 1850.

Beulach Ban Falls, Cape Breton Highlands National Park

Map labels

GULF OF ST. LAWRENCE
BLACKROCK PT
ST. LAWRENCE BAY
CAPE NORTH
MONEY PT
Meat Cove
Capstick
Bay St. Lawrence
Salmon River
Sugarloaf Mountain
24
ASPY BAY
CABOT'S LANDING PROV PK
North Harbour
Cape North
Dingwall
WHITE PT
CAPE EGMONT
Smelt Brook
17.5
Big Intervale
Red River
29
South Harbour
Aspy R
Middle Aspy
Cabot Trail
Neil's Harbour
Halfway Brook
Black Brook Cove
68.5
BEULACH BAN FALLS
North Aspy
Black Brook
41.5
16
CAPE BRETON HIGHLANDS NAT PK
Warren Brook
Warren Lake
Ingonish
8
KELTIC LODGE
Ingonish Beach
Ingonish Ferry
6.5
CAPE SMOKEY
CAPE BRETON ISLAND
CAPE SMOKEY
This majestic 365-metre-high headland is best seen from Middle Head (within Cape Breton Highlands National Park), on the other side of South Bay Ingonish. It is named for the white mist that often shrouds its top. The Cabot Trail climbs—with hairpin turns—to the cape's summit, which has picnic grounds and a lookout with a fine view of Cape Breton and the Atlantic.
Mc Leod Brook
Wreck Cove
18.5
42.5
French River
Skir Dhu
Briton Cove
8
North Shore
BIRD ISLANDS
Barachois R
9.5
Indian Brook
Tarbotvale
ST. ANNS BAY
Cabot Trail
9.5
312
North River Bridge
5
34.5
ST. ANNS HAR
Englishtown
St. Anns
10.5
9.5
105
North Gut St. Anns
South Gut St. Anns
105
Big Harbour

Canada's Scotland by the Sea Bids '100,000 Welcomes'

Cape Breton Island

Highland piper, Iona

WHYCOCOMAGH

This resort town is actually two communities—a village established by 19th-century Scottish settlers and a Micmac Indian Reserve—which are separated by the Skye River. (The name of the town is Micmac for "head of the waters.") At the reserve, local craftsmen sell their work—baskets, wood carvings and other objects.
□ At nearby Whycocomagh Provincial Park, lookouts at the summit of 300-metre-high Salt Mountain provide superb views of the surrounding region. There are nature trails through a dense forest of beech, horse chesnut, maple, pine and spruce.
□ The Whycocomagh Summer Festival in July features Scottish music and dance, and sports events.

IONA

The Nova Scotia Highland Village Museum overlooks Bras d'Or Lake from a 17-hectare hillside site here. Dedicated to the preservation of local Scottish culture, the museum has nine restored buildings, including a carding mill, crofter's cottage, forge, schoolhouse and country store. A summer highlight is Highland Village Day, held in early August, which celebrates traditional Scottish music.

CANSO CAUSEWAY

Opened in 1955, the 1,370-metre-long Canso Causeway links the Nova Scotia mainland with Cape Breton Island. Reputedly the world's deepest, the causeway rises 65 metres from the depths of the Strait of Canso. The base is 244 metres wide and the 24-metre-wide surface has a highway, a rail line and a walkway. Some 10 million tonnes of rock used to build the causeway block the annual ice drift from the Northumberland Strait and St. Georges Bay, creating a year-round, 16-kilometre-long harbor. This is a major benefit to all the Strait of Canso communities south of the causeway.
□ A lock near Port Hastings allows oceangoing vessels to pass through the causeway. A major oil refinery at Point Tupper has a 600-metre-long, deep-water terminal dock that can accommodate supertankers.
□ At Creignish, north of the Canso Causeway, 260-metre-high Creignish Mountain offers a fine view of St. Georges Bay and the Strait of Canso.

Oil refinery at Point Tupper, near Port Hastings

ARICHAT

Settled by Acadians in the mid-1700s, Isle Madame is ringed by rocky coves and picturesque villages, such as Arichat, which is the oldest community in the region.
□ When Thomas LeNoir came from the Magdalen Islands in the early 1800s, Arichat was a prosperous shipbuilding town. The forge that he and his family built at nearby Petit-de-Grat served the builders and trained new craftsmen; eventually the LeNoirs established Nova Scotia's first blacksmith school. When shipbuilding declined, so did the forge, but it was restored in 1967 as a museum with exhibits of ship chandlery and anchor making.
□ Arichat's twin-towered, wooden L'Assomption Church, built in 1838, was a cathedral until 1886, when the diocesan seat was moved to Antigonish. The original bishop's palace is now a hospital.

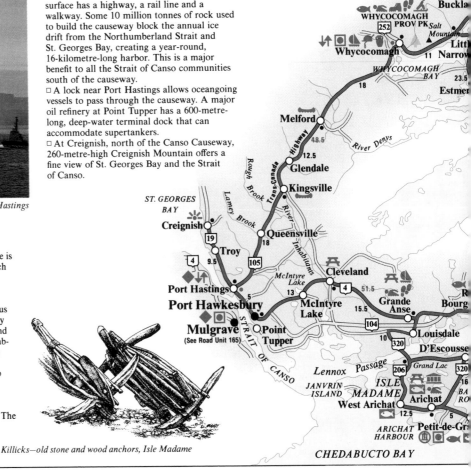

Killicks—old stone and wood anchors, Isle Madame

When the Strait of Canso was bridged by a 1,370-metre causeway in 1955, one Nova Scotian wrote to a newspaper, claiming that the link would unify Canadians from Atlantic to Pacific. "For now," he declared, "we're all Cape Bretoners."

After crossing the causeway, the Trans-Canada Highway sweeps around sparkling Bras d'Or Lake, a 1,098-square-kilometre inland sea that almost splits Cape Breton Island. Encircled by superb highland scenery, the virtually tideless lake resembles a Scottish loch. To the south, a strip of land about a kilometre wide (now traversed by St. Peters Canal) separates Bras d'Or Lake from the sea. To the north, the Atlantic comes and goes on both sides of Boularderie Island. Low mountains rise behind the channels, bays and harbors, and the salty lake has excellent fishing, sheltered anchorages and scores of fine beaches.

This is Scottish Nova Scotia, fiercely proud of its heritage—the Gaelic language (which is still taught and spoken here); the local Highland games, which feature sword dances and caber tossing; and, above all, the ancestral virtues of industry and thrift. This is the region where Scottish-born inventor Alexander Graham Bell chose to spend his summers at *Beinn Breagh* near Baddeck Bay.

Nestling by the shore of Bras d'Or Lake, towns named Iona and Ben Eoin speak of Scottish origins. Gaelic signs bid visitors "100,000 welcomes," and kilted pipers skirl "Will Ye No Come Back Again?"

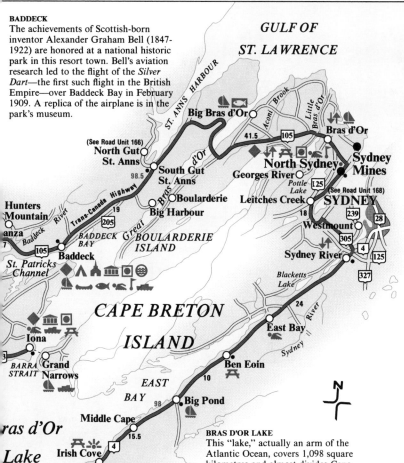

BADDECK
The achievements of Scottish-born inventor Alexander Graham Bell (1847-1922) are honored at a national historic park in this resort town. Bell's aviation research led to the flight of the *Silver Dart*—the first such flight in the British Empire—over Baddeck Bay in February 1909. A replica of the airplane is in the park's museum.

The Genius of *Beinn Breagh*

The 10-hectare Alexander Graham Bell National Historic Park contains a museum (*above*) that mirrors many facets of the Scottish-born inventor's genius. Bell's interests extended beyond the telephone to aviation, marine engineering and medical science. The museum displays Bell's early telephone equipment, as well as his other inventions, such as the *Silver Dart* airplane, the HD-4 hydrofoil boat, and the "vacuum jacket" (an early version of the iron lung).

Bell first visited Baddeck in 1885. Seven years later he built a summer home, *Beinn Breagh* (Gaelic for beautiful mountain), on a headland overlooking Baddeck Bay. There he did much of his research. He died at *Beinn Breagh* in 1922 and was buried on the summit of his beautiful mountain, amid scenery that had reminded him of Scotland. (Bell's descendants still reside at *Beinn Breagh*, which is closed to the public.)

BRAS D'OR LAKE
This "lake," actually an arm of the Atlantic Ocean, covers 1,098 square kilometres and almost divides Cape Breton in two. At the north end, two narrow channels—Great Bras d'Or and St. Andrews, on either side of Boularderie Island—are natural links to the Atlantic. At the south end, the St. Peters ship canal provides another—man-made—link. The lake, which is ringed by high hills, offers fine fishing and water sports.

ST. PETERS
The kilometre-wide strip of land separating Bras d'Or Lake from the Atlantic, where St. Peters now stands, was the site of a fort established in 1650 by French explorer Nicholas Denys. Across this land Denys constructed a road of skids over which boats were hauled by oxen. Built about 1669, the road survived until the 1850s, and the spot became known as "Haulover Isthmus." A local museum honors the explorer's achievement.
□ St. Peters Canal, built between 1854 and 1869, offered a route through Cape Breton Island that was safer and shorter than the one around it. Improvements to the canal continued until 1917. Some 1,600 ships used it annually during its heyday (1880-1940). Today the waterway—the Maritimes' only heritage canal—is used by pleasure craft.

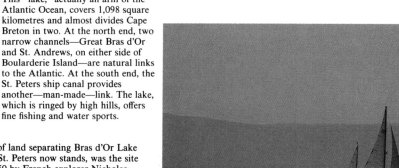

Sailing on Bras d'Or Lake, near Baddeck

'Impregnable' Louisbourg…
and Towns Built by Coal

Cape Breton Island

The Fortress of Louisbourg, a great gray ghost on the rocky Cape Breton coast, was built to guard the Gulf of St. Lawrence and France's dwindling empire in the New World. Begun in 1720, it was ringed with three-metre-thick stone walls nine metres high, armed with 148 cannon, and built at such cost that Louis XV said he expected to see the towers of Louisbourg rising over the Paris horizon.

Yet, as a stronghold it was a failure. In 1745 a ragtag army of 4,000 Yankee volun-

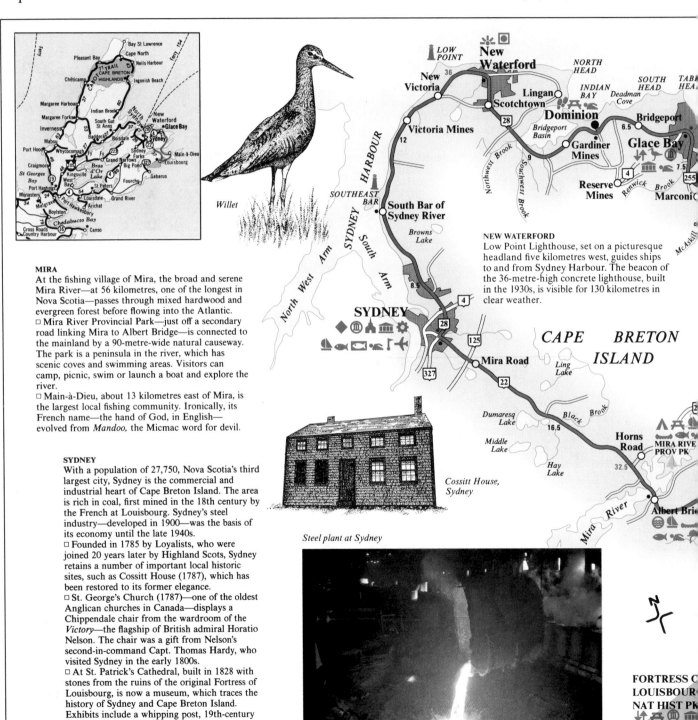

Willet

Cossitt House, Sydney

Steel plant at Sydney

MIRA

At the fishing village of Mira, the broad and serene Mira River—at 56 kilometres, one of the longest in Nova Scotia—passes through mixed hardwood and evergreen forest before flowing into the Atlantic.
□ Mira River Provincial Park—just off a secondary road linking Mira to Albert Bridge—is connected to the mainland by a 90-metre-wide natural causeway. The park is a peninsula in the river, which has scenic coves and swimming areas. Visitors can camp, picnic, swim or launch a boat and explore the river.
□ Main-à-Dieu, about 13 kilometres east of Mira, is the largest local fishing community. Ironically, its French name—the hand of God, in English—evolved from *Mandoo,* the Micmac word for devil.

SYDNEY

With a population of 27,750, Nova Scotia's third largest city, Sydney is the commercial and industrial heart of Cape Breton Island. The area is rich in coal, first mined in the 18th century by the French at Louisbourg. Sydney's steel industry—developed in 1900—was the basis of its economy until the late 1940s.
□ Founded in 1785 by Loyalists, who were joined 20 years later by Highland Scots, Sydney retains a number of important local historic sites, such as Cossitt House (1787), which has been restored to its former elegance.
□ St. George's Church (1787)—one of the oldest Anglican churches in Canada—displays a Chippendale chair from the wardroom of the *Victory*—the flagship of British admiral Horatio Nelson. The chair was a gift from Nelson's second-in-command Capt. Thomas Hardy, who visited Sydney in the early 1800s.
□ At St. Patrick's Cathedral, built in 1828 with stones from the ruins of the original Fortress of Louisbourg, is now a museum, which traces the history of Sydney and Cape Breton Island. Exhibits include a whipping post, 19th-century Gaelic bibles, and clothing from the Confederation era.

NEW WATERFORD

Low Point Lighthouse, set on a picturesque headland five kilometres west, guides ships to and from Sydney Harbour. The beacon of the 36-metre-high concrete lighthouse, built in the 1930s, is visible for 130 kilometres in clear weather.

CAPE BRETON ISLAND

0 1 2 3 4 5Miles
0 2 4 6 8Kilometres

teers, backed by three British ships, captured Louisbourg in seven weeks—only to see it returned to the French in 1748. Ten years later, the British took it again, and two years after that, in 1760, they blasted the fortress to rubble.

Some of Louisbourg's massive fortifications have risen again at the original site in an ongoing re-creation of the garrison area and the enclosed town. An impressive reflection of 18th-century New France, the Louisbourg site contains restored stone bastions and wooden houses and barracks. The tools, materials and methods of the past are used wherever possible to mirror the tiniest historical detail. Uniformed officers stroll along the cobblestone, fishermen salt and dry their catch, soldiers patrol the bastions, and costumed staff hold auctions, launder clothes, bake bread, mold bullets, and operate taverns and blacksmith shops.

Though short-lived, Louisbourg was a toehold for settlement in eastern Canada. Rich seams of bituminous coal—first mined in 1720 to supply the garrison at Louisbourg—were discovered under much of northeastern Cape Breton. Full-scale mining operations began in the 1850s, and the names of such towns as Sydney, Glace Bay, Dominion, Donkin and New Waterford became synonymous with coal.

Today these highland and harbor towns supplement traditional trades with manufacturing and tourism. But their heritage—a rich blend of French and English traditions—is reverently preserved.

GLACE BAY
This industrial city of 20,000—known to the French as *Baie de Glace* (Ice Bay)—is proud of its coal-mining past. At Quarry Point, the Miners' Museum has coal-mining equipment, a model of a Sydney and Louisbourg Railway coal train, and even a coal mine, the Ocean Deeps Colliery. Retired miners conduct tours through three levels of the colliery where visitors, using mining machinery, can dig coal samples as souvenirs. Also on the site is the Miner's Village, containing a late 1800s coal miner's house.

LOUISBOURG
This fishing village—at the head of Louisbourg Bay—is flanked on both sides by the Fortress of Louisbourg National Historic Park. Besides the fortress, the village has many other attractions, including the Atlantic Statiquarium; the restored Sydney and Louisbourg Railway station; and the Louisbourg Craft Workshops.
□ The 1923 lighthouse on the eastern arm of Louisbourg Harbour can be reached by car from the village. It is near the site of Canada's first lighthouse, built by the French in 1730-33.

A Fortune From the Deep

For 236 years the cold Atlantic near the Fortress of Louisbourg hid a fortune in gold and silver coins. The treasure—pay for the French army in Quebec—had been strewn over the rocky ocean floor in 1725 when the 48-gun naval transport *Le Chameau*, seeking refuge from a sudden gale, was wrecked on a reef.

In 1961, skin diver Alex Storm found a silver coin with the bust of Louis XV and the date 1724. Convinced that he had stumbled upon *Le Chameau*, Storm mapped a system of grids to search, in water 22 to 30 metres deep, more than 250,000 square metres of sea bottom. Finally, on Sept. 22, 1965, the bulk of the treasure was discovered. Within days some $300,000 in silver and gold coins was recovered—the largest treasure find in Canadian history.

Alex Storm (above right) with treasure from Le Chameau

FORTRESS OF LOUISBOURG NATIONAL HISTORIC PARK
A re-creation of an 18th-century fortified French town is the centerpiece of this 6,700-hectare park. Begun in 1961, the work remains the largest ongoing historical reconstruction in Canada. Visitors are welcomed at a reception center, 1.5 kilometres from the village of Louisbourg, and taken by bus to the fortress site. This covers more than 50 hectares and re-creates Louisbourg as it appeared in 1744. Roughly a quarter of the original town has been reconstructed.
□ Among some 50 buildings are barracks, dwellings, storehouses and taverns. The impressive three-story King's Bastion includes the governor's luxurious 10-room suite, the officers' quarters, chapel, prison and artillery school. Massive stone and earth fortifications enclose the site.
□ Drawings and plans of the original fortress—as well as historic accounts of the sieges of 1745 and 1758—are on display. Costumed staff reenact the daily life of 18th-century Louisbourg and uniformed guides interpret the site for visitors. The Hôtel de la Marine, L'Épée Royale and two other restaurants serve 18th-century meals.

King's Bastion Barracks, Louisbourg

Costumed staff re-create the past at Louisbourg

Coastal Barrens, a Bay of Islands and a World-Famous Salmon Stream

Southwestern Newfoundland

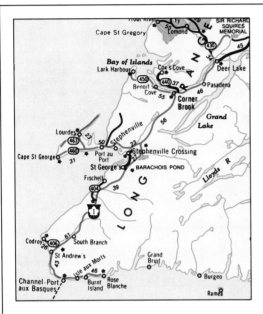

PORT AU PORT PENINSULA
Here live descendants of French fishermen who used the peninsula as their base of operations as early as 1713.
□ Evidence of forces that shaped this region some 500 million years ago is seen in layered, folded and faulted rock in cliffs along the peninsula's south shore. Mostly dolomite and limestone, the formations contain fossils of marine animals. Wind and waves batter Cape St. George, the peninsula's westernmost point.
□ At Piccadilly Head Provincial Park visitors dig for clams from the sand flats at low tide. A walking trail leaves the beach and penetrates a forest of balsam fir. Some limestone cliffs in the park drop more than 12 metres to the sea. Blue- and green-winged teal may be seen here in the fall.

Cape St. George, Port au Port Peninsula

CODROY VALLEY
Migrating Canada geese—as many as 500 at a time—stop on the banks of the Grand Codroy River, near Grand Codroy Provincial Park.
□ In Mummichog Provincial Park, 12 kilometres south, a lagoon supports the tiny mummichog, a fish found in few other places in Newfoundland. The lagoon is a mixture of fresh water from the Little Codroy River and salt water from the Atlantic. Great blue herons and American woodcocks are seen in the park.

Rose Blanche

CHANNEL-PORT AUX BASQUES
A monument commemorates 133 persons who died in 1942 when a German submarine torpedoed the ferry *Caribou*. A scenic, 40-kilometre drive leads east to the picturesque fishing village of Rose Blanche.
□ A sandbar shelters a saltwater inlet from the Atlantic's thundering surf, northwest of Channel-Port aux Basques at John T. Cheeseman Provincial Park. Surrounding the park are the desolate barrens of Cape Ray. Strong winds funnel down from Table Mountain and across a dry gulch at nearby Red Rocks; the winds have frequently upset railway cars.
□ Car ferries connect Channel-Port aux Basques with North Sydney, N.S.

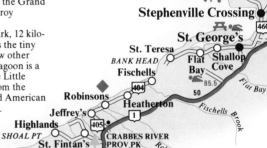

Newfoundland pine marten

BARACHOIS POND PROVINCIAL PARK
A 3.2-kilometre self-guiding nature trail climbs through a forest of birch, spruce and fir to the barren summit of Erin Mountain. Moose, caribou and, occasionally, the rare Newfoundland pine marten, are sometimes spotted. The 305-metre peak provides a panoramic view of the surrounding area.

| 0 | 3 | 6 | 9 | 12 | 15 Miles |

| 0 | 6 | 12 | 18 | 24 Kilometres |

Southwestern Newfoundland is a region of stark coastal barrens, broad headlands pounded by surf, placid wilderness lakes and densely forested mountains. East of the ferry terminus at Channel-Port aux Basques is Newfoundland's sparsely settled south coast, a vast area served only by boat. Ships from the port travel 400 kilometres east to Terrenceville, stopping at remote fishing villages.

The Trans-Canada Highway goes north from Channel-Port aux Basques, past the desolate barrens of Cape Ray, to Red Rocks and McDougall Gulch. Farther on is the Codroy River valley, a bird-watcher's paradise in spring and fall; and the Crabbes River, where salmon anglers can try their luck in June and early July. A trek to the summit of Erin Mountain in Barachois Pond Provincial Park will reward hikers and photographers with a spectacular view of sea and shore—and perhaps a glimpse of a moose or a caribou. To the west, farms and fishing hamlets line the coast of the Port au Port Peninsula—where residents speak French with a Newfoundland accent.

Still farther north, nestled in the lush valley of the Humber River, is the pulp mill city of Corner Brook. Some of Newfoundland's finest scenery is west of the city, where towering cliffs rise sharply out of the water on both sides of Humber Arm and in the Bay of Islands.

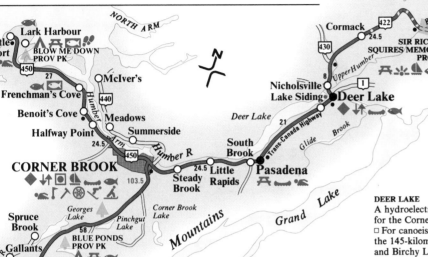

SIR RICHARD SQUIRES MEMORIAL PROVINCIAL PARK
During summer visitors can watch spawning salmon try repeatedly to jump over Big Falls on the Humber River. Fishing near the falls is among the best in Newfoundland. North of the park the Upper Humber flows between narrow canyon walls up to 90 metres high. Farther upstream are wilderness lakes, turbulent rapids and shoreline forests of spruce and white birch. A canoe route from the park leads downstream to Corner Brook.

DEER LAKE
A hydroelectric station at the town of Deer Lake supplies power for the Corner Brook paper mill.
□ For canoeists, there is magnificent scenery south of here along the 145-kilometre waterway formed by Grand Lake, Sandy Lake and Birchy Lake. A short portage extends the waterway into Sheffield Lake, set amid heavily forested mountains.
□ From Deer Lake roads lead northwest to Bonne Bay and Gros Morne National Park, then north 420 kilometres to the tip of Newfoundland's Great Northern Peninsula.

BAY OF ISLANDS
Blow Me Down Provincial Park provides a stunning view of this bay. Wooden stairs, set in a steep rock overhang, lead to a lookout tower. Woods Island lies at the head of the bay. Guernsey, Tweed and Pearl islands are strung across the horizon at the bay's outer reaches. The densely forested park is reputed to have buried treasure.

CORNER BROOK
Worldwide demand for newsprint has made Corner Brook the second largest city in Newfoundland: its population is now approaching 23,000. On one of several hills overlooking the city, a cairn honors Capt. James Cook, who sailed up the Humber River as far as Deer Lake in 1767 and made the first detailed map of Newfoundland's west coast. From the cairn one has a fine view of the Corner Brook paper mill, one of the world's largest with a capacity of more than 500,000 tonnes a year.
□ Among the city's striking buildings is the 10-story Government Building. The Centennial Arts and Culture Center contains a theater, a swimming pool, an art gallery and exhibition areas.
□ Humber Valley salmon streams and big-game hunting are easily accessible from Corner Brook. Parks include Margaret Bowater Park (in the city) and the Bowater Park at South Brook, 24 kilometres northeast. Blue Ponds Provincial Park, 13 kilometres southwest, contains two lakes whose limestone bottoms account for their deep turquoise color.

Atlantic Salmon— Surviving All Obstacles

Revered by sportsmen and esteemed by gourmets, the Atlantic salmon (*below*) is world renowned as a game fish and a commercial species.

The Atlantic salmon is the classic migratory fish. After spawning in the freshwater streams of Newfoundland in October and November, the adults head for the sea. (Unlike Pacific salmon, Atlantic salmon usually survive after spawning and may return to spawn more than once.) The young remain in fresh water for two or three years, then descend to the sea to spend one or more years feeding and growing before coming back to the streams of their birth to spawn.

The ability of the salmon to surmount falls and other obstacles on their return is a fascinating sight. At Sir Richard Squires Memorial Provincial Park, spawning salmon can be seen leaping out of the water as they attempt to scale Big Falls.

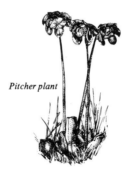

Pitcher plant

Corner Brook

The Misty Heights of Gros Morne... and (Perhaps) the Norse Vinland

Northwestern Newfoundland

Along the craggy coast of Bonne Bay in Gros Morne National Park, the peaks of some of the most spectacular mountains in eastern North America drop sharply to long narrow fjords. Close to the bay, tiny fishing hamlets dot the sloping landscape.

Highway 430 presents travelers with many spectacular views of this west coast of Newfoundland's Great Northern Peninsula. The brooding, flat-topped Long Range Mountains rise dramatically from a low coastal

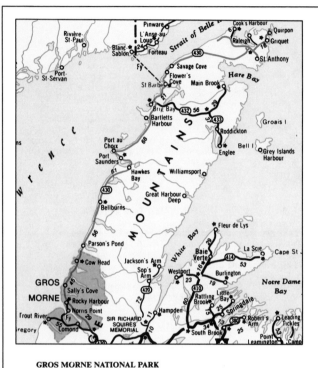

RIVER OF PONDS PROVINCIAL PARK
On the shore of a freshwater lake fringed by sand beaches and a forest of softwood, River of Ponds Provincial Park provides facilities for camping, swimming, hiking, canoeing and fishing (for Atlantic salmon and brook trout).
□ The skeletal features of a whale are described in a park display which includes whale bones an estimated 7,000 years old. The bones, found at nearby sites, offer proof that this part of Newfoundland's west coast was once submerged.

The Arches, north of Gros Morne National Park

ST. BARBE
A car ferry connects this fishing hamlet with Blanc-Sablon, Que., on the Labrador border 35 kilometres across the Strait of Belle Isle. (The ferry service operates from May to December.)
□ Pinware River Provincial Park on Labrador's southeastern coast offers salmon, trout and cod fishing. On nearby Amour Point is a burial mound 24 metres in circumference. It was built by Early Maritime Archaic Indians about 5500 B.C.

GROS MORNE NATIONAL PARK
Set in the most spectacular portion of the Long Range Mountains, this 1,943-square-kilometre park is named for Newfoundland's second highest peak, Gros Morne (806 metres), which dominates the Bonne Bay area. In recognition of its unique features—the geologically interesting landforms and the tundralike vegetation that grows on the high plateaus—the park was declared a United Nations World Heritage Site in 1988.
□ South of Bonne Bay is the Serpentine Tableland, a barren upland plain littered with ocher-brown volcanic boulders.
□ North of the bay, between the sea and the mountains, lies a low coastal plain crisscrossed by small rivers and covered with bogs and grassland. Along the shore are sand dunes up to 12 metres high. Rock cliffs tower above Western Brook Pond, one of several fjordlike lakes cradled in river gorges that were deepened by glaciers during the last ice age.
□ The arctic hare, usually found in the far north, and the Newfoundland caribou (one of the largest of its kind in the world) inhabit the park. Other native mammals include the black bear and lynx. Common and arctic terns, herring gulls and great black-backed gulls are found along the coast; willow and rock ptarmigan, on heathlands and barrens.

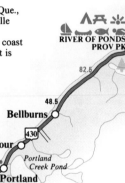

Arctic hare

Arctic rhododendron

Red Paint People, *a mural at Port au Choix National Historic Park*

plain. Along Gros Morne's rugged 65-kilometre coastline are fine beaches and broad expanses of shifting dunes. Inland are dense forests, narrow mountain lakes, a tidal inlet, and streams noted for salmon.

Past Gros Morne's northern boundary, travelers may return to the dawn of recorded Canadian history. In L'Anse aux Meadows, at the northern tip of Newfoundland, is the only known site of Viking settlement west of Greenland. Norsemen came to these rocky shores about A.D. 1000 and

established what may have been the first European colony in North America.

Another important archaeological site is at Port au Choix. An interpretive center displays skeletons and relics of "red paint people" who lived here 5,000 years ago.

A memorable side trip begins at Black Duck Cove, where summer travelers can take a car ferry across the Strait of Belle Isle and explore the southern coast of Labrador.

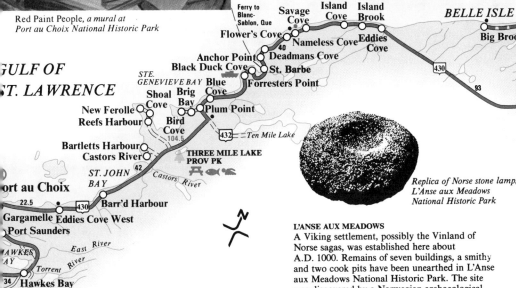

Replica of Norse stone lamp, L'Anse aux Meadows National Historic Park

PORT AU CHOIX
Skeletons and relics of "red paint people" who roamed between Maine and Labrador some 5,000 years ago are displayed in an interpretive center at Port au Choix National Historic Park. Burial sites uncovered here in the late 1960s tell most of what is known about the red paint people. Graves were lined with red ocher and contained bundles of artifacts for use by the dead in the afterlife. Weapons of slate, bone and ivory show that the red paint people lived by hunting and fishing. Awls, gouges, axes and cutting tools show there was a well-developed wood-carving industry, and fine bone needles demonstrate the existence of sewn garments. Also on display are relics of Dorset Inuit who lived on nearby Pointe Riche about A.D. 100.
□ Picnic grounds at Pointe Riche lighthouse provide fine sunset views of the Gulf of St. Lawrence.

Western Brook gorge, Gros Morne National Park

L'ANSE AUX MEADOWS
A Viking settlement, possibly the Vinland of Norse sagas, was established here about A.D. 1000. Remains of seven buildings, a smithy and two cook pits have been unearthed in L'Anse aux Meadows National Historic Park. The site was discovered by a Norwegian archaeological team in 1960 and was declared a United Nations World Heritage Site in 1978. Research has left a pattern of shallow, sod-covered diggings approximating the layout of the original Norse buildings. Displays in the park's interpretive center include the floorboard of a Norse boat, iron rivets excavated at the site, and soapstone flywheel used for spinning wool. The flywheel, the earliest European household article unearthed in North America, is identical to those found at Viking sites in Greenland, Iceland, Norway and Sweden.

ST. ANTHONY
This community is a beacon of hope for the people of northern Newfoundland and Labrador. It is headquarters of the Grenfell Mission, which provides medical aid along a bleak 2,400 kilometres of coast. Sir Wilfrid Grenfell founded the mission in 1893. He died in 1940, aged 75, and is buried here. Grenfell's work goes on here and in a network of clinics and nursing stations linked by ships and aircraft. Ceramic murals by Jordi Bonet adorn the foyer of Curtis Memorial Hospital, named for Dr. Charles S. Curtis, another devoted missionary. Handcrafted items sold at St. Anthony include embroidered parkas and soapstone carvings.

When Seafaring Norsemen Found the New World

About A.D. 800, Norwegians began voyages of exploration in the North Atlantic, and eventually settled in Iceland. In A.D. 982 an Icelander named Erik the Red murdered a man and was banished for three years. He spent his exile exploring the shores of Greenland, where he established two colonies. Men from these settlements sailed farther west. One ship was driven off course in 986 and sighted strange new wooded lands—apparently Newfoundland and Labrador.

Leif Eriksson, son of Erik the Red, heard of the discovery. Attracted by the possibility of timber close to Greenland, he sailed (about A.D. 995) and landed at a fertile spot he called Vinland. He remained there for a year. Archaeologists have proved there was a Norse settlement at L'Anse aux Meadows. But was it Eriksson's Vinland or the settlement of Norsemen who came after him? That question will probably tantalize scholars for years to come.

A'Road to the Isles' and a World-Famous Airport

Central Newfoundland

About midway along the Newfoundland portion of the Trans-Canada Highway lies Grand Falls. The town was established in 1909 when Lord Northcliffe, the British newspaper magnate, acquired forests in the

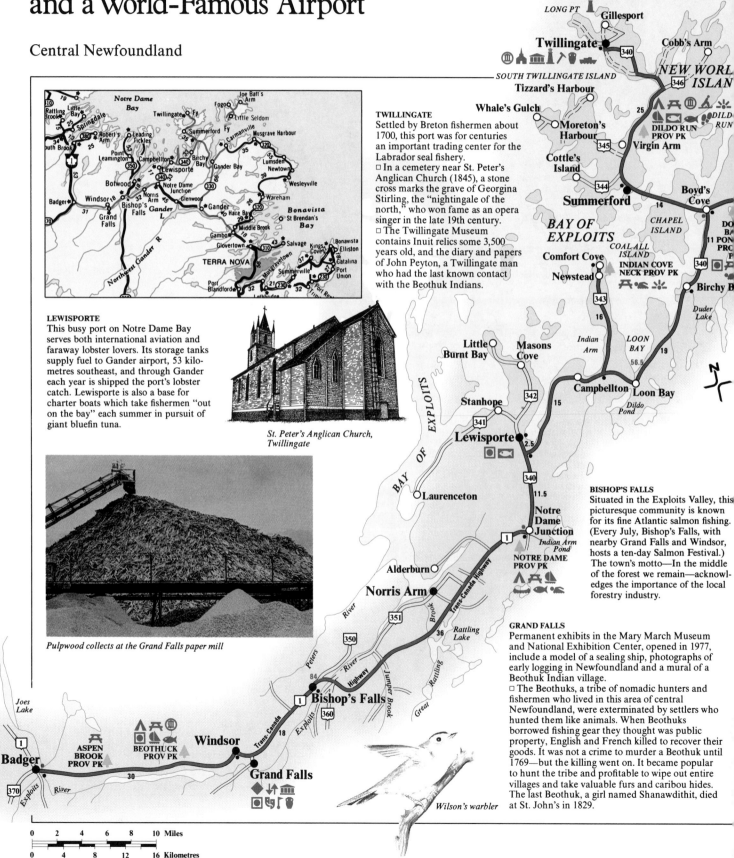

TWILLINGATE
Settled by Breton fishermen about 1700, this port was for centuries an important trading center for the Labrador seal fishery.
□ In a cemetery near St. Peter's Anglican Church (1845), a stone cross marks the grave of Georgina Stirling, the "nightingale of the north," who won fame as an opera singer in the late 19th century.
□ The Twillingate Museum contains Inuit relics some 3,500 years old, and the diary and papers of John Peyton, a Twillingate man who had the last known contact with the Beothuk Indians.

St. Peter's Anglican Church, Twillingate

LEWISPORTE
This busy port on Notre Dame Bay serves both international aviation and faraway lobster lovers. Its storage tanks supply fuel to Gander airport, 53 kilometres southeast, and through Gander each year is shipped the port's lobster catch. Lewisporte is also a base for charter boats which take fishermen "out on the bay" each summer in pursuit of giant bluefin tuna.

Pulpwood collects at the Grand Falls paper mill

BISHOP'S FALLS
Situated in the Exploits Valley, this picturesque community is known for its fine Atlantic salmon fishing. (Every July, Bishop's Falls, with nearby Grand Falls and Windsor, hosts a ten-day Salmon Festival.) The town's motto—In the middle of the forest we remain—acknowledges the importance of the local forestry industry.

GRAND FALLS
Permanent exhibits in the Mary March Museum and National Exhibition Center, opened in 1977, include a model of a sealing ship, photographs of early logging in Newfoundland and a mural of a Beothuk Indian village.
□ The Beothuks, a tribe of nomadic hunters and fishermen who lived in this area of central Newfoundland, were exterminated by settlers who hunted them like animals. When Beothuks borrowed fishing gear they thought was public property, English and French killed to recover their goods. It was not a crime to murder a Beothuk until 1769—but the killing went on. It became popular to hunt the tribe and profitable to wipe out entire villages and take valuable furs and caribou hides. The last Beothuk, a girl named Shanawdithit, died at St. John's in 1829.

Wilson's warbler

Map labels (Fogo Island):
16, 334, Tilting, Barr'd Islands, Joe Batt's Arm, Fogo, Shoal Bay, 8, 333, FOGO ISLAND, Hare Bay, Deep Bay, 10, 5, Wild Cove, 4, CHANGE ISLAND, Little Seldom, Island Harbour, Seldom, 8, Stag Harbour

Tizzard's Harbour, New World Island

Map labels (mainland):
HAMILTON SOUND, ROCKY BAY, Frederickton, Noggin Cove, Beaver Cove, Carmanville, 332, 330, Rodger's Cove, 331, 27, Victoria Cove, Main Point, Mann Point, GANDER BAY, 24, Wings Point, 330, Clarke's Head, Gander Bay, Weir's Pond, 69, Gander River, 26, JONATHAN'S POND PROV PK, 330, 16, Jonathan's Pond, Gander, 1, Gander, Lake, Trans-Canada Highway, 17, Benton, 40, Soulis Pond, Butts Pond, DAVID SMALLWOOD PROV PK, 320, FRESHWATER BAY, 1, 23, Middle Brook, Square Pond, SQUARE POND PROV PK, Dark Cove, Gambo, First Burnt Pond

area and started a pulp and paper plant. Today Grand Falls is one of the major producers of newsprint for papers around the world.

From Grand Falls, highways 1 and 340 lead northeast to the bustling commercial center of Lewisporte, also a popular tuna-fishing base. Farther on, at Boyd's Cove, the "Road to the Isles" begins—a series of bridges and causeways crossing Dildo Run, linking the mainland with Chapel, New World and South Twillingate islands. In June and July, north of the historic town of Twillingate, giant icebergs off Long Point Lighthouse appear menacing when they loom through fog, enchanting when they sparkle in bright sunshine.

Farther south lies Gander Bay, the starting point for hunting and fishing expeditions up the Gander River. East of Gander and its famed international airport is the village of Gambo, set in prime hunting and fishing country, a popular base for campers and canoeists.

FOGO ISLAND
A car ferry crosses Hamilton Sound, linking Fogo Island with the mainland village of Farewell. (Farewell can be reached by taking Highway 335 north from Highway 331.) Fishing is an important industry on Fogo Island, where a shipbuilders' and fish producers' cooperative contributes greatly to the island economy.

Arctic char

GANDER
In the heart of one of North America's finest hunting and fishing areas, a town of some 10,000 has grown up near Gander International Airport. The British Air Ministry chose Gander as a transatlantic base in the mid-1930s and the airport opened in 1938.
□ In the modern terminal are *Flight and Its Allegories,* a striking 22-metre mural by Kenneth Lochhead. An aviation museum exhibits a four-bladed wooden propeller from the twin-engine Vickers Vimy biplane that was used by British aviators Capt. J. W. Alcock and Lt. A. W. Brown on the first nonstop transatlantic flight, from St. John's, Nfld., to Clifden, Ireland, in June 1919.
□ Outside the terminal is the Atlantic Ferry Pilot Memorial, a huge cairn surmounted by a Lockheed Hudson bomber in wartime camouflage. It is identical to one that on Nov. 10-11, 1940, made the first transatlantic crossing from Gander. That flight was the first of thousands by pilots of the Atlantic Ferry.

GANDER BAY
In long, narrow Gander Bay boats, guides lead hunters and fishermen upstream on the Gander River in search of moose, salmon and arctic char. Descended from Old Town canoes imported from Maine, the boats are made of spruce, larch and fir and equipped with light outboard motors.

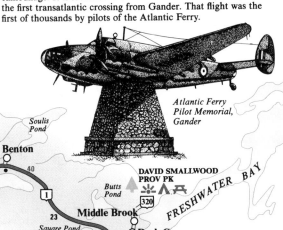

Atlantic Ferry Pilot Memorial, Gander

A Stately Parade of Towering Icebergs

The highlight of a visit to Twillingate is often the sight of icebergs drifting south with the Labrador Current until midsummer. Huge masses of curiously eroded ice, as high as 45 metres, are frequently seen off nearby Long Point. A few are islands of ice almost two kilometres long. Others are smaller—about the size of a cathedral or a castle and shaped somewhat the same, with soaring towers, turrets, buttresses and battlements. The bergs' colors range from deep blue to pale green.

Icebergs off the Newfoundland coast

GAMBO
Nearby Square Pond is the habitat of the largest landlocked arctic char in Newfoundland. Canoe routes from Gambo lead to Indian Bay, 64 kilometres northeast, and to Gander Bay, 137 kilometres northwest. Lakes and rivers along these routes are fringed by forests of white birch and balsam fir.

Timeless Terra Nova Park and Rockbound Outports

Central Newfoundland

Terra Nova National Park, overlooking the rugged shores of Bonavista Bay, is a good base for sight-seeing in central Newfoundland. Peace seems to reign here in sheltered bays, numerous lakes and streams and in dense forests.

A trip from Glovertown, near the park's northern boundary, leads to Salvage, at the tip of the Eastport Peninsula. Here, in one of Canada's oldest outports, travelers visit a snug museum containing early artifacts of the Newfoundland fishing industry. Like

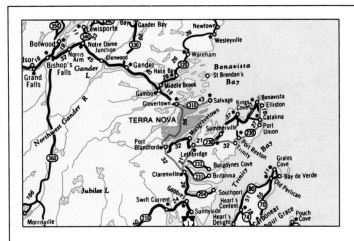

GLOVERTOWN
This town is the main service center for visitors to nearby Terra Nova National Park. Small craft can sail safely here. Glovertown is sheltered by a score of islands which extend almost 30 kilometres into Alexander Bay—one of the many great glacier-carved indentations in the shoreline of Bonavista Bay.

Lobster

Terra Nova National Park

TERRA NOVA NATIONAL PARK
Icebergs in the cold Labrador Current drift off Terra Nova's coast in early summer. Atlantic breakers crash against towering headlands, boil along sheltered sounds and roll up long, deserted beaches. Pilot, minke and humpback whales may be seen inshore; bay and harp seals, offshore. Dolphins and killer whales cruise in Bonavista Bay, which is also the habitat of squid up to 15 metres long. Shellfish abound in the park's bays and inlets. Quiet beaches give way to gently rolling hills and dense forests dotted with ponds, streams, bogs, myriad wildflowers and lichens. Among the park's 350 plant species are several rare bog orchids, including dragon's-tongue and spotted coralroot. Nature trails lead into marshes and forests inhabited by moose, black bears and red foxes.

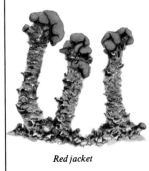

Red jacket

CLARENVILLE
Like other towns on the western shore of Trinity Bay, Clarenville began as a woodcutters' camp in the mid-1800s, supplying lumber to fishing settlements on the barren eastern shore.
□ A plaque in nearby Milton commemorates William Epps Cormack, who in 1822 completed a 58-day trek across the unmapped Newfoundland interior to study flora, fauna and geology. Cormack later founded a Beothuk institute and shared his home with Shanawdithit, the last known member of her tribe, before her death in 1829.

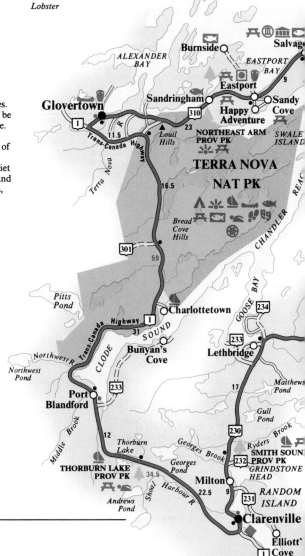

neighboring villages, Salvage provides coastal scenes of dramatic beauty. Locally smoked salmon and capelin are to be had, and in the nearby village of Happy Adventure fresh lobsters can be purchased until late July. Also close by is one of Newfoundland's finest beaches, at Sandy Cove. The farming community of Eastport is another popular stopover.

Clarenville is the starting point for an excursion to Cape Bonavista, possibly the site of John Cabot's landfall in 1497. Along the way is Trinity, where Newfoundland's first Court of Admiralty convened in 1615. Like many early Newfoundland settlements, Trinity was harassed by pirates and seized by the French in the early 1700s. The remains of fortifications and guns dating from 1706 can still be seen. In the graveyard of St. Paul's Church (1734), the oldest tombstone is dated 1744. Farther north lies the busy commercial fishing port of Bonavista, settled in the 1600s. A few kilometres north of the town is a lighthouse whose beacon has guided fishermen around Cape Bonavista for more than a century.

Salvage

SALVAGE

This village at the tip of the Eastport Peninsula is the oldest settlement in this region. It was isolated for almost 300 years: until a road was built after the Second World War, its only contact with the outside world was by boat.
□ In a restored century-old frame dwelling, the Salvage Fisherman's Museum displays local artifacts. The floor of a kitchen in the museum is covered with canvas sails—in accordance with an old Newfoundland custom.

BONAVISTA

One of Newfoundland's oldest settlements, Bonavista has a population of 4,600 and has been called the largest all-fishing town in the province. Its important cod industry has a drying plant and cold-storage facilities. Deep-sea fishermen take tuna and swordfish in Bonavista Bay.
□ A stone statue of John Cabot is at Cape Bonavista, which may have been the explorer's landfall in 1497. The lighthouse here began operating in 1842; it is open to the public in summer.
□ At Spillers Cove, near Cape Bonavista, water erosion has formed a double grotto called The Dungeon.

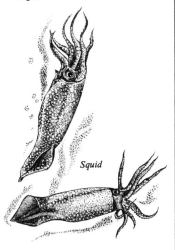

Squid

PORT UNION

Sir William Coaker founded this town as headquarters of his Fishermen's Protective Union in 1914. A bust of the labor leader, who died in 1938, is at the head of his tomb, on a platform with marble railing. Sir William's union organized a political party, and trading, light-and-power, publishing, shipping, shipbuilding and cold-storage companies. But Coaker never realized his dream of political and economic control of Newfoundland.

Codfish: Big Business Since the 16th Century

Cod fishing takes place in a narrow belt along the eastern shore of Newfoundland and, to a lesser extent, on the Grand Banks, the rich fishing grounds southeast of the island. The harvest peaks in July and August, when cod swarm to bays and inlets to feed on capelin. (Squid, used as cod bait, appear in Newfoundland waters between mid-July and late October.)

The cod fishery has been a big business since the 16th century when fleets from France, England, Portugal and Spain flocked to Newfoundland's waters. French ships worked the Grand Banks in spring; leather-clad fishermen stood in barrels behind wind barriers, and caught one fish at a time. French catches were dressed on deck and stored in the hold between thick layers of salt. English fishermen, lacking much salt, dried cod on shore, using open-air flakes—wooden racks like those still found in Newfoundland outports.

St. Paul's Church, Trinity

TRINITY

Newfoundland's first Court of Admiralty was held at Trinity in June 1615. A plaque honors John Clinch, a medical missionary who administered the first smallpox vaccination in North America here in 1800. Another plaque is near the ruins of a three-story Georgian-style brick house built in 1821 by John Bingley Garland, the first speaker in Newfoundland's House of Assembly.
□ Ship models dating from the 1830s, used for reference and measurement in the building of trawlers and sealers, are displayed at the Trinity Museum along with British bluebacks (19th-century Admiralty charts).

Where Dories and Long-Liners Brave a Wave-Battered Shore

Avalon Peninsula

A narrow arm of lichen-crusted rock and stunted spruce and fir links the Avalon Peninsula with the rest of Newfoundland. Dense fogs are frequent here, and the weather is often "mausey" (a Newfoundland word describing misty rain); but when the sun shines there are fine views of both Placentia and Trinity bays.

Scorning the life of the "angishore" (someone too lazy to fish), fishermen of Avalon's west coast brave rough seas in dories, skiffs and five-man long-liners, hand-jigging

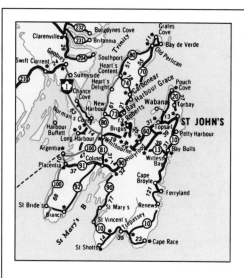

Cod Tongues, Jiggs Dinner and Figgy Duff

Many ingredients in Newfoundland cooking—hardtack biscuits, dried peas, salt beef and fish—were staple foods of the English and Irish seamen who fished here four centuries ago.

When Newfoundlanders speak of fish, they mean only one kind: cod. Boiled and baked, in soups and pies, cod appears in hundreds of island recipes. "Fish and brewis" consists of boiled salt cod and hardtack softened in water, garnished with "scrunchions" of crisped salt pork. Cod tongues are a delicacy: sliced and fried, they taste like scallops. Though the ocean's yield is abundant, other food must be imported, either canned, salted, dried or smoked. "Jiggs dinner" is a stew of salt beef, salt pork, potatoes, carrots, turnips and cabbage. Side dishes include peas pudding (mashed split peas) and figgy duff (raisin and molasses pudding).

COME BY CHANCE
In recent years a huge oil refinery has brought supertankers to this quiet village at the head of Placentia Bay. On clear days, a lookout in the neighboring fishing settlement of Sunnyside provides a view of Trinity Bay to the east and Placentia Bay to the west—two of Newfoundland's most productive inshore fishing grounds.
□ South of Come By Chance, at Jacks Pond Provincial Park, a stream meanders between grassy banks, then tumbles over a small falls into Jacks Pond. Activities in the park include canoeing and fishing for brook trout.

Atlantic pilot whale

PLACENTIA
In Castle Hill National Historic Park are the ruins of fortifications from which the French directed forays against the first British settlements in Newfoundland. The French built Fort Royal here in 1692 and attacked the British in St. John's and elsewhere until the 1713 Treaty of Utrecht ceded the fortress to England. In the inner fort are the remains of guardrooms, barracks, a powder magazine and the foundations of a British blockhouse. An interpretation center documents the history of Placentia.
□ A car ferry connects nearby Argentia with North Sydney, N.S., during the summer.
□ A plaque at Argentia commemorates the Atlantic Charter, signed by Churchill and Roosevelt aboard a British warship anchored offshore in August 1941.

Gannet colony, Cape St. Mary's Sea Bird Sanctuary

CAPE ST. MARY'S
A sanctuary here shelters a vast seabird colony. Thousands of gannets crowd cliffs on Bird Rock, a 150-metre-high sea stack. The streamlined, snow-white birds have wingspans up to two metres. Common and thick-billed murres and black-legged kittiwakes also nest here in densely populated colonies.

for cod or hauling gill and trap nets from many fathoms down. Heavy trawlers with crews of 10 to 15 scour the stormy Grand Banks. The coast is almost a continuous chain of fishing villages—many settled by people of Irish descent. These Newfoundlanders have the lilting accents of Galway and County Clare. They are great talkers and the yarns they spin are laced with the supernatural.

Placentia, the old French capital of Newfoundland, is in a superb setting flanked by two fjords that reach inland for 10 kilometres. Behind it, atop steep hills, brood the ruins of old forts that once made Placentia a formidable stronghold.

Off the tip of Cape St. Mary's looms Bird Rock, a vast half-dome awash with nesting gannets, murres and kittiwakes. The birds cling to every ledge and cranny, bowing and cackling, stealing pieces of each others' nests, performing elaborate courtship rituals and—as is the way of life here—ceaselessly commuting between land and sea.

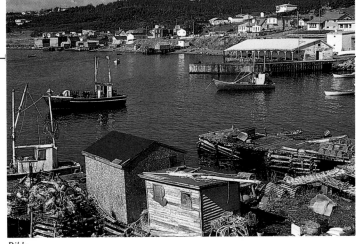
Dildo

Black-legged kittiwakes

BELLEVUE BEACH PROVINCIAL PARK
Blue mussels can be picked in a saltwater pond here, protected from pounding waves by a *barachois,* a natural sand and gravel breakwater. Other shellfish found along the shore include barnacles, periwinkles and tortoise shell limpets. Black-legged kittiwakes and black guillemots are among the seabirds spotted here.

Tortoise-shell limpet

HEART'S CONTENT
North America's first cable relay station is now a provincial historic site. The cable ship *Great Eastern* landed the first successful transatlantic telegraph cable here in July 1866, linking Newfoundland with Ireland. A series of stations across Nova Scotia relayed messages from here throughout North America. The cable station, which saw 92 years' service, contains early equipment used for receiving and relaying telegraph messages. The oldest section of the building is furnished as it was when built in 1873. Staff in period costume guide visitors through the site. There are displays explaining the key role that Heart's Content stayed in transatlantic communications.

Over a Great Cable, at Last: 'All Right'

The ship was the largest in the world; in her hold lay coiled the longest cable ever made, 4,447 kilometres of insulated copper. The 1866 excursion of the *Great Eastern* was the fifth attempt to lay a telegraph cable from Ireland to Newfoundland. The transatlantic cable had cost American businessman Cyrus Field 13 years of effort. Three earlier cables had broken en route; a fourth operated briefly, then failed. The fifth attempt proved successful. For two weeks the *Great Eastern* had steamed across the Atlantic, lowering cable more than three kilometres to the ocean floor. After the ship arrived at Heart's Content (depicted here by Rex Woods), a message sent to Ireland on July 26, 1866, read simply, "All right."

CHAPEL ARM
The whaling industry once flourished here and in the neighboring villages of New Harbour and Dildo. Dorymen would "herd" large schools of Atlantic pilot whales into shallow water where they were slaughtered for their valuable oil and meat, which found a ready market in Europe. (The meat was also used as food for mink farms.) The Canadian government imposed a moratorium on pilot whaling in 1973.

Memories of an 'Iron Isle' and a Thousand Tall Ships

Avalon Peninsula

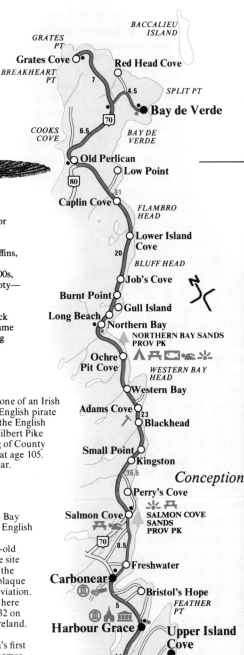

Cod-fishing boats at Port de Grave, near Hibbs Cove

Storm petrel

BAY DE VERDE
This large fishing community has an artificial harbor created by blasting down a hill of solid rock and dumping it into the Atlantic to form a breakwater.
□ Offshore is Baccalieu Island, a nesting site for puffins, storm petrels, gannets, gulls, black guillemots, kittiwakes, murres and razorbacks. In the early 1900s, two kegs of Spanish gold—believed to be pirate booty—were dredged up from a small cove here by local fishermen.
□ John Cabot may have inscribed his name on a rock at nearby Grates Cove in 1497. At one time, the name IO CABOTO and other words were legible; nothing now remains of the inscription.

CARBONEAR
In a private garden here is the gravestone of an Irish princess who wed (and reformed) an English pirate after being kidnapped from a ship in the English Channel. "Sheila Na Geira, wife of Gilbert Pike and daughter of John Na Geira, King of County Down," reads the stone, died in 1753 at age 105. She lived much of her life in Carbonear.

HARBOUR GRACE
This historic town overlooking Conception Bay was settled about 1550 and fortified by the English pirate Peter Easton around 1610.
□ The Conception Bay Museum, a century-old brick and stone former customhouse on the site of Easton's fort, has an exhibit chronicling the history of transatlantic flight. Outside is a plaque commemorating Harbour Grace's role in aviation. Wiley Post began a round-the-world flight here in 1931, and Amelia Earhart took off in 1932 on a solo flight to Londonderry in Northern Ireland.
□ Other plaques honor the Rev. Laurence Coughlan, who established North America's first Wesleyan mission here in 1765; and Sir Thomas Roddick, a Harbour Grace native who was deputy surgeon-general in the expeditionary force that suppressed the Northwest Rebellion in 1885, president of the British Medical Association, a Canadian MP, and dean of medicine at McGill University in Montreal.

HIBBS COVE
Artists and photographers are attracted to the west shore of Conception Bay by picturesque fishing villages and by some of the most striking coastal scenery in Newfoundland.
□ Large, square wooden houses crowd the tiny, rock-ringed harbor of Hibbs Cove, the embodiment of the Newfoundland outport. The Fishermen's Museum here displays handmade furniture, tools and artifacts used by the peninsula's early settlers. The museum's art center, in an old two-story frame house, exhibits works produced in a children's art school.

CUPIDS
John Guy led 39 English colonists here in 1610 and established Sea Forest Plantation, Newfoundland's first official settlement. They built a fort and a battery of three guns but disbanded the colony after 18 years of pirate raids and the opposition of fishermen.
□ Nearby Brigus, a great cod-fishing and sealing center in the 1800s, is the birthplace of Arctic explorer Capt. Robert Abram "Bob" Bartlett. He commanded ships in the polar expeditions of Lt. Robert Edwin Perry and Vilhjalmur Stefansson in the early 1900s.

0 1 2 3 4 5Miles

0 2 4 6 8Kilometres

B rooding cliffs and bright fishing ports give the road around Conception Bay its special character. At Pouch Cove, where impressive surf piles up along the shore, fishing dories are winched out of the water on skids. The stages and flakes (fish-drying racks) perched on stilts above the rocks here, once a familiar sight along Newfoundland's coast, are now rare.

Cape St. Francis is a dark headland surrounded by treacherous shoals and white-ringed islands. Topping this crest, the road makes a breathtaking plunge into the surf-battered cove at Bauline. Atop a hill overlooking the town stands a huge iron "barking" kettle still used to cure fishing nets for use in salt water.

Between Portugal Cove and St. Phillips, the bay is dominated by the frowning bulk of Bell Island—the "Iron Isle" as it was called for generations. The precipitous chunk of rock, nine kilometres long and three kilometres wide, had for half a century the largest iron mine in the world.

North and west of Holyrood, the harborless cliffs of the east bay are replaced by a continuous series of deep, fjordlike inlets. A thousand tall ships once plied these waters—and made Newfoundland one of the world's great seafaring centers in the last century. Along the coast, pastures, hay-fields and vegetable gardens climb the slopes to the forest, but the houses face the sea, for fish and seals and foreign trade gave all these towns their birth.

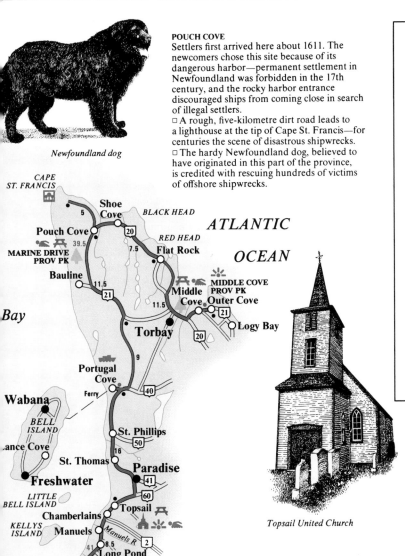

Newfoundland dog

POUCH COVE
Settlers first arrived here about 1611. The newcomers chose this site because of its dangerous harbor—permanent settlement in Newfoundland was forbidden in the 17th century, and the rocky harbor entrance discouraged ships from coming close in search of illegal settlers.
□ A rough, five-kilometre dirt road leads to a lighthouse at the tip of Cape St. Francis—for centuries the scene of disastrous shipwrecks.
□ The hardy Newfoundland dog, believed to have originated in this part of the province, is credited with rescuing hundreds of victims of offshore shipwrecks.

The Hellion of Harbour Grace

For three years, Peter Easton—the "Pirate Admiral"—terrorized Canada's east coast. A veteran of the English navy, he turned to piracy in 1604 and arrived in Conception Bay around 1610. From an embattled fort in Harbour Grace (*above*), with ships manned by fishermen he recruited or pressed into his service, Easton soon controlled the western North Atlantic.

Easton plundered coastal villages, looted French and Portuguese fishing boats off the Grand Banks, and raided English vessels in St. John's Harbour. In 1612 he sailed from Ferryland (south of St. John's) to attack what was then the Spanish colony of Puerto Rico. His ships returned laden with gold.

In 1613 Easton left for the Mediterranean. He bought a palace in France, became a marquis, and ended his days as one of the world's richest men.

Topsail United Church

TOPSAIL
The village offers fine views of Conception Bay and Bell, Little Bell and Kellys islands. Huge iron-ore deposits were mined at Bell Island from 1893 to 1966. Kellys Island is named after a pirate who is said to have made his headquarters there some three centuries ago.
□ At the mouth of the Manuels River are the fossil remains of countless trilobites. The prehistoric marine creatures lived on the floor of a shallow sea approximately 320 million years ago.
□ The Topsail United Church (1870)—"The Church by the Side of the Road"—has a churchyard dating from 1837.

HOLYROOD
Delightful scenery and excellent sailing and fishing have made Holyrood a popular summer resort. Area streams yield Atlantic salmon and brook trout, and Conception Bay is famous for giant bluefin tuna. Close by are jigging grounds where fishermen use jiggers (grouped hooks with radiating points) to catch squid—used as bait in cod fishing.
□ Off the Trans-Canada Highway near Holyrood is Butter Pot Provincial Park. A lookout atop 305-metre Butter Pot Hill provides scenic views of Conception Bay.

Conception Bay between Topsail and Kelligrews

A Storied Harbor, Silent Cannons and a Rock Called Signal Hill

One of North America's oldest cities, St. John's—Newfoundland's capital, chief port and commercial center—is situated on an almost landlocked harbor. The origin of the city's name is obscure. A popular legend says John Cabot anchored here on the feast day of St. John the Baptist (June 24) in 1497. Local settlement was well underway when Sir Humphrey Gilbert claimed Newfoundland for England in 1583.

The bustling, successful port of today preserves much of its historic core. With its brightly painted wooden dwellings and numerous narrow streets, old St. John's has changed little since it was rebuilt after a devastating city fire in 1892.

The narrow entrance to St. John's harbor is protected by the majestic rock of Signal Hill, whose silent cannons and fortifications recall the turbulent times when British and French contended for this strategic location. St. John's storied harbor still welcomes ships of all nations as it has since seafarers and settlers first arrived in the 16th century.

Alcock and Brown Historic Site (3)

Several plaques and monuments mark the site where Capt. J. W. Alcock and Lieut. A. W. Brown began the first transatlantic flight on June 14, 1919. Roughly 16½ hours later, the British aviators landed their Vickers Vimy biplane at Clifden, Ireland.

Arts and Culture Centre (5)

Built as a Centennial project in 1967, the St. John's Art and Culture Centre is a focal point of the visual and performing arts. It contains Memorial University's art gallery and a 1,000-seat auditorium.

Basilica of St. John the Baptist (9)

The 42-metre-high twin spires of this Roman Catholic cathedral (Newfoundland's largest church) have dominated St. John's skyline since the mid-19th century.

Bowring Park (4)

This 80-hectare park has a replica of the Peter Pan statue, taken from the same mold as the famous statue in Kensington Gardens, London. A full-size bronze caribou and a statue of a soldier, known as *The Fighting Newfoundlander*, honor the men of the Royal Newfoundland Regiment who died in the First World War.

Cape Spear National Historic Park (6)

North America's most easterly point (roughly ten kilometres from downtown St. John's) is the site of Newfoundland's first coastal lighthouse, restored to the way it was in 1838-40. The old lighting equipment has been installed in a nearby modern tower.

C.A. Pippy Park (1)

This 1343-hectare park includes the Memorial University Botanical Gardens (at Oxen Pond), hiking trails, playgrounds, two golf courses, a children's farm, a trailer park and a picnic area. The Confederation Building, the Newfoundland and Labrador Museum of Transportation, provincial government offices, Memorial University, and the Newfoundland Freshwater Resource Centre are also within the park.

Cathedral of St. John the Baptist (10)

This Anglican cathedral, designed by British architect Sir Gilbert Scott (1811-78), is regarded as one of the finest Gothic Revival structures in North America. (The cathedral is a national historic site.) The cornerstone was laid in the 1843. The cathedral was destroyed by a fire that devastated St. John's in 1892. Reconstruction began almost immediately and continued for many years.

Commissariat House (13)

Between 1821 and 1870, this three-story wooden building served as living and working quarters for the senior officer in charge of pay, food and supplies for the British garrison in St. John's. The interior of the restored structure, now a provincial historic site, has been decorated with 1830 furnishings.

Commissariat House

Confederation Building (8)

Overlooking downtown St. John's, the Confederation Building consists of two blocks. The 12-story East Block, opened in 1960, houses Newfoundland's legislative assembly; the six-story West Block (1985), provincial government offices.

Fort Amherst (16)

For centuries, forts and lighthouses have occupied this site at the south side of the entrance to St. John's harbour. A modern lighthouse has replaced the one built in 1812. Nearby are the remains of a Second World War fortification.

Government House (12)

Built in 1830, this Georgian-style stone Government House is the official residence of Newfoundland's lieutenant governor.

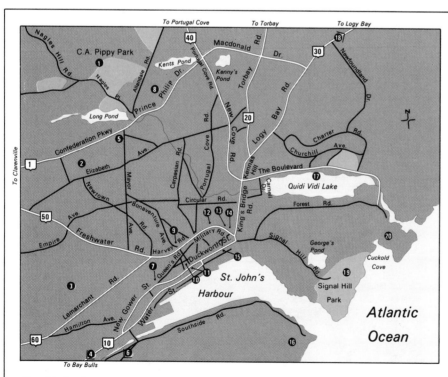

St. John's

1 C.A. Pippy Park
2 Memorial University of Newfoundland
3 Alcock and Brown
4 Bowring Park
5 Arts and Culture Centre
6 Cape Spear National Historic Park
7 Tourist Information
8 Confederation Building
9 Basilica of St. John the Baptist
10 Cathedral of St. John the Baptist
11 Newfoundland Museum
12 Government House
13 Commissariat House
14 Old Garrison Church
15 Provincial War Memorial
16 Fort Amherst
17 St. John's Regatta
18 Logy Bay
19 Signal Hill Park
20 Quidi Vidi Battery

Old Garrison Church (above). Cuckold Cove (below), viewed from Quidi Vidi Battery.

Newfoundland's capital is an attractive mixture of past and present. Modern office blocks add a new element to St. John's waterfront (above). But some of the oldest streets in North America (right) still survive just a few steps from the harbor.

Logy Bay (18)

The Ocean Research Laboratory, operated by Memorial University at Logy Bay (five kilometres east of St. John's), specializes in cold ocean biology and oceanography. Guided tours are available in summer.

Memorial University of Newfoundland (2)

Founded in 1925, the university was first called Memorial College (as a tribute to the men of Newfoundland who died during the First World War) and became a degree-conferring institution in 1949. Today the campus accommodates more than 15,000 students each year.

Newfoundland Museum (11)

The museum depicts 9,000 years of Newfoundland and Labrador history. Exhibits describe the life-styles of native peoples, settlers, seafarers and townspeople. Another

branch of the museum at the Murray Premises—a restored 19th-century building on St. John's waterfront—houses maritime, military and natural history collections.

Old Garrison Church (14)

One of St. John's oldest wooden churches, the Old Garrison Church (St. Thomas' Anglican) was built in 1836. A royal coat of arms from that time is a feature of the church's interior.

Provincial War Memorial (15)

This 7.6-metre-high granite memorial—topped by a statue of *Freedom*—was unveiled in 1924. A plaque near the memorial marks the site where the explorer Sir Humphrey Gilbert (1537-83) claimed Newfoundland for England in 1583.

Quidi Vidi Battery (20)

Overlooking Quidi Vidi Village, the battery was built by French troops during their brief occupation of St. John's in 1762. British forces reconstructed the fortification in 1780 and manned it until 1870. The battery has been restored to its 1812 condition.

St. John's Regatta (17)

Reputedly North America's oldest continuous annual sports event, the St. John's Regatta is a rowing race, held on Quidi Vidi Lake in early August. (The first recorded race occurred in 1826.) During the race, four long, fixed-seat rowing shells—each with six oarsmen—cover a 2.6-kilometre course.

'Fort Impregnable' Guards St. John's

Cabot Tower, Signal Hill

Once known as "Fort Impregnable," Signal Hill (19) rises 152 metres from the sea at the entrance to St. John's Harbour. Seafarers used the headland as a signaling post, and early settlers used it as a defense base against incursions by enemy ships. During the Seven Years' War (1756-63), French forces breached local defenses, but were routed by the British in September 1762 at the Battle of Signal Hill—the last conflict of the war in North America. Now a national historic park, Signal Hill preserves its military past at the Queen's Battery, a fortification dating from 1812. Another Signal Hill attraction is the Cabot Tower (*left*), built in 1897 to commemorate the 400th anniversary of John Cabot's discovery of Newfoundland. From a spot near the tower, the Italian inventor Guglielmo Marconi (1874-1937) received the first transatlantic wireless signal in December 1901.

An Enduring Seafaring Life at Canada's Eastern Tip

Avalon Peninsula

The wrecks of thousands of ships—dashed onto rocky headlands or ripped by hidden shoals—dot the shore between St. John's and Cape Race. In many coves rotting beams and rusted iron hulls can be seen at low tide. The fogs, storms and tides that doomed these ships are a point of pride to Newfoundlanders, who boast about their erratic weather. Despite the dangers fishermen endure, few choose to exchange their way of life for city jobs, preferring the traditional isolation of the outports.

SALMONIER NATURE PARK
A two-kilometre nature trail winds through forests of balsam fir and birch, along boardwalks, over bogs thick with pitcher plants, round-leaved sundews and sphagnum moss, and past marshes where orchids and wild roses bloom. Mammals typical of Newfoundland—moose, arctic hares and foxes, beavers and caribou—roam fenced enclosures. Blackpoll and myrtle warblers, owls, ospreys and bald eagles can also be seen.

Fox sparrow

Thorny skate

TREPASSEY
The first plane to cross the Atlantic Ocean from west to east left here in 1919. Three U.S. Navy seaplanes attempted the trip. Two were forced down at sea, but the third touched down in the Azores and flew on to Portugal.
□ In 1928 aviatrix Amelia Earhart left Trepassey on her first transatlantic flight—as a passenger. The thrill of that crossing convinced her to make aviation her career.
□ Holyrood Pond near St. Vincent's provides a saltwater home for a wide variety of marine species. A beach separates the 23-kilometre-long lake from the sea, and ocean perch, sculpins, haddock and thorny skates inhabit its depths.

CAPE RACE
An arm of the ocean cuts between ancient cliffs near Cape Race. The world's richest find of Precambrian fossils—a record of animals that flourished some 500 million years ago—was made at nearby Mistaken Point in 1968. The area has been declared an ecological reserve to preserve this find.

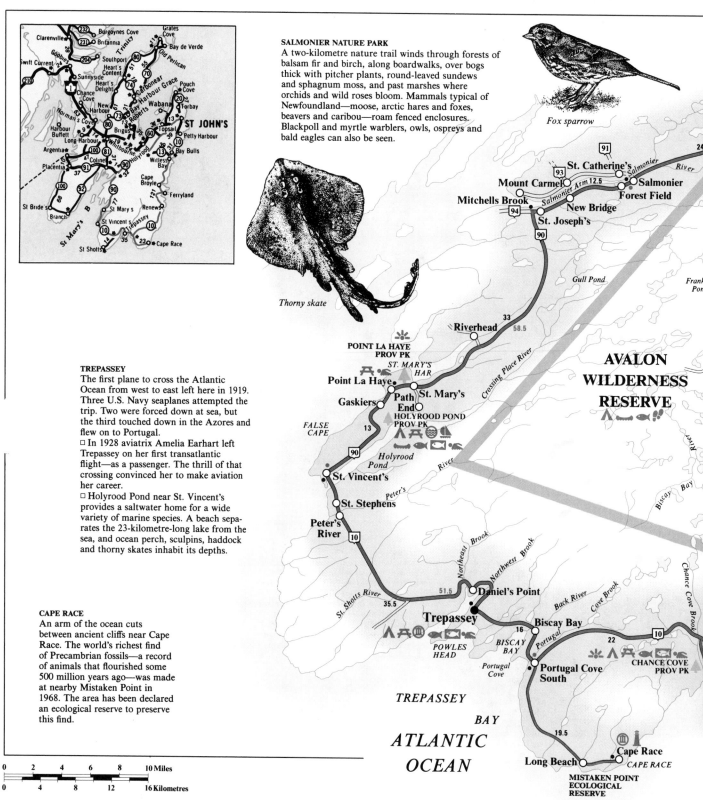

0   2   4   6   8   10 Miles
0   4   8   12   16 Kilometres

Change comes slowly to these villages. Fishermen in such towns as Petty Harbour and Renews set out each morning in wooden dories to jig for cod with hooks and lines. Some preserve their catch as their forefathers did, spreading the salted fish on flakes (wooden racks) to dry in the sun. Many villagers still speak with an Irish brogue.

Newfoundland's east coast is rich in history. Here were pirates' lairs, great sea battles and some of the first permanent settlements in Canada. The Avalon Peninsula was named by the first Lord Baltimore, who in 1621 founded a colony at Ferryland. But colonists found farming hard—the interior mountains, forests, bogs and barrens discouraged a pastoral life.

Most who live here turn to the sea—and the sea rewards their labor. Each day fishermen brave chill waters and stiff ocean breezes, and return at sundown in boats laden with fish.

Petty Harbour

PETTY HARBOUR

Wooden houses in this fishing community cling precariously to a steep hill that rises from the sea. Skiffs, dories and long-liners (fishing boats with four- or five-man crews) set out from Petty Harbour's busy wharves each morning during spring and summer. The fishermen jig for cod by hand, or haul up heavy gill nets set in deep water the day before.

BAY BULLS

One of Newfoundland's oldest settlements, Bay Bulls was repeatedly attacked by the French and the Dutch, and several times was destroyed by fire. A hint of the village's stormy history is in the four old cannon used as gateposts at the Roman Catholic church. Bronze statues of saints Patrick, Paul, Joseph and Theresa stand atop the upright cannon.
□ Enormous flocks of seabirds nest on three small islands in nearby Witless Bay. Parts of Gull Island are honeycombed with the burrows of some 1,500,000 Leach's storm petrels. Black-legged kittiwakes, herring gulls and some 500,000 common puffins also nest here. Green Island supports gulls, black guillemots and Atlantic murres; puffins and Leach's storm petrels inhabit Great Island. Charter boats circle the islands, which teem with birds during nesting season (mid-June through early July).

AVALON WILDERNESS RESERVE

A herd of woodland caribou feeds on the lichens that thrive in this protected region. Dwarf spruce and balsam fir grow here, too. The reserve attracts hikers, canoeists, wilderness campers, and anglers casting for brook trout. Visitors must obtain permits from the Department of Culture, Recreation and Youth in St. John's before entering the area.

Ferryland

Bronze statues atop cannon, Bay Bulls

FERRYLAND

In 1621, a colony was established at Ferryland by Sir George Calvert, the first Lord Baltimore. Because of repeated French attacks and the harsh climate, he quit Newfoundland in 1629 and transferred his colony to Virginia. A later settlement under Sir David Kirke also failed, and cod fishermen, formerly ousted by colonists, returned to Ferryland.
□ In the 18th century, Ferrylanders built fortifications on Bois Island at the mouth of the harbor and repulsed several attacks by French naval squadrons. Earthworks can still be seen on the island.

Sir George Calvert's coat of arms preserved in an old stone church at Ferryland

Map labels

CONCEPTION BAY

Donovans
Mount Pearl
Maddox Cove
Goulds
Petty Harbour
HEART PT
SHOAL BAY
LONG PT
THE SPOUT
Bay Bulls Big Pond
Middle Pond
BULL HEAD
SOUTH HEAD
GULL I
GREEN I
Bay Bulls
Witless Bay
Mobile
Tors Cove
Burnt Cove
Bauline East
WITLESS BAY ECOLOGICAL RESERVE
GREAT I
CAPE NEDDICK
Shore's Cove
Cape Broyle
Brigus South
BRIGUS HEAD
Calvert
Ferryland
BLACK HEAD
Fermeuse
BALD HEAD
FERMEUSE HAR
Renews
BEAR COVE HEAD
Cappahayden
BURNT PT
Seal Cove

La Manche R.
LA MANCHE VALLEY PROV PK
Mount Carmel Pond
Cape Pond
Paradise Pond

Hawke Hills
Butter Pot
BUTTER POT PROV PK
(see Road Unit 174)
COCHRANE POND PROV PK
Trans-Canada Highway
Manuels River
FATHER DUFFY'S WELL PROV PK
SALMONIER NATURE PK

North to the Arctic on an Adventure Highway

Yukon Territory/Northwest Territories

The Dempster Highway starts near Dawson and stretches 740 kilometres across the Yukon and the Northwest Territories, linking muskeg and mountain, forest and barren, frontier town and Inuit community. And, at the end of the highway, travelers can venture farther—by air from Inuvik to Tuktoyaktuk on the Beaufort Sea, where offshore rigs are tapping Arctic oil reserves.

The Dempster is Canada's most northerly public highway—and the only one to cross the Arctic Circle. It is named for RCMP

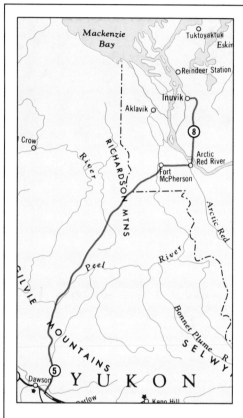

Midnight sun (time-exposure photograph)

ARCTIC CIRCLE
North of Kilometre 403 on the Dempster Highway—the Arctic Circle—the summer sun never sets but appears to circle the top of the world. During the long winter, the midday sun is only a pastel streak on the southern horizon.
□ About 44 kilometres north of the Arctic Circle is the Cornwall Campground, which provides Dempster Highway travelers with a good stopping place and protection against the unpredictable weather in this region.

Ogilvie Mountains

TOMBSTONE CAMPGROUND
This campground is located at the tree line where the last sparse stands of spruce and poplar give way to tundra and the stark, soaring Ogilvie Mountains.
□ Some 2.5 kilometres farther north, travelers on the Dempster Highway can see the wedge-shaped peak of the 2,192-metre-high Tombstone Mountain. Long before the Dempster was built, the mountain was a reliable landmark for prospectors, trappers and RCMP who had lost their way.
□ About five kilometres farther along the highway is North Fork Pass, whose 1,289-metre height rivals passes in the Banff and Jasper regions.

RICHARDSON MOUNTAINS
This somber range of mountains, part of the Rocky Mountain chain, is named for surgeon and naturalist Sir John Richardson who, with Sir John Franklin, traveled through the Yukon to the Canadian Arctic in 1819-22 and 1825-27.

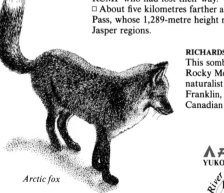

Arctic fox

EAGLE PLAINS
"Plains" here is a misnomer. This area is, in fact, a high mountain valley dividing the Ogilvie and Richardson mountains.
□ At the community of Eagle Plains—the halfway point on the Dempster Highway—historic photos recall the tragic "Lost Patrol," a group of Mounties who lost their way on the Peel River in the winter of 1910-11. Another display recounts the story of "Mad Trapper" Albert Johnson, the object of a famous 1932 manhunt. Johnson was cornered by the Mounties and killed near a bridge nine kilometres north of here.

0   10   20   30   40   50 Miles

0   20   40   60   80 Kilometres

Insp. W.J.D. Dempster (1876-1964). His 1911 dogsled journey across wintry wastes in search of the "lost patrol" (four Mounties who perished on the trail) is commemorated

Pingo, Tuktoyaktuk

A Deep Freezer in a Permafrost Pingo

Volcano-shaped pingos, huge mounds of solid ice pushed out of the flat tundra by permafrost pressure, are common in the Mackenzie Delta. A thin covering of moss and turf insulates the clear, blue ice from the summer sun.

Two pingos, about 30 metres across and 12 metres high, are in the town of Tuktoyaktuk. One has been hollowed by residents to form a natural deep freezer. A food supply of caribou, geese, ducks and fish lies stiffly frozen inside a glistening ice chamber lit by electric light.

FORT McPHERSON
The Loucheux Indian community at Fort McPherson dates from 1852 when a HBC trading post was established here. About that time Fort McPherson became also the center for Anglican Church work in the western Arctic. By 1900 it had become an important RCMP post. A local monument commemorates the "Lost Patrol" (see Eagle Plains), which set out from here for Dawson in 1910.

at two main stopping places—Eagle Plains and Fort McPherson.

The highway was begun in 1959 to reach the remote regions (and resources) of the Yukon and the Northwest Territories. Its construction in a scenic—but often inhospitable—land took 20 years and $100 million. Two major rivers—the Eagle and the Ogilvie—were bridged. And most of the route had to be elevated on gravel "berms" to insulate the road from permafrost and prevent excess thawing. But today it is the main supply route for Inuvik and the Mackenzie River delta.

Travel on the Dempster is best between June and September. But even then weather can be unpredictable; heavy rains, high winds and blizzards can occur! And, although the highway itself is well maintained, accommodations and services en route are limited. Drivers should be well outfitted for emergencies, because traffic is light and phones are few.

TUKTOYAKTUK
Located on a sandspit on the shore of the Beaufort Sea, Tuktoyaktuk (Inuit for "resembling a cariboo") was once a whale-hunting community of the Karngmalit Inuit. Today "Tuk" is a government administration center and a base for offshore oil exploration.
□ Visitors can tour *Our Lady of Lourdes,* a 15-metre schooner, which served as a supply ship for a local Catholic mission between 1931 and 1957.
□ Beluga and bowhead whales, which summer in the Beaufort Sea, can be seen in Kugmallit Bay.

Beluga whale

INUVIK
This town is the most northerly point in Canada you can reach by public highway. Inuvik—its Inuit name means "place of man"—was founded in 1954 to replace Aklavik, a town on the west side of the Mackenzie Delta, which was endangered by erosion and floods.
□ Virtually all Inuvik's buildings are raised above ground on piles embedded in permafrost. The town's heat, sewer and water pipes—housed in giant aluminum conduits called "utilidors"—are also above ground to prevent them from freezing.
□ Visitors to Inuvik can arrange tours of the Mackenzie Delta and flights to Tuktoyaktuk on the Beaufort Sea.

ARCTIC RED RIVER
Although traders and explorers had been in contact with the Loucheux (Kutchin) Indians of the Arctic since the 18th century, the first permanent contact was made when a Catholic mission was established here in 1868. A trading post was set up in the 1870s. The local Loucheux Indians still earn their living hunting and fishing. It is in Arctic Red River that northbound travelers on the Dempster Highway first see the Mackenzie Delta.

Map labels:
BEAUFORT SEA
MACKENZIE BAY
ELLICE ISLAND
RICHARDS ISLAND
KUGMALLIT BAY
TOKER PT
Tuktoyaktuk
LANGLEY ISLAND
MACKENZIE DELTA
EAST CHANNEL
River
Parsons Lake
Eskimo Lakes
Inuvik
Noell Lake
Campbell Lake
297
Richardson Mountains
Stony
Fort McPherson
Indian Village
8
122
48
Arctic Red River
Vittrekwa River
Peel River
Red River
NWT YT
PEEL RIVER GAME RES
Martin House
Arctic Circle
YT NWT
Arctic

Inuvik

A 'City of Gold' Whose Gaudy Ghosts Live On

Yukon Territory

Battered by fate and slowed by age, Dawson wears the proud marks of its flaming youth as the Yukon's "City of Gold." The fewer than a thousand permanent residents live nostalgically among the ghosts of 25,000 who flocked to Dawson in 1897-98. Here, along creaking boardwalks, once strolled the gaudy characters of the Klondike Gold Rush—Silent Sam Bonifield, Swiftwater Bill Gates, Glass-Eyed Annie and Overflowing Flora—past rowdy dance halls, swinging-door saloons and gambling

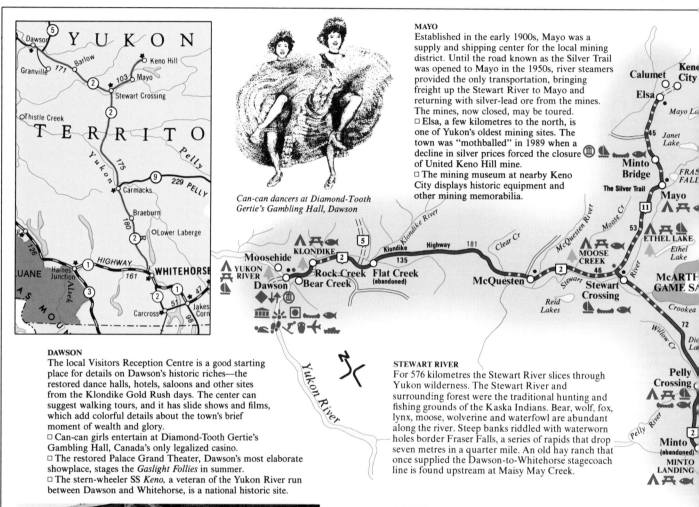

Can-can dancers at Diamond-Tooth Gertie's Gambling Hall, Dawson

MAYO

Established in the early 1900s, Mayo was a supply and shipping center for the local mining district. Until the road known as the Silver Trail was opened to Mayo in the 1950s, river steamers provided the only transportation, bringing freight up the Stewart River to Mayo and returning with silver-lead ore from the mines. The mines, now closed, may be toured.
□ Elsa, a few kilometres to the north, is one of Yukon's oldest mining sites. The town was "mothballed" in 1989 when a decline in silver prices forced the closure of United Keno Hill mine.
□ The mining museum at nearby Keno City displays historic equipment and other mining memorabilia.

DAWSON

The local Visitors Reception Centre is a good starting place for details on Dawson's historic riches—the restored dance halls, hotels, saloons and other sites from the Klondike Gold Rush days. The center can suggest walking tours, and it has slide shows and films, which add colorful details about the town's brief moment of wealth and glory.
□ Can-can girls entertain at Diamond-Tooth Gertie's Gambling Hall, Canada's only legalized casino.
□ The restored Palace Grand Theater, Dawson's most elaborate showplace, stages the *Gaslight Follies* in summer.
□ The stern-wheeler SS *Keno,* a veteran of the Yukon River run between Dawson and Whitehorse, is a national historic site.

STEWART RIVER

For 576 kilometres the Stewart River slices through Yukon wilderness. The Stewart River and surrounding forest were the traditional hunting and fishing grounds of the Kaska Indians. Bear, wolf, fox, lynx, moose, wolverine and waterfowl are abundant along the river. Steep banks riddled with waterworn holes border Fraser Falls, a series of rapids that drop seven metres in a quarter mile. An old hay ranch that once supplied the Dawson-to-Whitehorse stagecoach line is found upstream at Maisy May Creek.

Main street of Dawson

Robert Service— Poet of the Gold Rush

Robert Service's poems immortalized the Klondike Gold Rush even though he took no part in it. "The Yukon was the source of my first real inspiration," he said, "I bubbled verse like an artesian well."

In 1904 Service, a young bank teller, arrived in Whitehorse. Three years later he published *Songs of a Sourdough,* which was an immediate success. It contained his best known poem, *The Shooting of Dan McGrew*—suggested one Saturday night by sounds of barroom revelry. *Ballads of a Cheechako* appeared two years later, after Service had moved to Dawson. Now a successful writer and financially independent, he resigned from the bank and wrote a novel, *The Trail of '98,* in a log cabin on a Dawson hillside. The cabin is a national historic site.

0   5   10   15   20   25 Miles

0   10   20   30   40 Kilometres

casinos where the motto was "never refuse a drink or kick a dog."

Gold was discovered southeast of Dawson on Bonanza Creek, a tributary of the Klondike River, in 1896. Word of the strike reached the outside world in 1897, touching off the Klondike Gold Rush—three years of hardship and greed, starvation and lavish spending. Dawson and other boom towns along the Yukon River system sprang up almost overnight. Between 1896 and 1904, the creeks yielded more than $100 million in gold. But as the more accessible gold was removed, the population dwindled. Cabins, claims, even whole towns were deserted. Huge dredges became part of the landscape they had furrowed and scarred.

Upriver, Whitehorse not only survived, but has prospered since the 1890s. The city lies at a bend in the Yukon River, north of the wild rapids that were once the most hazardous stretch of the Trail of '98. Modern Whitehorse is a capital city and busy commercial center. Where eager cheechakos (greenhorns) once boarded sternwheelers headed north, river barges now unload washing machines, television sets and other trappings of modern living.

Dawson on the Yukon River

YUKON RIVER
North of Lake Laberge, the Yukon River surges through a winding channel bordered by sand-and-gravel cliffs up to 90 metres high. At Five Finger Rapids four 15-metre-high sandstone columns divide the river into five streams. Near Carmacks is 210-metre-high Eagle's Nest Bluff and north of Minto are black basalt cliffs towering 135 metres. Abandoned cabins—many built during the Klondike Gold Rush—and beaches, sandbars and wooded islands provide excellent campsites for canoeists paddling the 960-kilometre stretch from Lake Bennett, B.C., to Dawson.

McARTHUR GAME SANCTUARY
This preserve was established to protect the Fannin sheep, once considered near extinction. Golden eagles, blue grouse, kingfishers and loons are also found in the sanctuary.

Kingfisher

PELLY CROSSING
The 400-kilometre Pelly River canoe route from Ross River to Fort Selkirk crosses the Klondike Highway here. Northwest of the Faro Bridge the river meanders past 1,800-metre Rose Mountain; some 60 kilometres downstream are 2,000-metre Mount Hodder and Tay Mountain. The river races through three sets of rapids in Granite Canyon, six kilometres long and up to 75 metres deep.

WHITEHORSE
Now Yukon's largest city, with a population of more than 15,000, Whitehorse began in 1898 as a stopping place for thousands of gold seekers on their way to the Klondike goldfields. It became the territorial capital in 1953.
□ Displays at the MacBride Museum describe Yukon history from the earliest native Indian cultures to the construction of the Alaska Highway. Exhibits in the Old Log Church Museum, which is housed in one of the city's oldest permanent structures, shows the Church's role in this region.
□ SS *Klondike II,* the last stern-wheeler to operate on the Yukon River, houses a river-transport museum.
□ MV *Schwatka* offers daily excursions through spectacular Miles Canyon, where rapids have been tamed by a hydroelectric project.
□ In February Whitehorse celebrates Yukon Sourdough Rendezvous. A range of contests—beard growing, dogsled and snowshoe racing, sawing and wrestling—are open to residents and visitors. Sourdough pancake breakfasts start the day right, and the Old Time Fiddle Show gets toes tapping during festivities.

MONTAGUE
The remains of a roadhouse, built in the late 1890s to accommodate Klondike gold seekers, can be seen here. It is one of several constructed at 32-kilometre intervals along the road between Whitehorse and Dawson.

CARMACKS
This community is named for George Washington Carmacks, who discovered coal here in 1895 and set up a local trading post. (George Carmacks is best remembered as the codiscoverer of Klondike gold in 1896.) During the 1890s, the trading post became a stopping place on the Dalton Trail and the Whitehorse-Dawson winter road. It was also a fueling station for Yukon River steamers.

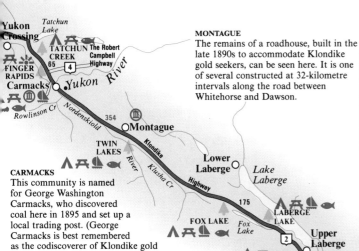

Whitehorse

Where Canada's Highest Peak Looms Above a Lofty Mountain Range

Yukon Territory

In almost every way the southwest corner of the Yukon is a place of superlatives. Kluane National Park, the second largest of Canada's national parks, preserves a wilderness almost four times the size of Prince Edward Island. Within the park are the St. Elias Mountains—the largest and loftiest of Canada's ranges—dominated by our highest peak, the 5,951-metre Mount Logan.

Hikers who are experienced enough to explore Kluane's rugged interior find stunning mountain vistas. The vast Kaskawulsh

DESTRUCTION BAY
This community began as a construction camp on the Alaska Highway. It was named Destruction Bay after a fierce storm wrecked the campsite of the army crew that was working on a nearby stretch of the highway.

KLUANE LAKE
The 60-kilometre-long lake is hemmed in by the Kluane Range of the St. Elias Mountains. Dall sheep, grizzly bears, moose and wolves inhabit the mixed spruce-aspen forests surrounding the lake. Canada geese, loons, ducks, and trumpeter and whistling swans summer here.

Arctic loon, Kluane Lake

BURWASH LANDING
The community was established by tw French brothers, Louis and Jean Jacquot, who constructed trading pos on the creeks where miners gathered t hunt for gold. When the dream of rich died, the Jacquots stayed on as outfitte Their descendants still live locally.
□ The Kluane Museum of Natural History at Burwash Landing exhibits more than 50 animal species (some ar displayed in dioramas) and a collectio of local Indian costumes and artifacts.

Dall sheep, Kluane National Park

BEAVER CREEK
For eight months road-builders had labored on the Alaska Highway. Work continued seven days a week, in temperatures which ranged from subtropical heat to well below freezing. On Oct. 20, 1942, the construction crews working south from Alaska and north from Whitehorse met at Beaver Creek. Two bulldozer operators heard the drone of each other's machine in the distance. They bulldozed through the forest separating them, and clasped hands. Formal ribbon-cutting ceremonies opening the highway took place a month later on Soldier's Summit.

KLUANE NATIONAL PARK
Mountains and glaciers dominate this 22,000-square-kilometre park. Established in 1972, it contains Canada's highest and largest mountains—the St. Elias. These mountains are split by the Duke Depression into two ranges—the Icefield to the west and the Kluane to the east. The Icefield ranges have the giant peaks, which include 5,951-metre Mount Logan (Canada's highest), 5,488-metre Mount St. Elias, and 5,290-metre Mount Lucania. The Kluane ranges, which average 2,500 metres in height, are visible from the Alaska Highway, which follows Kluane's eastern edge. At the mountains' upper levels are the world's most extensive nonpolar icefields. From the icefields, glaciers—the 65-kilometre-long Lowell, for example—spread out over Kluane. Where the glaciers end, fens, forests and floodplains, marshes and meadows begin. Dall sheep, caribou, mountain goats and grizzly bears inhabit Kluane—a combination of animals found in no other national park.
□ Although Kluane has been recognized as a United Nations World Heritage site (1979), it remains a wilderness with few amenities. A trail system (still under development) permits exploration. Some trails—for example, the walk to St. Elias Lake or the self-guiding Rock Glacier Trail—are easy for day hikers. Overnight hikers and climbers must register with park officials.

St. Elias Mountains

Glacier is a five-hour hike from the Slims River bridge at Kilometre 1688 of the Alaska Highway; two rivers that begin at the glacier end hundreds of kilometres apart. Other hiking trails lead to the King's Throne, a grassy expanse adorned with wildflowers, and to Silver City, a ghost town of rotting sluice boxes and sod-and-log cabins.

Wildlife is abundant in and around the park. Along willow-edged rivers visitors may sight some of the largest moose on the continent. The giant mountain caribou is less plentiful, although one band has been sighted occasionally near Burwash Flats, outside the park but near the Alaska Highway. Forests and meadows shelter mountain goats, grizzlies and black bears.

The landscape constantly astonishes. The grasslands of the Slims River delta could have been borrowed from the Canadian Prairies. Million Dollar Falls cascades 60 metres into the frothing Takhanne River, one kilometre west of the Haines Highway.

Snow blankets the higher peaks year round.

Soldier's Summit, overlooking Kluane Lake, commemorates a man-made feature of the northern landscape. On Nov. 20, 1942, the Alaska Highway was officially opened here. Military and civilian workers had pushed a highway through 2,200 kilometres of wilderness, completing in eight months an engineering feat which would normally have taken five years. Today the highway is an artery of northern commerce and a magnet for sportsmen and campers.

Bannock, Hardtack and Jerky

The traditional fare of old-time woodsmen and prospectors is still popular with campers. Fresh bread—sourdough, bannock and hardtack—can be baked easily over an open fire; jerky and pemmican are practical ways to preserve meat.

Sourdough, a spongy mixture of flour, water and yeast, is used as a "starter" to ferment dough for bread or flapjacks. Klondike prospectors became known as "sourdoughs" for this staple food. On winter nights they kept their starter next to their bodies so that it wouldn't freeze.

Bannock, made from flour, water, baking powder and lard, is baked to a golden brown in a greased skillet. Hardtack is simplest of all: a flat cake of flour and water baked until dry and hard.

Jerky is lean meat—moose, deer or caribou—cut into strips and dried in the sun. For pemmican, an Indian specialty, jerky is shredded and mixed with hot animal fat. Jerky and pemmican will keep for months without refrigeration.

Teslin Lake

TESLIN
Rolling, forested hills and the peaks of the Big Salmon Range form a backdrop to the clear, deep waters of Teslin Lake. The Nisutlun Bridge, longest water span of the Alaska Highway (575 metres), crosses an arm of the lake here.

HAINES JUNCTION
This community at the junction of the Alaska and Haines highways is the headquarters of Kluane National Park and a center for trail-riding, photographic and mountain climbing expeditions.

WATSON LAKE
Here are some 1,300 signs with the names of faraway places. The first were erected by homesick soldiers building the road in 1942; tourists have kept up the tradition.

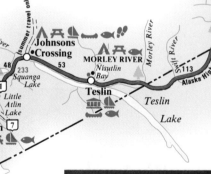

CARCROSS
This village's original name, Caribou Crossing, was abbreviated in 1904 to avoid being confused with places in British Columbia and Alaska.
□ In 1896 George Washington Carmack and his Indian brothers-in-law, Skookum Jim and Tagish Charlie, set out from here to search for gold. Their find at Bonanza Creek began the Klondike gold rush. Skookum Jim, Tagish Charlie and Kate Carmack (George's wife) are buried in Carcross cemetery. (Skookum Jim's headstone reads "James Mason," Tagish Charlie's is marked "Dawson Charlie.")
□ A local attraction is the old stern-wheeler SS *Tutshi*, which has been beached on the shore of the narrows between Bennett and Nares lakes since 1955.

Gold nuggets from the Yukon

Signposts, Watson Lake

A 'Golden Triangle' Gilded by Wheat and Water Power

Northeastern British Columbia

Northeastern British Columbia is a rough triangle bordered by the Yukon and Northwest Territories, Alberta, and the high spine of the Rocky Mountains.

The "Golden Triangle"—an area larger than Great Britain—is unique in western Canada. Although much of the landscape is rolling and often mountainous, several thousand square kilometres are an exten-

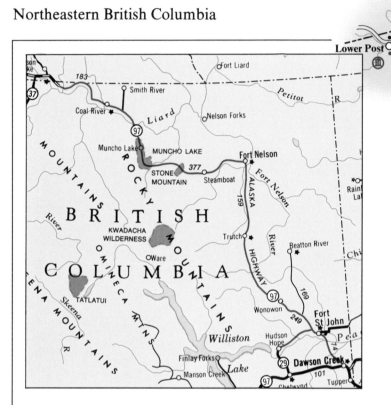

LOWER POST
A Roman Catholic mission and an Indian residential school are located in this former Hudson's Bay Company trading post.
□ In 1898 a North West Mounted Police party labored northward through Lower Post, blazing an overland route from Edmonton to Dawson City and the Klondike goldfields. More than a year later the trip was completed, but the scheme proved impractical and the "Yukon Trail" was abandoned.

LIARD RIVER
Visitors to Liard River Hot Springs can soak or swim in a natural pool, which is fed by water flowing at the rate of 2,900 litres per minute. The reputedly therapeutic water has an average temperature of 43°C. The area has an abundance of southern plants such as lobelia, scarlet monkey flower, ostrich fern, cow parsnip and dogbane—all unusual blooms for this latitude. (Liard River Hot Springs is on the 56th parallel.)

Heroic Labor on an Epic Road

More than 1,900 kilometres of the 2,436-kilometre Alaska Highway are in Canada. The highway between Dawson Creek and Fairbanks was built by 16,000 U.S. Army and American and Canadian civilian personnel as a supply road to bases in Alaska during World War II.

Work continued seven days a week, day and night, in conditions that ranged from sub-zero cold to stifling heat. No time was wasted on niceties of engineering. The road was looped over hills to save blasting and rammed through the forest with bulldozers. Overhead, aerial reconnaissance planes photographed the next section to be attacked. The highway was completed in November, 1942, only eight months after construction began.

Alaska Highway near Muncho Lake

Red monkey flower

MUNCHO LAKE PROVINCIAL PARK
Thick forests of white spruce and lodgepole pine carpet most of the park's deep valleys. Scrub alpine spruce clings to the slopes near the timberline.
□ Stone sheep, caribou, mountain goat and moose frequent a small area where calcium and magnesium are exposed in loamy soil. (By licking at the minerals, the animals have hollowed out holes in cliffs and pillars.) Photographers can often approach within close range of feeding animals here.
□ A 12-kilometre trail follows Nonda Creek, near the park's eastern boundary, past dwarf alpine plants, mosses, lichens and showy wildflowers.

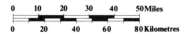

Dogsled Races,
Fort Nelson

sion of the Prairies. Grain elevators and the great sweep of farmland near Fort St. John confirm this impression.

Dreams of furs, gold, wheat and oil have ebbed and flowed in this corner of British Columbia since Alexander Mackenzie's search for an overland route to the Pacific. Crossing the region in 1793, the explorer marveled at the abundant resources, which were to remain untapped for 150 years. Simon Fraser followed in Mackenzie's wake in the 1800s, establishing trading posts for

the North West Company along the rivers.

Despite the toehold of the fur trade, and later the Klondike Gold Rush, the Golden Triangle remained a sparsely populated expanse of forest, prairie and muskeg until the Alaska Highway was built in 1942. With this link to the south, the region boomed. Grain farms flourished along the Peace River. The first oil well in British Columbia was wildcatted near Fort St. John. At Hudson's Hope, tons of earth were blasted and bulldozed into Canada's largest dam.

FORT NELSON
A North West Company post built here around 1800 was destroyed and some of the inhabitants were massacred by Indians in 1813. In 1865 the Hudson's Bay Company founded a second post which is still in operation.
□ Once the town center, Old Fort Nelson is now an Indian settlement. Willow, birch and fireweed have swallowed up many of the settlement's abandoned boats and buildings.
□ Fort Nelson offers a Welcome Visitors Program of Alaska Highway travel information four or five nights a week from June to August. Items relating to construction of the highway can be seen at Fort Nelson Historical Museum.

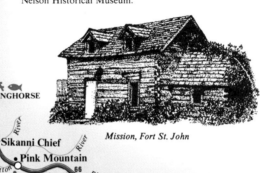

Mission, Fort St. John

FORT ST. JOHN
With a population of more than 13,000, Fort St. John is the largest community north of Prince George. Some claim it is the oldest non-white community in British Columbia. Explorer Alexander Mackenzie traveled on the Peace River through this area on his journey to the Pacific in 1793. The original fur trading post—Rocky Mountain Fort—was built about 1798, then renamed Fort St. John. Several forts of this name were constructed locally at different sites during the fur trade period.
□ Items relating to the city's pioneer days, the construction of the Alaska Highway and the development of local oil deposits are housed at the Fort St. John-North Peace Museum.
□ Local events include a rodeo in July and North Pine Fall Festival in August.

TAYLOR
The community is set in a scenic, thickly wooded valley. Local refineries "scrub" (refine) billions of cubic feet of natural gas and millions of gallons of gasoline each year.
□ The Peace Island Park Museum displays pioneer furnishings and tools, an Indian dugout and a birchbark canoe.
□ There is a gold-panning contest and a canoe race in September.

Stone sheep,
Stone Mountain Provincial Park

STONE MOUNTAIN PROVINCIAL PARK
Eroded pillars of sand and gravel—some are 18 metres high—stand near 1,265-metre-high Summit Pass, the highest point on the Alaska Highway.
□ Glacial sediment in Summit Lake gives the water an iridescent green hue, a striking contrast with the birch and willow trees along the shore.
□ A six-kilometre trail leads from the Alaska Highway along the North Tetsa River to Flower Spring Lake. Stone sheep and migrating caribou are sometimes sighted grazing in the meadows near the lake.

(Map labels)
Fort Nelson — 64.5 — Alaska Highway
Kledo Cr
TETSA RIVER PROV PK — 84 — Steamboat — 261
Summit Lake
Summit Lake
STONE MOUNTAIN PROV PK
ANDY BAILEY REC AREA
159.5
PROPHET RIVER REC AREA — Prophet River
Trutch — 97 — 253 — Trutch Cr
BUCKINGHORSE RIVER
93.5
Mason Creek — Sikanni Chief — Pink Mountain — 66
Wonowon — 143 — 77 — Montney — Rose Prairie
CHARLIE LAKE
Halfway R — Fort St. John — Baldonnel
10
Attachie — 82 — Taylor — 74 — KISKATINAW PROV PK
Farrell Creek — 84
PEACE CANYON DAM — 29 — Farmington — 97 — 49
W.A.C. BENNETT DAM — 15 — Progress — Dawson Creek — Pouce Coupe
Hudson's Hope — 2
Williston Lake

(see Road Unit 181)

Peace River Powerhouse
Williston Lake—the largest body of fresh water in British Columbia—was formed when the W.A.C. Bennett Dam—one of the world's largest earth-fill structures—was completed in 1967. The lake, at the source of the Peace River, occupies 1,660 square kilometres, extends for 360 kilometres, and has 1,770 kilometres of shoreline. From a lookout, visitors can see the panorama of the dam, the reservoir and the surrounding mountains. The dam and the powerhouse, 150 metres underground, may be toured. The Peace Canyon Dam, 22 kilometres downstream from the Bennett Dam, has obliterated the Peace Canyon rapids—once a treacherous obstacle for explorers and fur traders.

W.A.C. Bennett Dam

HUDSON'S HOPE
Explorer Simon Fraser founded a trading post here in 1805. The foundations of the original settlement—Rocky Mountain Portage—can be seen near the ferry landing.
□ Until the decline of the fur trade, the community was an important trading post and head of navigation for steamboats plying the Peace River. In the 1960s, the construction of the nearby W.A.C. Bennett Dam revived the community.
□ Hudson's Hope Museum houses items from the community's past.
□ Local events include a rodeo (June), Explorer Days (August) and a canoe race (September).

A Joseph's Coat of Crops
on Canada's Northernmost Farmland

Peace River Valley

Rolling foothills, a patchwork of forest and plains and some of the world's richest farmland are found in the Peace River country. Crystal lakes are hidden in groves of aspen, meandering streams nestle in pastoral valleys, and badlands are filled with the strange shapes of erosion.

The landscape is a Joseph's coat of colorful crops—the brown of oats and barley, the green and gold of wheat, the blue of flax, the yellow of rapeseed, the earthy tones of blocks of summer fallow. In late

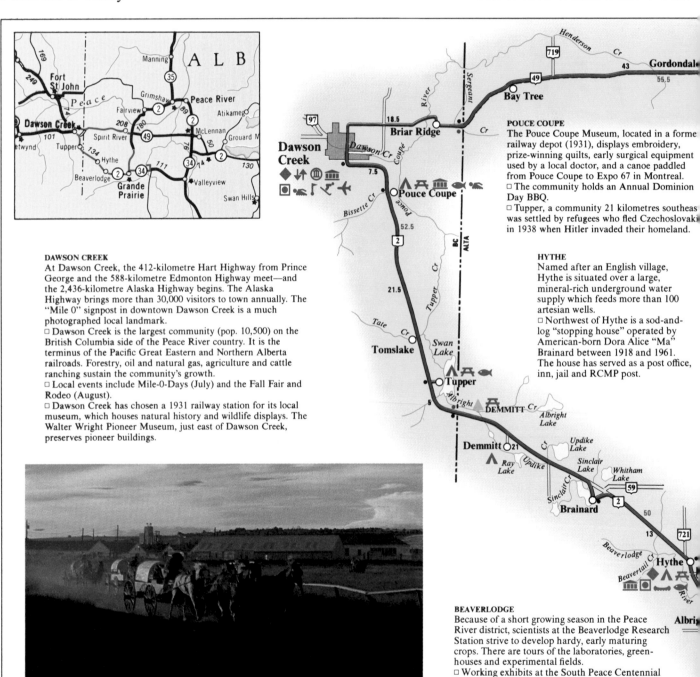

Chuck-wagon races, Dawson Creek, B.C.

DAWSON CREEK

At Dawson Creek, the 412-kilometre Hart Highway from Prince George and the 588-kilometre Edmonton Highway meet—and the 2,436-kilometre Alaska Highway begins. The Alaska Highway brings more than 30,000 visitors to town annually. The "Mile 0" signpost in downtown Dawson Creek is a much photographed local landmark.
□ Dawson Creek is the largest community (pop. 10,500) on the British Columbia side of the Peace River country. It is the terminus of the Pacific Great Eastern and Northern Alberta railroads. Forestry, oil and natural gas, agriculture and cattle ranching sustain the community's growth.
□ Local events include Mile-0-Days (July) and the Fall Fair and Rodeo (August).
□ Dawson Creek has chosen a 1931 railway station for its local museum, which houses natural history and wildlife displays. The Walter Wright Pioneer Museum, just east of Dawson Creek, preserves pioneer buildings.

POUCE COUPE

The Pouce Coupe Museum, located in a former railway depot (1931), displays embroidery, prize-winning quilts, early surgical equipment used by a local doctor, and a canoe paddled from Pouce Coupe to Expo 67 in Montreal.
□ The community holds an Annual Dominion Day BBQ.
□ Tupper, a community 21 kilometres southeast, was settled by refugees who fled Czechoslovakia in 1938 when Hitler invaded their homeland.

HYTHE

Named after an English village, Hythe is situated over a large, mineral-rich underground water supply which feeds more than 100 artesian wells.
□ Northwest of Hythe is a sod-and-log "stopping house" operated by American-born Dora Alice "Ma" Brainard between 1918 and 1961. The house has served as a post office, inn, jail and RCMP post.

BEAVERLODGE

Because of a short growing season in the Peace River district, scientists at the Beaverlodge Research Station strive to develop hardy, early maturing crops. There are tours of the laboratories, greenhouses and experimental fields.
□ Working exhibits at the South Peace Centennial Museum (some of which were used to build the museum) include early gas and steam tractors, plows, a threshing machine and a reconstructed sawmill.
□ A 128-kilometre road into British Columbia leads to the South Pine River and Kinuseo Falls, 90 metres wide and 60 metres high.

summer, columns of harvesters mobilize against the rippling, ripened grain.

Salty inland seas covered this area several times. Farms that checkerboard the countryside are on the bed of prehistoric Lake Agassiz. In the Kleskun Hills, erosion has scoured the glacial till, exposing dinosaur tracks and aquatic fossils.

The human history of the Peace River district is a recent one. Except for a few Indians, trappers and prospectors, the region remained an unpeopled wilderness until the end of the last century.

Since then, homesteaders have carved the most northerly farming belt in Canada. Bush receded to be replaced by sweeping fields of grain and rapeseed. Trails became roads, and roads became highways.

Despite this new prosperity—and the prospect of extensive oil and gas activity, mining and forestry—much of "the Peace" retains a genuine pioneer spirit, original and unspoiled.

Short-eared owl

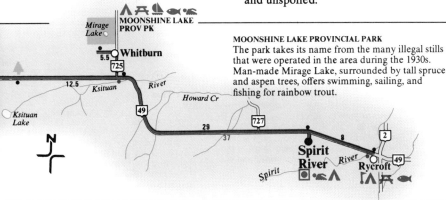

MOONSHINE LAKE PROVINCIAL PARK
The park takes its name from the many illegal stills that were operated in the area during the 1930s. Man-made Mirage Lake, surrounded by tall spruce and aspen trees, offers swimming, sailing, and fishing for rainbow trout.

RYCROFT
Often seen perched on fence posts and tree stumps in Rycroft and throughout the region, the short-eared owl is a crow-sized bird of prey. Unlike most owls, it is active in daylight and inhabits open spaces rather than woodlands. With buoyant wingbeats, the short-eared owl flies over meadow and marsh, pausing to pounce on unwary mice. Like most owls, it is an efficient and valuable destroyer of rodent pests.

From a Little-Known Seed, Lubricant and Cooking Oil

Ripening rapeseed

One of the most remarkable success stories of the Peace River country is the development of the ubiquitous but little-known rapeseed. Introduced during the Second World War to supply lubricating oil for ships, rapeseed also proved useful in products as varied as cooking oil, shortening, margarine, soap, varnish and printing ink.

A short growing season offset by rich soil and long midsummer days resulted in yields as high as 366 kilograms of seed per hectare, with oil contents of 40 percent. When a major market for rapeseed oil was discovered in Japan in the 1960s, production doubled, then tripled to present levels, assuring that seas of banana-colored rapeseed will continue to wave in the Peace River district.

GRANDE PRAIRIE
Situated in a region rich with agricultural, oil and timber resources, Grande Prairie is the business and transportation capital of the Peace River country.
□ Grande Prairie Regional College is set in spacious parkland in the center of the city, overlooking a man-made reservoir. The five college buildings flow into each other without formal passageways, and the curved, earth-colored walls that echo the contours of the prairie enclose an "academic street."
□ The city's Pioneer Museum presents items of historic interest, and the Prairie Gallery displays the work of local artists.
□ Big local events include a stampede in May and a Frontier Days celebration in August.

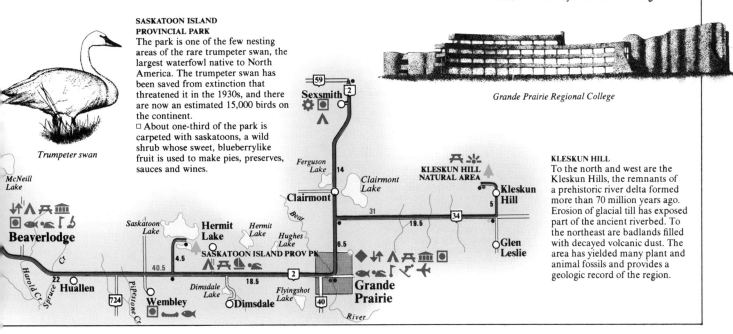

Grande Prairie Regional College

SASKATOON ISLAND PROVINCIAL PARK
The park is one of the few nesting areas of the rare trumpeter swan, the largest waterfowl native to North America. The trumpeter swan has been saved from extinction that threatened it in the 1930s, and there are now an estimated 15,000 birds on the continent.
□ About one-third of the park is carpeted with saskatoons, a wild shrub whose sweet, blueberrylike fruit is used to make pies, preserves, sauces and wines.

Trumpeter swan

KLESKUN HILL
To the north and west are the Kleskun Hills, the remnants of a prehistoric river delta formed more than 70 million years ago. Erosion of glacial till has exposed part of the ancient riverbed. To the northeast are badlands filled with decayed volcanic dust. The area has yielded many plant and animal fossils and provides a geologic record of the region.

An Ancient River Valley
Where 'Twelve-Foot' Davis Settled

Peace River Valley

The Peace River, together with its connecting rivers and lakes, forms one of the largest river systems in the world. Rising in the Rocky Mountains of British Columbia, the Peace flows east through the plains of northern Alberta, winding more than 1,600 kilometres to its junction with the Athabasca River. Together they form the Slave River, ultimately joining the Mackenzie and flowing north to the Beaufort Sea.

The broad Peace River cuts the Alberta prairie to a depth of 300 metres in places

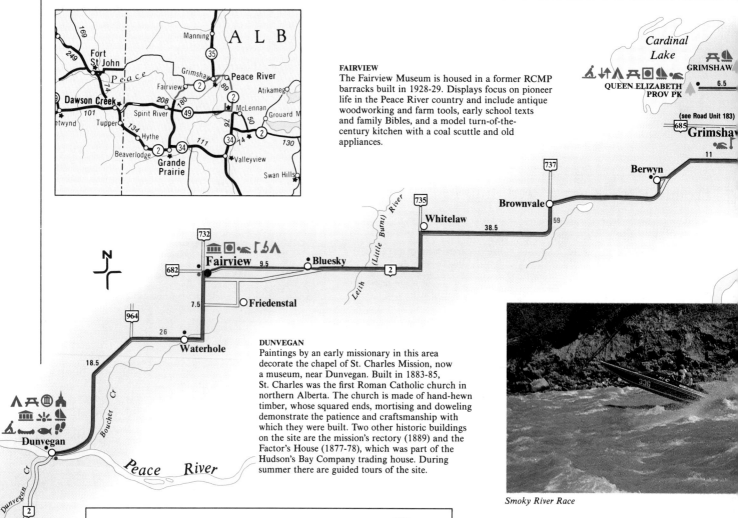

FAIRVIEW
The Fairview Museum is housed in a former RCMP barracks built in 1928-29. Displays focus on pioneer life in the Peace River country and include antique woodworking and farm tools, early school texts and family Bibles, and a model turn-of-the-century kitchen with a coal scuttle and old appliances.

DUNVEGAN
Paintings by an early missionary in this area decorate the chapel of St. Charles Mission, now a museum, near Dunvegan. Built in 1883-85, St. Charles was the first Roman Catholic church in northern Alberta. The church is made of hand-hewn timber, whose squared ends, mortising and doweling demonstrate the patience and craftsmanship with which they were built. Two other historic buildings on the site are the mission's rectory (1889) and the Factor's House (1877-78), which was part of the Hudson's Bay Company trading house. During summer there are guided tours of the site.

Smoky River Race

SMOKY RIVER
Competitors in boats ranging from rubber rafts to 1,100-horsepower twin-engine jet boats brave rapids, rocks and gravel bars during the Smoky River Race between Grande Cache and Peace River. Teams from as far away as New Zealand compete in the five-day, 608-kilometre event each July.
□ The 80-kilometre Smoky River canoe route from Watino to Peace River meanders past 180-metre-high sandstone cliffs and striking hoodoo formations. Spruce, birch and poplar cover the high banks. Tracks of bears, coyotes and deer are seen on the numerous sandbars, and waterfowl are abundant.

Every Man's Friend
Who Never Locked His Door

The tombstone of Henry Fuller "Twelve-Foot" Davis, on a hill overlooking the junction of the Peace and Smoky rivers, records that "he was every man's friend and never locked his cabin door." A statue in Peace River represents Davis as a towering giant. He was really a little man, an American who joined the Cariboo Gold Rush in 1858.

Davis discovered two claims that exceeded regulation width, claimed the 12-foot space between them for his own and mined over $15,000 in gold. Later, in the Peace River country, he was a trader and explorer whose kindness was legendary. As he lay near death in 1900, he was asked whether he was afraid. Said Davis: "I never kilt nobody, I never stole from nobody, and I kept my house open for travelers all my life. No, I ain't afraid to die."

0 1 2 3 4 5 Miles

0 2 4 6 8 Kilometres

and forms a valley 3 to 11 kilometres wide. It is an ancient river—one of the few to survive the ravages of the last ice age. Dinosaur tracks millions of years ago have been unearthed along the river's course.

During the winter of 1792-93, the explorer Sir Alexander Mackenzie wintered in the Peace River valley on his journey to the Pacific. In Mackenzie's wake came fur traders, trappers, prospectors, missionaries and homesteaders. Most settlers found the country an uncompromising, rough-hewn wilderness, but a few of these persevered and prospered here. Despite a short growing season, the 230,000-square-kilometre region on both sides of the Peace River has become famous for its fine barley, wheat, oilseed, and oversize fruits and vegetables.

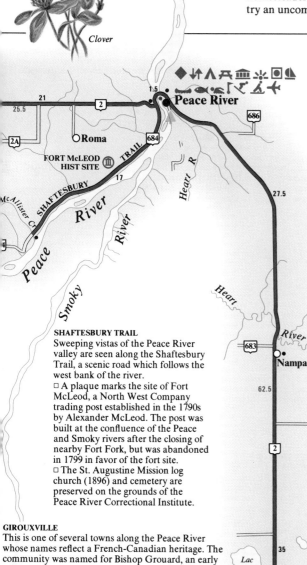

Clover

PEACE RIVER

In the Peace River Centennial Museum is a model of Fort Fork, the trading post where Alexander Mackenzie wintered in 1792-93 on his journey to the Pacific Ocean. The fort's fireplace has been reconstructed with stones from the original. Also displayed is a rare Hudson's Bay Company fur press, used to compact raw furs into bales for shipment.
□ A natural gas fire burns day and night on the Peace River downstream from the town. When an old well was capped in the 1950s, gas was forced up through the riverbed 11 kilometres away, where it ignited and has burned ever since.
□ A 12-passenger boat plies the Peace River on two-day, 60-kilometre sightseeing cruises.

SHAFTESBURY TRAIL

Sweeping vistas of the Peace River valley are seen along the Shaftesbury Trail, a scenic road which follows the west bank of the river.
□ A plaque marks the site of Fort McLeod, a North West Company trading post established in the 1790s by Alexander McLeod. The post was built at the confluence of the Peace and Smoky rivers after the closing of nearby Fort Fork, but was abandoned in 1799 in favor of the fort site.
□ The St. Augustine Mission log church (1896) and cemetery are preserved on the grounds of the Peace River Correctional Institute.

GIROUXVILLE

This is one of several towns along the Peace River whose names reflect a French-Canadian heritage. The community was named for Bishop Grouard, an early missionary to the Peace River country, who ministered to the Indians, then encouraged farmers from Quebec to settle in northern Alberta.
□ The Girouxville Museum, operated by the Oblate Fathers, displays more than 2,000 artifacts, including fossils, wood carvings, two millstones from an 1895 flour mill, and personal effects of Bishop Grouard. A replica of a trapper's log cabin contains pioneer furniture, clothing and tools.

The junction of the Peace and Smoky rivers

FALHER

This town claims to be the "Honey Capital of Canada." Some 35,000 beehives in the region produce more than two million kilograms of honey per year. Along the highway are vast fields of fragrant clover.
□ St. Jean Baptiste Mission (1914) is a hand-hewn log building covered with cedar shingles. Two stories high, it combines both church and priest's residence.

Honey bee, Falher

Through Forest and Flying Gravel to the World's Largest Park

Alberta/Northwest Territories

Louise Falls, Hay River

HAY RIVER

With a population of roughly 3,000, Hay River is one of the largest communities in the Northwest Territories. The town is also the center of the Great Slave Lake commercial fishing industry. Lake trout and whitefish are the major catches.
□ Near Hay River, the Mackenzie Highway passes scenic Alexandra Falls, a 90-metre-wide cataract that plummets 30 metres. Three kilometres away a trail leads to 14-metre-high Louise Falls and, below it, a steep-walled gorge and five kilometres of rapids. To the northwest are the 75-metre-wide Lady Evelyn Falls.

HIGH LEVEL

The town is situated on the height of land that separates the northward flowing Hay River from the eastward flowing Peace River. Once little more than a bus stop on the Mackenzie Highway, High Level has become the jumping-off point for the oil fields at Rainbow Lake to the east. It is also a grain and timber shipment center.
□ Fort Vermilion, once accessible only by boat or plane, is linked to High Level by road. The community, which began as a fur trading post, is surrounded by one of the oldest farming areas in Alberta.

NORTH STAR

The Charles Plavin Homestead (1918), one of the oldest remaining farms in northern Alberta, is being restored as a historical site by the provincial government. The hand-hewn log buildings, sauna and barns reflect the craftsmanship and ingenuity of the early Latvian settler. On display are handmade tools and farm implements.

GRIMSHAW

This is Kilometre Zero of the Mackenzie Highway, a system of northern roads through dense forests, across spongy muskeg, past duck-filled sloughs and lakes, over and alongside swift rivers. It has opened vast tracts of northern wilderness and, when completed, will stretch more than 2,000 kilometres to Tuktoyaktuk on the Beaufort Sea. Road conditions are generally good during the summer, although dust and flying gravel are a constant annoyance. Campsites, food, fuel and supplies are available along the route.

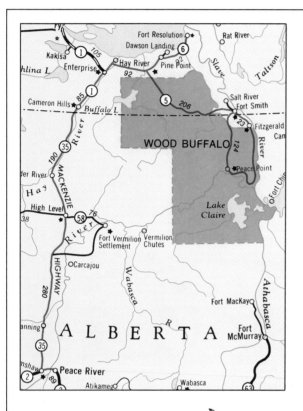

A Northern Sanctuary for a Rare Bird

The magnificent whooping crane, North America's rarest bird, probably has never existed in great numbers. About a century ago there were an estimated 1,500 birds but by 1941, because of man's encroachment, only 15 remained. Now, with protecting legislation, and a Canadian-American breeding program, approximately 100 whooping cranes survive.

Standing erect, the whooping crane is about 150 centimetres tall. Its black beak, wing tips and legs contrast with its glistening white plumage and brilliant red crown. It has a loud, clear buglelike call.

Whooping cranes are thought to mate for life. The eggs are laid after the spring migration to Wood Buffalo National Park from the birds' winter range in the Aransas National Wildlife Refuge on the Texas coast.

0 10 20 30 40 50 Miles

0 20 40 60 80 Kilometres

From Grimshaw, Alta., the Mackenzie Highway reaches north across 940 kilometres of prairie and forest to Fort Simpson, N.W.T. North of Grimshaw the hills and ridges level off to flat alluvial forest land—a dense bush of spruce, poplar, jack pine and tamarack. Occasionally the long stretches of forest, gravel and dust are interrupted by roadside towns. Farming, forestry, mining (and now tourism) are the mainstays of the communities; many residents are descendants of the original British, Mennonite, Ukrainian and Métis settlers of a century ago.

At Hay River, N.W.T., a key northern port and railhead, a secondary highway turns east along Great Slave Lake to Wood Buffalo National Park. The world's largest national park—only slightly smaller than Nova Scotia—was established in 1922 to protect North America's last herd of wood bison. Four migratory flyways overlap in the park and there is an abundance of birdlife. Some 100 whooping cranes—more than half the world population of that rare bird—nest in Wood Buffalo National Park each summer.

The plains near the Slave River are crisscrossed by saline streams. Evaporation has formed salt mounds up to 20 metres across and a metre high. Throughout the park are huge sinkholes where runoff has eroded underlying soft rock. One sinkhole measures 36 metres across and 24 metres deep. Dominating the landscape is the vast expanse of the Peace-Athabasca Delta.

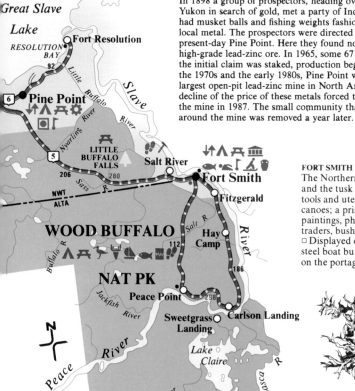

PINE POINT
In 1898 a group of prospectors, heading overland to the Yukon in search of gold, met a party of Indians who had musket balls and fishing weights fashioned from local metal. The prospectors were directed to a site near present-day Pine Point. Here they found not gold, but high-grade lead-zinc ore. In 1965, some 67 years after the initial claim was staked, production began. During the 1970s and the early 1980s, Pine Point was the largest open-pit lead-zinc mine in North America. The decline of the price of these metals forced the closure of the mine in 1987. The small community that grew up around the mine was removed a year later.

FITZGERALD
Riverboats on the Mackenzie River had a clear, 2,440-kilometre run to the Beaufort Sea except for rapids on the Slave River—the most formidable named the Rapids of the Drowned—which extends 22 kilometres from Fitzgerald, Alta., to Fort Smith, N.W.T. At Fitzgerald the freight for the north country was unloaded from the Athabasca-Slave River barges and hauled, originally by ox- and horse-drawn wagons, later by truck and tractor, to Fort Smith. There it was reloaded onto a second fleet of barges bound for Aklavik on the Mackenzie Delta.

FORT SMITH
The Northern Life Museum displays dinosaur bones and the tusk of a mammoth; early Indian and Eskimo tools and utensils; moosehide and spruce-bark canoes; a printing press brought north in 1873, and paintings, photographs and mementos of trappers, traders, bush pilots and missionaries.
□ Displayed outdoors are the *Radium King*, the first steel boat built here (1937), and an old tractor used on the portage between Fort Smith and Fitzgerald.

Closed gentian

Reindeer moss

Salt plains, Wood Buffalo National Park

Wood bison

Sink hole, Wood Buffalo National Park

WOOD BUFFALO NATIONAL PARK
This 44,900-square-kilometre park, which straddles the Alberta–N.W.T. border, was established in 1922 to protect the last remaining herd of wood bison in North America. Three years later, some 6,000 plains bison were shipped from a protective compound at Wainwright, Alta., to the park. Disease and crossbreeding almost wiped out the wood bison. Today, the park supports a hybrid population of more than 5,000 free-roaming bison.

Modernity in the 'Land of the Midnight Sun'

Northwest Territories

Winding through lush forests, past duck-filled sloughs and lakes, and alongside swift rivers, the Mackenzie Highway is a delight to the visitor craving wilderness.

Once in the Northwest Territories, the highway branches into an enticing system of roads, generally in such good condition as to surprise travelers. Along much of its length the route crosses a flat land treed with poplar, spruce, tamarack and jack pine. Wild raspberries hang in red clusters, al-

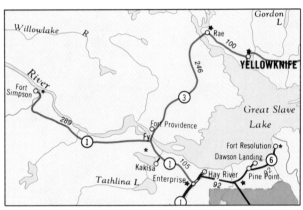

Mountain avens

Kildeer

FORT SIMPSON

The great Liard River fights for survival here after joining the mightier Mackenzie. Downstream from the confluence the Mackenzie River is often dark and laden with debris that the Liard has carried from the mountains of the Yukon and British Columbia. Gradually the Mackenzie swallows all trace of the tributary.

□ Fort Simpson is on an island with a commanding view of Gros Cap, a 67-metre-high promontory where the rivers meet. The first fort here was the North West Company's Fort of the Forks (1804). The post was renamed by the Hudson's Bay Company in 1821 for George (later Sir George) Simpson, a HBC governor.

□ A notable local attraction is the Papal site, which commemorates the visit of Pope John Paul II to this northern community in September 1987.

□ From Fort Simpson, visitors can charter floatplanes that fly to Nahanni National Park, which was recognized as a United Nations World Heritage Site in 1979.

Mackenzie River

FORT PROVIDENCE

A Roman Catholic mission and a HBC trading post, both established in the 1850s, attracted the Slavey Dene Indians, whose community grew up nearby. Fort Providence, a center of Slavey culture, is well known for the exceptional quality of its crafts.

Beads, Quills and Tufted Moose Hair

Most Inuit and northern Indians once hunted, fished or trapped for a living—and often went hungry. Today many are self-employed in thriving co-ops, producing traditional crafts for sale in other parts of Canada.

Handmade parkas, gloves, mittens and mukluks are prized for their warmth and decoration. Skilled seamstresses embroider garments in bright cottons; some sew on beads (*right*) or dyed porcupine quills. Footwear made by Fort Providence Indians is ornamented with intricate designs in tufted moose hair.

As the demand for northern prints and soapstone carvings has increased, many co-ops have stepped up production. Their crafts—far more than souvenirs of the North—are now a recognized art form.

MACKENZIE RIVER

Spanning three time zones and draining one-fifth of Canada, the Mackenzie and its tributaries rank as one of the world's largest river systems.

The Mackenzie rises in the British Columbia Rockies 4,200 kilometres from its outlet at the Beaufort Sea. One by one the Parsnip, Peace, Athabasca and Slave pour into the system. In the northwest corner of Great Slave Lake, the Mackenzie proper begins. From here, fed by innumerable streams, the Mackenzie snakes northward to the Arctic Ocean.

Canada lynx

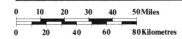

most as thick as the persistent clouds of mosquitoes and black flies. Trophy-size walleye, northern pike and Arctic grayling ply roadside lakes, rivers and streams.

During July and August, when the daytime temperatures are pleasantly mild, the southern part of the Northwest Territories receives 20 hours of sunshine. Throughout the short summer this "Land of the Midnight Sun" bustles with activity. The Mackenzie River and Great Slave Lake are busy with supply barges bound for remote settlements and oil camps. Adventurous visitors sail these waters in canoes and motorboats.

Like the varied scenery, the former fur-trade posts linked by the Mackenzie Highway take southerners by surprise. Most visitors to Yellowknife, the capital of the Northwest Territories, expect a primitive mining town. (Yellowknife owes its existence to a 1934 gold strike.) What they are not prepared for is the modernity of this northern city, with its high-rise buildings and its vital way of life.

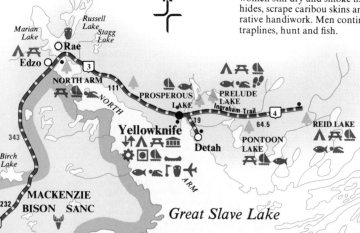

Drying fish, Rae

RAE

The original Fort Rae, built in 1852 and named after explorer Dr. John Rae, was a seasonal hunting and fishing camp of the Dogrib Indians. In 1902-06 the camp became a permanent settlement; the twin community of Edzo was founded in 1965.

Today the towns are a blend of traditional and modern life-styles. Older women still dry and smoke fish, tan moose hides, scrape caribou skins and do decorative handiwork. Men continue to run traplines, hunt and fish.

Eskimo dogs

Last of the Hardy Husky?

At one time every northern household owned at least half a dozen sled and work dogs. The four common breeds are the Eskimo, Malamute, Samoyed and Siberian husky. These sturdy, hardy dogs are referred to as "huskies" by southerners.

Northern dogs were indispensable. Hunters, forced to travel for days to find caribou, piled sleds with gear and hitched up the dogs in sealskin traces. The teams could reach speeds of 30 kilometres an hour, but averaged a steady trot that covered eight kilometres an hour. Snowmobiles are now replacing the huskies. But there is a disadvantage to this modern form of transport: "You can eat your dog if you're hungry," say the old-timers.

GREAT SLAVE LAKE

This vast lake, the fifth largest in North America (eleventh in the world), is in a transition zone between the boreal forest of the Canadian Shield and the grasses of the Arctic tundra.
□ The Lockhart River drops a total of 200 metres, through rapids and over falls—including 40-metre Parry Falls—in the last 400 kilometres of its descent to the lake.
□ The challenging 480-kilometre Camsell River canoe route winds from Great Slave Lake to Great Bear Lake.

YELLOWKNIFE

The capital of the Northwest Territories and its largest city (with a population of about 12,000) is named for the Indian peoples who lived locally for thousand of years. Yellowknife's modern history begins with the gold rush of the mid-1930s. The rough-and-ready boom town has long since given way to the enterprising northern capital of today, although traces of the past are apparent in the surviving gold rush buildings and the local Dene community. Within the city, there are a number of notable attractions: the Prince of Wales Northern Heritage Centre, which houses Inuit, Indian and Métis artifacts, and the 313-seat Globe Theatre in the Northern Arts and Cultural Centre.
□ The annual Caribou Carnival in March features a wide range of contests—igloo-building, log-sawing, skiing and snowshoeing competitions.
□ East of Yellowknife, the scenic Ingraham Trail offers excellent camping and fishing.

Yellowknife

Index

Road unit numbers are given with all references. Numbers in **boldface** signify major references to specific sites and subjects; those in regular typeface, incidental references. A number followed by the letter P means a site or subject is pictured in the road unit. A number in *italics* is a map reference. A roman numeral is a bird's-eye view reference.

Picture Credits

The abbreviations used here are these:

AH	Allan Harvey
BD	Barbara K. Deans
BS	Brian Stablyk
CH	Chic Harris
DB	Dunkin Bancroft
DW	Daniel Wiener
FP	Freeman Patterson
JdV	John de Visser
MF	Menno Fieguth
NS	Nova Scotia Communications and Information Centre
PG	Pierre Gaudard
PK	Peter M. Keane
PM	Patrick Morrow
PvB	Paul von Baich
RV	Richard Vroom

The credits are arranged according to the road unit numbers, unless otherwise indicated. They are given from left to right, top to bottom, across the two-page unit, with additional information as needed. Four city units—Vancouver (**11**), Toronto (**96**), Ottawa (**105**), and Montreal (**112**)—have four pages each. In these instances, the first two pages are marked A, and the second two pages, B.

Title page: Bryce Flynn; Hans L. Blohm; Road Unit Atlas: DB; Northern Adventure Roads: PvB. Road Units: **1** Clifford A. Fenner; PvB; **2** Nina Raginski; Bert Hoferichter; Robert Herger; JdV; BD; Canadian Postal Museum; **3** Anna Neilson; Allan Harvey; Clifford A. Fenner; **4** PvB; MF; PvB; **5** Peter Tasker (top) British Columbia Government (left); MF; **6** Mildred McPhee (top); PvB; Fred Bruemmer; **7** PvB (3); **8** Gerry Deiter (top); J. David Dennings (2); British Columbia Government (left); **9** BS (top); MF; Ted Spiegel (left); **10** Alan Zenuk (top); David Clark; **11A** Bob Clarke/Image Finders; Gar Lunney; Joe Munroe/Photo Researchers; **11B** AH; JdV; AH (2); Bob Crosby; Don McPhee; BS; **12** Bill Collins/Image Finders; JdV; Robert Herger (bottom); **13** Henry Kalen; Don McPhee (right); Valerie J. May; **14** Jim Babchuk (top); PvB; BS; **15** Nancy Anderson (top); Fred Chapman/Image Finders; Alan Zenuk; **16** BS; Dennis Schmidt; MF; **17** Clifford A. Fenner; Creston Valley Wildlife Centre; **18** Nancy Anderson; Valerie J. May; PvB; **19** PvB; British Columbia Government (2); **20** PvB (top); Dan Guravich (left); Canadian Pacific; PvB; **21** John G. Woods; Parks Canada; E.M. Segall; **22** Parks Canada; Tom W. Hall (right); Valerie J. May; **23** Patrick Morrow (top); Neil G. Carey; UBC Museum of Anthropology. From *Indian Masterpieces* (The Walter and Marianne Koerner Collection) published by UBC Press, 1975; Allan Harvey (right); **24** Richard Wright; PvB; **25** British Columbia Government (left); BS (2); **26** British Columbia Government; PvB; Peter Tasker; **27** Vancouver City Archives (right); PvB (left); JdV; **28** Native Sons of British Columbia, post no. 2; PvB (left); BS; **29** Richard Wright; Jack Fields/Photo Researchers; Peter Tasker; **30** Gerald Dumont (left); Victor Last; BD; **31** Egon Bork (2); **32** Hälle Flygare; J.A. Kraulis; **33** Karvonen Films Ltd. (right); Peter Tasker; J.A. Kraulis (left); **34** Peter Tasker (2); Thomas Kitchin (right); **35** Paolo Koch/Photo Researchers; Don Beers; Colin Michie; **36** E. Otto/Miller Comstock; Glenbow Alberta Institute; Robin White/Fotolex; Toby Rankin/The Image Bank; **37** Deena Soicher; Hazel Hudson; R.B. Walter Kerber; **38** Nicholas Morant (2); Colin Michie; **39** Prairie Farm Rehabilitation Administration (top); Stock Photos Unlimited; Donald R. Gunn (left); Kay McGregor; **40** Egon Bork (top); RV (center); Mary Hampson; Hälle Flygare; **41** JdV (top); Peter Benison; **42** Thomas Kitchin; Doug Leighton (right); Jim Martin; **43** Edgar T. Jones; Deena Soicher (right); Wilhelm Schmidt; **44** George Tingle; **45** Deena Soicher (right); Lowell J. Georgia/Photo Researchers; **46** JdV; Reynolds Museum; **47** PG; PM; **48** Paolo Koch/Photo Researchers (right); Robert N. Smith; **49** PM; **50** Stony Plain Farmers Market; BS; **51** Thomas Kitchin; BS (center left); Provincial Museum of Alberta; Lowell J. Georgia/Photo Researchers (2); **52** BS; Wilfried Schurig; S.R. Cannings; **53** Patrick Morrow (top); Ukrainian Women's Association of Canada; PM; **54** Egon Bork (2); **55** Department of Indian and Northern Affairs; PM; **56** MF (top); Bob Hewitt; Saskatchewan Historic Parks (left); Saskatchewan Government; **57** B. Hoferichter/Miller Comstock; PvB (top right); Robert Baillargeon (2); Parks Canada, Battleford National Historic Park (2); **58** MF (2); Richard Knelsen (left); Saskatchewan Government; **59** Manitoba Government Travel (2); MF (left); **60** Gar Lunney; Parks Canada; Richard Knelsen; **61** Ken Patterson (top); RCMP; Saskatchewan Archives; **62** MF (2); RV (left); **63** Lorne Scott; RCMP; Bryce Flynn; **64** Ken Patterson; Gordon Knight; MF; **65** Government of Saskatchewan (5); Gar Lunney; **66** MF; RV; **67** Manitoba Government Travel (2); Douglas C. Harvey (left); Freshwater Institute, Environment Canada; **68** Dr. L. Syms (2) (right); Fred Waines (left) Manitoba Government Travel; **69** Fred Clark; Manitoba Government Travel; Department of National Defence; Henry Kalen; **70** Jack McKinnon; L.B. Shilson (center left); Henry Kalen; Manitoba Government Travel; **71** Bryce Flynn (top); Henry Kalen; JdV; **72** JdV; Manitoba Government Travel (2); Parks Canada, Lower Fort Gary; **73** JdV (2); Colin Hay; **74** MF (2); **75** JdV (top); Bert Hoferichter; Kryn Taconis/Magnum; **76** Vic Robinson (top); Pierre St-Jacques/Miller Comstock (right); courtesy Elinor Barr Collection (inset); Dennis Smyk; **77** JdV; Elaine Edwards (center right); Victor C. Last; JdV; **78** Dawn Goss/First Light (center); National Gallery of Canada, Ottawa; **79** Algoma Central Railway; JdV (right); Sheila Naiman; **80** Parks Canada (right); CH; **81** JdV; Rudi Christl; Sheila Naiman; **82** Bill Lowry (top); Victor C. Last; George Hunter; **83** Victor C. Last (right); C.P.S. Film Productions; **84** RD (right); JdV/Masterfile; Brian Swales/courtesy Orangeville Raceway; **85** Richard J. Urysz (right); Texasgulf; **86** J.D. Taylor; Quints Museum; John R. Hunt; Sheila Naiman; **87** CH; Atomic Energy of Canada Ltd.; Parks Canada; **88** JdV (top); Oliver J. Dell; **89** Terry W. Self/Canapress; Environment Canada Parks Service, Fort Malden N.H.S.; Harvey Medland; **90** Victor Aziz; The Stratford Shakespearean Festival Foundation of Canada/photo Robert C. Ragsdale; **91** Robert Baillargeon (right); C.P.S. Film Productions; **92** Helmut Schade; JdV; J.D. Taylor; **93** C.W. Perkins (top); E. Otto/Miller Comstock (left); Tom Bochsler; **94** JdV; George F. Long; Ontario Tourism; **95** Courtesy The McMichael Canadian Collection (top); Photo Librarium; Lowry Photography (left); **96A** Randy Bulmer (top); David Prichard/First Light; **96B** Allan Harvey (center right); Jim Russell/First Light (left); Gera Dillon/First Light (top right); courtesy Pantages Theatre (center left); Lorraine Parrow/First Light (bottom left); **97** Lowry Photography (3); **98** Courtesy Dr. J. Wendell MacLeod, Bethune Memorial Foundation (top); Courtesy The McGill Daily; Mary Ferguson; **99** Art Gallery of Ontario; Ontario Tourism (right); JdV; **100** Kryn Taconis; JdV; George Long; **101** RV (center); courtesy Serpent Mounds Provincial Park; JdV; **102** William R. Wilkins (top); BD (center); Ontario Tourism; **103** W. Griebeling/Miller Comstock; JdV; Helmut W. Schade (left); Sheila Naiman; **104** R. Tait McKenzie Memorial Museum and Mill of Kintail; Ontario Tourism; **105A** Harold Clark; Kenneth Ginn; **105B** Allan Harvey (top left); JdV; Ted Maginn; JdV (2); P. Brunet/Publiphoto; JdV (2); **106** Crombie McNeil; Hans L. Blohm; Tibor Bognar/Réflexion; **107** Oliver J. Dell; C.P.S. Film Productions; JdV; **108** Roland Weber/The Image Bank; Diana Lafleur; Hans L. Blohm; **109** Ontario Tourism (center); courtesy the Department of Rare Books, McGill University/photo Mike Haimes; RV; **110** National Archives of Canada (right); Peter Benison; Sean O'Neill/Réflexion; **111** DW; PG; Peter Benison; **112A** J. Boutin/Publiphoto (top); George Zimbel/Publiphoto; **112B** Perry Mastrovito/Réflexion (2); Bernard Martin/Alpha Diffusion (center); JdV; Michel Gagné/Réflexion; Cadel Ettore (center top); MUCTC; Thomas Kitchin; **113** Impart/The Image Bank; Michel Bleau; DW; **114** Cynthia Chalk (right); PG; **115** Claude Lavigne; Parc Safari Africain, Hemmingford; **116** Serge Laurin; Surveys and Mapping Branch, Department of Energy, Mines and Resources; CH; **117** Diana Lafleur (2); CH; **118** Pedro Rodriguez (2); **119** Denis Plain; J. Boutin/Publiphoto; DW; **120** PG; Conseil de développement de la Chaudière; Paul G. Adam/Publiphoto; **121** Fred Bruemmer (right); Mia and Klaus; Pierre Kandalaft; Montreal Municipal Library/Gagnon Collection; **122** Roger Tessier; Galerie d'Art Pierre Labrecque, Trois-Rivières; **123** Yves Tessier; Paul Gélinas; PG; **124** Jim Hutchison and Margo Pfeiff; Mia and Klaus; DB; Denise Beha (bottom left); Sylvain Majeau; **125** Adelaide Leitch; Pierre Kandalaft; Paul E. Lambert; **126** Paul E. Lambert (top); Art Gallery of Ontario, gift of the family of Sir Edmund Walker, 1926; Jules Rochon; **127** Paul E. Lambert (top); DB; Denise Beha; Photo Librarium; **128** National Gallery of Canada, Ottawa; Photo Librarium (right); BD; **129** C.P.S. Film Productions (top); JdV (2); CH; JdV; **130** Société zoologique de St-Félicien Inc.; Photo Librarium; **131** DB (top); Roland Weber; Ivan Boulerice; **132** Fred Bruemmer; Sheila Naiman; Gil Jacques/Réflexion; **133** Karl Somerer; CH; JdV; **134** Roland Weber (left); Karl Sommerer; **135** Sheila Naiman; Fred Bruemmer; JdV; **136** New Brunswick Tourism (right); FP; **137** G. Michaud (2); L.J. Michau **138** National Archives of Canada PA-26647 (top); T. Cliffo Hodgson (left); New Brunswick Tourism (right); Malak, Ottaw **139** New Brunswick Tourism (2); **140** Military Compound Boar **141** Harold Clark (top); JdV; **142** Théâtre du Rideau Vert; Rc Stears; RV; **143** T. Clifford Hodgson (top); New Brunswick Tou ism; Wambolt Waterfield (left); **144** Doris Mowry; Elmer N. Wi cox; **145** JdV (top); Michael Saunders/Miller Comstock; T. Cliffor Hodgson; **146** FP (2); **147** Charles Steinhacker/Black Star (right Robert Baillargeon; **148** RV (top); P.E.I. Tourism, Parks and Cor servation; RV; **149** P.E.I. Tourism, Parks and Conservation (top RV; Jean-Claude Hurni; **150** JdV (top); Canadian Government O fice of Tourism; Dr. Stewart MacDonald (center); P.E.I. Tourism Parks and Conservation; **151** CH (left); Canadian Governmer Office of Tourism; Gord Johnston; **152** RV (2); **153** Canadian Go ernment Office of Tourism (top); P.E.I. Tourism, Parks and Conse vation; PK; **154** Tim Randall; JdV (right); DW (left); PK; **155** DV (2); Kejimkujik National Park (left); FP; **156** Tim Randall; G.V Condon; Tim Randall; **157** Tim Randall; Grand Pré National His toric Park; Nova Scotia Public Archives (center); NS; **158** Joh Pohl; PK; **159** Charles Steinhacker/Black Star (right); NS; Ga Lunney; **160** NS; Sherman Hines; Albert Lee; DW; **161** Dan Gura vich (right); FP; PK; **162** PK (right); NS; **163** PK (3); **164** N (right); Bob Brooks; Tim Randall; **165** NS; Bob Brooks; **166** NS; Ji Baillargeon (right); DB; **167** DB (2); Stephen Homer; **168** Bo Brooks (top); Mary Primrose; PK; Jean-Claude Hurni; **169** PK Mary Primrose; PK; **170** PK; Rick Filler; **171** Nicholas Devore III Bruce Coleman Inc.; CH; Parks Canada; **172** JdV (2); **173** R. Har rington/Miller Comstock; JdV; Confederation Life Collection; **17** Conception Bay Museum; Nicholas Devore III/Bruce Colema Inc.; Rick Filler; **175** Gary N. Corbett; Dan Guravich (right); CH DW; **176** Robert Baillargeon; JdV; Dan Guravich; **177** Governmen of the Northwest Territories (top); C. Bruun/NFB; Hans L. Blohm Richard Fyfe; **178** Roy Ooms/Creative Stock; PvB (left); Yuko Archives; K. Dudley; **179** PvB, J.D. Taylor (left); PvB; **180** PvB (2 **181** Anne Soicher (right); Kenneth H. Seto; **182** Deena Soiche (right); Charles E. McManis, Las Vegas; **183** René Fumoleau; Park Canada (2); **184** Government of Northwest Territories; William J Carpenter/Eskimo Research Foundation; Richard Fyfe (left) Bryce Flynn.

Front cover E. Otto/Miller Comstock; Back cover RV (top); Thom as Kitchin (center); Paul G. Adam/Publiphoto.

ILLUSTRATORS: Lea Daniel, Louise Delorme, Jean-Claude Gagnon André Pierzchala, Jocelyn Veillette

COLOR ILLUSTRATIONS: Jim Bruce (170), Diane Desrosiers, Anke Odum (41, 97)

DIAGRAMS: Réal Lefebvre (22, 60, 81)
CUTAWAYS: Georges Buctel (10, 30, 32, 94)

Illustration source for 81: Courtesy of The Mining Association of Canada
Illustration sources for 12 and 83: Elaine Sears

Film work: R.P.J. Litho Inc.
Printing: Pierre DesMarais Inc. and Litho Prestige
Binding: T.H. Best Printing Company
Paper: Rolland inc.

Canadian Book of the Road contains non-acid paper to ensure durability. The paper and other materials used to make the book are recyclable.

Distances in Kilometres Between Major Metropolitan Centers

	Chicoutimi-Jonquière	Calgary	Edmonton	Halifax	Hamilton	Kitchener	London	Montreal	Oshawa	Ottawa	Quebec	Regina	St. Catharines-Niagara	Saint John	St. John's	Saskatoon	Sudbury	Thunder Bay	Toronto	Vancouver	Victoria	Windsor	Winnipeg
Chicoutimi-Jonquière		4220	299	4973	3502	3543	3612	3743	3354	3553	4014	764	3571	4664	6344	620	3057	2050	3434	1057	1162	3241	1336
Calgary	4220		4241	977	1083	1124	1198	476	934	666	206	3455	1152	649	2329	3713	1160	2169	1015	5277	5382	1381	2884
Edmonton	299	4241		5013	3523	3564	3638	3764	3375	3574	4035	785	3592	4704	6384	528	3078	2071	3455	1244	1349	3262	1357
Halifax	4973	977	5013		1856	1897	1971	1249	1708	1439	982	4228	1925	309	1989	4485	1935	2942	1788	6050	6154	2153	3656
Hamilton	3502	1083	3523	1856		61	110	607	148	467	877	2737	69	1547	3227	2995	355	1452	68	4559	4664	319	2166
Kitchener	3543	1124	3564	1897	61		107	648	189	491	918	2779	130	1588	3268	3036	463	1473	109	4601	4705	290	2208
London	3612	1198	3638	1971	110	107		722	263	583	992	2853	203	1662	3342	3110	547	1545	183	4675	4779	190	2282
Montreal	3743	476	3764	1249	607	648	722		459	190	270	2979	676	940	2620	3236	686	1693	539	4801	4905	904	2408
Oshawa	3354	934	3375	1708	148	189	263	459		319	729	2590	217	1399	3079	2847	380	1376	80	4412	4516	449	2019
Ottawa	3553	666	3574	1439	467	491	583	190	319		460	2789	536	1130	2810	3046	494	1503	399	4611	4715	764	2218
Quebec	4014	206	4035	982	877	918	992	270	729	460		3249	946	673	2353	3507	956	1963	809	5071	5176	1175	2678
Regina	764	3455	785	4228	2737	2779	2853	2979	2590	2789	3249		2807	3919	5519	257	2280	1286	2670	1822	1926	2477	571
St. Catharines-Niagara	3571	1152	3592	1925	69	130	203	676	217	536	946	2807		1616	3296	3064	505	1521	137	4628	4733	388	2235
Saint John	4664	649	4704	309	1547	1588	1662	940	1399	1130	673	3919	1616		1727	4176	1626	2633	1479	5741	5845	1844	3347
St. John's	6344	2329	6384	1989	3227	3268	3342	2620	3079	2810	2353	5519	3296	1727		5856	3306	4313	3159	7421	7525	3524	5027
Saskatoon	620	3713	528	4485	2995	3036	3110	3236	2847	3046	3507	257	3064	4176	5856		2538	1543	2927	1677	1782	2734	829
Sudbury	3057	1160	3078	1935	355	463	547	686	380	494	956	2280	505	1626	3306	2538		1001	388	4102	4206	735	1722
Thunder Bay	2050	2169	2071	2942	1452	1473	1545	1693	1376	1503	1963	1286	1521	2633	4313	1543	1001		1384	3108	3212	1289	715
Toronto	3434	1015	3455	1788	68	109	183	539	80	399	809	2670	137	1479	3159	2927	388	1384		4492	4596	369	2099
Vancouver	1057	5277	1244	6050	4559	4601	4675	4801	4412	4611	5071	1822	4628	5741	7421	1677	4102	3108	4492		105	4299	2232
Victoria	1162	5382	1349	6154	4664	4705	4779	4905	4516	4715	5176	1926	4733	5845	7525	1782	4206	3212	4596	105		4403	2337
Windsor	3241	1381	3262	2153	319	290	190	904	449	764	1175	2477	388	1844	3524	2734	735	1289	369	4299	4403		1905
Winnipeg	1336	2884	1357	3656	2166	2208	2282	2408	2019	2218	2678	571	2235	3347	5027	829	1722	715	2099	2232	2337	1905	

(100 kilometers = 62 miles)

Map Features and Symbols

ROADS

Road unit route

Multilane highways

Multilane highways (Under construction)

Principal and secondary highways

Principal and secondary highways (Gravel surface)

Principal and secondary roads

Point-to-point distances .... ● 5 km ● 5 km ●

Accumulated distances .... ● 10 km ●

TOWNS AND CITIES

Towns or villages under 1,000 .... O

Towns or cities over 1,000 (These may be located with either a black dot or a shaded area according to the scale of the map) ●

Under 1,000 .... Nobel

1,000 to 25,000 .... **Hillsborough**

25,000 to 100,000 .... **BRANTFORD**

(The provincial capital of P.E.I., Charlottetown, with a population of 16,500, is the exception.)

100,000 to 500,000 .... **REGINA**

500,000 and over .... **MONTREAL**

PARKS

Small park or outdoor area

Large park

Small park within a large park

Other large outdoor areas

Other special areas

OTHER MAP FEATURES

Ferry (Road unit ferry rides are marked in red)

Railways

Provincial boundaries

International boundary

SITES

Airfield (regular service)

Aquarium

Battle site

Bird sanctuary, waterfowl park

Botanical garden

Hotel/motel accommodation

Campsite

Covered bridge

Craft center

Ferry

Forest reserve, arboretum, tree nursery

Fort

Historic or important building or sites

Historic or important church

Historic water mill

Historic windmill

Industrial site, industrial tour

Lighthouse

Lookout

Mountain

Museum, art gallery

Picnic site

Research station, experimental farm, fish hatchery

Summer school

Theater

Tourist information center

Wildlife preserve

Zoo, menagerie

ACTIVITIES

Alpine skiing

Aquatic activities*

Boating

Canoeing

Caving

Climbing

Cross-country skiing

Deep-sea fishing

Fishing

Golfing

Hiking

Horseback riding

Local events (fairs, festivals, sporting events, etc.)

Rock hounding

Skin diving

Swimming

Winter sports (general)

*This general symbol includes boating, canoeing, fishing and swimming. There are specific symbols for these activities. A specific symbol appearing with the general symbol indicates an area where a particular aquatic activity is outstanding.